Dutch and Flemish Literature as World Literature

Literatures as world literature

Literatures as World Literature takes a novel approach to world literature by analysing specific constellations – according to language, nation, form, or theme – of literary texts and authors in their world-literary dimensions. World literature has been mapped and theorized in the abstract, but the majority of critical work, the filling in of what has been traced, lies ahead of us. **Literatures as World Literature** begins the task of filling in the devilish details by allowing scholars to move outward from their own area of specialization. The hope is to foster scholarly writing that approaches more closely the polyphonic, multiperspectival nature of the world literature we wish to explore.

Series Editor:
Thomas Beebee

Editorial Board:
Eduardo Coutinho, Federal University of Rio de Janeiro, Brazil
Hsinya Huang, National Sun-yat Sen University, Taiwan
Meg Samuelson, University of Cape Town, South Africa
Ken Seigneurie, Simon Fraser University, Canada
Mads Rosendahl Thomsen, Aarhus University, Denmark

Volumes in the Series

German Literature as World Literature
Edited by Thomas Beebee
Roberto Bolaño as World Literature
Edited by Nicholas Birns and Juan E. De Castro
Crime Fiction as World Literature
Edited by David Damrosch, Theo D'haen, and Louise Nilsson
Danish Literature as World Literature
Edited by Dan Ringgaard and Mads Rosendahl Thomsen

From Paris to Tlön: Surrealism as World Literature
By Delia Ungureanu
American Literature as World Literature
Edited by Jeffrey R. Di Leo
Romanian Literature as World Literature
Edited by Mircea Martin, Christian Moraru, and Andrei Terian
Brazilian Literature as World Literature
By Eduardo F. Coutinho
Dutch and Flemish Literature as World Literature
Edited by Theo D'haen
Afropolitan Literature as World Literature (forthcoming)
Edited by James Hodapp
Modern Indian Literature as World Literature (forthcoming)
By Bhavya Tiwari
Francophone Literatures as World Literature (forthcoming)
Edited by Christian Moraru, Nicole Simek, and Bertrand Westphal
Persian Literature as World Literature (forthcoming)
Edited by Mostafa Abedinifard, Omid Azadibougar, and Amirhossein Vafa
Philosophy as World Literature (forthcoming)
Edited by Jeffrey R. Di Leo
Bulgarian Literature as World Literature (forthcoming)
Edited by Mihaela P. Harper and Dimitar Kambourov

Dutch and Flemish Literature as World Literature

Edited by
Theo D'haen

BLOOMSBURY ACADEMIC
NEW YORK • LONDON • OXFORD • NEW DELHI • SYDNEY

BLOOMSBURY ACADEMIC
Bloomsbury Publishing Inc
1385 Broadway, New York, NY 10018, USA
50 Bedford Square, London, WC1B 3DP, UK
29 Earlsfort Terrace, Dublin 2, Ireland

BLOOMSBURY, BLOOMSBURY ACADEMIC and the Diana logo
are trademarks of Bloomsbury Publishing Plc

First published in the United States of America 2019
This paperback edition published in 2021

Volume Editor's Part of the Work © Theo D'haen, 2019
Each chapter © of Contributors

Cover design by Simon Levy / Levy Associates

All rights reserved. No part of this publication may be reproduced or transmitted in any form or by any means, electronic or mechanical, including photocopying, recording, or any information storage or retrieval system, without prior permission in writing from the publishers.

Bloomsbury Publishing Inc does not have any control over, or responsibility for, any third-party websites referred to or in this book. All internet addresses given in this book were correct at the time of going to press. The author and publisher regret any inconvenience caused if addresses have changed or sites have ceased to exist, but can accept no responsibility for any such changes.

Library of Congress Cataloging-in-Publication Data
Names: Haen, Theo d', editor.
Title: Dutch and Flemish literature as world literature / edited by Theo D'haen.
Description: New York, NY : Bloomsbury Academic, 2019. | Series: Literatures as world literature | Includes bibliographical references and index.
Identifiers: LCCN 2019011686 (print) | LCCN 2019017691 (ebook) | ISBN 9781501340130 (ePub) | ISBN 9781501340147 (ePDF) | ISBN 9781501340123 (hardback :alk. paper)
Subjects: LCSH: Dutch literature–History and criticism. | Flemish literature–History and criticism.
Classification: LCC PT5061 (ebook) | LCC PT5061 .D88 2019 (print) | DDC 839.3/109–dc23
LC record available at https://lccn.loc.gov/2019011686

ISBN:	HB:	978-1-5013-4012-3
	PB:	978-1-5013-7196-7
	ePDF:	978-1-5013-4014-7
	eBook:	978-1-5013-4013-0

Series: Literatures as World Literature

Typeset by Integra Software Services Pvt. Ltd.

To find out more about our authors and books visit www.bloomsbury.com and sign up for our newsletters.

CONTENTS

List of Figures ix
List of Tables xi
Notes on Contributors xii

Introduction 1

1   A King and Two Foxes: Middle Dutch Literature on European Crossroads   *Geert H.M. Claassens* 5

2   John of Ruusbroec (1293–1381), Celebrated Mystagogical Author of *The Spiritual Espousals*   *Kees Schepers* 19

3   *Die Rose* by Heinric of Brussels, the Brabantine Version of the Old French *Romance of the Rose*   *Anne Reynders* 35

4   Courtly Literature in the Low Countries and Germany: Jacob van Maerlant and Rudolf von Ems   *Bart Besamusca* 44

5   The Many Returns of Elckerlijc: Every Man's Mirror of Salvation   *Geert Warnar* 54

6   Joost van den Vondel (Cologne 1587 Amsterdam 1679) as Writer/Translator: Literacy in Transit   *Marco Prandoni* 68

7   Multatuli – His Work Through the World   *Jaap Grave* 82

8   How a Flemish Writer Turned Global: The Nineteenth-century Journey of Hendrik Conscience's Early Novellas   *Lieven D'hulst* 104

9 Louis Couperus in Translation *Ruud Veen* 122

10 Dutch Literature and the Global System of Indentured Labour, 1900–1940 *Saskia Pieterse* 146

11 Towards a History of Russian Translations of Dutch Literature: Herman Heijermans and His Play *The Good Hope* in Russia *Irina Michajlova and Sergei Tcherkasski* 161

12 Rescuing Something Fine: Huizinga's *Herfsttij der Middeleeuwen* (The Waning of the Middle Ages) as World Literature *Elke Brems and Orsolya Réthelyi* 183

13 'Glimpses of a poetic genius': Paul van Ostaijen (1896–1928) and World Literature *Geert Buelens* 206

14 Dutch Interbellum Poetry and/as World Literature *Theo D'haen* 218

15 Reinventing the Modernist Novel: Louis Paul Boon and Hugo Claus *Kris Humbeeck* 230

16 Small Amsterdam and the World Beyond: The Case of the Magazine *Barbarber* *Bart Vervaeck and Dirk de Geest* 248

17 Post-war Dutch Fiction *Hans Bertens* 260

18 Expansions Without Affect; Identities Without Globality: Global Novels in Dutch from an Agonistic Perspective *Hans Demeyer* 271

19 Orpheus in the Trenches: Modes of Translation in Stefan Hertmans' *War and Turpentine* *Frank Albers* 284

20 At the Edge of the World and Other Stories: Dutch-Australian Emigration Literature, c. 1945–1990 *Ton van Kalmthout* 295

Index 312

LIST OF FIGURES

11.1 Herman Heijermans 163

11.2 Michael Chekhov (Cobus), Lidya Deykun (Kniertje), Grigory Khmara (Geert), Vera Soloviova (Jo) and Leo Bulgakov (Barend) in *The Good Hope* by Heijermans. The First Studio of Moscow Art Theatre, 1913 169

11.3 Vera Soloviova (Jo), Ivan Lazarev (Bos), Lidya Deykun (Kniertje) and Grigory Khmara (Geert) in *The Good Hope* by Heijermans. The First Studio of Moscow Art Theatre, 1913 170

11.4 Anna Popova (Saart) and Michael Chekhov (Cobus) in *The Good Hope* by Heijermans. The First Studio of Moscow Art Theatre, 1913 171

11.5 Shipwreck scene from *The Good Hope* by Heijermans. St Petersburg Theatre Arts Academy, Tcherkasski's Studio, 2015 174

11.6 Lyubov Konstantinova (Jo), Maria Papashvili (Truus), Anna Khristich (Saart) and Dmitriy Frolov (Bos) in *The Good Hope* by Heijermans. St Petersburg Theatre Arts Academy, Tcherkasski's Studio, 2015 174

11.7 Lyubov Konstantinova (Jo) and Darya Lenda (Kniertje) in the final scene of *The Good Hope* by Heijermans. St Petersburg Theatre Arts Academy, Tcherkasski's Studio, 2015 175

11.8 *'The Good Hope' on Mokhovaya Street – 100 years later: Reconstruction of Actor Training at the First Studio of the Moscow Art Theatre* (St Petersburg: Baltic Seasons Publishing, 2016: 104 pages, 195 colour photos) 177

12.1 Translation Timeline for *Herfsttij der Middeleeuwen* 185

19.1 Diego Velázquez, *Rokeby Venus*, c. 1647–1651 291

LIST OF TABLES

9.1 Survey translations of books until 1973 124

9.2 Number of literary translations from the Dutch to other languages (1900–1949) 126

9.3 Publications in papers, magazines and anthologies in language areas with number of titles and passages until 1973 129

NOTES ON CONTRIBUTORS

Frank Albers studied philosophy at the University of Ghent and literary theory at the University of Oxford, under the supervision of Terry Eagleton. He holds a PhD in Comparative Literature from Harvard, where he worked with Sacvan Bercovitch. Albers teaches American literature and philosophy of culture at the University of Antwerp. His research focuses on nineteenth-century American romanticism. Albers is also a novelist and the author of several Dutch Shakespeare translations.

Hans Bertens is Distinguished Emeritus Professor of the Humanities at Utrecht University, the Netherlands, and Past President (2013–2016) of the International Comparative Literature Association. He has published mainly on post-war American literature, postmodernism and literary theory. His most recent books include *The Idea of the Postmodern: A History* (1995), *Contemporary American Crime Fiction* (2001; with Theo D'haen), *Literary Theory: The Basics* (3rd revised edition 2013) and *American Literature: A History* (2013; with Theo D'haen). He is currently working on a book on twenty-first-century literature.

Bart Besamusca is Professor of Middle Dutch Textual Culture from an International Perspective at Utrecht University and at the Utrecht Centre for Medieval Studies. He has published widely on medieval narrative literature, manuscripts and early printed editions. He manages the research tool Arthurian Fiction in Medieval Europe (www.arthurianfiction.org) and is currently supervising the research project 'The Multilingual Dynamics of the Literary Culture of Medieval Flanders, c. 1200–c. 1500'.

Elke Brems is Associate Professor at the Faculty of Arts KU Leuven. She is the head of the Research Unit of Translation Studies at the University of Leuven (KU Leuven). Her research interests include Dutch literature, reception studies and translation studies. She has published on contemporary Dutch poetry, literature and poetics during the interwar period, the relation between Dutch culture and other cultures, cultural identity and literature. She is a member of the Board of CETRA (Centre for Translation Studies www.arts.kuleuven.be/cetra). She is also a member of the editorial boards of *Zacht Lawijd* (www.zachtlawijd.be) and of *Poeziekrant* (www.poeziecentrum.be).

Notes on Contributors

Geert Buelens is Professor of Modern Dutch Literature at Utrecht University, Guest Professor of Dutch Literature at Stellenbosch University, South Africa, and Kluge Fellow at the Library of Congress (2008). His research deals primarily with the intersections between literature and society. He has published widely on the Flemish avant-garde writer Paul van Ostaijen and on twentieth-century avant-garde poetry, nationalist literature and poetry of the First World War (*Everything to Nothing: The Poetry of the Great War, Revolution and the Transformation of Europe*, 2015). He is editor of *Avant Garde Critical Studies*.

Geert H.M. Claassens studied Dutch at the University of Nijmegen and Old-French at the University of Utrecht. In 1993 he obtained his PhD with a dissertation on 'De Middelnederlandse kruisvaartromans'. From 1992 to 1995 he served as 'Lektor für Niederländisch' at the Rheinische Friedrich-Wilhelmsuniversität in Bonn. Since 1995 he has been teaching medieval Dutch literature at the University of Leuven (KU Leuven). He has published widely on medieval Dutch literature.

Dirk De Geest is Professor of Modern Dutch Literature at the University of Leuven (KU Leuven). He has published widely on modern Dutch literature, and on theory of literature, especially genre theory.

Hans Demeyer is Assistant Professor in Dutch and Comparative Literature at University College London and an editor of the literary journal *nY*. He wrote his PhD on corporality and affect in Dutch fiction of the 1960s, and is currently preparing, together with Sven Vitse, a book on twenty-first-century literature from the perspective of an affective crisis.

Theo D'haen is Emeritus Professor of English and Comparative Literature at the University of Leuven (KU Leuven), Emeritus Professor of English and American Literature at Leiden University, and Distinguished Visiting Professor at Shanghai Jiao Tong University and Changjiang (Yantgtze River) Professor at the University of Sichuan. His most recent English-language publications comprise: *American Literature: A History* (2014; with Hans Bertens), *Crime Fiction as World Literature* (2017; co-edited with Louise Nilsson and David Damrosch), *Cosmopolitanism and the Postnational: Literature and the New Europe* (2015; co-edited with César Domínguez) and *Major versus Minor? Languages and Literatures in a Globalized World* (2015; co-edited with Iannis Goerlandt and Roger Sell).

Lieven D'hulst is Professor of French and Francophone Literature and of Translation Studies at the University of Leuven (KU Leuven), where he heads the Research Group 'Translation and Intercultural Transfer'. He is a member of the editorial board of *Target. International Journal of Translation Studies*, and the co-director of the series 'Traductologie' at Artois Presses Université. His most recent publications include *Histoire des traductions en langue française. 19e siècle* (2012; co-edited with Yves Chevrel and Christine Lombez), *Essais d'histoire de la traduction. Avatars de Janus*

(2014) and *Politics, Policy and Power in Translation History* (2016; co-edited with Carol O'Sullivan and Michael Schreiber).

Jaap Grave teaches at the University of Münster in Germany. He obtained degrees in the Netherlands and Germany, and a PhD at the University of Ghent, with 'Zulk vertalen is een werk van liefde. Bemiddelaars van Nederlandstalige literatuur in Duitsland 1890–1914'. He has taught at universities in Berlin, Jakarta, Leipzig, Münster, Nagasaki and Padua. He has published on modern literature, the history of science and cultural transfer. From 2002 to 2012 he served as editor of the journal *Over Multatuli*, and he co-edited *150 Jahre Max Havelaar. Multatulis Roman in neuer Perspektive* (*150 Years Max Havelaar. Multatuli's Novel from New Perspectives*, 2012).

Kris Humbeeck is Professor of Modern Dutch Literature at the University of Antwerp, co-director of the Instituut voor de Studie van de Letterkunde in de Nederlanden (ISLN) and a regular member of the Koninklijke Academie voor Nederlandse Taal- en Letterkunde (KANTL). He is editor-in-chief of the *Verzameld werk van L.P. Boon* (2005–), and has published widely on Dutch literature of the nineteenth and twentieth centuries, including on Boon, Nicolaas Beets, Hendrik Conscience, Conrad Busken Huet, de Tachtigers, Gerard Walschap and Hugo Claus.

Ton van Kalmthout is a senior researcher in literary history at the Huygens Institute for the History of the Netherlands, Amsterdam. His research is concerned with various forms of cultural transmission in national and international contexts, including the import of foreign literature in the Netherlands and the worldwide circulation of Dutch literature. His most recent publications include *Beatrijs de wereld in. Vertalingen en bewerkingen van het Middelnederlandse verhaal* (*Beatrijs into the World. Translations and adaptations of the Middle-Dutch story*, 2013; co-edited with Orsolya Réthelyi and Remco Sleiderink) and *Doing Double Dutch. The International Circulation of Literature from the Low Countries* (2017; co-edited with Orsolya Réthelyi and Elke Brems).

Irina Michajlova is a professor of Dutch language, literature and culture at the Department of Scandinavian and Dutch Philology, Faculty of Philology, St Petersburg State University. Her translations from Dutch include prose (fiction and non-fiction), children's books and poetry. In 2005, she was awarded the NLPVF Vertalersprijs. In 2011, she received the RusPrix Award (an initiative conducted under the patronage of the Embassy of the Russian Federation, the Netherlands) for her personal contribution to the cultural exchange between Russia and the Netherlands. In 2015, she was elected a foreign honorary member of the Royal Academy of Dutch Language and Literature, Ghent.

Saskia Pieterse is an assistant professor and postdoctoral researcher at Utrecht University, currently working in the fields of postcolonial studies, economic criticism and imagology. She is completing a postdoctoral project on 'Domesticated Capitalism', in which she analyses the historical formation of the 'domestic' Dutch national self-image in the context of the country's colonial and capitalist enterprises. She studied at Utrecht University and obtained her PhD at the University of Amsterdam in 2008, with her thesis titled 'De buik van de lezer. Over spreken en schrijven bij Multatuli' ('In the Belly of the Reader: On Speaking and Writing in the Work of Multatuli').

Marco Prandoni teaches at the University of Bologna. His research focuses on interconfessional and intercultural dynamics in Early Modern drama and contemporary literature. He served as an editor of *Harba lori fa!* (2012). His recent publications include *Backlighting Plots. The 'Protestant' Patriarch Cyril Loukaris* (2015), *Se fossi in te andrei in Olanda. Letteratura della migrazione nei Paesi Bassi contemporanei* (2015), *Il segno elusivo. La traduzione italiana della poesia in neerlandese (e afrikaans) del XX e XXI secolo* (2016; with Herman van der Heide) and *De glans van Vondels Lucifer. Culturele herinnering, vertalingen, opvoeringen* (2018; with Marijke Meijer Drees and Rita Schlusemann).

Anne Reynders is Associate Professor at the Faculty of Arts of the University of Leuven (KU Leuven), Campus Antwerp. She lectures in Dutch Literature and Translation (and Interpreting) Studies. Her research focuses on descriptive translation studies, literary translation and especially on Middle Dutch translations of Old French source texts.

Orsolya Réthelyi is Associate Professor of Literature at the Department of Dutch Studies of the Eötvös Loránd University of Budapest (ELTE). She is also affiliated as a researcher in literary history to the Huygens Institute for the History of the Netherlands. Together with Ton van Kalmthout and Elke Brems she coordinated the international research project CODL – an International Network Studying the Circulation of Dutch Literature. The results of the project, edited by the three coordinators, were published in 2017 in the volume *Doing Double Dutch. The International Circulation of Literature from the Low Countries*. At present, she coordinates the NWO-FWO project Eastbound.

Kees Schepers is Associate Professor at the Ruusbroec Institute of the University of Antwerp. He has published critical editions of several late-medieval mystical and spiritual texts, both in the vernacular and in Latin. Most notable are the Latin translation of John of Ruusbroec's *Spiritual Espousals*, and the fifteenth-century Middle Dutch miscellany known as the Wiesbaden codex. His current research interests are sixteenth-century mystical culture in the Low Countries and the neighbouring Rhineland, and sixteenth-century intellectual culture in the monasteries of the Bois de Soignes near Brussels. He is preparing a critical edition, with English translation, of the Arnhem Mystical Sermons.

Sergei Tcherkasski is a theatre director, theatre researcher (PhD, DSc) and Head of the Acting Studio at the Russian State Institute of Performing Arts/Saint Petersburg Theatre Arts Academy, Russia (est. 1779). He has directed more than three dozen productions, two of them – *Dangerous Liaisons* and *Great Catherine* – ran in St Petersburg for twelve and sixteen years respectively. He is an internationally known acting teacher and expert on actor training and the Stanislavsky System. He has led workshops for actors and directors in forty major theatre schools in seventeen countries. Tcherkasski's publications include *Stanislavsky and Yoga* (2016); *Sulimov's School of Directing* (2013, in English 2016) and the award-winning *Acting: Stanislavsky – Boleslavsky – Strasberg. History, Theory and Practice* (2016).

Ruud Veen started his career with L.J. Veen Publishers, a publishing company founded by his grandfather in 1887. Later, he specialized in educational and science publishing, and worked for several publishers. In the 1980s he co-founded, and later owned, LEMMA Publishing. Upon retirement he started researching the foreign editions of the works of Couperus. He completed a PhD on the German publishers of Couperus in 2015 and on the reception of translations of Couperus in Germany. Now he researches translations and editions of Couperus in language areas other than German.

Bart Vervaeck is a professor of Dutch literature and narrative theory at the University of Leuven. He has published widely on postwar Dutch fiction and on narratology.

Geert Warnar is a senior lecturer at the Leiden University Centre for the Arts in Society, where he teaches medieval Dutch Literature. His publications cover forms of interaction between Dutch textual culture and religious and intellectual traditions of the Middle Ages.

Introduction

In most surveys of world literature, Dutch-language literature, that is to say literature written in the territory that comprises the present-day Netherlands and the northern part of Belgium known as Flanders, counts for little. Never has a Dutch-language author won the Nobel Prize. In Comparative Literature studies Dutch-language literature hardly ever enters into the equation. One could say, then, that Dutch-language literature, either considered as a whole or in its constituent parts of Dutch literature, the literature of the Netherlands, and Flemish literature, definitely is a 'minor' or 'small' literature. Yet, in the European context Dutch is not really a 'small' language when it comes to number of speakers. With some 22 million speakers in the Netherlands and Flanders, Dutch is outnumbered only by Russian, German, French, Italian, English, Polish and Spanish. All the Scandinavian languages and most Slavic languages are (often considerably) smaller in numbers of speakers. Even Portuguese is smaller within Europe, although of course not when one includes its former colonies.

Nor can it legitimately be said that 'Netherlandic' culture is 'minor' in a European context. In painting, we have the so-called Flemish Primitives, now usually referred to as Early Netherlandic Painting, with the Brothers Van Eyck, Rogier van der Weyden and Hans Memling, and from later ages Hieronymus Bosch, the Breughels, Rubens, Van Dyck, Jordaens, Rembrandt, Vermeer, and later still Van Gogh, Ensor, Mondriaan and Appel. Similar achievements can be signalled in music, with Flemish polyphony, and in book printing and production, with the great printing house of Plantin (Plantin himself being originally French but having established himself in Antwerp, the greatest European commercial metropolis of the fifteenth and sixteenth centuries). If in all these fields, then, as also in philosophy and science, with the likes of Erasmus, Mercator, Dodenius, Justus Lipsius, Spinoza, Van Leeuwenhoeck, Boerhaave and others, Netherlandic culture has had at least some impact on the wider world, the same cannot be said of its literature.

Next to the relative European weight of Dutch in terms of numbers of speakers, the very central position of the Dutch-speaking regions in the heart of Europe, located right in between what are – or at least over the more recent centuries have been – the three major cultures and literatures of Europe, French, English and German, would lead one to assume that its literature would at least find some echo in these major cultures. In fact, little of the kind has ever happened, perhaps with the very recent exception of the success of some Dutch-language authors in German translation, and much less so in English and French translation. To be sure, writings in Dutch, especially sermons, philosophical literature and to a certain extent also the work of Holland's major seventeenth-century playwright Joost van den Vondel, made it across the North Sea to Britain, mostly because of Protestant affinities, and also because throughout much of the sixteenth and seventeenth centuries Dutch, because of the importance of Flemish and especially Holland and Zeeland shipping, functioned as a kind of lingua franca around the North Sea. Yet this very centrality in geographical and even cultural terms never translated into anything equivalent in the realm of literature.

The Danish critic Georg Brandes, in his brief essay on world literature from around the turn of the twentieth century, ranged Dutch-language authors, along with their colleagues from a number of other smaller European nations or ethnicities, among those least likely to ever achieve fame with works written in their native language, as opposed to their counterparts having the good fortune to be native users of French, German, English or Russian. Yet if we look more closely, Scandinavian literature, and Slavic literatures, on the contrary, do feature on the world literature map – suffice it to think of Andersen, Ibsen, Strindberg and Hamsun, or Miłosz, Szymborska, Kundera, Andrić, Kiš and Pavič. Perhaps part of the explanation resides in the fact that although Dutch literature geographically sits in the heart of Europe, its very enclosure by the three major literatures mentioned earlier also means that it has no 'natural' allies in the sense of a larger regional constellation of minor literatures such as, precisely, the Scandinavian, Central- and East-European, Slavic, Balkan or Baltic ones. Even otherwise linguistic outliers such as Finnish or Hungarian literature can still count on regional 'backing'. Dutch-language literature even looked at from this perspective stands out because of its absence.

And yet … and yet … Dutch-language literature DOES have significant links with, and to, other European literatures, and to the literature of the world beyond Europe. It does so by what over the centuries it has absorbed from other literatures and how it reflects wider developments in European literature, how it refracts major literary traditions and itself contributes to them. Sometimes these contributions are barely acknowledged or even ignored. An example in case is the Middle-Dutch *Elckerlyc*. Malgorzata Dowlaszewicz, in her article 'Hoe Nederlands is Elckerlyc? De verwijzingen naar de Nederlandse oorsprong in de Poolse receptie van de Middelnederlandse tekst' (How Dutch is Elckerlyc? The references to its Dutch origin in the Polish reception of the Middle-Dutch text), published in *Werkwinkel* 11 (2), 2016, pp. 91–107, shows that the two Polish 'translations' (1921 and 1933) were made from the sixteenth-century English *Everyman* or from Hugo von Hofmannsthal's 1911 *Jederman*, a German adaptation of the English *Everyman*. Referring to earlier research, Dowlaszewicz stresses that Latin translations of the Dutch original were known in Poland during the sixteenth century, but without any knowledge of the Dutch morality play itself. In the twentieth-century Polish translations/adaptations the German and English versions of Everyman are seen as the 'originals', without any mention or apparent knowledge of a Dutch origin.

The present volume looks at these links: how Dutch-language literature served as an important originator and mediator in a European context in the Middle Ages and Early Modernity, how it reflected on colonialism before this happened in most other European cultures, how it counted some 'world authors' in the time of Brandes, how one of its most celebrated historians decisively influenced the world's image of the Middle Ages, how one of its most popular turn-of-the-twentieth-century dramatists became a favourite in Communist Europe, and how its twentieth-century poets and novelists related to other European, American and Asian literatures. Dutch-language literature truly participates in 'world literature'.

1

A King and Two Foxes: Middle Dutch Literature on European Crossroads

Geert H.M. Claassens

Introduction

King Arthur is a constant feature in medieval European literature: for some three-and-a-half centuries the legendary king forms the centre of an ever-expanding world of stories. It all began in the middle of the twelfth century, with a Latin text by Geoffrey of Monmouth, the *Historia regum Brittanniae* (*c.* 1135). This is the oldest text to contain a more or less complete description of the life of Arthur as part of a history of the kings of Britain written by Geoffrey for the Anglo-Norman dynasty then ruling the British Isles. The book initiated a literary fashion that left traces in many European languages – in Italy it even led to a medieval Arthur romance in Hebrew.[1] Notwithstanding its popularity with the aristocracy, the world of Arthur at the same time came in for criticism. In the thirteenth century Geoffrey's work was already branded as untrue and a lie, and the historicity – or what somewhat anachronistically we might label the 'fictionality' – of the Arthurian epics remained a bone of contention.

In this contribution two works that may stand as testimony to the Arthurian vogue also in Middle Dutch literature are dealt with in some detail: the *Spieghel historiael* (A Mirror of History, *c.* 1283–1288) by the Flemish poet Jacob van Maerlant (see also the contribution on Van Maerlant elsewhere in this volume) and the Flemish *Roman van Walewein* (Romance of Walewein, *c.* 1230–1260) by Penninc and Pieter Vostaert.

'Fictionality' is an important factor in both texts. As the *Roman van Walewein* features the talking fox Roges we at the same time bridge the gap to the animal epic and *Van den vos Reynaerde* (Of Reynaert the Fox, 1230–1260) and its later continuation *Reinaerts historie* (History of Reynaert, c. 1430–1460). These two texts also stand in a widely disseminated European tradition with Latin roots – the *Ecbasis captivi* (c. 1100) and the *Ysengrimus* (1140) – and a rich Old French stem, the *Roman de Renart*, the oldest branch of which dates from around 1174. The fact that most characters in these epics are animals acutely raises the problem of fictionality: as talking animals do not exist, any story in which they occur is by definition untrue.

A tour of these four texts not only opens a window on fictionality as a highly controversial issue in medieval literature but also proves that medieval Low Countries literature is open to influences from other literatures, assimilates them and adds original works to existing traditions, which then are exported into other literatures.

Medieval literature was decidedly transnational: plots, motifs, themes and characters effortlessly moved from one language area to another, though we also have to note the strong cultural dominance of France.[2] In the Middle Ages literature does not move across borders via more or less faithful translations but rather via absorption and adaptation or what is commonly referred to as acculturation. In this process the medieval Low Countries played a central role because here language borders did not coincide with political borders. The County of Flanders is Dutch-speaking in principle, but as it is (for the most part) a fief of the French crown, the Flemish high nobility will most probably have used French as its literary and cultural language, different from the rest of the population. The (large) Duchy of Brabant was part of the (German) Holy Roman Empire but also contained a French-speaking southern region, part of the so-called *Reichsromania*. Until the thirteenth century Brabantine high nobility also used French as their main language of culture, but under the reign of Duke Jan I (r.1267–1294) there was a decided turn toward Middle Dutch. The important thing is that the cultural make-up of the southern part of the then Low Countries – roughly coinciding with the northern part of present-day Belgium and part of the southern regions of the present-day Netherlands – greatly facilitated literary exchange and osmosis.

The true king Arthur (Jacob van Maerlant's *Spieghel historiael*)

For Jacob van Maerlant, King Arthur himself was not a 'historical problem'; so much is clear from his *magnum opus*, the *Spieghel historiael* (A Mirror of History). Maerlant started upon this very ambitious chronicle of world history in rhyming couplets around 1283. His main source was the *Speculum historiale* of the French Dominican Vincent of Beauvais (d.1264). Whenever he thought necessary, however, he added material from other sources.[3] Maerlant had planned his chronicle in four parts or *partien*, subdivided into books and chapters, but was unable to complete his work as such. He did complete the first and third parts and the first three books of the fourth part, bringing the work up to 1113. Why he skipped the second part remains a mystery, but his giving up on the fourth part most probably was due to his advanced age, although here again considerable doubt remains.[4] What we do know for certain is that Maerlant wrote his chronicle for the high aristocracy of the County of Holland – he dedicated his work to Count Floris V of Holland (d.1296), son and successor to Count Willem II (d.1256). As its title indicates, the chronicle was meant as a mirror, in this case a mirror of history from which a ruler might glean the do's and don'ts of a good sovereign.

Given all this it is no coincidence that Maerlant devotes a good number of verses to King Arthur: a little over five chapters in book 5 of part 3, altogether 574 lines, and some shorter references to Arthur's rule in other parts.[5] He opens the main passage on Arthur as follows: 'Thus Arthur was lord of the realm and ruled in great honour for more than seventy five years. His equal never appeared in later years nor was found in earlier times amongst the Christian kings.'[6] Maerlant does not cover all of Arthur's rule. He concentrates on Arthur's war with the Romans under the Emperor Lucius, who claims the tribute the Britons are due to Rome since Julius Caesar. Needless to say, the Romans are defeated, but as a man of honour Arthur makes sure that the dead Emperor Lucius receives a fitting burial. Maerlant ends his history of King Arthur upon the following rather surprising note: 'Of Perchevael, of Galyot, of Egravein and Lanceloet, or of King Ban of Benowijc and Behoerd, as well, and of many other fabricated names I found no mention, however brief, in Latin: therefore it seemed a wasted effort for me to reveal anything about them here, for I hold everything in French to be but fabrications.'[7]

What Maerlant in fact is saying here is that he is quite ready to look upon King Arthur as a true historical figure, but that he considers many of the stories linked to him, and which have the knights here mentioned as protagonists, humbug. Determining is the source: because Maerlant is familiar with many of these stories from French sources only he considers them untrue; if supported by Latin sources he considers them true history. Maerlant here assumes the role of a historian practicing sources criticism, using language as his main criterion: a Latin text he finds more trustworthy than a French one. In fact, his oeuvre contains more passages that lead to the same conclusion.[8] In this case, however, he is hoist with his own petard: for his history of Arthur Maerlant has traded in his main source, Vincent of Beauvais's *Speculum historiale*, for … Geoffrey of Monmouth's *Historia regum Brittanniae*.[9] What Maerlant failed to consider is that in Latin one may lie as competently as in French or any other vernacular.

Lancelot is not mentioned in Geoffrey's *Historia* and consequently does not make it into Maerlant's history of Arthur. Another knight does, though: Walwanius, whom Maerlant – and this goes for Middle Dutch Arthur epic in general[10] – calls 'Walewein'. In the wider European tradition Walewein is one of the most important, if not uncontroversial, Knights of the Round Table, although he usually goes by another name: in Old French it is 'Gauvain', in Middle English 'Gawain' and in German 'Gawan'. The fact that 'Walewein' is the name most commonly used in Middle Dutch may well point to a very early connection between the County of Flanders and Anglo-Norman England. Indeed, the resemblance to Geoffrey's 'Walwanius' is at the least remarkable and Walewein's presence in Geoffrey's *Historia* is sufficient reason for Maerlant to treat him as a historical figure: 'About Lancelot I cannot write, nor about Perchevael or Eggravein, but the good Walewein I found included in his history [Geoffrey's *Historia*].'[11]

The *Roman van Walewein*

Walewein features in all Middle Dutch Arthur Romances.[12] Many of these are translations/adaptations of Old French texts, but there are also a number of original Middle Dutch texts, such as the *Moriaen*, the *Roman van den riddere metter mouwen* (The Romance of the Knight with the Sleeves) and the *Walewein ende Keye* (Walewein and Kay). Of these original Middle Dutch Arthurian romances the *Roman van Walewein* (11,198 lines) is the most important.[13] From the prologue we know that the romance was begun by the otherwise unknown poet Penninc and the epilogue tells us that it was completed by the further equally unknown Pieter Vostaert – like Penninc originating from Flanders. We do not know why Penninc stopped around line 7,840 and left the remaining 3,300 lines to Vostaert. We also have no definite idea what the intended audience was – most probably though the lower Flemish nobility. Vostaert claims to have completed the romance 'as best as he could according to the text that he found which Penninc left behind' (vss. 11,178–11,179), but his narrative style is very different from that of Penninc. Penninc is more interested in the courtly rituals enacted at the courts Walewein visits while Vostaert focuses on Walewein's martial encounters.

The structure of the romance largely corresponds with that of the fairy tale type Aarne-Thompson number 550, the best-known representative is probably *Der goldene Vogel*, number 57 in the Grimm corpus. Like the fairy tale, the *Roman van Walewein* consists of a series of interlocking tasks/quests.

When a richly decorated flying chessboard briefly appears at the court of King Arthur, the latter would like to gain possession of it. In first instance none of the knights is interested, but when Arthur promises his crown to who delivers him the chess board Walewein rises to the challenge. Walewein's pursuit of the chessboard first takes him to a mountain of light where he is attacked by a dragon that he only defeats by using great effort. Next stop is the court of King Wonder, who is the owner of the chess board and who is willing to grant it to Walewein in exchange for the magical, because invincible, Sword-with-two-Rings, the possession of King Amoraen of Castle Ravensteen. While traveling to Ravensteen Walewein succours a squire who has just been robbed. He even lends him his horse Gringolet. When the same young man, who in the meantime has been knighted by King Arthur, fights the murderer of his brother in front of the castle of King Amadijs, and is beset by an entire army, Walewein again comes to his rescue. Walewein then seeks out Amoraen, who is willing to give up the Sword-with-two-Rings if Walewein will travel to far-away Endi, to secure him the wonderful beauty Ysabele as his bride. Walewein is allowed to take along the magical sword as the latter has chosen Walewein as its 'ideal host'. The trip to Endi brings many more adventures, but the greatest adventure of all is Endi itself. The city is guarded by a burning river that can only be crossed by a bridge of swords. Finally, it is the speaking fox Roges – in fact an enchanted prince – who leads Walewein to the far side of the river via a tunnel. The castle Endi itself is ringed by twelve walls, each of them manned by eighty knights. Walewein fights his way in, but is finally beaten by King Assentijn, Ysabele's father. When the princess sets eyes on Walewein she is immediately smitten – the *coup de foudre* in fact is mutual. She asks her father to be allowed to personally vent her ire on Walewein but this is just a ruse to be alone with him and give in to her burning desire for him. When Assentijn finds out he intends to punish them both. However, the lovers manage to escape and together with Roges they travel to the court of King Amoraen. He turns out to have died in the meantime, which releases Walewein from his obligation to give up his beloved Ysabele for the Sword-with-two-Rings. From Ravensteen they set out for the court of King Wonder. On their way they are beset by an unknown knight, whom Walewein defeats. Eventually he will turn out to be Estor, Lancelot's brother. They also find the squire to whom Walewein lent his horse Gringolet besieged in his castle. It is only when Walewein once more has intervened decisively on behalf of the squire that he, Ysabele and Roges can continue to King Wonder. There, the gathering of the king, his son Alidrizonder, Ysabele and Walewein breaks the spell that was cast upon Roges, and the fox changes into a prince again. The Sword-with-two-Rings is exchanged for the chessboard, which Walewein can now finally take to Arthur. For the festive finale to the story, King Assentijn appears at the court, as do King Roges of Ysike, the father of Roges and Estor. Whether Walewein will after all marry Ysabele and wear the crown of Arthur is left open.

Obviously, this summary cannot do justice to what is a long and intricate romance, but what should be clear is that the epithet 'original' only applies in the sense of this particular text not being a translation or adaptation of any other such Arthurian romance in another language. Several of the motifs used in the *Walewein* are known from other Arthurian romances, such as the bridge of swords spanning the burning river, which also occurs in the *Lancelot* of Chrétien de Troye. There are also links to the *Lancelot en prose* and to Gerbert de Montreuil's continuation of Chrétien's *Perceval*. The fox Roges in his role as animal helpmate to the hero has roots in the fairy tale tradition. Yet, even though the *Roman van Walewein* is grafted onto Old French Arthurian materials, it also shows traits very much its own. The romance appears meant to enhance the status and reputation of Walewein as an Arthurian hero and as an example of chivalry in a period in which Gauvain's repute in the Old French Arthurian tradition was far from unblemished.[14] In fact, a tendency to rehabilitate Walewein in comparison to the Old French tradition is a *leitmotiv* in the Middle Dutch Arthurian epics.[15] It is tempting to link this tendency to the influence of the 'historiographer' Geoffrey of Monmouth, precisely because with him too Walwanius is a knight without blemish. With such suppositions, however, we move into the realm of speculation.

The prominent role of the fox Roges – an enchanted young man – raises the question whether the medieval audience may have regarded the romance as an amusing and perhaps instructive fiction or whether after all it was ready to accept it as 'true history'. And mind, Roges is not the only miraculous phenomenon: normally speaking, chessboards do not sail through the air of their own accord, nor do swords choose their owners themselves. This touches upon the thorny question of the position of fiction, and its acceptability or not, in medieval *Schrifttum*, an issue I cannot go into in detail in the space here available.[16] Still, the *Roman van Walewein* contains a passage we perhaps may interpret as a relevant pointer. In the prologue the poet Penninc appeals to the gods to help him complete the work upon which he is engaging: 'May the Lord, who for our sake was born, and who made bread from stone, grant me as much wisdom as this book demands so that I may acquit myself of the task, from start to finish, without mishap!'[17] The God Penninc here invokes to shield him from making errors in his story is defined by a miracle he in fact never performed. In all probability Penninc thus wanted to warn his audience: 'Watch out, in this story that strives to be true (plausible), you may expect to encounter strange things.' It would be extremely interesting to know whether Maerlant was familiar with the *Roman van Walewein* – unfortunately we have no means of ascertaining this – and whether the miraculous phenomena in the story would have carried greater weight in his evaluation of the romance than Walewein's being vouched for as a historical figure via Geoffrey's *Historia regum Brittanniae*.

Real foxes, real problems: *Van den vos Reynaerde* and *Reinaerts historie*

The role of Roges in the *Roman van Walewein* refers to the miraculous, the magical. In animal epics, however, we encounter 'real' animals that speak and reason. Though this leads us into the territory of the counter-natural, this has never hampered the popularity of the stories about Reynard the Fox, not in the Middle Ages nor in later times.

The medieval Low Countries had a very rich Reinaert tradition. There is, for instance, the *Ysengrimus* of the twelfth-century magister Nivardus of Ghent. This animal epic has links to Ghent not only via its author but also through its content – the story is set at least partially in the abbey of Blandinium in Ghent – but it is in Latin. The same thing goes for the late thirteenth-century *Reynardus vulpes* (before 1279), produced in Flanders by Balduinus Iuvenis, but this goes back directly upon the vernacular Reinaert tradition as it is a translation/adaptation of *Van den vos Reynaerde*.[18]

The magnificently inventive *Van den vos Reynaerde* is the work of Willem die Madocke maecte.[19] Nothing more is known about him, notwithstanding this self-confident auto-presentation in the first line of his poem, which suggests that in his own time he must have been quite well known. Most likely, we have to situate Willem in the County of Flanders: the language of his poem points that way as well as the many Flemish toponyms (Ghent, Belsele, Hyfte, Elmare, etc.). His easy familiarity with the topography of the Ghent region makes it very probable that this is where he originated from. This probably also says something about his intended audience: if Willem draws upon such specific toponyms does this not mean that he also assumes they are familiar to his audience? Still, its specifically Flemish background has never prevented *Van den vos Reynaerde*'s widespread dissemination.

We can gauge the period in which Willem wrote his work in several ways, but with a clear *terminus post quem* of 1179, the date of writing of Willem's most important source – the first branch of the Old French *Roman de Renart*, with the title Le Plaid ('the trial') or Le Jugement ('the judgment') – and an equally clear *terminus ante quem* of 1279, the latest year in which the earlier-mentioned *Reynardus vulpes* may have been written. Attempts have been made to arrive at more precise dates, and there now seems to be a consensus to date the work *c.* 1250–1260, mostly on the grounds of Willem's use of an Old French compilation of the *Roman de Renart* (after 1205), his specific versification and the fact that Jacob van Maerlant in his *Scolastica* from 1271 is thought to refer to Willem's text.[20]

When compared to the *Roman van Walewein*, *Van den vos Reynaerde* has been very well preserved, with two complete manuscripts and fragments from three more manuscripts. If we add the two manuscripts of *Reinaerts historie* (see below), we arrive at seven manuscripts, originating from almost all corners of the then Dutch-language area: Flanders, the County of Holland, Limburg and the easterly Middle Dutch region around Guelder-Cleves (now part of Germany).[21]

The plot of the story is very straightforward. When King Nobel, the lion, is holding court, many animals come forward to complain about Reinaert, who himself is absent. The complaints are so serious (theft, rape, violence) that the king decides to summon Reinaert to court. He chooses Bruun, the bear, as his emissary. However, the bear fails in his mission. Reinaert astutely exploits Bruun's craving for honey to trap him and deliver him to the villagers who severely beat him. Bruun barely escapes with his life. The second emissary, Tybeert the tomcat, fares little better. He is undone by his desire for fat mice. Grimbeert the badger does succeed in bringing Reinaert before Nobel. He avoids being trapped by Reinaert because he is a relative of the fox, his nephew. On their way to court Reinaert confesses a whole series of misdeeds to his nephew, but his obvious lust for a bunch of chickens reveals that his repentance is nothing but fake.

At court, Reinaert is tried and condemned to death. Facing the gallows, Reinaert now wants to make a full confession, which he is allowed to do. But just as he earlier tricked the bear and the cat, he now does the same with King Nobel and his wife. He confesses that he knows about a conspiracy against the life of the king and names not only Ysingrijn the wolf, Bruun the bear and Tybeert the tomcat, but also his own (deceased) father and his nephew Grimbeert the badger as conspirators. He adds that he has succeeded in stealing the treasure the conspirators meant to use to finance their *coup*, and that he has hidden it at Kriekeputte well, close to Hulsterloe. None of the accused are present at court to gainsay Reinaert. The king fears for his life, but he also covets the treasure, and at the same time hesitates about whether to believe Reinaert. In a scene reminiscent of the Fall of Man (Genesis 3), the queen leads her husband to believe Reinaert's story, citing Reinaert's accusing his own father and nephew as co-culprits as proof of his sincerity. Reinaert is pardoned in exchange for the treasure. When the king pressures him to guide him to the treasure, Reinaert promises to give him precise directions but adds that he himself cannot come along as he has been excommunicated by the pope and now urgently has to go on a pilgrimage. Moreover, the king should not involve himself with an excommunicated subject.

When the wolf and the bear return (they had gone to raise the gallows for Reinaert) they are taken prisoners. From the skin of the bear a piece is cut to make a pilgrim's purse, and Ysingrijn and his wife have to furnish the skin to make Reinaert a pair of shoes – a cruel punishment Reinaert wreaks upon his enemies. When Reinaert wants to leave the court Belijn the ram and Cuwaert the hare are assigned to him as companions. At his lair Malpertuus Reinaert lures the hare inside, where he is immediately killed and devoured. Belijn impatiently waits outside, but eventually he is given Reinaert's pilgrim's purse, with what he believes is an important letter for King Nobel, but which in fact contains the head of the unfortunate hare. Reinaert informs Belijn that he may present himself to the king as co-author of the supposed letter, which puffs up the vanity of the illiterate ram. When the king opens the pilgrim's purse Reinaert's trickery is beyond doubt. The king realizes that because of his own naivety and greed he has estranged his two most powerful barons, the wolf and the bear. The leopard Fyrapeel then brings about a reconciliation by which the wolf and the bear, in exchange for their loyalty, are given permission to hunt and kill all members and descendants of the families of Reinaert and Belijn. Thus, peace seems restored.

It is no more than just that *Van den vos Reynaerde* is part of the world literary canon. It is a perfectly composed text, with supple versification, irony, sarcasm and humour effortlessly upholding a story that runs along smoothly according to a perfect plot. The fox outsmarts all other animals by slyly manipulating them: catering to their deepest cravings he succeeds in trapping them again and again. Bruun falls victim to his unbridled desire for honey; with Tybeert the mice do the trick, and the royal pair cannot resist the lure of big money. Reinaert exposes how at court what matters is keeping up appearances: the courtiers are not who they pretend to be, and royal justice is but a pretence too. But Reinaert ruins his enemies with such grotesque humour that we risk forgetting that the fox is the greatest scoundrel of them all. His unmasking of the moral decadence of the court relegates his own completely immoral behaviour to the background. And whoever reading the tale or listening to it identifies with the sly fox (and who doesn't?) afterwards really should pose themselves the question whether the purpose always does justify the means. Whoever wants to be Reinaert will have to take this decadence in their stride.

In essence, *Van den vos Reynaerde* is the story of a trial, but a trial that completely misfires because of the moral failure of the characters involved and of the failure of justice itself. However, the text also forms a sharp medieval commentary on the use – and especially the abuse – of language: Reinaert does not make use of physical violence to defeat his adversaries but words. Language, the prime marker of (human) reason (ratio), here very effectively serves the pursuit of (animal) desires and lust and does not serve as a God-given instrument to enable its users to jointly pursue the *beata visio pacis* and to adapt their attitude to life accordingly. Obviously, it is not the animals that are held accountable for their moral merits – for the divine order of creation it is completely acceptable that animals live according to their instincts and drives. This corresponds to their place in that divine order. Rather, if a story features talking animals, these of necessity function as stand-ins for human beings (for whom language and reason are the distinctive qualities) and it is the latter that are being addressed.

A story in which animals can talk (but at the same time continue to also possess animal qualities) is problematic in the Middle Ages: talking animals do not exist in reality and thus a story with talking animals can only be defined as fiction. For us fiction is completely acceptable, but for medieval man fiction is equivalent to lying. That is a very serious sin. In the oldest Dutch-language poetics, 'Hoe dichters dichten sullen ende wat si hantieren sullen' ('How poets should write and what they should practise'), the fifteenth chapter of the third book of *Der leken spiegel* (A mirror for laymen, 1325–1330) of the Brabantine poet Jan van Boendale (*c.* d.1351), we find a passage that leaves no doubt of how objectionable lying is: 'Holy Scripture states clearly that lies lead the soul to damnation and that we shall have to answer for all idle talk when the just Judge will pass judgement on this entire world.'[22] We might tend to understand this as a general moral maxim rooted in religion if it weren't for Boendale saying this in a poetical context. He lashes out against anyone lying in writing and in this respect refers to hagiographers and historiographers: 'Should it be found out that his [a poet's] writings are not true he will, quite justly, never again be believed; he has forfeited the right to write and lost the title of writer, and will consequently forever stand in ill repute.'[23] Still, Boendale is also familiar with animal epics and raises the matter of the fables of Aesop and Avianus, and of the stories of Reinaert. He unhesitatingly admits their untrue (non-referential) character by pointing out that animals cannot talk, and as animals cannot talk in reality these stories can only be labelled untrue. But for Boendale this does not yet mean that they are complete lies: on the level of their link to extra-literary reality they are untrue (because impossible), but on the level of ethics they are true, because they contribute to an understanding of moral matters. He puts it as follows: 'These [stories about Reynaert] have been composed entirely for the purpose of instruction and wisdom, as I told you before, for a meaning that is difficult to grasp can be elucidated by instructive examples; after all, God himself couched the sermons that he preached in parables.'[24] Reinaert for certain is not a repentant sinner, but in Boendale's poetics his literary hide nevertheless is saved by the Jesus of the Gospels precisely because although he does not exist in reality he offers us a saving insight.

From a literary-theoretical perspective the medieval fox stories may have been controversial but this in no way has hampered their triumphant march through European literature. This certainly holds for *Van den vos Reynaerde* and its direct successor *Reinaerts historie*. The latter was written sometime between 1430 and 1460 by an otherwise unknown poet who in the first line of his work announces himself as *Willam*.[25] It is possible that he in fact was called 'Willem,' but his mention of that name could also follow from his incorporating almost the entire text of *Van den vos Reynaerde* in his own work. To the latter he added some 4,300 more lines, again focusing on conflicts between Reinaert and the other animals. Another (plausible) reference in the text points to Flanders as the place of origin of *Reinaerts historie*: at the end of this text we again find an acrostichon, which in this case reads *dismwde*, 'Diksmuide', which may be a reference to the powerful family of the Diksmuides from Ieper (Ypres). Diksmuide is also the name of a town in Flanders. More we do not know, and of course we have to be open to the possibility that although the poet may have originated from the County of Flanders he may have worked somewhere else entirely – as we know to have been the case of for instance Hendrik van Veldeke and Jacob van Maerlant. Two manuscripts of *Reinaerts historie* have come down to us, both of them produced in the northern Netherlands. This has led to the origins of this particular work being sought in the north, but the language and the toponyms featured rather point to the County of Flanders. If Willem primarily relied on the first branch of the *Roman de Renart* as the main source for *Van den vos Reynaerde*, the poet of *Reinaerts historie* in the first instance turned to branch VI (*Le Duel Judiciaire*). Thus, in his continuation the confrontation of Reinaert with his accusers does not remain on the level of the verbal; in a duel with Ysegrim Reinaert he has to defend himself also physically. Again Reinaert gains the upper hand, and again he does so by a ruse, but unlike in *Van den vos Reynaerde* the story does not end with his having to flee with his wife and children. Instead he is promoted to bailiff of King Nobel and thus rises to a powerful position at court – the poacher has turned sheriff.

The main reason for paying some more attention to the continuation of *Van den vos Reynaerde* is that via *Reinaerts historie* the Dutch-speaking fox has come to play an important role on the European literary scene. In the earliest days of book printing in the Low Countries (sometime between 1487 and 1490) the text, illustrated with woodcuts, was put to the press by the famous printer Gheraert Leeu. It was also subdivided into chapters by Hinrek van Alckmer, and synoptic chapter titles and explicit moralizing passages in prose were added. As far as we know nothing was changed to the text itself. What we know about this can be deduced in the first instance from the prologue to a Low German printed adaptation of this rhyming incunable, *Reynke de vos*. This edition from Lübeck (1498) is no direct descendant of Leeu's Antwerp incunable, but of a lost edition that must have dated from in between the Antwerp and the Lübeck editions. For the rest, the Lübeck edition features the same adaptations as that of Gheraert Leeu: woodcuts, chapter titles, and moralizing passages in prose.

We cannot here go into detail as to how the Lübeck edition leads to a much wider dissemination. We can only trace some main lines.[26] The Low German text was reprinted until 1660 but was also translated into High German in 1544 and into Danish in 1555. The latter served as a source for translations into Icelandic and Swedish. The High German translation remained in print until 1617 – with at least twenty-one printings – and itself 'fathered' a number of subgroups in the wider tradition. For instance, we have a group of seven Latin editions from the period 1567–1612. Needless to say, the prose translation by Johan Christoph Gottsched in 1752 was of immense importance, as some forty years on it served as the basis for Goethe's hexameter *Reineke Fuchs, In zwölf Gesängen*. Like many other works by Goethe this text of his also was translated and adapted in many languages, leading to yet more branches on the Reinaert tree. This, however, is where we have to stop pursuing our fox.

Conclusion

King Arthur entered Middle Dutch literature via the door opened by Geoffrey of Monmouth. We could even say that he came, saw, and triumphed, given the many stories that were told about him and his Knights of the Round Table in the Low

Countries as in other parts of Europe. But unlike with for instance Charlemagne, Julius Caesar or Alexander the Great, there always clung an air of scepticism to Arthur. Even if his historicity was not in doubt, the same thing did not apply to the stories surrounding him. It is tempting to ask ourselves whether precisely its flirtation with fictionality was (one of) the (many) reason(s) why Arthur vanished from Dutch-language literature at the end of the Middle Ages,[27] but we simply lack sufficient data to support this hypothesis. Reinaert was successful in the Low Countries via Old French literature, although most probably he was already a native of these regions before, as demonstrated by Nivardus of Ghent's *Ysengrimus*. The fictionality of the world of Reinaert could not be denied, but found a counterbalance in its ethical charge, and via the Middle Dutch *Reinaerts historie* set out on a triumphant march through German and Scandinavian literature. Most likely it is precisely because of its undeniable fictional character that 'the matter of the fox' has succeeded in remaining alive in European literature: because it is not in thrall to any time in particular it is of all times.

Notes

1. See Smith and Henley (in press), especially the contribution of David F. Johnson, 'The Middle Dutch Reception of Geoffrey of Monmouth'. For the Hebrew Arthur Romance see Leviant 1969.
2. See Claassens, Knapp and Pérennec 2010-2015.
3. The most important survey of Maerlant's life and work is undoubtedly Van Oostrom (1996), but also the older work by Te Winkel ([1892] 1979) retains its interest.
4. Maerlant's younger contemporary Philip Utenbroeke wrote the second *partie*, and Maerlant's self-declared successor Lodewijc van Velthem completed the fourth *partie* and added a fifth *partie*. Fully completed the *Spiegel historiael* covers from Creation to 1316 and counts some 184.000 lines of verse, of which some 90.000 by Jacob van Maerlant.
5. Jacob van Maerlant, *Spiegel historiael*, Part III, Book V, chs 48 (from vs. 63)-54. Cf. De Vries and Verwijs 1861-1879: vol. 2, 333-343. In book VI, chs 29-30, Maerlant describes the civil war between Arthur and Mordred and the fatal battle on the Salisbury plain (De Vries and Verwijs 1861-1879: vol. 2, 386-388).
6. Jacob van Maerlant, *Spiegel historiael*, Part III, Book V, ch. 49, vss. 1-6. Cf. De Vries and Verwijs 1861-1879: vol. 2, 333.
7. Jacob van Maerlant, *Spiegel historiael*, Part III, Book V, ch. 54, vss. 51-60. Cf. De Vries and Verwijs 1861-1879: vol. 2, 343.
8. Earlier Maerlant had already produced some Arthurian texts based on Old French sources. Later he renounced this, because they were untrue. See Claassens and Johnson 2000: 1-5.
9. On Maerlant's use of the *Historia regum Brittanniae* in *Spieghel historiael* see Gerritsen 1981; specifically on the war against the Romans see Gerritsen 1970.
10. Only in the *Ferguut* (c. 1250), a translation/adaptation of the Old French *Fergus* by Guillaume li clers, we find the name 'Gawein' for this character. In line 4325 there is mention of a 'Walewein', but this is a different character. For *Ferguut* see Johnson and Claassens 2000a, an edition with an English translation.
11. Jacob van Maerlant, *Spiegel historiael*, Part III, Book V, ch. 49, vss. 18-21. Cf. De Vries and Verwijs 1861-1879: vol. 2, 333.

12 For an English-language survey of the Middle Dutch Arthurian epics see Claassens and Johnson 2000.
13 Middle Dutch text with English translation in Johnson and Claassens 2000b. The romance is available in a complete manuscript (Leiden, Universiteitsbibliotheek, Ltk. 195, which according to the colophon dates from 1350 and linguistically can be situated in the western part of Flanders). There are also a few pages from a second manuscript, some 388 lines in toto, also dating back to the fourteenth century (Ghent: Universiteitsbibliotheek, 1619).
14 See Johnson and Claassens 2000b: 5.
15 See for example Hogenbirk 2000 for the role of Walewein in *Walewein ende Keye*, another original Middle Dutch Arthurian epic.
16 From the rich scholarly literature, I just mention three publications that have been important to me: Knapp 1980, Olson 1982 and Otter 1996. For a discussion of fictionality in a specifically Middle Dutch context, see Claassens 2005.
17 *Roman van Walewein*, vss. 14-18 (cf. Johnson and Claassens 2000b: 28-29). The so-called miracle recalls that performed by Jesus during the wedding at Canaan, where he changed water into wine (John 2: 1-12), but also the miraculous multiplication of the loaves, when five thousand people are nourished with five loaves of bread and two fishes (Matthew 14: 13-21, Mark 6: 31-34, Luke 9: 10-17 and John 6: 5-15). A final possibility is that in these lines reference is made to the temptations of Jesus, in which the devil among other things taunts him to turn stones into bread, but which Jesus refuses to do (Matthew 4: 1-4 and Luke 4: 1-4). What is remarkable is that we encounter a similar reference in another original Middle Dutch text, *Karel ende Elegast* (vs. 185). This too is a story in which the (historical) Charlemagne takes centre stage, but in which his 'sidekick' Elegast proves a master of witchcraft. For some this made *Karel ende Elegast* a controversial text (see Claassens 2005: 248-249).
18 A good introduction to *Van den vos Reynaerde* is Bouwman and Besamusca 2009, which on facing pages features an edition of the original text and an English translation by Thea Summerfield.
19 At the end of the text, in an acrostichon covering the final nine lines, he presents himself one more time: *bi willeme*. *Van den vos Reynaerde*, vss. 3462-3469. Cf. Bouwman and Besamusca 2009: 244. Of the other work by Willem, that is the *Madocke* he refers to as the work for which he is primarily known, nothing has been preserved and we have no other means of identifying him, although there have been numerous attempts to do so, in vain.
20 Cf. Bouwman and Besamusca 2009: 15-16.
21 Cf. Bouwman and Besamusca 2009: 34-35.
22 Jan van Boendale, *Der leken spieghel*, Book III, ch. 15, vss. 113-118 (De Vries 1844-1847, III: 161; translation Gerritsen et al. 1994: 255.
23 Jan van Boendale, *Der leken spieghel*, Book III, ch. 15, vss. 61-67 (De Vries 1844-1847, III, 161; translation Gerritsen et al. 1994: 254.
24 Jan van Boendale, *Der leken spieghel*, Book III, ch. 15, vss. 192-198 (De Vries 1844-1847, III: 166; translation Gerritsen et al. 1994: 256.
25 The most recent edition of *Reinaerts historie* is in Schlusemann and Wackers 2005, which also provides a German translation on facing pages.
26 See Menke 1992 and (specifically for the *Nachleben* of the Middle Dutch texts) Wackers 2000.

27 In all, there is only one Arthurian romance that has come down to us from the early days of book printing. We have two quires from a Middle Dutch *Merlijn* but this is not a direct descendant of the Middle Dutch manuscript Arthurian tradition. Its direct source is the Middle English *Of Arthour and of Merlin*, of which the printed *A lytel treatyse of ye byrth and prophecye of Marlyn* (London: Wynkin de Worde, 1510) is the only extant full edition. See Pesch 1985.

References

Bouwman, A. and B. Besamusca, eds (2009), *Of Reynaert the Fox. Text and Facing Translation of the Middle Dutch Beast Epic Van den vos Reynaerde*, Amsterdam: Amsterdam University Press. Available online: http://open.org/search?identifier=340003 (accessed 25 February 2019).

Claassens, G.H.M. (2005), 'The "Scale of Boendale." On Dealing with Fact and Fiction in Vernacular Mediaeval Literature', in W. Verbeke, L. Milis and J. Goossens (eds), *Medieval Narrative Sources. A Gateway into the Medieval Mind*, 231–250, Leuven: Leuven University Press [Mediaevalia Lovaniensia, 34].

Claassens, G.H.M. and D.F. Johnson (2000), 'Arthurian Literature in the Medieval Low Countries: An Introduction', in G.H.M. Claassens and D.F. Johnson (eds), *King Arthur in the Medieval Low Countries*, 1–34, Leuven: Leuven University Press [Mediaevalia Lovaniensia, Series I, Studia XXVIII].

Claassens, G.H.M., F.P. Knapp and R. Pérennec, eds (2010–2015), *Germania Litteraria Mediaevalis Francigena. Handbuch der deutschen und niederländischen mittelalterlichen literarischen Sprache, Formen, Motive, Stoffe und Werke französischer Herkunft (1100–1300)*, 7 vols, Berlin: De Gruyter.

Gerritsen, W.P. (1970), 'L'épisode de La Guerre Contre Les Romains Dans La Mort Artu Néerlandaise', in *Mélanges de Langue et de Littérature Du Moyen Age et de La Renaissance Offerts à Jean Frappier*, vol. 1, 337–349, Geneve: Droz.

Gerritsen, W.P. (1981), 'Jacob van Maerlant and Geoffrey of Monmouth', in K. Varty (ed.), *An Arthurian Tapestry. Essays in Memory of Lewis Thorpe*, 368–388, Glasgow: D.S. Brewer.

Gerritsen, W.P., H. van Dijk, O.S.H. Lie and A.M.J. van Buuren (1994), 'A Fourteenth-century Vernacular Poetics: Jan van Boendale's "How Writers Should Write" (with a Modern English Translation of the Text by Erik Kooper)', in E. Kooper (ed.), *Medieval Dutch Literature in its European Context*, 245–260, Cambridge: Cambridge University Press.

Hogenbirk, M. (2000), 'A Perfect Knight: Walewein in the *Walewein ende Keye*', in G.H.M. Claassens and D.F. Johnson (eds), *King Arthur in the Medieval Low Countries*, 163–172, Leuven: Leuven University Press [Mediaevalia Lovaniensia, Series I, Studia XXVIII].

Johnson, D.F. and G.H.M. Claassens (2000a), *Ferguut*, Woodbridge: Boydell & Brewer [Arthurian Archives VII, Dutch Romance II].

Johnson, D.F. and G.H.M. Claassens (2000b), *Roman van Walewein*, Woodbridge: Boydell & Brewer [Arthurian Archives VI, Dutch Romance I].

Knapp, F.P. (1980), 'Historische Wahrheit und poetische Lüge. Die Gattungen weltlicher Epik und ihre theoretische Rechtfertigung im Hochmittelalter', *Deutsche Vierteljahrsschrift für Literaturwissenschaft und Geistesgeschichte* 54 (4): 581–635.

Leviant, C. (ed. and trans.) (1969), *King Artus, a Hebrew Arthurian Romance of 1279*, Assen: Van Gorcum.
Menke, H. (1992), *Bibliotheca Reinardiana*, I: *Die Europäische Reineke Fuchs-Drucke bis zum Jahre 1800*, Stuttgart: Hauswedell.
Olson, G. (1982), *Literature as Recreation in the Later Middle Ages*, Ithaca, NY: Cornell University Press.
Oostrom, F.P. Van (1996), *Maerlants wereld*, Amsterdam: Prometheus.
Otter, M. (1996), *Inventiones. Fiction and Referentiality in Twelfth-century English Historical Writing*, Chapel Hill: University of North Carolina Press.
Pesch, P.N.G. (1985), 'Het Nederlandse volksboek van *Merlijn*: bron, drukker en datering', in F. de Nave (ed.), *Liber Amicorum Leon Voet*, 303–328, Antwerp: voor de Vereeniging der Antwerpsche Bibliophielen door het Gemeentekrediet van België.
Schlusemann, R. and P. Wackers, eds and trans. (2005), *Reynaerts historie (Mittelniederländisch-Neuhochdeutsch)*, Münster: Agenda Verlag [Bibliothek mittelniederländischer Literatur, vol. 2].
Smith, J.B. and G. Henley, eds (in press), *A Companion to Geoffrey of Monmouth*, Leyden: Brill.
Vries, M. de, ed. (1844–1847), *Der leken spieghel, leerdicht van den jare 1330, door Jan Boendale, gezegd Jan de Clerc, schepenklerk te Antwerpen*, 3 vols, Leiden: D. Du Mortier en zoon.
Vries, M. de, and E. Verwijs, eds (1861–1879), *Jacob van Maerlant's 'Spiegel Historiael', met de fragmenten der later toegevoegde gedeelten, bewerkt door Philip Utenbroeke en Lodewijc van Velthem*, 4 vols, Leiden: Brill.
Wackers, P. (2000), 'The Printed Dutch Reynaert Tradition. From the Fifteenth to the Nineteenth Century', in K. Varty (ed.), *Reynard the Fox. Social Engagement and Cultural Metamorphoses in the Beast Epic from the Middle Ages to the Present*, 73–103, New York: Berghahn Books [Polygons. Cultural Diversities and Intersections, I].
Winkel, J. te ([1892] 1979), *Maerlant's werken beschouwd als spiegel van de 13de eeuw*, 2nd, rev. edn, Utrecht: HES.

2

John of Ruusbroec (1293–1381), Celebrated Mystagogical Author of *The Spiritual Espousals*

Kees Schepers

Introduction

If successful works of art, music and literature would light up on a digital map of late-medieval Europe, the Low Countries would shine brightly with a multitude of coalescing lights. The densely populated Low Countries, then as now a hub of trade and commerce, with highly developed urban centres and infrastructure, boasting a literate class of commoners, bourgeoisie and nobility, constituted the fertile substrate for a manifold artistic production to grow from. The relatively small coastal region had, for example, a disproportionately large share in the composition of polyphonic music – the Franco-Flemish School – and in panel painting – the equally renowned Flemish primitives. Less known, but equally remarkable is the significant role authors in the Low Countries played in the development of vernacular mystical literature in western Europe. The context of a dense network of formal religious institutions, such as monasteries, priories and charterhouses, and of less formal groups of fervently religious people, such as beguines and beghards, and the early adherents of the *Devotio Moderna*, favored the development of this textual genre. Several authors attained fame – or notoriety – in their own time, a fame that was forgotten for a very long time, only to be rediscovered in the late nineteenth century. Authors who have obtained a firm place in international discourse on spiritual literature are Hadewijch, Marguerite Porete (d.1310), Geert Grote (1340–1384) and John of Ruusbroec. The latter, a fourteenth-century priest and later canon regular, is the subject of this chapter.¹ My focus will be on one of his works, *Die geestelike brulocht* (The Spiritual Espousals), a treatise he was and remains famous for (Alaerts 1988).

John of Ruusbroec (1293–1381)

John of Ruusbroec was born in the vicinity of Brussels, in the small village of Ruisbroek from which he takes his name.² He became a priest at St Goedele Church, in the centre of Brussels. In 1343 he chose to go and live the life of a hermit in the Forêt de Soignes (Zoniënwoud), south of Brussels, together with two of his friends. In 1350 their early settlement was converted into a priory of regular canons of St Augustine, of which Ruusbroec became the first prior. This Groenendaal priory was the centre of a short-lived fourteenth-century flowering of mystical literature in the vernacular, manifested by the works of, besides Ruusbroec, lesser-known authors such as Jan van Leeuwen (d.1378) and Willem Jordaens (d.1372).

During his lifetime Ruusbroec acquired fame as a teacher, receiving guests from near and far asking for spiritual guidance. Among them were Geert Grote, the founder of the *Devotio Moderna*, from the northern part of the Low Countries, and John Tauler (1300–1361), the famed preacher from Strasbourg, in the south of Germany.

Ruusbroec wrote his treatises both in Brussels and later in Groenendaal. His oeuvre comprises eleven texts that are for the most part mystagogical, describing the path towards a mystical union with God.³ Nowadays, *Die geestelike brulocht* is undisputedly regarded as Ruusbroec's *opus magnum*.⁴ The clarity of its structure, combined with the width and depth of Ruusbroec's phenomenological description of mystical life, makes the *Brulocht* stand out as a monument of mystical expertise and experience. Among Ruusbroec's contemporaries, however, *Vanden gheesteliken tabernakel* (The Spiritual Tabernacle) seems to have been more popular (Mertens 2006). They probably found it to be a more easily accessible text for the same reason modern day readers have a problem with it: the *Tabernakel* provides spiritual exegesis through an elaborate and detailed allegorical reading of the chapters in the book of Exodus that are devoted to the building instructions for the tabernacle.

Die geestelike brulocht describes what Ruusbroec sees as three stages of the spiritual life: the active life, the yearning life and the contemplative life. Ruusbroec uses the phrase: *Ecce/sponsus uenit/exite/obuiam ei* ('See/the bridegroom cometh/go out/to meet him', Mt. 25:6) as a structuring device. In three books, covering the three 'lifes', Ruusbroec extensively interprets the four elements of the phrase as referring to the four stages within each of the lives. Through the use of the scriptural theme *Ecce sponsus venit* ... Ruusbroec's treatise is linked to the sermon tradition.

Mystagogical texts as literature

In the case of medieval Middle Dutch texts – with regard to Ruusbroec more specifically mystagogical treatises – it is imperative to first address the concept of 'literature' before we can consider such texts as *world* literature (Damrosch 2003; D'haen 2011).

The common concept of 'literature' in the modern sense – esthetically appealing and/ or innovative, inspiring and meaningful as opposed to merely 'a good read' – was alien to medieval readers of Middle Dutch texts, and hence the question whether a text was considered literature is irrelevant. However, it is important to note that the situation for Latin was different, where the arts of poetry and prose provided prescriptive poetics, and one could argue that texts following these guidelines might be labelled 'literature'. Poetics were almost entirely absent from Dutch vernacular texts; a notable exception being a chapter in *Der leken spiegel* (The Laymen's Mirror), a work by the Brabantine clerc and author John of Boendale (1279-1350) (Gerritsen 1994: 245-260). The gist of Boendale's 'poetics' is that authors should have a training in Latin grammar and rhetoric, before they can write rhyming texts in Dutch; in other words, they should be steeped in Latin culture. Boendale distances himself from vernacular authors without a solid training. Furthermore, authors must be truthful; Boendale abhors fiction. Finally, authors should be morally irreprehensible. All these prescripts have no bearing on spiritual literature, and therefore a de facto division exists in this regard between secular texts of every kind and spiritual texts. Secular texts, if they aim at stylistic sophistication, can be placed against the background of the arts of poetry and prose in Latin, and as such they are ultimately linked to classical authors such as Cicero, Ovid and Virgil (Kelly 1991). For spiritual texts, on the other hand, the only classification that matters is based on the – highly influential – division that Bonaventura made between scribes, compilers, commentators and authors.[5] In other words, whereas secular texts are for the most part judged by their style and content, spiritual texts are organized on the basis of the role of the producer of the text. Following this categorization Ruusbroec firmly established himself as an author.

International context

Ruusbroec was not a shooting star on the firmament of medieval spiritual literature. In the past the criticism has been raised – with some validity – that in twentieth-century scholarly literature Ruusbroec's works were studied with himself as *sui interpres*. That is no longer the case: through extensive research the network of influences he underwent has been charted, and the influence he himself exerted has also been explored. Ruusbroec's works sprang forth from a vibrant local mystical culture using the vernacular, while it was influenced by Latin texts from twelfth-century monastic culture. There have been attempts, later dismissed, to suggest that the Brabantine mysticism of Ruusbroec was influenced by the Rhineland mysticism of Meister Eckhart (1260-1327). Both mystics, Ruusbroec and Eckhart, spearhead two mutually independent traditions, following separate trajectories of development. The mysticism that comes to a climax in Ruusbroec is love mysticism for which the foundations were laid by the Cistercians saint Bernard of Clairvaux (1090-1153) and William of Saint-Thierry (*c*.1080-1148), as well as by authors from the Augustinian abbey of Saint Victor in Paris, commonly labelled the Victorines. Prominent among them were Hugh of Sint-Victor (*c*.1091-1141), born in Saxony, and Richard of Sint-Victor (1110-1173), originally from Scotland. In the twelfth century the theme of spiritual love came to the fore. The theme was developed by applying the language of love – especially in the form of nuptial imagery as found in the Song of Songs – to the relationship between God and man. The love of the soul for God is described in worldly, affectionate terms; this love, however, must be purified, to become essentially dispassionate. Ruusbroec was heavily influenced by this type of mysticism, and it is therefore fitting that he named his main work *The Spiritual Espousals*.

The Rhineland type of mysticism, on the other hand, peaks with Eckhart. His main followers were John Tauler and Heinrich Suso (1295–1366). This mysticism is more speculative and philosophical, carefully executing a balancing act on the dividing line between Christian mysticism and philosophical Neo-Platonism. Eckhart especially describes a highly intellectual way of emptying the self in order to allow one's innermost being to reconnect to the ultimate being from which it sprang forth and from which it continues to depend. He does so both in his Latin works aimed at a learned audience and in his vernacular works – particularly sermons – that he addressed to convent sisters (Eckhart 1958–). His daring language in the German sermons were the main reason he got into doctrinal trouble with ecclesiastical authorities, leading, ultimately, to his works being condemned as heretical. To the extent that he knew about Eckhart's works, Ruusbroec distanced himself from his approach and his most provocative statements. It can fairly be stated that Ruusbroec did not undergo any influence from Eckhart.

Dissemination and influence

Texts of medieval spiritual literature often managed to find circulation on their own textual merit, rather than the fame of the author. The international dissemination of Ruusbroec's *Spiritual Espousals* in Latin is a good case in point. The early Latin translation *De ornatu spiritualium nuptiarum* found its way to other regions and later periods, even though several scribes and printers clearly knew little or nothing about the author. In three Italian manuscripts of *De ornatu* the text is introduced thus: 'Epistola dompni Johannis primi prioris uallis uiridis ad fratres Cartusienses de capella rosan in Flandria super interpretatione libri sequentis'[6] (Letter of master John, the first prior of vallis viridis to the Carthusian fathers from the Charterhouse of Rosan(!) in Flanders, on the translation of the following book). This sentence is riddled with errors and vagueness. Apparently the scribes did not know the last name of 'John', who was indeed the first prior of Groenendaal (*viridis vallis*), but not of *vallis viridis*, a name that likely refers, given the context of the sentence, to the charterhouse of Vauvert (*vallis viridis*) in Paris. The letter was addressed to the Cistercians of Ter Doest (Thosan) not to the Carthusians of Rosan – a non-existent place. In sum, the scribes only knew that the author was some 'John'. However, notwithstanding the apparent obscurity of the author, there are more extant copies of *De ornatu* from Italy than from any other region, which shows that the text was considered significant and worthwhile outside of its own Brabantine context.

In describing the dissemination and influence of Ruusbroec and his works, it is useful to distinguish three different phases. The first phase is that of the unbroken 'tradition', literally the 'passing on', of his works from one group or monastery to the next up until the early sixteenth century. This phase involves the transmission of Ruusbroec's works both in the vernacular and in early Latin translations. I will first address Ruusbroec's influence on the spiritual literature of the Low Countries.[7] My attention will then turn to the early Ruusbroec translations. The second phase is that of Ruusbroec's influence in the early modern period in several European literatures, occasioned, for the most part, by the availability of his entire oeuvre in the translation of Laurentius Surius (more on him later). Ruusbroec thus influenced Spanish mysticism of the sixteenth century, the French mystical movement of the seventeenth century, and even German pietism in the eighteenth century. The third phase, finally, entails modern interest in his works, starting with their rediscovery in the late nineteenth century after they had remained dormant in libraries for some two centuries.

Influence of Ruusbroec in the Low Countries

Ruusbroec directly influenced other authors from the fourteenth to the sixteenth century. In his own Groenendaal monastery, he was much admired by the cook Jan van Leeuwen (d.1378) – someone without formal scholarly training – who himself became a prolific writer of ardent, albeit unpolished mystical treatises. Geert Grote, the founder of the *Devotio Moderna* had a high esteem for Ruusbroec the mystagogue, although he kept his distance from the more daring aspects of his teaching. Hendrik Mande (d.1411) and Gerlach Peeters (d.1431), two authors of mystical treatises, also underwent direct influence from Ruusbroec's treatises. They were both canons regular belonging to the Congregation of Windesheim, the monastic branch of the *Devotio Moderna*. Finally, Henry Herp (d.1478), who became a Franciscan later on in life, was deeply imbued with the mysticism of Ruusbroec. He came to be an internationally recognized mystical author in his own right, especially in the Roman cultural sphere. His six most important works were published in Latin translation by the Cologne Carthusians under the title *Theologica Mystica*.[8]

The immense but diffuse and hard to pinpoint influence of Ruusbroec can furthermore be detected in countless spiritual texts from the fifteenth century from the Low Countries and the German regions.

Ruusbroec's influence becomes clearly recognizable again in the early sixteenth century, during what has been labelled the sixteenth-century mystical renaissance (Schepers 2015: 84–123; McGinn 2012: 141–175). All of the most important Middle Dutch mystical treatises from that era reveal precise knowledge and understanding of the more lofty aspects of Ruusbroec's teaching. These texts – *Die evangelische peerle* (The Evangelical Pearl), *Vanden tempel onser sielen* (The Temple of our Soul) and *The Arnhem mystical sermons* – are remarkable in that they not only draw on Ruusbroec but also on the Rhineland mystics, thus bringing together the two mains strands of mystical thought from the fourteenth century.

Early translations of Willem Jordaens and Geert Grote

We are all aware – witness this volume – that in today's world the English language provides almost the sole linguistic entrance to global academic discourse; it is perhaps difficult to imagine that in the Middle Ages the dominance of Latin was even greater. The only way, therefore, for the works of John of Ruusbroec to gain access to and have an influence on contemporary discourse on mystical theology and on the experiential aspects of mysticism was to have them translated in Latin. This inevitability was first brought home to the Canons Regular of Groenendaal when the Cistercians from the Flemish abbey of Ter Doest asked for a Latin translation of Ruusbroecs *Espousals*. The Cistercians claimed they could only perceive 'a faint hint of the full flavour' of Ruusbroec's vernacular text, and asked for a text in a more accessible language.[9] Only then would they be able to receive the full benefit of the text.[10] The request of the Ter Doest monks was the first impulse for a Latin translation of one of Ruusbroec's works (Schepers 2014: 237–285). Ruusbroec's learned fellow-brother Willem Jordaens (d.1372) took on the task. He had probably become master of theology at the University of Paris (Schepers 2004: 10–19). It was his intention – and that of the Groenendaal community – to insert Ruusbroec's works into fourteenth-century Latin discourse. In the introductory letter Jordaens addresses the Ter Doest Cistercians, and through them the larger Latin world. He writes in the first person plural, thus suggesting that Ruusbroec himself wrote the letter.[11]

> we gave in to your pleas, or rather, obeyed to the demands of love, and we have translated the book you wrote about in Latin, or rather, we have dressed the meaning of the book in Latin garments.[12]

Jordaens is explicit about his translation strategy: he wants to respect the peculiar nature of the target language: the *interpretantis linguae proprietas*. He takes the meaning of the original text and dresses this meaning in Latin garments; in his own words: *latinis vestivimus indumentis*. With tacit reference to Jerome (and Quintillian), he describes his mode of translating as *sensus de sensu*, as opposed to *verbum e verbo* (word for word), respecting the stylistic demands of, in this case, Latin. This inevitably leads to what we would call a 'free translation'. Jordaens thus hopes to meet the anticipated stylistic demands of his readership, in the first place, the lofty sociocultural milieu of Cistercian monks. His text was definitely not intended for *sciolis* – the beginners in either language.

Jordaens was not the only contemporary of Ruusbroec to translate his works into Latin. The earlier-mentioned Geert Grote, too, produced translations of some key works. Interestingly, both Jordaens and Grote translated *The Espousals* – among other works – only a mere twenty years apart. Jordaens wrote his *De ornatu spiritualium nuptiarum* somewhere between 1353 and 1365; Grote's *Ornatus spiritualis desponsationis* was produced c.1383/1384 (Hofman 2000). The reason Grote decided to translate *The Espousals* as well is not only that he deemed Willem Jordaens's free rendering in *De ornatu spiritualium nuptiarum* to be inadequate, but also because he thought that it would not reach the kinds of readers he aimed for, in particular the more down-to-earth adherents of the *Devotio moderna*. He strictly applied the *verbum e verbo* technique, as he explains in his introduction. In doing so he implicitly criticizes *De ornatu* for being too free and stylistically too ornate:

This book, originally written in the Germanic vernacular, was then translated into Latin, not by a translation of sense for sense, nor of sentence for sentence, but almost word for word, without embellishment of style. For this was both convenient for the translator and not unprofitable for the common and unlearned readership. Also, while translating, he [i.e. the translator Grote] did not dare add grace to the style, for fear that in these matters exceeding his experience, he would be seen to add to or remove something from his exemplar.[13]

Stylistically the translations of Jordaens and Grote could not have been more different, and they resulted in very diverging dissemination patterns. Grote's very literal translations found their way mostly in the German cultural sphere, while the Roman cultural sphere proved impenetrable; Jordaens's refined translations were appreciated in the Roman cultural sphere, but not in the German world. The German and the Roman worlds seem to have had a different *Erwartungshorizont* with regard to style, influencing textual preferences. The combined result of Jordaens's and Grote's efforts was that Ruusbroec's works were disseminated from Great-Britain to Poland, and from Italy to Austria.

The Gerson censure

The dissemination of Ruusbroec's *Espousals* was brought to a grinding halt shortly after 1398, because of the censure by John Gerson (1363–1429), the chancellor of the University of Paris. It apparently caused a long hiatus in the circulation of both Jordaens's and Grote's translation. The censure of Gerson thus proved to be the strongest impediment yet – although not lasting – for Ruusbroec's widening international fame as a mystical writer. How did this censure come about? The text was probably brought to the attention of Gerson, with great pride, by Bartholomew, a Carthusian from Herne near Brussels. If this was done hoping to get Gerson's stamp of approval for *The Espousals*, and thus to make the work more widely known, the Carthusians may well have regretted their move in view of its consequences. After an initial cursory reading, Gerson carefully read *The Espousals* a second time, and he was shocked to find in the third book propositions that could possibly lead to heretical views among its readership. He therefore sent a sternly worded letter to Bartholomew, who then had to relay the bad news to his community – and that of Groenendaal.[14] A carefully crafted rebuttal by John of Schoonhoven (1356–1432), a fellow-brother of Ruusbroec, who had also studied in Paris, did not have the intended result.[15] In fact, it incensed Gerson even more, who then wrote a very curt second letter, in which he affirmed his earlier rejection of *The Espousals*.[16]

The 1512 printed edition: Paris, Henri Estienne

The effect of Gerson's censure lasted for a very long time. As a consequence, when the publisher Henri Estienne decided to put Ruusbroec's *Espousals* into print in the early sixteenth century, he still felt the need to be apologetic about this project and to find a way to deflect Gerson's criticism.[17] Estienne must have feared that the potential readers might not welcome Ruusbroec's *Espousals* because Gerson had pronounced such a harsh verdict. Jacques Lefèvre d'Étaples (Jacobus Faber Stapulensis, c.1450–1536), who played an important role in the spread of Christian humanism in France, wrote a dedicatory letter in which he dealt with this problem (Rice 1972: 276–280). Lefèvre's way to explain Gerson's censure is that the chancellor must have come across a corrupted version of the text.[18] He contends that the right version of the text will surely demonstrate that Ruusbroec was a literate and admirable man. He thus uses the well-known difficulties of any manuscript tradition of a text to account for the problems that Ruusbroec's *opus magnum* had encountered.

Translation of Ruusbroec's *Opera omnia* by Laurentius Surius

One could visualize the dissemination of Ruusbroec by way of the early translations of Grote and Jordaens as thin lines inching forward from Brussels into most of western Europe, but without any noticeable radiating effect. Individual manuscript copies slowly multiplied from one introverted monastic community to the next. This dissemination mode changed dramatically with the Ruusbroec translation by Laurentius Surius (1522–1578). The Lübeck-born Cologne Carthusian translated the entire oeuvre of Ruusbroec, and it was published in one sturdy printed volume in Cologne in 1552.[19] The publication of these *Opera omnia* compares to a blot on the map bleeding its effect to all sides. The edition had a double objective: on the one hand making Ruusbroec's works accessible to new audiences, on the other hand trying to roll back the tide of Lutheranism, by providing admirable texts emanating from earlier 'catholic' spirituality. Ruusbroec's *Opera* were received in every cultural sphere, by monks, priests and laymen alike, and all over western Europe. The Ruusbroec edition was part of a concerted publication offensive of the Cologne Carthusians, a failed attempt to halt the spread of Lutheranism through this and numerous other editions. The Surius edition did, however, provide the material for Ruusbroec-translations in several European languages that were to follow. The authoritative Surius translation itself was reprinted in 1608 and 1692.

Early Modern and Modern translations in West European vernaculars

Ruusbroec was translated into several vernaculars, at different times and with different effects. I will briefly mention the main facts.

It is not known how extensive the knowledge of Ruusbroec was, directly or indirectly, in sixteenth-century Spain (Behiels and Ubarri 2004). The fact is, however, that copies of the 1512 Latin edition of Ruusbroec's *Espousals* are still extant in Spanish libraries. It is also a fact that Herp's *Theologia mystica* already influenced Spanish mystics in the sixteenth century, and hence Ruusbroec was a source of influence via Herp. However, the exact extent of Ruusbroec's influence on the Spanish mystics of the Golden Age of mysticism (1500–1650) has yet to be determined. Only in the late seventeenth century are we on solid ground again, when the first complete translation of Ruusbroec's works, based on the Surius edition was published in Madrid.[20]

In Italy, even more so than in Spain, the dissemination and influence of Ruusbroec's works is second to that of Henry Herp. Interestingly, two translations of individual works, both attributed to Willem Jordaens, were already published in print in Italy in 1538.[21] The texts were edited by the Bologna priest Nicolaus Bargilesius. In an introductory letter he says that he had received the manuscript texts on which he based his edition from Carthusians in the Bologna charterhouse. Testimony to Ruusbroec's influence – along with that of Tauler and Herp – is the 1557 decree from Everard Mercurian, Superior General of the Jesuit Order. He placed all three writers on a list of authors that members of the Jesuit Order were forbidden to read.[22]

The Spiritual Espousals was the first work of Ruusbroec to be printed in French. It was translated by a Paris Carthusian, most likely Richard Beaucousin, and appeared in 1606 in Toulouse; it was reprinted in 1612, 1613 and 1619, in an identical edition but with a different title page.[23] Beaucousin had a special interest in Dutch mysticism, judging from the fact that he also made a translation of *The Evangelical Pearl*, which was published in 1602.[24] He played an important role in the genesis of the seventeenth-century French school of spirituality, of which Cardinal Pierre de Bérulle (1575–1629) is considered to be the founder. This movement was strongly influenced by texts from the Low Countries and the Rhineland, with Herp and Tauler again taking precedence over Ruusbroec.

In the German empire Ruusbroec's work were received in both catholic and protestant circles. The latter reception is remarkable: apparently Ruusbroec's teachings easily made the transition into some quarters of the protestant word. They were particularly well received among seventeenth- and eighteenth-century pietists; to name the most important: Daniel Suderman (d.1631), Gottfried Arnold (d.1714) and Gerhard Tersteegen (d.1769). Suderman edited two of Ruusbroec's treatises on the basis of manuscripts, both published in 1621.[25] Arnold prepared the first complete translation of Ruusbroec's works in German, again a translation of the Surius edition.[26]

A remarkable case is Johann Scheffler (d.1677), better known as Angelus Silesius. Raised a protestant, he converted to Catholicism after having studied mystical treatises from the Low Countries and France, among which some of Ruusbroec's texts. He remains famous for his treatise, *Der Cherubinischer Wandersmann* from 1657, a work that testifies to these influences.

Probably due to the problematic circumstances in England, Ruusbroec's works did not cross the Channel in the sixteenth century. Only in the seventeenth century was there a modest rediscovery of Ruusbroec's works, mainly as a consequence of contact with British exiles in France and the Southern Low Countries.

Fast forward, finally, to the Modern era. In the last decades the complete works of Ruusbroec have been re-edited with an accompanying English translation (Jan van Ruusbroec 1988–2006).[27] Thus the treatises of the Brabant mystic have become available to a much wider public. In the United States in particular, Ruusbroec's works have found a new audience. At the opposite side of the globe, *The Spiritual Espousals* are now available in Chinese and Korean translations. Furthermore, there are translations of individual treatises into Russian, Polish, Hungarian and Japanese. Ruusbroec has thus become the author who – after Anne Frank – has been translated in the largest number of languages. In sum, from the confines of his fourteenth-century monastic cell Ruusbroec has now attained global recognition.

Nineteenth- and twentieth-century perceptions of Ruusbroec

There is no lack of appraisals of the works of Ruusbroec as literature from the nineteenth and twentieth centuries; unfortunately, almost all of them suffer from the application of either very subjective or era-specific criteria for what good literature should be like (cf. Noë 2014: 100–129). Virtually no effort is made to relate Ruusbroec's works to contemporaneous views on what literature in the vernacular should be like. Nevertheless, it is interesting to see how Ruusbroec's works were perceived. The following telling – and often contradictory – appraisals comment on the style, composition or content of his treatises.

The Flemish author – but writing in French – Maurice Maeterlinck (1862–1949), winner of the Nobel Prize in 1911, was so fascinated by *The Espousals* that he made a translation from Middle Dutch into French (Maeterlinck 1891). As a member of the francophone bourgeoisie in Flemish-speaking Ghent, he knew Dutch well enough to also understand Middle Dutch. His fascination with the content of Ruusbroec's work did not prevent him from delivering a harsh verdict on Ruusbroec's style:

> Je connais peu d'auteurs plus maladroit; il s'égare par moments en d'étranges puérilités [...]. Il n'a extérieurement aucun ordre, aucune logique scolastique. Il se répète souvent, et semble parfois se contredire. [...] Il a une syntaxe tétanique qui m'a mis plus d'une fois en sueur. Il introduit une image et l'oublie. Il emploie même une certain nombre d'images irréalisables. (Maeterlinck 1891:1–2)[28]

Maeterlinck also warns his readership: 'Il ne faut pas s'attendre à une œuvre littéraire' (2). From a romantic perspective, caring little for historic accuracy, Maeterlinck seems to long for a world of serenity and simplicity, and this he finds in Ruusbroec:

> (Ruusbroec) ignorait le grec et peut-être le latin. Il était seul et pauvre. Et cependant, au fond de cettte obscure forêt brabançonne, son âme, ignorante et simple, reçoit, sans qu'elle le sache, les aveuglants reflets de tous les sommets solitaires et mystérieux de la pensée humaine. (2)

If the style of Ruusbroec is considered to be rather plain – which *can* be seen as something laudable – the composition receives more unanimous praise. Especially the composition of his *Espousals* is habitually compared to the architecture of a medieval cathedral. Friedrich

Böhringer, for example, calls it 'die kunstreichste mystische Schrift der germanischen Mystik des Mittelalters, ein wahrhaft architektonisches Gebäude' (Böhringer 1855: 455).[29]

Among the twentieth-century campaigners for the fame of Ruusbroec, as the early members of the Ruusbroec Institute might well be labelled, was the Jesuit Jozef van Mierlo. His praise of authors was often phrased in such a forceful way that it seems to have been intended to preclude deviating views. He lavishes praise on Ruusbroec:[30]

> But from the whole boundless creation he filled the barns of his imagination with a rich stock ... He stood amidst nature, under the rustling leaves of the expansive Zoniën forest ... what fresh, delightful images from the simple nature around him, from the daily beauty of flower, and fish, and bird, and water, and animals of the Flemish lands.

For Van Mierlo, Ruusbroec is first and foremost a Flemish author, firmly rooted in Flemish culture. A priest, moreover, who deserves to be defended from views from the outside, that is, the non-Catholic world. In a book review of Wauter D'Aygielliers he informs the reader that 'I see it as my duty to warn catholic readers against it.'[31]

How different does Maeterlinck portray Ruusbroec. Profiting from the great distance, both temporal and cultural, from his object, Maeterlinck places Ruusbroec unwittingly within a context of 'world literature' (understood as dealing with comparable subject matter in different times and cultures), thus pulling it out of its religious, doctrinal and cultural confines:

> [Ruusbroec] sait, à son insu, le platonisme de la Grêce; il sait le soufisme de la Perse, le brahmanisme de l'Inde et le bouddhisme du Thibet.' [...] Je pourrais citer des pages entières de Platon, de Plotin, de Porphyre, des livres Zends, des Gnostiques et de la Kabale, dont la substance presque divine se retrouve, intacte, dans les écrits de l'humble prêtre flamand. (Maeterlinck 1891: 11–12)

Thus, in my opinion, Maeterlinck points to one important way for Ruusbroec's work to remain relevant. As the number of devout readers of Ruusbroec's works dwindles, and the intellectual readership is almost completely without religious beliefs, Ruusbroec can continue to inspire as a teacher of interiority. His works can be fruitfully read as a testimony of the search for contact with the divine or sublime, and they can be studied in connection with analogous works from other cultures that his work does not have a genetic relationship with.

Notes

1 See Arblaster and Faesen (2014) for a recent overview of numerous aspects of Ruusbroec's life and work.
2 An important study of the works of Ruusbroec and their context is Warnar (2007). Important overviews of Ruusbroec life and works are Ruh (1999: 26–82) and McGinn (2012: 5–61).

3 See the Bibliography for the complete list of works.
4 There is an ongoing debate on the date of composition of *Die geestelike brulocht*. For a long time, the *opinio communis* held that Ruusbroec wrote his *Espousals* while living in Brussels, that is to say, before 1343. Fairly recently, the hypothesis has been brought forward that he started writing the *Espousals* when he lived without a specific religious rule in the woods, and finished and published it as a regular canon in 1350. A definitive conclusion of this discussion has not yet been reached; see Kienhorst and Kors (2001: 69–101).
5 'A man might write the works of others, adding and changing nothing, in which case he is simply called a "scribe" (*scriptor*). Another writes the works of others with additions which are not his own; and he is called a "compiler" (*compilator*). Another writes both others' works and his own, but with others' works in principal place, adding his own for purposes of explanation; and he is called a "commentator" (*commentator*) ... Another writes both his own works and others' but with his own work in principal place, adding others' for purposes of confirmation; and he is called an "author" (*auctor*)', quoted from Eisenstein (1979: 121–122).
6 The three manuscripts are from Monte Cassino (2) and Subiaco; see Schepers (2004: 203 fn).
7 Within the context of 'world literature' I will leave aside a description of the extensive 'local' manuscript tradition in Middle Dutch. For this tradition see *Jan van Ruusbroec* (1981).
8 *Theologia mystica, cum speculativa, tum praecipue affectiva ... per Henricum Harph, ... Opus nunc primum typis excussum* (Cologne: Novesianus, 1538).
9 *Ioannis Rusbrochii De ornatu spiritualium nuptiarum, Wilhelmo Iordani interprete* (Schepers 2004: 22–24, 203).
10 It is likely that the request had more to do with the lower status of the vernacular in a sophisticated textual culture of the Cistercians than with the alleged incomprehensibility of the text.
11 Which subsequently led to confusion with John Gerson, as we will see.
12 'Acquievimus itaque petitionibus uestris, ymmo iubenti paruimus caritati, et ipsum de quo scripsistis librum transtulimus in latinum, seu potius, sensum libri latinis vestiuimus indumentis.' For a translation of the whole letter see Schepers (2010: 525–558).
13 'postea in latinum non interpretatione sensus ex sensu, nec sententie ex sententia, sed verbi fere ex verbo sine stili lepore translatus est. Nam et hoc transferenti fuit facile et communitati seu ruditati legentium non inutile. Nec ausus fuit transferens stilo decus tribuere, ne in tantis rebus suam experientiam excedentibus exemplari quicquam addere vel detrahere videretur'; *Ioannis Rusbrochii Ornatus spiritualis desponsationis, Gerardo Magno interprete* (Hofman 2000: 3–4).
14 (1398/1399, Paris), Jean Gerson, *Epistola I ad fratrem Bartholomaeum* (Combes 1945: 615–635).
15 (1406/1408, Groenendaal), Johannes van Schoonhoven, *Epistola responsalis* (Combes 1945: 717–772).
16 (1408, Paris), Jean Gerson, *Epistola II ad Bartholomaeum* (Combes 1945: 790–804).
17 *Deuoti et venerabilis patris Ioan[n]nis Rusberi ... De ornatu spiritualium nuptiarum libri tres* (Paris: Henricus Stephanus, 1512). Note that the author's name is spelled incorrectly. See Moreau (1977, no. 448: 159).
18 'Arbitror igitur Gersoni, probo quidem viro, id accidisse, quod in corruptum codicem inciderit. Quod et alias michi accidit. Vbi autem incidi in verum et emendatum, quem

iudicaveram illiteratum, mutata sententia cepi admirari. Simili igitur ratione eum allucinatum puto (...) Lege ergo securus que et ipse Gerso securus legisset et etiam delectabiliter.' (I therefore think that what happened to Gerson, who certainly is an honorable man, is that he came across a corrupted text. Which also happened to me at some time. But when I found a true and emendated one, after a change of mind I started to admire whom I first thought of as illiterate. For the same reason I think therefore that he [Gerson] was mistaken (...). Therefore read without worry what Gerson himself would have read without worry and even with joy.); see Rice (1972: 276–280).

19 *D. Ioannis Rusbrochii summi atque sanctissimi viri, quem insignis quidam theologus alterum Dionysium Areopagitam appellat, opera omnia. Nunc demum post annos ferme ducentos e Brabantiae Germanico idiomate reddita Latine per F. Laurentium Surium. Carthusiae Coloniensis alumnum* (Cologne: Ex officina haeredum Ioannis Quentel, 1552).

20 *Traducción de las obras del iluminado doctor y venerable padre D. Juan Rusbroquio ... en ... castellana con adiciones por el padre Blas López* (Madrid: Melchor Álvarez, 3 vols., 1696–1698).

21 *D. Ioannis Ruisbroici canonici regularis libelli duo, vere divini. Prior, De septem scalae divini amoris, seu vitae sanctae gradibus. Posterior, De perfectione filiorum Dei. Nuper inventi, et nunc primum in lucem aediti* (Bologna: Parmensis and Carpensis, 1538).

22 For the critical edition of the text of the ordinance, see Leturia (1957: vol. 2, 365–367).

23 Jan van Ruusbroec, *L'ornement des nopces spirituelles ... Traduict en François par un religieux chartreux de Paris. Avec la vie de l'autheur à la fin du livre* (Toulouse: veuve J. Colomiés et R. Colomiés, 1606). The reprints come from the same printing house.

24 *La perle évangelicque, trésor incomparable de la sapience divine. Nouvellement traduict de latin en francois par les PP. Chartreux lez Paris* (Paris: Vefve Guillaume de la Noue, 1602).

25 *Ein edles Büchlein, des Johann Taulers. Wie der Mensch möge ernsthafftig, innig, geistlich unnd Gottschawende werden* (n.p., 1621). In this edition Suderman attributed Ruusbroec's *Vanden blinckenden steen* (The Sparkling Stone) to Tauler. *Ein alt und werdes Büchlein von der Gnade Gottes, genommen auss dem Anfang des Hohen Liedts Salomonis ... von Johan. Rüsebruch ...* (n.p., 1621). This edition was based on manuscript compilation from *The Spiritual Espousals*.

26 *Des Johannis Rusbrochii ... Schriften ...* (Offenbach am Main: Bonaventura de Launoy, 1701).

27 This trilingual edition also includes the Latin translation by Surius.

28 Cited in Willaert (1995: 49–64, here 49).

29 Cited in Willaert (1995: 49). It should be noted that nineteenth-century German scholars had little qualms about simply considering Dutch literature to be 'German'. Maeterlinck applies the same metaphor, but with a quite different qualification, to Ruusbroec's œuvre: 'ce temple sans architecture' (p. 3).

30 Jozef van Mierlo, quoted in *Jan van Ruusbroec: leven, werken* (1931: 212): 'Maar uit geheel de wijde schepping heeft hij de schuren van zijn verbeelding gevuld met rijken voorraad ... Hij heeft gestaan te midden van de natuur ... onder de ruischende boomen van het wijde Zoniënbosch ... Wat al frissche, verrukkelijke beelden uit de eenvoudige werkelijkheid om hem heen, uit de dagelijksche schoonheid van bloem en visch en vogel en water en dier der Vlaamsche gouwen.'

31 In a review of A. Wautier d'Aigalliers, *Ruysbroeck l'Admirable* (Paris: Perrin, 1923), Van Mierlo writes, among other things (my translation): 'This book is such that I consider it my duty to warn Catholic readers against it' (Van Mierlo 1925: 714–721, here 714).

References

Jan van Ruusbroec critical edition

Van Ruusbroec, J. (1981–2006), *Opera Omnia*, ed.-in-chief G. de Baere, *Studiën en tekstuitgaven van Ons Geestelijk Erf*, 20/*Corpus Christianorum Continuatio Mediaevalis*, 101–110, 10 vols, Tielt: Lannoo/Turnhout: Brepols.
Vol. 1.Baere, G. de, ed. (1981), *Boecsken der verclaringhe* [Little Book of Explanation].
Vol. 2.Baere, G. de, ed. (1981), *Vanden seven sloten* [The Seven Enclosures].
Vol. 3.Alaerts, J, ed. (1988), *Die geestelike brulocht* [The Spiritual Espousals].
Vol. 4.Alaerts, J., ed. (2002), *Dat rijcke der ghelieven* [The Realm of Lovers].
Vol. 5/6.Mertens, Th., ed. (2006), *Van den geesteliken tabernakel* [The Spiritual Tabernacle].
Vol. 7/7A.Kors, M.M., ed. (2000), *Vanden XII beghinen* [The Twelve Beguines].
Vol. 8.Baere, G. de, ed. (2001), *Een spieghel der eeuwigher salicheit* [A Mirror of Eternal Salvation].
Vol. 9.Faesen, R., ed. (2003), *Vanden seven trappen* [Seven Rungs].
Vol. 10.Baere, G. de, Th. Mertens and H. Noë (1991), *Vanden blinkenden steen* [The Sparkling Stone], *Vanden vier becoringhen* [The Four Temptations], *Vanden kerstenen ghelove* [The Christian Faith], *Brieven* [Letters].

Secondary literature

Arblaster, J. and R. Faesen, eds (2014), *A Companion to John of Ruusbroec*, Brill's Companions to the Christian Tradition, 51, Leiden: Brill.
Behiels, L. and M.N. Ubarri (2004), 'Nederlandse bronnen van de Spaanse mystiek uit de Gouden Eeuw', special issue of *Ons Geestelijk Erf* 78 (2): 131–136.
Böhringer, F. (1855), *Die deutschen Mystiker des vierzehnten und fünfzehnten Jahrhunderts*, Zürich: Meyer & Zeller.
Combes, A. (1945), *Essai sur la critique de Ruysbroeck par Gerson*, Études de théologie et d'histoire de la spiritualité, 4, vol. 1: *Introduction critique et dossier documentaire*, Paris: Librarie Philosophique J. Vrin.
D'haen, T. (2011), *The Routledge Concise History of World Literature*, London: Routledge.
Damrosch, D. (2003), *What is World Literature?*, Princeton, NJ: Princeton University Press.
Eckhart, Meister (1958–), *Die deutschen und lateinischen Werke*, Stuttgart: Kohlhammer.
Eisenstein, E. (1979), *The Printing Press as an Agent of Change: Communication and Cultural Transformation in Early-Modern Europe*, Cambridge: Cambridge University Press.
Gerritsen, W.P., H. Van Dijk, O.S.H. Lie and A.M.J. van Buuren (1994), 'A Fourteenth-century Vernacular Poetics: Jan van Boendale's "How Writers Should Write" ... ', in E. Kooper (ed.), *Medieval Dutch Literature in its European Context*, 245–260, Cambridge: Cambridge University Press.
Hofman, R., ed. (2000), *Ioannis Rusbrochii Ornatus spiritualis desponsationis, Gerardo Magno interprete*, *Corpus Christianorum Continuatio Mediaevalis*, 172, Turnhout: Brepols.

Jan van Ruusbroec 1293-1381 (1981) [exhibition catalogue], Brussels: Koninklijke Bibliotheek Albert I.

Jan van Ruusbroec: leven, werken (1931), ed. Ruusbroec-genootschap, Mechelen: De Spieghel/Het Kompas.

Kelly, D. (1991), *The Arts of Poetry and Prose, Typologie des sources du Moyen Âge Occidental*, vol. 59, Brepols: Turnhout.

Kienhorst, H. and M.M. Kors (2001), 'De chronologie van Ruusbroecs werken volgens de Groenendaalse codex', *Ons Geestelijk Erf* 75: 69-101.

Leturia, P. de (1957), *Estudios Ignacianos*, Rome: Institutum Historicum Societatis Iesu.

Maeterlinck, M. (1891), *L'Ornement des noces spirituelles de Ruysbroeck l'Admirable, traduit du flamand et accompagné d'une introduction*, Brussels: Paul Lacomplez (repr. 1990).

McGinn, B. (2012), *The Varieties of Vernacular Mysticism (1350-1550)*, The Presence of God: A History of Western Christian Mysticism, 5, New York: Crossroad.

Mierlo, J. van (1925), 'Ruysbroeck in Frankrijk', *Dietsche Warande en Belfort* vol. 25, (8/9): 714-721.

Moreau, B. (1977), *Inventaire chronologique des éditions parisiennes du 16e siècle, d'après les manuscrits de Philippe Renoaurd*, vol. 2, Paris: Imprimerie Municipale.

Noë, H. (2014), 'Ruusbroec the Author', in J. Arblaster and R. Faesen (eds), *A Companion to John of Ruusbroec*, Brill's Companions to the Christian Tradition, 51, 100-129, Leiden: Brill.

Rice, E.F. (1972), *The Prefatory Epistles of Jacques Lefèvre d'Etaples and Related Texts*, New York: Columbia University Press.

Ruh, K. (1999), *Die niederländische Mystik des 14. Bis 16. Jahrhunderts, Geschichte der abendländischen Mystik*, 4, Munich: Beck.

Schepers, K., ed. (2004), *Ioannis Rusbrochii De ornatu spiritualium nuptiarum, Wilhelmo Iordani interprete, Corpus Christianorum Continuatio Mediaevalis*, 207, Turnhout: Brepols.

Schepers, K. (2010), 'Literary Style as Cultural Code. A Case Study of the Early Ruusbroec Translations by Willem Jordaens and Geert Grote', in K. Schepers and F. Hendrickx (eds), *De letter levend maken, Opstellen aangeboden aan Guido de Baere bij zijn zeventigste verjaardag, Miscellanea Neerlandica*, 39, 525-558, Leuven: Peeters.

Schepers, K. (2014), 'Ruusbroec in Latin. Impulses and Impediments', in J. Arblaster and R. Faesen (eds), *A Companion to John of Ruusbroec*, Brill's Companions to the Christian Tradition, 51, 237-285, Leiden: Brill.

Schepers, K. (2015), 'The Arnhem Mystical Sermons and the Sixteenth-Century Mystical Renaissance in Arnhem and Cologne', in S.S. Poor and N. Smith (eds), *Mysticism and Reform, 1400-1750*, 84-123, Notre Dame, IN: University of Notre Dame Press.

Warnar, G. (2007), *Ruusbroec: Literature and Mysticism in the Fourteenth Century*, trans. Diane Webb, Brill's Studies in Intellectual History, 150, Leiden: Brill.

Willaert, F. (1995), 'Is Ruusbroecs *Brulocht* literatuur?' in T. Mertens (ed.), *Siet, de brudegom comt. Facettten van 'Die geestelike brulocht' van Jan van Ruusbroec (1293-1381)*, 49-64, Kampen: Kok.

Early printed books (chronological)

Deuoti et venerabilis patris Ioan[n]nis Rusberi ... De ornatu spiritualium nuptiarum libri tres (1512), Paris: Henricus Stephanus.

Theologia mystica, cum speculativa, tum praecipue affectiva ... *per Henricum Harph,* ... *Opus nunc primum typis excussum* (1538), Cologne: Novesianus.

D. Ioannis Ruisbroici canonici regularis libelli duo, vere divini. Prior, De septem scalae divini amoris, seu vitae sanctae gradibus. Posterior, De perfectione filiorum Dei. Nuper inventi, et nunc primum in lucem aediti (1538), Bononiae impraessum ex officina Vincentii Bonardi Parmensis, et Marci Antonii Carpensis.

D. Ioannis Rusbrochii summi atque sanctissimi viri, quem insignis quidam theologus alterum Dionysium Areopagitam appellat, opera omnia. Nunc demum post annos ferme ducentos e Brabantiae Germanico idiomate reddita Latine per F. Laurentium Surium. Carthusiae Coloniensis alumnum (1552), Cologne: Ex officina haeredum Ioannis Quentel.

La perle évangelicque, trésor incomparable de la sapience divine. Nouvellement traduict de latin en francois par les PP. Chartreux lez Paris (1602), Paris: Vefve Guillaume de la Noue.

van Ruusbroec, J. (1606), *L'ornement des nopces spirituelles* ... Traduict en François par un religieux chartreux de Paris. Avec la vie de l'autheur à la fin du livre, Toulouse: veuve J. Colomiés et R. Colomiés.

Ein alt und werdes Büchlein von der Gnade Gottes, genommen auss dem Anfang des Hohen Liedts Salomonis ... von Johan. Rüsebruch (1621), n.p.

Ein edles Büchlein, des Johann Taulers. Wie der Mensch möge ernsthafftig, innig, geistlich unnd Gottschawende werden (1621), n.p.

Traducción de las obras del iluminado doctor y venerable padre D. Juan Rusbroquio ... en ... castellana con adiciones por el padre Blas López
(1696-1698), 3 vols, Madrid: Melchor Álvarez.

Des Johannis Rusbrochii ... Schriften ... (1701), Offenbach am Main: Bonaventura de Launoy.

3

Die Rose by Heinric of Brussels, the Brabantine Version of the Old French *Romance of the Rose*

Anne Reynders

Introduction: The radiance of the French *Rose*

The Old French *Romance of the Rose* was probably the most successful and influential text of the French Middle Ages (Kay 1995: 9). It is a narrative poem about the art of love in the format of an allegorical tale in a dream setting. The narrator retells a dream that he had five years earlier. In this dream he fell in love with a rosebud he wanted to pick and in the end he did so. But before he conquered the rose, he met a whole series of allegorical characters, who either helped or hindered him. They instructed him as well; in the first place about love, but also about a variety of other more or less related topics.

The Old French *Rose* is generally seen as the work of two poets. Around 1230, Guillaume de Lorris wrote the first part, which comprises around 4,000 verses, to which Jean de Meun added a continuation of more than 17,000 verses some forty years later (10). Both parts are very different in character. The first part by Guillaume de Lorris is very much influenced by the doctrine of courtly love or *fin'amors*, whereas Jean de Meun's is full of irony about love, marriage and relations between men and women. There is a lot of description in Guillaume de Lorris's section, whereas in Jean de Meun's part discourse is more important. The latter section is essentially made up of long speeches delivered by the allegorical characters, who no longer limit themselves to topics related to love (24–28).

The use of allegory in a secular work and the format of an autobiographical narrator recounting his own experience (i.e. his dream) made *The Romance of the Rose* a highly innovative text (Uitti 1978: 211–212; Van der Poel 1989: 145). Exceptional also for a work in the vernacular was the bulk of classical Latin philosophy and learning offered by the allegorical figures, especially by the figures in Jean de Meun's section (Fleming 1992: 81–100, especially 85).

The *Romance of the Rose* had a profound influence on French literature and in the century following Jean de Meun's continuation it was translated into Italian, twice into English and twice into Dutch (Badel 1980; Huot 2008). One Middle Dutch version originated in the county of Flanders around 1290 and the other in the duchy of Brabant before 1325 (Van der Poel 1989: 18–20). These Middle Dutch versions are independent from one another – that is, neither is a reworking or a retranslation of the other, and they are very different in many respects (61–65 and 82–143).

The Flemish *Rose* is a free adaptation and has an unmistakable conservative bias. The most important innovative element of the French source, i.e. the use of allegory, is cast in a different frame. The allegory is no longer presented as the narrator's account of a dream but as the history of a happy couple that the narrator meets at the beginning of the story. This new frame was probably meant as a kind of stepping stone to smooth the introduction to the allegorical tale (Van der Poel 1989: 162–199; Van der Poel 1992).

The Brabantine translation or *Die Rose* is generally considered a faithful, though abridged, translation. However, this is an old label that dates back to a nineteenth-century edition of the text (Verwijs 1868: XIV–XXI), and since the publication of this edition *Die Rose* has hardly attracted any scholarly attention. The Flemish *Rose*, on the other hand, has been the object of study more frequently (e.g. Heeroma 1958; Van der Poel 1989; Van Driel 2007). Tellingly, the only scholar who devoted attention to *Die Rose* in the twentieth century did so in a monograph on the Flemish *Rose*. Van der Poel (1989) used *Die Rose* as a kind of third element in the comparison of the Flemish and Old French versions. She made many interesting remarks on *Die Rose*, but it was not the main focus of her research.

It is quite surprising that there has been so little interest in *Die Rose* during recent decades. Since the last quarter of the twentieth century, the field of Middle Dutch Studies has been booming and has manifested a keen interest in translations. However, the attention has been very focused on the creativity and on the agency of the medieval translators. Consequently, creative adaptations have been much more appealing to researchers than translations that are thought to closely follow their source texts. *Die Rose* is highly likely to have suffered from being labelled a faithful translation (Reynders 2018: 27–29).

The surviving manuscripts, however, strongly suggest that in the Middle Ages the Brabantine version was much more appreciated than the Flemish one. To begin with, the Flemish *Rose* survives only in fragments totalling not even 3,000 lines from no more than two manuscripts (Van der Poel 1989: 56–62), whereas *Die Rose* survives in three complete manuscripts and in seven fragments, which probably derive from five other codices (21–22). Second, *Die Rose* has been copied over a much longer period than the Flemish *Rose* and spread over a much wider geographical area. The fragments of the

Flemish *Rose* stem from a manuscript from the beginning of the fourteenth century and a manuscript from the middle of the same century, both of which originated in Flanders (Heeroma 1958: 84). On the other hand, a famous manuscript of *Die Rose* (Stuttgart, WLB, Cod. Poet. phil. 2° 22) shows that the text was still being copied at the beginning of the fifteenth century (Brinkman and Mulder 2003). This happened in Ghent, a city in Flanders. It was quite exceptional at that time that a Brabantine text – be it an original or a translated work – found its way to Flanders.

There is quite some evidence that the medieval Low Countries did not form a single literary system but were composed of two different systems, which were unequal in prestige. F. Willaert (2010) thinks that the county of Flanders may have harboured a literary and cultural system that was different from that in the rest of the Low Countries. The Flemish cultural and literary system was probably the more prestigious of the two: B. Caers (2011) has demonstrated that a large number of Flemish romances were copied all over the Low Countries, whereas Flemish copies of Middle Dutch romances that originated elsewhere in the Low Countries are rare. *Die Rose* seems to be a most notable exception. Although parts of it were reformulated and retranslated (Brinkman in press), it travelled against this flow and crossed an important cultural border.

Last but not least, the fragments of the Flemish *Rose* do not mention an author's name, whereas the translator of the Brabantine *Rose* is credited in all three complete manuscripts, even in the fifteenth-century Ghent manuscript. Moreover, the translator, who presents himself as Heinric of Brussels, does so with a self-assurance which is quite exceptional for the period (Reynders 2015). He repeats his name several times and adds a short biography. He tells his audience that he is a priest living near Leuven and that he is quite renowned as an author. Nevertheless, although authors' names are rare in Middle Dutch literature and authorship contribution has come to the fore in Middle Dutch Studies recently (Kestemont 2013), nothing can be said with certainty about the profile and oeuvre of Heinric of Brussels. The most recent studies of the author's oeuvre date back to the late 1950s. The problem is, first of all, that quite a lot of works which originated in Brabant around the turn of the thirteenth century name 'Heinric' as their author and, second, that Heinric was a very common name at the time. It remains unclear whether all these works can be attributed to one and the same author (Van der Poel 1989: 16–17).

The Brabantine *Rose* undoubtedly still offers plenty of opportunities for further research and merits more scholarly attention, not in the least because it seems to have enjoyed considerable and enduring success in the Middle Ages. The following section aims to contribute to this research by focusing on the way *Die Rose* relates to its famous French source.

Die Rose: A faithful but abridged translation?

As already noted, *Die Rose* is generally considered to be a faithful, though abridged translation. Even in the most recent history of medieval Dutch literature it is described in these terms (Van Oostrom 2013: 354). However, this is a somewhat paradoxical label, especially when we take into account that *Die Rose* is abridged substantially. It consists of 14,412 verses (Verwijs 1868), as opposed to the 21,780 verses of the French text (Langlois 1914–1924). Although the verse forms of the Old French *Rose* and the Brabantine *Rose* are different, they do not differ very much in length. The Old French *Rose* is versed in octasyllabic rhyming couplets, whereas Heinric used the verse form in which most Middle Dutch literature is written, i.e. rhyming couplets with three to five stresses.

More importantly, it is Jean de Meun's continuation which is abridged, for Guillaume de Lorris's section has almost exactly the same length in Heinric's translation. In the Old French *Rose* Guillaume de Lorris's part counts 4,058 verses, whereas Heinric's translation of it counts 4,056 verses. Given the fact that both sections of the French poem differ considerably in tone and theme, a pattern such as this could well result from a planned design, and from the intent not to translate faithfully but rather to adapt the source text in one way or another. The best way to uncover such a design is through an analysis of the effect of the omissions on the overall structure of the poem.

According to current research, the abridgement of *Die Rose* can be attributed to two different kinds of shifts. There are small omissions of a limited number of verses, often in descriptions or in speeches, which have a streamlining effect and which tend to make the macrostructure easier to follow. These omissions occur in the translation of both parts of the romance. Next to these small omissions, there are the so-called major omissions. These omissions, which change the macro-level substantially, only occur in the translation of Jean de Meun's part (Van der Poel 1989: 30–53).

The most striking example is the treatment of Nature and Genius, two allegorical characters introduced by Jean de Meun (50–52). In *Die Rose* both characters are absent and so is most of their discourse (Langlois, 15,891–20,682). Only a very small part of Genius's sermon, i.e. a fierce diatribe against women (Langlois 16,323–16,706), has not been omitted, but is launched by the narrator. This operation results in the deletion of approximately 4,500 verses. The most notable effect of the omission of Nature and Genius is that the macrostructure of the story comes more to the fore. In the last verses of Guillaume de Lorris, Bel Accueil (Fair Welcome), the allegorical character who represents the willing disposition of the loving lady towards her lover, is punished for granting a kiss to the dreamer-lover and imprisoned in a vast castle by Jealousy. In Jean de Meun's continuation, which is essentially made up of long monologues, the frame story becomes very thin: it is, in fact, limited to the assault and the destruction of Jealousy's castle. During the long sermons of Nature and Genius the preparations for the attack on the castle recede completely into the background. In the Brabantine *Rose* the imminent attack is never far off.

A second and related effect is that *Die Rose* is more exclusively a treatise about love than the French *Rose*. As K. Brownlee (1985) has shown, Jean de Meun's continuation on the whole offers a critical rewriting of Guillaume de Lorris's part, which is essentially a treatise about the courtly love code and the pleasures and the sufferings that (courtly) love entails. The fiercest critic of Guillaume de Lorris's courtly love code is undoubtedly Genius. His speech is primarily a plea for procreation and it is cast in an irreverent discourse combining the registers of sexual activity and Christian spirituality. Nature, who lectures on different scientific theories and theological debates, also stresses the importance of procreation and, as such, she criticizes the sterile *fin'amors* as well, albeit more implicitly. On the other hand, she attacks the aristocratic world of hereditary noblemen quite openly: according to her, men of learning are of higher esteem (Kay 1995: 43–44, 96–101 and 107–108). Without Nature's and Genius's sermons Guillaume de Lorris's courtly love tale is much less criticized and the theme of love remains in the forefront.

Other speeches are not omitted entirely but shortened. An example is La Vieille's sermon, which is about 31 per cent shorter in *Die Rose* (Van der Poel 1989: 45–47). La Vieille, or the old woman, is not really an allegorical character; she is rather a type. She is the prototype of the old woman who regrets the loss of her youth, her beauty and the men of her youth, and even more of the money of her former lovers. La Vieille is the guardian of Bel Accueil while he is being kept as a prisoner in Jealousy's castle, and she sermonizes him in order to help him.

Bel Accueil is a male character, but as he represents an aspect of the loving lady, the old woman's sermon is addressed to women, especially to those in love. Essentially, La Vieille encourages women to enjoy men and sex while they are young and, above all, to fleece their lovers. At times, her sermon is rather subversive, because it sheds a dubious light on herself and on women in general. In the passage where La Vieille discusses good table manners, for instance, she explains to Bel Accueil how to behave when eating and drinking, but she also describes at length how not to behave (Langlois 13,385–13,474).

These descriptions of ill-mannered women are at times longer and more colourful than the advice itself. This ironic playfulness is typical of Jean de Meun's continuation (Kay 1995: 62–63) but does not seem to have amused Heinric so much. He often renders these descriptions in a reduced way, omitting the most disgraceful scenes. When it comes to drinking habits, for instance, Heinric includes La Vieille's advice that women should not drink too much (Langlois 13,449; Verwijs 12,345), but leaves out the description of women pouring wine straight down their throats in large quantities and falling dazed from their stools to the ground (Langlois 13,443–13,448 and 13,463–13,466).

The way Heinric renders la Vieille's sermon also shows more respect for marriage, faithful love and courtliness. When towards the end of her sermon La Vieille explains in great detail how women can cheat their lovers, Heinric omits a passage of 269 verses altogether (Langlois 14,161–14,430). Other smaller passages in which La Vieille makes fun of marriage or faithful lovers are left untranslated as well (e.g. Langlois 14,139–14,147). As a result, the didactic function of this sermon is less perverted by cynical and licentious digressions than in the Old French source text: the advisory function of la Vieille's speech can be taken more seriously.

This may well have been a conscious strategy, because Heinric made some additions reinforcing the didactic function. To give an example, he added a passage concerning 'courtly' conversation, 'courtly' being a word that does not even appear in the corresponding Old French text. While La Vieille is being cynical about women's tears, which dry so quickly, Heinric insists instead on the virtue of a nice conversation:

Ere vrouwen steet oec wale
Scone spreken ande suete tale
Ende heblec te sine overal
Ende hovesch: dat maecse liefgetal
(It makes a good impression when women speak beautifully and suavely and behave elegantly and courteously in every situation: it makes them attractive.)
(Verwijs 1868: vv. 12,297–12,300; my translation)

The rationale underlying the shifts in La Vieille's sermon seems to be in tune with the omission of Nature's and Genius's discourse. Jean de Meun's cynical and humorous rewriting of Guillaume de Lorris's exalted ideal of courtliness and courtly love has been toned down. Consequently, the duality of the French *Rose* is attenuated and *Die Rose* becomes a more unified and more serious art of love.

This hypothesis can also help to explain why Heinric did not reduce Raison's speech as much as La Vieille's (Raison's sermon is only 15 per cent shorter than its Old French counterpart, see Van der Poel 1989: 37–38). Raison warns the lover, who is desperately unhappy at that moment, of the pain caused by passionate love for women and offers a warm plea for the benefits of friendship. As such, her good advice is exempt from the licentiousness that regularly appears in the advice of the other main allegorical figures in Jean de Meun's continuation.

The famous midpoint of the French *Rose* was adapted in the same vein. At the exact midpoint of the conjoint texts of Guillaume de Lorris and Jean de Meun, the God of Love addresses the troops that are about to attack Jealousy's castle. In this speech the names of both authors are mentioned: we are told that Jean de Meun will continue the romance begun by Guillaume de Lorris. The God of Love even cites the last verses of Guillaume and the first verses of Jean. At that very moment, the audience realizes that they have been reading (or listening to) Jean de Meun's continuation for quite some time: his continuation starts around verse 4,000 and the midpoint is situated around verse 10,500. At the same time, it becomes clear that the romance is no longer told by the dreamer-lover himself. Jean is a clerk-narrator and the dreamer-lover Guillaume has become his protagonist (Uitti 1978: 213–214).

In *Die Rose* neither of the French authors is mentioned, and the whole idea of a first part written by a lover-dreamer-poet continued by someone else, who is no longer relating his own experience, has disappeared as well. The only author who is mentioned is Heinric, the translator. Again, we seem to see Heinric's design to offer a more homogenous rendition of his source. The whole idea of the continuator ironizing the ideology of the first author has been omitted.

Seen from this vantage point, the old label of 'a faithful, though abridged translation' becomes somewhat problematic. The substantial shortening of Jean de Meun's continuation alters not only the structure, but also the tone and the function of the French *Rose*. Still, it is important to note that this is a matter of gradation. The irony of Jean de Meun is certainly not completely absent: Heinric may have toned it down to a certain extent, but he preserved a great deal of the playful humour as well.

Conclusion: The testimony of the miscellanies

The shifts that Heinric of Brussels applied while translating the French *Rose* seem to spring from his wish to offer his audience an art of love which was more homogeneous, less ironic, and less licentious than his source text. Still, he enriched the Brabantine literature and culture with several new literary devices and a whole range of philosophical ideas about love and life. Together with the fact that he so proudly presents himself, this seems indicative of a literary and cultural system that welcomed foreign influences as important and enriching. The co-texts of *Die Rose* in the two oldest extant miscellanies confirm this impression.

The two oldest miscellanies containing a version of *Die Rose* were both written in the fourteenth century in Brabant. The oldest (The Hague KB, KA XXIV) dates from around 1325 (Lieftinck 1951: 17). The more recent (Brussels KBR, II. 1171) consists of two parts. Still, as both these parts have a similar size and layout, they are likely to have been designed to be used together from the beginning. The first part was probably written in the second quarter of the fourteenth century. The second part possibly dates from around the same time or from around 1350 (Deschamps and Mulder 2007: 40–41).

In The Hague KB, KA XXIV, *Die Rose* is followed by what is commonly called *The Romance of Cassamus*, a series of courtly scenes from a Dutch translation of *Les Voeux du Paon*, and *Die Frenesie*, a short satirical text in which a Parisian student talks about his lazy life in that city. Shortly after, this codex was joined to codices containing didactic work by Maerlant: notably his *Best of Nature*, a Dutch translation of Cantimpré's *De natura rerum*, and his *Verse Bible*, a Dutch adaptation of Comestor's *Historia Scolastica* (Lieftinck 1951: 17).

In Brussels KBR, II. 1171 the longest and most important co-text of *Die Rose* is the first part of Maerlant's *Mirror of History*, a Dutch adaptation of Vincent of Beauvais's *Speculum historiale*. The other co-texts are much shorter and comprise a Dutch version of the misogynist *Seven sages of Rome* and some satirical works.

What do these miscellanies reveal about the reception of the French *Rose* in fourteenth-century Brabant and the literary climate of the time? First of all, the predominance of translated texts is striking: all major texts are translations of French or Latin sources. The openness towards foreign influences comes clearly to the fore. Non-translated texts seem to be included only to fill the remaining space in the last quires. Still, the satirical nature of most of these short texts fits in well with the satirical and misogynist strands in the French *Rose*, which were attenuated, but surely not entirely omitted from *Die Rose*. The courtly scenes of *The Romance of Cassamus*, on the other hand, echo the courtly world of Guillaume de Lorris. In this respect, the co-texts also confirm the fact that, notwithstanding the shifts which Heinric applied, several formative characteristics of the French *Rose* were transmitted in Heinric's version and recognized by the compilers.

Even more significant is the fact that the largest and most prominent co-texts are all works by Maerlant. Maerlant was a thirteenth-century poet and a very prolific translator. He translated, or rather adapted, a whole series of Latin works of learning, in order to make these accessible to a lay audience. His patrons belonged to high aristocratic circles, but in the fourteenth century his works were widely disseminated (Van Oostrom 2009: 29–33).

In the fourteenth century, moreover, Maerlant was seen by other authors as a kind of founding father of Middle Dutch didactic literature (33). By the end of the thirteenth century and throughout the fourteenth century, book production in the Low Countries was booming and books containing didactic works in Dutch were produced on an unprecedented scale. Laymen seem to have discovered books in the vernacular as a means of access to learning, which previously had been accessible only in Latin (Warnar 2008). In this respect, it is important to note that neither of the two Brabantine miscellanies show traces of Latin, not even in marginal notes, as is often the case in the manuscripts of the French *Rose* (Huot 1993: 40–46 and 48–55).

As such, these two miscellanies tend to show that the Brabantine *Rose* was part of this movement in Middle Dutch literature that offered instruction and learning to a lay audience, and to this end it drew extensively on foreign sources. It is even conceivable that Heinric reckoned with the taste or the expectations of an audience used to more serious didactic works, such as those written by the celebrated Maerlant, and that his wish to contribute to this new movement explains to some extent the shifts he applied while translating the French *Rose*.

References

Badel, P.-Y. (1980), *Le Roman de la Rose au XIVe siècle. Étude de la réception de l'œuvre*, Geneva: Droz.
Brinkman, H. (in press), 'Entering the Commercial Scriptorium. History of the Book at the Crosssection of Codicology and Textual Scholarship', in P. Stoop (ed.), *Writing for Third Parties*, Turnhout: Brepols.
Brinkman, H. and H. Mulder (2003), 'Recht, historie en schone letteren: het arbeidsterrrein van een Gents kopiistencollectief. Hs. Brussel kb 16.762-75 en het Comburgse handschrift', *Queeste* 10 (1): 27–78.
Brownlee, K. (1985), 'Jean de Meun and the Limits of Romance. Genius as Rewriter of Guillaume de Lorris', in K. Brownlee and M.S. Brownlee (eds), *Romance Generic Transformation from Chrétien de Troyes to Cervantes*, 114–134, Hannover: University Press of New England.
Caers, B. (2011), 'Een buchelin inn flemische. Over ontstaan en verspreiding van de ridderepiek in de Nederlanden (ca. 1150–1450)', *Tijdschrift voor Nederlandse Taal- en Letterkunde* 127 (3): 223–251.
Deschamps, J. and H. Mulder (2007), *Inventaris van de Middelnederlandse handschriften van de Koninklijke Bibliotheek van België (voorlopige uitgave)*, vol. 9, Brussels: Koninklijke Bibliotheek.
Driel, J.M. van (2007), 'Vlaamse meesters. Vergi, Rose, Aiol en anderen', *Neerlandistiek. nl* 07.13. http://dspace.library.uu.nl/handle/1874/28433 (accessed 17 April 2018).
Fleming, J.V. (1992), 'Jean de Meun and the Ancient Poets', in K. Brownlee and S. Huot (eds), *Rethinking the Romance of the Rose: Text, Image, Reception*, 81–100, Philadelphia: Pennsylvania University Press.

Heeroma, K., ed. (1958), *De fragmenten van de Tweede Rose*, Zwolle: N.V. Uitgevers-Maatschappij W.E.J. Tjeenk Willink.

Huot, S. (1993), *The Romance of the Rose and its Medieval Readers: Interpretation, Reception, Manuscript Transmission*, Cambridge: Cambridge University Press.

Huot, S. (2008), 'The *Roman de la Rose* in translation in Medieval Europe', in H. Kittel, A.P. Frank and N.G. Norbert (eds), *Übersetzung. Translation. Traduction*, vol. 2, 1366–1370, Berlin: De Gruyter Mouton.

Kay, S. (1995), *The Romance of the Rose*, London: Grant & Cutler.

Kestemont, M. (2013), *Het gewicht van de auteur: stylometrische auteursherkenning in Middelnederlandse literatuur*, Gent: Koninklijke Academie voor Nederlandse Taal- en Letterkunde.

Langlois, E., ed. (1914–1924), *Le Roman de la Rose par Guillaume de Lorris et Jean de Meun*, Paris: Champion.

Lieftinck, G.I. (1951), 'Drie handschriften uit de librije van de abdij van Sint-Bernards opt Schelt (Brussel KB 19545, 19546 en Kon. Ned. Akad. v. Wetensch. XXIV)', *Tijdschrift voor Nederlandse Taal- en Letterkunde* 69 (1): 1–30.

Oostrom, F. van (2009), 'The Middle Ages until circa 1400', in T. Hermans (ed.) *A Literary History of the Low Countries*, 1–61, Rochester: Camden House.

Oostrom, F. van (2013), *Wereld in woorden. Geschiedenis van de Nederlandse literatuur 1300–1400*, Amsterdam: Prometheus.

Poel, D.E. van der (1989), *De Vlaamse Rose en Die Rose van Heinric: Onderzoekingen over twee Middelnederlandse bewerkingen van de Roman de la Rose*, Hilversum: Verloren.

Poel, D.E. van der (1992), 'A Romance of a Rose and Florentine: The Flemish Adaptation of the Romance of the Rose', in K. Brownlee and S. Huot (eds), *Rethinking the Romance of the Rose. Text, Image, Reception*, 304–315, Philadelphia: University of Pennsylvania Press.

Reynders, A. (2015), 'Die Rose, de Brabantse vertaling van de Roman de la Rose. Heinric van Brussel en zijn vertaling in de proloog en het betoog van de God van Minnen', *Queeste* 22 (2): 139–164.

Reynders, A. (2018), 'Middle Dutch Literary Studies and Translation Studies', *Translation Studies* 11 (1): 17–32. doi: 10.1080/14781700.2017.1334581.

Uitti, K.D. (1978), 'From *Clerc* to *Poète*: The Relevance of the *Romance of the Rose* to Machaut's World', in M. Pelner Cosman and B. Chandler (eds), *Machaut's World: Science and Art in the Fourteenth Century*, 207–216, New York: The New York Academy of Sciences.

Verwijs, E., ed. (1868), *Die Rose van Heinric van Aken, met de fragmenten der tweede vertaling*, Leiden: Maatschappij der Nederlansche Letterkunde.

Warnar, G. (2008), 'Leringhen in den boeken. De tekst en de drager in de Nederlandse literatuur van de veertiende eeuw', *Spiegel der Letteren* 50 (2): 155–171.

Willaert, F. (2010), *De ruimte van het boek: Literaire regio's in de Lage Landen tijdens de middeleeuwen*, Leiden: Stichting Neerlandistiek Leiden.

4

Courtly Literature in the Low Countries and Germany: Jacob van Maerlant and Rudolf von Ems

Bart Besamusca

This chapter is concerned with the oeuvre of the thirteenth-century Middle Dutch poet Jacob van Maerlant (*c.* 1235–*c.* 1295), who was doubtless the most prolific and influential author of the medieval Low Countries (Van Oostrom 2006: 502–549). His romances and didactic works are discussed here as examples of courtly literature. A range of meanings are attached to the notion 'courtly'. The adjective may indicate a type of text in which an idealized world is presented, or may refer to the stylized language of certain works (Johnson 1999: 5–7). Here, yet another meaning of 'courtly' is applied: the texts which will be the object of our attention were written for audiences that belonged to aristocratic courts. It should be noted in this context that a court was not identical to a household. Whereas a noble household was an institution, serving as the court's backbone in providing domestic services, the court itself, in medieval times in essence an itinerant body, was the ruler's 'environment, both a place, normally of unfixed location, and an assemblage of people' (Vale 2001: 15–33, 31). For Jacob van Maerlant, this court consisted of the high nobles who belonged to the inner circle of Count Florens V of Holland and Zeeland. In the first section of this chapter, the poet's literary production will be discussed in relation to this court. The second section compares Jacob's activities as a court poet to that of Rudolf von Ems, who composed his texts for German aristocrats.

Jacob van Maerlant and the Court of Florens V

In 1248, Count William II of Holland and Zeeland (r.1234-1256) was elected as Holy Roman Emperor (Blok et al. 1982: 294-299; Van Oostrom 1996: 103-107). To confirm his high status, he started to build a princely palace in The Hague, which he had selected as his main residence (Hourihane 2012: vol. 3, 270-272). One may suspect that his preference for The Hague was connected to the abundant possibilities to hunt in the area around the town (Smit 1991: 118). However, William II was not granted much time to rise to European prominence. Just six years after his election, in 1256, he was killed in battle against the Frisians. His son Florens, at that time only a year and a half, was placed under the guidance of William's brother, also called Florens, but this guardian died in tournament in 1258. Then the young boy came under the supervision of his aunt Aleide of Hainault, who was his guardian between 1258 and 1263 (Blok et al. 1982: 299). It is likely that Florens grew up in the company of Aleide's children and the young heirs of the Lords of Voorne and Cats from Zeeland, who strongly supported Aleide (Van Oostrom 1996: 107-111). In 1266, Florens V started to rule his county. He became a powerful prince, who improved the administration, built castles and added an impressive ceremonial hall, the Ridderzaal (Knight's Hall), to the buildings in The Hague's Inner Court, inspired by Westminster Hall in London and Salisbury Cathedral (Blok et al. 1982: 300-303; Mekking 1991; Hourihane 2012: vol. 4, 423). In 1296, Florens V was murdered by a number of high-placed nobles as a consequence of his decision to join the French king in his political conflict with the English sovereign (Blok et al. 1982: 303).

The court of Florens V provided the literary patronage for a substantial number of Jacob van Maerlant's texts. Writing in the second half of the thirteenth century, Jacob was the most important author in the Dutch-language area. Born in Flanders around 1235, he may have attended Bruges' famous chapter school of Saint Donatian (Van Oostrom 1996: 29-36). His intellectual training was already apparent in the text that scholars assume to be his debut, *Alexanders geesten* (Alexander's great deeds), because a school text, Gautier de Châtillon's *Alexandreis*, served as the main source for this verse text about Alexander the Great (Van Oostrom 1996: 19-29). Since he mentions in his epilogue that he completed his adaptation of fourteen thousand lines in half a year's time (Franck 1882: X, lines 1530-1531), we may safely conclude that the poet was an extremely hard worker (cf. Van Oostrom 1984). The patron of this text is thought to be Aleide of Hainault. Although Jacob refrains from directly mentioning the name of his benefactor, in his epilogue he points out that his audience may identify the noble lady who supported him by studying the anagram that he made of the initial letters of the ten parts of his romance (Franck 1882: X, lines 1516-1520). 'Aleide' is the most convincing solution of Jacob's riddle (Van Oostrom 1996: 112-113, Van der Meulen 2012: 56-57).

It has been argued that Aleide asked Jacob to write *Alexanders geesten* for the education of the young Florens (Van Oostrom 1996: 113-127). This assumption, which implies that Jacob wrote his text around 1258, is supported by a remarkable textual deviation from the Latin source. At the moment that Alexander is preparing himself for a battle against

Darius, Jacob adds a description of the hero's shield (Franck 1882: IV, lines 1617–1619), which corresponds to the coat of arms of the county of Holland (Van Oostrom 1996: 117–118; Van der Meulen 2012: 58). This passage strongly suggests that *Alexanders geesten* was meant to inspire Florens by presenting him the story of a young prince, who lost his father untimely and performed great deeds (Van Oostrom 1996: 118–119).

Around 1261, Jacob lived in Voorne, an island on the border between Holland and Zeeland. As he states in the prologue to his *Graal-Merlijn*, he was employed there. The poet makes himself known as 'Jacob de coster van merlant / Den gij to voren hebbet bekant / Jn des koninges Allexanders Jeesten'(Jacob, the sexton of Maerlant, whom you have met in King Alexander's deeds) (Sodmann 1980: lines 37–39). His position as verger of the church of Saint Pieter in the village of Maerlant evidently allowed him to compose extensive texts such as the *Graal-Merlijn*, which he dedicated to 'hern alabrechte / Den heer van vorne wal myt rechte' (Lord Albrecht, the rightful prince of Voorne) (Sodmann 1980: lines 15–16). For this young viscount of Zeeland, whose father Hendrik died in 1259, Jacob adapted French prose versions of Robert de Boron's *Joseph d'Arimathie* and *Merlin*. These Arthurian romances inform their readers about the history of the Grail and tell about a young boy, Arthur, who became king of Britain with help of the magician Merlin. It is likely that these subjects had the interest of young noblemen like Albrecht, who, due to Jacob's additions to his source, also learned about, for instance, good behaviour and trustworthy counselors. The romance was not only meant to entertain the readers and listeners, but had a didactic purpose as well (Van Oostrom 1996: 127–129; Besamusca and Brandsma 1998).

Frits van Oostrom (1996: 127–136) has argued persuasively that *Alexanders geesten* and the *Graal-Merlijn* functioned as part of a scheme, initiated by Aleide, for the education of Florens, her own children and some young nobles from Zeeland, including Albrecht. This so-called 'literature program of Voorne' (Van Oostrom 1996: 135) may have included at least three other texts, albeit that nothing is known about their patronage. Around 1262, Jacob used a French Arthurian romance, *Torrez, chevalier au cercle d'or*, to write *Torec*, which tells about the hero's quest for a precious diadem stolen from his grandmother. In the course of his adventures, he defeats a large number of King Arthur's knights, and listens to conversations on virtues, good behaviour and love in the mysterious Chamber of Wisdom. Around 1264, Jacob adapted another French source, Benoît de Saint-Maure's *Roman de Troie*, Virgil's *Aeneid* and various other texts to compose his voluminous *Historie van Troyen*. In this romance, the history of the Trojan War is preceded by the story of the Argonauts and followed by the founding of Rome by Aeneas. About 1266, in the period that Florens V began his reign as count of Holland and Zeeland, at the age of twelve, Jacob completed his translation of the *Secret secretorum*. This *Heimelijkheid der heimelijcheden* (Secret of secrets) is a mirror of princes, allegedly consisting of the advice that Aristotle gave to his pupil Alexander the Great. It is striking that all these five romances are concerned with young men who develop into great rulers. This joint focus reinforces the idea that they were used for educational purposes. The teacher of the young aristocrats may have been Jacob himself. It is, however, as likely that Aleide's learned chaplain Bette van Zierikzee was in charge of their education and not a cleric from the lower orders such as Jacob (Van der Meulen 2000: 52–53, 67–71).

Jacob's connections with the high nobles of Holland and Zeeland did not come to an end with the installation of Count Florens V in 1266. Although the poet returned to Flanders, these aristocrats continued to show an interest in his work. Living in Damme, Bruges' seaport, Jacob may have been employed as secretary to the aldermen of the town, or as toll collector in the service of Nicolaas van Cats, Lord of North-Beveland, and one of Florens's closest advisors (Van Oostrom 1996: 137, 143–146). Around 1270, the poet produced a verse rendition of Thomas of Cantimpré's *De natura rerum*, adapting the Latin learning to suit the needs of his lay audience. In the prologue of this biological encyclopedia, *Der naturen bloeme* (The Best of Nature), Jacob states right at the beginning that the work was meant 'omme te sendene tere gichte'(to send as a present) (Verwijs 1878: l. 2). At the end of the prologue, we read that the receiver of the gift was Nicolaas van Cats, who is said to have requested the text (Verwijs 1878: lines 147–149). It has been assumed that this nobleman also commissioned Jacob's *Rijmbijbel* (Verse Bible), which was completed in 1271 (Van Oostrom 1996: 145–146). It certainly makes sense to situate the *Rijmbijbel* in the context of the Holland-Zeeland patronage of Jacob's didactic texts, but it should be noted that evidence for this claim is lacking. The poet just mentions that his lengthy account of biblical history, based on Petrus Comestor's *Historia scholastica* and Flavius Josephus's *De bello Judaico*, was ordered by someone whom he calls 'my dear friend' (Postma 1991: 57).

Count Florens V himself, finally, also acted as Jacob's patron. His name is related to the poet's *magnum opus*, which he produced at the end of his career. Between circa 1284 and 1289, Jacob adapted Vincent of Beauvais's *Speculum historiale*. After having written more than 90,000 lines, the poet was unable to complete this huge world chronicle, due to reasons of health or growing tensions between Holland and Flanders (Van Oostrom 1996: 370–371). At the end of the prologue of his *Spiegel historiael* (Mirror of history), he offers 'Grave Florens, coninc Willems sone' (Count Florens, King William's son) (De Vries and Verwijs 1861–1879: l, 93) his work ('Ontfaet dit werk', [Receive this work] l. 94), and states: 'Ghi waert de ghone / Die mi dit dede anevaen'(You were the one who made me undertake this work) (lines 94–95). In the context of the Holland-Zeeland patronage of Jacob's oeuvre, it is apt that the prince of that county commissioned Jacob's most ambitious work, even though the *Spiegel historiael* turned out to be the poet's swan song.

The quantity, quality and scope of Jacob's oeuvre make him a unique figure in the history of medieval Dutch literature. Looking for European counterparts, Frits van Oostrom (1996: 437–439) has suggested that, on account of his literary production and his patrons, one outstanding and prolific author in particular, Rudolf von Ems, merits a comparison with the Flemish poet. This suggestion will be followed in the next section.

Jacob van Maerlant and Rudolf von Ems

Since neither Jacob nor Rudolf are attested in historical documents, our knowledge of these authors is based on the information they and other writers have provided in their works. The German author was born some decades earlier than Jacob, and was active in the period between circa 1210 and 1250. While Jacob mentions that he was a verger, Rudolf calls himself, in his *Willehalm von Orlens*, 'knappe' and 'dienest man zu Muntfort' (Von Ertzdorff 1967: 50). This means that Rudolf was, like the famous poet Hartmann von Aue, a member of the knightly class of *ministeriales*, serving the counts of Montfort (Bumke 1986: 684). 'Knappe' indicates that he was not knighted (Von Ertzdorff 1967: 53). According to the author who continued Rudolf's unfinished *Weltchronik* (Chronicle of the world), the poet was from Ems, meaning that he came from a *ministeriales* family whose ancestral castle was situated above present-day Hohenems, south of Bregenz (Bumke 1986: 122; Andersen 2006: 225). The continuator also mentions that Rudolf passed away in Italy, which may indicate that he was in the retinue of the Hohenstaufen King Konrad IV, who died in Lavello, near Melfi, in 1254 (Heinzle 1984: 48; see for a different opinion Brackert 1968: 196–198).

Jacob and Rudolf were both men of learning, as their abundant use of Latin source material indicates. It has been suggested that Rudolf was educated either at the Benedictine monastery of St Gallen or the cathedral school of Constance (Von Ertzdorff 1967: 59–60; Andersen 2006: 229). In spite of their scholarly background, both Jacob and Rudolf composed their works in the vernacular. Moreover, they only wrote verse texts, probably due to the literary tastes of their audiences (Besamusca 2013: 474). Both authors were prolific and enjoyed extensive literary patronage. According to his own statements, Rudolf composed four commissioned texts (Bumke 1979: 512–518, 648–650, 660–661). There is general agreement about the order in which Rudolf wrote these texts and his *Alexander*, which does not name a patron (Brackert 1968: 11–23). This relative chronology will be followed here.

Rudolf's first work is assumed to be *Der guote Gêrhart* (Good Gerhard), composed in the 1210s or around 1220 to 1225 (Benz 2017: 116–119). It is the story of the humble merchant Gerhard, who, by relating his extraordinary adventures, makes the emperor Otte aware of his presumptuousness. In his epilogue, Rudolf states that a man from Austria had given the source text to Rudolf von Steinach, who asked the poet to produce a German verse translation (Bumke 1979: 512, text 43). Whereas this Latin(?) source is no longer extant – that is to say, if it ever existed – there is historical evidence of Rudolf's patron, dating from the period 1209–1221. Rudolf von Steinach was an esteemed *ministerialis*, serving the Bishop of Constance (Von Ertzdorff 1967: 67–70; Brackert 1968: 25). *Der guote Gêrhart* was commissioned by a peer with whom the poet was acquainted, as is suggested by the intimate way in which he addresses his fellow *ministerialis* and patron (Bumke 1986: 674–675). Comparing the circumstances of Rudolf's debut with those of Jacob, it is striking that the Middle Dutch poet seems to have been supported by a high aristocrat, Aleide of Hainault, who not only was of very high standing but who also did not live in Jacob's surroundings. These observations make one wonder how the contact between Aleide and Jacob was established.

It is likely that Rudolf was also familiar with his second patron (Bumke 1986: 681–682), for whom he composed *Barlaam und Josaphat* around 1225 to 1230. This story tells of a prince of India, Josaphat, who converts to Christianity under the influence of the hermit Barlaam's instructions about Christian history and doctrine. Rudolf wrote this text at the request of Wido, who was abbot of the Cistercian monastery at Kappel near Zürich between 1223 and 1232 (Von Ertzdorff 1967: 80-83; Brackert 1968: 25-26). The abbot provided the poet with a Latin source, written by John of Damascus, who in his turn had translated a Greek text (Bumke 1979: 648-650, text 184; Green 1986: 170-172). This example of non-secular patronage results in a parallel between Rudolf and Jacob. Like Rudolf, the Middle Dutch poet did not only produce texts for courtly circles. Around 1275, he composed a, now lost, life of St. Clare, maybe at the request of the Poor Clares monastery near Bruges, and between 1276 and 1282 he wrote a life of St. Francis, *Sinte Franciscus Leven*, commissioned by the Utrecht Franciscans (Van Oostrom 1996: 142). It is noteworthy that the ideal of poverty advocated by the saint's life did not keep Jacob from being astonishingly explicit about his financial motivation for writing the text. He states in his prologue that he accepted the invitation of the Utrecht Franciscans to translate St. Bonaventura's *Life of St Francis* because he loves 'de bidders enten patroon' (the requesters and their saint) (Maximilianus 1954: l. 79-80), and he 'beghert den loon' (desires the reward) (Maximilianus 1954: l. 80; Van Oostrom 1996: 143).

Highly interesting for the purposes of this chapter is that both Jacob and Rudolf wrote an Alexander romance. The two authors based their accounts of the life of Alexander the Great on various Latin texts. Whereas Jacob's principal source was Gautier de Châtillon's *Alexandreis*, Rudolf used this text to augment his main sources by Leo of Naples and Quintus Curtius Rufus (Brackert 1968: 13-14; Andersen 2006: 229). Scholars agree that Rudolf's *Alexander* came into being in two phases. The German poet started to write the text around 1230, interrupted his work for over a decade, perhaps due to the composition of *Willehalm von Orlens* (see below), and then continued the work in the 1240s but never finished it (Von Ertzdorff 1967: 98-100; Brackert 1968: 16-18). Although Rudolf's *Alexander* does not mention a patron, the text has been related to the royal Hohenstaufen court in Swabia, and in particular to the young kings Heinrich VII, born in 1211, and Konrad IV, born in 1228 (Von Ertzdorff 1967: 98-101; Heinzle 1984: 45). While firm evidence for these patrons or dedicatees is lacking, a parallel to Jacob's *Alexanders geesten* is apparent. Dutch scholars argue, after all, that Jacob's Alexander romance was written to present young Florens with the portrait of an inspiring princely predecessor. Both *Alexander* and *Alexanders geesten* could have been appreciated for their instructional value for young nobles.

The connection of Rudolf's fourth work, *Willehalm von Orlens*, to the Hohenstaufen court is irrefutable (Brackert 1968: 28-29). Written between 1235 and 1240, this verse romance recounts the adventures of the orphan Willehalm, who is raised as an exemplary courtly knight, falls in love with a princess at the English court, marries her eventually, and succeeds to the throne of both his adoptive father and his father-in-law. In various passages, Rudolf refers to nobles who were part of the Hohenstaufen circles (Bumke 1979: 513-518, texts 45-49). He deplores the death of Count Konrad II von Öttingen (d.1241-1242), informs the reader that the Swabian *ministerialis* Johannes von Ravensburg brought the French source with him to Germany, and acknowledges that Konrad von Winterstetten (d.1243) commissioned *Willehalm von Orlens* (Von Ertzdorff 1967: 89-94; Brackert 1968: 26-27). This patron was a very influential noble at the Hohenstaufen court. He served as imperial cup bearer, and, highly interesting in the context of this chapter, as tutor and advisor to the young kings Heinrich VII and Konrad IV. This state of affairs makes it likely that Konrad von Winterstetten saw in *Willehalm von Orlens* much more than an entertaining romance about love. The text may have served as a means to educate future Hohenstaufen princes (Brackert 1968: 220–224; Benz 2017: 110). This line of reasoning definitely brings the assumed didactic role of Jacob's Middle Dutch romances to mind. These texts were, after all, part of the 'literature program of Voorne', according to Van Oostrom (1996: 135). Jacob's Arthurian romance *Torec* is particularly interesting in this context. Based on a now lost French source, like *Willehalm von Orlens*, *Torec* tells of a young prince who goes in quest of a precious diadem stolen from his grandmother, visits the Chamber of Wisdom to listen to the conversations of wise people, and marries his beloved after having defeated all the knights of the Round Table in a tournament (Johnson and Claassens 2003: 562–727). Both *Willehalm von Orlens* and *Torec* may have quickened the minds and the hearts of young high-placed noblemen in Germany and the Low Countries.

Rudolf's fifth and final work was the *Weltchronik*, a chronicle of the world which he wrote in the period around 1250. For this voluminous text, he did not restrict himself to a single principal source, as did Jacob for his *Spiegel historiael*, based on the *Speculum historiale*. Next to a series of other texts, Rudolf made use mainly of the Vulgate Bible and Comestor's *Historia scholastica* (Von Tippelskirch 1979: 27–60; Andersen 2006: 228–229). For the *Weltchronik*, the German poet enjoyed royal patronage (Von Ertzdorff 1967: 101–106; Brackert 1968: 27). He states that he was commissioned by King Konrad IV, who promised him a considerable reward (Bumke 1979: 660–661, text 197). This patronage of the *Weltchronik* is one of the many aspects that link the German chronicle to Jacob's *Spiegel historiael*. In both cases, the poet's final work was requested by his most highly positioned patron (Konrad IV, Florens V). Both poets were asked to write a world chronicle in vernacular verses. Both set out to fulfil their daring task, wrote large parts of their text, but were unable to complete their work. Rudolf managed to produce around 30,000 lines, describing the turmoil of history up to the death of King Solomon (Bumke 1979: 252). Jacob stopped writing after around 90,000 lines, when he had reached the First Crusade (Van Oostrom 1996: 369). Both chronicles were continued by other medieval authors, and were highly popular texts in medieval times, as is attested by the dozens of copies that have come down to us (Von Tippelskirch 1979: 6; Biemans 1997). Quite a number of the *Weltchronik* copies are illustrated, and some of them belong to the most beautiful manuscripts that were made in the German Middle Ages (Von Tippelskirch 1979: 172). Most of the *Spiegel historiael* manuscripts are rather modest, unillustrated copies, the one spectacular exception being the luxurious early fourteenth-century manuscript that was probably made in Ghent and contains just Jacob's part of the *Spiegel historiael* (Janssens and Meuwese 1997).

The comparison of the literary production and patrons of Rudolf and Jacob is rewarding for our view on the Middle Dutch poet. He was not as unique as Dutch scholars are inclined to think when they look at him in linguistic isolation. Both Jacob and Rudolf were prolific authors, who wrote for courtly circles. They depended on literary patronage and had to cater to the wishes of their commissioners, both in terms of form (writing vernacular verses) and content. The two authors did not only use French source material, like their fellow court poets, but also appropriated texts that were part of the clerical Latin tradition. Their texts may have entertained their audiences, but in both cases there are strong indications that they were also asked to write for educational purposes. Both authors, finally, positioned themselves in the vernacular literary traditions of their times. Twice, in *Willehalm von Orlens* and *Alexander*, Rudolf lists his predecessors, and comments on their work (Von Ertzdorff 1967: 394–414). Jacob admiringly acknowledges that he fully incorporated an earlier Middle Dutch Troy romance, by Segher Diengotgaf, in his *Historie van Troyen*, and places his *Der naturen bloeme* in the literary tradition by claiming that his text, based on a Latin source, surpasses the biological encyclopedia of Willem Utenhove, because this priest from Aardenburg followed an unreliable French source (Van Oostrom 1996: 256, 435–436).

Comparing the literary production and patrons of Rudolf and Jacob also brings a number of Jacob's special characteristics to the fore. Two of them sharpen Jacob's profile as drawn in Dutch scholarship. First, it is remarkable that nearly his whole oeuvre can be related to the literary patronage of nobles in the entourage of Florens V. A prolific author like Rudolf had to look for comparable commissions at various places, both secular and religious, in order to be able to produce his extensive works (Benz 2017: 123). Jacob wrote even more and longer texts than Rudolf: he produced a staggering total of around 300,000 lines (Van Oostrom 1996: 11), while the German poet wrote around 100,000 verses (Benz 2017: 123). Jacob was nevertheless focused almost exclusively on just a single aristocratic circle. This phenomenon may have to do with Jacob's limited possibilities to find aristocratic patrons. Whereas noble commissioners of German literature abound in the Middle Ages (Bumke 1979), high-placed patrons of Middle Dutch literature were rather scarce in Jacob's times (Sleiderink 2017). He had few to choose from, so it seems.

The second characteristic is concerned with Jacob's scope of subject matter. Even in comparison to Rudolf, who is a giant among the medieval authors when his oeuvre is taken into account, Jacob's corpus of texts is astonishing. Like his German counterpart, he wrote romances and didactic texts. While Rudolf's factual texts are restricted to the *Alexander*, if seen as a historiographical work, and the *Weltchronik* (Andersen 2006: 231), Jacob attracted vernacular audiences by writing a whole series of informative texts in the vernacular. One way or another, he was successful in securing patronage for a treatise on princely conduct (*Heimelijkheid der heimelijcheden*), a lengthy account of biblical history (*Rijmbijbel*), an encyclopedia of nature (*Der naturen bloeme*) and a world chronicle (*Spiegel historiael*). It is due to the impressive variety of his oeuvre that he can claim a chapter in this volume on Dutch literature as world literature.

References

Andersen, E.A. (2006), 'Rudolf von Ems', in W. Hasty (ed.), *German Literature of the High Middle Ages*, 225–233, Rochester, NY: Camden House.

Benz, M. (2017), 'Heteronomien und Eigensinn. Die Werke Rudolfs von Ems im Spannungsfeld von Politik, Religion und Kunst', in B. Bastert, A. Bihrer and T.

Reuvekamp-Felber (eds), *Mäzenaten im Mittelalter aus europäischer Perspektive: von historischen Akteuren zu literarischen Textkonzepten*, 105–124, Göttingen: V&R Unipress.

Besamusca, B. (2013), 'The Prevalence of Verse in Medieval Dutch and English Arthurian Fiction', *Journal of English and Germanic Philology* 112: 461–474.

Besamusca, B. and F. Brandsma (1998), 'Jacob de Maerlant, traducteur vigilant, et la valeur didactique de son *Graal-Merlijn*', in J. Claude Faucon, A. Labbé and D. Quéruel (eds), *Miscellanea Mediaevalia. Mélanges offerts à Philippe Ménard*, 2 vols, vol. 1, 121–131, Paris: Champion.

Biemans, J.A.A.M. (1997), *Onsen Speghele Ystoriale in Vlaemsche. Codicologisch onderzoek naar de overlevering van de Spiegel historiael van Jacob van Maerlant, Philip Utenbroeke en Lodewijk van Velthem, met een beschrijving van de handschriften en fragmenten*, 2 vols, Leuven: Peeters.

Brackert, H. (1968), *Rudolf von Ems. Dichtung und Geschichte*, Heidelberg: Winter.

Bumke, J. (1979), *Mäzene im Mittelalter. Die Gönner und Auftraggeber der höfischen Literatur in Deutschland 1150–1300*, Munich: Beck.

Bumke, J. (1986), *Höfische Kultur. Literatur und Gesellschaft im hohen Mittelalter*, 2 vols, Munich: Deutscher Taschenbuch Verlag.

Blok, D.P. et al., eds (1982), *Algemene geschiedenis der Nederlanden*, 2: Middeleeuwen, Haarlem: Van Dishoeck.

Ertzdorff, X. von (1967), *Rudolf von Ems. Untersuchungen zum höfischen Roman im 13. Jahrhundert*, Munich: Fink Verlag.

Franck, J., ed. (1882), *Alexanders Geesten van Jacob van Maerlant*, Leiden: Sijthoff.

Green, D. (1986), 'On the Primary Reception of the Works of Rudolf von Ems', *Zeitschrift für deutsches Altertum und deutsche Literatur* 115: 151–180.

Heinzle, J. (1984), *Wandlungen und Neuansätze im 13. Jahrhundert (1220-30-1280/90)*, II: Geschichte der deutschen Literatur von den Anfängen bis zum Beginn der Neuzeit, Vom hohen zum späten Mittelalter/2, Königstein: Athenäum.

Hourihane, C.P., ed. (2012), *The Grove Encyclopedia of Medieval Art and Literature*, 6 vols, Oxford: Oxford University Press.

Janssens, J. and M. Meuwese (1997), *Jacob van Maerlant, Spiegel Historiael. De miniaturen uit handschrift Den Haag, Koninklijke Bibliotheek, KA XX*, Leuven: Davidsfonds.

Johnson, L.P. (1999), *Die höfische Literatur der Blütezeit (1160/70-1220/30)*, II: Geschichte der deutschen Literatur von den Anfängen bis zum Beginn der Neuzeit, Vom hohen zum späten Mittelalter/1, Tübingen: Niemeyer Verlag.

Johnson, D.F. and G.H.M. Claassens, with the Assistance of K. De Bundel and G. Pallemans, eds (2003), *Dutch Romances III: Five Interpolated Romances from the Lancelot Compilation*, Cambridge: Brewer.

Maximilianus, P., ed. (1954), *Sinte Franciscus Leven van Jacob van Maerlant*, 2 vols, Zwolle: Tjeenk Willink.

Mekking, A.J.J. (1991), 'De "Grote Zaal" van Floris V te Den Haag. Een onderzoek naar de betekenis van het concept', in D.E.H. de Boer, E.H.P. Cordfonke and F.W.N. Hugenholtz (eds), *Holland in Wording. De ontstaansgeschiedenis van het graafschap Holland tot het begin van de vijftiende eeuw*, 65–90, Hilversum: Verloren.

Meulen, J.F. van der (2000), 'Avesnes en Dampierre of "De kunst der liefde." Over boeken, bisschoppen en Henegouwse ambities', in D.E.H. de Boer, E.H.P. Cordfunke and H. Sarfatij (eds), *1299: één graaf, drie graafschappen. De vereniging van Holland, Zeeland en Henegouwen*, 47–72, Hilversum: Verloren.

Meulen, J.F. van der (2012), 'Vrouwen van Avesnes. Een nieuwe Alexander in de Lage Landen', in A. Faems and M. Hogenbirk (eds), *Ene andre tale. Tendensen in de Middelnederlandse late ridderepiek*, 55–81, Hilversum: Verloren.

Oostrom, F.P. van (1984), 'Hoe snel dichtten middeleeuwse dichters? Over de dynamiek van het literaire leven in de middeleeuwen', *Literatuur* 1: 327–335.

Oostrom, F.P. van (1996), *Maerlants wereld*, Amsterdam: Prometheus.

Oostrom, F.P. van (2006), *Stemmen op schrift. Geschiedenis van de Nederlandse literatuur vanaf het begin tot 1300*, Amsterdam: Bert Bakker.

Postma, A. (1991), 'Voor wie schreef Jacob van Maerlant zijn *Rijmbijbel*?' in Jaap van Moolenbroek, Maaike Mulder (eds.), *Scolastica willic ontbinden. Over de Rijmbijbel van Jacob van Maerlant*, 53–70, Hilversum: Verloren.

Sleiderink, R. (2017), 'Mäzene in der mittelniederländischen Literatur: Versuch einer Bestandsaufname', in B. Bastert, A. Bihrer and T. Reuvekamp-Felber (eds), *Mäzenaten im Mittelalter aus europäischer Perspektive: von historischen Akteuren zu literarischen Textkonzepten*, 201–221, Göttingen: V&R Unipress.

Smit, J.G. (1991), 'De graven van Holland en Zeeland op reis. Het grafelijk itinerarium van het begin van de veertiende eeuw tot 1425', in D.E.H. de Boer, E.H.P. Cordfunke, F.W.N. Hugenholtz (eds), *Holland in Wording. De ontstaansgeschiedenis van het graafschap Holland tot het begin van de vijftiende eeuw*, 91–124, Hilversum: Verloren.

Sodmann, T. (1980), *Historie van den Grale und Boek van Merline. Nach der Steinfurter Handschrift*, ed. T. Sodmann, Koln: Bohlau Verlag.

Tippelskirch, I. von (1979), *Die 'Weltchronik' des Rudolf von Ems. Studien zur Geschichtsauffassung und politischen Intention*, Göppingen: Kümmerle Verlag.

Vale, M. (2001), *The Princely Court: Medieval Courts and Culture in North-West Europe 1270–1380*, Oxford: Oxford University Press.

Verwijs, E., ed. (1878), *Jacob van Maerlant's Naturen Bloeme*, Groningen: Wolters (repr. Arnhem: Gijsbers & Van Loon, 1980).

Vries, M. de and E. Verwijs, eds (1861–1879), *Jacob van Maerlant's Spiegel Historiael*, 4 vols, Leiden: Brill (repr. Utrecht: HES, 1982).

5

The Many Returns of Elckerlijc: Every Man's Mirror of Salvation

Geert Warnar

The late fifteenth-century Dutch morality play *Elckerlijc*, printed for the first time in 1495, owes its ongoing international fame to the allegorical arrangement of a universal theme: man's confrontation with mortality.[1] Having been summoned by Death to do reckoning, Elckerlijc – or Everyman in the contemporary English translation – is left on his own by his friends, family and the material goods that were deer to him in his earthly life. Virtue has been neglected so completely by Elckerlijc that she is too weak to accompany him. Only *Kennisse* (knowledge, self-reflection) goes with Elckerlijc, advising him how to obtain salvation through confession and penitence. This helps Elckerlijc's Virtue to recover and escort him to the grave, while beauty, strength, prudence and senses leave him. Accepting the fleeting nature of earthly life, Elckerlijc dies peacefully. Hence the original title of the play: *Spyeghel der Salicheyt van Elckerlijc*, which can be translated both as 'Everyman's Mirror of Salvation' or 'Mirror of Everyman's Salvation'.

The sacramental turn takes *Elckerlijc* to devotional spheres that now are hard to reconcile with modern notions of literature, drama and other forms of artistic imagination. It comes as no surprise that many modern interpretations of *Elckerlijc* take the text as a parable of materialism or man's inevitable decay, leaving out or even ignoring the religious discourses of accountability and redemption that have shaped the medieval original. The most recent and significant case in point is Philip Roth's American novel *Everyman*, which closely follows its medieval precursor although for the principal character 'religion was a lie that he had recognized early in life' (Roth 2006a: 51). Roth's twenty-first century Everyman is an art director in the commercial world of advertising. For this businessman there is no hereafter. Still, there is much in Roth's novel that reminds us of *Elckerlijc*: in the struggle with an inevitable end, when family nor friends, wealth nor physical strength can help to prolong life. Although this new Everyman is no longer an allegorical archetype like Elckerlijc, Roth's anonymous protagonist is more than an individual. His characteristics exemplify a generation, a set of beliefs, illusions and disillusions that everyone has to face. In this sense, Roth's novel is a modern American response to a Netherlandish medieval morality, welcoming a specimen of Dutch literature as world literature.

Therefore, when Roth's novel *Everyman* was translated into Dutch (Roth 2006b), there was still enough of *Elckerlijc* in this *Alleman* to claim that the late medieval morality play had returned to its original language. This was not for the first time – neither was it the first time that this required a number of intermediaries. Philip Roth must have consulted the sixteenth-century English translation of *Elckerlijc* – meaning there were at least three stages before *Elckerlijc* became *Alleman*. Many of the earlier returns of *Elckerlijc* in Dutch literature were the result of similar detours – and like Roth's adaptation: these new Elckerlijcs were not always immediately recognizable as descendants of their medieval ancestor. With some we might even ask if there is a direct connection. Do we really see the wide circulation of a Dutch text, or rather the recurrence of a theme? And if so, what was it that made Elckerlijc return in so many guises? Is it inevitable? The Dutch literary scholar Asselbergs (1968: 5 and 8) observed that Elckerlijc, being one of the most significant Netherlandish contributions to the international history of literature, presents a challenge for every author, actor, playwright or director that one way or the other had to turn this abstract figure into a character in a novel or on stage. Every choice or option was a step away from the original. The nineteenth-century rediscovery of *Everyman* resulted in new drama productions both in Europe and America (Potter 1975: 222–245; Schreiber 1975) that were successful but made at least one scholar wonder 'to what extent did the original play of Everyman become lost in the process?' (Potter 1975: 222).

The modern appeal of *Elckerlijc* may make us think that the play was meant to be world literature, which is all but true. Originally composed as a play to be performed in the competitions of the South-Netherlandish rhetoricians, the *Elckerlijc* was not even aimed at a reading audience.[2] A wider circulation only became possible after the play had been turned into a text for reading. All editions announce a 'boecxken ghemaect in den maniere van eenen speele ofte esbatemente op elckerlijc mensche' (booklet made in the manner of a play or drama on every human being) (Davidson, Walsh and Broos 2007).[3] The three printed editions of the Dutch *Elckerlijc* – published over a period of about twenty-five years (*c.* 1495–1525) – suggest a relatively substantial interest in the text, the more so because there is no earlier rhetorician's play in print.[4] Also, the four printed editions of the English translation in the same period were an unprecedented international success for Dutch literature (Freeman 2008: 397–407), even though 'success' is a very anachronistic term. Moreover, two Latin adaptations were produced in the next decade: *Homulus* (Roersch 1903) by the Maastricht schoolmaster Ischyrius, or Christiaan Stercken, and *Hecastus* (Bolte 1927: 63–160) by the more famous humanist Georgius Macropedius, or Joris van Lanckveldt. These Latin versions generated the international circulation of the Elckerlijc theme and a series of translations and adaptations back in vernacular languages (Bloemendal 2013: 148–154).

The stories of Elckerlijc's lineage have been told quite often and from various perspectives. In German studies it was what happened previously to *Jedermann*, the early twentieth-century play by Hugo von Hoffmannsthal that is still being performed (Dammer and Jeßing 2007). In English studies it was the question whether *Elckerlijc* was prior to *Everyman* (King 1994: 255–258). In neo-Latin studies it was the interaction between Latin and vernacular drama. This article looks at the sixteenth-century returns of Elckerlijc in Dutch drama and literature, to understand the continuous interest in an anonymous allegorical figure.

Some of Elckerlijc's descendants are hard to identify, for instance in the rather obscure *Comedie vanden bekeerden coopman* (*Comedy of the converted merchant*), by a certain Frans Leerse from the Flemish city of Aarschot. The text survives only in one copy of a printed edition from Antwerp of 1583.[5] The title figure appears as the prototype of a greedy tradesman in all respects. Much more than Elckerlijc, and also more explicitly, he has disregarded the things that he should care about. In this case not Virtue but Conscience has been neglected. She is the wife of the merchant, but he has literally shown her the door. Outside her house she is greeted by *Straffe Godts* (God's Punishment). To him Conscience complains of the merchant that she has lived with him for many years but now he favours a whore called *Onghestadighe Fortuyne* (Fickle Fortune), that bore him the child *Gewin* (Profit), although he is called *Woeker* (Usury) by the servants in the house.

Inside, the merchant gives a demonstration of his avarice. Preparing for a new business trip, he instructs his servant in the dirty tricks of book keeping and deceit that have made him a prosperous man. However, just before his departure, God's Punishment knocks on the door, with the message that it is time to settle other affairs:

Sdoots herout ben ick, ick en derfs niet sweren
En bevele u te laten u leven,
Goet, rijckdom, eere, ghewin touwen verneren
Op dat ghy ter stont rekeninghe compt gheven
Voor Gode den richter van dat ghy hebt bedreven.

(I am Death's herald, I do not need to swear an oath
And I command you to leave behind your life,
Goods, riches, honour, profit for your consumption
In order that you do reckoning right away
Of what you have done for God the judge.)

(Comedie 1583: 26)

These last verses seem to echo the *Elckerlijc*, where Death tells the allegorical protagonist that God 'begheert dat ghi voer hem coemt toghen u rekeninghe van dat ghi hebt bedreven' (wants you to come before Him to show your reckoning of what you have done) (Davidson, Walsh and Broos 2007: lines 140–141; cf. Vanderheyden 1930: 203).

The verbatim correspondence between the texts does not exceed these two lines, and may very well be coincidental – or both may be related to conventional ideas on *memento mori*. However, Elckerlijc and the merchant have more in common. Both protagonists find themselves suddenly faced with death or God's punishment summoning them to account for their deeds; and they fall in a similar state of despair. Around 1495 Elckerlijc complains: "Allendich arm katijf, o wach! Nu en weet ick mijns selfs ghenen raet' (Miserable poor wretch, o woe! Now I don't know what to do) (Davidson, Walsh and Broos 2007: lines 115–115) and almost a century later the merchant says: 'Och, ick, arm cattijf, beghin my te ververen' (O, I, poor wretch, begin to fear) (Comedie 1583: 26). In both cases the reason for the sudden despair is obvious: neither Elckerlijc nor the merchant is prepared to do reckoning.

From this point onward the plays move to completely different positions. The medieval *Elckerlijc* follows the standard medieval trajectory to salvation passing through the stages of remorse, confession, mercy, penance and sacraments. The *Comedie vanden bekeerden coopman* is a Protestant play, with its principal character not benefitting but suffering from the Catholic rites, provided by the priest who is ridiculed to the extreme. The patient can only be cured after the apostles Paul and Luke – as medical doctors – have replaced the swindler-priest to look after the merchant and literally purge him from all sacraments, rosaries and indulgences.

In spite of the sharp contrast – or rather because of this contrast – Elckerlijc and the merchant are directly related. The *Comedie vanden bekeerden coopman* is a Dutch adaptation of the Latin play *Mercator* (Bolte 1927: 161–319; Roloff 1982) by the German theologian and playwright Thomas Kirchmayer, or Naogeorgus, one of the more prominent reformed authors in sixteenth-century Germany. Kirchmayer must have modelled his *Mercator* deliberately after another play: *Hecastus*, by the Utrecht schoolmaster Macropedius, for whom the *Elckerlijc* was the principal source (Bloemendal 2013: 153–154). *Hecastus* was printed for the first time in 1539 in Antwerp; Kirchmayer published his *Mercator* only one year after *Hecastus*. Both texts were popular, both in the Latin original and in vernacular translations. Before the end of the sixteenth century the *Mercator* was translated into German (four times) and into French. This *Marchant Converti* by Jean Crespin was the text used by Frans Leerse.[6]

The transformation from Elckerlijc to the converted merchant required three intermediaries, with *Mercator* being an aggressive reaction to *Hecastus* rather than a loyal adaptation. Although the original *Elckerlijc* theme of man's unexpected confrontation with death was still recognizable, we witness an intertextual engagement (in terms of adaptation theory [Hutcheon 2013: 8]) that uses the original plot for religious discussions.[7] Most of the Early Modern *Elckerlijc* reworkings respond to the changes generated by the Reformation (or Counter-Reformation).[8] Jean Crespin claimed to have translated *Mercator* into French for the Netherlandish francophone Huguenot community in Frankfurt (Bouteille-Meister 2014: 4–5) and the *Comedie van de bekeerden coopman* was printed during the years of the Calvinist republic in Antwerp.[9] A direct translation of Kirchmayer's *Mercator* in Dutch is even more explicit about its religious concerns. The author was Doede van Amsweer, a reformed mayor from the Northern province of Groningen in exile in Emden. The *editio princeps* of his text was printed in Bremen in 1593. To his translation Van Amsweer added an appendix addressed to the local government (*Provintiale Staten*) of Groningen in which he argued for a new unity based on Reformation principles, taking his Christian Tragedy (*christelijcke tragedia*) as a point of reference for political theory (Steenbeek 1966: 38–42).

Reflecting the religious changes of the Reformation, the sixteenth-century Elckerlijc characters were involved in processes of conversion that were still absent in the medieval period from which the original play had emerged. However, to understand how Elckerlijc turned into a converted *merchant* we also have to trace how the main figure grew into a personification of wealth, worldliness and materialism. Some years before the *Comedie van de bekeerden coopman* was published, the Dutch Humanist author Dirck Coornhert had written his *Comedie van de Rijckeman* (*Comedy of the Rich Man*) (Van der Meulen 1955: 15–79), a play that moves along the same lines as *Hecastus* and *Mercator*, but without any strict statement on Catholic or Reformed religion.[10] Coornhert focused on the effects and the consequences of wallowing in lust and riches. The title figure is similar to Mercator: he also has sent his Conscience away, after which she has been molested by *Landtzeede* (Country's customs/morals) and *Waenschijns Zoon* (Illusion's Son). When Conscience (re)appears on the stage, she is carrying the mirror of self-knowledge and the candle of the light of truth. Both attributes are taken away from her by her former attackers. They manage to convince Conscience to be redressed in allegorical garments like *Eigen Behagen* (self-congratulation) to reconcile her with the Rich Man. In the end of the play, no longer hindered by his conscience, the protagonist turns out to be the rich man of the New Testament parable, who goes to hell for not having taken care of the poor Lazarus. What is left of *Elckerlijc* – or better: what connects Coornhert's rich man to the medieval morality play – is the confrontation with death, but now with a completely different and bitter outcome: arrogance and materialism lead the protagonist far from Elckerlijc's road to salvation. The focus has shifted to social critique, discussing the morals of the merchant (Vandommele and Bussels 2014).

A similar story of adaptation and translation, and no less complicated, is the play *Homulus* (Serrure 1857), performed in the Dutch cities of Nijmegen (1553) and Arnhem (1554) (Van Bemmel 1989: 130, 132), and printed by Peter van Elzen in 1556 in Nijmegen. This *Homulus* was the Dutch version of *Der sünden loin ist der Toid* [Sin's reward is death] by the Cologne printer Jasper van Gennep (Norrenberg 1873). The title of Van Elzen is closer to Van Gennep's original subtitle: 'Comedia Homuli, gemehrt und gebessert mit personen und sprüchen. Dairin angezeigt wirt was loins die sündt gibt, nemlich den Toid, und wie den menschen dan all creaturen verlaissen, Alleyn syn Duigt stät ym dan by. Gar nützlich und lieblicht zu lesse' (The Comedy of Homulus, extended and improved with characters and sayings. In the play is shown the reward of sin, namely death, and how man is then left on his own by all other creatures. Only Virtue stays with him. Very profitable and lovely to read).

Van Gennep, who would publish three editions of this play, had also printed the *editio princeps* of the Latin *Homulus* by the Maastricht schoolmaster Ischyrius (Roersch 1903: XVII). This was the first Latin translation of the *Elckerlijc*. According to Van Gennep's preface to *Der sünden loin*, he himself had translated *Homulus* back into the German vernacular to perform the play in Cologne (Norrenberg 1873: 35). The reactions of the audience had made Van Gennep rework his German *Homulus* – adding material that strengthened the message. In his own words: 'The plot of the play I have taken from the Latin comedy by Peter of Diest [whom Van Gennep seems to take for the author], but many things, out of which man may learn the deceptiveness of this life, I have collected from other books'.[11] These other books included the *Hecastus*, meaning Van Gennep also knew the second translation of *Elckerlijc* (Norrenberg 1873: 40-41). Moreover, it is clear from the German text that the Cologne printer was even familiar with the original Dutch play. When the German text was recast in Dutch by Peter van Elzen, some verses still echo the original *Elckerlijc*.[12]

Compared to his ancestor, this Dutch *Homulus* has changed almost as much as the merchant of Frans Leersse, or the rich man of Coornhert. When this Homulus enters the stage, at the opening of the play, he is boasting about his wealth, a beautiful wife, children and a large family, an attic full of wheat, a cellar full of wine, chests full of money and gold. These fortunes have made him over-confident:

Daerom, mijn siel, zijt wel gemoet,
Gebruyct met vruechden dijn grote goet;
Laet u niet verschricken, noch ververen
Van den die u willen sterven leren,
Ende seggen: 'Men moet God rekening geven
Hoe men zijn goet gebruyct in zijn leven.'
Dat ys vrylick gedacht ende ghelogen;
Die papen hebben ons sus lange bedrogen.

(Therefore, my soul, be happy
Enjoy and delight in your great wealth
Do not be frightened by those
that want to teach you how to die
and who say: 'One has to do reckoning for God
of what one has done with his goods.'
This is being invented and made up freely.
The priests have lied to us for so long.) (Serrure 1857: 7)

After this self-satisfied monologue, Homulus bullies his wife, who wonders why she has to prepare dinner parties every night for the friends of her husband. Her attempts to make him leave his worldly pleasures behind are in vain. When Homulus is addressed by a hermit and a friar, he sees no reason to turn to things of higher importance. For the duration of the first two acts of the play (six acts in total) Homulus parties with his friends and the whore Melusina. None of these tavern scenes are found in the *Elckerlijc*, nor in the English *Everyman* or the Latin *Homulus*. Van Gennep had looked at *Hecastus* for this portrait of an arrogant protagonist. Macropedius had turned the allegorical *Elckerlijc* into a man of the world, who was exposed to all its temptations but also responded to them all too willingly. Jasper van Gennep thought – as he said himself – that the added opening scene helped to make his audience aware of the *betrieglichkeit dises lebens* (deceptiveness of this life).

The changes in the Elckerlijc character had to do with new concerns for the protagonist's position in life. Over time, the protagonists were represented more and more as revelling in luxury and riches, boasting their good fortunes, confident that their material wealth would protect them from any harm. What is suggested or left to the imagination in the *Elckerlijc* is presented in detail in later versions like the German *Homulus* adaptations. The *Elckerlijc* starts with God speaking from his throne in anger because mankind has chosen earthly wealth instead of Him; he sends Death to summon every man to do reckoning – in God's prologue *elckerlijc* still refers to everyone and not to the individualized personification. The sixteenth-century versions present the materialism as almost inseparable from the profession of the merchant, the businessman. In the comedy of the converted merchant, Conscience enters the stage, exclaiming: 'Och, ick arme wijf, watten armen cattijf / Bin ick gheworden door mijns mans bedrijf' (What a wretched creature I have become because of my husband's business).[13] Coonhert's *Comedie van de Rijckeman* is even more outspoken in its social critique on commercialism. The main reason that the Rich Man in Coornhert's comedy goes straight to hell is his total neglect of charity. Blinded by greed, he has forgotten his moral duty of sharing his wealth with the poor – who are represented by the figure of Lazarus.[14]

A rhetoricians' play by Jan vanden Berghe dated around 1550 – and again from Antwerp – shows a similar tendency of foregrounding the 'deceptiveness of life'.[15] Its main character is the Voluptuous Man, who enters the stage like *Homulus*, bragging about his wealth and good fortune and certain that nothing is out of his reach:

Heij, wie sal mijn lustighe naetuere dwingen
Die in allen dingen nu heeft voorspoedicheijt?
Mijn crachten tot alle solaesheijt dringen,
Wie sout mijn ontwringen oft tonder bringen,
Ick die van godt begaeft ben sonderlingen,
Rijckdom, schadt, wijsheijt en cloeckmoedicheijt
Omringen mijn in alder overvloedicheijt,
Gedient met behoedicheijt van maerten en knaepen.
Mijn selven regeer ick met alle vroedicheijt,
Weeldige woedicheijt is mijn betraepen,
Ick eete, ick drincke, ick stae op, ick gae slaepen,
Mijn goet is geschaepen daer ick mach op leven, siet.
Heij, laet mij godt hier, ick sou om den hemel geven niet. (Kruyskamp 1950: 98)

(Ha, who shall clip my sensuous wings,
I who in all things enjoy now prosperity?
My vigours direct me towards every jollity,
Who'd take it from me as if it never existed?
I who by God am singularly gifted,

And surrounded by wisdom and also valiance,
Wealth and riches in all their abundance.
Served by lackeys and maid-servants solicitous,
I look after myself extremely felicitous.
My sole aim in life is passionate pleasure.
I eat, I drink, I sleep at my leisure.
My fortune is made and life's just bliss.
Who cares about heaven, if life's like this?) (King 1986: 59)

This Voluptuous Man also ends up before God's throne, but the *pièce de resistance* of the play is a lengthy scene in the brothel called 'A handful of sunshine', supervised by the female keeper *Eertsche solaesheyt* (Earthly pleasure) with the pimp *begheerlicheyt der oghen* (concupiscence of the eyes) and the prostitutes *Luxurie* and *Overdaet* (Lust and Excess). The play highlights how man is being exposed to a world full of temptations, and even though the Voluptuous Man's plea and prayer for God's mercy is similar to Elckerlijc's there is a considerable shift from the original idea of the morality play as a Mirror of Salvation. Jan vanden Berghe's play of the Voluptuous Man is closer to *Hecastus* and Van Gennep's *Homulus* in its focus on the protagonist's delusions.

Although all the new sixteenth-century Elckerlijc's have to do reckoning, the faults and failures they have to deal with are more of this world than those of their forefather's. There are different explanations for the explicitness of the *expositio* in new versions of the Elckerkijc-theme. One is the changing idea of what drama should be in the sixteenth century: the medieval morality plays grew out of fashion after the rediscovery of classical models. Allegorical abstractions were replaced by individuals. Drama should demonstrate rather than tell what was happening (Verschelde 1983). However, even the late sixteenth-century comedies of the Converted Merchant and the Rich Man are deeply rooted in the conventional rhetoricians' tradition of personification and disputation (Ramakers 2006). The evolution of the Elckerlijc-theme as a turn to a more realistic setting would perhaps be better characterized as an attempt to bring theoretical discussions on salvation back to problems in daily life and provide answers to new questions. The deceptiveness of life no longer exclusively concerned the hereafter, but also had to be dealt with in the world of the living. Material wealth and worldly pleasures or the position of the merchant, his morals, reputation and social function were anxieties that no longer could be confronted exclusively in terms of eternal life.

Parallels in contemporary visual arts help to understand the shift from salvation to the situation of the sinner. Rhetoricians' plays, prints and paintings from Antwerp all address these dilemmas. The Antwerp painter Jan van Hemessen (active in the middle of the sixteenth century) is famous for his tavern scenes, which refer to biblical themes such as the Prodigal Son but highlight – and literally foreground – the feasting of a voluptuous man that Jan vanden Berghe portrayed in his play.[16] An earlier Antwerp painting by Jan Provoost (*c.* 1525) directly reflects Elckerlijc's confrontation with Death. It can be argued that Provoost really depicted the opening scene of the *Elckerlijc* (Warnar 2015). The painting by Provoost suggests that the interpretation of Elckerlijc as a rich merchant goes back to the days that the text was printed. As a painter Provoost was a member of the Antwerp guild of Saint Luke together with the printers Godevaert Bac and Willem Vorsterman that published editions of the *Elckerlijc* in the same period. Provoost's panels show a person, surrounded by his money bags and completely engaged in his account books – apparently unaware that he is facing death. His initial reaction seems to be to pay off Death, handing him some sort of receipt, exactly like Elckerlijc offers to buy off death with a thousand pounds (Davidson, Walsh and Broos 2007: l. 103).

The painting takes us back to the initial question: is the *Elckerlijc* theme a popular motif – that returns in various guises through the ages – or are the depicted and described confrontations between materialism and mortality really to be traced back to the medieval morality play? The play itself associated Elckerlijc's moral dilemmas with the deceptiveness of man's earthly riches, already in the opening lines when God speaks from His throne:

> Dat al dat is int smenschen persone
> Leeft uut vresen, onbekent.
> Oec sie ic tvolc also verblent
> In sonden, si en kennen mi niet voer God.
> Opten aertschen scat sijn si versot,
> Dien hebben si voer Gode vercoren,
> Ende mi vergheten.
>
> (that all that is of human kind
> lives without fear of God, ignorant.
> I see the people so blinded
> by sin, that they don't recognize me as God.
> They are enamored of worldly treasures,
> which they have chosen over God,
> and have forgotten me.) (Davidson, Walsh and Broos 2007: l. 2–8)

At the moment that Elckerlijc enters the stage – and suddenly transforms from everyone into an individual character – Death watches him coming and comments: He worships earthly goods above God, for which he will have to lack eternal joy (*Voer God aenbidt hi deertsche goet, Daer hy deeuwighe vreughde om derven moet*), as an affirmation that the character is no different from mankind (Davidson, Walsh and Broos 2007: lines 61–62).

It has been pointed out that Elckerlijc's social position is defined by his material wealth. The Dutch medievalist Max de Haan (1975) wrote a short article with the title and thesis: *Elckerlijc is niet iedereen* (Everyman is not everyone), arguing that the title figure of the morality play was represented as the successful businessman. Other researchers have demonstrated how the English *Everyman* is rooted in mercantile metaphors (Ladd 2007) and a spiritual economy (Harper and Mize 2006) that was based on a traditional religion and defined in the terms of an accountability tuned to the practices of the commercial class. The Dutch original repeatedly uses the metaphor of *rekeninghe doen*, which has both the meaning of actual bookkeeping and the act of reckoning (Warnar 2015: 278–279). Here, the secular and sacred are interlocked rather than opposed.

The real confrontation of mortality and materialism takes place when Elckerlijc turns to his riches. Left on his own by family and friends, he asks his goods to accompany him on his last journey. He is turned down by personified Good in the most bitter way; and now reckoning almost literally becomes (spiritual) bookkeeping:

Neen, Elckerlijc, ic mocht u letten daer.
Ic en volghe niemant tot sulcker reisen.
Ende al ghinghe ic mede, wilt peisen,
So soudi mijns te wors hebben grotelic,
Bi redenen ic salt u segghen blotelijc:
Ic heb zeer u pampier verweert.
Want al u sinnen hebdi verteert
Aen mi, dat mach u leet zijn.
Want u rekeninghe sal onghereet zijn
Voer God Almachtich, mits minen scouwen.

(No, Everyman, I might hinder you there.
I follow no man on such a journey.
And even if I went with you, do consider,
you would fare far worse off because of me,
for reasons I will tell you candidly:
I have botched your accounts terribly.
Since you have given your whole being
to me, for this you may be sorry.
Your reckoning will not be in order
before God Almighty, through my fault.) (Davidson, Walsh and Broos 2007: lines 372–381)

It is after this that *Elckerlijc* realizes his moral bankruptcy. He turns away from his wealth with a monologue that expresses his self-loathing and marks the beginning of his road to salvation with the assistance of Virtue and Self-Knowledge.[17]

The real turning point of the *Elckerlijc* is the protagonist's farewell to his material goods. The conversion to Virtue and Self-Knowledge here leads to a genuine mercantile salvation – but would be rewritten and rearranged in *Homulus, Hecastus* and the play of the Voluptuous Man; and eventually Elckerlijc would reappear as the advertising director in Philip Roth's American *Everyman*.

However, if we take the mercantile dilemma of mortality and materialism as the play's most distinctive element, world literature (if this term is appropriate for medieval textual culture) also found its way into *Elckerlijc*, but the story of the play's sources is similar to that of its reception: it remains hard to see when shared motifs could or should be redefined in direct relationship – especially concerning universal themes such as death, materiality and mortality. This is even problematic for parallels in Dutch literature, for instance in a fourteenth-century Dutch text: *Spiegel van sonden* (Mirror of sins). This treatise on the capital sins is an adaptation of the wide-spread Latin *Summa de vitiis* by the thirteenth-century French Dominican friar William Peraldus (an example of medieval world literature in itself). One of its many *exempla* tells a story of a rich man on his deathbed, who asks his riches to help him. When there is no response he sighs:

> O bedriegelike rijcheide,
> Hoe zeere heb ic di begheert,
> Ghemint met herten, ghehad so weert!
> Nu ne vindic cleen no groot
> Hulpe no raet ter meester noot!
> Wel schijnt dat ghi mi wilt laten,
> Ende niet volghen te mijnre baten.
> Alsic hier keeren sal ter erden.

(O deceitful riches, how I have I longed for you, loved you with all my heart with the highest respect. Now in my hour of need, I find no help or advice. It appears that you leave me and do not want to follow me for my benefit now that I will return to the earth.)
(Verdam 1900–1901: vol. 1, lines 3347–3370)

He decides to distribute his wealth among the poor; and he dies in peace.

Elckerlijc shares with the *exemplum* the direct address of riches/goods (although the conversation is one-way in the exemplum) in the final hour of need, the disillusion that gathering wealth is in vain and the turn to righteousness by giving riches to the poor (Elckerlijc distributes half of his goods among the poor). Like other *exempla* or parables that have been put forward as a possible source for *Elckerlijc*, this story of the rich man possibly has left some traces in the play, but not more than others. It only goes to show that also *Elckerlijc* was firmly rooted in a traditional religion of reckoning, sacraments – offered in the many books of everyman's salvation that circulated in late medieval culture. The comparison with the *exemplum* also shows the innovative strength of the play. The story of a rich man and his wealth is the kind of narrative evidence medieval *exempla* used to offer in addition to series of authorities and arguments. The unknown author of the *Elckerlijc* transformed this individual case to an allegorical archetype, mankind's struggle with the human condition and Everyman's mirror of salvation.

Notes

1 There are many good editions of the *Elckerlijc*, for instance Elslander (1985), available online. An edition of all Dutch Elckerlijc sources is De Haan and Van Delden (1979). An edition of the Dutch text, the sixteenth-century English translation and a modern English translation can be found in Davidson, Walsh and Broos (2007), that will be used for this contribution. This edition is also online. For an introduction to the later popularity of *Elckerlijc* see Parker (1970).
2 For *Elckerlijc* and its connection to the rhetoricians Brinkman (2004: 163–164) and Warnar (2015); on the communities of rhetoricians in general see Van Bruaene 2006).
3 On *Elckerlijc* as a text for reading see Coigneau (2001: 201).

4   Brinkman 2004: 163–164. An edition of all Dutch sources (three printed editions and a manuscript) in De Haan and Van Delden 1979.
5   'Een seer schoon comedie oft spel vanden bekeerden coopman, waer inne die warachtighe wel ghefondeerde ende oock die valsche onghefondeerde ende verkeerde religie oft kercke deen vanden anderen naer d'leven claer ghepresenteert ende af ghemaelt wordt: om te verstaen welck haerlieder viertuyt, cracht is. Om te bestryden elcx conscientie (die welcke daer sal gaen met eenen yeghelijcken ende hem volghen) ten uitersten oordeele ons Heeren Jesum Christi.' (Antwerp: Niclaes Mollyns, for Jasper Troyens, 1583). The only known surviving copy is Leiden University Library, 1096 H 93. Digital reproduction: http://www.let.leidenuniv.nl/Dutch/Ceneton/Facsimiles/BekeerdenCoopman1583/ (accessed 18 February 2019). On the text see Strengholt 1969.
6   On the French text see Bouteille-Meister 2014. I thank Marcus de Schepper (University of Antwerp) for pointing me to the French text as a possible source for the Dutch play.
7   On the figures of Death in the plays see Best 1981.
8   See Dammer and Jeßing 2007; Best 1987; and Valentin 1980.
9   On the Calvinist Republic see Marnef 1994.
10 On the text see Bussels 2008; see Strengholt (1969: 341–342) for the conections of *Mercator* and the *Comedie*.
11 'Das argument[t]e disz spyls hab ich zům mehrn teil ausz der Lateynschen comedien Petri Diesthemii genomen, aber vil dinges darausz der mensch betrieglichkeit dises lebens erlernen mag ausz andern büchern dar bey gesůcht und im trůck gemeyn gemacht.' Unfortunately, this passage was not edited in the edition (see Noorrenberg 1873: 37). The transcription is given here on the basis of a pdf-file of an unidentified copy of the first edition of *Homulus*, found on Googleplay: https://play.google.com/store/books/details/Homulus_Eyn_sch%C3%B6n_Spyl_in_w%C3%B6lchem_menschliches_Leb?id=YqZQAAAAcAAJ (accessed 18 February 2019).
12 For instance: *Waer sidi, mijn doot, die niemant en spaert* (Davidson, Walsh and Broos 2007: l, 46) and *Waer bistu, Doot, die niemant en spaert* (Serrure 1857: 27), or *Ay, Elckerlijc wat dede ic ye gheboren / Ick sie mijn leven al verloren* (Davidson, Walsh and Broos 2007: lines 163–164) and *O wee dat ick ye wert geboren! / Ick sie nu wael mijn leven is nu verloren* (Serrure 1857: 55).
13 *Comedie* 1583: 6. Bouteille-Meister (2014: 9–11) points at the *dénonciation des mauvaises pratiques commerciales du Marchant* in the French source.
14 Vandommele and Bussels 2014: 147–149.
15 Edition of the original Dutch text in Kruyskamp (1950: 91–144). English translation in King 1986.
16 On Van Hemessen's oeuvre in connection to *Elckerlijc, Homulus* and *Hecastus* in general, see Wallen (1983: 59–63). In particular on the painting of the Prodigal Son see Rothstein 2012.
17 On the role of Self-knowledge see Jambeck 1977.

References

Asselbergs, W.J.M.A. (1968), *De stijl van Elkerlijk*, Zwolle: Tjeenk Willink.

Bemmel, H. van (1989), 'Toneel in Arnhem van 1500 tot 1655', in G.R.W. Dibbets and P.W.M. Wackers (eds), *Wat duikers vent is dit! Opstellen voor W.M.H. Hummelen*, 121–138, Wijhe: Quarto.
Best, T.W. (1981), 'Heralds of Death in Dutch and German Everyman Plays', *Neophilologus* 81: 397–403.
Best, T.W. (1987), '*Everyman* and Protestantism in the Netherlands and Germany', *Daphnis* 16: 13–32.
Bloemendal, J. (2013), 'Similarities, Dissimilarities and Possible Relation Between Early Modern Latin Drama and Drama in the Vernacular', in P. Ford and A. Taylor (eds), *The Early Modern Cultures of Neo-Latin Drama*, 141–158, Leuven: Leuven University Press.
Bolte, J., ed. (1927), *Drei Schauspiele vom sterbenden Menschen*, Leipzig: Hiersemann.
Bouteille-Meister, C. (2014), 'Le Marchant converti (1558) ou la mise en scène scatologique du débat sotériologique contemporain: comment se rapprocher d'un public à convaincre. Théâtre et polémique religieuse'. Available online: http://umr6576.cesr.univ-tours.fr/publications/polemique/fichiers/pdf/03-BOUTEILLE.pdf (accessed 18 February 2019).
Brinkman, H. (2004), 'De const ter perse. Publiceren bij de rederijkers voor de Reformatie', in H. Pleij et. al. (eds), *Geschreven en gedrukt. Boekproductie van handschrift naar druk in de overgang van Middeleeuwen naar Moderne Tijd*, 157–176, Gent: Academia Press.
Bruaene, A.-L. van (2006), '"A wonderfull tryumfe, for the wynnyng of a pryse": Guilds, Ritual, Theater, and the urban Network in the Southern Low Countries, ca. 1450–1650', *Renaissance Quarterly* 59: 374–405.
Bussels, S. (2008), 'Hoe overtuigt Coornherts *Comedie vande Rijckeman? Enargeia* en het opvoeren van personificaties', *Spiegel der Letteren* 50: 1–40.
Coigneau, D. (2001), 'Drama in druk tot circa 1540', in H. van Dijk, B. Ramakers et. al. (eds), *Spel en spektakel. Middeleeuws toneel in de Lage Landen*, 201–214, Amsterdam: Prometheus.
Dammer, R. and B. Jeßing (2007), *Der Jedermann im 16. Jahrhundert. Die Hecastus-Dramen von Georgius Macropedius und Hans Sachs*, Quellen und Forschungen zur Literatur- und Kulturgeschichte 42, Berlin: De Gruyter.
Davidson, C., M.W. Walsh and T. Broos, eds (2007), *Everyman and Its Dutch Original, Elckerlijc*, Kalamazoo: Medieval Institute Publications.
Elslander, A. van, ed. (1985), *[Den] spyeghel der salicheyt van Elckerlijc*, Antwerp: De Nederlandsche Boekhandel.
Freeman, A. (2008), '*Everyman* and others, part II: The Bandinel Fragments', *The Library*, ser.7, 9 (4): 397–427.
Haan, M.J.M. de (1975), 'Elckerlijc is niet iederéén', in M.J.M. de Haan et. al. (eds), *In navolging, Een bundel studies aangeboden aan C.C. de Bruin bij zijn afscheid als hoogleraar te Leiden*, 286–291, Leiden: Brill.
Haan, M.J.M. de and B.J. van Delden, eds (1979), *[De] spiegel der zaligheid van Elckerlijk naar de bewaarde bronnen uitgegeven*, Leiden: Vakgroep Nederlandse Taal- en Letterkunde.
Harper, E., and B. Mize (2006), 'Material Economy, Spiritual Economy, and Social Critique in Everyman', *Comparative Drama* 40: 263–311.
Hutcheon, B. (2013), *A Theory of Adaption*, 2nd edn, Londen: Routledge.
Jambeck, T.J. (1977), 'Everyman and the Implications of Bernardine Humanism in the Character "Knowledge"', *Medievalia et Humanistica* 8: 103–123.
King, P.M. (1986), 'The Voluptuous Man, Jan van den Berghe', *Dutch Crossing*, 28: 53–107.

King, P.M. (1994), 'Morality Plays', in R. Beadle and A.J. Fletcher (eds), *The Cambridge Companion to Medieval English Theatre*, 240–264, Cambridge: Cambridge University Press.
Kruyskamp, C., ed. (1950), *Dichten en spelen van Jan van den Berghe*, The Hague: Martinus Nijhoff.
Ladd, R.A. (2007), '"My Condicion is Mannes Soule to Kill" – Everyman's Mercantile Salvation', *Comparative Drama* 41 (1): 57–78.
Marnef, G. (1994), 'The Changing Face of Calvinism in Antwerp, 1550–1585', in A. Pettegree, A. Duke and G. Lewis (eds.), *Calvinism in Europe, 1540–1620*, 143–159, Cambridge: University Press.
Meulen, P. van der, ed. (1955), *Het roerspel en de comedies van Coornhert*, Leiden: Brill.
Norrenberg, W., ed. (1873), *Homulus (Der Sünden Loin ist der Toid). Geistliches Schauspiel von Jaspar von Gennep*, Wiersen: Meyer.
Parker, J.J. (1970), *The Development of the Everyman Drama from Elckerlyc to Hofmannsthal's Jedermann*, Doetinchem: Ratio.
Potter, R.A. (1975), *The English Morality Play. Origins, History, and Influence of a Dranmatic Tradition*, London: Routledge.
Ramakers, B. (2006), 'Dutch Allegorical Theatre. Tradition and Conceptual Approach', in E. Strietman and P. Happé (eds), *Urban Theatre in the Low Countries, 1400–1625*, 12: Medieval texts and cultures of Northern Europe, 127–147, Turnhout: Brepols.
Roersch, A., ed. (1903), *Chr. Ischyrius: Homulus*, Gent: La Librairie Neerlandaise.
Roloff, H.-G., ed. (1982), *T. Naogeorgus: Sämtliche Werke II: Dramen II: Tragoedia alia nova Mercator mit einer zeitgenössischen Übersetzung*, Berlin: De Gruyter.
Roth, P. (2006a), *Everyman*, London: Cape.
Roth, P. (2006b), *Alleman*, Amsterdam: De Bezige Bij.
Rothstein, B. (2012), 'Beer and Loafing in Antwerp', *Art History* 35: 886–907.
Schreiber, E. G. (1975), 'Everyman in America', *Comparative Drama* 9: 99–115.
Serrure, C.P., ed. (1857), *Van Homulus, een schoene comedie daer in begrepen wort hoe inder tijt des doots der menschen alle geschapen dinghen verlaten dan alleene die duecht die blijft by hem vermeerdert ende ghebetert*, Gent: Annoot-Braeckman.
Steenbeek, B.W. (1966), *Doede van Amsweer. Bijdrage tot de kennis van de geschiedenis der Reformatie in de provincie Groningen*, Wageningen: Veenman.
Strengholt, L. (1969), 'Kooplui in conflict met hun geweten', *De Nieuwe Taalgids* 62: 340–343.
Valentin, J.-M. (1980), 'Die Moralität im 16. Jahrhundert: Konfessionelle Wandlungen einer dramatischen Struktur', *Daphnis* 9: 769–788.
Vanderheijden, J.F. (1930), *Het thema en de uitbeelding van den dood in de poëzie der late Middeleeuwen en der vroege renaissance in de Nederlanden*, Gent: Liedeberg.
Vandommele, J. and S. Bussels (2014), '"Cooplieden die rechtveerdich handelen eenpaer." Coornhert en het zestiende-eeuwse Antwerpen over handel en rijkdom', in J. Gruppelaar and J. Pieters (eds), *'Un certain Holandois'. Coornhert en de vragen van zijn tijd*, 143–166, Hilversum: Verloren.
Verdam, J., ed. (1900–1901), *Spiegel der sonden*, Leiden: Brill.
Verschelde, B. (1983), 'Macropedius' Hecastus (1539), Ischyrius' Homulus (1536) en Elckerlijc', *Handelingen van de Koninklijke Zuid-Nederlandse Maatschappij voor Taal- en Letterkunde en Geschiedenis* 37: 235–254.
Wallen, B. (1983), *Jan van Hemessen. An Antwerp Painter between Reform and Counter-Reform*, Ann Arbor, MI: UMI Research Press.
Warnar, G. (2015), '*Elckerlijc* in beeld. Jan Provoosts *Rijkaard en de dood*', *Spiegel der letteren* 57: 273–289.

6

Joost van den Vondel (Cologne 1587 Amsterdam 1679) as Writer/Translator: Literacy in Transit

Marco Prandoni

> Van den Vondel, a poets' pearl,
> Possessed by a stronger spirit than most,
> Glory of the Amstel, a leader of the guild
> That spent its time with dreams on Parnas [...]
> The fustigator of pure preachers' pulpits [...]
> That Vondel, I say, that highly famous Vondel,
> In whom we find all clustered together
> A treasure of art we could only search in many,
> Belonged at first to Menno's simple people,
> Either by choice or in the footsteps of his parents.[1]

In this poem praise is mixed with satire. Physician and poet – translator as well – Jacob Westerbaen sketches Joost van den Vondel's life up to the present, in 1648.[2] More specifically, he concentrates on Vondels transconfessional trajectory: born as a Mennonite in 1587, he supported the Arminian-Remonstrant religious and political party in the 1620s, then converted to Roman Catholicism around 1640. A militant Remonstrant himself, who has fought like Vondel for religious tolerance and against any dogmatism from the Calvinist or Catholic side, Westerbaen cannot understand this fluctuation and concludes sharply: Vondel's first name allows one to prophesize he will eventually turn Jewish ... you only need to swap the last two letters, Joost/Joots (Jew)!

In this chapter I will connect Vondel's different confessional stances with his changing social environment and his networks inside and outside the – still fluid and somewhat in progress – borders of the young Republic of the United Provinces. Through those connections he absorbed and included transnational literary models by means of an intense translation practice, accompanied by reflection on translation and on his own role of intercultural negotiator.

The young Vondel and France

Westerbaen's witty poem gives us a glimpse of the multi- and transconfessional landscape of the Republic of the United Provinces around 1650 and especially of its informal capital, Amsterdam. A city where despite the presence of a public church – the Dutch Reformed, which never became a state church in the Republic – many Protestant denominations lived beside a large Catholic (or crypto-Catholic) population and a community of Askhenazi and Sefardi Jews (Nadler 2003), with a multi-shaded grey area of converts, religious dissidence and cross-confessional fluidity (Pollmann 2012: 88). The latent political-religious tensions burst out on some occasions, for instance around 1620 between Remonstrants and Contraremontrants, capital years for both Vondel and Westerbaen. However, the more general note in the ensuing decades was one of interconfessional conviviality based on practical tolerance that was prompted by the well-to-do elite of merchants-regents, regardless of religious leanings or political differences (Frijhoff and Spies 2004).

Despite his somewhat awkward status in the eyes of many Protestants like Westerbaen or Constantijn Huygens after his conversion to Roman Catholicism, in 1648 Vondel enjoyed a vast reputation: the most prominent literary exponent of the city of Amsterdam. Few could have foreseen this exceptional integration story – let alone his conversion to Catholicism! – when eight-year old Joost Jr. migrated with his parents from Cologne to the city on the river Amstel. They fled from religious persecutions because of their Mennonite faith. The family came originally from Antwerp but had moved to the free city of Cologne, major transport hub on the Rhine, probably for economic reasons. In Amsterdam they settled in the Warmoesstraat, a lively neighbourhood where Protestant migrants from the Southern Netherlands clustered together. They kept tight bonds with Cologne and participated in the exceptional economic boom of Amsterdam around 1600: the Vondels traded in silk and had international connections, which would lead Joost for instance twice to Copenhagen (Grit 1994: 29–51). Outside their work, they socialized mainly with fellow-members of the Anabaptist communities: Joost married a girl, Maeyken de Wolff, from the same street and confession (and with connections in Cologne) and deployed his first literary and theatrical activities inside the Chamber of Rhetoric *The*

White Lavender (*Het Wit Lavendel*), founded in 1598 by Protestant migrants from the Southern Netherlands. Karel van Mander, an Anabaptist like the young Vondel, participated in its activities during his last years, which he spent in Amsterdam, surrounded by fellow-literati of southern origin such as schoolteacher Peeter Heyns and his son Zacharias (Molkenboer 1950: 84). The latter was a poet, translator and publisher and had worked with the humanist printer Plantin (Plantijn) in Antwerp before moving to Cologne and eventually to the Warmoesstraat in Amsterdam. They were all imbued with a large international culture, were multilingual, shared the experience of exile and migration and showed a complex loyalty: to the city where they lived and its municipal culture, to the Dutch Republic, where they had settled, and to broad and diffused border-crossing confessional communities. Their literary practice is very telling in this respect: it reflects both their commitment to the shaping of what we might call a proto-national literary landscape in wording and their rootedness in a cross-border literary and religious culture, that of Protestantism, in the first place Calvinism and Anabaptism. Moreover, people like Karel van Mander participated both in the municipal, regional and intraregional network of the Chambers of Rhetoric in the vernacular language and in the national and international *res publica literarum* in Latin and, especially inside the circles of southern intellectuals at Leiden University, in French (Lash and Meerhoff 2010: 46).[3]

In 1610 Vondel wrote his first play, *Het Pascha* (*The Passover*, 1927). The biblical subject-matter, the exodus of the Jews from slavery, foreshadowed mankind's delivery from sin by Christ but also the successful independence struggle of the United Provinces against Spain, as Vondel stressed in a poem that accompanied the printed edition of the play (WB 1: 261–263).[4] Old Testament tales of struggle for freedom were actualized as prefigurations of contemporary tales of oppression, martyrdom and liberation that broadly circulated in the circles to which Vondel belonged, based in Amsterdam but with material and ideal ramifications all over Protestant Europe, especially where prosecuted minorities had fled and created memory communities. The Dutch Revolt had a wide resonance in Protestant Europe, also due to the exiled communities in Germany and London. Vondel's literary models were mostly to be traced back to works by French Huguenots, like Garnier's drama *Les Juives* (*The Jewish Women*, 2007) and Du Bartas's biblical epos *Les sepmaines* (*The Weeks*, 1979). At the time, France formed a transit-space for the spread of Renaissance forms and ideas in the Republic: many classic and Italian models reached the Netherlands through French mediation (Van Leeuwen 2004). Vondel was not as imbued with French literature or as proficient in the French language as were other intellectuals in the Brabantine chamber of rhetoric who were often bilingual (like playwright Abraham de Koningh) or French schoolteachers (Molkenboer 1950: 150). However, the orientation of his young years is unequivocal (Thys 1987: 28).

Since the publication of his very first poems in 1607 Vondel used the 'modern' syllabotonic verse, influenced by Romance – and specifically French – isosyllabic metrics but based also on a regular alternation of stressed and unstressed syllables as in the old Germanic tradition, since 'the Netherlands lay at a cultural crossroads between France and England, and both practices were well known' (Gasparov 1996: 166). Moreover, this versification could be considered a plausible equivalent to classic quantitative metrics: it could then be passed on to Germany, to Scandinavian literatures, to Eastern and Balkan Europe. The French metrics carried with them Renaissance forms (sonnets, odes, epistles, etc.) and practices: Marot and the Marotiques, Ronsard and the Pléiade, the Calvinist translation of the Psalms by Marot and De Bèze. Vondel was immediately receptive of these new poetic forms, partially elaborated by migrant poets in exile, and stood in the tradition of Francophile Protestant exiled poets like Lucas d'Heere, Jan van der Noot, Marnix van St Aldegonde (Porteman and Smits-Veldt 2008: 123–128; Prandoni 2016). For him this meant first and foremost a great fascination for the poetry of Guillaume Du Bartas: a modern poet, admired throughout reformed Europe, translated by both Van Mander and Zacharias Heyns. Du Bartas expressed in pure Renaissance alexandrines and musical lines the world-view of Calvinism (Verwey 1927: 16–21).

In the paratext accompanying the printed edition of his first play, Vondel addressed in a poem a friend of his, a fellow-merchant migrated from Antwerp like himself (WB 1: 167–170, see Thys 1987: 25). The text is in French, the language use drawn from intense reading of Du Bartas (Beekman 1912: 56). In the ensuing years, Vondel would translate and rearrange a number of French works but not Du Bartas until 1616. In 1620 he rendered an episode from the second week of *Les sepmaines* (1584–1591), *La Magnificence de Salomon* (*De Heerlyckheyd van Salomon*), with an entertaining foreword.

> I have considered many times, Reader, to get a hold with my clumsy hands of this pure work, but fear made me always hesitate, as I was afraid to touch this Ark with unconsecrated fingers […] My feelings were confirmed in this by the commendable testimony of the best connoisseurs of this excellent work, as among others its exegete Simon Goulart who exceptionally praises it with the following words: *s'ensuit la MAGNIFICENCE ou seconde partie* […] That is: *the MAGNIFICENCE follows, or the second part* […] Thus it was not without reason that I was afraid to commit a sin. However, even though fear did me sometimes shy away, a secret passion compelled me to consider how I could embellish and adorn this French Venus with a Dutch garment and costume […]. I surrendered. I ventured in. Reader, […] do not be surprised if we waste some time with translation: a poor household often needs to borrow something from others. And if you object with the funny fable of the magpie that bragged with borrowed feathers among peacocks, we feel we are touched where it hurts the most, as we are showing off with what is not ours. But before you get annoyed at our rhymes, I beg you to consider the following points in a row: 1. that we are delivering you a translation and not our own creation; 2. that we could have flowed more fluently were it not that we wanted to remain close to the text; 3. that my mother did not teach me better Dutch.[5]

The 'sacred' beauty of Du Bartas's poem refers at the same time to its biblical topic and to its aesthetic perfection. The scholar Vondel refers to as an *auctoritas* and quotes is Simon Goulart, in French, who exceptionally provided the text of a living author with commentary, contributing to its canonization (Lash and Meerhoff 2010: 46). Goulart was a French Reformed theologian and humanist in Genève and the father of a preacher who lived in the Republic. Between Genève, France and the United Provinces there existed a web of connections made up of personal contacts, exchange of correspondence and books: a transnational linguistic and religious community (Frijhoff 2017: 124). Many humanists and theologians – teachers and students – operating at Leiden University were for instance of southern origin, in some cases French.

In this preface, the cultural import from France by means of translation is judged positively: what we might call a defective attitude towards a culture felt as superior (Burke 2004: 122). The lengthy quotations, in translation *and* in the original language, from Goulart and from Montaigne in the dedicatory letter, show deep admiration. Moreover, Vondel states that his work is not an original but a *translation* (Hermans 1996: 11) and asks his reader to reflect on that: a humble stance but at the same time showing an awareness of the status of his own work and of the otherness with respect to the original. Although Vondel confirms the idea of 'the derivative nature of the translated text' (Hermans 1985), with Lawrence Venuti we can say that the translator's labour does not collapse into the foreign author's (Venuti 2004). It is an adaptation, no cultural substitution. Vondel focuses on his own translation practice as well as on his role of 'cultural go-between' (Venuti 2004). He communicates his genuine emotion in facing this challenge, his doubts, his fear – or certainty (Hermans 1985) – of failure in his undertaking. He justifies his own choices, for instance to stick closely to the original text, at a time when the borders between translation and creative imitation were mostly blurred, and 'borrowings' undeclared.

The text contains the witty remark: 'my mother did not teach me better Dutch'. A joke, but also the reality of a transnational identity of a young man born in Cologne from Brabantine parents who migrated to Amsterdam to a neighbourhood where most people were not autochthonous, and multilingual, as we can read in the contemporary comedy the *Spanish Brabander* (*De Spaansche Brabander*, 1982) by G.A. Bredero.

Vondel and humanist culture

Bredero and Vondel met at the gatherings and the performances of the Dutch Academy (De Nederduitsche Academie) founded by physician and poet Samuel Coster in order to provide the young elite of the city with education in the vernacular. Vondel set himself to learn Latin and got rapidly acquainted with the classics, Seneca in the first place, as the Senecan tragedy dominated the repertoires. In 1620 Vondel put on stage his *Hierusalem verwoest* (*Jerusalem Destroyed*, 1929), based for the historical subject on Flavius Josephus and for the literary modelling on Seneca's *Troades*. Garnier's *Les Juives* and *La Troade* still resonated too, together with the classics (Smit 1956–1962: vol. 1, 89–93).

Vondel's bonds with the Mennonite community began to loosen, even if the process of estrangement was gradual (Paijmans 2017). He retired as deacon and faced a period of depression, of which we are informed by his later biographer Brandt (1932: 11–12). Brandt was a supporter of the Remonstrant faction inside the Calvinist church, and of the party of the merchants-regents against the Contraremonstrants and Prince Maurice of Nassau (Maurits van Nassau). Vondel had belonged to the same Remonstrant faction and participated in the theological-political struggle. After Maurice's death in 1625 and the victory of the moderate liberal faction, the situation calmed down considerably for the poet.

Vondel made new acquaintances in humanist circles: P.C. Hooft, Bredero, Laurens Reael, Roemer Visscher and his daughters Anna and Maria who animated a lively literary salon. This was a very different milieu from that in which Vondel had been raised, less preoccupied with sin and imbued with classic learning. For Vondel this meant catching up with the young intellectual elite of Amsterdam characterized by an aversion to religious fanaticism and confidence in the feasibility of a new society and of literature in the vernacular. They were also engaged in the shaping of a standardized written language – a supra-regional civilized sociolect of the elite – pushed by the drive to demonstrate that it could compete with any other vernacular. In a society that was politically fragmented, particularistic, with a culturally and linguistically diverse population, divided along confessional lines, largely multilingual (see Frijhoff 2017), and so all but homogeneous, they shared a concern about shaping the discursive space of Dutchness in the literary language. No wonder they tried to purify this language from French and Latin 'bastardized' loanwords, as we can read in Bredero's paratexts (see Hermans 1996: 89–90). A new, assertive tone prevailed.

Together with his friends, Vondel studied, discussed, wrote – and translated. In the foreword to his translation from Du Bartas, he wrote that he 'wasted some time' with it, but that was an understatement. Translation formed most certainly an essential part of the learning program, as Vondel himself would write in 1650: 'Knowledge of foreign languages is a great advantage, and translating the illustrious Poets will help the aspiring Poet in the same way that the Painter's apprentice may benefit from copying great masterpieces.'[6] However, it would be too simplistic to say that the derivative, imitative practice of translation for him formed the first step before original creation, even if in fact it often came down to this. To him translating was a core literary practice alongside others. What translation, being a place of negotiation between different cultures, certainly did was to help him reassess his orientation and often mark the discontinuities of tradition and of the imagined community he wanted to inscribe himself in, as the dedicatees of his paratexts show. It helped him to shape new configurations of the world.

In the early 1620s he shared the general enthusiasm for Seneca whose tragedies were edited many times in Latin throughout learned Europe, and also in the Republic, which was becoming the most important staple market for books as well as for many other goods.[7] Vondel could get access to classic scholarship for the first time without mediation in other vernaculars, albeit with the help of erudite friends. He then set up to study Seneca, and translate him, inside a collective, equally interested in rendering the Roman author – for the book market and for the stage – and in molding the translating language into a new standard. Seneca's *Trojan Women* (*Troades*) was adapted into *The Amsterdam Hecuba* (*De Amsteldamsche Hecuba*) in 1626: the naturalizing title reveals the desire to absorb the humanist tradition in a new context but is somewhat misleading, as the translation is conducted with scrupulous philological care and preservation of the cultural otherness of the original. The cover contains an untranslated quotation, in Greek, from Euripides' *Hekabe*. The foreword is addressed to Antonis de Hubert, a man holding Leiden degrees in law and the classics, and author of a recent translation of the Psalms. Together with the top politician Laurens Reael – Governor-General of the Dutch East Indies from 1616 to 1619 – and probably with P.C. Hooft, De Hubert was one of the *verscheyde vaders* (different fathers) of this *kind* (child), in Vondel's own words (WB 2: 533).

During the 1620s and 1630s Vondel put a lot of intellectual energy in translation projects including Seneca, Horace and Juvenalis. Also Tasso, from the *Gerusalemme Liberata*, despite his almost non-existing knowledge of Italian (Van den Vondel 2013): as he was working on a Christian epos on Constantine the Great he needed to deepen his understanding of the paradigmatic modern epic of Christianity, alongside the venerated Virgil. The world-renowned scholar Hugo Grotius, whom he met during Grotius' short secret visit to the Republic from Paris, where he had escaped to at the time of the turmoil between Remonstrants and Contraremonstrants, urged him to realize this epic (Smits-Veldt and Spies 2012: 67). It appeared to him functional to his own strife to unite all Christians beyond confessional barriers on the common denominator of the faith of early Christianity (Posthumus Meyjes 1984). An Irenicist stance to which Vondel himself was growingly committed.

Even when he eventually abandoned the epic and turned again, and for good, to tragedy, Vondel first translated a Latin play by Grotius and then dedicated to him, in exile, the history drama *Gysbreght van Aemstel* (2018). The play was intended to officially inaugurate, in 1637, the first stone theatre in the Republic: the classicist Schouwburg built after the Renaissance model of Palladio and Scamozzi in Vicenza. Its aim was to compete with ancient Rome or even surpass it, as Vondel stated in the paratexts of the printed edition (Van den Vondel 2018: 100), published by Willem Blaeu – known not only for his navigational maps but also for his literary publications – Vondel's new publisher since his 'humanist turn': the self-aware posture of the intellectual elite of the Republic.

The play dealt with an obscure episode of the history of Amsterdam but aimed at a complex reconsideration of past traumas: in the first place, the end of the medieval Catholic plenitude of a communitarian religious experience after the city had officially joined the side of the Reformation (Prandoni 2013; Sierhuis 2016). The historic subject was intertextually shaped after the model of Virgil's second book of the *Aeneid*. This was a grandiose humanist intellectual achievement at the heart of the social life of the Republic which Grotius commented upon in a letter from Paris to Vondel: this play will be *onsterffelyk* (immortal, Brandt 1932: 32). Vondel was writing a classic in his turn, according to Grotius. Literature and drama in Dutch could compete with the work of the ancients.

The Catholic Vondel and the translations from Virgil

About a decade later, in 1646, Vondel published a complete Virgil translation in prose. The book was dedicated to Constantijn Huygens, secretary of the Prince of Orange, and sent directly to P.C. Hooft. Huygens and Hooft were among the most refined intellectuals in the Republic of the time, both old acquaintances of Vondel's. However, their relation to Vondel had cooled considerably after his conversion to Roman Catholicism around 1640. From Grotius' Irenicism Vondel grew to the acceptation of the one, and universal, Church of Rome. He was helped in this spiritual evolution by the active pastor of the Catholic Church in Amsterdam Leonardus Marius and other connections in the still flourishing Catholic Amsterdam: a hidden elite which had lost the political power but still remained rich (Parker 2008: 160) and active in various fields, like charity institutions and the theatre – many of the trustees of the Schouwburg were in fact Catholic. This was a self-conscious minority with tight connections with Catholic lands and lands where Catholic minorities lived. In the same year 1646 Vondel issued a tragedy on the execution of Mary Stuart, presented as a martyr, and translated as early as 1672 in Saxony (Van de Poppe 2017). His *auctoritates* were from now on among others the Church Fathers, medieval theologians and modern intellectuals from Catholic Europe.

In a later poem, Vondel would look back upon this step and say that he had 'discovered, at a better day, / the pearl that had been hidden / [...] Happy is he who chooses the best'.[8] This choice was simply not understood by many of his acquaintances, and seen with dismay by Huygens. The hostility against the new convert and his apologetic zeal would surface one year later, in 1647, when the Remonstrant Westerbaen and Brandt (his future biographer!) discredited Vondel by issuing a new edition of his collected poems. They added the texts with the harshest tone that had not been included in the first anthology published three years earlier. In 1648 Westerbaen would write the satirical poem quoted at the beginning of this contribution. Vondel had to work patiently in order to restore his network of connections and the Virgil-translation was a strategic move in that direction. First of all, he tried to regain the patronage of the Oranges at the court in The Hague. Second, he showed a respectful attitude towards men of letters such as Huygens and Hooft, after years of reciprocal alienation (Reinders and Blom 2011). This strategy would prove successful. In 1648 he was asked to compose a play for the city theatre to celebrate the end of the war with Spain. In 1653 he was crowned Prince of Dutch Poets by the guild of St Lucas.

The foreword to the Virgil translation is very interesting also in other respects. It contains views on translation which can be considered exceptional for Vondel's time.

> For if, as some would claim, there is some secret of meaning or sound concealed beneath every word, syllable and letter, how much will then not be necessarily spoilt and lost due to the inequalities between the two languages, and their unequal nature and proprieties, and the differences in names and words, which are signs of the things they signify; also indeed in terms of the flowers and fragrance of eloquence – apart from the fact that verse and prose differ from each other like a trumpet blast and the unaided voice, and verse is like the sound of the voice being energetically forced through a trumpet with three coils. For this reason the translator would be better advised to render [Virgil] in rhyme and metre: but how many more feathers would he not have lost if his spirit had been squeezed and pressed into the narrow straits of rhyme and metrical feet, and from sheer need distorted and tampered with, and of necessity covered all over with the borrowed plumes of stopgaps for

the sake of the verse. To put the translated text to rhyme without adding or taking away is scarcely possible, indeed impossible, and nearly always strays to a smaller or larger extent from what has been translated. So I saw no way of rendering him more accurately or more faithfully except in prose, so as to impress Maro's soul all the more directly on the Dutch reader, to serve him [i.e. the Dutch reader] better, and also the student of Latin, who may find the Latin more accessible when he sees the properties of the Roman tongue matched as closely as possible with our language, and the style and expression rendered as smoothly as possible.[9]

Reading this reflection on translation, I cannot agree with the central assumption in a recent article by Madeleine Kasten. According to her, Vondel considered – the dominant paradigm in the Early Modern period, before Romanticism – 'perfection in translation' as 'an attainable goal' (Kasten 2012: 255), as *verba* (words) may differ from one language to another, but 'their referents [*res*] were regarded as universal and unchangeable'. An outlook that would imply 'a relationship of full, unproblematic equivalence between the individual languages' and that the 'preservation of meaning' was 'as a priori guaranteed' (253).

On the contrary, Vondel appears to be painfully aware of the impossibility to render a text properly in another language without losing *meaning* (*zin*) and sound (*klanck*) hidden behind each word, syllable, letter[10] – let alone a literary text with its stylistic embellishment. Language shapes reality and Vondel states clearly that source and target language are 'unequal' and the loss in translation irreparable. He is fully aware that 'a translation can never be identical to the foreign text or communicate it in some direct, untroubled manner', as Lawrence Venuti (2004) puts it.

Also, his choice to render the classic author *par excellence* during the Renaissance, Virgil, in prose is remarkable (Hermans 1985; Reinders and Blom 2011). Prose translations of poetic originals did circulate, especially for the stage – from successful Spanish plays for instance: they were made by professional translators, often from Sephardic Jewish circles in the case of Spanish, whose versions were afterward rhymed by playwrights (Blom, Jautze and Álvarez Frances 2016). Vondel himself used to make unpublished prose translations as an exercise (Hermans 1985). But the choice to translate the stylistically venerated Virgil in prose was unprecedented. Vondel did it in order to stick as closely as possible to the foreign text and its structures, a preoccupation he had had since his first Du Bartas's translations, even if his versions became freer with time, 'from a strongly source-oriented to a target-oriented approach' (Hermans 1985). He preferred to avoid the drastic manipulation that a translation in rhymed alexandrines with its formal constraints would imply.[11] Vondel knew that his Virgil would reach a wide and diverse audience in the receiving culture: there was demand for it (Geerts 1932: 49; Reinders and Blom 2011). He addressed both Dutch readers with no specific or little knowledge of Latin and the *classici*, a small elite of men (around 3.5 per cent of the population, Frijhoff 2017: 132) using the ancient language as sociolect (108). In this preface, he says that even those scholars (or pupils) can appreciate his prose translation for they get the chance to compare the two languages: thus they can enjoy it as a *translation*, at a meta-level. He is not saying that his translation will provide those readers with the same experience as the foreign text, not in the least. Venuti notes: 'A translation ought to be read differently from an original composition precisely because it is not an original' (2004).

New (re)translations and reorientations

Vondel would never stop writing – or translating. He eventually re-translated Virgil in rhymed alexandrines, probably feeling the urge, despite his perplexities, to give him a stylistically adequate form in Dutch, and the desire to be confronted with this text again. With Ovid's *Metamorphoses*, another capital text for the Renaissance culture, he did the same: a prose translation, turned into verse years later. For what concerns the theatre, he reverted thanks to the 'Aristotelic' Vossius to the ancient Greek models as soon as 1639, somewhat anticipating Racine and other European playwrights: first with a translation from Sophocles' *Elektra*, then with his own original creations. *Lucifer* (1990) can be considered one of his masterpieces. The tragedy about the fallen angel was dedicated to none other than the Holy Roman Emperor Ferdinand III, clearly stating that earthly hierarchies are 'not only analogous to the heavenly order, but, like his art, reflections of it, drawing their "light," or power, directly from God' (Van Dijkhuizen and Helmers 2012: 386–387). Like most biblical plays by Vondel, history is staged very daringly (Korsten 2009). In this baroque drama, multiple voices resonate and destabilize God's plan, in the first place Lucifer's who pleads his case with passion and lucid argumentation.[12] However, the insistence on the sacrality of the government of the Emperor testifies to a new absolutist religious and political stance. Vondel had moved very far indeed from where he had started his journey.

In 1667, aged 81, Vondel devoted one of his last tragedies, *Zungchin* (1937), to the collapse of the Ming dynasty. Recent events, as the poet underlines, concerning the Chinese world in 1644 (WB 10: 326, 327). In the seventeenth-century Republic Chinese objects like porcelain grew popular thanks to the growing interconnectedness with China (Brook 2007). Vondel was interested in the history of the Jesuit missions in Asia, as his preface to Cornelis Nobelaer – an acquaintance of his who had two brothers in the Jesuit Order – shows. But he must have drawn a lot of inspiration also from Johan Blaeu's publication of several editions of the *Atlas Sinensis* by the missionary Martino Martini whom he probably met in Amsterdam (Minderaa 1963: 125). His curiosity for 'other' cultures and his drive to mediate and negotiate them in a transnationally oriented literacy, participating in border-crossing developments, never decreased, even inside his newly acquired world view of Catholicism.

Notes

1 'Van Vondelen, een parel der poëten, / van sterker geest dan anderen bezeten, / des Amstels roem, een hoofdman der gilde / dat op Parnas zijn tijd met dromen spilde / [...] de geselaar der zuiv're predikstoelen, / [...] die, zeg, die zo hoog beroemde Vondel,

/ bij wie men vindt gelijk in ene bondel, / wat schat van kunst bij velen is te zoeken, / bevond zich eerst bij Menno's slechte broeken, / hetzij door keur of voorgang zijn'er ouderen' (Westerbaen 2001: 82–83; modern spelling).
2. Bloemendal and Korsten 2012 is an excellent reader to Vondel.
3. French slowly but surely overshadowed Latin as the international lingua franca in the second half of the century (Burke 2004: 43–60; Frijhoff 2017: 128).
4. Throughout this chapter the abbreviation *WB* refers to Van den Vondel 1927–1940.
5. 'Ick hebbe, Lezer, meermaels voorgehad mijn plompe handen aan dit zuyvere te slaen, maer vreeze heeft my altijd doen aerzelen, om dat ick ontzag, met ongewyde vingeren deze Arcke aen te tasten [...] Mijn gevoelen hier in wierd versterckt vermids het loflijck getuygenisse dat de aldertreffelijcxste verstanden van dit Puyckjen gaven: gelijck dan neffens andere zynen Uytlegger Simon Goulart hier van luydskeels trompettet in deze woorden: *s'ensuit la MAGNIFICENCE ou seconde partie* [...] Dat is: *volght de HEERLYCKHEYD of het tweede deel* [...] Het was dan niet zonder oorzaeck dat ick my hier aen vreesde te bezondigen. Maer gelijck my vreeze zomtijds dede deynzen, alzoo noopte my wederom een heymelijcke hertstocht om eenmael te zien hoe ick deze fransche Venus met een neerlands gewaed en hulsel zoude mogen toijen en opsmucken [...] Ick wiekte. Ick waeghde 't. Lezer, [...] latet u oock niet vreemd toeschynen dat wy wat tijds met vertalen spillen: een beroyd huysraed moet veeltijds van anderen wat te leen bezitten. En zoo ghy ons voorwerpt die boertery van d'Exter die onder de Paeuwen met geleende veeren dacht te proncken, wy voelen dat wy heerlijck getackt, en op ons zeer geraeckt zijn, want wy brageren met het gene eens anders is. Maer eer ghy u aen onze rymen ergert, zoo bidde ick dat ghy eerst deze dingen op de ryge overweeght: 1. dat wy u een vertalinge en geen eygen vindinge ter hand stellen. 2. dat wy zoetelijcker hadden mogen vloeijen zoo wy ons niet naeuwer aende texst wilden binden. 3. dat mijn moeder my geen beter nederduyts geleert heeft' (WB 2: 228–230).
6. 'Kennis van uytheemsche spraecken vordert niet weinigh, en het overzetten uit vermaerde Poëten helpt den aenkomende Poeet, gelijck het kopieeren van kunstige meesterstucken den Schilders leerling' (WB 5: 488, translation by M. Kasten in Kasten 2012: 255).
7. See Geerts 1932: 20–21.
8. 'ontdeckt wiert, in een' schooner dagh, / De Perle, die verborghen lagh, / [...] Geluckigh die het beste kiest' (WB 5: 492, translation by J. Pollmann in Pollmann 2012: 95).
9. 'want indien, gelijck zommigen drijven, onder elck woort lettergreep en letter eenige geheimenis van zin of klanck schuilt; wat moet 'er nootzaeckelijck door d'ongelijckheit der beide talen, en heuren ongelijcken aert en eigenschappen, en het verschil van namen en woorden, die tekens der betekende zaecken zijn, gespilt worden en verloren gaen, oock zelf aen bloemen en geuren van welsprekentheit; behalve dat dicht en ondicht, of vaers en onvaers onderling verschillen, gelijck trompetklanck en bloote stem, en het vaers een stem, door een drieboghtige trompet krachtig uitgewrongen, gelijck is. Hierom mogdt de vertolcker liever Augustus Hofzwaen in rijm en op maet leeren opzingen: maer hoe veel meer had'er de Mantuaen van zijn vederen moeten laten, indien men zijnen geest door benaeutheit van voeten en rijm bestont te prangen en te knijpen, en uit verlegenheit te rucken, te plucken, en ter noot doorgaens met geleende pluimen van rijm-en-noodige stopwoorden te decken. Het vertaelde te rijmen, zonder afdoen of toedoen, is qualijck mogelijck, ja onmogelijck, en dwaelt meest al min of meer af van het vertaelde. Ick zagh hem dan niet nader nochte eigentlijcker dan door onvaerzen en onrijm uit te beelden, om

den Nederlander te levendiger Maroos ziel in te boezemen, hem te beter te dienen, en met een den Latynist, wien het Latijn nu misschien smaeckelijcker wil vallen, wanneer hy d'eigenschappen der Roomsche met onze moederlijcke spraecke zoo na overeengebrocht, en den stijl en rede zoo vlack en effen gevlijt ziet, als my mogelijck was' (WB 6: 43–44, translation by Theo Hermans in Hermans 1985).
10   'A reference, presumably, to the unbroken tradition of detailed and multi-layered exegesis and commentary of Virgil's poetry' (Hermans 1985).
11   Like Jacob Westerbaen would do after him (Hermans 1996: 124).
12   Forbidden after two performances because of the protests of Calvinist preachers, *Lucifer*'s extraordinary success story would begin with Romanticism, first as a literary work and later as drama, both in the Low Countries and abroad (see Beltrami et al. 2017).

References

Beekman, A. (1912), *Influence de Du Bartas sur la littérature néerlandaise*, Poitiers: Université de Poitiers.
Beltrami, C., M. Meijer Drees, M. Prandoni and R. Schlusemann (2017), 'The Splendour of Vondel's *Lucifer*. Canonicity and Cultural Memory', E. Brems, T. van Kalmthout and O. Réthelyi (eds.), *Doing Double Dutch. The International Circulation of Literature from the Low Countries*, 153–174, Leuven: Leuven University Press.
Bloemendal, J., and F.-W. Korsten, eds (2012), *Joost van den Vondel (1587–1679). Dutch Playwright in the Golden Age*, Leiden: Brill.
Blom, F.R.E., K. Jautze and L. Álvarez Frances (2016), 'Spaans theater in de Amsterdamse Schouwburg (1638–1672). Kwantitatieve en kwalitatieve analyse van de creatieve industrie van het vertalen', *Zeventiende Eeuw* 32 (1): 12–39.
Brandt, G. (1932), *Het leven van Joost van den Vondel*, ed. P. Leendertz, 's Gravenhage: Martinus Nijhoff.
Bredero, G.A. (1982), *The Spanish Brabander*, ed. H.D. Brumble, Binghamton, NY: Center for Medieval & Early Renaissance Studies.
Brook, T. (2007), *Vermeer's Hat. The Seventeenth Century and the Dawn of the Global World*, London: Bloomsbury Publishing.
Burke, P. (2004), *Languages and Communities in Early Modern Europe*, Cambridge: Cambridge University Press.
Dijkhuizen, F.J. van and H. Helmers (2012), 'Religion and Politics – *Lucifer* (1654) and Milton's *Paradise Lost* (1674)', in J. Bloemendal and F.-W. Korsten (eds), *Joost van den Vondel (1587–1679). Dutch Playwright in the Golden Age*, 377–405, Leiden: Brill.
Du Bartas, G. de Saluste (1979), *The Divine Weeks and Works*, eds. J. Sylvester and S. Snyder, 2 vols, Oxford: Clarendon Press.
Frijhoff, W. (2017), 'Multilingualism in the Dutch Golden Age. An Exploration', in W. Frijhoff, M.-C. Kok Escalle and K. Sanchez-Summerer (eds), *Multilingualism, Nationhood, and Cultural Identity. Northern Europe 16th–19th Centuries*, 95–168, Amsterdam: Amsterdam University Press.
Frijhoff, W. and M. Spies (2004), *Dutch Culture in a European Perspective. 1650: Hard-won Unity*, Assen: Van Gorcum.
Garnier, R. (2007) *Les Juives*, ed. M. Jeanneret, Paris: Gallimard.

Gasparov, M. (1996), *A History of European Versification*, Oxford: Clarendon Press.
Geerts, A.M.F.B. (1932), 'Vondel als classicus bij de humanisten in de leer', PhD diss., University of Utrecht.
Grit, D. (1994), *Driewerf zalig Noorden. Over literaire betrekkingen tussen de Nederlanden en Scandinavië*, Maastricht: UPM.
Hermans, T. (1985), 'Vondel on Translation', *Dutch Crossing* 26 (1): 38–72.
Hermans, T. (1996), *Door enen strengen hals. Nederlandse beschouwingen over vertalen 1550-1670*, 's, Gravenhage: Stichting Bibliographica Neerlandica.
Kasten, M. (2012), 'Translation Studies – Vondel's Appropriation of Grotius' *Sophompaneas* (1635)', in J. Bloemendal and F.-W. Korsten (eds), *Joost van den Vondel (1587-1679). Dutch Playwright in the Golden Age*, 249–269, Leiden: Brill.
Korsten, F.-W. (2009), *Sovereignty as Inviolability. Vondel's Theatrical Explorations in the Dutch Republic*, Hilversum: Verloren.
Lash, W. and K. Meerhoff (2010), 'Olivier – Guevara – Poupo: drie opmerkelijke bronnen voor Van Manders *Wtlegghingh op de Metamorphosis*', *De zeventiende eeuw* 26 (1): 21–52.
Leeuwen, C. van (2004), 'De Franse inspiratiebronnen van Joost van den Vondel', in G. Janssens, S. Sereni and E. Spinoy (eds), *n/f Onderzoek en praktijk in de Franstalige neerlandistiek*, 23–39, Liège: Association des Néerlandistes de Belgique francophone.
Minderaa, P. (1963), 'Het treurspel Zungchin belicht vanuit zijn vermoedelijke groei', *Tijdschrift voor Nederlandse Taal- en Letterkunde* 79: 115–134.
Molkenboerm, B.H. (1950), *De jonge Vondel*, Amsterdam: Meulenhoff.
Nadler, S. (2003), *Rembrandt's Jews*, Chicago: University of Chicago Press.
Paijmans, M. (2017), 'Rhetorics of the Dutch Republic: *Parrhesia* in the Complications Surrounding Vondel's *Palamedes* (1625)', *Tijdschrift voor Nederlandse Taal- en Letterkunde* 33 (1), 109–133.
Parker, C. (2008), *Faith on the Margins. Catholics and Catholicism in the Dutch Golden Age*, Cambridge, MA: Harvard University Press.
Pollmann, J. (2012), 'Vondel's Religion', in J. Bloemendal and F.-W. Korsten (eds), *Joost van den Vondel (1587-1679). Dutch Playwright in the Golden Age*, 85–100, Leiden: Brill.
Poppe, C. Van de (2017), 'Nach dem Holländischen Joost van den Vondel', *Nederlandse Letterkunde* 22 (1): 1–23.
Porteman, K. and M.B. Smits-Veldt (2008), *Een nieuw vaderland voor de Muzen. Geschiedenis van de Nederlandse literatuur 1560-1700*, Amsterdam: Bert Bakker.
Posthumus Meyjes, G.H.M. (1984), 'Grotius as an Irenicist', in *The World of Hugo Grotius (1583-1645)*, 43–63, Amsterdam: APA-Holland University Press.
Prandoni, M. (2013), 'Staging the History of Amsterdam in Vondel's *Gysbreght van Aemstel*: A Non-Confessional Dramatic Contribution to the Narrative of the Dutch Revolt', in J. Bloemendal, P.G.F. Eversmann and E. Strietman (eds), *Drama, Performance and Debate. Theatre and Public Opinion in the Early Modern Period*, 297–310, Leiden: Brill.
Prandoni, M. (2016), 'Vive la France, A bas la France! Contradictory Attitude Toward the Appropriation of French Cultural Elements in the Second Half of the Sixteenth Century: The Forewords of 'Modern' Poetry Collections', in B. Noak (ed.), *Wissenstransfer und Auctoritas in der frühneuzeitlichen niederländischsprachigen Literatur*, 179–194, Göttingen: Vandenhoeck & Ruprecht.

Reinders, S. and F.R.E. Blom (2011), 'Men zou Virgilius zien opgaen in zijn' tolck': de functie van Vergilius in het artistiek ondernemerschap van Joost van den Vondel', *Zeventiende Eeuw* 27 (2): 194–213.

Sierhuis, F. (2016) 'Performing the Medieval Past: Vondel's *Gysbreght van Aemstel*', in J. Bloemendal and N. Smith (eds), *Politics and Aesthetics in European Baroque and Classicist Tragedy*, 102–131, Leiden: Brill.

Smit, W.A.P. (1956–1962), *Van Pascha tot Noah. Een verkenning van Vondels drama's naar continuïteit en ontwikkeling in hun grondmotief en structuur*, 3 vols, Zwolle: Tjeenk Willink.

Smits-Veldt, M.B. and M. Spies (2012), 'Vondel's Life', in J. Bloemendal and F.-W. Korsten (eds), *Joost van den Vondel (1587–1679). Dutch Playwright in the Golden Age*, 51–83, Leiden: Brill.

Thys, W. (1987), *Vondel et la France*, Lille: Presses Universitaires de Lille.

Venuti, L. (2004), 'How to Read a Translation', *Words Without Borders*, July. Available online: https://www.wordswithoutborders.org/article/how-to-read-a-translation (accessed 25 February 2019).

Verwey, A. (1927), *Vondels vers*, Santpoort: C.A. Mees.

Vondel, Joost van den (1927), *Het Pascha*, ed. H.W.E. Moller, in J. van den Vondel, *De werken. Volledige en geïllustreerde tekstuitgave*, eds J.F.M. Sterck, H.W.E. Moller, C.G.N. de Vooys and C.R. de Klerk, 10 vols, vol. 1, 159–264, Amsterdam: De Wereldbibliotheek.

Vondel, Joost van den (1929), *Hierusalem verwoest*, ed. H.W.E. Moller, in J. van den Vondel, *De werken. Volledige en geïllustreerde tekstuitgave*, eds J.F.M. Sterck, H.W.E. Moller, C.G.N. de Vooys and C.R. de Klerk, 10 vols, vol. 2, 74–215, Amsterdam: De Wereldbibliotheek.

Vondel, Joost van den (1937), *Zungchin*, ed. H.W.E. Moller, in J. van den Vondel, *De werken. Volledige en geïllustreerde tekstuitgave*, eds J.F.M. Sterck, H.W.E. Moller, C.G.N. de Vooys and C.R. de Klerk, 10 vols, vol. 10, 323–390, Amsterdam: De Wereldbibliotheek.

Vondel, Joost van den (1927–1940), *De werken. Volledige en geïllustreerde tekstuitgave*, eds J.F.M. Sterck, H.W.E. Moller, C.G.N. de Vooys and C.R. de Klerk, 10 vols, Amsterdam: De Wereldbibliotheek.

Vondel, Joost van den (1990), *Lucifer*, ed. N. Clark, Bath: Absolute Classics.

Vondel, Joost van den (2013), *Tassoos Godefroy of Hierusalem verlost*, ed. D. van der Mark, DBNL.

Vondel, Joost van den (2018), Gysbreght van Aemstel. Il criollo di Amsterdam in una tragedia del Secolo d'Oro olandese, eds S. Brunetti and M. Prandoni, Bari: Edizioni di Pagina.

Westerbaen, J. (2001), *Gedichten. Bloemlezing uit het werk van een levensgenieter*, ed. J. Koppenol, Amsterdam: Griffioen.

7

Multatuli – His Work Through the World

Jaap Grave

In the relatively brief period between 1860 and 1877, Eduard Douwes Dekker (Amsterdam 1820 – Nieder-Ingelheim 1887), using the pseudonym 'Multatuli' (Latin for 'I have suffered a lot', probably inspired by Horace), published a number of works that were influential not only in Dutch literature – and on then prevailing views on colonialism – but also abroad, especially after Multatuli's death. These works were influential because of the issues they dealt with and due to their innovative and refreshingly straightforward language. The best-known and most frequently translated of his works is the 1860 novel *Max Havelaar, of de koffiveilingen der Nederlandsche Handelmaatschappy* (*Max Havelaar Or the Coffee Auctions of the Dutch Trading Company*). In 2002 the members of the Maatschappij van Nederlandse Letterkunde (Society for Dutch Literature – a more than 250-year-old literary society that is very highly reputed in the Dutch-language area) hailed this novel the most important work in Dutch literary history. The book has been adapted for film and theatre, as a musical, as a cartoon and as a linguistic update. Between 1950 and 1995 Multatuli's *Volledig Werk* (Complete Works) appeared in twenty-five volumes, eighteen of which were volumes of letters and documents. Following upon the publication of the *Max Havelaar* there further appeared during Multatuli's lifetime; *Minnebrieven* (*Love Letters*: 1861), *Ideën I–VII* (*Ideas I–VII*, including *The History of Woutertje Pieterse*, 1880 in book form: 1862–1877) and *Millioenen-studiën* (*Millions Studies*: 1870–1873). Multatuli himself called his 1,282 *Ideën*, which were often reactions to contemporary events, 'de *Times* van myn ziel' (The *Times* of my soul). After 1877 he did not publish any new works but kept on working on emendations, additions and reprints of his earlier work. His birthplace in Amsterdam is now a museum dedicated to his memory, and as of 1978 a journal devoted to his life and work has been going strong.

Life and work

Eduard Douwes Dekker was the fifth of six children in a Mennonite family. His father was a ship's captain, his mother a housewife. He attended Latin School (the highest form of secondary schooling) until the age of 15, then worked for a while in an office, and in 1838 he sailed with his father to Batavia, present-day Djakarta in the then Dutch Indies, present-day Indonesia. From 1839 to 1856 he served the colonial administration in various functions. In 1846 he married, in Indonesia, baroness Everdine (Tine) van Wijnbergen. They had a son and a daughter. After Tine's death in 1874 he married Mimi Hamminck Schepel, with whom he had already been living for quite some time. They adopted a son.

Dekker's civil service career started off auspiciously, but in 1842 to 1843, when he was stationed in Natal (Sumatra), he was found short in his financial bookkeeping, and he was discontinued. In his next station, Lebak, in 1856, he had served only three months when he became convinced, after having conducted an investigation into the matter, that his predecessor had been murdered and that the local regent was mistreating the population. Accordingly, he brought a complaint against the ruler. The Dutch governor of the region tried to make Dekker change his mind. The Governor-General finally judged that Dekker had acted rashly and unjustly and decided to transfer him again. Instead of accepting, Douwes Dekker resigned. This event plays a major role in the novel *Max Havelaar* and continues the subject of polemics. Some are of the opinion that Douwes Dekker acted rashly because he was unfamiliar with the *adat*, the common (unwritten) norms and laws of the Javanese, and moreover because he had brought a complaint against the local ruler bypassing the regional Dutch governor. In 1857 he returned to Europe, and in 1860 he published *Max Havelaar*. One of the most common misunderstandings about *Max Havelaar* concerns the mission of the novel: Multatuli was not against colonialism itself, but he was of the opinion that the local population should not be exploited.

Max Havelaar is best seen as a plea for rehabilitation on the part of Douwes Dekker. The character Max Havelaar is an idealized personification of Douwes Dekker himself. The novel's publication history is checkered: as Douwes Dekker had no contacts in the world of publishing, he contacted Van Hasselt, one of his freemason acquaintances, who informed the Minister of Colonies. Van Hasselt was then given the manuscript, which he passed on to the well-known author and lawyer Jacob van Lennep. Van Lennep bought the rights from Douwes Dekker and made a significant number of changes to the text: indications of specific years were blurred, the book was divided into chapters, and place and proper names were partially replaced with dots. The end, though, with its indictment of the Dutch king, was kept. Douwes Dekker had offered to forego publication if he was rehabilitated and decorated, an end would be put to the oppression of the Javanese, and he himself would be reinstated. The Minister of Colonies offered him a position in the West Indies, but Douwes Dekker wanted to be nominated to the Council of the East Indies.

After the publication of *Max Havelaar* Multatuli claimed that reviewers appreciated the book but that the demands he voiced in the text were not met. Research by Nop Maas proves this not to have been the case, though: reviewers thought *Max Havelaar* a masterpiece, praised its style, but some of them also regretted the novel's many digressions. Still, the bulk of the attention went to what Multatuli himself found most important: the mistreatment of the Javanese population. Some reviewers doubted whether Multatuli had told the truth, but that he disapproved of any mistreatment and thought that if it occurred it had to be brought to an end. They also thought it was a good thing that Multatuli had made it clear that there was a big difference between the official reports disseminated in the Netherlands and colonial reality (Maas 2000: 7-49).

Multatuli's work has always had prominent admirers and readers: Alfred Russel Wallace in his 1869 *The Malay Archipelago* referred to *Max Havelaar*. Wallace's book was a favourite of Joseph Conrad. Conrad therefore is thought to have read *Max Havelaar* and the protagonists of *Almayer's Folly* (1895) and *Lord Jim* (1900) are supposed to resemble Havelaar. Sigmund Freud in 1907 listed Multatuli as one of the ten most important writers, Lenin read parts of *Max Havelaar* and D.H. Lawrence wrote a postscript to the English translation in 1927 (Multatuli 1927). He compared *Max Havelaar* to Harriet Beecher Stowe's *Uncle Tom's Cabin*, to which Multatuli himself referred in his novel. Lawrence labelled the novel a 'satire' and Multatuli a 'satirical humourist'. However, he thought that 'As far as composition goes, it is the greatest mess possible.' It is other things that for Lawrence make this book the only true masterpiece of Dutch literature: 'The great dynamic force in Multatuli is as it was, really, in Jean Paul and in Jonathan Swift and Nicolai Gogol and in Mark Twain, hate, a passionate, honourable hate.' *Max Havelaar* also made a great impression on the American author James Albert Michener (1907-1997). Moses Nxumalo, in *The Covenant* (1980), reads Multatuli's novel and identifies with Saïdjah, the protagonist of one of its most famous passages. Konstantin Paustovsky (1892-1968) in 1925 in 'Gollandskaja koroleva' (The Queen of Holland, 1972) did not hide his enthusiasm for Multatuli. Paustovsky's story is 'about a sailor who, irate over Multatuli's fate, hurls a stone at the carriage of Queen Wilhelmina. The story is deeply marked by an anti-colonialist, anti-monarchist and anti-capitalist mood'. From Paustovsky's decription of Douwes Dekker's life in his 1956 novella *Zolotaja roza* (The Golden Rose) it is clear that he knew *Max Havelaar* and *Minnebrieven* (Hinrichs 1995: 3-5). Pramoedya Ananta Toer (1925-2006), the most important prose writer of the Indonesian 'Generation of '45', as well as in other places in his work, mentions Multatuli in his *Buru Quartet* (1980-1988). After Multatuli's death there were always writers who were at the centre of the Dutch literary system that stood up for him: E. du Perron (*De man van Lebak*, 1937) and W.F. Hermans (*De raadselachtige Multatuli* 1976) are only two of the more telling examples. However, Rob Nieuwenhuys argues that in *De mythe van Lebak*, Douwes Dekker did not take into account the social structure of Lebak, and that he was not the only colonial administrator to complain about the mistreatment and oppression of the native population (Nieuwenhuys 1987).

During Multatuli's own lifetime *Max Havelaar* was translated into German, French and English, three languages central to the wider European and therefore also the 'world' literary system. We can divide the translation activity into three periods: during his lifetime, around 1900, and after 1945. Translation into German and French was essential to the dissemination of Multatuli's work. In what follows I explore some avenues that were of importance for the dissemination of his work in the world. By looking at translations within language groups certain patterns in the sequence of translations and stopovers emerge. With language groups I simply and pragmatically refer to sets of related languages that are grouped under common umbrellas such as Germanic, Scandinavian, Romance and Slavic languages (Grave 2013: 163–178). It will immediately become clear that at least for Dutch-language literature Paris, at variance with what Pascale Casanova (2007) claims, was not a major centre. It is undeniable though that central languages such as German and French played, and play, an essential role in the dissemination also of Dutch literature. These central languages often serve not only as mediating languages for translations into other languages, the reception in these language areas is frequently also crucial for the reception in further language areas. On the contrary, the reception in the Dutch-language area itself played only a minor role in the dissemination of Multatuli's work. An important role in the dissemination of Dutch-language literature is played, though, by bi- or multilingual countries: in the first instance Belgium, which has always played a central role in transfers to the French language area. But parts of the population of countries with frequently changing borders, or who have been occupied by foreign powers, such as Poland, or that have been part of a larger unit with a different administrative language, such as the Austro-Hungarian Empire, often are bilingual. Indonesia, a former Dutch colony and the setting of *Max Havelaar*, occupies a special position: the more highly educated elite spoke and read Dutch. In part this also applies to South Africa. We should also mention Yiddish here, a language that is not tied to any specific national borders. Translations into English follow a trajectory of their own and play only a minor role in the translation history of Multatuli's work.

During Multatuli's lifetime

During Multatuli's lifetime *Max Havelaar* was translated directly from the Dutch into three major languages: English (1868), German (1875) and French (1876). Under the title 'A Dutch Political Novel' *The North British Review* in 1867 published a review that also included a few passages of *Max Havelaar* in translation (anonymous 1867). The reviewer to a certain extent agreed with Multatuli's critique of Dutch colonialism but criticized the end of the novel and the style of the Saïdjah-story. A first complete translation of the novel followed in 1868, the work of Alphonse Nahuys (1840–1890), a Dutchman himself (Multatuli 1868). He abridged certain passages but also collaborated with Multatuli. For this reason, his translation was the first edition in which Van Lennep's changes were overturned. In his preface he referred, as did

Multatuli in his novel, to Harriet Beecher Stowe's *Uncle Tom's Cabin* (1852). The English version was well received (Salverda 2010: 4-16). In Germany, the first article on Multatuli, along with some translations, among which a chapter from *Max Havelaar* and 'Saïdjah and Adinda', appeared in 1862. In 1875 there appeared *Max Havelaar oder die Holländer auf Java* in a translation by Theodor Stromer (Multatuli 1875). Multatuli was not involved in this endeavour, and he pointed out a significant number of errors in the translation. One year later *Max Havelaar* made it into French, translated by Henri Crisafulli and the Dutchman A.J. Nieuwenhuis, 'saint-simonist, free thinker and freemason', and uncle to the socialist Ferdinand Domela Nieuwenhuis. For A.J. Nieuwenhuis *Max Havelaar* was 'a weapon in the struggle against colonial abuses' (Andringa 2007: 39-50).

1890-1914

The cultural and social climate underwent a change in Europe at the turn of the twentieth century. In many European countries there arose movements that urged (cultural) renewal, and that were characterized by an anti-bourgeois attitude, a critical, anarchist or revolutionary spirit emphasizing anti-clericalism, the importance of better education for children, the labouring classes and women, anti-colonialism and interest in the exotic. The market for newspapers, periodicals and books grew expansively, which also created a demand for literature translated from minor languages. The mediators and translators of Multatuli's work largely originated from left-leaning circles. Around 1910, though, cosmopolitanism and the leftist, anarchist movements saw their position in the literary field weakening, with nationalist tendencies gaining on them.

In Germany many translations of work by Multatuli found their way into newspapers and periodicals or found favour with publishers: in 1888 to 1889 *Max Havelaar* appeared in peridocials in a translation by the anarchist Carl Derossi, and between 1899 and 1906 Wilhelm Spohr (1868-1959) published eleven volumes of Multatuli. For the first volume, the anthology *Multatuli. Auswahl aus seinen Werken, eingeleitet durch eine Charakteristik seines Lebens, seiner Persönlichkeit und seines Schaffens* (1899), Spohr provided an extensive and very positive 133-page introduction. Spohr, an anarchist from the 'Friedrichshagener Dichterkreis', a group of left-leaning publicists comprising amongst others Wilhelm Bölsche, Bruno Wille, Gustav Landauer and Erich Mühsam, got to know Multatuli's work through a French translation by Alexander Cohen (Beekman 1996; Cohen 1997; Grave 2001). Spohr tightly collaborated with Multatuli's widow. Through his extensive network and his many activities (he toured Germany and abroad) his translations were much commented on and the picture of Multatuli he had painted in his introduction to *Multatuli. Auswahl* became the dominant one. The eight volumes Karl Mischke translated between 1900 and 1904 were cheaper than Spohr's but received less attention. Various works also appeared in translations by other translators (amongst others Paul Seliger, Paul Raché, Regina Ruben and the race theoretician Otto Hauser). This was possible because the Netherlands did not sign the Berne Convention until 1912 (Vanrusselt 1982; Van Uffelen 1993a, 1993b; Grave 2001, 2003).

Multatuli's Danish translators were close to the literary renewal movement in Denmark. Most famous in this regard is Georg Brandes, who in 1871 with his lectures on cultural renewal prepared the ground for the *moderne gennembrud* (modern breakthrough). Alfred Ipsen and Mads Jepsen, prominent reviewers of Multatuli's work, were early supporters of Brandes. *Saïdjah. En Kjærlighedshistorie fra Java* appeared in 1880 in a translation by Gustav (Henrik Andreas) Budde-Lund (1846–1911), probably via the French (Multatuli 1880). The leftist liberal Carl Michelsen (1842–1911), who mostly translated from French, published *Max Havelaar eller Det hollandske Handelsselskabs Kaffeauktioner* (Multatuli 1901a). The Danish reception primarily was filtered through German sources, though: we know that Jepsen mostly relied on German publications (Larsen 2007: 24–38).

The issues Multatuli addressed found a ready response in the Swedish cultural climate at the turn of the century. They fitted the tenets of the Swedish Eighties' authors with their interest in socialism and the exotic. With Swedish intellectuals almost without exception being fluent in German at the time, here again the reception was mostly based on German sources. Multatuli was compared to Swedish authors such as August Strindberg and C.J.L. Almqvist, and to foreign writers like Charles Dickens, Mark Twain, Friedrich Nietzsche, Heinrich Heine and Gustave Flaubert. 'Auktoritet', from *Minnebrieven*, and the very first translation of work by Multatuli into Swedish, appeared in 1899 in *Svenska Dagbladet*. It was probably based on Spohr's anthology (1899). Petrus Hedberg (1849–1926), who also translated work by Walter Scott, Mark Twain and Leo Tolstoy, translated *Max Havelaar* from a Danish translation by Michelsen (Wikén Bonde 2007: 8–23).

In 1904, *Walter Pieterse: A story of Holland* appeared in English translated by the Canadian writer and journalist Hubert Evans (1892–1986) (Multatuli 1904). It was reprinted in the USA in 2008. In the anthology *The Humour of Holland* (1893, reprinted in 1908 and 1923), a volume translated and introduced by the German Africanist Alice Werner (1859–1935), Multatuli features with twelve contributions. Werner thought *Max Havelaar* 'one of the most exasperatingly inartistic books ever written' (Salverda 2010: 4–16).

In the Slavic language area Polish, Czech and Russian are most important for translations of Multatuli, with Spohr's translations, and his anthology, often serving as sources. The two periods in which Multatuli was most frequently translated into Polish were the turn of the twentieth century and after 1945. Influential in both eras was Julius Baltazar Marchlewski (1866–1925), the founder of the Social-Democrat Party of the Kingdom of Poland and Lithuania, co-founder of the Spartakusbund (1916, Spartacus League) in Germany, diplomat in the service of the Soviet-Union, economist and publicist. During a stay in Munich he became acquainted with Multatuli's work, wrote about it and translated 'Geschiedenissen van Gezag' (Histories of Authority) from *Minnebrieven* on the basis of Spohr's translation (Marchlewski 1901a, 1901b, 1901c). Between 1901 and 1907 four book-length translations of Multatuli saw the light. For her 1901 selection and introduction Maria Feldman (Multatuli 1901b) drew on the Spohr edition (1899). In 1903 there appeared another anthology, in a translation by Malwina Posner-Garfeinowa (Multatuli 1903b, repr. 1906), with an introduction again based on Spohr (1899). In the same year *Max Havelaar* was published in a translation by Bronisława Neufeldówna (Multatuli 1903a), and in 1907 an edition of 'Idee 448' in a translation by Izabela Zielińska (Multatuli 1907). Characteristic for the Polish translators, critics and mediators of Multatuli is their leftist commitment, the use of German as an intermediary language, and that for the book-length editions of 1901 to 1907 they were all women (Koch 2008: 20–47).

Versions in Czech started in 1899 with translations in a periodical, probably based on Spohr (1899), and a review in 1903 of the latter's translation of *Max Havelaar*. The image of Multatuli presented to the Czech readership corresponded with Spohr's (1899) and with the translation in Poland around 1900: he was compared to Ibsen and Nietzsche, and pictured as a saint. The 1899 review was by František V. Krejčí (1867–1941), a social-democrat and a 'protagonist of the literary wing of the so-called *Česká moderna*, a current that stressed individualism and non-conformism' (Krejčí 1899). For her anthology *Výbor ze spisův, jež napsal Multatuli* (Multatuli 1903a), Krista Nevšimalová (1854–1935), translator, publicist and feminist, again used Spohr (1899). In 1911 another anthology appeared, probably by the same translator (Engelbrecht 2011: 2–41). 'Saïdjah and Adinda', along with 'Idee 229' and '518' appeared in Hungarian in 1899, in the periodical *Budapesti Szemle*, translated by the assimilated Jewish literary scholar, translator and docent Ignác Gábor (1868–1945) (Multatuli 1899). Again, probably Spohr (1899) served as an intermediary. In 1901 these same pieces appeared in book form as *Szaidzsa és egyéb elbeszélések* with Lampel Róbert, who carried a list of Hungarian and world literature (Gera 2013: 97–112).

In Russia too, translations started to appear in this period. In 1903, W.W. Bittner published an article and a biographical sketch as 'Multatuli and his oeuvre', in which he claimed that Multatuli fought 'all forms of restriction of personal freedom, freedom of thought and of speech, because he ridiculed narrow prejudices and launched a call for support of the downtrodden' (Couvée 2006: 29). In his bibliography of Russian translations of Multatuli, Scheltjens lists forty editions up to 2003 (Scheltjens 2003: 214–222).

Bilingual Belgium plays a central role in the transfer of Dutch-language literature to the French language area and – indirectly – to other Romance languages. Kolenberg lists some sixty translations already in the nineteenth century; in newspapers, periodicals and in book form. In the nineteenth century Multatuli for 'young French intellectuals [served] as the great revolutionary, the prophet of times to come. Anti-clericals, opponents to colonialism, socialists and anarchists used … and abused his work in their struggle with the powers that were' (Kolenberg 1971a: 85; Kolenberg 1971b: 16–49, 153–177, 270–309). Also important in the final two decades of the nineteenth century were Belgian periodicals such as *La Société Nouvelle*, the *Revue des deux Mondes* and the *Mercure de France*, in which Cesar de Paepe, Louis van Keymeulen and Theodor de Wyzewa published their work. They thought Multatuli's work of minor interest from a literary point of view: Van Keymeulen (1892) regarded Multatuli as an anarchist, whose ideas were rooted in the eighteenth-century philosophes, while De Wyzewa thought only 'Saïdjah and Adinda' as of literary value. The Dutch anarchist Alexander Cohen, who translated Zola and Gerhart Hauptmann, succeeded in placing a lot of work by Multatuli in periodicals such as the *Revue Blanche* and the *Mercure de France*. He also published an anthology, *Pages Choisies* (1901c), with a preface in which Anatole France called Multatuli the Dutch Voltaire. Other important mediators were Julian Pée, Henry Meyners d'Estrey, Roland de Marès and Emile van Heurck. Pée was a socialist who wrote a PhD dissertation about Multatuli, Meyners d'Estrey and De Marès were journalists; the former a Frenchman, the latter a Belgian (and the director of *L'Indépendance belge*) (Andringa 2007: 39–50). Multatuli's popularity reached its zenith in the period 1890–1914, particularly 'in free thinking, that is to say liberal or socialist circles' and here too he was compared to Ibsen and Nietzsche. Here, as in other countries, it was mostly utopians, reformists and anarchists that read him, translated him, and wrote about him and his works in anarchist periodicals such as the *Revue des deux mondes* and the *Mercure de France*. This leftist reception of his work mostly resonated with French-language intellectuals at the Université Libre de Bruxelles. But the Flemish-minded young August Vermeylen (who in any case moved easily in both French- and Dutch-language circles in Belgium) and Emmanuel de Bom also knew and admired Multatuli, who in Belgium, as in the Netherlands, was very popular in working-class milieus and with primary school teachers. In the 1920s and 30s prominent Flemish authors such as Willem Elsschot, Paul van Ostaijen, Gerard Walschap and Louis-Paul Boon read Multatuli (Vandevoorde 2008: 4–19).

In 1907 there appeared *Die minhogiem* (De Zeden) in Yiddish. It contains translations of a number of 'Ideën' and the second, third and fourth 'Geschiedenis van Gezag' from *Minnebrieven*. This edition appeared in New York with Vek-Ruf, and the back cover refers to publications in an English and two anarchist Yiddish periodicals. In 1908 this is followed by *Gekliebene meysch'lich* (an anthology primarily of pieces from *Ideën* and *Minnebrieven*), put together by the translator, critic and essayist Baruch Rivkin (1883–1945), who also frequently contributed to the anarchist *Fraye Arbayter Shtime*, a publication of A. Golub in London. These were probably all translated from Spohr (1899). In 1911 the prominent anarchist Abraham Frumkin (1872–1946) translated *Liebes-brief* (*Minnebrieven*), with a foreword by Rudolf Rocker, and published it in London with Arbayter Fraynd (Multatuli 1911). Rocker calls the novel 'one of the most original works of world literature'. He probably knew the work of Multatuli via Spohr. In Kiev there appeared *Saaid oen Adinde* (Multatuli 1925), a children's edition by Lipe Reznik (1890–1944), author, translator and teacher of Yiddish. Finally, in 1937 *Sajid oen Adinda oen a Peroe'aner maisse'le*, appeared in Warsaw in the periodical *Kinder-Frajnd*, with a preface by the translator-editor Moyshe Taichman (Multatuli 1937), who probably used a German or English source. There is no translation of *Max Havelaar* in Yiddish (Daniëls-Waterman 2011: 4–18).

1914–1945

In Germany there are some new translations and reprints of *Max Havelaar*: in 1920 Spohr and Mischke were reprinted, and in 1927 the publication of a new translation by Erich M. Lorebach.

The second English-language *Max Havelaar* came out with Knopf in New York in 1927, in a translation by the Dutchman Willem Siebenhaar (1863–1936) (Multatuli 1927). Like many of his German and French companion translators at the end of the nineteenth century, he was an anarchist who in 1891 had emigrated to Australia. In 1922 he met D.H. Lawrence there, 'whom he gave the inspiration for the character of the labour union activist Willie Struther in the novel *Kangaroo*' (1923). A third English-language *Max Havelaar* appeared in 1967, this time in a translation by Roy Edwards (1931–) (Multatuli 1967b). This latter translation first appeared in the *Bibliotheca Neerlandica* of Sijthoff and Heinemann, but in 1982 it was republished in the *Library of the Indies* of the American scholar E.M. Beekman and in 1987, with an introduction by Reinder P. Meijer, in the *Penguin Classics*. The Beekman edition has been reprinted as of 1993 by Periplus in Singapore. In 1926 'The Story of Saïdjah' featured in *Great Short Stories of the World* (Multatuli 1926b) (Salverda 2010: 4–16).

Remarkable, but also typical for the dissemination and ideological reception of Multatuli in former Czechoslovakia, is that two social-democrat politicians in 1919 in parliament referred to him, with one of them even doing so with respect to *Max Havelaar* of which no Czech translation was yet available. This is convincing proof that Czech intellectuals mastered German, a minority language in post-1918 Czechoslovakia. As the Czech social-democrats during the First World War had entertained good relations with the Netherlands it is even possible that they knew the novel in Dutch. Between the two world wars the *Geschiedenis van Saïdjah en Adinda* (*O věrné lásce Saidjaha a Adindy* 1926a, reprinted in 1927 and 1931) appeared in a translation by Josef Veselý. Interest in Indonesia increased in Czechoslovakia in the interbellum, as the Netherlands recruited Czech engineers for the Dutch colony. This might be an explanation for why *Woutertje Pieterse* was translated in 1932 (Multatuli 1932; repr. 1953 and 1963), by the Romance and Germanic scholar Lida Faltová (1890–1944), who also published in liberal and social-democrat periodicals. The mystic Emanuel Lešetický z Lešehradu (1877–1955), an important translator during the interbellum, made a selection from the *Ideën*, published in 1933 in a collection that was mainly devoted to French authors such as Verlaine and Mallarmé (Engelbrecht 2011: 2–41). In 1924 *Max Havelaar* appeared in Hungarian, translated, most probably not directly from the Dutch, by Zoltán Bartos (1890–1982), who translated mainly from English, and with an introduction by József Migray (Gera 2007: 51–67).

In the beginning of the twentieth century Multatuli pretty much disappears below the French literary horizon. In 1937, commemorative of Multatuli's death fifty years earlier, he again receives some attention, but the ideological approach to his work remains dominant. In the foreword to an anthology put together by the Belgian Lode Roelandt, Henry Poulaille compares Multatuli to Proudhon, Max Stirner and Bakunin. There also appears an introduction to Multatuli by Julian Pée (Andringa 2007: 39–50). In Spain there appears, in 1927, *Páginas Selectas de Multatuli*, put together, while in prison, by the journalist, writer and anarchist Felipe Alaiz de Pablo (1887–1959) (Multatuli 1947b), who also translated Max Nettlau and Dos Passos. According to Van Raemdonck Alaíz de Pablo's novel *Quinet* is based on Multatuli's work. In the first chapter of his Multatuli anthology he draws a picture of the Dutch writer, focusing on the latter's humour. Van Raemdonck suspects that the translator worked from a French version. The final chapter of the anthology is by Rudolf Rocker, who compares Multatuli to Doctor Stockman in Ibsen's drama *An Enemy of the People* (1882) and with the devil in *Le diable boiteux* of Alain-René Lesage (1707) (Van Raemdonck 2007: 68-82).

After 1945

In Communist countries translations of Multatuli's works routinely featured pre- or postscripts that looked at the man and his work from a communist ideological perspective. The general tenor is as follows: Multatuli opposed the capitalist system but did not have an eye for the working classes and the class struggle. Print runs are strikingly large. In the GDR *Max Havelaar* was published in translations by Erich Stück (1948b, reprinted in a version adapted and emended by the German scholar of Dutch literature Gerhart Worgt in 1972) and Spohr (Multatuli 1952). *Woutertje Pieterse* (1955) was translated by Hans Bruck, who in an extensive foreword called the novel a 'satire critical of society' (Multatuli 1955). There were also several translations of 'Saïdjah and Adinda' (the first print run of 1951 counted 40,000 copies; reprinted in 1988). In the German Federal Republic Spohr's *Max Havelaar* translation was republished in 1965. In 1988 there appeared *Erzählungen, Parabeln und Ideen des niederländischen Autors*, with a postscript by the translator Manfred S. Fischer (Multatuli 1988).

In Denmark *Max Havelaar eller Det hollandske Handelskompagnis kaffeauktioner* was published in 1981. The translation was the work of Grete Bentsen and Gerard Cruys, based on the most unadulterated Dutch original extant (Multatuli 1949), that is to say without the changes wrought by Van Lennep and also without the footnotes later added by Multatuli himself. *Drømmen om Insulinde* (1969) contains a selection from Multatuli's letters, selected and translated by Ingeborg Buhl (1890-1982), a well-known Danish author and translator (Larsen 2007: 24-38). For Wikén Bonde the renewed interest in Multatuli in Sweden in the 1940s is the work of the Dutch literaterary scholar Martha A. Muusses (1894-1981). In 1945 *Max Havelaar* was published in one volume together with Joseph Conrad's *Lord Jim* in a prestigious series, in a translation by Hedberg and with a postscript by the author Artur Lundkvist (Multatuli 1945). Finally, *Max Havelaar* in 1979 was re-issued in a translation by Wikén Bonde. The latter, a scholar of Dutch literature, also provides an introduction, while the postscript is a translation of the text D.H. Lawrence wrote to accompany the 1927 English translation. Wikén Bonde sees the novel as perfectly fitting a time in which interest in politically committed literature was at a high point (Wikén Bonde 2007: 8-23).

In post-1945 Poland Marchlewski was held in high regard, and his pre-1914 Multatuli translation was reprinted in 1953. In 1949 two editions of *Max Havelaar* appeared, based on the Neufeldówna translation (Multatuli [1860] 1903), and in 1950 the novel was adapted for the stage. Jerzy Koch, one of the most noted contemporary Polish scholars of Dutch (and Afrikaans) literature, argues that there is no real difference between the first and second periods of Multatuli-reception in Poland: 'translators, mediators and critics [...] all infused multatulian ideas into their own projects, be they artistic, cultural or public' (Koch 2008: 39). In 1994 Koch himself gave a new translation of *Max Havelaar*, with an extensive introduction.

The diplomat and freemason Rudolf Jordan Vonka (1877–1964) translated *Max Havelaar* (Multatuli 1947a) into Czech, directly from the Dutch, with an initial print run of 10,000. The Czech *Woutertje Pieterse* was reprinted with a new postscript in which Multatuli and his work were measured with a communist ideological ruler: in *Max Havelaar* Multatuli is said to have outlined the 'barbaric foundations of Dutch prosperity', but he remained 'a prisoner [...] of the idealist errors of his class and time'. Júlia Májeková (1919–1991), who had studied German and Dutch in Bratislava, Leipzig and Leiden, and who translated directly from Dutch, produced the first Slovak translation of *Woutertje Pieterse*. In 1960 she also translated *Max Havelaar*. Olga Krijtová (1931–2013), Professor of Dutch in Prague, in 1987 translated a number of aphorisms of Multatuli for the periodical *Světová literatura* (World Literature). In 1963 she also curated a new edition of Faltová's translation of *Woutertje Pieterse*. In 1974 *Max Havelaar* also appeared in a translation by Miroslav Drápal (1916–1991), with a postscript by the Romance scholar Vladimír Brett, an 'ideologue who had to lend political support for the work', according to Krijtová (Engelbrecht 2011: 2–41).

The second translation of *Max Havelaar* into Hungarian appeared in 1950 with a print run of 12,000 (Multatuli 1950). There is no mention of the name of the translator and Gera suspects that they had either become the victim of political disfavour or that it was a re-run of the first translation, as the same mistakes are repeated (Gera 2007: 53). Five years later, in 1955, the novel was re-issued again, this time translated by the poet György Faludy (1910–2006), using the 1949 Dutch edition as the source text, with a foreword by the literary scholar and cultural historian Géza Hegedűs (1912–1999). Finally, *Max Havelaar* also appeared in the series Highlights of World Literature, with the 1949 Stuiveling Dutch edition once again as the source text and Péter Balabán translating from English not from Dutch. The philologist Béla Szondi, who amongst other works also translated *De Kapellekensbaan* (Chapel Road) of the Flemish novelist L.P. Boon, edited the text, while Ilona Róna provided a postscript (Gera 2007: 51–67).

In 1936 there appeared in Russia *Istorija Edvarda Dekkera* (*De Geschiedenis van Eduard Dekker*; The History of Eduard Dekker, 1936) by Emma Iosifovna Vygodskaya (1899–1949), children's author and translator from German, English and French. The book covers Multatuli's life up to and including the publication of *Max Havelaar*. The work was meant for secondary school pupils and had a print run of 25,000 copies. An abridged version with the title *Plamja gneva* (Flame of Ire, 1949) was published in 1949. Between 1952 and 1955 this was translated into German in the GDR – once for a publisher in Moscow and another time for a GDR publisher – as *Flamme des Zorns. Die Geschichte des Eduard Dekker* (Flame of Ire. The History of Eduard Dekker, Wygosskaja 1953). What stands out in the texts of Vygodskaya, Paustovsky and much later also Viktor Astafjev (1924–2001) is that they think that Multatuli was not appreciated in his own country, but this is probably based on the image of him sketched by Spohr in 1899 (Couvée 2006: 29–36).

Marija Grubešlieva (1900-1970), figure head of socialist poetry in Bulgaria, translated *Max Havelaar* (Multatuli 1953), not directly from Dutch. In 1984 the novel was translated anew by Stefan Načev, who did work directly from Dutch, and with a foreword by Nešo Davidov (Multatuli 1984). The latter in the 1930s had gotten to know some of Multatuli's parables in translations made by the poet Dimčo Debeljanov in 1910. Debeljanov had also translated *Minnebrieven* in 1918 (Multatuli 1918). Davidov compares Multatuli to authors such as Heine, Swift, Gogol and Twain, and he characterizes him as a combatant against the capitalist system of the Dutch bourgeoisie. He also claims that Multatuli did not pay attention to the 'importance of the working class', and that he is related to 'the great humanists and the people of the Enlightenment'. Furthermore, he calls him a 'living encyclopedia', something that will later again crop up with respect to his poetics (Smeets-Sirakova 1986: 27–31).

Already at the start of the twentieth century passages of Multatuli appeared in Romanian periodicals. During the interbellum, 'Saïdjah and Adinda' appeared in a translation by N.N. Botez, who primarily translated from German and in this case too probably relied on a German source (Multatuli n.d.). De Editura de Stat (State Publishing House) published *Max Havelaar* in 1948 in a translation by Silvia Mărgărit (Multatuli 1948a). As Spohr is mentioned as the author of the endnotes, her translation most probably used Spohr's German translation as its source. De Editura de Stat provided a postscript completely in line with leftist and communist ideology: 'He has been revenged by History which has lit the fires of liberation in the colonies and which has made the people of Indonesia rise up in a heroic war for independence. He has been revenged by the Indonesian republicans who, with each bullet, with each advancing step, remind the Dutch of some page or other of "Havelaar"'. In 1967 *Max Havelaar* was translated from the Dutch by H.R. Radian (1907–1992), who, although trained as an architect, made his living as a translator from Dutch, Spanish and Portuguese (Bos 2009: 55–59).

In 1973 *Max Havelaar* appeared in Estonia in a translation by Rein Sepp (1921–1995), a poet and translator of German epic literature. The translation had a print run of 18,000 copies and featured a postscript that focused on protesting against the colonial system and the policies of the Dutch bourgeoisie, meant to maximize profits (Multatuli 1973). The same year fifteen of Multatuli's aphorisms, translated from a non-Dutch source, appeared in the periodical *Kultuur ja Elu* (Prosa 1994: 58–61).

There are several translations of Multatuli into Serbo-Croat, Slovene, Macedonian and Serbian. *Parabolen* (1920) is a selection from Multatuli's *Ideën*. It is a translation of a German edition by the Austrian race theoretician, translator, author and publicist Otto Hauser (1876–1944), whose racist foreword is likewise included. Translations of 'Saïdjah and Adinda' appeared in Serbo-Croat (1924, 1939, 1945, 1955), Slovene (1947) and Macedonian, in book form or in newspapers and periodicals. A passage from *Max Havelaar* appeared in Serbo-Croat in a newspaper in 1946 and in Serbian in a periodical in 1993. Finally, the complete *Max Havelaar* appeared in 1939 (reprinted in 1946 and 1965) in Slovene, in 1946 in Serbo-Croat and in 1996 in Serbian. The Slovene translation was by Mirko Košir, using a German source. He criticized Dutch colonialism and considered Multatuli a 'hero of the communist working-class ideology. That is why the ideas of Multatuli constitute an important heritage in the world of internationalism and of the proletariat' (Nikolić 2008: 51). The 1946 Serbo-Croat translation was made by Ivo Hergešić, Professor of Comparative Literature in Zagreb, and was based on Spohr. Finally, in 1996 there appeared a translation into Serbian by Jelica Novaković-Lopušina, a scholar of Dutch literature (Nikolić 2008: 48–61).

In French, three more translations of *Max Havelaar* should be mentioned: in 1943, 1968 and 1991 (the latter with a foreword by the translator Philippe Noble, who sees Multatuli as a representative of Romanticism). The Spanish author, poet, essayist, translator and academic Francisco Carrasquer (1915–2012) translated *Max Havelaar, o las subastas de café de la compañía comercial Holandesa* (1975), with footnotes and an introduction (Multatuli 1975a). Carrasquer was an anarchist who suffered prison, fled to France, and studied and worked at Dutch universities. Carrasquer also dedicated a poem to Multatuli. He regarded Multatuli as equal to Cervantes and the Brazilian nineteenth-century novelist Machado de Assis, and also relates him to the Cuban writer José Martí (Van Raemdonck 2007: 68–82). In 2017 there appeared a new translation, *Max Havelaar* (*Max Havelaar, o las subastas de café de la Compañía Neerlandesa de Comercio*), by Malou Van Wijk Adan, with an introduction by the Belgian literary scholar Van Raemdonck (Multatuli 2017b). Italian translations of Multatuli were slow to appear. The literary scholar Bernardini Marzolla translated and introduced *Max Havelaar* for the series 'I grandi scrittori stranieri' (The Great Foreign Writers) (Multatuli 1965). In 2007 his translation was re-issued, now with a postscript by the academic and translator Fulvio Ferrari (Multatuli 2007). In 1997 Giorgio Faggin translated the *Ideën* (Multatuli 1997b). In the meantime, there had also appeared a Portuguese translation of *Max Havelaar: ou os leiloes de café da companhia holandesa de comércio*, the work of Daniel Augusto Gonçalves, in 1976 (Multatuli 1976). The pattern is clear: the Spanish, Italian and Portuguese translations followed the French ones.

After the fall of the Berlin Wall there appeared in Germany an anthology (*Auswahl aus seinen Schriften*, 1992), *Millioenenstudiën* (1992), *Minnebriefe* (1993b) and *Max Havelaar* (1993a, the latter two in a translation by Martina den Hertog-Vogt, 1997a), and *Die Abenteuer des kleinen Walther* (1999, an adaptation of the Spohr-translation). In 1995 *Briefe aus dem Rheingau* and *Ingelheimer Briefe, 1881–1887*, were published by the Internationale Multatuli-Gesellschaft (Multatuli 1995a, 1995b).

In English *Saïdyah and Adinda* appeared in a translation by Siebenhaar in the collection *Great Love Stories of All Nations* (Multatuli 1970), next to *The Oyster and the Eagle: Selected Aphorisms and Parables* in a translation by the Dutch-American literary scholar E.M. Beekman (Multatuli 1974) and *The Stone Cutter's Dream*, translated by Gustav Rueter.

Max Havelaar further also was published in Lithuanian (1982, translator Laima Breslavskien), Urdu (1983, translator Ghulam Ahmed Bashir, Lahore), Hebrew (1998, translator Ran HaCohen), Sardinian (2014, translator Giovanni Antioco Cappai), Turkish (2015, translator Erhan Gürer) and Arabic (from the English, by Musa al-Halool, 2017a).

Asia

In 1924 Zhou Shuren (1881-1936), the 'father of modern Chinese literature', using the penname Lu Xun, translated two parables from *Ideën* (Multatuli 1924),with as their source the second edition of Spohr's anthology (1902). He had learnt German in order to be able to go and study medicine in Japan, where this course of studies was inspired by the German system and used German manuals. Like all other mediators/ translators around the turn of the twentieth century, Lu Xun was an idealist, who wanted to serve the people by improving their living conditions as a physician and their spiritual condition via literature (Sun and Praamstra 2013: 11-24). *Max Havelaar* appeared in 1987 in Chinese as *Magesi Hafula'er de qiyu* (The Adventure of Max Havelaar, Multatuli 1987) in a translation by Shi Huiye (1941-), the son of Chinese Indonesians, whose name was Dutchified as Jaap Sie, and who had returned to China. He himself explains the translation of *Max Havelaar* – of which several pirate editions circulate – as follows: as far as the nineteenth century is concerned three texts circulated in China – *Das Kapital, Uncle Tom's Cabin* and *Max Havelaar* – that addressed the 'three greatest sins of mankind [...]: capitalism, slavery and colonialism' (Leerdam and Van Waterschoot 2009: 16-17). Japan has seen three translations of *Max Havelaar*. The first appeared in 1942, the year in which Japan occupied Indonesia, as *Ran in ni seigi o sakebu Makkusu Haferaru*. The two other translations appeared in 1989 and 2003 with the title *Makkusu Haferaru*. In 1994 the translator and literary scholar Myong-Suk Chi published a Korean translation with a Seoul publisher. She argued that the Korean literary system is almost inaccessible for works from minor or smaller literatures, but that Korean readers, because of their own occupation by Japan, are interested in a topic like colonialism. From the two reviews of the novel it is clear that 'Saïdjah and Adinda' is considered the highlight of the novel which is said to be 'highly appreciated by Europeans' for its literary style, and Multatuli is compared to Shakespeare and said to have influenced Conrad (Chi 1996: 68-74). *Max Havelaar* in 2004 also appeared in Vietnamese.

South Africa

In his survey of the reception of Multatuli in South Africa, Van Zyl starts out by posing the important question whether it is possible 'for a South African writer [...] to admire Multatuli without adopting his critique of a divisive colonial social system based on race'? When Multatuli's name was first mentioned in South Africa in 1872 it was in a negative evaluation of his critique of colonialism. C.J. Langenhoven (1873-1932), who shared Multatuli's struggle against a written language dictated by the authorities, in 1922 published an Afrikaans translation of 'Derde Sprookje' (Third Fairy Tale) from *Minnebrieven*. The influence of Multatuli can also be traced in the same author's novel *Herrie op die ou tremspoor* (*Trouble on the Old Tramway*, Langenhoven 1925). The poet, playwright and physician C. Louis Leipoldt (1880-1947) is the second important mediator of Multatuli's work in South Africa; he translated 'Saïdjah and Adinda', published several articles on the Dutch author, and in 1932 published *Uit my Oosterse dagboek* (*Pages from my Eastern Diary*, Leipoldt 1932), about a trip he made to Java in 1912. In 1942 there appeared *Bloemlesing uit die werke van E. Douwes-Dekker (Multatuli)* (*Anthology of Works by E. Douwes-Dekker [Multatuli]*, Buning 1942) with passages from *Max Havelaar, Vorstenschool* and *Ideën*. André P. Brink (1935–2015) – a professor at Cape Town University and a world-famous author, in Afrikaans and in English, and one of the central figures of the so-called *Die Sestigers* (*The Sixty-ers*), a generation of authors that brought about a complete renewal of Afrikaans literature – called *Max Havelaar* the fore-runner of the 'nieuwe roman' (the new novel, meaning here the new novel in Afrikaaans, not the French 'nouveau roman') (Brink 1967). In his own novel *n Droë wit seisoen* (*A Dry White Season*, 1979) there are traces of Multatuli. In her 1997 *Gordel van smarag,'n reis met Leipoldt* (*Emerald Belt; A Trip with Leipoldt*, Joubert 1997) Elsa Joubert (1922–) chronicles a trip she made to Indonesia in the footsteps of Leipoldt, in which she quotes from and refers to Multatuli's work, and wonders whether Leipoldt might have been the South African Multatuli (Van Zyl 2007: 83–96).

Indonesia

It goes without saying that for Indonesia Multatuli's message is all important. Still, the first translation of *Max Havelaar* in Bahasa Indonesia, the common language of all of Indonesia, which counts many 'regional' languages, the most important of which is Javanese, only saw the light in 1972. It was the work of Hans Bague Jassins (1917–2000) and featured a foreword – and this shows the book's importance – by Mashuri, the then Indonesian Minister of Education (Snoek 2010: 35–45). The Indonesian author Sitor Situmorang (1923–2014) claims that *Max Havelaar* at the end of the nineteenth century was an important source of information on 'the reality of the colonial system and also a denouncement of their own intellegentsia' for the 'first generation of Western-educated Indonesian intellectuals on Java'. The 'leaders of the Indonesian nationalist movement' considered Havelaar 'an anti-colonial co-combattant' (Situmorang 1990: 3, 5). In 1999 Pramoedya Ananta Toer in *The New York Times* called *Max Havelaar* 'The Book That Killed Colonialism' (Toer 1999). Here too, Indonesian communists saw Multatuli as an 'anti-imperialist' and 'proletarian humanist'.

There are several translations and adaptations of 'Saïdjah and Adinda' (1921, 1951, 1954 and 1975b). The first appeared as a serial in the newspaper *Neratja* in a translation by the Sumatran Muhammad Jamin, who as of 1932 would be a leading member of Soekarno's Partai Indonesia. In 1948, when the Dutch tried to suppress the Indonesian struggle for independence, a radio play on 'Saïdjah and Adinda', written by Urip Tjitrosuwarno, was aired. In 1951 there appeared an illustrated translation, in Sundanese, made by the former native ruler R.T.A. Sunarja. In 1954 a theatre version by Bakri Siregar was put out in print. In 1975 Kamajaya published it in book form, but the text, with some aditions and excisions, was taken from the 1972 *Max Havelaar* translation (Snoek 2010: 35–45).

The first Indonesian translation of *Max Havelaar* in book form, then, appeared late. It had a print run of 5,000 moderately priced copies, subsidized by the Dutch authorities as a result of the Cultural Agreement the two countries had concluded in 1968. In order to reach as many readers as possible the third edition was an abridged one, especially adapted to secondary school pupils, but also the fourth and fifth editions underwent adaptations. Up to and including the eighth edition published in 2000 a total of 40,000 copies have been sold. In 2008 there appeared a new translation, by Andi Tenri Wahyu, which, according to Snoek, is based on the English translation of Roy Edwards. The release of the movie *Max Havelaar* in 1987 in Indonesia led to numerous reactions: some critics thought that Multatuli had gone too far in his critique of the local ruler and had disregarded the common law of *adat* while others drew parallels between the present times and those of Multatuli: abuse of power, corruption and nepotism were exposed (Snoek 2010: 35-45).

From this survey it should be clear that the academic study of Dutch literature, in the Netherlands itself but perhaps even more so elsewhere (e.g. Anderson 2006: 449-462), pays ever more attention to Multatuli: many academics translate him, others write forewords and/or postscripts, or do research on how his work has been received worldwide. We here should make mention of some important studies that hitherto have not yet been cited: Sötemann investigated the structure of *Max Havelaar* (1966), Oversteegen concentrates on the poetics (Oversteegen 1987), Koch the reception in Poland (1991), Vermoortel how Multatuli used parables (1994), Beekman discussed Dutch-Indonesian colonial literature from an international perspective (1996), Termorshuizen situated Multatuli in the context of Dutch-Indonesian colonial literature (2002), Van der Meulen wrote a biography of Multatuli (2002), Gera looked at gender aspects in his work (2001), Pieterse took a closer look at the *Ideën* (2008) and Honings chronicled Multatuli's public career (2016). Finally, the proceedings of several important international symposia and conferences on Multatuli have been published: on *Max Havelaar* (Grave, Praamstra and Vandevoorde 2012), on various parts of his work (Bel, Honings and Grave 2018) and on lists in his work (Neven and Vervaeck 2018).

References

Anderson, B. (2006), '*Max Havelaar* (Multatuli 1860)', in Franco Moretti (ed.), *The Novel, Volume 2: Forms and Themes*, 449-462, Princeton, NJ: Princeton University Press.

Andringa, K. (2007), 'Van anarchist tot altermondialist. Multatuli in Frankrijk', *Over Multatuli* 29 (59): 39-50.

Anonymous (1867), *The North British Review* 46 (92): 319-342.

Beecher Stowe, H. (1852), *Uncle Tom's Cabin; or, Life Among the Lowly*, Boston, MA: John P. Jewitt.

Beekman, E.M. (1996), *Troubled Pleasures: Dutch Colonial Literature from the East Indies, 1600-1950*, Oxford: Clarendon Press.

Bel, J., R. Honings and J. Grave, eds (2018), *Multatuli nu. Nieuwe perspectieven op Eduard Douwes Dekker en zijn werk*, Hilversum: Verloren.

Bos, J.W. (2009), 'Nederlandstalige literatuur in het Roemeens – een succesverhaal', *Filter. Tijdschrift voor vertalen* 16 (2): 55-59.

Brink, A.P. (1967), *Aspekte van die Nuwe Prosa*, Pretoria: Academica.
Buning, T.J. (1942), *Bloemlesing uit die werke van E. Douwe-Dekker (Multatuli)*, Pretoria: J. van Schaik.
Casanova, P. (2007), *The World Republic of Letters*, trans. M.B. DeBevoise, Cambridge, MA: Harvard University Press.
Chi, M.-S. (1996), 'Multatuli in Korea', *Over Multatuli* 19 (37): 68–74.
Cohen, A. (1997), *Brieven 1888–1961*, ed. R. Spoor, Amsterdam: Prometheus.
Couvée, P. (2006), 'Van de Indische archipel tot de Goelag: Multatuli's heldendom in Rusland', *Over Multatuli* 28 (57): 29–36.
Daniëls-Waterman, M. (2011), 'De Multatuli van het Jiddisch. Een prosopografische bespreking', *Over Multatuli* 33 (67): 4–18.
Engelbrecht, W. (2011), 'Een strijder tegen het onrecht. De receptie van Multatuli in Tsjechië en Slowakije', *Over Multatuli* 33 (66): 2–41.
Gera, J. (2001), *Van een afstand. Multatuli's* Max Havelaar *tegendraads gelezen*, Amsterdam: Veen.
Gera, J. (2007), 'De vier levens van Multatuli in het Hongaars', *Over Multatuli* 29 (59): 51–67.
Gera, J. (2013), 'De intrede van Multatuli in Hongarije', *Werkwinkel* 8 (2): 97–112.
Grave, J. (2001), *Zulk vertalen is een werk van liefde. Bemiddelaars van Nederlandstalige literatuur in Duitsland 1890–1914*, Nijmegen: Vantilt.
Grave, J. (2003), *"Verdammt sei, wem das nicht heilig ist." Die Korrespondenz von Wilhelm Spohr mit Mimi Douwes Dekker und dem J.C.C. Bruns' Verlag*, Auswahl Kommentar and Nachwort J. Grave, edition friedrichshagen 6, Berlin: Müggel-Verlag.
Grave, J. (2013). '"But you can't do that!" Een andere visie op onderzoek naar Nederlandse literatuur in vertaling', in E. Besamusca, C. Hermann and U. Vogl (eds), *Out of the Box. Über den Wert des Grenzwertigen*, 163–178, Vienna: Praesens Verlag.
Grave, J., O. Praamstra and H. Vandevoorde, eds (2012), *150 Jahre* Max Havelaar. *Multatulis Roman in neuer Perspektive/150 Years* Max Havelaar. *Multatuli's Novel from New Perspectives*, Frankfurt am Main: Peter Lang.
Hermans, W.F. (1976), *De raadselachtige Multatuli*, Amsterdam: De Bezige Bij.
Hinrichs, J.P. (1995), 'Paustovskij en Multatuli', *Over Multatuli* 17 (34): 3–5.
Honings, R. (2016), *De dichter als idool*, Amsterdam: Bert Bakker.
Joubert, E. (1997), *Gordel van smarag, 'n reis met Leipoldt* (Emerald Belt; A Trip with Leipoldt), Kaapstad: Tafelberg.
Keymeulen, L. van (1892), 'Multatuli, un écrivain hollandais', *Revue des Deux Mondes*, 15 April 1892: 791–819.
Koch, J. (1991) 'Multatuli in Polen. Proeve van een literair-historische analyse van het verloop van de receptie in de periode van de eeuwwisseling', PhD diss., K.U. Leuven, Leuven.
Koch, J. (2008), 'Het wel en wee van de receptie. De ontvangst van Multatuli in Polen', *Over Multatuli* 30 (60): 20–47.
Kolenberg, J. (1971a), 'Multatuli in Frankrijk', *Ons Erfdeel* 14 (3): 85–89.
Kolenberg, J. (1971b), 'Multatuli en France (1860–1901)', *Les Lettres Romanes*, February: 16–49; May: 153–177, August: 270–309.
Krejčí, F.V. (1899), 'Multatuli', *Rozhledy* 9 (5) (1 December): 185–190.
Langenhoven, C.J. (1925), *Herrie op die ou tremspoor*, Kaapstad: Nasionale Boekhandel.
Larsen, N.-E. (2007), 'De door vrouwen zo zinloos verwende man. Multatuli in het Deens', *Over Multatuli* 29 (59): 24–38.
Leerdam, G. and J. Van Waterschoot (2009), '*Das Kapital, Uncle Tom's Cabin* en *Max Havelaar*. Interview met Shi Huiye', *Over Multatuli* 31 (62): 15–21.

Leipoldt, C.L. (1932) *Uit my Oosterse dagboek* (Pages from my Eastern Diary), Kaapstad: Nasionale Pers.
Maas, N. (2000), '"Dat boek is meer dan een boek – het is een mensch." Reacties op *Max Havelaar* in 1860', in N. Maas, (ed.), *Multatuli voor iedereen (maar niemand voor Multatuli)*, 7–49, Nijmegen: Vantilt.
Marchlewski, J.B. (1901a), 'Aforyzmy z dzieła pt. "Idee"', *Prawda, tygodnik polityczny, społeczny i literacki* 37: 447–448 (Polish trans. of amongst others Idea 2, 57, 48, 507, 337, 346, 213, 425, 411, 345, 141, 142, 59, 104, 223).
Marchlewski, J.B. (1901b), 'Multatuli', *Prawda, tygodnik polityczny, społeczny i literacki* 36: 440–441.
Marchlewski, J.B. (1901c), 'Z dzieł Multatuli (Douwes-Dekker). Opowieści o powadze', *Prawda, tygodnik polityczny, społeczny i literacki* 36: 434–436; 37: 446–447 (Polish trans. of 'Geschiedenissen van gezag' from *Minnebrieven*).
Meulen, D. van der (2002), *Multatuli, leven en werk van Eduard Douwes Dekker*, Amsterdam: Sun.
Multatuli (n.d.), *Saida și Adinda*, trans. N.N. Botez.
Multatuli ([1860] 1903), *Maks Havelaar (Max Havelaar)*, trans. B. Neufeldówna, Biblioteka Dzieł Wyborowych Nos. 297 and 298, Warsaw: A.T. Jezierski.
Multatuli (1861), *Minnebrieven* (Love Letters), Amsterdam: F. Guenst.
Multatuli (1862–1877), *Ideën I–VII* (Ideas I–VII), Amsterdam: R.C. Meijer.
Multatuli (1862), *Ideën I* (Ideas I), Amsterdam: R.C. Meijer.
Multatuli (1865), *Ideën II* (Ideas II), Amsterdam: R.C. Meijer.
Multatuli (1867), *Max Havelaar*, trans. by A.J. Nieuwenhuis and H. Crisafulli, Rotterdam: J. van der Hoeven, Paris: E. Dentu.
Multatuli (1868), *Max Havelaar or the Coffee auctions of the Dutch Trading Company*, trans. A. Nahuys (with maps), Edinburgh: Edmonston & Douglas.
Multatuli (1868), *Max Havelaar or the Coffee auctions of the Dutch Trading Company*, trans. from the original manuscript by Baron Alphonse Nahuys, Edinburgh: Edmonston & Douglas.
Multatuli (1870), *Ideën III* (Ideas III), Amsterdam: Van Helden.
Multatuli (1870–1873), *Millioenen-studiën* (Millions Studies), Delft: J. Waltman Jr.
Multatuli (1872–1873), *Ideën IV* (Ideas IV), Amsterdam: G.L. Funke.
Multatuli (1873a), *Ideën V* (Ideas V), Amsterdam: G.L. Funke.
Multatuli (1873b), *Ideën VI* (Ideas VI), Amsterdam: G.L. Funke.
Multatuli (1874–1877), *Ideën VII* (Ideas VII), Amsterdam: G.L. Funke.
Multatuli (1875), *Max Havelaar oder die Holländer auf Java*, trans. T. Stromer, Berlin: G.M.F. Müller.
Multatuli (1880), *Saïdjah. En Kjærlighedshistorie fra Java*, trans. G. Budde-Lund, Kjøbenhavn: E.L. Thaarups Forlag.
Multatuli (1899), 'Szaidzsa: Maláj történet', trans. I. Gábor, *Budapesti Szemle* 27 (275): 276–279.
Multatuli (1901a), *Max Havelaar eller Det hollandske Handelsselskabs Kaffeauktioner*, trans. C. Michelsen, København: Gyldendalske Boghandels Forlag.
Multatuli (1901b), *Osobistość jego i wybór pism* (wybór pism), trans., selection and introduction by M. Feldman, supplement to the magazine 'Przeglądu Tygodniowego', Warsaw: Wydawnictwo 'Przeglądu Tygodniowego'.
Multatuli (1901c), *Pages Choisies*, selected and trans. by A. Cohen, preface by A. France, Paris: Société du Mercure de France.

Multatuli (1903a), *Výbor ze spisův, jež napsal Multatuli*, trans. K. Nevšímalová, Praha: Josef Pelcl.
Multatuli (1903b), *Wybór pism*, trans. M. Posner-Garfeinowa, Warsaw: Ksiegarnia Naukowa (Repr. 1906).
Multatuli (1904), *Walter Pieterse: A story of Holland*, trans. H. Evans, New York: Friderici & Garcis. (Repr. Whitefish, MT: Kessinger Publishing, 2008.)
Multatuli (1907), *Kto z was bez winy... – Rzecz napisana i ogłoszona drukiem w formie listu otwartego w 1863 r. nastepnie pomieszczona w książce 'Myśli' t. II. (Idee 448, 1863)*, trans. I. Zielińska, Warsaw: Ksiegarnia Naukowa.
Multatuli (1911), *Liebes-brief (Minnebrieven)*, trans. A. Frumkin, preface by R. Rocker, London: Arbayter Fraynd.
Multatuli (1918), *Pritci i paraboli*, trans. D. Debeljanov, Sofija: B & S.
Multatuli (1920), *Parabole*, trans. unknown: Zagreb.
Multatuli (1921), 'Saidjah dan Adinda', in *Neratja; penjokong dan pembantoe kemadjoean jang lajak bagi Bangsa dan Tanah Air dengan djalan jang patoet*, vol. 5, trans. S.M. Jamin, 19 February–10 March 1921.
Multatuli (1924), 'Two parables from the *Ideas*', trans. Lu Xun, *Jingbao fukan*, 7 and 16 December 1924.
Multatuli (1925), *Saaid oen Adinde*, trans. L. Reznik, Kiev: Kultur-Lige.
Multatuli (1926a), *O věrné lásce Saïdjaha a Adindy. Vesnická povídka z Jávy*, trans. J. Veselý, Prague: Společnost Československého červeného kříže.
Multatuli (1926b), 'The Story of Saidjah', in B.H. Clark and M. Lieber (eds), *Great Short Stories of the World*, 576–586, London: William Heinemann.
Multatuli (1927), *Max Havelaar; or, The Coffee Sales of the Netherlands Trading Company*, with an introduction by D.H. Lawrence, New York: Knopf.
Multatuli (1932), *Příběh malého Waltra Pieterse*, trans. L. Faltová, Prague: Družstevní práce.
Multatuli (1937), *Sajid oen Adinda oen a Peroe'aner maisse'le*, trans. M. Taichman, Warschau: Kinder-Frajnd.
Multatuli (1945), *Max Havelaar*, in *Modern Världslitteratur: de levande mästerverken*, 22, trans. P. Hedberg, postscript by A. Lundkvist, 325–566, Stockholm: Natur och kultur.
Multatuli (1947a), *Max Havelaar (Drážební řížení v holandské obchodní společnosti)*, trans. R.J. Vonka, Prague: Nakladatelství Svoboda.
Multatuli (1947b), *Páginas Selectas de Multatuli*, trans. and selection by F. Alaiz, biography by R. Rocker, Toulouse: Tierra y Libertad.
Multatuli (1948a), *Max Havelaar*, trans. S. Mărgărit, București: Editura de Stat.
Multatuli (1948b), *Max Havelaar oder die Kaffeeauktionen der Niederländischen Handelsgesellschaft*, trans. E. Stück, afterword P. Wiegler, Berlin: Aufbau Verlag.
Multatuli (1949), *Max Havelaar*, in the authentic writing, issued and introduced by G. Stuiveling, Amsterdam: G.A. van Oorschot.
Multatuli (1950), *Max Havelaar*, Budapest: Szikra.
Multatuli (1951), *Saidja; Karangan Multatuli*, trans. R.T.A. Sunarja, Djakarta: Balai Pustaka.
Multatuli (1952), *Max Havelaar oder die Kaffeeauktionen der Niederländischen Handelsgesellschaft*, trans. W. Spohr, Berlin: Verlag der Nation.
Multatuli (1953), *Maks Havelar*, trans. M. Grubeslieva, Sofija.
Multatuli (1954), *Saidjah dan Adinda; Lakon 3 babak*, theatre play by B. Siregar, Medan: Sasterawan.

Multatuli (1955), *Woutertje Pieterse. Die Geschichte eines holländischen Jungen*, trans. H. Bruck, Berlin: Neues Leben.

Multatuli (1965), *Max Havelaar ovvero le aste del caffè della Società di Commercio Olandese*, trans. P.B. Marzolla, Turin: Unione Tipografico Editrice Torinese (I grandi scrittori stranieri; 272).

Multatuli (1967a), *Max Havelaar în Indiile Olandeze*, trans. H.R. Radian, Bucureşti: Pentru Literatura (Biblioteca Pentru Toti; 413).

Multatuli (1967b), *Max Havelaar or The Coffee Auctions of the Dutch Trading Company*, trans. R. Edwards, introduction by D.H. Lawrence, ed. and introduced by R. Edwards, Leyden: Sijthoff; London: Heinemann; New York: London House & Maxwell.

Multatuli (1970), *Saïdyah and Adinda*, in *Great Love Stories of All Nations*, trans. W. Siebenhaar.

Multatuli (1973), *Max Havelaar*, trans. R. Sepp, Tallinn: Kirjastus Eesti Raamat.

Multatuli (1974), *The Oyster and the Eagle: Selected aphorisms and parables*, trans. E.M. Beekman, Amherst: University of Massachusetts Press.

Multatuli (1975a), *Max Havelaar, o las subastas de café de la compañía comercial Holandesa*, introduction, trans. and notes by F. Carrasquer, Barcelona: Colección Los Libros De La Frontera.

Multatuli (1975b), *Saijah dan Adinda*, trans. Kamajaya, Yogya: Penerbit University Press Indonesia.

Multatuli (1976), *Max Havelaar: ou os leiloes de café da companhia holandesa de comércio*, trans. D. Augusto Gonçalves, Porto: Livraria Civilizacao.

Multatuli (1982), *Maksas Havelaras*, trans. L. Breslavskien, Vilnius: Vaga.

Multatuli (1983), *Max Havelaar*, trans. G. A. Bashir, Lahore: Maktaba Meri Library.

Multatuli (1984), *Maks Havelar*, trans. S. Načev, foreword by N. Davidov, Sofija: Narodna Kultura.

Multatuli (1987), *Makesi Hafulaèr de qiyu*, trans. H. Shi - P. Xinliang, Beijing: People's Literature Publishing House.

Multatuli (1988) *Erzählungen, Parabeln und Ideen des niederländischen Autors*, trans. and postscript M.S. Fischer, Frankfurt: Ullstein.

Multatuli (1992), *Auswahl aus seinen Schriften*, trans. W. Spohr, Munich: Verena Franke.

Multatuli (1993a), *Max Havelaar oder Die Kaffeeversteigerungen der niederländischen Handelsgesellschaft*, trans. M. den Hertog-Vogt, Köln: Bruckner & Thünker.

Multatuli (1993b), *Minnebriefe*, trans. M. den Hertog-Vogt, Köln: Bruckner & Thünker.

Multatuli (1995a), *Briefe aus dem Rheingau*, trans. E. Leibfried, Fernwald: Litblockín (Mitteilungen der Internationalen Multatuli-Gesellschaft Ingelheim; III).

Multatuli (1995b), *Ingelheimer Briefe, 1881-1887*, trans. E. Leibfried, Fernwald: Litblockín (Mitteilungen der Internationalen Multatuli-Gesellschaft Ingelheim; IV).

Multatuli (1997a), *Max Havelaar, oder Die Kaffeeversteigerungen der Niederländischen Handelsgesellschaft*, trans. M. den Hertog-Vogt, Berlin: Ullstein (Ullstein-Buch; 24166).

Multatuli (1997b), *Pensieri*, trans. G. Faggin, Faenza: Mobydick.

Multatuli (1998), *[Max Havelaar]*, trans. R. HaCohen, Bnei Brak: Hakibbutz Hameuchad.

Multatuli (1999), *Die Abenteuer des kleinen Walther*, trans. W. Spohr, Köln: DuMont.

Multatuli (2007), *Max Havelaar ovvero le aste del caffè della Società di Commercio Olandese*, trans. P.B. Marzolla, postscript by F. Ferrari, Milan: Iperborea.

Multatuli (2014), *Max Havelaar*, trans. G. A. Cappai, Cagliari: Condaghes.

Multatuli (2015), *Max Havelaar. Hollanda Ticaret Şirketinin Kahve Borsalan*, trans. E. Gürer, Istanbul: Aylak Adam Yayınları.

Multatuli (2017a), [(*Max Havelaar*)], trans. M. al-Halool, Abu Dhabi: Kalima.
Multatuli (2017b), *Max Havelaar o las subastas de café de la Compañia Neerlandesa de Comercio*, trans. M. Van Wijk Adan, introduction by A. Van Raemdonck, notes by A. Van Raemdonck and M. Van Wijk Adan, Madrid: Ediciones Cátedra (Letras universales; 528).
Neven, E. and B. Vervaeck, eds (2018), *Lijsten in Literatuur. Verslagen & Mededelingen van de Koninklijke Academie voor Nederlandse Taal- en Letterkunde* 127 (2-3), Gent: KANTL.
Nieuwenhuys, R. (1987), *De mythe van Lebak*, Amsterdam: G.A. van Oorschot.
Nikolić, S. (2008), 'De toekomst zal anders zijn, de toekomst zal mooier zijn!' *Over Multatuli* 30 (60): 48–61.
Oversteegen, J.J. (1987), *De redelijke Natuur. Multatuli's literatuuropvattingen*, Utrecht: HES.
Paustovsky, K. (1956), 'Inscription on a Rock', in *The Golden Rose. Literature in the Making* (*Zolotaja roza*), trans. S. Rosenberg, Moscow: Foreign Language Publishing House.
Paustovsky, K. (1972),'Gollandskaja koroleva' (The Queen of Holland), in *Rasskazy. Očerki i publicistika. Stati'i i vystuplenija po voprosam literatury i iskusstva*, 51–55, Moscow: Chudožestvennaja literatura.
Perron, E. du (1937), *De man van Lebak. Anekdoten en Dokumenten betreffende Multatuli*, Amsterdam: Em. Querido's Uitgevers-Mij N.V.
Pieterse, S. (2008), *De buik van de lezer. Over spreken en schrijven in Multatuli's Ideën*, Nijmegen: Vantilt.
Prosa, K. (1994), 'Multatuli in Estland', *Over Multatuli* 16 (32): 58–61.
Raemdonck, A. van (2007), '*Páginas Selectas* en *Max Havelaar*. Multatuli in Spanje', *Over Multatuli*, 29 (59): 68–82.
Salverda, R. (2010), '"A Dutch Political Novel." Over *Max Havelaar* in het Engels', *Over Multatuli* 33 (65): 4–16.
Scheltjens, W. (2003), *Bibliografie van de Nederlandse literatuur in Russische vertaling*, St Petersburg: Aleteja.
Situmorang, S. (1990), 'Multatuli en de Indonesische cultuur. Een terugblik op zijn Sumatraanse periode', *Over Multatuli* 12 (24): 3–15.
Smeets-Sirakova, N. (1986), 'Multatuli in het Bulgaars', *Over Multatuli* 8 (16): 27–31.
Snoek, K. (2010), '*Max Havelaar* in Indonesië: constanten en variabelen', *Over Multatuli* 33 (65): 35–45.
Sötemann, A.L. (1966), *De structuur van Max Havelaar. Bijdrage tot het onderzoek naar de interpretatie en evaluatie van de roman*, Groningen: Wolters Noordhoff.
Spohr, W. (1899), *Multatuli. Auswahl aus seinen Werken, eingeleitet durch eine Charakteristik seines Lebens, seiner Persönlichkeit und seines Schaffens*, with portraits and handwritten supplement; title drawing of Fidus, Minden: J.C.C. Bruns' Verlag.
Spohr, W. (1902), *Multatuli. Auswahl aus seinen Werken, eingeleitet durch eine Charakteristik seines Lebens, seiner Persönlichkeit und seines Schaffens*, with portraits and handwritten supplement, title drawing of Fidus, 2nd edition, Minden: J.C.C. Bruns' Verlag.
Sun, Y. and O. Praamstra (2013), 'De eerste vertaling van Multatuli in het Chinees', *Over Multatuli* 35 (71): 11–24
Termorshuizen, G. (2002), '"Indië is ook in het litterarische eene melkkoe." Indisch-Nederlandse letterkunde van de negentiende eeuw', in *Europa buitengaats. koloniale en postkoloniale literaturen in Europese talen*, T. D'haen (ed.), 98–132, Amsterdam: Bert Bakker.

Toer, P.A. (1980-1988), *Buru Quartet* (for the individual volumes see the following entries)
Toer, P.A. (1982), *This Earth of Mankind* (Bumi manusia, 1980), trans. and introduced by M. Lane, Ringwood, VIC: Penguin.
Toer, P.A. (1982), *Child of All Nations* (Anak semua bangsa, 1980), trans. and introduced by M. Lane, Ringwood, VIC: Penguin.
Toer, P.A. (1990), *Footsteps* (Jejak langkah, 1985), trans. and introduced by M. Lane, Harmondsworth: Penguin.
Toer, P.A. (1992), *House of Glass* (Rumah kaca, 1988), trans. and introduced by M. Lane, Ringwood, VIC: Penguin.
Toer, P.A. (1999), 'The Book That Killed Colonialism', *New York Times*, 18 April 1999.
Uffelen, H. van (1993a), *Moderne niederländische Literatur im deutschen Sprachraum 1830-1990*, Niederlande-Studien; 6, Münster: Waxmann Verlag.
Uffelen, H. van (1993b), *Bibliographie der modernen niederländischen Literatur in deutscher Übersetzung 1830-1990*, Niederlande-Studien; 7, Münster: Waxmann Verlag.
Vandevoorde, H. (2008), 'Multatuli in het land van Leopold II. Een geval van "histoire croisée"', *Over Multatuli* 30 (60): 4-19.
Vanrusselt, R. (1982), 'Multatuli in het Duitse cultuurgebied. Een receptiestudie', PhD diss., Leuven University.
Vermoortel, P. (1994), *De parabel bij Multatuli. Hoe moet ik u aanspreken om verstaan te worden?* Gent: Koninklijke Academie voor Nederlandse Taal en Letterkunde.
Vygodskaja, E.I. (1936), *Istorija Edvarda Dekkera*, Moscow.
Vygodskaja, E.I. (1949), *Plamja gneva*, Moscow: Detgiz.
Wallace, A.R. (1869), *The Malay Archipelao. The land of the orang-utan, and the bird of paradise. A narrative of travel, with studies of man and nature.* London: Macmillan and Co.
Werner, A. (1893), *The Humour of Holland*, trans. with an Introduction by A. Werner, illustrations by D. Hardy and others, London: Walter Scott Publishing; New York: Charles Scribner.
Wikén Bonde, I. (2007), 'Eeuwige strijd tegen het kwaad. De receptie van *Max Havelaar* in Zweden', *Over Multatuli* 29 (59): 8-23.
Wygodskaja, E. (1953), *Flamme des Zorns. Die Geschichte des Eduard Dekker* (Flame of Ire. The History of Eduard Dekker), Moscow: Verlag für Fremdsprachliche Literatur Moskau.
Zyl, W. van (2007), 'Genie en vijand. Multatuli in het land van de Apartheid', *Over Multatuli* 29 (59): 83-96.

8

How a Flemish Writer Turned Global: The Nineteenth-century Journey of Hendrik Conscience's Early Novellas

Lieven D'hulst

Introduction

Belgium has for more than a century cherished, honoured and remembered its Flemish writer Hendrik Conscience (1812–1883) as the author of *De Leeuw van Vlaanderen* (*The Lion of Flanders*, 1838), a romantic rewriting of the Battle of the Golden Spurs, a fourteenth-century episode in the medieval French-Flemish war. Yet, in recent times Conscience and his *Lion* have dissolved into vague metonyms, pointing less at the prolific writer of novels, short stories and historical works or at a specific set of themes and styles, than at a conglomerate of images and stereotypes, among which 'the most Flemish of all authors', or 'the man who taught his people how to read', are perhaps the most tenacious. And although many historians of Flemish[1] literature regard Conscience's *Lion* as the foundational narrative of Flanders' literature, 135 years after his death not one of his more than a hundred novels, including *The Lion of Flanders*, is reprinted, available in bookshops or even in public libraries.[2] What's more, in a recent book with the title *De grote onleesbare* (The Great Unreadable, by Humbeeck, Absillis and Weijermars 2016), influential Flemish critics consider his work to have become unreadable in our time, because of the gap that separates Conscience's language and style from present-day literary Dutch, the intimate but old-fashioned and moralizing themes of his work, the grandiloquence of his patriotism and the reluctance of twenty-first-century readers to embrace the exaltation of national ideologies.

The process of Conscience's rise and decline in his home country parallels to a large extent his international trajectory. Once read all over Europe and across the Atlantic, Conscience's work now has disappeared from the international canon, bookshops and libraries, while Wikipedia and other easily accessible or open resources reproduce without further notice and in many languages the same images and stereotypes that prevail in Belgium. Understandably, national and international trends mutually determine one another: Conscience, as 'the chief' of the then new Flemish literature (Calis 2013: 305), the Flemish Walter Scott, served as an example of the emergent national literatures of the nineteenth century, and his international image boosted his prestige in his home country.

However, the principle of mutual determination does not account by itself for the very process of rise and decline. The essential theme of Conscience's major historical novel, which is the Flemish liberation from the French yoke, is the elevation of the Battle of the Golden Spurs, during which Flemish foot militia defeated the French king's knights, into a crucial symbol of upcoming national identity. Yet, in contradistinction with the powerful European tradition of historical novels stemming from Walter Scott, *The Lion of Flanders* was less successful through most of the nineteenth century, in and outside of Belgium, than most of Conscience's later, and especially minor, narrative work. If not a paradox, this case of reverse popularity (the *Lion* getting more attention from the end of the nineteenth century on, at the detriment of his later work) is at least surprising. But what is even more striking, perhaps, is the fact that the success of this later and minor work was not confined to his home country, but embarked on the contrary on a still unparalleled international journey as far as a Flemish author is concerned.

The central question becomes obvious: why did a nineteenth-century Flemish author, using a minor language, and abandoning the more prestigious genre of the historical novel endowed with nationalist functions in favour of minor prose forms, evolve into one of the most prosperous novelists of his time, equaling Dickens's popularity in major languages such as French, German and Spanish? This question entails a second: why did all of Conscience's work rapidly fade into oblivion during the twentieth century, and particularly so after the Second World War, contrary to the fate of evergreens such as Dickens, Sand or Dumas, and even a Dutch novelist such as Multatuli, who has more solidly stood the test of time?

In this contribution, I will focus on the first question, and limit the time scope to the second half of the nineteenth century.[3] Successful literary circulation depends on a number of issues, three of which I will look at in some detail. The first issue is literary: after the Napoleonic era, some of the smaller emergent European literatures tried to free themselves from French and German cultural and literary hegemony by embarking on new literary genres that explicitly pointed at popular forms fitting specific ethnic groups and local identities. The second issue is sociological: Conscience's work swiftly made its way in many languages thanks to its repackaging by an efficient, international network of mediators, in which publishers, critics and translators, but also the author himself, played a role (D'hulst et al. 2014). The third issue is ideological: Conscience's early work exalted models of Christian morality and group identity embodied by a large range of Flemish characters, going against the grain of the rapidly expanding liberalism and socialism mainly represented by French realism. This world view was shared by many smaller emergent cultures in Europe. Needless to say, all issues are intertwined.

In search of a new genre

There is no dissemination without texts. Viewed in retrospect, Conscience's narrative work falls roughly divided into three genres: the historical novel, the narrative of manners and the rural story. Conscience's first and second books, *In 't Wonderjaer* (The Year of Wonders, 1837) and *De Leeuw van Vlaanderen* (1838) embrace the historical novel, a genre still widespread and vivid some twenty years after Walter Scott had introduced it. Nineteenth-century Flemish readers and critics keenly recognized these two novels as working in Scott's tradition and at the same time renewing it. They acknowledged the strengthening of the epic dimension, the weight given to local folklore, the oral tone of telling, etc. Yet they also noted the global decline of the genre and welcomed, a few years later, Conscience's adopting two genres to which the Flemish author contributed more innovatively, i.e. the narrative of manners and the rural novel.

The narrative of manners constituted a reaction against recent mutations of the historical novel, notably the growing intrusion of whimsical plots, elusive spatio-temporal settings, and the portrayal of exalted heroes. It also responded to the upcoming French vogue of *littérature facile* (easy literature) or *littérature industrielle* (industrial literature) represented by melodrama, fantastic tales and other short stories that seemed deprived of literary grandeur and moral standards, and were accused of pursuing no other goal than fame and profit (Vaillant 2005). Still, these popular genres massively penetrated the Belgian and European literary market by means of cheap and successful pirate editions. Belgian institutional players such as journalists, literary critics, and the Church, considered these features unfit to serve the exemplary ethic and civic functions they likely assigned to literature, next to its nation-building function. The latter, however, was less urgently solicited some twenty years after Belgian independence.

Conscience and several of his contemporaries zeroed in on the growing demand for shorter narratives, such as sketches, novellas or tales, in which urban and, later on, rural settings allowed for the realistic depiction of conflicting social interests and values embodied by rudimentary and even Manichean characters. The narrator of such fictions adopts a committed and paternalistic stance, employs a highly accessible language and gives preference to a dialogic mode that recalls contemporary melodrama. Abundantly illustrated, the narrative of manners solicits empathic reading and adhesion to the social, religious and literary values propagated among the middle classes and backed by social, educational and religious institutions. Conscience's work succeeded in addressing a large public composed of adolescent and adult readers, while its success was underpinned and even amplified thanks to numerous techniques of recycling, in particular adaptations in other media, such as theatre (later on film), opera and painting, as well as for children. Intermedia transfer as well as the transfer of isolated themes and figures may very well have improved the international dissemination of Conscience's work.

Three shorter works of less than one hundred pages each, issued in the early 1840s, and often published together in translation, best represent Conscience's generic turn from the historical novel to the story of manners: *Hoe men schilder wordt. Eene ware geschiedenis van eenen schilder die nog leeft* (How to Become a Painter. The True History of a Painter Still Alive Now, 1843a); *Wat eene moeder lyden kan. Eene ware geschiedenis* (What a Mother Can Endure. A True History, 1843b); and *Siska van Roosemael. Ware geschiedenis van eene jufvrouw die nog leeft* (Siska van Roosemael. The True History of a Woman Still Alive Now, 1844). The referential character is foregrounded in the three titles, in the chronotopes and many detailed descriptions of concrete places and customs. All of these stories are set in Antwerp, the city where Conscience lived most of his life. The first story narrates the laborious path of a gifted but poor boy who aspires to become a painter and through hard work, and in spite of many deceptions, sees his dream come true. In the second story a needy labourer's family threatened by mendicancy receives help from an upper-class young lady, who discovers the tragedy of poverty and the blessings of Christian charity. The last story features the daughter of a poor Antwerp grocer. Seduced by her neighbour's son she flees to corrupt Paris. She returns to obtain her dying father's forgiveness for her sins and continues her life in repentance and religious devotion.

The peculiar flavour of a style far remote, it seems, from upcoming European modernity, may be illustrated by the following example, i.e. the excipit of *Siska Van Roosemael*, narrating the return of the prodigal daughter:

> Shall I now describe the last solemn hour of the father, and the despair of the daughter? Shall I show you Siska, – with tearful eyes and disheveled hair, heart-broken and frantic with grief! Shall I tell you how she strikes her head against the deathbed of her father, until the blood gushed forth! How she endeavors to destroy her beauty, and lacerates her cheeks with her nails! How she tears into pieces, tramples upon, and destroys all the marks of her vanity and thoughtlessness! Oh! no! This spectacle is too painful, too touching.
>
> Behold! the father dies! – but an expression of happiness brightens his countenance like that of a saint: his dying eyes, with a consolatory look, are fixed upon the bedside. There Siska kneels, clinging round her mother with both her arms, kisses her affectionately, and entreats for mercy; the doctor stands opposite, and sheds tears of emotion. The dying man beholds this scene! he raises his feeble hand over the side of the bed – and lets it drop on the head of his child; then he speaks, whilst his soul unfolds its wings and soars from the earth to heaven, 'My blessing upon thee, Siska! my child!'

> The shop of a hundred years' standing is now shut up. Mother and daughter lead a life of solitude and repentance; with horror they think of the cause of their misery, and to their litany they add the significant prayer, – 'From the French degeneracy, deliver us, O Lord!'
> I venture to hope, indulgent reader, that this true narrative may have engaged your attention, and you are, perhaps, anxious to see Siska. (Conscience 1846: 86–88)

The narrative of manners endows literary resources with ethical and didactic functions, and with an anti-French ideology (made explicit in *Siska Van Roosemael*), in a way that was deemed innovative in comparison with the derivative and outdated but higher ranked historical novel. Thus, Conscience deliberately altered his earlier strategy: bypassing the criticism levelled at the historical novel, even if the genre continued to flourish in the peripheral literary system of Belgium or Flanders, he fashioned a genre in which simplification and downsized prestige go hand in hand with originality of theme and style. This combination has no direct correlate in French, German or British literature, the literatures that at the time played a central role in the European literary system. According to Calis, who refers to Even-Zohar's polysystem theory (1990), 'the rather conservative choices Conscience made with respect to the Flemish market, a weak literary system conditioned by strong ethical and didactic constraints, gave his work a universal appeal to similar audiences abroad' (2013: 297; my translation). Among these similar audiences, one may think of audiences belonging to major adjacent literatures who were looking for another type of popular repertoire, as well as of those of other peripheral literatures at the time, such as for instance Spanish literature. More than French critics, their Spanish counterparts openly acknowledged the innovative character of Conscience's prose, and the genre of the novella, for which, according to one Spanish critic, there is not even a linguistic equivalent available. At the same time, it was welcomed as an alternative to the historical and social novel genres (Saguer 2013: 323).

The story of manners with an urban setting coalesced smoothly with the upcoming rural or village novella, to which Conscience extensively contributed during the 1850s and later, relocating minor heroes, moral norms and national pride within local communities, in which nature is bestowed with a healing power with regard to the social, political and moral tensions between individuals and groups. Popular initiators of the genre, often translated, were the German novelists Zschokke and Auerbach (cf. Zellweger 1941). The focus is on rituals and customs, language variation, play, carnival, etc., in line with the rise of folklore studies and the growing and nostalgic awareness that certain parts of society were fast disappearing (Van den Berg and Couttenier 2009: 448 *ff*). A case in point is Conscience's *De loteling* (The conscript, 1850), the story of a poor peasant who enlists as a conscript in the army. When he returns as a blind vagrant, he is affectionately welcomed back home. French author Alexandre Dumas, in a novel ironically entitled *Conscience l'innocent* (Conscience the innocent, published in Brussels in 1852), blatantly plagiarized two chapters of this novel. Two years later, as a form of reparation, he issued a translation of Conscience's original in his journal *Le Mousquetaire* (Dumas 1854), becoming a mediator for the Flemish author in the French market and beyond.

From Flanders to the world

Between Conscience and the world stand dozens of such mediators, who dialectically channeled the former into the latter.[4] One may think of translators, of course, of agents, publishers, critics, but also of teachers or adaptors for different audiences and media. All take part in the process of the intercultural circulation of literature. I will sketchily present the main phases of this process and then briefly elaborate on publishers' policies or strategies to embed translated texts in the target literatures.

Two rhizomes

Networks are not always confined to language areas, but may extend beyond, depending on individual taste or publishers' strategies. Literary taste is not incompatible with commercial success, it may even be a condition for the latter, while one would be tempted to see their relation as the fruit of hazard. Conscience's narrative of manners' international fate has a starting point outside Belgium, from where it will expand along a rhizomatic pattern, of which we are unable to reconstruct more than bits and pieces.[5] This starting point is an article by an acquaintance of Conscience, the Flemish critic Ferdinand Snellaert, published in the *Augsburger Allgemeine Zeitung* in July 1844 with the title: *Die flämische Literatur und ihre hervorragenden Schriftsteller* (Flemish literature and its prominent writers, 1844). The *Augsburger Allgemeine Zeitung* was a regional newspaper, located in the Bavarian city of Augsburg, close to the Austrian Empire and even Italy. Still, it was one of the most prestigious and widely distributed newspapers of the nineteenth century (Fischer 2003), which may help to understand the rapid spread of Conscience's work in Germanophone Europe. Snellaert's article apparently made a deep impression on Melchior Baron von Diepenbrock, the Catholic prince-bishop of Breslau, at that time a German city.[6] Diepenbrock was born at the German-Dutch border and spoke Low-German, a dialect close enough to Flemish to allow him to read Conscience in the original. Upon having read and appraised Conscience's work,[7] he decided to translate the three *Genreschilderungen* (genre paintings), which Snellaert refers to as quite successful in their mother tongue: 'man [kann] von ihre Absätze wirklich sagen [...] sie seien nicht "ausverkauft" sondern "ausgefochten" worden [...] ein unerklärbarer Zauber hängt an seiner Feder, an seinen Lippen'[8] (1844: 1540). Von Diepenbrock quotes this passage in the *Vorrede* (Foreword) of his translation published in 1845 with the title *Flämisches Stillleben, in drei kleinen Erzählungen* (Flemish still lifes, in three small tales).[9] He also mentions the latter's lehrreich (didactic) and nützlich (useful) properties.

The laudatory article by Snellaert, issued in the major language of German, in a major journal of that time, its lengthy quotation in the Foreword that further expands on the main theme of the article, and the translation itself of the three novels by an institutionally influential translator in the same major language,[10] are the starting points of the international trajectory of Conscience. On a temporal scale, they launch a 'viral' chain (Leerssen 2011) of a quick concatenation of retranslations and new translations (making up *Kometenschweife*, i.e. comet tails, Frank and Schultze 2004) in German and also in other languages.[11] Von Diepenbrock's translation was first reprinted in German, and new translations followed rapidly with different publishers in different locations: for 1846 alone, we arrive at fourteen editions in more than twenty volumes printed for seven different publishers (Hermans 2014: 164). Surprisingly, the same year, Von Diepenbrock's translation is used as a source text for translations into Czech, English and Italian, followed, later on, by translations into Hungarian (1858) and Polish (1875). In England, in 1845, Nicholas Trübner – a German translator and later London publisher, who also happened to be the son-in-law of a Flemish writer, translator and acquaintance of Conscience, Octave Delepierre – retranslated Von Diepenbrocks's *Flämisches Stillleben* for Longman, with the title *Sketches from Flemish life in Three Tales* (1845b). Translations of other stories followed in 1854 and 1855 by different translators, with different publishers, probably based on earlier French or German versions. And so, as conveyed by the German and English titles, the image of the first international Conscience is that of a Flemish writer of local short novels with a manner endowed with strong moral and religious functions. The local becomes the token of the universal.

Coming after this first rhizome of translation and dissemination, a second one developed, following a different path, which others adopted in turn. In France, it seems, the start began with translations of short passages of Conscience published in the influential *Revue des Deux Mondes* in 1854 as well as translations of the novellas in a journal of the aforementioned Dumas in the same year. Dumas also stressed his mediating role while announcing the upcoming *Œuvres complètes* by Parisian publisher Michel Lévy frères:

> Nous annonçons avec grand plaisir à nos lecteurs que, grâce aux trois nouvelles flamandes publiées dans notre journal, le nom de notre confrère Conscience a acquis assez de publicité et de retentissement en France pour que M. Michel Lévy lui achetât non-seulement la propriété de tout ce qu'il avait fait jusqu'à présent, mais encore de tout ce qu'il ferait dans l'avenir.[12] (Dumas quoted in Andringa 2013: 280)

These translations served in turn as source texts for translations into Spanish, Portuguese (Huylebrouck 1984: 303) and, again, English. And so English became the language through which the first rhizome encountered and merged with the second one. Whether German or French was chosen as the mediating language depended on factors such as the agents' contacts, the translator's mastery of the language, no doubt also the prestige of the publisher, as well as financial considerations.[13]

From England, Conscience's work travelled to the United States (Wellens 1982, Calis 2013). Already in 1846, Trübner's version of *What a Mother Can Endure* appeared in the New York religious magazine *The Young Churchman's Miscellany: A Magazine of Religious and Entertaining Knowledge*. Later on, British publishers Lambert & Burns set up a joint venture with John Murphy in Baltimore to distribute translations of Conscience. Others followed. A decade later, Murphy reprinted and also adapted these translations (for which he used the term 'translated expressly for this edition') in view of his own edition of *Hendrik Conscience's Short Tales* in thirteen volumes (1856-1875).

All in all, what had started as an individual if not isolated undertaking by an atypical German translator turned into a massive rhizomatic growth, extending across national borders as well as across the entire literary field (through intermediary adaptations for the theatre, opera and iconography, through adaptations for children, anthologies with a didactic purpose, etc.[14]). In many languages, the zeal to benefit from these dynamics is attested to by the fact that Conscience was the first author of the Dutch language area to be translated: this is the case in Danish, Norwegian, Swedish, Hungarian, Slovak and Czech. Also, Conscience is one of the earliest Dutch writers to be translated into English and Polish, and, so far perhaps, the most successful Dutch writer ever in French and German (Engelbrecht 2016: 239).

Publishers' strategies

The first image of this internationalized Conscience is that of a regional Flemish writer of short novels of manners, gifted with patriotic, moral and didactic ideals. To some extent, it was also nationalized or re-nationalized, by translators and publishers, in order to fit specific expectations or norms of reading groups within national literatures. This is a seemingly paradoxical undertaking, since, for example, French and German translations of Conscience's work address readers in many places, including Belgium and the Netherlands, next to remote parts of Europe. In addition, translations in both languages often serve as pseudo-originals for translations in other languages (these translations being called 'indirect' translations, as occurs with the already mentioned retranslations of Diepenbrock's versions). But nationalizing or target-oriented trends are equally conspicuous in the efforts of translators, notably when it comes to designing and applying techniques that assist the incorporation of the source text in the target literature, such as free renderings, or changing names of characters and places (D'hulst 2013), next to the foregrounding of generic affinities between translations and original work in the target literature.

However, it is impossible to adequately ascertain the material success of both the national and international images of Conscience, simply because there are not enough comparable data offered by the many language areas that carry them. Be that as it may, the available information about numbers of titles and print copies for separate languages is in itself quite telling. For instance, a list of translated titles in German for the period 1845-1990, covering new translations and reprints, has been established by Van Uffelen (1993b: vol. II, 83-132). The total of both amounts to 461 titles, unequally spread over the periods 1845-1900 (297 titles) and 1901-1990 (164 titles), the number of reprints being much higher for the second period: clearly, translations are concentrated in the nineteenth century.[15]

More interesting, perhaps, is the number of copies printed by publishers, when the information is available. Such is the case with the French translations of fifty-three titles of the *Œuvres complètes de Henri Conscience* issued by M. Lévy frères between 1856 and 1884 (Mollier 2005). The 53 titles generate a total of 682,300 printed copies, corresponding to an annual average of 24,237 copies, a result which probably makes Conscience into one of the most successful foreign writers in France of that very period (D'hulst 2013). Not surprisingly, perhaps, the title with the largest number of copies printed is the first of the series: the *Scènes de la vie flamande* (1856), containing the three novellas already grouped by Von Diepenbrock a decade earlier. This volume reaches 35,200 copies, while the average title does not exceed 6,000 copies (this applies notably to the *Lion des Flandres*).

The literary circulation of Conscience's work was steered by publication strategies that were gradually expanding, from issues of mediation and literary assimilation to full-fledged policies. To start with, publishers sustained or designed networks of mediators: translators were suggested by agents, even by the author, and contacted publishers or, conversely, were recruited by publishers on the basis of their supposed aptitude to convey a literary form and, if necessary, to adapt it to target culture specifics. Diepenbrock is, again, a case in point: solicited by an agent and by the author, he himself took care of the distribution of his work. Conversely, French publisher Lévy solicited Conscience's guidance in finding suitable Belgian translators in French (D'hulst 2013: 258–260).

Secondly, publishers strove for a gradual containment if not assimilation of Conscience's work in the target cultures. They contributed to this by weakening or disguising the reference to the author's foreign extraction, or by suppressing the translator's name. This happened with Lévy in France. In 1857, the title page of one of the novels reads as follows: 'Henri Conscience / traduction Léon Wocquier / *Le démon de l'argent*' (Henri Conscience / translation Léon Wocquier / The demon of money, 1857). In 1869, another translation is presented as follows: '*La Fiancée du maître d'école* / par / Henri Conscience' (The fiancée of the schoolmaster / by / Henri Conscience, 1869). The same occurs in Italy, no doubt because of the French assimilation strategy (Dagnino 2013: 336), as well as in the United States (Boyden and Vandenbussche 2012: 27). As numerous letters witness, the author himself sustained adaptation by encouraging changes to be made by the translators, by allowing selective groupings of his works, to some extent also by preformatting his own writing in view of fitting the image already established.[16] The effect was a smooth integration, as noted by French lexicographer Larousse, who mentions thematic and stylistic affinities between the source and target literatures:

> Tous ses livres, et nous le constatons malgré le dédain de M. Conscience pour notre langue, tous ses livres, bien que portant en eux le parfum du terroir, et marqués au cachet d'une originalité native incontestable, sont français par bien des côtés, n'en déplaise à leur auteur, et principalement par le tour vif et rapide du récit, la grâce des caractères, le brillant des descriptions, et l'intérêt savamment ménagé de la composition. C'est pourquoi la littérature française a adopté M. Conscience, non comme un étranger, mais comme un enfant prodigue longtemps absent du foyer paternel et dont on fête le retour.[17] (Larousse 1869: 970)

From the 1850s onwards, publishers made use of vertically integrated strategies, which become the norm and were copied internationally. An example of such a strategy is that designed by Michel Lévy frères (cf. Mollier 2005). It applies four criteria: (1) attract well-established authors, (2) offer high quality translations,[18] (3) sell at a reasonable price that is lower than average before the 1850s (think of Lévy's *Collection à un franc*, i.e. a collection of books that cost one franc each), and (4) put together strong literary collections. Let us consider the last two criteria. Low prices guarantee high sales figures. To lower production costs, the quality of the paper, typography and cover are downsized, as is the format of the book. Additional income is generated by publicity on the back cover or in a quire. Obviously, such measures bring about a depreciation of the book, a consequence that correlates with the repositioning of the genre and the author within the field of popular literature as well as with the changing status of the material object and reading habits: literature becomes portable (to be carried on the train, hence called *littérature de gare* or railway literature[19]).

The effect of assembling books in collections is considerable, as witnessed by the *Œuvres complètes de Henri Conscience*. Similar groupings burgeon elsewhere, for example in Germany, Italy and England. In England, for instance, publisher Lambert & Co issued a set of volumes labelled *Conscience's Tales and Romances* in the series *The Amusing Library*, presenting them as 'neat pocket volumes for home or railway, also for presents or prizes, containing original tales; also translations and reprints of popular works' (quoted in Calis 2013: 301). In the same vein, numerous German publishers group translations of Dutch or Flemish literature from the late 1840s on, such as the *Sammlung der neuesten flämischen Romane und Novellen* (Collection of the newest Flemish novels and novellas), the *Niederländische Bibliothek*, (the Dutch Library), etc. English collections sport a broader range of authors, for example the *Miscellany of Foreign Literature, Half-hours with Foreign Authors, Duffy's Popular Library*, etc. Similarly, in Italy, publisher Sonzogno's series in which Conscience was associated with a group of French authors seems particularly attractive (Dagnino 2013: 341-346), to the extent that Sonzogno acquired the monopoly to publish translations of French authors that were members of the Société des Gens de Lettres (Society of Men of Letters). He looked for close collaboration with other publishers, and created a subsidiary in Paris. Clearly, exchanges between publishers need further investigation.[20]

A syncretic identity?

The third issue to be addressed briefly here is ideological: during the 1840s and 1850s Conscience shaped an urban and a rural subgenre of the story of manners, exalting models of Christian morality, putting up resistance to the growing tides of liberalism and socialism, defending his Flemish cultural minority against massive French literary imports and cultural hegemony. These features are common ground, being reproduced from culture to culture, while additional elements are added or foregrounded according to the situation in hand.

Early critics, publishers and translators, like Von Diepenbrock, suggest a high degree of cultural and historical affinity between Flanders, the Netherlands and Germany, if not a comprehensive sort of pan-Germanism that may extend as far as to include Scandinavia (Broomans 2013). The suggestion of a historically engrained and shared cultural identity empowers the claims for recognition by the smaller and peripheral ethnic and language communities that are part of it. As we know, these claims are political and cultural, but in their early phase they focus predominantly on cultural issues (Hroch 1985). Hence, Flemish literature promoting a Flemish identity opposed to French domination was attractive to many young European nations. But alliances change: invoking and translating Flemish literature was a way for Czech national identity to affirm itself against German domination, as happened with Czech translator Jakub Malý when referring in his 1846 translation of *Siska van Roosemael* to the Latin saying: *Mutatis mutandis de te fabula narratur* (with the necessary changes, the story applies to you; quoted in Engelbrecht 2016: 84). Translating Conscience is claiming acknowledgement: like Flemish identity, Czech identity bears on a national language and literature.

In Italy, German translations are accepted as tokens of recognition of Flemish literature. The Italian translations are not framed as antidotes to French cultural domination. After all, Italian literature is less of a 'periphery' than is its Flemish counterpart. Translations of Conscience are also supposed to embody values of morality, veracity and recognizability. These were already at the heart of Manzoni's *Promessi sposi* (1840): *vero* (true), *interessante* (interesting) and *utile* (useful), and are repeatedly put forward by translators Tommaso Gar and Nicola Negrelli (Dagnino 2013: 338–339).

Across the Atlantic, the rhizomatic pattern of expansion and replication applied almost identically to ideology, i.e. texts were transferred together with the functions already attributed to them in England, and as we have seen those were already aggregated by German translations. As occurred within smaller European spaces, translations, their readings and valuations spread rapidly through numerous reprints. Both *Graham's Magazine* and *The Living Age* in 1852 reused Mary Howitt's translation of Conscience's *Blind Rosa* issued the same year by Sharpe's *London Magazine*. As a consequence, the early image of the Flemish nationalist and conservative writer lasted much longer than that of the later Conscience, that of his liberalist and social turn of the 1850s: it was based on a small set of elements strongly embedded in many cultures, thanks to efficient publishing policies. In spite of his own liberalist turn of the 1850s, Conscience will be confined in the posture of a regional writer of novels of manners and one historical novel. No doubt the solidity of this image explains its lack of flexibility and hence Conscience's rapid oblivion once other literary models and ideologies took over.

And what about the fate of Conscience in his own language area? In the Netherlands, his work was welcomed and even reached broad reading circles. Yet he was also criticized as being too Flemish, too Catholic and too insignificant in both social and literary terms, a writer at best comparable to Dutch writers using a regional dialect (Van Kalmthout 2013: 406). As to Belgium, Conscience no doubt acquired a strong national function in both the Flemish and francophone regions, united against

French cultural hegemony (cf. D'hulst 2013). One may point out differences between the reception in the north and south, but they are overruled by the awareness of the international recognition of a small and vulnerable but courageous nation. Conscience thus became a forerunner of the famous *âme belge* (Belgian soul), i.e. the myth of a syncretic identity composed of Germanic and Romance features, one that propelled Belgian literature into the limelight of the European literary and cultural scene around the turn of the century, by the less forgotten generation of Symbolist poets Maurice Maeterlinck, Georges Rodenbach and Emile Verhaeren.

Conclusion

Conscience's international career seems to contradict a well-known thesis of translation sociology, i.e. that the relation between intranslation and extranslation is an asymmetrical one: the more a language in-translates, the more its position among other languages is peripheral; the more it ex-translates, the more its position is central.[21] Conscience is one of the most ex-translated authors of the second half of the nineteenth century, although his mother tongue is one of the more peripheral national languages of Europe. Unquestionably, one should not forget that the translations made into the central languages, German and French, actually serve as source texts (or indirect translations) in view of the broader European and North American dissemination of the Flemish originals. Be that as it may, there are no other examples of Flemish or even Dutch writers turning global during the same period. Does that make Conscience a unique case?

In fact, the thesis referred to above derives from an analysis of contemporary translation flows. We do not have access to similar data for the nineteenth century. The same remark applies to the book industry and publishing and distributing practices: they resist transhistorical generalizations. And so it is worthwhile to launch a comparative perspective, testing modern sociology or book history driven methods against past practices, for example the transnational novel and theatre circulation in Europe during the eighteenth and nineteenth centuries (e.g. Moretti 2006; Charle 2012). Such a perspective naturally will have to be contextualized, i.e. historicized.[22] Many issues need specific attention. To name but a few: strong changes in print technology during the second half of the century; unequal establishment and application of copyright and translation rights over cultures; the evolution of the hierarchy of higher and lower literatures, the distinctions between literature and other media, and between adult and children's literature, alongside the very status of literature, the spread of literacy and readership, etc.

In addition, religious, political or didactic institutions influence publishers' and other mediators' decision-making processes as to which books they select for translation or how translations should be carried out, distributed, at what cost and so forth.[23] Correlatively, the distinction between the three levels of literary circulation, made by amongst others Van Es and Heilbron,[24] may be maintained on the condition that one assumes that none of the three possesses the same amount or type of stability, organization and autonomy that one may attribute to them within a field approach that is particularly familiar with translations published or circulating at the end of the twentieth and the beginning of the twenty-first centuries.

As this study may have shown, there is a sequence of intertwined effects at all levels. The language system is the macro-level: German and French are the dominant European languages at the time and serve as de facto carriers of Conscience's work. At the meso-level, dissemination is facilitated if not enabled by an efficient publishing system that extends beyond national borders. At the micro-level, agents mediate across languages and areas. Yet deeper inquiry into translated texts is needed, and in particular the underlying poetics and politics. These may be seen as effects of the other levels but also as serving other purposes. In this respect, the cross-cultural position of many translations is quite interesting: they operate either as substitutes, or second-hand translations or even as originals in their own right. Likewise, the mobility and incorporation of translations in national literatures that share the same language (such as francophone Belgium, France or Switzerland, England and America, Flemish Belgium and the Netherlands) become original topics of study. They may bring us a step closer to a better understanding of the history of global circulation through translation.[25]

Notes

1. I will adopt throughout this chapter the most commonly used term during the nineteenth century, i.e. 'Flemish', to indicate the southern variant of the Dutch language and its literature. In addition, and with regard to the terms 'Flanders' and 'Belgium', it is good to take into account that Belgium's independence in 1830 created a multilingual state, and thus a complex environment in which national belonging entered into conflict with the unequal language status of Flemish and French (amongst others see Witte and Van Velthoven 1998). In a sense, Conscience's work was at the same time a binding element between both communities and a claim for recognition of the subjugated Flemish language and literature.
2. Curiously enough, since his work has fallen into the public domain, digital libraries such a Kindle, iBooks, Google Books, The Internet Archive, Project Gutenberg, etc. offer open access to older editions of Conscience's work, in many languages.
3. I am indebted to the considerable previous work that has been achieved on the reception of Conscience in different languages and literatures.
4. To some extent also vice versa: exchanges with publishers and translators have impacted on later auctorial postures. Our focus here will be on the first direction.
5. As we know, the rhizome metaphor had been introduced by Deleuze and Guattari (1980), as a shortcut for a conception of knowledge that rejects a binary and hierarchic or tree-like way of representing reality. By extension, it may qualify as a principle of connection and multidirectionality that features complex translation flows (see also D'hulst 2018a).
6. It became Wroclaw, in Western Poland, after the Second World War. There isn't space in this chapter to unfold the broader set of mediating relations in which this pattern emerged and took form. For instance, a few years before Diepenbrock discovered

Conscience and published his translations, Hoffmann von Fallersleben had issued, also in Breslau, a collection of Dutch songs and theatre texts testifying to the strong historical and cultural bond between Germany, the Netherlands and Belgium (D'hulst 2018b).

7 According to George Eekhoud, the author of a biography resulting from a long interview with the author, the three books were given to Diepenbrock by a certain Countess Von Dornabey (1881: 66–67), while Conscience himself engaged in an epistolary exchange with Von Diepenbrock (Nowack 1933: 399). Another, more plausible name, suggested by Herbert van Uffelen (1993a: 54, 81, is that of German poet Luise von Plönnies, who travelled in Belgium and visited Conscience, to whom she dedicated a volume of *Reise-Erinnerungen aus Belgien* issued in Berlin in 1845 (https://dlbt.univie.ac.at/digital-libraries-and-bibliographies/showcases/hendrik-conscience-flaemisches-stillleben/publication-history/ (accessed 3 September 2018).

8 'One may truly say that these booklets were not "sold off", but actually 'fought for. An inexplicable charm pends from his pen, from his lips' (my translation).

9 The very first translation in German was published in 1842 in a small journal *Die Grenzboten*, published in Brussels, by Ignaz Kuranda, a correspondent of the *Augsburger Allgemeine Zeitung* (Ceuppens 2013: 238–329). It is unclear whether there is a link between Kuranda and Von Diepenbrock.

10 As an influential member of the church, Diepenbrock favoured the dissemination of his translations in Catholic Germany, as well as the Austrian Empire, most notably by freely distributing 14,000 copies of his translation (Engelbrecht 2016: 246).

11 The recently designed DLBT (Digital library and bibliography for literature in translation, https://dlbt.univie.ac.at/) contains an impressive database of translations of amongst others Concience's work, including a well-documented showcase of Diepenbrocks' *Flämisches Stillleben* (https://dlbt.univie.ac.at/digital-libraries-and-bibliographies/showcases/hendrik-conscience-flaemisches-stillleben/ (accessed 3 September 2018)).

12 'We announce with great pleasure to our readers that, thanks to the three Flemish novellas published in our journal, the name of Conscience has acquired enough publicity and stir in France to make M. Michel Lévy buy not only the rights of all his writings, but also of all his future writings' (my translation).

13 These are less known, but one may safely assume that arrangements with author and translator vary greatly (see amongst others Keersmaekers 2009), at least before the signing of the Berne Convention of 1886, mandating major aspects of copyright law.

14 This process of interdisciplinary spill-over or transfer requires further analysis, more so since it is also cross-cultural.

15 Still, one has to wait until 1920 to see Conscience replaced by Felix Timmermans as the most translated Flemish author in German.

16 In this respect, it would be interesting to look more closely at the content of conferences and letters by Conscience himself, with regard to his work and its distribution. See also Hermans 2011: 30 *ff.*

17 'All his works – and we ascertain this in spite of the disdain of M. Conscience for our language – are French in more than one respect, even if they carry the perfume of their native land and bear the marks of an undeniable native originality: principally because of the vivid and swift stroll of the narration, the grace of the characters, the brilliant descriptions, and the skilful composition. These are the reasons why French literature has adopted Henri Conscience, not as a stranger, but as the prodigal son celebrated on his return home after a long absence' (my translation).

18 Baudelaire is the translator of Poe, Pichot of Dickens, Guizot of historical works. Translators get a contract with Lévy. In Conscience's case, royalties paid to the author equal those paid to the translator (Keersmaekers 2009: 84).
19 Publisher Hachette created a *Bibliothèque des chemins de fer* (Library of the railways) in 1852 (cf. Parinet 1993: 96 *ff.*). See also Lambert 1980.
20 The same holds for reading rooms and lending libraries, which played an influential role in Germany according to Van Uffelen (1993a: 59).
21 Cf. Heilbron and Sapiro: 'While dominant countries "export" their cultural products and translate little into their languages, dominated countries export little and import a substantial number of foreign books, principally by translation' (2016: 381). See also A. de Swaan 2001.
22 As acknowledged from a theoretical viewpoint by Van Es and Heilbron with regard to the access of peripheral Dutch literature to the centre: 'The involvement of (to varying extents) transnational intermediary actors, events and institutions such as international publishers, literary agents and book fairs such as the *Frankfurter Buchmesse*, is indispensable for Dutch authors to be able to transcend the boundaries imposed on each of the aforementioned levels in order to become consecrated into the English-language literary field' (2015: 298).
23 Not to forget the issues of production and distribution techniques, copyright, censorship, reading, second-hand libraries, etc. (Mollier 2015).
24 'The macro level pertains to the center-periphery structure of the global translation system and the balance of power between the language groups and countries that form this system. The meso level concerns the predominantly national publishing fields and the strategies different publishing houses use to acquire translation and publishing rights. The micro level, finally, concerns the role of the various actors who are effectively involved in the selection (publishers, editors), translation (translators) and framing (publishers, literary critics) of particular books' (Van Es and Heilbron 2015: 298).
25 Bibliographies like those established by Arents (1931, 1944, 1950) and Van Uffelen (1993b) need to be resumed for many other languages. I sincerely thank Heleen van Gerwen for her careful language revision.

References

Andringa, K. (2013), 'Grote scheppen zoete broodpap: de receptie van Hendrik Conscience in Frankrijk', *Verslagen & mededelingen van de KANTL* 123 (2–3): 273–296.
Arents, P. (1931), 'Hendrik Conscience: vertalingen in het Fransch', *Mededeelingen van de Stedelijke Hoofdbibliotheek* 4 (1–2): 110–121.
Arents, P. (1944), *De Vlaamsche schrijvers in het Duitsch vertaald*, Brussels: De lage landen.
Arents, P. (1950), *De Vlaamsche schrijvers in het Engels vertaald 1781–1949*, Gent: Koninklijke Vlaamse academie voor taal- en letterkunde.
Berg, W. van den and P. Couttenier (2009), *Alles is taal geworden. Geschiedenis van de Nederlandse literatuur, 1800–1900*, Amsterdam: Uitgeverij Bert Bakker.

Boyden, M. and L. Vandenbussche (2012), 'Translating the American West into English: The Case of Hendrik Conscience's *Het Goudland*', *Western American Literature* 47 (1): 22-44.
Broomans, P. (2013), 'De Leeuw van Vlaenderen en ander werk van Henrik Conscience in het Noorden. De invloed van literaire ontwikkelingen op contemporaine en late vertalingen', *Verslagen & mededelingen van de KANTL* 123 (2-3): 367-387.
Calis, K. (2013), 'Meer melk dan vlees? Sporen van Hendrik Conscience in Engeland en Amerika', *Verslagen & mededelingen van de KANTL* 123 (2-3): 297-319.
Ceuppens, J. (2013), 'De Germaanse leeuw. Consciences *Leeuw van Vlaenderen* als inzet van Duits-Vlaamse betrekkingen 1840-1918', *Verslagen & mededelingen van de KANTL* 123 (2-3): 233-247.
Charle, C. (2012), 'Circulations théâtrales entre Paris, Vienne, Berlin, Munich et Stuttgart (1815-1860). Essai de mesure et d'interprétation d'un échange inégal', in N. Bachleitner and M.G. Hall (eds), '*Die Bienen fremder Literaturen*'. *Der literarische Transfer zwischen Großbritannien, Frankreich und dem deutschprachigen Raum im Zeitalter der Weltliteratur (1770-1850)*, 229-260, Wiesbaden: O. Harrassowitz.
Conscience, H. (1838), *De Leeuw van Vlaenderen of de Slag der Gulden Sporen*, Antwerp: De Cort.
Conscience, H. (1843a), *Hoe men schilder wordt. Eene ware geschiedenis van eenen schilder die nog leeft*, Antwerp: J.E. Buschmann.
Conscience, H. (1843b), *Wat eene moeder lyden kan. Eene ware geschiedenis*, Antwerp: J.E. Buschmann.
Conscience, H. (1844), *Siska van Roosemael. Ware geschiedenis van eene jufvrouw die nog leeft*, Antwerp: J.E. Buschmann.
Conscience, H. (1845a), *Flämisches Stillleben, in drei kleinen Erzählungen* von Heinrich Conscience. Aus dem Flämischen übersetzt von Melchior Diepenbrock, Regensburg: Friedrich Pustet.
Conscience, H. (1845b), *Sketches from Flemish life in Three Tales*, trans. N. Trübner, London: Longman.
Conscience, H. (1846), 'Siska van Roosemael', in *Sketches from Flemish Life, in Three Tales: Translated from the Flemish of Hendrik Conscience*, trans. N. Trübner, 1-88, London: Longman.
Conscience, H. (1850) *De loteling*, Antwerp: J.E. Buschmann.
Conscience, H. (1856-1875), *Hendrik Conscience's Short Tales*, Baltimore: John Murphy & Co.
Conscience, H. (1857), *Le démon de l'argent*, Paris: Lévy frères.
Conscience, H. (1869), *La Fiancée du maître d'école*, Paris: Lévy frères.
Dagnino, R. (2013), 'Een genoeglijk avontuur. De Italiaanse vertalingen van 'Enrico' Conscience (1846-1967)', *Verslagen & mededelingen van de KANTL* 123 (2-3): 335-366.
Deleuze, G. and F. Guattari (1980), *Mille Plateaux*, Paris: Les Éditions de Minuit.
D'hulst, L. (2013), 'Over de negentiende-eeuwse Belgische en Franse vertalingen van Consciences verhalend proza', *Verslagen & mededelingen van de KANTL* 123 (2-3): 249-272.
D'hulst, L. (2018a), 'Translation and Space. A Historical Viewpoint and a Case Study', in A.J. Escher and H.C. Spickermann (eds), *Perspektiven der Interkulturalität. Forschungsfelder eines umstrittenen Begriffs*, 197-212, Heidelberg: Universitätsverlag Winter.
D'hulst, L. (2018b), 'Mediating Flemish Folk Songs Across Cultural Borders During the Nineteenth Century: From Patrimonial Monuments to Musical Propaganda', in

D. Roig-Sanz and R. Meylaerts (eds), *Literary Translation and Cultural Mediators in 'Peripheral' Cultures*, 235–262, Dordrecht: Springer Verlag.

D'hulst, L., M. Gonne, T. Lobbes, R. Meylaerts and T. Verschaffel (2014), 'Towards a Multipolar Model of Cultural Mediators Within Multicultural Spaces. Cultural Mediators in Belgium, 1830-1945', *Revue belge de philologie et d'histoire/Belgisch Tijdschrift voor Filologie en Geschiedenis* 92 (4): 1255–1275.

Dumas, A. (1852), *Conscience l'innocent* (Conscience the innocent), Brussels: C. Muquardt.

Dumas, A. (1854), *Le Mousquetaire, Le journal d'Alexandre Dumas*, 4–11 January 1854.

Eekhoud, G. (1881), *Henri Conscience*, Brussels: Lebègue.

Engelbrecht, W. (2016), 'De Tsjechische Conscience', in K. Humbeeck, K. Absillis and J. Weijermars (eds), *De Grote Onleesbare. Hendrik Conscience herdacht*, 239–263, Gent: Academia Press.

Es, N. van and J. Heilbron (2015), 'Fiction from the Periphery: How Dutch Writers Enter the Field of English-Language Literature', *Cultural Sociology* 9 (3): 296–319.

Even-Zohar, I. (1990), 'Polysystem Studies', special issue of *Poetics Today*, 11 (1).

Fischer, B., ed. (2003), *Die Augsburger 'Allgemeine Zeitung' 1798–1866*, Berlin: De Gruyter.

Frank A.P. and B. Schultze (2004), 'Historische Übersetzungsreihen I: Kometenschweifstudien', in A.P. Frank and H. Turk (eds), *Die literarische Übersetzung in Deutschland. Studien zu ihrer Kulturgeschichte in der Neuzeit*, 71–92, Berlin: Erich Schmidt.

Heilbron, J. and G. Sapiro (2016), 'Translation: Economic and Sociological perspectives', in V. Ginsburgh and S. Weber (eds), *The Palgrave Handbook of Economics and Language*, 373–402, London: Palgrave Macmillan.

Hermans, T. (2011), '"Tusschen europeaensche vermaerdheden": het vertalen van Hendrik Conscience', *Filter, tijdschrift over vertalen*, 18 (3): 27–34.

Hermans, T. (2014), "The Highs and Lows of Hendrik Conscience', *The Low Countries* 22: 162–9.

Hroch, M. (1985), *Social Preconditions of National Revival in Europe. A Comparative Analysis of the Social Composition of Patriotic Groups among the Smaller European Nations*, Cambridge: Cambridge University Press.

Humbeeck, K., K. Absillis and J. Weijermars, eds (2016), *De Grote Onleesbare. Hendrik Conscience herdacht*, Gent: Academia Press.

Huylebrouck, R. (1984), 'Conscience in het Portugees', *Ons Erfdeel* 27 (2): 301–303.

Kalmthout, T. van (2013), 'Een meester in het minder grootse genre der novelle. Het onthaal van Hendrik Conscience in Nederland, 1849–1883', *Verslagen & mededelingen van de KANTL* 123 (2-3): 389–412.

Keersmaekers, A. (2009), *Hendrik Conscience. De Muze en de Mammon*, Gent: Koninklijke Academie voor Nederlandse Taal- en Letterkunde.

Lambert, J. (1980), 'De verspreiding van Nederlandse literatuur in Frankrijk: enkele beschouwingen', *Ons Erfdeel* 23 (1): 74–86.

Larousse, P. (1869), *Grand Dictionnaire universel du XIXe siècle*, vol. IV, Paris: Administration du Grand Dictionnaire universel.

Leerssen, J. (2011), 'Viral Nationalism: Romantic Intellectuals on the Move in Nineteenth-century Europe', *Nations and Nationalism* 17 (2): 257–271.

Mollier, J.-Y. (2005), 'Les réseaux de libraires européens au milieu du XIXe siècle: l'exemple des correspondants de la maison d'édition Michel Lévy Frères, de Paris', in F. Barbier (ed.), *Est-Ouest: Transferts et réceptions dans le monde du livre en Europe, XVII*ᵉ*-XX*ᵉ *siècle*, 125-139, Leipzig: Leipziger Universitätsverlag.

Mollier, J.-Y. (2015), 'L'histoire de l'édition, du livre et de la lecture en France de la fin du XVIIIᵉ siècle au début du XXIᵉ siècle: approche bibliographique', *HAL, Archive ouverte en Sciences de l'Homme et de la Société*. Available online: https://halshs.archives-ouvertes.fr/halshs-01164765 (accessed 25 April 2018).

Moretti, F., ed. (2006), *The Novel*, 2 vols, Princeton, NJ: Princeton University Press.

Nowack, A. (1933), 'Brieven van Hendrik Conscience aan Melchior Baron von Diepenbrock, prinsbisschop van Breslau, uit het Erzbischöfliches Diözesan-Archiv te Breslau', *Verslagen en mededelingen van de Koninklijke Vlaamse Academie voor Taal- en Letterkunde*, June 1933: 399-415.

Parinet, É. (1993), 'Les bibliothèques de gare, un nouveau réseau pour le livre', *Romantisme* 80: 95-106.

Saguer, E. (2013), 'Hoe Hendrik Conscience Spanje veroverde', *Verslagen & mededelingen van de KANTL* 123 (2-3): 321-334.

Snellaert, F.A. (1844), 'Die flämische Literatur und ihre hervorragenden Schriftsteller', *Augsburger Allgemeine Zeitung*, 11 July: 1539-1540.

Swaan, A. de (2001), *Words of the World: The Global Language System*, Cambridge: Polity Press.

Uffelen, H. van (1993a), *Moderne niederländische Literatur im deutschen Sprachraum 1830-1990*, Munich: LiT.

Uffelen, H. van (1993b), *Bibliographie der modernen niederländischen Literatur in deutscher Übersetzung, 1830-1900*, Munich: LiT.

Vaillant, A. (2005), *La Crise de la littérature: romantisme et modernité*, Grenoble: ELLUG.

Wellens, O. (1982), 'De kritische receptie van Conscience in Engeland', *Handelingen van de Koninklijke Zuidnederlandse Maatschappij voor Taal- en Letterkunde en Geschiedenis* 36: 259-271.

Witte, E. and H. van Velthoven (1998), *Strijden om taal. De Belgische taalkwestie in historisch perspectief*, Brussels: VUBpress.

Zellweger, R. (1941), *Les debuts du roman rustique: Suisse-Allemagne-France, 1836-1856*, Geneva: Droz.

9

Louis Couperus in Translation

Ruud Veen

Introduction

In his own time Louis Couperus (1863–1923) was one the most frequently translated Dutch-language authors. This was due not only to the quality of his work. Other elements played a role as well. In most research concerning the place an author occupies in the field of world literature the focus lies on the author himself, the quality of his work, and how the latter has been received. In my own research into the reception of Couperus in Germany I looked, rather, at the role translators and publishers played (Veen 2015). This led to a different perspective: after all, it is the publishers that decide whether or not they want to publish a particular work. It turned out that the role of the translator was much more important than the name of the original author or the quality of his or her work. In the period from 1880 until the Second World War, and especially so in the more important or larger language areas, it is not the publishers that take the initiative to have one or other work translated. It is the translators that take the risk and expense upon themselves of making a translation, which they then try to place with a publisher. In smaller language areas, comparatively speaking, more works in translation were published than in larger language areas such as the English area. One of the reasons is that in those larger language areas there are simply more highly qualitative native works available. The reason larger language areas still felt the need for translated work is in large part due to newspapers and periodicals running *feuilletons* or serials of complete works. I will return to this. First, I offer a survey of Couperus translations. I then briefly discuss Couperus and his work. Subsequently I turn to who took the initiative to translate Couperus. Finally, I address why publishers took on translations.

The first translations

Couperus was just short of 25 years old when in 1887 the first German translation of one of his work appeared: the sonnet 'Indisches dolce far niente' from his first volume of poems, *Een Lent van Vaersen* (A Ribbon of Verse). As far as we know, this sonnet, an item in the final chapter, 'Anthologie aus den Dichtern der Gegenwart', of Lina Schneider's *Geschichte der niederländischen Litteratur* (1887: 839) is also the very first translation of anything by Couperus. His first novel to be translated was *Noodlot* (Fate) which appeared in English in both the UK and the USA in 1891, and in German the following year. Since then Couperus has been translated into numerous languages. *Noodlot* and *Majesteit* (Majesty) top the list as his most frequently translated works.

Table 9.1 shows that up to 1973 Couperus had been translated into twelve languages, covering thirty-one of the forty-seven titles Couperus has to his name. In the last decade of the nineteenth century translations appeared in various languages. The bulk of translations however appeared between 1914 and 1930. Except for some reprints, nothing more appears until 1945. After the Second World War and until 1973 only four titles were published in new translations. In 1973 the copyright to Couperus's works expired, and from then on some new translations started appearing, but they fall outside the scope of the present article.

Table 9.1 also shows that in Germany twelve out of the twenty-three translated titles were reprinted at least once. The most successful title in Germany was *Heliogabal* (*De berg van licht*). In the United States pride of place went to 'Small Souls', the first part of *De boeken der kleine zielen* (The Books of Small Souls). Some interesting conclusions can be drawn from Table 9.2. The so-called 'Haagse romans' (The Hague novels) – *Eline Vere*, *De boeken der kleine zielen* and *Van oude menschen, de dingen, die voorbij gaan* (Of Old People the Things that Pass) – remained unpublished in Germany, while two of these were reprinted at least once in the USA. This lends support to findings that literary taste and culture differ from country to country (Fraser and Hammond 2008). To gauge the significance of Couperus in translation Table 9.2, the data for which I take from Johan Heilbron, Wouter de Nooy and W. Tichelaar (1995), and Barbara Kastner (2005), is revealing.

From Table 9.2 it is clear that German was the main target language for Couperus translations, and that the 1920s mark the highwater point of Couperus translations into various languages. In English, most translations appeared between 1910 and 1929. It should be mentioned that in this table no account has been taken of anthologies in which work by Couperus may have featured. Overall, though, the number of translations is rather scant, and consequently the influence of Couperus seems to have been restricted. Still, the fact that translations of Couperus were available in German, English, Hungarian and Norwegian shortly after the publication of the Dutch originals is remarkable. A possible explanation might be that readers in the countries involved felt a need for innovative fiction from abroad.

Table 9.1 Survey translations of books until 1973

Year Dutch	Title in Dutch	German	English GB	English USA	French	Finish	Italian	Spanish	Hun.	Czech	Croat	Polish	Norwegian	Swedish	Number of Languages
1889	Eline Vere		1892	1892									1893		2
1891	Noodlot	1892	1891[2]	1891[3]					1893	1897	1915	1903		1900	7
1892	Extaze	1894[2]	1892[2]	1919											2
1892	Eene Illusie*	1897													1
1893	Majesteit	1895[2]	1894	1895[2]	1898		1900[2]	1904					1895	1895	7
1895	Wereldvrede	1895[2]			1899		1902[3]					1906		1915	5
1896	Hooge troeven*	1897													1
1898	Psyche	1924	1908		1923[5]				1925						4
1899	Fidessa								1927						1
1900	Langs lijnen	1921	1921[2]	1920[2]											2
1900	De stille kracht	1902[4]	1922	1921[2]									1916		3
1901	Babel	1920[3]													1
1901	Boeken kleine zielen 1		1914	1914[8]											1
1902	Boeken kleine zielen 2		1915	1915[4]											1
1903	Boeken kleine zielen 3		1917	1917[3]											1
1904	Boeken kleine zielen 4		1918	1918[2]											1
1904	Dionyzos	1920[2]													1

Year Dutch	Title in Dutch	German	English GB	English USA	French	Finish	Italian	Spanish	Hun.	Czech	Croat	Polish	Norwegian	Swedish	Number of Languages
1905	Berg van het licht	1916[8]						1946	1918[2]	1922					4
1906	Van oude men-schen		1918[6]	1918[3]	1973	1924	1946					1966			5
1908	Aan de weg der vreugde	1920													1
1911	Antiek toerisme	1920[4]	1920	1920											2
1912	Lucrezia (from: Schimmen)	1926													1
1913	Herakles	1923													1
1915	De ongelukkige	1921													1
1917	Komedianten	1919[3]	1926	1926					1921						3
1918	De verliefde ezel	1920[3]									1923				2
1919	Xerxes	1919[2]		1930											2
1920	Iskander	1925[5]													1
1922	Het zwevende schaakbord	1921[3]													1
1924	Oostwaarts	1926	1924	1924											2
1925	Nippon	1929	1926[2]	1926											2
	Number per language	23	16+1 18 titles	16	4	1	3	2	5	2	2	3	3	3	69

Note: *Together in one German collection. In England in 1924 a book published with the four parts of *The Book of the Small Souls*, reprinted in 1942. Superscript number means the number of reprints. In case of the four books of the *Small Souls* it is excluding the complete book with the four parts. book was published with short stories from several books of Couperus. In the USA in 1932 a complete book published with the four parts.

Table 9.2 Number of literary translations from the dutch to other languages (1900–1949)

Language	Before 1900	1900–09		1910–19		1920–29		1930–39		1940–49		Total	
	C		C		C		C		C		C	1900–49	C 1900–49
German	-5	80	-1	32	-3	78	-14	114		90		656	-18
English	-4	8	-1	20	-7	40	-7	67	-1	51		243	-16
Finnish		0		0		1	-1	15		9		25	-1
French	-2	14		2		8	-1	19		39		139	-1
Italian		4	-2	0		5		6		12	-1	37	-3
Spanish		0	-1	0		0		1		1	-1	22	-2
Hungarian	-1	1		1	-1	3	-3	7		5		24	-4
Czech	-1	3		3		3	-1	25		24		63	-1
Croat		nb		nb	-1	nb	-1	nb		nb		nb	-2
Polish		3	-2	1		0		17		3		31	-2
Norwegian	-2	0		2	-1	3		11		33		95	-1
Swedish	-1	5	-1	3	-1	11		48		45		165	-2
Total	-16	118	-8	64	-14	151	-28	315	-1	303	-2	1500	-53

Note: C = Couperus.

Louis Couperus

Louis Marie-Anne Couperus was born on 10 June 1863 and died on 16 July 1923. His father was a high civil servant in the Dutch East-Indies. Couperus spent part of his youth in Batavia, present-day Djakarta. It is there that he met his niece Elisabeth Baud (1867–1960), whom he married in the Netherlands in 1891. As of 1883 his poems appeared in newspapers and periodicals. A first collection, *Een Lent van Vaersen*, appeared in 1884 (Couperus 1884). A second collection, *Orchideeën* (Orchids, 1886) contained, next to poems, short stories. *Eline Vere*, his first novel, was serialized in *Het Vaderland* in 1888, and appeared in book form in 1889 (Couperus 1889). He first made contact with L.J. Veen, who would become his main publisher, in 1890. Couperus had to earn a living with his writing, and he kept up a steady production: from 1892 to his death there appear one or more new titles every year. He also served as editor of *De Gids* (The Guide), a leading cultural journal at the time, and he was involved with the founding of *Groot Nederland*, another influential magazine. Much of his work first appeared in the latter magazine before being published in book form. Soon after his marriage Couperus started travelling extensively. Except for the First World War he resided abroad for most of his life, mostly in the South of Europe. After the war he travelled to North Africa and the Far East. His many travels and his residence abroad gave Couperus a very international outlook and facilitated extensive contacts with translators and publishers, as well as with other authors.

Couperus was a versatile writer, and his work touches upon a wide array of subjects and genres. Else Otten, in her bibliography in the German edition of *Het zwevende schaakbord* (The Floating Chessboard), follows a categorization of Couperus's works first devised by André de Ridder (Ridder 1917):

Contemporary novels (13)
Eline Vere, 1889; *Noodlot*, 1890; *Eene illuzie*, 1892; *Extaze*, 1892; *Majesteit*, 1893; *Wereldvrede*, 1895; *Hooge troeven*, 1896; *Metamorfoze*, 1897; *De stille kracht*, 1900; *Langs lijnen van geleidelijkheid*, 1900; *De boeken der kleinen zielen*, 4 parts, 1901–1903; *Van oude menschen, de dingen, die voorbij gaan*, 1906; *Aan den weg der vreugde*, 1908.

Historical novels and stories (10)
De berg van licht, 3 parts, 1905–1906; *Antieke verhalen*, 1911; *Antiek toerisme* 1911; *Schimmen van schoonheid*, 1912; *De ongelukkige*, 1915; *De komedianten*, 1917; *Het zwevende schaakbord*, 1918; *De verliefde ezel*, 1918; *Xerxes of de hoogmoed*, 1919; *Iskander, de roman van Alexander de Grote*, 1920.

Mythological novels (3)
God en goden, 1903; *Dionyzos*, 1904; *Herakles*, 1913.

Symbolical and allegorical tales (4)
Psyche, 1898; *Fidessa*, 1899; *Babel*, 1901; *Over lichtende drempels*, 1902.

Serials (8)
Korte Arabesken, 1911; *De zwaluwen neergestreken*, 1911; *Van en over mijzelf en anderen*, 4 parts, 1910–1917; *Van en over alles en iedereen*, 5 parts, 1915; *Legende, mythen en fantazie*, 1918; *De ode*, 1919; *Het snoer der ontferming en Japanse legenden*, 1924; *Proza*, 3 parts, 1923–1925.

Travelogues (5)
Reisimpressies, 1894; *Uit blanke steden, onder blauwe lucht*, 2 parts, 1912–1913; *Met Louis Couperus in Afrika*, 1921; *Oostwaarts*, 1923; *Nippon*, 1925.

Poems (3)
Een Lent van Vaerzen, 1884; *Orchideeën*, 1886; *Willeswinde*, 1895.

Translations (1)
De verzoeking van den H. Antonius, 1896.

There are significant differences between the German and English language areas, the most important ones when it comes to Couperus translations. In both we find translations of nine of Couperus's 'contemporary' novels, but the lists are not identical. Of the historical novels only one has not been translated into German, whereas seven remain untranslated in English. When it comes to other language areas we find that only a few novels have been translated and that comparison is difficult. Hungary takes the lead with five titles. *Noodlot* and *Majesteit* found their way into five smaller language areas. It is important to mention, though, that in addition to book form, translations of work by Couperus also appeared in newspapers, periodicals and anthologies. As more and more of this material is digitized it becomes easier to also trace these translations. We know, for instance, of translations in book form in Hungarian, Spanish and Croat, but currently of no other forms of publication in these languages (Table 9.3).

Instigators and disseminators of translations

In most cases the initiative to translate some text was taken by a translator, and in rare cases by a publisher or by the author himself. From the correspondence of L.J. Veen is it is clear that this publisher took the initiative for translations of *Majesteit* and *Wereldvrede* (World Peace) (Veen 2013). The fact that these titles were available in German and English probably inspired translators of other languages to also tackle them. Couperus was an innovative writer at the turn of the twentieth century, with a literary style all of his own. Once an author had been translated into a major target language, translation into so-called minor languages followed almost automatically. In some cases it is not clear whether translation was from the original Dutch or from the German or English. The Italian translation of *Van oude menschen, de dingen, die voorbij gaan* was made from the English version (Couperus 1946b), including the foreword by Stephen McKenna (1888–1967).

Table 9.3 Publications in papers, magazines and anthologies in language areas with number of titles and passages until 1973

Language	Anthologies	Magazines	Papers	Number of Book Titles	Number of Stories, Poetry and Passages
Catalan		1		2	
Danish	1				1
German	7	8	1	5	21
English	4	2		1	8
Finnish		1			1
French	2	12	2	4	11
Indonesian	1				1
Italian	4				6
Norwegian	1				1
Polish	1				1
Russian		1		4	
Serbian		1			1
Czech	1				1
Swedish			1		1
14	22	26	4	16	54

Two translators stand out from the rest. Else Otten (1873–1931) was born in the Netherlands but moved with her parents abroad and eventually ended up in Germany, where she finished her studies and entered a successful career as a translator. Alexander Teixeira de Mattos (1865–1921) was also born in the Netherlands, moved with his parents to England when he was nine years old, and worked in the publishing industry. In other countries Couperus's works were handled by various translators and by various publishers.

In many countries there flourished around the turn of the twentieth century literary-historical and cultural periodicals that serialized complete novels. Sometimes these were independent ventures. Alternatively, they were part of larger publishing concerns that also published books and newspapers. These periodicals were always in search of high-quality materials, and this led to their interest in translated works of literature. Translators with a good professional network thus had easy access to editors of publishing houses. They also took their cue from one another. *Noodlot* was a favourite with many translators: it appeared in German, English, Hungarian, Czech, Croat, Polish and Swedish. *Majesteit* was also translated into seven languages, and *Wereldvrede* into five. From Table 9.1 we can see that most of these translations appeared around 1900. We also see the same stories returning in different languages in newspapers and periodicals.

After these first successes Couperus's popularity abroad entered a lull in the major language areas. After twelve years there was a revival in Germany with the translation of *De berg van licht* (The Mountain of Light) by Else Otten. She had undertaken this translation on her own initiative, and in 1916 succeeded in placing it with the then well-known Berlin publisher Rütten & Loening (Couperus 1916a). In English, a revival took place with the translation of *De boeken der kleine zielen* (Small Souls) in 1914 in the United States (Couperus 1914a), followed by reprints. This was largely the work of Alexander Teixeira de Mattos, and a result of the collaboration with the publishers Dodd, Mead and Company in New York. This success led to other translators also trying to place works by Couperus with different publishers. As Table 9.1 shows, this strategy achieved some moderate success. As mentioned before, not only editions in book form have to be taken into account when measuring how an author's work is received in a particular language area. Publications in anthologies, newspapers and periodicals also count (Table 9.3). Until 1912 translations from the Dutch enjoyed very little copyright. Hence the possibility for several translators to translate the same work, and place it with different publishers, as happened for instance in the German language area.

The German Language Area

Although Austria and part of Switzerland together with Germany make up the German language area, only German publishers took on work by Couperus. Earlier I mentioned that Lina Schneider included a poem by Couperus in her 1887 *Geschichte der niederländischen Litteratur*. The first translation of a volume by Couperus was done by Paul Bernhard Raché (1869–1939) (Couperus 1892g). He took the initiative to translate *Noodlot*. Paul Bernhard Raché (1869–1939) was the most important champion of Dutch literature, and particularly of Couperus (Grave 2001), in Germany. In the period 1891–1897 he wrote eleven articles on Dutch literature for *Die Gesellschaft*, eight for *Das Magazin für die Litteratur des In- und Auslandes* between 1890 and 1898, and ten for *Das litterarische Echo* between 1898 and 1907, as well as some more for several other newspapers and periodicals. Raché also published original work and translated not only from the Dutch but also from English. In the end, he was more interested in writing articles than in doing translations. Raché translated only two books by Couperus. In 1892 he translated *Noodlot* as *Schicksal* (Couperus 1892g). This translation was first published in *Aus fremden Zungen*, a periodical completely dedicated to translated literature, and published by Deutsche Verlags-Anstalt in Stuttgart. Later the same year it also appeared in book form in a series with the same name as the periodical. Requested to do so by Veen, Couperus's Dutch publisher, he also translated *Wereldvrede* as *Weltfrieden*, published in 1895 by Minden in Dresden (Couperus 1895e). His translation of 'Een Zieltje', from *Eene illuzie*, appeared as 'Ein Seelchen' in the anthology *Addio von Neera und andere Novellen* with Deutsche Verlags-Anstalt in 1894 (Couperus 1894a). In *Aus fremden Zungen* there also still appeared, in 1901, the poem 'Kleopatra' from *Een lent van vaerzen*, in a translation by Otto Hauser (1876–1944) (Couperus 1901a). Hauser also translated many other poems collected in *Die niederlandischen Lyrik von 1875–1900* (Dutch Poetry 1875–1900) (Couperus 1901b). In 1906 his translations also featured in *Die Lyrik des Auslandes in neuerer*

Zeit (Modern Foreign Poetry, Couperus 1906a). He also wrote several articles on contemporary Dutch literature.

Several other translators preceded Else Otten before she became Couperus's dedicated translator. In 1894 Freia Norden translated *Extaze* as *Extase. Ein Buch vom Glück* for Verlag von Alexander Beyer in Dresden (Couperus 1894b). Little is known of Norden except her name. Her translation of *Extaze* was reviewed very negatively by both Couperus and Raché. A year later the same title appeared with Deutsche Verlags-Anstalt as *Ekstase – Roman* in a translation by Ida Frick (Couperus 1895b). The Norden translation had not been authorized but at that time translations from Dutch were not legally protected in Germany. For the translation by Frick, Couperus had given his consent. Frick (1824–?), though born in Germany, had lived a few years in Rotterdam before moving to Munich in 1889. She supported herself by novel writing, under the penname J. Fremann, and producing translations. Couperus's Dutch publisher placed translations of *Majesteit* and *Wereldvrede* with Minden in Dresden. The translation of *Majesteit* as *Majestät* in 1895 was probably the work of V. Heiden (Couperus 1895c). Her name is not listed in the book, but this was a not unusual practice at the time. *Weltfrieden* also appeared in 1895 (Couperus 1895e). Both books were reprinted once. In 1902, and also with Minden, there appeared a translation of *De stille kracht* as *Stille Kraft* (Couperus 1902f). This was the work of Mark von Wengstein, in reality the pseudonym of Marie Luise Wanda Olga Gräfin von Wengersky (1864–1928). Under the same penname she also published novels in 1914, 1915 and 1920. She herself had taken the initiative to translate Couperus's novel and to offer it to Minden, who by then had already published two other novels by the Dutchman. *Stille Kraft* went through four reprints. One year earlier the translation had already appeared in *Aus fremden Zungen*, but apparently Deutsche Verlags-Anstalt did not judge publication in book form profitable, unlike what had happened with *Schicksal*.

Else Otten stepped in on her own initiative when already four titles of Couperus's had appeared in German translation. Eventually, she would deliver eighteen of the twenty-three translations of Couperus in Germany. Otten was multitalented. She had a good voice, was a talented musician, and also mastered, next to German and Dutch of course, French, Spanish and English. She translated professionally from all of these languages, earning a good living. She started on Couperus in 1894, with a translation of *Eene Illuzie*, a collection of stories published in 1892 with Veen (Couperus 1892b). She tried to place the separate stories in periodicals. She may have translated 'Uitzichten' (Views), but apparently did not succeed in getting it accepted for publication. The other stories, and those from another collection, *Hooge troeven* (High Trumps), appeared in various periodicals. In *Die Gegenwart*: 'Kinderseele' (1896), 'Eine Illusion' (1896), 'Die Marquise' (1898), 'Kleine Lebensräthsel' (1900) and 'Hohes Spiel' (1900). In *Neue Deutsche Rundschau*: 'Marquise d'Yéména' (1895) and 'Eine Illusion' (1896). *Das Magazin für die Litteratur des In- und Auslandes* published 'Kleine Rätsel' (1896) and 'Verkündigung' (1898). *Monatsschrift für neue Litteratur und Kunst* serialized 'Hohe Trümpfe' (1897). *Die Zeit* published 'Ein Verlangen' in 1905/1906. In *Welt-Literatur* there appeared 'Ein Seelchen', 'Ein Verlangen' and 'Kleine Rätsel', in 1920. *Novellen* appeared with Verlag Siegfried Cronbach in 1897.

After this first wave, it would take until 1916 before Otten succeeded in placing another novel by Couperus. *Heliogabal*, her translation of *De berg van licht* was accepted by Literarische Anstalt Rütten und Loening in Frankfurt (Couperus 1916a). Over the next two years the novel was reprinted three times. This would lead one to expect this publisher to have more work by Couperus. In fact, the twenty-three works by Couperus that appeared in German translations did so with nineteen different publishers. From 1919 onward, Otten succeeded in placing another title almost every year. In 1919 *Die Komödianten* appeared with Müller (Couperus 1919a) and *Xerxes oder der Hochmut* with Borngräber (Couperus 1919d). *Die Komödianten* was reprinted three times, the last one with Zenith Verlag in 1928, while the second and ultimate reprint of *Xerxes* appeared in 1926 with Oestergaard.

In 1920 there appeared five new titles: *Am wege der Freude* with Ullstein & Co (Couperus 1920a), *Aphrodite in Ägypten* (Couperus 1920b) and *Babel* with Rowohlt (Couperus 1920c), *Dionysos* with Wunderlich (Couperus 1920e) and *Der verliebte Esel* with Borngräber (Couperus 1920d). The first of these was never reprinted, the second went to Reclam in 1926; where it was reprinted three times, the final one in 1930. *Babel* was reprinted twice that same year but not again. *Dionysos* did very badly. Fortunately, the publisher sold the remaining 1,500 copies to the book club Bücherfreunde, where it was repackaged and distributed to its members in 1928. *Der verliebte esel* changed publishers too. It appeared in 1927 with Reclam and was reprinted twice, the last time in 1957.

In 1921 there appeared *Die Lebenskurve* with Vobach (Couperus 1921d), no reprint; *Der Unglückliche* with Müller (Couperus 1921b), no reprint; and *Das Schwebende Schachbrett* with Rowohlt (Couperus 1921a), reprinted in 1923 and 1928 with Zenith Verlag. In 1923, the year Couperus died, VdB Wegweiser, a book club, brought *Herakles*. *Psyche* appeared in 1924 with Feuer Verlag (Couperus 1924e). Reclam in 1925 published *Iskander* (Couperus 1925a), five times reprinted, followed in 1926 by *Lucrezia Borgia* (Couperus 1926d) and *Aphrodite in Ägypten* (Couperus 1926a), the latter transferred from Rowohlt. *Lucrezia Borgia* had earlier appeared in *Reclams Universum, Moderne illustrierte Wochenschrift* (Couperus 1925–1926), introduced by Hans Lebene. It also appeared as number 6,641 in the well-known series *Reclam's Universal Bibliothek*. That same year also saw the publication of *Unter Javas Tropensonne* with the book club DBG (Couperus 1926g). The last new title to appear was *Japanische Streifzüge*, with Oestergaard in 1929 (Couperus 1929a). *Eline Vere* is the only novel of Couperus's to have been published in a newspaper. This happened, in abridged form, in 1893 in the *Magdeburger Zeitung* (Couperus 1893b), and was repeated in 1930.

The English language area

The English language area covers not just the United Kingdom and the United States, but also all and sundry countries where English is spoken. Many of the latter, though, for the longest time could boast but few publishers, and they were served by the established UK publishers catering to the international market. Early on agreements had been reached as to how to divide the market between UK and US publishers. It was the custom that works translated into English appeared more or less simultaneously in the UK and the USA. When the translator had contracted with a UK publisher the latter looked for a partner in the USA and vice versa.

As in Germany with Otten, so too with de Mattos in England. He too was not the first to translate Couperus into English. The first work by Couperus to appear in English is *Noodlot*. Translated by Clara Bell (1834-1925) under the title *Footsteps of Fate* it was brought out in England by Heinemann in London in 1891 (Couperus 1891), and a year later in the United States by D. Appleton and Co., in New York, under the title *Fate* (Couperus 1892f). It was probably Edmund Gosse (1849-1928), who served as editor with Heinemann, who initiated the translation. Gosse was acquainted with the Dutch author Frederik van Eeden (1860-1932), and the latter drew his attention to *Noodlot* when Gosse announced his intention to bring Dutch works in his 'Heinemann's International Library'. The titles in said library were adopted by UK and US book clubs. *Fate* in 1906 came out in one volume together with Hendrik Conscience's *The Lion of Flanders*, and in identical editions, with P.F. Collier & Son in New York and The Cooperative Publication Society in London. In 1892, *Eline Vere* (1889) appeared with Chapman and Hall in London (Couperus 1892c) and Appleton in New York (Couperus 1892d), in a translation by J.T. Grein (1862-1935). Probably requested to do so by the publishers, Grein abridged Couperus's novel by excising a few chapters.

Alexander Teixeira de Mattos (1865-1921) surfaced with a translation of *Extaze* as *Ecstasy - A Study of Happiness*, which appeared in 1892 with Henry and Co in London (Couperus 1892a), reprinted in 1897, and with Dodd, Mead and Company in New York (Couperus 1919b), no reprints. Teixeira de Mattos had collaborated with John Gray on the translation of *Extaze*. The first Couperus translation he undertook alone was *Majesteit*. *Majesty* appeared in 1894 with T. Fisher Unwin in London (Couperus 1894c), a business relation of Couperus's Dutch publisher L.J. Veen, and in 1895 with Appleton in New York. The latter of course already had another book by Couperus in his catalogue. Teixeira de Mattos preferred to be called de Mattos in daily life - his friends called him 'Tex'. Before he could make a living by his translations he had worked for a publishing house, probably that of Grein. He had good contacts in the London literary world. However, before de Mattos became the almost sole translator of Couperus into English there appeared a translation by another translator.

Benjamin Shepherd Berrington (1845-1934) translated *Psyche* in 1908 for Alston Rivers Ltd in London (Couperus 1908). This edition sported twelve illustrations by Dion Clayton Calthrop (1878-1937). The latter drew the attention of L.J. Veen, who bought the reproduction rights and in 1909 he incorporated these illustrations in the 250 remaining copies of the third Dutch printing (1904) of the novel. After this, interest in Couperus died out in the English language area. Not until 1914 did Dodd, Mead and Company, in collaboration with Heinemann, dare publish Couperus again, once more in translations by de Mattos. That year, Part one of *De boeken der kleine zielen* appeared under the title *Small Souls* (Couperus 1914a, 1914b). In the United States the volume was reprinted eight times in 1917, twice in 1918, and one time each in 1919, 1920, 1923, 1926 and 1930. In the UK the entire series was printed only once. Part 2, *The Later Life*, appeared in 1915 (Couperus 1915a), with US reprints in 1916, 1920 and 1923. Part 3, *The Twilight of Small Souls*, appeared in 1917 (Couperus 1917a, 1917b), reprinted in 1919 and 1920. Part 4, *Dr. Adriaan*, was published in 1918 (Couperus 1918a, 1918b) and reprinted in 1921. Complete editions appeared in 1932 (Couperus 1932) and 1942. These volumes remain by far Couperus's most popular and longest running success in the United States.

De Mattos entertained good relations with Couperus's US publisher, with whom, next to the four parts of *De boeken der kleine zielen*, there appeared six more titles, while *Majesty*, which had earlier appeared with Appleton, received a reprint. *Old people and the Things that Pass* appeared in 1918 with Dodd (Couperus 1918d) and in 1919 with Thornton Butterwoth in London (Couperus 1919c). In the United States the volume was reprinted two times, in 1919 and 1920; in England five times, in 1920, 1923, 1924, 1926 and for university purposes in 1963. Dodd also brought *Ecstasy: A Study of Happiness. A Novel* (*Extase*) in 1919 (Couperus 1919b), with as UK partner Henry and Co. (1892a). *The Inevitable* (*Langs lijnen van geleidelijkheid*) appeared in 1920 (Couperus 1920f), reprinted 1921, with UK partner Thornton Butterworth (Couperus 1921g), *The Tour* (*Antiek tourisme*) in 1920 (Couperus 1920h), with the same UK partner (Couperus 1920i), and in 1921 *The Hidden Force*, (*De stille kracht*; Corperus 1921e), with Jonathan Cape in London (Couperus 1922a). How important translators are is clear from the fact that after the death of de Mattos it took quite a while before other translators succeeded in getting further work by Couperus published. Dodd had considerable success with Couperus but when sales declined steeply he refused to take on further Couperus translations.

After de Mattos's death other translators stepped up to the plate. Jacobine Menzies-Wilson (1878–1960) and Ms C. C. Crispin in 1924 translated *Eastward* (*Oostwaarts*). They successfully placed it with Hurst & Blackett in London (Couperus 1924b) and George H. Doran in New York (Couperus 1924a). Menzies-Wilson also published *The Comedians. A Story of Ancient Rome* (*De komedianten*) with Jonathan Cape in London (Couperus 1926c), and George H. Doran in New York (Couperus 1926b), in 1926. *Nippon* was translated by John de la Veletta, a nephew of Couperus, and published in 1926 by Hurst & Blackett (Couperus 1926f) and George H. Doran (Couperus 1926e). The later had replaced Dodd as Couperus's US publisher.

Couperus had greater success in the United States than in the UK. De Mattos therefore preferred to deal directly with the American publishers. From Table 9.1 we can also learn that there were more reprints in the United States. In rare cases the search for a transatlantic partner did not prove successful. *Psyche*, translated by Berrington, and published in 1908 with Alston Rivers Ltd. in London (Couperus 1908), and the collection *Eighteen Tales*, selected and translated by J. Kooistra, were published in the UK only, with F.V. White & Co. Ltd. in London (Couperus 1924c). *Arrogance* (*Xerxes*), in translation by Frederick Martens, only appeared in the United States, with Farrar & Rinehart, Inc. in New York (Couperus 1930). This was also the final title by Couperus to be published in English.

Let us now turn to Couperus translations in periodicals and anthologies. *The Fortnightly Review* in 1909 brought *Queen Carola*, a translation of *Hooge troeven* (Couperus 1909). In *The New World – Monthly and Allied International Review* there appeared 'The Kingdom of Arles' and 'Bébert the Butcher and André the Fisherman' in 1920 (Couperus 1920g).

Flowers from a Foreign Garden (Couperus 1902b) contained 'My Art', a translation by A.L. Snell of the poem 'Maar 't allerzoets ...' from *Orchideeën*. The 1929 anthology *The Great Literature of Small Nations* featured chapter XXII from *Old people and the Things that Pass* (Couperus 1929b). 'Old Trofime,' from *Korte Arabesken*, was part of the *Harvest of the Lowlands, An Anthology in English Translation of Creative Writing in the Dutch Language with Historical survey of the Literary Development*, compiled and edited by J. Greshoff (Couperus 1945). The name of the translator is not mentioned.

The Hungarian language area

Five titles by Couperus were translated into Hungarian. As far we are able to determine from existing correspondence in all cases the initiative lay with the translators. Couperus's first translator into Hungarian was Ignotus, pseudonym of Hugo Veigelsberg (1869-1949), who in 1893 published *Noodlot* as *Végzet* with Singer és Wolfner in Budapest (Couperus 1893c). Lendvai István (1888-1945) in 1918 translated *De berg van licht* as *Heliogabalus* for Kultura Könyvkiadó in Budapest (Couperus 1918c). The same publisher in 1921 also bought *Komédiások*, the translation of *Komedianten*, by Balla Ignác (1885-1945) (Couperus 1921f). The only one to translate two books of Couperus's into Hungarian was Balogh Barna (1903-?). He published *Psyche* with Franklin-Társulat Kiadása in Budapest in 1925 (Couperus 1925b). The foreword is dated 1922, an indication that it took him some time to find a publisher. *Fidessa* appeared in 1927 with Tolnai Nyomdai Müintézet es Kiadovallalat R.-T. Kiadasa in Budapest (Couperus 1927). I have been unable to establish whether any one of these translators also succeeded in getting work by Couperus published in newspapers or periodicals.

The French language area

Only four titles by Couperus appeared in French. We know though that translators tried unsuccessfully to place more than these four books. The first work by Couperus to appear in a French translation is *Majesteit*, which appeared in 1898 as *Majesté* with Librairie Plon in Paris (Couperus 1898a). The same publisher also brought out *Wereldvrede* as *Paix universelle* in 1899 (Couperus 1899a). Both books had been translated by Louis Bresson (1844-1918), the minister of the Walloon Church in Rotterdam. They had appeared previously in *La revue Hebdomadaire*, also by Plon (Couperus 1898b, 1899b). Apparently, the reactions to these periodical publications had been sufficiently positive for the publisher to venture a book publication. Couperus's works in France thus followed a trajectory already familiar to us from what we saw in Germany. After this it took until 1923 for another book by Couperus to appear in French.

In 1922 the publisher – Dutch by origin – of *Le monde nouveau* had brought a few chapters from *Psyche* into his journal. In 1923 he published the entire novel, under the title *Le cheval ailé*, as an extra to the journal (Couperus 1923a). The translator was

Felicia Barbier (1875–1931, pseudonym of F. Korpershoek). The book was reprinted five times. The Belgian newspaper *L'indépendance belge* in 1897 serialized *Extase* in a translation by Charles Sluyts. The latter had earlier translated 'Een verlangen' as 'Un désir' in the same newspaper in 1895. The same newspaper in 1902 published 'Jours et Saisons' (Van dagen en seizoenen).

In fact, quite a few stories and parts of novels appeared in French-language periodicals. 'Een zieltje' appeared as 'Une petite âme' in *La Vogue* (1900c), *La revue des revues* (1894d) and *Les Mille Nouvelles* (1910). 'Kleine raadsels' made it into *L'ermitage, Revue mensuelle de littérature* as '*Petites énigmes*' (1900b). *Le carnet historique & littèraire* published 'La princesse aux cheveux bleus' (1903a); *La Mèditerranée Illustrée* included 'Devant Carthage morte' (1921c); *Les marges* published 'Les courtisanes' (1923b); and *Les nouvelles littéraires* included 'Viervier et escade'(1923d).

Especially George Khnopff (1860–1927) knocked himself out in trying to place translations of Couperus. He only succeeded in bringing some stories from *Eene illuzie* in sundry periodicals. *L'Aube. Revue artistique, mensuelle, internationale* in 1896 published parts of *Majesteit* (*Majesté*) (Couperus 1896b). *Revue des deux mondes* published parts of *Wereldvrede* (*Paix universelle*) in 1896 (Couperus 1896d) and in 1897 parts of *Metamorfoze* (Couperus 1897c). In 1901 *Le matin* serialized 'La reine Alexandra' (*Hooge troeven*) (Couperus 1901c). *Le Monde Nouveau* (1922c) and *L'Afrique du Nord illustrée* (1923c) published parts of *Psyche*. After 1923 we have to wait until 1973 for a new translation to see the light: *Van oude menschen, de dingen, die voorbij gaan*, translated by S. Roosenburg as *Vieilles gens et choses qui passent*, with Editions Universitaires in Paris (Couperus 1973).

Finnish

'Een zieltje' appeared as 'Pieni ineheme' in the journal *Valvoja* in 1902 (Couperus 1902d). In 1924 *Van oude menschen, de dingen, die voorbij gaan* was published as *Kuusikymmentä vuotta sitten* with Kunstannuosakeyhtio Otava in Helsingissa (Helsinki), in a translation by Helmi Krohn (Couperus 1924d).

Italian

Anna Franchi (1867–1954) in 1900 translated *Majesteit* as *Maestà* for Fratelli Treves in Milan (Couperus 1900a, 1902a), with a reprint in 1906. The same publisher also brought *Pace Universale* (*Wereldvrede*) in 1902 (Couperus 1902c), twice reprinted in 1903, in a translation by F.G.A. Dina Castellassi comtesse di Sordevolo (1860–1945). This novel had already been serialized in the newspaper *L'Ora* in 1901. Not until much later, in 1946, there appeared with Caregaro editore, in Milan, *Vecchia gente e le cose passano* (*Van oude menschen, de dingen, die voorbij gaan*), translated by Adele Cortese Rossi (Couperus 1946b). In 1906 the story 'Un'illusione' had found its way into *Nuova antologia di lettere, arti e scienze* (Couperus 1906b).

Croat

Sudbina (*Noodlot*), translator unknown, appeared in 1915 with Nakladam Kr. Zem. Tiskara in Zagreb (Couperus 1915b). *Zaljubljeni magarac* (*De verliefde ezel*) followed in 1923 with Tisak i naklada M. Sek in Zagreb, probably translated by Milan Draganic (Couperus 1923e3).

Norwegian

Alb. Cammermeyer Forlag in Kristiania (Oslo), in 1896 brought *Majesteit* in a translation by the otherwise unknown translator 'F.N.' (Couperus 1896c). *Eline Vere* appeared in 1893 with the publisher of the newspaper *Morgenposten* (Couperus 1893a). Most probably the novel had earlier been serialized before being republished as a premium to the paper. In 1916 *Stille magt* (*De stille kracht*), translator unknown, came out with Chr. Schibsteds Bogtrykkeri in Kristiania (Oslo) (Couperus 1916b).

Polish

Przeznaczenie (*Noodlot*), translator unknown, appeared in 1903 with Dodatek da Kuriera Cadziennego in Warsaw (Couperus 1903b). It was followed in 1906 by *Władca pokoju* (*Wereldvrede*), translator again unknown, with Nakladen księgarni Stefana Kavki in Cracow (Couperus 1906c). Much later, in 1966, *Ludzie starzy i sprawy przemijające* (*Van oude menschen, de dingen, die voorbij gaan*), translated by Marciej Chelkowski, appeared with Instytut Wydawniczy in Warsaw (Couperus 1966). As far as I know only one story by Couperus, 'Markiza d'Yemena' from *Eene illuzie*, was serialized in Polish, in *Zycle* (Couperus 1897a).

Russian

No translations of Couperus in book form were published in Russian, but four of his novels were serialized in *Novyj zurnal inostrannoj literatury*: in 1902 *Psyche* (Couperus 1902e), in 1905 *Noodlot*, in 1906 *Majesteit* and in 1907 *Wereldvrede*.

Spanish and Catalan

Su Majestad (*Majesteit*), translated by Juan García Rodríguez, appeared in 1904 with La España moderna in Madrid (Couperus 1904). *Heliogábalo* (*De berg van licht*), in a translation by José Goldstein, appeared with Editorial Futuro in Buenos Airos in 1946 (Couperus 1946a). In 1901 *Majesteit* and *Wereldvrede* appeared in *Novelas catalanas y extrangeras* (Couperus 1901d, 1904), a periodical that specialized in complete novels.

Czech

Jaroslav Kamper (1871–1911) in 1897 translated *Osud* (*Noodlot*) for Nakladatatel in Prague (Couperus 1897b). Twenty-five years later the same publisher brought *Hora svetla* (*De berg van licht*), translated by Hugo Kosterka (1867–1956) (Couperus 1922b). The periodical *Lumír* published 'Dušicka', the translation of 'Een zieltje' (Couperus 1896a). The same story, but now as 'Ubohá dušicka', appeared in 1902 in *Moravská orlice* (Couperus 1902g) and in the same year there also appeared a translation from *Hooge troeven*, 'Vysoké trumfy,' in *Lidové noviny* (Couperus 1902h).

Swedish

The first novel by Couperus to be translated into Swedish, by Maritz Boheman (1858–1908), was *Majestät* (Majesteit), with Hugo Gebers Färloo in Stockholm in 1895 (Couperus 1895d). In 1899 *Under vänskapens ok* (*Noodlot* appeared with C & E Gernandts Förlags-Aktiebalag in Stokholm, in a translation by Gustaf Uddgren (1865–1927) (Couperus 1899c). *Världsfred* (*Wereldvrede*), translated by Eva Wahlenberg, appeares with Nordiska Förlaget in Stockholm in 1915 (Couperus 1915c). 'Een zieltje' – again! – appears in Swedish as 'Charlot' in the newspaper *Svenska Dagbladet* in 1895 (Couperus 1895a). This story is the obvious favourite with translators and publishers, as it appeared in five different languages.

Couperus criticism

Introductions to translations of Couperus may serve to give us some idea as to how Couperus was perceived by his contemporaries. Not surprisingly, such introductions in general strike a positive note. After all, they were intended to further the sales of the book! In several translations the introductions not only address Couperus but also Dutch literature in general. This was for instance the case with the introduction Edmund Gosse (1849–1928) provided for *Fate* (Couperus 1892e). This was one of the first texts in English to pay any sort of attention to modern Dutch literature, and it was reprinted in the American edition of *Eline Vere* (1892d). Stephen McKenna (1888–1967), in a foreword to *Old People and the Things that Pass* (Couperus 1919c), also situated the novel in a wider literary-historical perspective.

Reviews in newspapers and periodicals offer a more independent opinion. Most of these, especially in German and in English, were timed for new translations appearing. Again in general, though, most reviews were quite positive. Publishers also reproduced these in brochures and catalogues. A good yardstick to measure how Couperus was perceived in the English language area is the article 'Couperus in English' by J.A. Russell (1927). He opened with 'Louis Couperus is undoubtedly the most outstanding figure in modern Dutch prose.' On the occasion of the translation of *Small Souls* and *Old People* Katherine Mansfield (1888-1923) published extensive reviews in the 1919 December and 1920 June issues of *The Athenaeum A Journal of English and Foreign Literature, Science, the Fine Arts, Music, & the Drama*. These were reprinted in *Novels and Novelists* (Murry 1930: 205-208).

In German there regularly appeared reviews and survey articles by Conrat, Raché and Hauser. Here again publishers avidly reproduced the more positive remarks from these reviews and surveys. Occasionally, there is some criticism of Couperus's convoluted language, even though Otten took care to adapt her translations to German expectations in this regard to gain acceptance with German publishers. De Mattos also took into account matters of censure and moral decorum prevalent with the editors of the publishers to which he submitted his translations.

In the other language areas there is hardly any systematic research into reviews and articles dealing with Couperus available. This is understandable as in the languages concerned few translations from Couperus appeared, and moreover only at irregular intervals.

Conclusion

After the Second World War interest in Couperus abroad was minimal. In fact, the same thing even applied to the Netherlands itself. With very few exceptions, his works received no reprints. New translations were very rare and very sporadic, as attested to by Table 9.1 and my summaries of what happened in the various languages.

In 1973 international copyright on works by Couperus expired, and especially the Dutch Foundation for the Translation of Literary Works actively promoted, via financial support, translations of Dutch literature, and therefore also of Couperus. This led to translations into Arabic, Bulgarian, Chinese, Danish, Esperanto, Hindi, Indonesian, Macedonian, Romanian, Russian, Slovak, Turkish, Urdu and Vietnamese. Furthermore, print-on-demand made many older translations available again. All of this catapulted Couperus once again into the rank of world authors.

References

Couperus, L. (1884), *Een Lent van Vaersen*, Utrecht: J.L. Beijers.
Couperus, L. (1886), *Orchideeën. Een bundel poëzie en proza*, Amsterdam: A. Rössing.
Couperus, L. (1889), *Eline Vere. Een Haagsche roman*, Amsterdam: P.N. van Kampen & Zoon.

Couperus, L. (1891), *Footsteps of Fate* (*Noodlot.*), trans. C. Bell, introduction by E. Gosse, London: William Heinemann (Heinemann's International Library, 7).
Couperus, L. (1892a), *Ecstasy: A Study of Happiness*, trans. A. Teixeira de Mattos and J. Gray, London: Henry & Co.
Couperus, L. (1892b), *Eene illuzie*, Amsterdam: L.J. Veen.
Couperus, L. (1892c), *Eline Vere*, trans. J.T. Grein, London: Chapman and Hall Ltd.
Couperus, L. (1892d), *Eline Vere*, trans. J.T. Grein, with introduction by E. Gosse, New York: D. Appleton and Co. (Holland fiction series. 1).
Couperus, L. (1892e), *Fate* (*Noodlot.*), trans. C. Bell, with introduction by E. Gosse, New York: P.F. Collier.
Couperus, L. (1892f), *Fate* (*Noodlot.*), trans. C. Bell, with introdution by E. Gosse, New York: D. Appleton and Co. (Holland fiction series. 2).
Couperus, L. (1892g), *Schicksal Roman*, trans. P. Raché, Stuttgart: Deutsche Verlags-Anstalt.
Couperus, L. (1893a), *Eline Vere*, trans. for *Christiania Nyheds- og Avertissements-Blad* (*Morgenposten*).
Couperus, L. (1893b), '*Eline Vere*', *Magdeburger Zeitung*, 28 May 1893, in 46 parts.
Couperus, L. (1893c), *Végzet. Forditotta: Ignotius* [= Ignotus], vol. 17, Budapest: Singer és Wolfner, Könyvkereskedése. Egyetemes regénytár.
Couperus, L. (1894a), 'Ein Seelchen', in *Addio von Neera und andere Novellen von Louis Couperus, Stephan v. Barsony, V. Heidenstam*, trans. P. Raché, Stuttgart: Deutsche Verlags-Anstalt (Biblothek der Fremden Zungen, no. 20).
Couperus, L. (1894b), *Extase. Ein Buch vom Glück*, trans. F. Norden, Dresden: Verlag von Alexander Beyer.
Couperus, L. (1894c), *Majesty*, trans. A. Teixeira de Mattos and E. Dowson, London: T. Fisher Unwin.
Couperus, L. (1894d), 'Une petite ärne', trans. G. Khnopff, *Revue des revues* 5 (15), 15 June 1894.
Couperus, L. (1895a), 'Charlot' trans. unknown, *Svenska Dagbladet* (28) 2 February.
Couperus, L. (1895b), *Ekstase. Roman*, trans. I. Frick, Stuttgart: Deutsche Verlags-Anstalt.
Couperus, L. (1895c), *Majestät. Roman*, trans. [von (?) Heiden], Dresden: Verlag von Heinrich Minden.
Couperus, L. (1895d), *Majestät. Roman*, trans. M. Boheman, Stockholm: Hugo Gebers Förlag.
Couperus, L. (1895e), *Weltfrieden Roman*, trans. P. Raché, Dresden: Verlag von Heinrich Minden.
Couperus, L. (1896a), 'Dušička', trans. V. Kuneš (pseud. V. Hladik), *Lumír* 24 (16): 186–189.
Couperus, L. (1896b), *Majesté*, [parts], trans. L. Bresson, *L'aube Revue artistique, littéraire, mensuelle, internationale* 2 (5), July.
Couperus, L. (1896c), *Majestaet. Roman*, trans. F.N. Kristiania, Oslow: Alb. Cammermeyers Forlag / Lars Swanstrorn (*Cammermeyers Roman-Bibliothek*).
Couperus, L. (1896d), *Metamorfoze*, [parts], trans. T. de Wyzema, *Revue des deux mondes*, LXVIe annëe - Quatrième pérode, vol. 134 (April).
Couperus, L. (1896e), *Paix universelle*, [parts], trans. T. de Wyzema, *Revue des deux mondes*, LXVIe annëe - Quatrième pérode, vol. 67 (June): 939–946.
Couperus, L. (1897a), 'Markiza d'Yemena', trans. A. Nowaczyński, *Życle* (serial) 2 (2 October), 3 (9 October) and 4 (16 October).
Couperus, L. (1897b), *Osud.* (*Noodlot.*), vol. 2, trans. J. Kamper, Prague: Jos. R. Vilímek. Moderní knihy.

Couperus, L. (1898a), *Majesté*, trans. L.B. [L. Bresson], preceded by a study by M. Spronck, Paris: Librairie Plon. E. Plon, Nourrit et Cie., imprimeurs-éditeurs.

Couperus, L. (1898b), 'Majesté, par Louis Couperus', trans. L. Bresson, *La Revue Hebdomadaire*, 2nd ser., Romans – Histoire – Voyages, Septième année.

Couperus, L. (1899a), *Paix Universelle*, trans. L.B. [L. Bresson], Paris: Librairie Plon. E. Plon, Nourrit et Cie., imprimeurs-éditeurs (Bibliothèque à 1 Fr. Le vol. 16).

Couperus, L. (1899b), 'Paix universelle, par Louis Couperus', in *La Revue Hebdomadaire*, 2nd ser. trans. L. Bresson, Romans – Histoire – Voyages, Huitiéme année.

Couperus, L. (1899c), *Under vänskapens ok ("Noodlot")*, trans. G. Uddgren, Stockholm: C. & E. Gernandts Förlags-Aktiebolag.

Couperus, L. (1900a), *Maestà. Romanzo di Luigi Couperus*, 1st edn, preface by A. Franchi, Milan: Fratelli Treves, editori.

Couperus, L. (1900b), 'Petites Énigmes, par L. Couperus', in *L'ermitage, Revue mensuelle de Litterature*, trans. G. Khnopff. Onzièm année.

Couperus, L. (1900c), 'Une petite âme', *La Voque, Revue mensuelle*, trans. G. Khnopff. 15 February.

Couperus, L. (1901a), 'Kleopatra', trans. O. Hauser, *Aus fremden Zungen* 11 (2).

Couperus, L. (1901b), 'Kleopatra', 'Ein venetianisches Bild', 'Meine kunst', in *Die niederlandische Lyrik von 1875-1900*, study and trans. O. Hauser, Großenhain: Verlegt bei Baumert & Ronge.

Couperus, L. (1901c), 'La reine Alexandra', *Le matin*, 5–15 July.

Couperus, L. (1901d), 'Pau Universal', trans. L. Bartrina, 2nd part 'Magestat', in *Novelas Catalanas Y Extrangeras, Publicadas en 10 folletí de La Renaixensa* 485–590.

Couperus, L. (1902a), *Maestà. Romanzo di Luigi Couperus*, 2nd edn, preface by A. Franchi, Milan: Fratelli Treves, editori

Couperus, L. (1902b), 'My Art', in *Flowers from a Foreign Garden – Selections from the Works of Modern Dutch Poets*, trans. A. L. Snell, London: Love & Malcomson.

Couperus, L. (1902c), *Pace Universale. Romanzo di Luigi Couperus*, trans. D. Castellazzi di Sordevolo, with a preface by G. Verga, Milan: Fratelli Treves, editori.

Couperus, L., (1902d), 'Pieni ineheme', trans. H.I., *Valvoja*, 23, June, no. 5–6.

Couperus, L., (1902e), 'Psicheja', trans. E.N. Polovcova, *Novyj zurnal inostrannoj literary* 5–64.

Couperus, L. (1902f), *Stille Kraft. Roman*, trans. Gräfin Wengstein (pseud. M.L. Gräfin von Wengersky), Dresden: Verlag von Heinrich Minden.

Couperus, L. (1902g), 'Ubohá dušicka', Moravská orlice...

Couperus, L. (1902h), 'Vysoké trumfy', trans. R. Smrček, *Lidové noviny* 10 (November–December).

Couperus, L. (1903a), 'La princesse aux cheveux bleus', trans. M. Vlielander Hein en Renée d'Ulmês, *Le Carnet – Revue mensuelle illustrée* 6 (12).

Couperus, L. (1903b), *Przeznaczenie (Noodlot)*, trans. unknown, Warsaw: Dodatek da Kuriera Codziennego.

Couperus, L. (1904), 'Magestat', in *Novelas Catalanas Y Extrangeras, Publicadas en 10 folletí de La Renaixensa*, trans. J. García Rodríguez, Madrid: La España moderna.

Couperus, L. (1906a), 'Kleopatra', 'Meine kunst', in H. Bethge (ed.), *Die Lyrik des Auslandes in neuer zeit*, Leipzig: Max Hessen Verlag.

Couperus, L. (1906b), 'Un'illusione', trans. E. Wissenburgh-Lopes Suasso, in *Nuova antologia di lettere, arti e scienze*, vol. 122, fase. 822, 16 March 1906.

Couperus, L. (1906c), *Władca pokoju. Powieść*, Kraków: Nakladen ksiegarni Stefana Kavki.
Couperus, L. (1908), *Psyche*, trans. B.S. Berrington, with twelve illustrations by D. Clayton Calthrop, London: Alston Rivers, Ltd.
Couperus, L. (1909), 'Queen Carola, a Story', trans. A. Teixeira de Mattos, *The Fortnightly Review*, new. ser., 85 (January–June).
Couperus, L. (1910), 'Une petite âme', trans. G. Knoff, *Les Mille Nouvelles Nouvelles, Revue Mensuelle pour tous* 9 (October): 19–33.
Couperus, L. (1914a), *Small Souls*, trans. A. Teixeira de Mattos, New York: Dodd, Mead and Company.
Couperus, L. (1914b), *Small Souls*, trans. A. Teixeira de Mattos, London: William Heinemann.
Couperus, L. (1915a), *The Later Life*, trans. A. Teixeira de Mattos, London: William Heinemann.
Couperus, L. (1915b), *Sudbina. Roman nesretnih ljubavnika*, vol. III, bk 36, Zagreb: Nakladom Kr. Zem. Tiskara. Zabavna biblioteka.
Couperus, L. (1915c), *Världsfred. Roman*, trans. E. Wahlenberg, Nordiska Förlagets 25 öres böcker av världslitteraturens mästerverk, vol. 302, Stockholm: Nordiska Förlaget.
Couperus, L. (1916a), *Heliogabal. Roman*, trans. and ed. E. Otten, cover drawing by M. Schwerdtfeger, Frankfurt: Verlag der Literarischen Anstalt Rütten & Loening.
Couperus, L. (1916b), *Stille magt. Fortælling fra Java*, trans. for 'Aftenposten', Kristiania: Chr. Schibsteds Bogtrykkeri.
Couperus, L. (1917a), *The Twilight of the Souls*, trans. A. Teixeira de Mattos, NewYork: Dodd, Mead and Company.
Couperus, L. (1917b), *The Twilight of the Souls*, trans. A. Teixeira de Mattos, London: William Heinemann.
Couperus, L. (1918a), *Dr, Adriaan*, trans. A. Teixeira de Mattos, New York: Dodd, Mead and Company.
Couperus, L. (1918b), *Dr, Adriaan*, trans. A. Teixeira de Mattos, London: William Heinemann.
Couperus, L. (1918c), *Heliogabalus. Regény*, trans. L. István, A. Kultura regénytára, vol. 8, Budapest: Kultura Könyvkiadó Részvénytársaság.
Couperus, L. (1918d), *Old People and the Things that Pass*, trans. A. Teixeira de Mattos, New York: Dodd, Mead and Company.
Couperus, L. (1919a), *Die Komödianten, Roman*, trans. E. Otten, vol. 1–5 Tausend, Munich: Georg Müller.
Couperus, L. (1919b), *Ecstasy: A Study of Happiness. A Novel*, trans. A. Teixeira de Mattos, New York: Dodd, Mead and Company.
Couperus, L. (1919c), *Old People and the Things that Pass*, trans. A. Teixeira de Mattos, with a preface by S. McKenna, London: Thornton Butterworth Ltd.
Couperus, L. (1919d), *Xerxes oder der Hochmut; Aus den Büchem der ironischen Geschichte*, trans. E. Otten. Berlin: Wilhelm Borngräber.
Couperus, L. (1920a), *Am wege der Freude. Roman*, trans. E. Otten, Berlin: Verlag Ullstein & Co. (Ullstein-Bücher, Eine Sammlung zeitgenössischer Romane, no. 119).
Couperus, L. (1920b), *Aphrodite in Ägypten, Roman aus dem alten Aegypten*, trans. E. Otten, cover drawing by G.H. Mathey, vol. 1–8 Tausend, Berlin: Ernst Rowohlt Verlag.
Couperus, L. (1920c), *Babel*, trans. E. Otten, Berlin: Ernst Rowohlt Verlag.

Couperus, L. (1920d), *Der verliebte Esel. Roman*, trans. E. Otten, vol. 1–5 Tausend, Berlin: Wilhelm Borngräber.
Couperus, L. (1920e), *Dionysos. Roman*, trans. E. Otten, cover and heliogravures after drawings by R. Schott, Leipzig: Rainer Wunderlich Verlag.
Couperus, L. (1920f), *The Inevitable*, trans. A. Teixeira de Mattos, New York: Dodd, Mead and Company.
Couperus, L. (1920g), 'The Kingdom of Arles', with short introduction by W.F.C. Timmermans, *The New World - Monthly and Allied International Review* 2 (12).
Couperus, L. (1920h), *The Tour. A Story of Ancient Egypt*, trans. A. Teixeira de Mattos, New York: Dodd, Mead and Company.
Couperus, L. (1920i), *The Tour. A Story of Ancient Egypt*, trans. A. Teixeira de Mattos, London: Thornton Butterworth Ltd.
Couperus, L. (1921a), *Das Schwebende Schachbrett*, trans. and afterword by E. Otten, with bibliography, 1–4 Tausend, Berlin: Ernst Rowohlt Verlag.
Couperus, L. (1921b), *Der Unglückliche. Roman*, trans. E. Otten, 1–3 Tausend, Munich: Georg Müller.
Couperus, L. (1921c), 'Devant Carthage morte', trans. F. Barbier, *La Méditerranée Illustrée*, 13 August 1921.
Couperus, L. (1921d), *Die Lebenskurve, Roman*, trans. E. Otten, Berlin: Verlag von W. Vobach & Co.
Couperus, L. (1921e), *The Hidden Force. A Story of Modern Java*, trans. A. Teixeira de Mattos, New York: Dodd, Mead and Company.
Couperus, L. (1921f), *Komédiások, Regény*, trans. B. Ignác, A. Kultura regénytára, vol. 33, Budapest: A Kultura Könyvkiadó és Nyomda R.-T. Kiadása.
Couperus, L. (1921g), *The Law Inevitable*, trans. A. Teixeira de Mattos, Londen: Thornton Butterworth, Limited.
Couperus, L. (1922a), *The Hidden Force. A Story of Modern Java*, trans. A. Teixeira de Mattos, London: Jonathan Cape.
Couperus, L. (1922b), *Hora svetla* (Heliogabal), Román ve třech dílech, trans. H. Kosterka, vol. 199, Prague: Ios. R. Viltmek (Vilfmkova knihovna).
Couperus, L. (1922c), *Psyche* [Parts], *Le Monde Nouveau* 4 (7).
Couperus, L. (1923a), *Le cheval ailé*, trans. J. [= Félicia] Barbier, preface by J. Benda, *Le Monde nouveau*, suppl., 1 March 1923.
Couperus, L. (1923b), 'Les courtisanes', trans. P. Eyquem, *Les marges - Revue littéraire* 27 (109) (15 July).
Couperus, L. (1923c), 'Psyche' [parts], trans. F. Barbier, *L'Afrique du Nord illustrée* 18 (123), 8 September 1923: 9.
Couperus, L. (1923d), 'Vivier et cascade', with introduction by P. Eyquem, *Les nouvelles littéraires, artistiques et scientifiques - Hebdomadaire d'information, de critique et de bibliographie* 16 (June).
Couperus, L. (1923e), *Zaljubljeni magarac. Roman*, trans. M. Draganić, illustrated by M. Trepše, Zagreb: Tisak i naklada M. Sek.
Couperus, L. (1924a), *Eastward*, trans. J. Menzies-Wilson and C.C. Crispin, with frontispiece and thirty-six other illustrations, New York: George H. Doran Company.
Couperus, L. (1924b), *Eastward*, trans. J. Menzies-Wilson and C.C. Crispin, with frontispiece and thirty-six other illustrations, London: Hurst and Blackett, Ltd.

Couperus, L. (1924c), *Eighteen Short Stories (Tales) Delightful Tales of the Bleu Mediterranean Joy. Colour, Sunshine: Even Frivolity prevail Throughout Eighteen Tales*, trans. J. Kooistra, London: F.V. White & Co. Ltd.

Couperus, L. (1924d), *Kuusikymmentä vuotta sitten (Van oude menschen, de dingen, die voorbijgaan)*, trans. H. Krohn, Otavan uusi romaanisarja, 22, Helsinki: Kustannuosakeyhtio Otava.

Couperus, L. (1924e), *Psyche*, trans. E. Otten, with twenty-eight pen-and-ink drawings by P. Jordan, Die Freunde, 28, Leipzig: Feuer-Verlag.

Couperus, L. (1925a), *Iskander. Der Roman Alexanders des Grossen*, trans. E. Otten, cover drawing by W. Tiemann, Leipzig: Philipp Reclam jun.

Couperus, L. (1925b), *Psyche*, trans. B. Barna, Budapest: Franklin-Társulat Kiadása.

Couperus, L. (1925-1926), 'Lucrezia Borgia', in *Reclams Universum, Moderne illustrierte Wochenschrift*, vol. 2, trans. E. Otten, with introduction by H. Lebene 499-502.

Couperus, L. (1926a), *Aphrodite in Ägypten, Roman aus dem alten Aegypten*, trans. E. Otten, cover drawing by W. Tiemann, Leipzig: Philipp Reclam jun.

Couperus, L. (1926b), *The Comedians. A Story of Ancient Rome*, trans. J. Menzies Wilson, New York: George H. Doran Company.

Couperus, L. (1926c), *The Comedians. A Story of Ancient Rome*, trans. J. Menzies Wilson, London: Jonathan Cape Ltd.

Couperus, L. (1926d), *Lucrezia Borgia*, trans. E. Otten, with an afterword by H. Lebede, Reclams Universal-Bibliothek, no. 6641, Leipzig: Philipp Reclam jun.

Couperus, L. (1926e), *Nippon*, trans. J. de la Valette, with 24 illustrations, New York: George H. Doran Company.

Couperus, L. (1926f), *Nippon*, trans. J. de la Valette, with 24 illustrations, London: Hurst & Blackett.

Couperus, L. (1926g), *Unter Javas Tropensonne*, trans. E. Otten, with an introduction by H.K. Heiland, Berlin: Deutsche-Buch-Gemeinschaft G.m.b.H.

Couperus, L. (1927), *Fidessa. Az örök hűség legendája*, trans. B. Barna, Tolnai regénytára, Budapest: Tolnai Nyomdai Müintézet és Kiadóvállalat R.-T. Kiadása.

Couperus, L. (1929a), *Japanische streifzüge*, trans. E. Otten, Berlin: Peter J. Oestergaard Verlag.

Couperus, L. (1929b), 'Old People and the Things that Pass', in *The Great literature of small nations - Vol. VIII of Columbia University Course in Literature, based on The world's best literature*, New York: Columbia University Press.

Couperus, L. (1930), *Arrogance. The Conquests of Xerxes*, trans. F.H. Martens, decorations by T. Nadejen, New York: Farrar & Rinehart, Inc.

Couperus, L. (1932), *The Book of the Small Souls*, including 'Small Souls', 'The Later Life', 'The Twilight of the Souls' and 'Dr. Adriaan', trans. A. Teixeira de Mattos, New York: Dodd, Mead & Company.

Couperus, L. (1945), 'Old Trofime', in *Harvest of the Lowlands*, compiled and ed. J. Greshoff, New York: Querido.

Couperus, L. (1946a), *Heliogábalo. Los fuegos fatuos de la decadencia romana*, trans. J. Goldstein, illustrated by O. Pierri, Buenos Aires: Editorlal Futuro.

Couperus, L. (1946b), *Vecchia gente e le cose passano [Romanzo.]*, with a preface by S. McKenna, Italian version of A. Cortese Rossi, Milan: Caregaro editore/Edizioni Alpe.

Couperus, L. (1966), *Ludzie starzy i sprawy przemijające*, trans. M. Chełkowski, Warszawa: Instytut Wydawniczy Pax.

Couperus, L. (1973), *Vieilles gens et choses qui passent*, trans. S. Roosenburg, Paris: Éditions Universitaires.

Fraser, R. and M. Hammond (2008), *Books without Borders, The Cross-national Dimension in Print Culture*, 2 vols, Basingstoke: Palgrave Macmillan.

Grave, J. (2001), *Zulk vertalen is een werk van liefde. Bemiddelaars van Nederlandstalige literatuur in Duitsland, 1890-1914*, Nijmegen: Uitgeverij Vantilt.

Heilbron, J., W. de Nooy and W. Tichelaar, eds (1995), *Waarin een klein land, Nederlandse cultuur in internationaal verband*, Amsterdam: Prometeus.

Kastner, B. (2005), 'Der Buchverlag der Weimarer Republik 1918-1933, Eine statistische Analyse', diss., Munich: Ludwig Maximilians University.

Murry, J.M., ed. (1930), *Novels and Novelists by Katherine Mansfield*, London: Constable.

Ridder, A. de (1917), *Bij Louis Couperus*, Amsterdam: L.J. Veen.

Russell, J.A. (1927), 'Couperus in English', *De nieuwe gids* 42.

Schneider, L., ed. (1887), *Geschichte der niederländischen Litteratur*, Leipzig: W. Friedrich.

Veen, R. (2013), '"All those requests for translations without a fee" – The Flying Start of Louis Couperus (1863-1923) in Germany', *Quaerendo* 43 (3): 238-268.

Veen, R.K. (2015), *Couperus bij de buren, Een onderzoek naar de uitgaven van het werk van Louis Couperus bij Duitse uitgevers tussen 1892 en 1973*, Culemborg: Stichting Couperus-collectie.

10

Dutch Literature and the Global System of Indentured Labour, 1900–1940

Saskia Pieterse

In the course of the nineteenth century, the British, Dutch, French and Spanish colonial administrations replaced chattel slavery with systems of indentured labour. This global system of migrant labour encompassed South and Southeast Asia, the Caribbean, Eastern and Southern Africa, Australia, the Central and Southern Pacific, and Central and South America. Millions of colonial subjects (African, Chinese, Indian, Japanese, Javanese, Melanesian) were bound by a signed or forced contract to work for a fixed amount of time – usually three to seven years. While the vast majority of these indentured men and women laboured on coffee, tea, sugar, or rubber plantations, others were put to work as miners – for example mining for gold in the South African Transvaal region and guano in Peru or constructing railways in East Africa and the Andes (Northrup 1995).

The effect this global system of indentured labour had on world literature is as wide-ranging as the system itself. Today, postcolonial authors reflect on the experiences and traumas of communities in diaspora (Carter and Torabully 2002; Pirbhai 2009; Sarwal 2017). Historically, the theme of indentured labour began to feature in fiction from the first half of the nineteenth century. However, thus far, an anthology of this global network of (post)colonial literary responses to indentured labour is lacking, as most case studies focus on just a single author or geographical area. I present a tentative, initial exploration of the topic. I limit myself to indenture in Asia and focus primarily on the situation in the Dutch East Indies, British India and China, from around 1900 until the beginning of the Second World War. Fictional accounts of indenture in literature from the West Indies, the Americas and South Africa are therefore not discussed – although it should be noted that the different systems of indenture were interconnected and thus shaped each other. Yet, accepting the limited scope of this essay, the selected literary works do shed substantial light, both on the globalizing forces that shaped the system of indentured labour itself, and on the literature that thematized this colonial practice.

In British and Indo-Anglian fiction, authors such as Joseph Conrad (1857-1824) and Mulk Raj Anand (1905-2004) gave fictionalized accounts of the lives of the marginalized – albeit from very different points of view. In Dutch literature, during the first decades of the twentieth century, the lives of 'coolies' – the derogatory colonial term used for these indentured labourers – became a recurring literary theme. In this essay I will discuss the colonial literary works of two often translated authors – Louis Couperus (1863-1923) and Madelon Székely-Lulofs (1899-1958) – and place their treatment of indentured labour side by side to those of Conrad and Anand respectively. Colonial administrations liberalized the labour market, and thus created the circumstances for a new and international corporate capitalism. In this way, indenture attested to a new phase in the global economy (Stoler 1995).

Franco Moretti defines the system of world literature as 'one, but unequal'. He compares world literature to capitalism, both are global systems bound together 'by growing inequality' (2000: 44-55). He proceeds to argue that 'the modern novel first arises not as an autonomous development but as a compromise between a western formal influence (usually French or English) and local materials' (58). With Moretti's hypothesis as a starting point, I will discuss how fictional accounts of indenture relate to two fundamental types of modernity: a new phase in capitalism (creating a new type of political-economic modernity); and literary modernism. I will highlight how authors used 'local materials' in their fictional accounts of indenture, and how this relates to their position in the centre or on the periphery of empire. I will discuss the forces of globalization at work, both within the system of indenture and in the literature that represented it. However, before I discuss the literary works themselves, I will start with a short comparison between the British and the Dutch public debates on indenture, as this provides the necessary context for the developments that took place within literature.

The beginning and ending of indenture

Following the British abolition of slavery in 1833, abolitionists shifted their focus to oppose the introduction of indenture. Contract labour provided plantation owners with a cheap labour force, and this of course continued to threaten the living conditions of those formerly enslaved (Major 2017). In 1838, the moral, social and economic implications of indenture were fiercely debated in both India and Britain (Drescher 2009: 39) – a debate that would continue into the latter decades of the nineteenth century. Effective opposition against indenture finally came to the fore in the twentieth century, with Mahatma Gandhi's passive resistance against discriminatory laws, and an anti-indenture campaign driven by, among others, Indian nationalist Gopal Krishna Gokhale. This anti-imperial activism finally led to the abolition of indenture in 1917, an act that came into force in 1920. However, even after abolition, the term 'coolie-labour' was still used to describe unskilled and underpaid labour (Kumar 2017: 205–240).

In the Dutch case, both the introduction and the abolition of indentured labour was a much more belated affair. Dutch abolitionists had to maneuver in a public space that left very little room for radical dissident voices (Janse 2015). The most effective lobby for the abolition of slavery came from a group of conservative Protestants, for whom a moderate pace of change was preferable to swift abolition. As a consequence, slavery was only abolished in 1863 when indenture replaced slavery in the Dutch Caribbean, with Javanese, Chinese and Indian workers being transported mostly to Surinam. In the Dutch East Indies, when the government-controlled cultivation system was abandoned around 1870, the colonial government decided to allocate substantial plots of land to private investors. Deli, a district of Sumatra on the island's east coast, soon became a site of unregulated capitalist enterprise. The first pioneering planters experimented with the cultivation of tobacco, which proved to be very successful. The success of these tobacco plantations was soon followed by a boom in rubber plantations and this plantation economy was built on the institutional use of indentured labour. Men and women were mainly recruited in Java, but there were also a considerable number of Chinese indentured labourers (Clerkx and Wertheim 1991: 8–9).

The situation on the east coast of Sumatra was very similar to that on the west coast of Malaya. In both cases, investment houses bought out the smaller plantations, creating vast commercial enterprises. The flow of capital grew to exceed the boundaries of the European empires. British investment firms were the first to arrive in Deli, followed by an influx of American capital around 1910. Indeed, the Sumatran east coast was often referred to as 'the Dollar land of Deli' (Stoler 1995: 18). There were also Japanese, German and Swiss capital investors in Deli, albeit to a much lesser extent (19). Ann Stoler points to the fact that the international flow of capital created a new type of corporate structure, with a 'multi-national and multi-ethnic resident population' (19). Plantation production was organized along military industrial lines, with up to 1,000 workers housed in so-called coolie lines or barracks. The militarization and financialization of the plantations leads Amarjit Kaur (2014) to speak of a 'plantation complex' in Malaya and Sumatra. Deli thus became one of the first sites in world history where a new type of corporate capitalism manifested itself and many of the structures first created in Deli were to become crucial to the world economy in the twentieth century.

Specific to the situation in Sumatra was the introduction of the 'penal sanction' section of the 'coolie ordinance' introduced in 1880. This ordinance stipulated that a plantation owner could punish his workers in any manner he saw fit. Brutal corporal punishments thus became an inherent feature of the Dutch 'plantation complex', with almost no governmental regulation. Protests in the press were put aside as 'socialist slander' (Breman 1992: 4), while English-language pamphlets criticizing 'Dutch cruelty' in Deli were snubbed by Dutch politicians as 'little English books' (Gouda 2008: 32). While the Dutch government policy effectively marginalized Dutch critics, it operated with outright violence towards Indonesian dissident voices. Although there was no Indonesian mass movement equivalent to Ghandi's passive resistance, a growing number of students were inspired by worldwide anticolonial nationalist movements. Up until the Second World War, Dutch colonial rule allowed for very little activism and political organizing. Many Indonesian nationalists were either banished to the Banda Islands or sent to the Netherlands, effectively gagging the oppositional press (Maters 1998: 149-220). A growing political consciousness did lead to a communist revolt in Java and Sumatra in 1926; however, it was violently repressed by the Dutch colonial government – so violently that it caused international indignation (Taselaar 1992: 264).

The effective and structural oppression of anti-imperial activism meant that the Dutch colonial administration could continue its policy of not intervening in the exploitation of contract labourers without risking political turmoil. Only when, in 1929, the United States Congress prohibited imports of tobacco from East Sumatra because they were the product of unfree labour (Clerkx and Wertheim 1991: 3) did the lobby for the abolishment of penal sanctions gain more traction. However, it took the Great Depression to end indenture. Hitting Deli in 1929 with massive force, Stoler describes how ultimately, the reasons for abolition were purely economic:

> Workers had to be fired on a massive scale; the forced retrenchment was used as a rationale for abolishing indenture. Between 1930 and 1935 150.000 workers, nearly 50 % of the workforce, were dismissed as their contracts expired. [...] The first were those suspected of being 'dangerous', 'extremist elements', while the most docile and hard-working were retained. (Stoler 1986: 135)

Penal sanctions were only completely abolished in the whole of the Dutch East Indies in 1942 (Stoler 1995: 45).

Joseph Conrad and Louis Couperus: Reflecting and repressing colonial capitalism

Joseph Conrad joined the British merchant navy in 1877. In his early novels, often situated on the Malay Archipelago, he writes of a colonial world in which European entrepreneurs from different nationalities intermingle. In his debut novel *Almayer's Folly* (1895), the Dutch merchant Almayer is the main character. It was serialized in the Dutch Newspaper *Het Nieuws van den Dag* (The News of the Day) in 1896 (Steltenpool n.d.). Conrad weaves many of the military conflicts on the archipelago into his early work, one of which was the Aceh-war. This war, which lasted from 1873 until 1914 (with many eruptions of violent protest long after 1914), was one of the clearest manifestations of Dutch imperialist ambitions. Conrad's fiction reflects the violent and decentralized forces that were unleashed during this period of new imperialism.

As Ross Forman (2004) shows, Conrad's novella *Typhoon* ([1902] 1986) reflects the ways in which destabilizing forces of free market capitalism were at work in the system of indenture. The story revolves around the crew of the Nan-Shan, a ship owned by a Swiss businessmen based in Bangkok. Sailing under the flag of Siam, the ship has an Irish captain, an English crew, and is transporting a group of coolies back to their homes in Fo-kien (Fujian) following the end of their seven-year contracts in an unspecified Southeast Asian colony. These coolies signed their contracts with the Bun Hin Company, a private company that profits from the flow of human capital between China and the Dutch and British colonies. As Forman argues, the narrative testifies to the 'flexibility that allowed Britain to reap profits from diffuse networks of affiliation (and at times, intra-European solidarity)' (2004: 402). Conrad does not tell this story in a straightforward fashion but, rather, through various narrative frames and devices: the diffusion in power thus translates itself into a new type of storytelling.

The Chinese men are kept below deck and are physically separated from the European crew. The Nan-Shan sails into a hurricane. During the storm, the boxes containing the hard-earned wages of the Chinese men are smashed and their money becomes scattered all over the floor, resulting in a scramble to retrieve the cash. Above deck, the crew fears the chaos and anger this creates amongst the Chinese might turn into an uprising against the ship's commanders. While this evokes the specter of a slave revolt, at the same time, power no longer manifests itself in a clear-cut fashion: who pays for what, who owns the ship, the contracts, the money? The captain decides to end the chaos – not by violence, but with an administrative ruse. He orders all the money to be collected, and then redistributes to each worker the exact same amount of cash.

Conrad was not the only writer to thematize the fear of revolting coolies. W. Carlton Dawe's story 'Coolies' ([1895] 1985) and James Dalziel's story 'Dead Reckoning' (1907) are also situated on merchant ships transporting Chinese labourers. All of these narratives convey a feeling of dread and terror towards 'human cargo'. The main protagonists are always white Europeans, whereas their contract labour 'cargo' is described in dehumanized and de-individualized terms, such as 'incomprehensible brutes' or 'swarming bees' (Yun 2008: 230). However, in Dalziel's story the Chinese men protest against the terrible circumstances on board. The presence of reformers from the Young China Party plays a crucial role in the kindling of this protest (Forman 2004: 401). In the ensuing mutiny, almost all the white men on board are killed. These stories do not just connect indenture to slavery but also show how, in the age of indenture, strong political counterforces were at work, creating a whole new set of fears for European colonizers.

In contrast, for Chinese authors the uprooting of vast amounts of people – and the racist policies that buttressed this system – became a focal point for the articulation of what Elizabeth Weber labels an 'awakening of activist subjectivity' (2016: 300) – the articulation of an anti-imperialist nationalism. She discusses two anonymously published Chinese novels, *Bitter Society* (1905) and *Golden World* (1907). Both novels detail the misery of Chinese labourers during transpacific journeys and the discrimination and exploitation they faced in the United States, where the 1882 Chinese Exclusion Act had created a hostile atmosphere for Chinese immigrants. Weber explains how the story's path is one of political awaking. The migrant's experiences range from humiliation at sea and in the Americas to a 'triumphant depiction of erstwhile laborers returning from abroad to lead activist efforts' (Weber 2016: 300). The specific trajectory of the coolies functions as a symbol for China's political situation at large: the return of the migrants can be read as 'a plea to readers to stand together and reclaim whatever power they could' (300). These two books did not constitute isolated literary incidents: according to Wen Jin, they 'appeared in the midst of a maelstrom of writings (novels, poetry, plays, and journalism) that offered firsthand testimonies to the persecution of Chinese laborers in the Americas' (2014: 105).

Similar stories of the transpacific journey of indentured workers are difficult to find in Dutch-language literature. Moreover, up until the 1930s, very few literary works were situated in Deli. An early exception is *Hans tongka's carriere* (Hans Tongka's Career, Délilah 1898) from Dé-lilah (a pseudonym of Lucie van Renesse). She was an Indo-European woman married to a Deli planter and thus knew the situation in Sumatra firsthand. Her novel details many of the abuses we also find in Van den Brand's pamphlet (Dharmowijono 2009: 248–253). However, Van Renesse's work made little impact; it was of little literary merit and, as she had no connections to the literary establishment in the Netherlands, her work was largely ignored by the mainstream press.

One of the most influential and critically acclaimed novelists of this period was Louis Couperus. He rose to prominence around the same time as Conrad and was loosely connected to a group of young Dutch authors that had gathered around the magazine *De Nieuwe Gids* (The new guide). They strove for the modernization of Dutch literature. Couperus situated many of his writings in the Dutch East Indies and is often compared to Conrad (Bel 2006), although the differences between the two writers are at least as instructive as their similarities. Couperus only started writing about indenture during the 1920s. In order to gain a better understanding of his literary treatment of the issue, we first need to examine his wider engagement with slavery. Black slaves are a recurring theme in Couperus's oeuvre (Van Luxemburg 1991). Yet they do not populate his colonial novels but, rather, appear in his fiction situated in antiquity, such as his 1911 work *Antiek toerisme* (Antique tourism). Thus, the issue of slavery is detached from the recent history of Western colonial capitalism and presented as an element of the Roman Empire (where, as Van Luxemburg [1991] points out, there were hardly any black enslaved people). In his historical fiction, Couperus eroticizes the black body and strongly emphasizes the unrepressed and immediate availability of black sexuality. A similar type of detachment from Dutch colonialism occurs when Couperus writes about coolies. The 1924 story 'De koelie' (The Coolie) is situated in premodern Japan. The narrator depicts the Japanese coolies as 'rough, simple, happy beasts' (Couperus [1924] 1995: 152–153).[1] His descriptions focus on the men's bodies: their 'statuesque' muscles ('statueske schoonheid'), their tattoos (153). They are represented as a merry, carefree lot, who like to sing songs in which they praise the aristocratic masters they carry around. However, one coolie has a different physique – a refined and noble face (156). He was orphaned and, as it transpires, is a child of noble parents. Of importance here is the way in which the story represents the existence of 'coolies' as an inevitability: some people are on a physical level born for nobility, while others are born for coarse physical labour. Compared to Conrad, who situated his novella *Typhoon* within the context of economic modernity, Couperus presents his readers with an eroticized and aestheticized version of history, in which modernity seems absent and hierarchies are a 'natural' phenomenon. Moreover, Couperus plays with the genre of the ancient oriental folk tale. The literary form thus mirrors this circumventing of modernity by means of an aestheticized past.

In his non-fiction, Couperus explicitly defends the system of indentured labour. He travelled extensively in Asia, and in 1921 his travelogues were published weekly in the Dutch journal *Haagsche Post* (The Hague Post). In 1923 the travelogues were collected under the general title *Oostwaarts* (Eastwards), in which the Dutch East Indies are depicted as prosperous, full of energy and self-evidently closely connected to the Netherlands (Nieuwenhuys [1972] 1978: 254). Visiting Deli, Couperus receives a warm welcome from the Governor of Sumatra Louis Constant Westenenk and fawns over the beauty and grandeur of the governmental palace. The building leads him to reflect on the incompatibility of democracy and beauty: 'Apparently, our democratic times have not erased all stature and joie de vivre in ordinary everyday things' (Couperus [1923] 1992: 38).[2] During his stay in the Dutch East Indies, he is carried around by coolies and, somewhat ironically, remarks that this hurts his modern, democratic sensibility, although emphasizing that the coolies themselves are merry and joyful – his description of them is quite similar to his depiction of coolies in the Japanese story he would write four years later (165).[3]

Couperus proceeds to argue that communism is alien to Sumatran people, 'because their instincts tell them the simple truth, namely, that equality cannot and will not exist' (284–285).[4] Again, reasoning from the assumption of an essentialist division between Oriental and Western people, Couperus considers the possibility of communism in the Dutch East Indies to be a 'Western' mirage and even though it might temporarily lead to mass protests in the Indies, this uproar would only be superficial: once calmed down, the Indonesian native would mourn for the old days of feudalism (258). Couperus admires Dutch imperial rule, both for its aesthetic grandeur, and for its innovative labour arrangements. On the heels of this economic modernity come democratic sensibilities, such as equality. Couperus, however, emphasizes that these modern sensibilities are *his* and are not shared at all by the coolies that carry him around. Thus, in *Oostwaarts* he claims that any improvements made to the circumstances of the coolies are the product of the Dutch, while abuses stem purely from Chinese and Javanese middlemen.

Mulk Raj Anand and Madelon Székely-Lulofs: High modernism and internationalism

Both the Dutch and British colonial administrations officially ended indenture in the 1930s. It is therefore striking that this was also the decade in which the abuses of unskilled and unorganized labourers became a dominant literary theme. As we shall see, the global political context is important here. The works of Madelon Székely-Lulofs and Mulk Raj Anand were written in the era of the Great Depression, and adopted a different, much more sober perspective on the economic boom of the 1920s. This boom had greatly accelerated the development of the 'plantation complex' in both empires. In the years following the financial crash, fascism was on the rise in Europe, and nationalist anti-colonial movements grew in strength in the colonies, which in turn also strengthened right-wing opposition to these movements. In this volatile political climate, writing a story from the perspective of a 'coolie' became a politically charged act – a demystification of imperial dreams held by the previous generation of intellectuals.

Anand was a vocal advocate for Indian autonomy and a key figure in the development of Anglo-Indian literature. Intellectually, his position is often described as on the intersection between Marxism and modernism. He studied philosophy in London in the 1920s and became acquainted with the Bloomsbury Set – a group of 'high' modernism's foremost practitioners, including, among others, Leonard and Virginia Woolf, T.S. Eliot, Edward Sackville-West, John Strachey and Dorothy Richardson (Cowasjee 1977: 27). As Sonali Perera (2014) demonstrates, Anand's writings do not fit easily within existing categories of literary history. The dominant interpretive frame reads his work as an expression of anticolonial nationalism. In *Coolie* ([1936] 1993) he charts the path of a 14-year-old boy called Munoo. The boy is continually displaced and forced to move: from a Kangra village in North West India to a small town (Sham Nagar), then to a city (Daulatpur) and onwards to the metropolis of Bombay. Although there are small moments of organized protest against the different systems of exploitation to which Munoo falls pray (he works in a factory, on a plantation and as a Rikshaw puller), the adolescent boy is battered over and over again and eventually dies. Anand envisioned *Coolie* as a counter-colonial narrative; a 'rewriting' of Kipling's *Kim* ([1900] 1956) – a combined boy's adventure story and celebration of empire. Anand was disturbed by the general admiration for Kipling's novel amongst the British elite (Perera 2014: 27–28). In *Conversations in Bloomsbury*, Anand characterized Kipling's *Kim* as 'a fairy tale' that glorified 'a fantasy boy' (1981: 39). Kim is a chameleon-like figure who adapts one regional dialect after another, has the agency to outwit authorities and acquires several benign father-figures along the way. In contrast, Munoo cannot escape the workings of an exploitative colonial-capitalist machinery. Thus, *Coolie* demystifies Kipling's vision of empire as a place of adventure and endless individual reinvention.

Perera (2014: 29) also notices a recent tendency to recuperate Anand as a modernist writer – to situate him among other canonized modernists. She then adds an important third lens through which to understand Anand's work: *Coolie* is not only a colonial counter-discourse and a modernist novel, but also an example of proletarian writing (Perera 2014). Thus, Anand's fiction can also be situated amidst 1930 internationalism, as his work reflects on the predicament of globalized capitalism after the crisis of 1929. If *Coolie* belonged to an internationalist tradition that aimed at giving voice to the proletarian voiceless, the novel at the same time made explicit why worldwide socialist solidarity was hindered by contradictions that proved so difficult to overcome. There are episodes in *Coolie* that evoke the structural disconnect between the working class in the British metropolis and the unschooled and unorganized labour forces in the colony: 'organized industrial action in England means short time for coolies in colonial factories in India' (Perera 2014: 28). Perera concludes that the novel 'is both a comment on the paradoxes of capitalist modernity – a modernity that must rely on backward, feudal institutions of indentured labor for the efficient extraction of surplus value – and a meditation on the paradoxes of trade unionist socialism' (28). These paradoxes are not just at work in the novel but also in its reception. They destabilize the categories used to place the novel either within a purely nationalist, modernist or internationalist framework.

Moving now to Székely-Lulofs, the colonial discourse in her novels does not fit squarely within the tradition of Dutch modernism, nor can her work be labelled as a conscious attempt at proletarian writing. Madelon Lulofs was born in the Dutch East Indies and accompanied her first husband to the Deli rubber plantations in 1918. However, in 1930 she divorced and married another Deli planter, László Székely, causing a scandal that forced them to leave Sumatra (Clerkx and Wertheim 1991: 2). As Stoler remarks, her novels are 'romanticized and voyeuristic' (1995: 33), while Meijer (1996: 124-169) points to the racial stereotypes in her work. At the same time, however, Stoler (1995) also notes that her descriptions of the plantation system are accurate. Sociologist Clerkx (1991) uses Székely-Lulofs's fiction to understand the sociological stratification of the Deli plantations. In other words: her work was of great documentary value and, in spite of its stereotypical elements, effectively demystified the image of the colonies as a place of Western self-realization and innovation.

Her debut novel *Rubber* (1932b) became an instant international bestseller and was translated into ten languages (Van Huffel 1939: 70-71). In the United States, the novel appeared under the title *White Money*. Prominent newspapers such as *The Herald Tribune*, *The Sun* and *The New York Times* wrote rave reviews and believed Hollywood might be interested in a movie-adaption (although this never came to be). In the Netherlands, *Rubber* was successfully adapted for the theatre and later, in 1936, turned into a movie (Praamstra 2006). Székely-Lulofs's subsequent novels, *Koelie* (*Coolie*, 1932a) and *De Andere Wereld* (*The Wealthy Beggar*, 1934) – both situated in Deli – were translated into several languages and were well received, especially in the United States. Her husband, László Székely, also wrote a novel about the lives of Deli planters, documenting the bonding of the white male planters through acts of racist violence and displays of white supremacy (Clerkx and Wertheim 1991: 55).

It is important to note that these Deli-inspired novels were not primarily intended as an indictment of indenture, but first and foremost depicted Deli as the site of an accelerating Americanization and modernization. The Netherlands had only slowly become industrialized, and for a long time the effects of economic modernization, such as a mobile middle class, were absent. Deli became the place where people could make 'easy money' and provided the conditions for an upward social mobility not yet feasible in the Netherlands itself. Moreover, the success of the rubber plantations can be seen in the growth of car ownership – the ultimate materialization of modern life. For example, the arrival of the American car plays a crucial symbolic role in *Rubber*. The growing wealth of the European planters is illustrated by their increasing hunger to possess the newest model of car. In the end, Dutch enterprises are taken over by American investors which, in Székely-Lulofs's novel, illustrates the loss of 'typical Dutch values', such as prudence and frugality. Yet it was not only Dutch writers that used these plantations as an example of capitalist modernity. In his book *The Life of the Automobile* ([1929] 1999) the Russian author Ilja Ehrenburg devotes an entire chapter to the rubber plantations.

Although *Rubber* was her greatest success, Székely-Lulofs's novel *Koelie* was her most innovative, as it was the first Dutch novel to feature a Javanese labourer as the protagonist. The story details the trials of a young Javanese boy named Roeki who, under false pretenses, signs a contract to work in Sumatra. Early on he is beaten into submission and the novel ends when he is an old man, still working on a Deli plantation and trapped in a system without an exit. Again, the tenor is not one of indictment and protest. The story is firmly situated in the past and the narrator explicitly states that in the 1930s the abuses suffered by Roeki as a child belong to the past. In an introduction to the English translation ('A Word to My British Readers'), Székely-Lulofs states that she was 'misunderstood' in Holland: 'they concluded that it was my intention to criticize a particular aspect of Dutch colonial policy, namely, the recruitment of contract coolies on the Island of Java for work on the plantations of Sumatra' (Székely-Lulofs 1936: v). She stresses that she did not want to write a 'political novel', stating that the system of indenture was 'more or less necessary', and she uses the rhetoric of colour blindness to claim that she wanted to tell a universal tale: 'A human being to me is a human being, whether white, brown, red, yellow or black' (v). She ends with an orientalist cliché reminiscent of Couperus's worldview: the novel details 'the soul of a strange race that remains mysterious to us in the west' (vi).

In the United States her work was critically read as a conscious departure from the Kipling tradition. A critic of the *New York Herald Tribune* remarked on *Rubber*: 'scorning the pompous platitudes of the Kipling school, Madelon Lulofs has written a candid and authentic novel of the daily lives of white men and their wives in the rubber plantations of Sumatra' (Poling 1933: h9). Three years later, the *New York Times* would go a step further and read her second novel *Coolie* as a politically charged debunking of Kipling's 'white man's burden':

> The white man's burden was, in the last analysis, nothing more than the very simple task of compelling the black man, the yellow man and the brown man to toil in what was actually – though unacknowledged – slavery. 'Coolie' is less a lament for a vanished Eastern simplicity than it is an excoriating exhibition of white brutality and degradation. (By 1936: br4)

In England the reception of *Coolie* was very different and much more in line with Székely-Lulofs's introduction to the British translation. John Beevers, a critic for *The Sunday Times*, stated that *Coolie* is 'no piece of left-wing reportage – a bitter attack on certain aspects of Imperialism' (1936: 10). To his relief, Lulofs does not resemble Marxist authors such as Egon Kisch; rather, Roeki's story is a universal 'human story' and not merely a 'facet of class-struggle' (10). It seems likely that the remarkable difference between the American and the British reception has everything to do with the two countries' different involvement in imperialism. Although American capital flowed into the Dutch colonies, officially the United States tried to ban Sumatran tobacco if it was harvested by coolies. The British had been deeply involved in the system of indenture themselves.

Székely-Lulofs's introduction to *Coolie* may have reflected her deeply felt poetical intention, but it could also be understood as a rhetorical move, prompted by the strong backlash her work provoked in the Netherlands. It was said that such books 'dragged European society through the mud' and that, rather than picturing colonial life as it really was, the novels were written with a premeditated slant (Nieuwenhuys 1982: 171). The Dutch Nazi-newspaper *Volk en Vaderland* (People and Mother Country) labelled her work as 'vile slander'. Conservative colonial journalists such as Henri Carel Zentgraaff wielded a similar rhetoric and characterized the fact that both husband and wife wrote novels as a 'case of infection within the family' (Pusztai and Praamstra 1997: 102).

Furthermore, there was a strong gendered element to all this disgust. Székely-Lulofs was not the only female author to write about Deli. Around the same time, Jo Manders, also the wife of a planter, wrote about the decadent lifestyle of the male planters. These female-authored novels provoked male critics to write 'counter-novels' that were meant to correct the impression of Deli society. In the introduction to his counter-novel, H. Veersema diagnosed the novels of Székely-Lulofs and Manders as a symptom of female boredom, and typical of women in the tropics. Worse still, their writings attested to a lack of female solidarity with the hard-working male planters (Veersema 1936: 3–4, cited in Clerkx and Wertheim 1991: 4).

And it was not only the right-wing press and the colonial community that lashed out. Dutch literary modernists (unlike the Bloomsbury Set) were an exclusively male group and cultivated a very negative attitude towards female authors. They structurally associated them with pandering to popular tropes and anti-intellectual domesticity (Van Boven 1992). Menno ter Braak was one of the most prominent literary critics in this circle of modernist writers. According to Ter Braak ([1934] 1949), Székely-Lulofs wrote 'ladies' prose', treating the tropics as merely a backdrop for clichéd stories of domestic life. Obviously, this criticism was not based on fact, as her novels would not have provoked such a strong reaction had they not documented the system of indenture in such a factual manner. Székely-Lulofs greatly admired Ter Braak, and the negativity of his review had a devastating effect on her (Van Boven 2010: 72).

Ter Braak preferred other colonial novels, for instance those of Louis Couperus, the nineteenth-century writer Multatuli, and his personal friend Eddy du Perron. These authors all put Western male individuality centre stage in their novels situated in the Dutch East Indies. Székely-Lulofs gave a very different account of masculinity under colonial capitalism, by showing how all the men went through the same military hazing ritual upon their arrival at the plantations, and how subsequently they all compensated for this humiliating initiation with violent acts towards the coolie labourers. The white men quickly understood that violence should be as depersonalized and unpredictable as possible, in order to create an atmosphere of terror. Thus, masculinity is not associated with subjectivity but with systemized violence. With this change of perspective, she confronted the Dutch audience with a demystification of what indenture entailed – a far cry from Couperus's travel stories.

If Anand highlighted the difficulty of a global solidarity amongst labourers, Székely-Lulofs's novels provoked anger because they were read explicitly (or implicitly) as a case of female betrayal. Because she herself claimed to have no political aims with her writings, one can hardly argue that her work should be read as an example of internationalist proletarian writing. Based on gendered arguments she was excluded from Dutch modernism. Though her novels were unrivaled by any other Dutch writer when it comes to international success and the ability to provoke discussion, her status in the Dutch literary canon remains ambivalent – unlike Couperus who, to this day, is considered to be one the most important Dutch writers of the twentieth century.

Conclusion

As the German poet Heinrich Heine supposedly quipped (apocryphal, as the reference has never been found): 'When the world ends I'll go to Holland, because everything happens there 50 years later.' The history of indenture seems to follow this pattern: compared to the British Empire, contract labour was introduced late in the Dutch East Indies and it was abolished only in 1931. This belatedness, however, should not be understood as the consequence of a 'typical Dutch' backwardness and slowness, but rather as the outcome of a specifically Dutch (and strategic) implementation of economic modernity. The Dutch strategically embraced economic modernization in very specific places such as Deli, under very specific militarized conditions, while simultaneously repressing any tendency towards democratization – debates were muffled, and local protests were violently suppressed.

As Moretti remarks, we can see world literature as a whole, but a whole which is structured around inequalities (2000: 44–55). The local differences in the treatment of indenture as a literary theme seem to illustrate his point. Conrad did not protest against the coolie trade, but he did situate indenture *within* the context of capitalist modernity, while Couperus imagined indenture as an essential element of premodern societies (and he considered the Sumatran people to be premodern). He thus legitimized that colonial regimes blocked democratization: the 'Western' striving for more equality would always remain alien to the local population.

We can identify a similar pattern in the 1930s. Although British imperialism was violent and repressive in its own right, it did leave room for a writer such as Mulk Raj Anand. In a manner very similar to Anand, the Indonesian writer Pramoedya Ananta Toer combined the poetical ambition to modernize Indonesian literature with a Marxist politics. His first writings, however, were published in 1947 – a decade after Anand, during the Indonesian War of Independence. The emergence of a writer like Pramoedya who showed how the racist laws of the Dutch colonial regime impacted the lives of the Javanese people, was simply impossible while the repressive Dutch colonial administration was still in place.

Female authors such as Dé-lilah, Jo Manders and Madelon Székely-Lulofs all experienced significant difficulty trying to enter the mainstream Dutch literary system because their work clashed not only with the male gatekeepers of high modernist sensibilities but also with the interests of the male European colonizers. Again, the difference with the British context is striking. The Bloomsbury Set was relatively open to outsiders such as Anand. The social climate in the Netherlands was quite different. Authors such as Menno ter Braak and Eddy du Perron cultivated a norm of masculine individuality that could only articulate itself in an exclusively male and heterosexual friendship (Bal 1991). In this masculine climate, polemical writing was considered to be the apex of intellectual honesty, and it resulted in the destruction of female literary reputations.

The international context opens up a different perspective. Especially in the United States, Székely-Lulofs's novels were understood as a debunking of Kipling's 'white man's burden', and Anand aimed for the exact same goal with his writings. Székely-Lulofs and Anand did not just happen to write a novel with the same title: their depiction of colonial capitalism points to a similar moment in colonial literature, after which the colonies can no longer be seen as the site of male self-realization and adventures.

Notes

1 'zij waren als ruwe, eenvoudige, vroolijke beesten'; translation Saskia Pieterse, as are all further quotations from Couperus.
2 'Onze demokratische tijd schijnt nog niet èlke voornaamheid en mooiheid van levenskunst in de gewone dagelijksche dingen te hebben uit gewischt.'
3 'Ik zet mijn scrupules van modern mensch-der-gelijkheid ter zijde; er is nu niets aan te doen aan het feit, dat acht koelies mij torsen.'
4 'Dat communisme voor hen een woord en een raadsel bleef en een Westersche hersenschim, die zij niet waardeeren omdat een instinct hen heeft doordrongen van de eenvoudige waarheid, dat gelijkheid nooit was en nooit zijn kan.'

References

Literature

Anand, M.R. (1981), *Conversations in Bloomsbury*, New Delhi: Arnold-Heinemann.
Anand, M.R. ([1936] 1993), *Coolie*, New Delhi: Penguin.
Bal, M. (1991), '"Door zuiverheid gedreven": het troebele water van *Het land van herkomst* van E. du Perron', in E. van Alphen and M. Meijer (eds), *De canon onder vuur. Nederlandse literatuur tegendraads gelezen*, 122–142, Amsterdam: Van Gennep.
Beevers, J. (1936), 'Adventures All round the Globe', *Sunday Times*, 9 February 1936: 10.
Bel, J. (2006), 'Racist or Anti-Colonial? A Comparison of *The Hidden Force* by Louis Couperus and *Heart of Darkness* by Joseph Conrad', in T.J. Broos, M. Bruyn Lacy and T.F. Shannon (eds), *The Low Countries: Crossroads of Cultures*, 165–176, Münster: Nodus Publikationen.
Boven, E. Van (1992), *Een hoofdstuk apart. 'Vrouwenromans' in de literaire kritiek 1898–1930*, Amsterdam: Sara/Van Gennep.
Boven, E. van (2010), 'Schandalen en successen: Madelon Székély-Lulofs (1899–1958)', in J. Bel and T. Vaessens (eds), *Schrijvende vrouwen: een kleine literatuurgeschiedenis van de Lage Landen, 1880–2010*, 97–101, Amsterdam: Amsterdam University Press.
Braak, M. ter ([1934] 1949), 'de roman als document', in M. van Crevel, H.A. Gomperts and G.H.S. Gravesande (eds), *Verzameld werk*, 5, Amsterdam: G.A. van Oorschot.

Breman, J. (1992), *Koelies, Planters en Koloniale Politiek. Het arbeidsregime op de grootlandbouwondernemingen aan Sumatra's Oostkust in het begin van de twintigste eeuw*, Leiden: KITLV.
By, P.H. (1936), 'An Affecting Tale of Coolie Life', *New York Times*, 16 February 1936: br4.
Carlton Dawe, W. ([1895] 1985), *Yellow and White*, London: J Lane.
Carter, M. and K. Torabully, eds (2002), *Coolitude: An Anthology of the Indian Labour Diaspora*, London: Anthem Press, Anthem South Asian Studies.
Clerkx, L.E. and W. F. Wertheim (1991), *Living in Deli: Its Society as Imaged in Colonial Fiction*, Amsterdam: VU University Press.
Conrad, J. (1895), *Almayer's Folly*, London: T. Fisher Unwin.
Conrad, J. ([1902] 1986), 'Typhoon', in Cedric Watts (ed.), *Typhoon and Other Tales*, Oxford: Oxford University Press.
Couperus, L. ([1923] 1992), *Oostwaarts*, H. T. M. van Vliet, J. B. Robert En and Gerard Nijenhuis (eds.), 6–277, *Volledige werken* 45, Amsterdam/Antwerp: L.J. Veen.
Couperus, L. ([1924] 1995), 'De koelie', in H.T.M. van Vliet and J.B. Robert (eds), *Het snoer der ontferming en Japansche legenden*, 148–165, Volledige werken 47, Amsterdam/Antwerp: L.J. Veen.
Cowasjee, S. (1977), *So Many Freedoms: A Study of the Major Fiction of Mulk Raj Anand*, Oxford: Oxford University Press.
Dalziel, J. (1907), 'Dead Reckoning', in *In the First Watch and Other Engine-Room Stories*, 153–154, London: T. Fisher Unwin.
Délilah (1898), *Hans Tongka's carrière; tabaksroman*, Utrecht: Honing.
Dharmowijono, W. (2009), 'Van koelies, klontongs en kapiteins: het beeld van de Chinezen in Indisch-Nederlands literair proza 1880–1950', PhD diss., University of Amsterdam.
Drescher, S. (2009), *Abolition: A History of Slavery and Antislavery*, Cambridge: Cambridge University Press.
Ehrenburg, I. ([1929] 1999), *The Life of the Automobile*, London: Serpent's tail.
Forman, R. G. (2004), 'Coolie Cargoes: Emigrant Ships and the Burden of Representation in Joseph Conrad's *Typhoon* and James Dalziel's "Dead Reckoning"', *English Literature in Transition, 1880–1920* 47 (4): 398–428.
Gouda, F. (2008), *Dutch Culture Overseas: Colonial Practice in the Netherlands Indies 1900–1942*, Jakarta: Equinox Publishing.
Huffel, J. van (1939), *Nederlandsche schrijvers in vertaling (van Marcellus Emants tot Jan Eekhout). Proeve van eene bibliographie*, Leiden: E.J. Brill.
Janse, M.J. (2015), 'Holland as a Little England? British Anti-Slavery Missionaries and Continental Abolitionist Movements in the Mid Nineteenth Century', *Past and Present: A Journal of Scientific History* 229 (1): 123–160.
Jin, W. (2014), 'Sentimentalism's Transnational Journeys: *Bitter Society* and Lin Shu's Translation of *Uncle Tom's Cabin*', *Modern Chinese Literature and Culture* 26 (1): 105–136.
Kaur, A. (2014), 'Plantation Systems, Labour Regimes and the State in Malaysia, 1900–2012', *Journal of Agrarian Change* 14 (2): 190–213.
Kipling, R. ([1900] 1956), *Kim*, New York: Doubleday.
Kumar, A. (2017), *Coolies of the Empire. Indentured Indians in the Sugar Colonies*, Cambridge: Cambridge University Press.
Luxemburg, J. van (1991), 'Zwarte slaven bij Couperus', *Literatuur* 8 (4): 210–216.
Major, A. (2017), '"Hill Coolies": Indian Indentured Labour and the Colonial Imagination, 1836-38', *South Asian Studies* 33 (1): 23–36.

Maters, M. (1998), *Van zachte wenk tot harde hand: Persvrijheid en persbreidel in Nederlands*-Indië *1906–1942*, Hilversum: verloren.
Meijer, M. (1996), *In tekst gevat. Inleiding tot een kritiek van representatie*, Amsterdam: Amsterdam University Press.
Moretti, F. (2000), 'Conjectures on World Literature', *New Left Review* 1: 54–68.
Mrázek, R. (1994), *Sjahrir: Politics and Exile in Indonesia, Cornell University*, Ithaca, NY: Southeast Asia Program, Cornell University.
Nieuwenhuys, R. ([1972] 1978), *Oost-Indische spiegel. Wat Nederlandse schrijvers en dichters over Indonesië hebben geschreven, vanaf de eerste jaren van de compagnie tot op heden*, Amsterdam: Querido.
Nieuwenhuys, R. (1982), *Mirror of the Dutch Indies, a History of Dutch Colonial Literature*, Amherst: University of Massachusetts Press.
Northrup, D. (1995), *Indentured Labor in the Age of Imperialism, 1834–1922*, Cambridge: Cambridge University Press.
Perera, S. (2014), *No Country: Working-Class Writing in the Age of Globalization*, New York: Columbia University Press.
Pirbhai, M. (2009), *Mythologies of Migration, Vocabularies of Indenture: Novels of the South Asian Diaspora in Africa, the Caribbean, and Asia-Pacific*, Toronto: Toronto University Press.
Poling, J.W. (1933), 'Some Leading Recent Fiction', *New York Herald Tribune*, 21 May 1933: h9.
Praamstra, O. (2006), 'Begraven en weer opgestaan. de literaire waardering van Madelon Székely-Lulofs', *Praagse perspectieven. Handelingen van het colloquium van de sectie Nederlands van de Karelsuniversiteit te Praag* 4: 47–59.
Pusztai, G. and O. Praamstra (1997), 'Een "lasterlijk geschrijf"; Kritiek en (zelf-)censuur in de Nederlands-Indische literatuur; De ontvangst van Laszló Székely's *Van oerwoud tot plantage*', *Indische Letteren* 12: 99–124.
Sarwal, A. (2017), *South Asian Diaspora Narratives: Roots and Routes*, Singapore: Springer Singapore.
Steltenpool, R. (n.d.), 'The First Serialization and Translation of Conrad: *Almayer's Folly* in *Het Nieuws van den Dag* (Amsterdam), May–July 1896'. Available online: http://www.conradfirst.net/conrad/scholarship/authors/steltenpool (accessed 18 February 2019).
Stoler A. (1986), 'Plantation Politics and Protest on Sumatra's East Coast', *The Journal of Peasant Studies* 13 (2): 124–143.
Stoler, A. (1995), *Capitalism and Confrontation in Sumatra's Plantation Belt, 1870–1979*, Ann Arbor: University of Michigan Press.
Székely-Lulofs, M.H. (1932a), *Koelie*, Amsterdam: Elsevier.
Székely-Lulofs, M.H. (1932b), *Rubber*, Amsterdam: Elsevier.
Székely-Lulofs, M.H. (1934), *De andere wereld*, Amsterdam: Elsevier.
Székely-Lulofs, M.H. (1936), 'A Word to My British Readers', in *Coolie*, trans. G.J. Renier and I. Clephane, ix–x, London: Cassell & co.
Taselaar, A.P. (1992), 'A.D.A. de Kat Angelino en de grondslagen van zijn koloniale theorie', *BMGN – Low Countries Historical Review* 107 (2): 264–84.
Veersema, H. (1936), *Delianen van de tafelronde*. Medan: Köhler.
Weber, E.E. (2016), 'Reimagining Coolie Trajectories: The Triumphant Return as Political Statement in Late Qing "Coolie Fiction"', *Literature Compass* 13 (5): 300–310.
Yun, L. (2008), *The Coolie Speaks: Chinese Indentured Laborers and African Slaves in Cuba*, Philadelphia, PA: Temple University Press.

11

Towards a History of Russian Translations of Dutch Literature: Herman Heijermans and His Play *The Good Hope* in Russia

Irina Michajlova and Sergei Tcherkasski

Dutch literature in Russian: A brief review of translations made before 1917

Getting acquainted with writers who wrote in Dutch was quite an uneven process for the Russian public, with translation activity depending not so much on the achievements of Dutch literature but rather on the situation in Russian culture. After the era of Peter I (the beginning of the eighteenth century) that established intense cultural ties between Russia and the Netherlands and saw the publication of the first Russian translation of a Dutch literary work – *Vorstelijke warande der dieren* (*The Princely Pleasure-Ground of Animals*) by Joost van den Vondel, which was translated as early as 1674 by the Russified Dutchman Andries Winius (Koreneva and Michajlova 2016) – there was a long pause before another translation occured. It was not until 1803 that another work of Dutch literature was published in Russian. This was a novel by Rhijnvis Feith, *Julia*, which was translated via an intermediary language.[1] *Julia* marks the beginning of the so-called 'Romantic translation' vogue accompanying the surge of interest in faraway little-known literatures (including Dutch literature), which was a characteristic feature of the Romantic Movement. However, after the Congress of Vienna (1814–1815) and the marriage of Grand Duchess Anna Pavlovna of Russia (Dutch: Anna Paulowna) to the heir to the Dutch throne (1816) the Netherlands was no longer one of those 'faraway little-known' countries and the interest in Dutch literature significantly increased. An important figure at the time was Petr A. Korsakov (1790–1844), a diplomat, censor and man of letters, who spent several years serving in the Russian diplomatic mission in the Netherlands and knew Dutch well. Korsakov penned three solid reviews of Dutch literature in general as well as of some individual writers: 'An outline of Dutch literature: its beginnings, development, and present state' (1838a), 'Joost van den Vondel' (1838b) and 'Jacob Cats. A poet, thinker, and man of wisdom' (1839). For the first of these reviews Korsakov was granted an audience with Anna Pavlovna. The swansong of Korsakov was an anthology of Dutch literature, the first in Russian history, with translations of both Northern Dutch and Flemish poets (1844).

After Korsakov's death there followed a period of translation inactivity that lasted for almost half a century. During this time only two translations from Dutch were published in Russia (in 1852 and 1859): a novel and a novella by Hendrik Conscience, who was very popular throughout Europe at the time.

It was not until the late nineteenth and early twentieth century that the situation changed and Russia saw a period of unprecedented translation activity in general. According to our data, through the 1890s and until 1917 more than 120 publications dealt with Dutch literature: translations, reviews, critical essays.

This explosion in translation activity could be accounted for by the democratization of literary life in Russia in general and the need for Russian culture to renew itself and find its own artistic voices and ways of expression. Painters, writers and composers looked for inspiration abroad. While translating foreign poetry Russian poets (Merezhkovsky, Balmont, Bryusov and others) sought to learn from European literature. Symbolism, focusing on a mystic 'Super Reality' and a specific ideal of beauty, became a major art movement of the Silver Age in Russian culture.

Most reviews of Dutch literature in Russian magazines of the time discuss 'the Eighties Movement', a highly influential group of writers in the Netherlands who professed to serve Beauty, embraced the idea of art for art's sake, and cultivated individualism in creative work. However, though it was in poetry that the writers of the Eighties Movement achieved a revolution, no Russian translations of poetry from Dutch were produced at that time. Russian publishers at the turn of the century opted for literary products that were more likely to enjoy success with the Russian readers.

Maarten Maartens (1858–1915), who wrote his adventure page-turner novels in English and now is almost completely forgotten, ranks first in the number of works published in Russian literary magazines (twenty-five novels) and the number of references (he was referred to as 'the Dutch writer whom everybody loves') in prefaces to other published translations from Dutch.

Multatuli (Eduard Douwes Dekker, 1820–1887) ranks second. According to our estimates more than a thousand pages of his works were translated into Russian at the time. Choice pieces from a number of his books (*De Japanse steenhouwer*, *Saïdjah en Adinda* and the stories about power from *Minnebrieven*) were published in dozens of magazines and newspapers all over the Russian Empire – from *Nizhegorodsky Listok*

(*Nizhny Novgorod News*) to *Sibirskaya Zhizn'* (*Siberian Life*), a Tomsk periodical, *Belorussky Vestnik* (*Byelorussian Courier*), and *Kavkaz* (*The Caucasus*), published in Tiflis. However, Multatuli's main work, the novel *Max Havelaar* (1860), was not published in Russia until 1916.

Herman Heijermans (1864–1924) – the main subject of this article – ranks third in number of pages (some seven hundred) translated into Russian during the same period. Translations of his works will be discussed in detail in the next section (Figure 11.1).

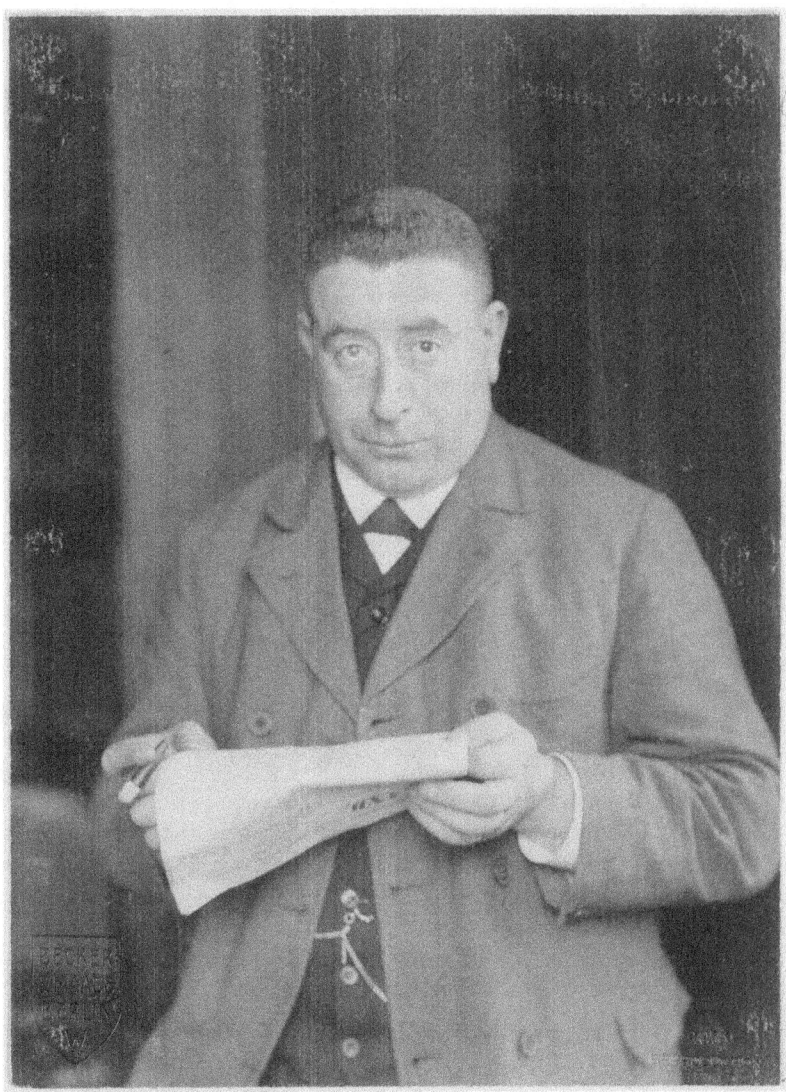

Figure 11.1 Herman Heijermans.

Louis Couperus (1863–1923) ranks fourth. From 1902 to 1907 *Noviy zhurnal Inostrannoy Literatury* (*The New Magazine of Foreign Literature*) published translations of *Psyche* (1902), *Noodlot* (*The Footsteps of Fate*) (1905), *Majesteit* (*Majesty: A Novel*) (1906), and *Wereldvrede* (*World Peace*) (1907).

Frederik van Eeden (1860–1932), the only writer of the Eighties Movement to be translated into Russian at the time, comes fifth. His symbolic fairy tale *De kleine Johannes* (*The Little Johannes*) (1887) was published in three different translations: in the magazines *Vestnik Evropy* (*Herald of Europe*) (1897) and *Russkaya Mysl* (*Russian Thought*) (1905), and in 1916 as a book.

Henriëtte Roland Holst-van der Schalk (1869–1952) ranks sixth. At the time, only her essays appeared in Russian translation: *Mysticism in Modern Literature, Maeterlinck*, and *Essays on Socialist Aesthetics*. The translations were made from German in 1905 to 1907. Her naïve socialist verse dramas were translated after the October Revolution of 1917.

The situation with regard to Flemish literature is quite interesting. In the early twentieth century Russian intellectuals saw Belgium, after the 1908 play Maurice Maeterlinck had written for the Moscow Art Theatre, as 'the country of *The Blue Bird*' – a mysterious and beautiful dream country. Russian intellectuals could read French and loved francophone Belgian Symbolist poetry, particularly that of Emile Verhaeren. Maeterlinck's plays enjoyed unwavering popular success in Russia, with his *Sister Beatrice* being staged in many Russian theatres. Charles de Coster, though he belonged to an earlier generation, also became fashionable at the time. Flemish literature was seen as even more romantic and remote through the lenses of these writers. In 1910 *Het sieraad der geestelijke bruiloft* (*The Adornment of the Spiritual Marriage*, 1910), by the Flemish mystic Jan van Ruusbroec (1293–1381), was translated via a French translation made by Maeterlinck, who also provided an eighty-page preface. The same journey – from an interest in Belgian francophone literature (and particularly the 1880s to 90s literary movement *La Jeune Belgique*) to a passion for Flemish literature – was made by the literary scholar Maria Veselovskaya. After writing a series of articles about francophone Belgian literature she turned to *Modern Flemish Literature* (1915).

After a forty-year break, Russian magazines in the 1890s also started publishing again works by Hendrik Conscience, who was already dead by that time: there appeared Russian translations of *De loteling* (*The Conscript*) (1892), *Blinde Rosa* (*Blind Rosa*) (1893) and *Moeder Job* (*Mother Job*) (1893).

Our brief review shows that translators and publishers were attracted by different types of literary work: those with social issue themes (Multatuli, Heijermans, H. Roland Holst), as well as artistic (Couperus), realistic (Heijermans), Symbolist (Couperus, Van Eeden) and mystic works (Ruysbroeck). However, most frequently translated were entertainment books (Maartens).

Translations of works by Herman Heijermans

It is appropriate to start discussing the Russian translations of Heijermans's works by recalling a mystification that the famous playwright made in 1893 when he published his play *Ahasverus* (*Agaspherus*) alleging it was a translation from the Russian (Michajlova 2013: 436). In his preface to the play Heijermans claimed its author to be Ivan Jelakovitch, a Russian Jew, who had suffered the persecution described in the play and who had died shortly after he had finished his work. Heijermans invented a biography for him: he had been born on 3 December 1864 (Heijermans date of birth) in Nizhny Novgorod, studied at the University of Kazan, and had written a novel *Zemstvo of Novgorod* 'which affects its readers so powerfully that it is reminiscent of Leo Tolstoy'. According to an American scholar S.L. Flaxman, *Agaspherus* shows Heijermans's familiarity with Leo Tolstoy's drama *The Power of Darkness* (Verdoes 1954: 336).

Heijermans resorted to mystification because of the failure of his first play *Dora Kremer*, which he published under his real name. It was not until after the work of the late Ivan Jelakovitch had met with the critics' approval that Heijermans revealed his authorship. From then on he published under his real name.

While *Agaspherus* never became known in Russia, *Ghetto* (subtitled *From the Life of Dutch Jews*) was published in a Russian translation in Vilno in 1903 and then again by two different theatre publishing houses in Moscow in 1904 (Heijermans 1903, 1904b, 1904c). This seems typical for the Russian translations of Heijermans's plays: most of them were published several times by a number of theatre publishing houses in various cities of the Russian Empire, which shows that there existed intense contacts in the Russian theatre world. For instance, in 1904 alone his play *Het zevende gebod* (*The Seventh Commandment*) was published twice by two different Moscow publishing houses, in a translation by M. Girshman under the title *Foundations of Marriage* and dedicated to Vera Komissarzhevskaya (Heijermans 1904d), and in another translation, by M. Gelrot, in Yalta under the title *The Seventh Commandment* (Heijermans 1904e). The famous Dutch critic L. van Deyssel traces echoes of *The Lady of the Camellias* by Dumas fils in the play (Van Deyssel 1901: 331–332). The main character, a young man from a wealthy family, is in love with the grisette Lotte Ricaudet and wants to marry her despite the opposition from his family. In the opinion of L. van Deyssel, the young man's relatives are portrayed with a talent worthy of Zola or Balzac. The fact that the play was published several times by different theatre publishing houses in Russia shows that Heijermans, on the basis of an all-too-familiar story, was able to create a topical play that dealt with issues resonating with the public not only in the Netherlands but in Russia as well.

According to our data, thirty-four editions of works by Heijermans, and a great many reviews of his plays, were published in Russia before 1917. Before we turn to a detailed discussion of the Russian publications and theatre productions of his most famous play *Op hoop van zegen* (literally: 'Hoping for the Best' but staged in English as *The Good Hope*, after the name of the ship that plays a major role in the play), which made the Dutch playwright's name an integral part of the history of Russian culture, we will briefly consider Heijermans's novels and novellas that were of interest to early twentieth-century Russian readers.

Heijermans's novel *Diamantstad* (*Diamond Town*) depicts the life of the poor inhabitants of the Jewish Quarter in Amsterdam. The Russian translation was published three times (1904a, 1920, 1922). Since the time of Spinoza diamond cutting had traditionally been an occupation of the Amsterdam Jews. For this reason the phrase 'Diamond Town' is immediately associated with Jewish Amsterdam. However, the title of the novel is poignantly sarcastic: the poverty and unsanitary conditions of the characters' lives are in stark contrast to the glitter of the jewels they work on. It is noteworthy that the editor of the translation and the author of the preface in the 1920 edition was a well-known Russian literary scholar of Jewish origin, A.G. Gornfeld, who studied the history of the Jewish people.

Heijermans was a committed socialist, and many of his writings were meant to raise awareness about the need to fight for freedom and a decent life. Yet, he also wrote works focused not so much on social issues but characterized rather by an entertaining plot, subtle humour and fantasy, and some of these were also translated. Good examples are the novellas *Gevleugelde Daden*, published in *Vestnik Inostrannoy Literatury* (*The Bulletin of Foreign Literature*) (1907), and *Joep's wonderlijke avonturen*, likewise published in *Vestnik Inostrannoy Literatury* (1910). *Gevleugelde Daden* is the story of a man named Zwaluw (swallow), who dreams of flying. This passion leads him to order a flying machine from the USA. For a long time he hides it from his neighbours. One day, he flies his family to the town belfry. However, when the flying machine burns because of an unextinguished cigarette, they cannot get down from the belfry. Zwaluw has to ask for help from the city services to rescue them. The family is taken down from the belfry but the secret comes to light. As a result, all the neighbours also buy flying machines. Flying becomes all the fashion, and Zwaluw is awarded the Nobel Prize for his contribution to the development of aviation.

Joep's wonderlijke avonturen is a science fiction novella about the wonders of modern science. In some ways it echoes H.G. Wells's novel *The Invisible Man*, which was translated into Russian in the same year 1910. In the beginning of the novella Joep, who had become blind as the result of an accident, meets a doctor experimenting with eye transplants. Thinking that he has nothing to lose, Joep agrees to be operated on and becomes the owner first of a pair of cat's eyes, and later of other animal eyes. He discovers that with his new eyes he not only sees the world around him differently but that he also perceives himself in a different way.

For reasons unknown, the witty short stories Heijermans wrote under the pen-name Samuel Falkland (known as *Falklandjes*), were not translated into Russian, as far as we know. This seems quite strange since Russian pre-revolutionary magazines were happy to publish all sorts of humorous short stories. Neither was the Russian public introduced to Heijermans's children books *Droomkoninkje* (1924) and *Vuurvlindertje* (1925), which remain popular in the Netherlands: after the October Revolution of 1917 the flow of translations from Dutch turned narrow and sometimes dried up altogether because only socially engaged books were selected for translation.

It was exactly in this way – as a socially engaged work – that Heijermans's play *Op hoop van zegen* (*The Good Hope*) (1900) for many years was received by most of the Russian public. Even the Russian translation of its title – *Gibel' 'Nadezhdy'* (literally: Wreck of 'Hope') – sounded like a social message. The plot is simple and provoking: the greedy ship-owner Clemens Bos sends a number of fishermen, among them widow Kniertje's two sons, to sea on a notoriously unsafe vessel to claim the insurance after its shipwreck. The play's powerful social agenda was one of the reasons for its popularity during the years when Russia 'was pregnant with the revolution'. And due to its conformity with the revolutionary ideology, the play was also allowed to be staged after the October Revolution of 1917.

As a result, *The Good Hope* broke many records: in the number of editions (to our knowledge, there were thirteen), in the number of languages it was translated from (German, French and probably Dutch), in the number of cities of the Russian Empire where the play was performed (Kazan, Kiev, Nizhny Novgorod, Odessa, Samara, Saratov, Kharkov, Kherson, Nikolayev, Sebastopol and Tiflis), in the glory and talent of the theatre directors who staged it and the actors who performed in it (Vsevolod Meyerhold, Konstantin Mardzhanov, Alexander Tairov, Michael Chekhov, Alexander Ostuzhev and many others), and, lastly, in the duration of the stage life of its most famous Russian production, which ran at the First Studio of the Moscow Art Theatre (since 1924 called Moscow Art Theatre-2) for more than twenty years (from 1913 to 1934) and was performed 648 times.

The Good Hope at the First Studio of the Moscow Art Theatre (1913)

The Good Hope as staged at the First Studio of the Moscow Art Theatre,[2] was radically different from all previous productions of the play: it was born as a result of a passionate pedagogical experiment in the course of which the Stanislavsky System was evolved. The First Studio itself was established in 1912 as a laboratory to study the nature of acting as objectively determined by human psycho-physiology. And in the first months of its existence one of the actors, Richard Boleslavsky, who by that time had played quite a few roles in the Moscow Art Theatre productions, came up with the initiative to stage a play on their own. He managed to talk Stanislavsky into giving him permission. The 23-year-old debut director chose to stage *The Good Hope*.

The work day of the Studio's members was busy: from 11.00 am to 1.00 pm they rehearsed the play independently without their teachers, in the afternoon they had the System classes with Stanislavsky, Sulerzhitsky, or Vakhtangov, and in the evening many of them performed in the Moscow Art Theatre productions. So, the Studio rehearsal work continued naturally at the classes, and the classes enriched the rehearsals. Thus Boleslavsky, while enjoying independence as a director, received priceless methodological support from Stanislavsky.

In fact, *The Good Hope* turned out to be ideal material for training: it provided plenty of opportunities to practice the basic skills of the Stanislavsky System. The characters in the play have to walk in the pouring rain and piercing wind, get drunk at the village feast, or see the first snow of the season. Thus, situations in the play offer the actors countless opportunities for checking out and developing their memory of sensory experiences. One would think that conveying the emotions of Dutch widows that have lost their husbands and sons at sea would make playing these parts too complex and challenging a task for the Studio's young actors. Yet they were able to come up with convincing performances thanks to the affective (emotional) memory exercises. Finally, while the actors have to go through some really tragic situations in the play, they are required not only to show an appropriate emotional response but also to control their muscle tension and retain attention focus – all the skills that formed the basis of Stanislavsky's teaching method. So, the actors of the Studio devoted themselves to the technical side of preparing themselves for the performance with great enthusiasm and a real passion.

The production premiered on 15 January 1913 (Figures 11.2 and 11.3). The work of the Studio's young actors and Boleslavsky's debut as a theatre director met with generally recognized success. The 'student work' became an important cultural event that surprised and excited the Moscow theatre world. It became apparent that the production developed something that could be a foundation for a new type of theatre. But what was it that made this production of *The Good Hope* so special?

Sofia Giatsintova, who played the part of Clementina, reminisced that the production was the triumph of 'a new method for providing insight into the nature of human feelings, the true reality of life and human emotions onstage, which was only made possible thanks to the Stanislavsky System' (Giatsintova 1989: 103).

In contrast to past productions, Boleslavsky didn't focus on the social themes of the play. What was foregrounded was the interaction of human beings with the powers of the sea, and so 'the sea was the unseen setting that determined the style of the production' (Markov 1974: 369). It was the sea, invisible but omnipresent, that determined the minute-to-minute existence of the actors onstage. The sea, almighty power and blind fate, could provide the means of livelihood or take a horrible toll by claiming the lives of the fishermen. The director focused on the minute details of the actors' existence onstage: 'the worthiness of living, grief, or happiness was conveyed by subtle details of behavior – by a look, a sob, a sudden cry' (369).

Boleslavsky's production brought to light quite a few emerging talents. The audiences reveled in Alexey Dikiy cast in the role of Barend, Kniertje's younger son, who has a horror of the sea. Traditionally, Barend had been portrayed as a neurotic, weakly and unhealthy-looking young man. Breaking with tradition, Dikiy made his character a strong, sun-tanned and sturdy man. In his memoirs he explained that he 'tried to reinforce this impression by choosing for Barend in the wardrobe department of the Moscow Art Theater a very bulky jacket, a thick cable knit sweater, rough baggy pants, and wooden clogs that produced a clattering sound when he walked' (Dikiy 1957: 225). On finding out that the fishing vessel is rotten all over and leaks, he implores his mother to not let him go aboard and to hide him. Instead, his mother hands him over to the gendarmes. This scene produced a stunning effect because of the contrast between the manly appearance of the robust healthy Barend as performed by Dikiy and his defenselessness, his animal fear of death.

Figure 11.2 Michael Chekhov (Cobus), Lidya Deykun (Kniertje), Grigory Khmara (Geert), Vera Soloviova (Jo) and Leo Bulgakov (Barend) in *The Good Hope* by Heijermans. The First Studio of Moscow Art Theatre, 1913.

Critics wrote a great deal about Serafima Birman, who revealed her gift for character roles playing the part of Mathilde, the ship-owner's wife, hypocritical and with affected manners. Birman had an exaggerated make-up, a pince-nez, paddings to make her figure look more massive, and a shrill raspy voice to boot. Her face was always twisted into an ugly grimace. As the actress wrote in her memoirs: 'Mathilde's stupid slobbery mouth, resembling a purse with a broken clasp, lays bare the true nature of that woman – all puffed up, with a duck-like figure, and also with brains like those of a duck' (Birman 1962: 84). All this made Mathilde – in Birman's interpretation

Figure 11.3 Vera Soloviova (Jo), Ivan Lazarev (Bos), Lidya Deykun (Kniertje) and Grigory Khmara (Geert) in *The Good Hope* by Heijermans. The First Studio of Moscow Art Theatre, 1913.

– one of the most important figures of the performance, though she doesn't appear onstage until the last act.

The central character of the performance was the widow Kniertje, played by Lidiya Deikun. In his memoirs Alexey Dikiy, who carefully observed the work of his stage partner, emphasizes how multifaceted her acting was:

> Her somewhat rough appearance hid tenderness and pain. Playing with Deikun in the scene when she herself sends her son to the fishing vessel destined to be wrecked, I witnessed each time the emotional flow of the scene going in the direction opposite to the action tasks. Kniertje breaks up Barend's resistance; she insists, more and more persistently, that he should go to the ship at once, and yet her heart is crying: 'Stay here! Don't go! I will not let my last son go to his death!' It is his mother's pain that eventually makes Barend give up; since his mother with all her love is telling him to go there, it means he should go. I felt my arms go weak and let go of the doorpost I was clutching to, and I allowed the hefty gendarmes to take me away. (Dikiy 1957: 224)

However, most attention in the press probably went to Michael Chekhov, for whom the part of Cobus, a sailor in the almshouse, was his first role both at the Studio and in the city of Moscow. Chekhov's Cobus was radiating love – for life and for people – in response to the harshness of life, adversity and social injustice. According to Dikiy, 'in Act Four Cobus comes to Bos's office several times to inquire about *The Good Hope*. Cobus didn't have any sons on board the ship yet his grief was so sincere and acute that not only

Figure 11.4 Anna Popova (Saart) and Michael Chekhov (Cobus) in *The Good Hope* by Heijermans. The First Studio of Moscow Art Theatre, 1913.

the audience but also we, the actors, felt our hearts breaking' (Dikiy 1957: 224). At the same time, Chekhov's acting was full of humour. To create this character of an old man, Chekhov used a bald cap (Figure 11.4); its description has become a textbook example:

> Chekhov pulled on a bald oversized wig with only a little cloud of thin gray hair on it as if it were an ear-flapped hat; he fastened it under his chin with a safety-pin, which

he didn't try to conceal and which he even stroked lovingly from time to time. Cobus' neck was wrapped with an old scarf that also became an integral part of acting: he would wrap it around him, unwrap it, get entangled in it, and weep into it. (224)

The performance enthralled not only the Moscow audiences. It attracted considerable attention in St Petersburg, where the Studio brought *The Good Hope* during their spring tours in 1913, 1914, 1915 and 1919. Sergei Volkonsky, an eminent theatre maker of the time, called the production 'rare' and admired the birthday scene in Act Two: 'it is all made up of tiny details, it is full of humor, simplicity, playfulness, laughter – and yet its seeming lightness is the sum result of a huge amount of work. This is "real life"' (Volkonsky 1914: 16). The renowned poet Alexander Blok wrote in his diary: 'Their acting is a true delight. It reminds you of the old days of the Moscow Art Theater. An ensemble' (Blok 1963: 246). And since Blok at that time was quite interested in the System actor training (another entry in his diary recounts his conversation with Stanislavsky about the basic acting exercises) he emphasized how effective this training was for preparing the actors of the Studio for their roles.

During the Studio's tours in St Petersburg *The Good Hope* was usually performed at the Theatre Hall of the famous Tenishev School on 33–35 Mokhovaya Street. This is where the Russian State Institute of the Performing Arts (until 2015 the St Petersburg State Theatre Arts Academy) is housed today and where – a remarkable coincidence – during the theatre seasons of 2014/15 and 2015/16 Heijermans's play was again presented to the Russian audience after a long, long time.[3]

A hundred years later

It all started when in 2012 an unusual four-year theatre research and training project was launched at Professor Sergei Tcherkasski's Acting Studio at the St Petersburg State Theatre Arts Academy. It was called 'Reconstruction of Actor Training at the First Studio of the Moscow Art Theatre', or as the students used to call it, 'Playing at Being the First Studio'.[4]

At the end of their first year of studies all the students of the Acting Studio received a task to find as material for their future études not some prosaic work of a classical Russian author, as custom had it, but pieces of *documentary prose*: actors' memoirs, diaries of rehearsals, stories about the artistic life of the First Studio of the Moscow Art Theatre, which had started its work exactly a hundred years earlier, in September 1912.

Then a 'casting' took place and every student was assigned an actor of the First Studio to research. Exploring their life (their family, their life experience before they came to the theatre, their major roles in the Studio and in the Moscow Art Theatre, as well as their subsequent artistic career), the modern-day students tried to draw parallels (not in an intellectual but in an emotional way) between themselves and those who were studying with Stanislavsky a hundred years ago. As it turned out, the challenges of acquiring acting skills, working out the ethics of a theatre company, and even the conflicts in a group of acting students now and a hundred years ago were very similar.

The students researched an enormous amount of literature. They travelled to Moscow to visit the Stanislavsky House Museum and Vakhtangov Memorial Apartment, to look into the mirror of Stanislavsky's dressing room at the Moscow Art Theater. They visited archives in St Petersburg, Moscow and even Vilnius. In their social media group on VKonakte (a Russian analogue of Facebook) and on Google drive the students downloaded dozens of photos of the First Studio's productions. They decorated the walls of their Studio at the Theater Academy with the portraits of the First Studio members (each portrait was labelled with the age when the actor entered the First Studio, and as often as not the students turned out to be of the same age).

Even the first professional examination in the students' lives – the presentation of their work to the faculty of the Academy's Acting Department– took place on 15 January 2013, that is exactly a hundred years after the First Studio presented *The Good Hope* to Stanislavsky and 'the elders' of the Moscow Art Theatre on 15 January 1913. And when the students showed their études during the second year of training (the academic year 2013/14) walking on-stage were 'Misha Chekhov', 'Richard Boleslavsky' and even 'Stanislavsky'.

Thus, some additional mechanisms of actor motivation were turned on. Thanks to that the students of today could discover for themselves the creative work of their famous predecessors and learn about the history and the artistic issues of the twentieth century Russian theatre in a new – and very personal – way. Every class would make them ask more and more probing questions about the essence of acting: Should I try and find myself in the other person or do that other person's feelings and thoughts already live in me? Do I fall in love, suffer, or get excited before going onstage in the same way as the young actors of the First Studio did when they felt love, hate, envy, or sacrificed themselves a hundred years ago? Why were Stanislavsky and the actors of the First Studio so much interested in Yoga? What can Yoga practice offer actors today?[5] And most importantly, why do I go onstage in the first place? The students worked hard to comprehend the creative work of Chekhov, Vakhtangov, Boleslavsky, Ouspenskaya, Sushkevich, Birman, Giatsintova, Dikiy and Smyshliaev; and eventually, behind the old photos in the albums and historical records, they were able to see the real people who had their strengths and weaknesses, who had happy but not easy lives devoted to the Theatre. Paradoxically, the students' efforts to recreate the epoch and life of a hundred years ago gave them a deeper understanding of themselves – both in their professional and personal lives.

The new production of *The Good Hope* premiered in February 2015, when the students were in their third year of training. Clearly, with its twenty-first-century aesthetics and staging, *The Good Hope* at St Petersburg Theatre Arts Academy turned out to be completely different from the production of the First Studio. A play about the life of one family of Dutch fishermen in the early twentieth century was now performed by twenty-eight modern students and turned into a story about the life of a whole maritime town. According to the reviews, the tragedy of its inhabitants was elevated to the level of philosophical generalization and became a poignant meditation about the eternal values of human life (Figures 11.5, 11.6 and 11.7).

The production was permeated with the studio spirit; it emerged from many études and stage tryouts of the students themselves. These were put together and directed

Figure 11.5 Shipwreck scene from *The Good Hope* by Heijermans. St Petersburg Theatre Arts Academy, Tcherkasski's Studio, 2015.

Figure 11.6 Lyubov Konstantinova (Jo), Maria Papashvili (Truus), Anna Khristich (Saart) and Dmitriy Frolov (Bos) in *The Good Hope* by Heijermans. St Petersburg Theatre Arts Academy, Tcherkasski's Studio, 2015.

Figure 11.7 Lyubov Konstantinova (Jo) and Darya Lenda (Kniertje) in the final scene of *The Good Hope* by Heijermans. St Petersburg Theatre Arts Academy, Tcherkasski's Studio, 2015.

by Sergei Tcherkasski and two other teachers of his Acting Studio – Natalia Lapina and Vitaly Lubskiy. For the head of the Acting Studio it was crucial to engage all the students and involve all the teachers in the staging process so that it would become their common child and not an expression of the will of just the director alone. The set was also created by joint efforts through the étude method, a process that implied a sequence of tryouts, clarifications and stylistic modifications suggested by the students, teachers and set designers (students of the Repin Academy of Fine Arts also contributed towards creating the set design as well as manufacturing it). It would be interesting to analyse how the process of developing the scenography went through various stages. Much effort was put into creating the walls and the beautiful Dutch window in Kniertje's room (quite a few interesting *mise-en-scènes* were developed when passersby looked through that window into the house). Still, these everyday details and solid walls were eventually rejected in favour of using fishing nets that wrapped all of the stage space to evoke the image of a maritime town. And the naturalistic barrier in the office of the shipowner Bos, which was initially constructed in the rehearsal room in accordance with the stage directions, was replaced – in line with the poetic conception of the production – by a wooden barrier/sail-yard on two ropes (drawn down as if on a ship), which eventually was equipped with a sail for the emotional final scene.

The Good Hope ran in the Academy Theater for two seasons and always played to full houses. It was shown more than thirty times in St Petersburg (alas, the stage life of student productions is short) and also in Moscow, at the international festival *Your Chance 2016*. Soon afterwards a TV version of the production was made by the students of the Department of TV Directing. However, the young actors that played in the production graduated from the Academy that spring, and they now work in different theatre companies in St Petersburg and Moscow. So today what is left of the production is a book with articles about the project and lots of photos (Figure 11.8),[6] but also, and most importantly, memories in the hearts of the spectators.

All those who were lucky enough to have seen the performance still remember it with a feeling of wonder (one of the co-authors of this article – Irina Michajlova – could attest to this, having watched the performance herself). It may seem improbable that a social drama, written on a subject that seemingly lost its relevance long ago, should still be able to carry the spectators away, strike a nerve in them and awaken their 'feelings of goodness'.

At the beginning spectators, who had not had the chance to see student productions before, may have been puzzled to see the young actress who played Clementine address as 'Daddy' the 25-year-old actor who played the part of the shipowner Bos, or to see that the sturdy young men Geert and Barend turn out to be the sons of an actress of the same age – Kniertje. However, after the first ten minutes of the performance the spectators stopped paying attention to the age of the actors and became immersed in what was happening onstage. In fact, the stage and the auditorium became one space. This happened in both a metaphorical and a literal sense, especially during the storm scene, when the sailors, who had had excellent acrobatic training, struggled with the furious wind and sea, and trying to fix the rigging, were flying on the ropes right above the heads of the spectators.

The production of *The Good Hope* staged at Tcherkasski's Acting Studio received lots of praise from theatre critics. Below are some quotations from reviews. Here's what Nikolai Pesochinsky writes in his article about the kind of staging opportunities the play offers to theatre directors:

> Heijermans' play could be staged (and indeed was staged in other theaters) in different ways. The simplest way is to stage it as a melodrama (shipwreck, death, despair resulting from the loss of the loved ones, cynicism of the rich). Another way could be to stage it as a modernist work, using metaphysics and psychoanalysis (the sea as a metaphor for the world, the unconscious fear of the future, human beings as playthings of the elements, the mystery of predetermined destiny). Yet another way to stage it would be to follow naturalistic theater tradition (the fishing village environment, country people smelling of the sea and with down-to-earth mentality, plain-spoken way of speaking, and simple feelings; the nature of human beings). This naturalistic aspect was to a certain extent of interest […] to the First Studio. However, both in 1913 and a hundred years later, the productions focused, primarily, on a way of life, human feelings that are easy to understand […] The play was interpreted as a piece of real life, as tangible elements of everyday routine comprised of chains of events and human emotions, with no place for ethnographic masks or details like in the paintings by the Lesser Dutch masters. (Pesochinsky 2016: 80–83)

Pesochinsky also explains how the young actor Grigory Nekrasov, while playing in the twenty-first century the part of the socialist Geert (who – in a traditional interpretation

Figure 11.8 *'The Good Hope' on Mokhovaya Street – 100 years later: Reconstruction of Actor Training at the First Studio of the Moscow Art Theatre* (St Petersburg: Baltic Seasons Publishing, 2016: 104 pages, 195 colour photos).

of the play – vehemently denounces the 'sharks of capitalism') was able to play this character in a convincing way, without placing him in the social criticism context: 'In contrast to Grigory Khmara in the 1913 production (who went down in Russian theatre history with his sharp interpretation of an embittered Geert), Grigory Nekrasov reveals in this young man the naïve enthusiasm of a truth-seeker' (83).

Another reviewer, Irina Boykova, when describing the characters created by the young actors, also draws attention to a subtle shift in Geert's personality: the director changes the emphasis, focusing on this character's quest for justice and his lyric aspects – as qualities common for all humans – instead of making him a revolutionary rebel:

> In Prof. Tcherkasski's Studio's production they opted for epic and poetic form, which allows the story to achieve a higher level of generalization. The same applies to their interpretation of the characters of the play. The young actress Darya Lenda interprets Kniertje, whose husband and two sons have drowned at sea, and who is going to lose her two other sons, as a strong heroic figure. In the play Geert, her elder son, is portrayed as a melodramatic misfit and revolutionary rebel, yet in the production he is interpreted as a polyphonic character who by no means could be summed up as a rebel [...]. During Kniertje's birthday party (live music, jokes, dances, everybody is in good spirits – here, as in all the other crowd scenes, the cast acts as an amazingly well-coordinated ensemble) Geert starts singing *La Marseillaise* [...], which for a moment arouses the sympathies of Kniertje's guests. However, those who have created this production today know only too well what the aftermath of a revolutionary rebellion is likely to be, hence the themes of social protest are not made prominent in the production. (Boykova 2016: 142)

The logic of the lyrical interpretation of the play led to adding an epilogue without words in the production. In Heijermans's play satirical overtones prevail in the last scene: on learning about her sons' deaths, Kniertje laments that she hasn't got anyone left but then she suddenly remembers that Jo is expecting a child from Geert. In response, heartless Bos starts talking about morality and says: 'What bad luck!' And though Kniertje does answer him: 'No, this is good luck,' her words get lost in what Bos goes on to say. So the last words in the play are, in fact, the words of a hypocritical letter that Kaps, an accountant, is writing routinely to ask for charitable assistance for the 'poor victims'. The widow Kniertje faces her misfortune alone, depressed and heartbroken.

The epilogue in the Theater Arts Academy's production develops what Kniertje says in the final scene of the play (Figure 11.7):

> We hear a child crying. Jo comes out from the back of the stage with a bundled-up baby in her arms. Some sailors rapidly run onto the stage. They are swaying again on the ropes right above the heads of the fishermen's wives. The scene is brilliantly staged and performed – it is obvious that the sailors are not in the same space where the women are; in the yellow diffused lighting their eyes never meet the eyes of those who are 'here and now', however, the presence of the sailors appears

to impart life to the living. The sailors' strong masculine hands effortlessly pick up and move forward the bench with the women sitting on it (and the women, as if sensing their support, exchange glances, smiling timidly). Thus the final *mise-en-scène* is arranged: Kniertje and Jo with the baby in her arms are in the center; Geert (who is invisible to them) carefully lifts a part of the baby's blanket to have a look at his child and then moves away, slightly swaying the lamp above the heads of his mother and wife; the lamp becomes bright and casts warm light onto the faces of the women. We experience a well-calculated effect of the open-end finale: dramatic and lyrical. The message is very clear: Hope (in the evangelical sense) does not die if Love is still alive. (Boykova 2016: 146)

Thanks to this epilogue and also thanks to the energy, talent, and enthusiasm of the young actors, the spectators leave the theatre in high spirits. After responding to the tragic events of the drama with the tears of compassion the spectators feel purified and enlightened.

Conclusion

Among many Dutch-speaking writers whose works were translated into Russian in the late nineteenth and early twentieth century Herman Heijermans was a major figure. The Russian public became acquainted in translation with more than a dozen of his works in various genres. However, as in other countries, it was his play *The Good Hope* (*Op hoop van zegen*) that became his most popular work.

It is possible to distinguish three periods in the stage life of *The Good Hope* in Russia. In the early twentieth century the play was produced in dozens of Russian theatres and always had a successful run thanks to the topical issues it raised. This anti-capitalist drama and its theater productions aimed at awakening compassion for the oppressed, stirring resentment towards the oppressors and the desire to fight for social justice.

In the 1912/13 season this play happened to be linked with a theatre experiment of great importance: *The Good Hope* was the first production to be staged by the First Studio at the Moscow Art Theater. In the words of Michael Chekhov, the Studio was 'an assembly of believers in the religion of Stanislavsky' (Chekhov 1995: 456). It was here in the First Studio that the fundamentals of the objective nature of acting were studied theoretically and used in practice; these discoveries continue to define professional actor training in many different parts of the world. The Studio's production premiered in January 1913. It revealed some new aspects of Heijermans's play and ran successfully for more than twenty years (from 1913 to 1934). During their tour in St Petersburg the Moscow Art Theater showed this production at the Theatre Hall of Tenishev School in Mokhovaya Street.

It was in this very building that a hundred years later Russian theatregoers could see the play again. It was produced as part of the project 'Reconstruction of Actor Training at the First Studio of the Moscow Art Theatre'. The students of the St Petersburg State Theatre Arts Academy (since 2015 the Russian State Institute of the Performing Arts) staged *The Good Hope* while playing at being the First Studio. The new production interpreted the play in a conceptually new way. The social themes of the play were raised onto a universal and existential level. The production revealed that Heijermans's play allows such an interpretation as well. And as in the past, not only did the play carry the spectators away and offer young actors great learning opportunities, it also helped the latter to master the fundamentals of acting and the Stanislavsky System.

As happened a hundred years ago, staging *The Good Hope* brought the Netherlands and Russia a little closer together. Remarkably, it was the theatre experiment led by the Russian director Stanislavsky that made the stage life of the Dutch play so long and exciting. So, after all, maybe it is no accident that Herman Heijermans's monument in Amsterdam is situated in Leidsebosje garden, just a hundred metres away from Stanislavsky Café in the lobby of the leading Dutch theatre Stadsschouwburg on the Leidseplein.

Another remarkable coincidence!

Notes

1   The information on Russian translations from Dutch here and further on is given on the basis of the Bibliography compiled by Scheltjens (2003).
2   The history of the production *The Good Hope* at the First Studio of the Moscow Art Theatre (1913) is discussed in more detail in the articles: Tcherkasski (2016a: 17–41) and Tcherkasski (2017: 85–110), and also in the book *Masterstvo aktera: Stanislavskii – Boleslavskii – Strasberg. Istoriia. Teoriia. Praktika* (Tcherkasski 2016c: 100–118).
3   After it was produced by the First Studio of the Moscow Art Theater *The Good Hope* was rarely staged in the Soviet Union. We know that it was staged at Krasny Fakel Theatre by the directors Dmitri Kramskoy and Nikolai Vent (Novosibirsk, 1938) and at the Lithuanian National Drama Theatre by the director Romualdas Juknevičius (Vilnius, 1940–1956).
4   Methodological approaches adopted in this theatre project are described in detail in the book *'Nadezhda' na Mokhovoy – 100 let spustia: Opyt rekonstruktsii teatral'noy pedagogiki Pervoy studii MKhT* (Tcherkasski 2016d), and in the articles: Tcherkasski (2016b: 53–65) and Tcherkasski (2017: 85–110), the latter is in English.
5   After Stanislavsky got acquainted with Hatha Yoga and Raja Yoga in 1911, largely through the Yogi Ramacharaka's books, Yoga-based exercises became an integral part of the Stanislavsky System's actor training. The curriculum of Tcherkasski's Acting Studio at St Petersburg Theatre Arts Academy also includes Yoga classes. For a more detailed discussion see the book *Stanislavsky and Yoga* (Tcherkasski 2015).
6   *'The Good Hope' on Mokhovaya Street – 100 years later: Reconstruction of Actor Training at the First Studio of the Moscow Art Theatre* (St Petersburg: Baltic Seasons Publishing, 2016: 104 pages, 195 colour photos).

References

Birman, S.G. (1962), *Put' aktrisy*, 2nd edn, Moscow: VTO.
Blok, A.A. (1963), *Sobranie sochineniy*, 8 vols, vol. 7, Moscow: Khudogestvennaya literatura.
Boykova, I. (2016), 'Vozvrashchenie "Nadezhdy"', *Voprosy teatra* 1-2: 141-146. Available online: http://theatre.sias.ru/upload/voprosy_teatra/2016_1-2_141-146_boykova.pdf (accessed 17 February 2019).
Chekhov, M.A. (1995), 'Za kulisami studii: [Interviews]', in M.A. Chekhov, *Litaraturnoe nasledie*, 2 vols, vol. 2, 456, Moscow: Iskusstvo.
Conscience, H. (1892), 'Rekrut', *Vestnik inostrannoy literatury* (October): 199-229, (November): 169-224.
Conscience, H. (1893), *Slepaya Roza. Matushka Job*. St Petersburg: Isdatel'stvo M.M. Lederle i Co.
Couperus, L. (1902), 'Psykhea', *Novyy zhurnal inostrannoy literatury* (1): 1-64.
Couperus, L. (1905), 'Fatum', *Novyy zhurnal literatury, iskusstva i nauki* (2): 1-17; (3): 33-48; (4): 49-64; (5): 65-77.
Couperus, L. (1906), 'Ikh velichestva', *Novyy zhurnal literatury, iskusstva i nauki* (1): 1-33; (2): 17-48; (3): 49-80; (4): 81-96; (5): 97-115.
Couperus, L. (1907), 'Mir vsemu miru', *Novyy zhurnal literatury, iskusstva i nauki* (1): 1-16; (2): 17-32; (3): 33-48; (4): 49-64; (5): 65-84.
Deyssel, L. Van (1901), 'Het Zevende Gebod. Burgerlijke Zeden-Komedie in vier Bedrijven door Herm. Heijermans Jr.', *Tweemaandelijksch Tijdschrift* 7 (1): 329-341. Available online: http://www.dbnl.org/tekst/_twe002190101_01/_twe002190101_01_0018.php (accessed 17 February 2019).
Dikiy, A.D. (1957), *Povest' o teatral'noy iunosti*, Moscow: Iskusstvo.
Eeden, F. Van (1897), 'Malen'kiy Johannes', *Vestnik Evropy* (5): 550-583; (6):177-247.
Eeden, F. Van (1905), 'Malen'kiy Johannes', *Russkaya Mysl* (4): 135-182; (5): 33-67; (6): 17-38.
Eeden, F. Van (1916), *Malen'kiy Johannes*. Moscow: Universal'naya biblioteka.
Giatsintova, S.V. (1989), *S pamiatiu naedine*, 2nd edn, Moscow: Iskusstvo.
Heijermans, H. (1900), 'Op hoop van zegen', fragment, *De jonge gids*: jrg. IV (1900-1901), 133-153. (Amsterdam: S.L. van Looy, 1901.)
Heijermans, H. (1903), *Lubov' v ghetto*, Vilno: Typografia A.G.Syrkina.
Heijermans, H. (1904a), 'Gorod brilliantov', *Russkoe bogatstvo* (9): 1-32; (10): 81-128; (11): 81-128; (12): 129-184.
Heijermans, H. (1904b), *Lubov' v ghetto*, Moscow: Teatra'naya biblioteka M.A. Sokolovoy.
Heijermans, H. (1904c), *Lubov' v ghetto*, Moscow: Teatra'naya biblioteka C.F. Rassokhina.
Heijermans, H. (1904d), *Osnovy braka*, Moscow: Teatra'naya biblioteka C.F. Rassokhina.
Heijermans, H. (1904e), *Sed'maya zapoved'*, Yalta, Typografia N.V. Bakhtina.
Heijermans, H. (1907), 'Na kryl'akh', *Vestnik Inostrannoy Literatury* (7): 7-46.
Heijermans, H. (1910), 'Glaza, ili Neobychaynye perezhivania', *Vestnik inostrannoy literatury* (1): 1-32; (2): 33-56; (3): 57-94.
Heijermans, H. (1920), *Gorod brilliantov*. Petrograd: Vsemirnaya literatura.
Heijermans, H. (1922), *Gorod brilliantov: 2-e izdanie*, Petrograd: Vsemirnaya literatura.
Heijermans, H. (1924), *Droomkoninkje*, Amsterdam: Van Holkema & Warendorf.
Heijermans, H. (1925), *Vuurvlindertje*, Amsterdam: Van Holkema & Warendorf.
Koreneva, M.Y. and I.M. Michajlova (2016), 'K voprosu o evropeiskikh istochnikakh "Zrelishcha zhitiia chelovecheskogo" (1674)', *Skandinavskaia filologia* 14 (1): 81-91.

Korsakov, P.A. (1838a), 'Gollandskaya literatura: yeye nachalo, khod i nyneshneye sostoyaniye', *Biblioteka dlya chteniya* 27: 49–140.
Korsakov, P.A. (1838b), 'Ioost fan den Fondel', *Biblioteka dlya chteniya* 28: 159–208.
Korsakov, P.A. (1839), *Iakov Kats. Poet, myslitel' i muzh soveta*, St Petersburg: V Tipografii Smirdina.
Korsakov, P.A. (1844), *Opyt niderlandskoy antologii*, St Petersburg: Bez Izdatel'stva.
Markov, P.A. (1974), 'Pervaia studiia MKhT: Sulerzhitsky – Vakhtangov – Chekhov', in P.A. Markov (ed.), *O teatre*, 4 vols, vol. 1, 347–418, Moscow: Iskusstvo.
Michajlova, I.M. (2013), 'Herman Heijermans', in P. Couttenier, I. Michajlova and K.Verheul (eds), *Van 'Reynaert de Vos' tot 'Godenslaap', Istoriia niderlandskoy literatury*, vol. 1, 434–442, St Petersburg: Alexandria.
Multatuli (1916), 'Max Havelaar', *Russkaya Mysl'* (6): 83–120; (7): 151–180; (8): 58–99; (9): 134–164; (10): 133–181; (11): 89–126; (12): 117–150.
Pesochinsky, N.V. (2016), 'Stoletie pedagogicheskoy idei', in S.D. Tcherkasski (ed.), *"Nadezhda" na Mokhovoy – 100 let spustia: Opyt rekonstruktsii teatral'noy pedagogiki Pervoy studii MKhT*, 80–86, St Petersburg: Baltic Seasons Publishing.
Roland Holst, H. (1905), *Mistitsizm v sovremennoy literature, Meterlink*, St Petersburg: Sovremennaya biblioteka.
Roland Holst, H. (1907), *Etyudy o sotsialisticheskoy estetike*, Moscow: Izdaniye P. G. Dauge.
Ruusbroec, J. Van (1910), *Odeyanie dukhovnogo braka*, Moscow: Knigoizdatel'stvo "Musaget".
Scheltjens, W. (2003), *Bibliografie van de Nederlandse literatuur in Russische vertaling*, St Petersburg: Aleteja.
Tcherkasski, S. (2015), *Stanislavsky and Yoga*, London: Routledge.
Tcherkasski, S.D. (2016a), "'Gibel' Nadezhdy" Pervoy studii MKhT', in S.D. Tcherkasski (ed.), *"Nadezhda" na Mokhovoy – 100 let spustia: Opyt rekonstruktsii teatral'noy pedagogiki Pervoy studii MKhT*, 17–42, St Petersburg: Baltic Seasons Publishing.
Tcherkasski, S.D. (2016b), 'Igra v Pervuiu studiiu', in S.D. Tcherkasski (ed.), *"Nadezhda" na Mokhovoy – 100 let spustia: Opyt rekonstruktsii teatral'noy pedagogiki Pervoy studii MKhT*, 53–65, St Petersburg: Baltic Seasons Publishing.
Tcherkasski, S.D. (2016c), *Masterstvo aktera: Stanislavskii – Boleslavskii – Strasberg. Istoriia. Teoriia. Praktika* [Acting: Stanislavsky – Boleslavsky – Strasberg: History, Theory and Practice], St Petersburg: RGISI.
Tcherkasski, S.D., ed. (2016d) *"Nadezhda" na Mokhovoy – 100 let spustia: Opyt rekonstruktsii teatral'noy pedagogiki Pervoy studii MKhT*, St Petersburg: Baltic Seasons Publishing.
Tcherkasski, S. (2017), 'Forward – to early Stanislavsky! or Reconstruction of Actor Training at the First Studio of the Moscow Art Theatre', *Stanislavski Studies* 5 (1): 85–110. Available online: https://www.tandfonline.com/doi/full/10.1080/20567790.2017.1298347 (accessed 17 February 2019).
Verdoes, P. (1954), 'Herman Heijermans. Een Amerikaanse dissertatie', *De nieuwe taalgids* 47 (6): 334–337. Available online: http://www.dbnl.org/tekst/_taa008195401_01/_taa008195401_01_0089.php (accessed 17 February 2019).
Veselovskaya, M. (1915), 'Sovremennaya flamandskaya literatura', *Golos minuvshego* (11): 99–111.
Volkonsky, S.M. (1914), *Otkliki teatra*, Petrograd: Typografia Sirius.
Wells, H. (1910), *Nividimka*, St Petersburg: Shipovnik.

12

Rescuing Something Fine: Huizinga's *Herfsttij der Middeleeuwen* (The Waning of the Middle Ages) as World Literature

Elke Brems and Orsolya Réthelyi

Introduction

In 2019, one century has passed since the Dutch historian Johan Huizinga published his international bestseller *Herfsttij der Middeleeuwen* (The Waning of the Middle Ages). Huizinga's much-discussed historical essay described the 'forms of life and thought' in the late Middle Ages (i.e. the fourteenth and fifteenth centuries) in France and the Burgundian Low Countries. In 1986, the leading medieval scholar Frits van Oostrom described the book as 'the most influential study [...] that was ever written by a Dutch "alpha"' (1986: 202).[1] Its influence reaches far beyond its national and linguistic borders. In fact, *Herfsttij der Middeleeuwen* by Johan Huizinga is world literature. American historian Sean Farrell Moran (2016: 423) stated that 'awareness of this book is a good touchstone for determining an educated person'; it is striking that he does not say that an educated person needs to have read the book, but only to be aware that it exists. Moran also indicates that twenty years earlier, in 1995, *Herfsttij der Middeleeuwen* 'was identified by a poll of writers as one of the "most influential books" since World War I in the Times Literary Supplement' (423). This article is thus concerned with the international dissemination of one of the most famous and successful Dutch texts and its position in what we call world literature.

According to David Damrosch, a work enters world literature by a double process: first by being read as literature; second, by circulating out into the broader world beyond its linguistic and cultural point of origin. A given work can enter world literature and then fall out of it again if it shifts beyond a threshold point along either axis, the literary or the worldly (Damrosch 2003: 4). If comic books, for example, are at a certain time considered literature, then *Tintin* can be part of world literature, or if an older book like John Williams's *Stoner* suddenly starts circulating in translation it can enter world literature. Damrosch's definition focuses on the processualism of becoming world literature, and indicates that declarations of such a nature are made in retrospect and based on investigations of the particular trajectory of certain texts (Helgesson and Vermeulen 2016: 7). We will adopt this retrospective perspective here to examine *Herfsttij*'s trajectory in the German- and English-speaking areas and in Central Europe (Czech, Slovak, Hungarian and Polish).[2]

There are of course many literary works that circulate beyond geographical and linguistic boundaries (the latter through translation) but that are never considered world literature. As Naaijkens states: some translated books are 'events' and others are 'incidents' (2010). Only the 'events' have a chance of making it into the realm of world literature: processes of canonization play a crucial role. And canons are dynamic, works can enter and exit the canon when literary, social and ideological standards alter. Accordingly, Herrnstein-Smith emphasizes that canons are comprised of 'works of art and literature (that) bear the marks of their own evaluation history' (Herrnstein-Smith 1983: 23). Translation, too, belongs to this evaluation history, as we will demonstrate.

Paratexts can likewise give the text a very different character each time it is published (either in the original language or in translation): in this case, forewords, footnotes, illustrations, etc. turn out to be very important in the presentation of the text, both in Dutch and in translation. These paratextual additions can help to canonize a text, to present it as literature, and to imbue it with an international character. Over the past 100 years, Huizinga's text has developed a timeless and placeless character, which is slightly paradoxical given that its subject is so specifically bound by time and place.

Three questions will guide our reconstruction of the trajectory of the book as part of world literature: did it circulate internationally, was it considered literature and how was it canonized?

Mapping the translation history of *Herfsttij*

Thanks to quantitative mapping, we can immediately answer the first question in the affirmative. *Herfsttij der Middeleeuwen* has been translated into twenty-six languages (Figure 12.1).[3] The book has even been published in two different versions in several of these languages (English, Hebrew, Italian, Polish, Portuguese).[4] Such retranslations

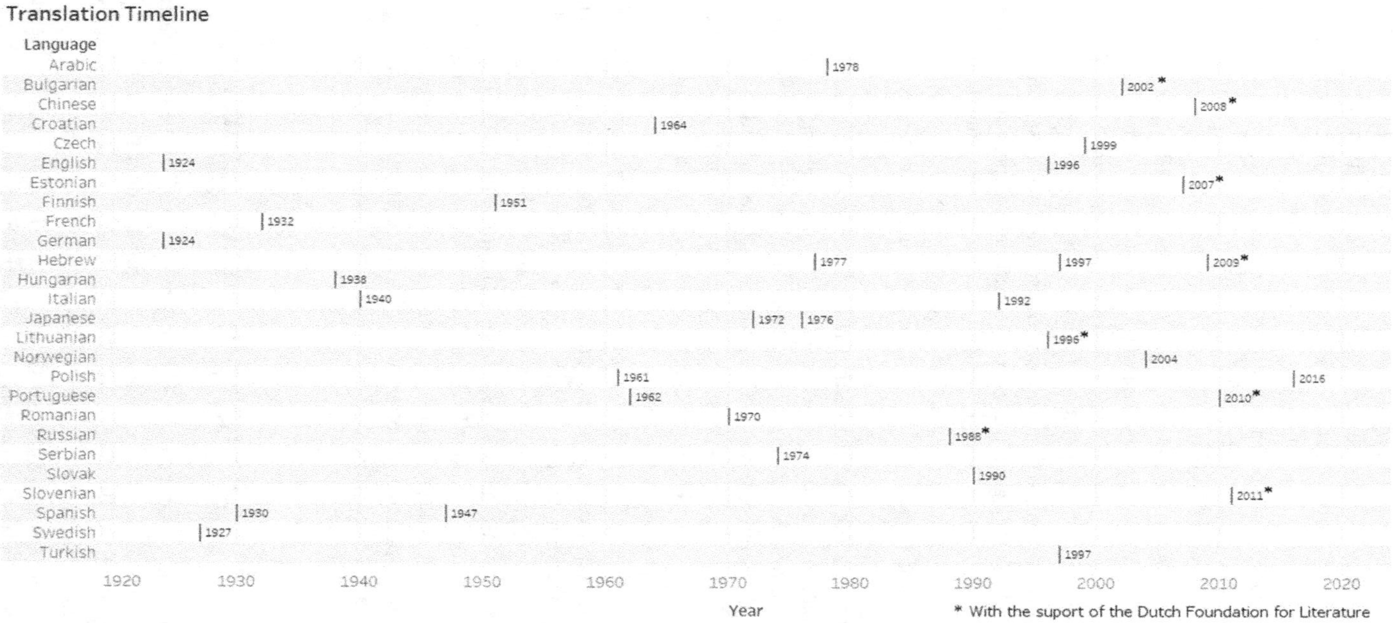

Figure 12.1 Translation Timeline for *Herfsttij der Middeleeuwen*.

are indicative of the enduring significance of *Herfsttij* and of the need to update the work for new readers. Koskinen and Paloposki have written the following in this regard, following Venuti: 'Retranslating and literary canon formations are indeed mutually dependent: retranslations help texts in achieving the status of a classic, and the status of a classic often promotes further retranslations' (Koskinen and Paloposki 2010: 295). A new German translation is currently being prepared by Annette Wunschel for a series of Huizinga editions by Wilhelm Fink Verlag and the book is currently also being retranslated into Spanish. A third English translation is likewise being prepared. The twenty-first century has seen several new translations of the work; the Bulgarian, Chinese, Estonian and Slovenian translations of *Herfsttij* were all published after 2000. The Dutch Foundation for Literature plays a prominent role in these projects. According to their own database, they have subsidized ten translations since 1995.[5] The Dutch government thus continues to promote the international dissemination of *Herfsttij* through this foundation. The Dutch Foundation for Literature promotes this book intensively because it considers *Herfsttij* to be the most important book of non-fiction ever written in Dutch and clearly a work of world literature.[6]

Surveying the impressive list of translations, it is striking that there are several indirect translations, based especially on the German and English versions. Due to the fact that the first English version differed significantly from the original, a text currently circulates internationally that is different (shorter and less florid) than the Dutch original. Van der Lem writes: 'It may seem sacrilegious, but even for the Dutch reader, *Herfsttij* may appear more accessible in German or English, translations in which the idiosyncrasies of the style have been resolved' (Van der Lem 1993: 143).[7] The Dutch Foundation for Literature considers the book a classic of Dutch language and subsidizes 100 per cent of the translation costs if certain conditions are met by the publisher (e.g. working from the Dutch original, involving an experienced translator with the necessary expertise, sufficient marketing). In the case of languages in which an experienced Dutch-target language translator cannot be found, it allows the use of the German edition as a source. It also supports second or third translations if there is sufficient reason (e.g. the original translation is dated or was based on the abridged English version). In practice, it is often very difficult to determine the language on which the translations were actually based, as will become evident from the reconstructions below.

Historiography or literature?

In terms of the content of the work, Huizinga aimed to offer a new perspective on the courtly culture of the late Middle Ages: he did not consider its riches and pageantry as evidence of the flourishing and wealth of its culture, but rather as purely external displays that masked the vacuity and decline of courtly culture. Huizinga's book was not primarily based on archival research, but on the visual arts and on literary sources and chronicles. This was highly exceptional in the historiography of his day, which championed a strict approach to source materials. Huizinga interpreted his sources and brought them together narratively in an almost literary essay.

The work was therefore not appreciated by Dutch historians of the period; it was deemed unscientific and even old-fashioned, while in hindsight it was in fact very innovative and even groundbreaking. Van der Lem writes that the 'appearance of Huizinga's Herfsttij [... was] an unusual event in Dutch historiography. The subjects and the way they are treated were completely new in comparison with the uniform tradition.' According to Van der Lem, the academic historians lacked the talent to judge the book on its merits (1993: 149).

A well-known story in the rejection of *Herfsttij* in the Netherlands is the statement of the archivist Samuel Muller in 1920, who judged Huizinga's book to be a failure (quoted in Van der Lem 1993: 149). Muller questioned 'whether Professor Huizinga has written history or literature, because literary praise is not appropriate for a historian'.[8] Matters were not helped by the fact that Dutch literary critics such as P.N. Van Eyck and Menno ter Braak did praise the work. While appreciation for the book as 'literature' was perceived negatively by historians, it is precisely this praise that enabled *Herfsttij* to become world literature. As indicated above, according to Damrosch, one of the conditions of this process is that a book is read as 'literature'.

Despite its mixed reception, three editions of *Herfsttij* were printed in relatively quick succession (1919, 1921, 1928). The second edition was also a revised edition. Under pressure from his publisher and readers, it was only in the third edition that Huizinga agreed to include illustrations and to translate the many quotations from late medieval French poetry, which he apparently assumed readers would simply understand.

Historiographers now generally consider the work to be groundbreaking. In 1990, Bouwsma attempted to describe why the book was so historiographically innovative: 'his rebellion against the tendencies dominant in the historical establishment of his time was fundamental; he rejected its scientific pretensions, its belief [...] in progress, and its naive confidence that the facts speak for themselves' (1990: 326). The historian himself was central to Huizinga's approach: he bore a responsibility with respect both to the past and the present through the questions that he posed to his sources and data, and these questions depended on the personal insights and personal imagination of the historian.[9]

The German reception

The book was and continues to be most popular in the German-speaking world. It was first published there in 1924 by Drei Masken Verlag, in a translation by Tilly Jolles-Mönckeberg, the former wife of one of Huizinga's best friends, André Jolles. Hugenholtz states that 'the book was reprinted much more often in Germany or Switzerland than in any other country outside the Netherlands' (1973: 91). Interest in Switzerland may be explained by the fact that *Herfsttij* is in a certain sense a response to the monumental work *Die Kultur der Renaissance in Italien* (1860) by the Swiss scholar Jacob Burckhardt. The German translation went through five editions during the interbellum alone (including the first 1924 print). Senger claims that the global success of *Herfsttij* is due to the German translation (2004: 6).¹⁰ The translation was immediately celebrated in Germany, for example by Hermann Hesse, who wrote that books like *Herfsttij* are rare 'as it is a rare stroke of luck, when a great scholar is at the same time a great writer' (quoted in Senger 2004: 7).¹¹ According to Krumm, who researched the German reception, there was a widespread consensus that *Herfsttij* was a masterpiece: 'Huizinga became a "highly respected" historian in Germany' (2011: 241–242).¹² He nevertheless notes that the work quickly became a monument, and people thus rarely engaged with it actively: 'Thus *Herbst des Mittelalters*, after only a few years, had become a monument of historical research, as inevitable as immovable.'¹³

Incidentally, the work's fate in Germany mirrored the reception in the Netherlands in that literary critics were initially more enthusiastic than historians, as is reflected in Hesse's reaction. In 2004, Senger concluded his article by stating that 'Mit seinem *Herbst des Mittelalters* hat sich Huizinga aber ganz gewiss ein bleibendes literarisches Denkmal gesetzt. Mit ihm durch das herbstelnde Mittelalter zu streifen lohnt sich noch immer, zumindest literarisch' (24).¹⁴

Two important changes in the 1924 German translation influenced the subsequent publication history of the work (including in other languages). The author and publisher agreed that there would be twenty-two chapters instead of the original fourteen, and they decided to include illustrations. Huizinga himself contributed to the translation significantly and he thus clearly supported these changes. He agreed with the critique that the length of the chapters varied excessively and that the chapter titles were unclear. He was also very conscious of translation problems, even between Germanic languages as similar as German and Dutch. He appears to have been a proponent of a so-called foreignizing translation. In his introduction to the German edition, he wrote: 'Why should we be so eager to obliterate fearfully the traces of what is foreign in that which is of foreign origin?' (quoted in Huizinga 1953: XIV).¹⁵

In 1953, Kurt Köster revised Jolles-Mönckeberg's translation to update it. In his foreword, he describes the 'untouchable' status of the work: 'A work that had great impact cannot really be judged any more.'¹⁶ Nevertheless, the fact that he updated an existing translation is an evaluation in itself: it signals that the book still needed to be 'actualized' in Germany, to be accessible to new generations.¹⁷

The English reception

While some might be convinced that *Herfsttij* has its German translation to thank for its international reputation, the English disagree. In 1973, Von der Dunk wrote the following about Huizinga: 'Had he uttered his first cry not in Groningen but in the English village of Bourton-on-the-Water, his work on the history of culture would have gained him an international reputation more quickly and more easily' (1973: 17). The fact that Huizinga wrote in Dutch was and continues to be perceived as a handicap. In this regard, Moran comments: 'He did face a major hurdle. It is important [...] to note that Huizinga was Dutch, and to reach a wider audience, he had perforce to have his works translated' (2016: 414). This is certainly an aspect that must be taken into account in surveying the canonization process: literary works from dominant cultures have a far greater chance of penetrating the international book market than works from peripheral cultures. A translation in a major language (English, German) may represent a kind of quality label, meaning translations in other languages will follow more quickly. Practical considerations also play a role: it is very difficult to find translators who can translate Dutch texts into all other languages. As mentioned above, many of the translations of *Herfsttij* are not based on the original Dutch text.

Huizinga himself was very concerned and involved in the international dissemination of his book. The idea of an English translation had already been voiced in 1920, at the University of Columbia in New York. A student of Adriaan J. Barnouw, who held the Queen Wilhelmina lectureship there at the time, was apparently interested in working on the translation, to Huizinga's great delight. On 13 July 1920, he wrote the following to Barnouw: 'As far as I am concerned, I would enjoy it very much if the book were to be published in English translation, and I am of course prepared to contribute to achieving this aim. The translation will not be easy, and I must hope that your student will muster the courage to undertake it' (Krul et al. 1989: letter 302). In that period, Huizinga was in the process of revising the book for its second edition, 'to clarify terse passages' (letter 319).[18] The American translation was never found.

In the meantime, however, through the mediation of Sir J. Rennell Rodd, a British publisher had expressed interest in an English translation. The problem was that the publisher, Edward Arnold, could not find anybody to evaluate the source text. He wrote to Huizinga on 1 March 1923: 'Unfortunately we do not know of any competent reader who is thoroughly conversant with the Dutch language, but I understand that your book is being translated into French, and if it was possible to see the French translation we could probably form an opinion more easily than from the original Dutch' (Krul et al. 1989: letter 465). Huizinga duly dispatched the French translation, but added the following: 'the book has been considerably abridged in the French translation and all the references left out. The Dutch edition is nearly one third larger than the French [...]. If there should be an English edition, I think it ought to be translated after the complete Dutch text, with all the references. Perhaps some details might be shortened' (letter 466). Huizinga backed down shortly afterwards, writing: 'I can agree in principle with the idea of an English edition of my book in the abridged form' (letter 472).[19]

In the foreword we read that it was 'not a simple translation of the original Dutch [...] but the result of a work of adaptation, reduction, and consolidation under the author's directions' (Huizinga 1924: v-vi). This all occurred under the auspices of Huizinga himself.[20] This translation history likewise entails an evaluation of the book:

the original text was deemed less appropriate for the English market than the first (unpublished) French translation. Huizinga was very flexible with regard to his text, given that there is not just one authorized version either of the source text or of the translated version.

As in Germany, the translation in English, made by Fritz Hopman, was well received both in the United Kingdom and the United States. In 1925, G.C. Sellery, for example, wrote in *The American Historical Review*: 'The breadth of its scholarship, the riches of its matter, afford ample pabulum for historical enlightenment and rumination upon the variety and persistence of human traits' (1925: 114).

Seventy years later, in 1996, Rodney J. Payton and Ulrich Mammitzsch ventured to retranslate the book. They used *Herfsttij* in their lectures and found the available text inadequate when compared to the original, which they thought was a far better book than the Hopman translation. In their introduction they described 'a certain feeling of being the rescuers of something fine that had been corrupted and undervalued' (Huizinga 1996: IX). They appreciated the first translation for bringing the book to the attention of the English-speaking world, but did not think that it did justice to the original. They were shocked that as a consequence, a book was circulating in the English-speaking world that was unrecognizable to Huizinga experts and readers: 'Is it possible that English-speaking historians have been discussing this book with their foreign colleagues without realizing that they were reading a significantly different text? If this is so, it is a primary justification for the present translation' (XIII). Mammitzsch – who had passed away by the time of publication – and Payton based their translation on the second Dutch edition of 1921: 'the second represents his thinking at its most seminal stage' (XVII), an evaluation that is of course entirely their own.

David Gary Shaw praised the retranslation in the specialist journal *History and Theory*: 'If a work is worth reading it is worth having translated every generation or so' (1998: 245). He described Huizinga's work as 'cutting-edge stuff' and wrote that 'the charm is still working, stirring people to the kind of commitment that few works of history achieve' (245).[21]

Nevertheless, the retranslation was also severely critiqued. The historian Walter Simons expressed appreciation about the availability of a complete translation of the book that 'hordes of undergraduates in America and Britain have read in the abridged and simplified version'. According to Simons (1997: 488), Hopman had given the text 'a Reader's Digest treatment'. Simons deeply regrets, however, that the new translators had no stylistic ambition whatsoever, and that Huizinga's rhetorical power had thus been completely lost. Simons's most substantial criticism is that 'the present translators appear ill at home in Dutch and southern Netherlandish (Belgian) history and culture' (489), as a result of which the new text contains many mistakes. Through a detailed comparison with the German translation, Simons demonstrates that the new English translation was primarily based on the German translation. His judgement of this fact is provocative: 'All of this makes for a sad story. At least Huizinga, who suffered quite enough during the Nazi occupation of the Netherlands, is no longer alive to see his own Herfsttij apparently treated as a

German book' (491).²² The new translation by Payton and Mammitzsch did ensure renewed interest in the book, and long reviews were published in academic journals, often accompanied by extensive critical assessments of its value and significance.²³ Everyone agreed that it had been profoundly influential. Peters and Simons (1999: 589) remarked that it has been particularly influential in the context of American academic curricula: 'In fact, at least in the United States, its wide use in large survey courses has made it a familiar component of the view of the later Middle Ages held by many people.'²⁴ In 2016, Moran brought the question of influence into sharp relief: 'Long after most monographs have been buried on library shelves, Huizinga continues to be read and nearly a century later, he still speaks to people' (413). This becomes even clearer when we consider that a new translation is currently being completed by Diane Webb. It is slated for publication in 2019 and is being entirely subsidized by the Dutch Foundation for Literature. They hope to further exploit this translation as an intermediate text for new translations into languages for which no translators who are proficient in Dutch can be found.

The Hungarian reception

An overview of the reception of *Herfsttij* in Central-Eastern Europe can best begin in Hungary, since Hungarian was the first language into which the book was translated east of Germany.²⁵ *Herfsttij* was first published in Hungarian in 1938 under the title *A középkor alkonya* (The Eve/Decline of the Middle Ages) by the Athenaeum publishing house in Budapest, in the series *Az európai kultúra története* (The History of European Culture), without illustrations, notes, a prologue or epilogue.²⁶ As stated on the cover, the book was translated by Antal Szerb and a note on the inner cover of the edition specifies that the translation was made from the 1937 English edition printed in London (Huizinga 1938a: i).

Despite these specifications, neither the source language, nor the identity of the translator is a straightforward case. According to the contract drawn up between Huizinga and the publishing house on 12 November 1937, both parties agreed that the Hungarian translation would be made on the basis of the English version and all further abbreviations should only be made with the permission of the author (Balogh 2009: 53). Balogh argues that it was probably the Hungarian publisher's decision to use the considerably abbreviated English version without an introduction or notes (even though this was already outdated at the time if compared to the third and latest German edition of 1931), because of the limitations of the series in which it was to be published, and the presumption that the shorter version would be more attractive to Hungarian readers. The contract should thus be interpreted as Huizinga's demand that at least no further abbreviations should be made (Balogh 2017: 51–53). The contract also specifies the name of the translator, Rudolf Szántó, a translator whose known translations are from German and French. It is not clear why the publishing house finally commissioned Antal Szerb, the renowned literary historian and novelist for the translation.²⁷

The picture is further complicated by the fact that the first chapter and a half of this edition, and parts of several further chapters were evidently translated from the German edition of 1931 (or later). Based on a detailed textual comparison, Balogh reaches several important conclusions: (1) There were (at least) two translators at work, initially using the German edition and later mainly relying on the English version as source text. (2) While the first chapter, translated from the German, is a vivid rendering of Huizinga's elaborate literary style, the majority of the text, translated from the English version, is bland, often careless and inconsistent. (3) The title, translated from the English, can most probably be attributed to Szerb. The identity of the translator is a key factor in the Hungarian reception of the work (Balogh 2017: 54–64). The figure of Antal Szerb, who continues even now to be an iconic figure in Hungarian literary history has in a way become merged with the Hungarian *Herfsttij* and plays an important role in the lasting popularity of the work in Hungary.

The Hungarian *Herfsttij* was reviewed positively in the contemporary Hungarian press (Törő 1999: 97–98).[28] *Herfsttij* is the first work in Huizinga's oeuvre to be published in Hungarian, but a Hungarian translation of his culture-critical study *In de schaduwen van morgen* (In the Shadow of Tomorrow, 1938b) was published in the same year, the popularity of which influenced the positive reception of *Herfsttij*. Hungarian intellectuals were aware of his earlier publications, since many of them were available in Hungary in German and French, and reviews of his monographs were systematically published in Hungarian philosophical and historical journals from the middle of the 1920s. The first review of *Herfsttij* (which predates the Hungarian translation), 'basically a paraphrase of the first chapter, at times a literal translation', was published in the journal *Korunk* (Balogh 2017: 10). Huizinga's fame in Hungary can also be attributed to his long-lasting personal contacts with Hungarian intellectuals. In 1936 he visited Hungary as a member of the Commission Internationale de Coopération Intellectuelle (CICI) for their annual meeting, which was held in Budapest, and he was elected an honorary member of the Hungarian Scientific Academy in 1939 (Van der Lem 1997: 192, Balogh 2002: 53–54).

Four decades after the 1938 edition, in 1976 the Magyar Helikon publishing house republished an ambitious new edition of *A középkor alkonya*: a beautiful hard cover book in large format with several appendices, including a rich section of ninety-nine pages with reproductions in black and white and colour (Huizinga 1976). Though the 1938 translation was reused and Antal Szerb is credited as the translator, this text was 'compared with the 1937 London edition of the work and supplemented by Gábor Dávid', as indicated on the inner cover (Huizinga 1976: 1).[29] It is not made clear what this comparison and supplementation implied, in any case Huizinga's preface of 1924 was also included. That again in this step of the reception process there was uncertainty about the translation is indicated by the comment on the new publication by the Hungarian poet and novelist Gyula Illyés in his diary: 'Evening: Gábor Dávid translated Huizinga's famous book, but on the cover, we see "compared the translations of Antal Szerb with the original". Why this false piety?' (Illyés 1992: 12, quoted in Kovács 1999: 328).[30] Significantly, the same tension between the 'untouchable status' of the work in Szerb's translation and the canonizing necessity for actualization is visible here, as in the case of Kurt Köster's revision of the German translation in 1953.

The introduction to the new edition was written by the medievalist Gábor Klaniczay, who in an erudite and elegant essay places *Herfsttij* and Huizinga's oeuvre in the context of European scholarship.[31] He made use of the afterword to discuss recent trends in intellectual history, which at the time were inaccessible to most Hungarians behind the iron curtain, but he also reflects on the Hungarian reception of *Herfsttij*. He discusses how Hungarian historical, intellectual-historical, literary and philosophical schools and individuals were influenced by Huizinga's writings, claiming that no other international historian's oeuvre had received a more enthusiastic reception in Hungary. Klaniczay argues that two people were instrumental in the acculturation of Huizinga's thought: Antal Szerb, both through the translation itself and by introducing Huizinga's scholarly attitude into his own *History of World Literature* (1941), and Gábor Halász.[32] Finally, Klaniczay reflects on an additional factor that may have made Huizinga popular in Hungary, the exemplary bravery with which Huizinga stood up against the National Socialists, and how – like Szerb and Halász in Hungary – he was persecuted by the fascists and did not live to see the end of the Second World War (Klaniczay 1976: 283). Even though Klaniczay defines his objective as separating 'legend' and inherent quality in the Hungarian reception of *Herfsttij*, his afterword not only analyses but also strongly reinforces the image of Huizinga as an exemplary humanist, scholar and man.

This prestigious edition, combining the text embedded in an extensive apparatus and information regarding its reception by leading and promising Hungarian experts in different fields, as well as the lavish appendix with reproductions, was an intellectual sensation in the seventies. Middle-class families strove to obtain a copy, despite its high price. This edition was followed by an unillustrated paperback copy in 1979.[33] In 1997, a hard cover illustrated edition, an unchanged reprint of the 1976 edition was published, followed by a digital edition in 2016 (Huizinga 2016a). All editions are readily available to this day in second-hand bookshops, and the historic first edition (1938) is available in a digitalized form from the Hungarian National Library (Huizinga 1938a).

The Polish reception

The first Polish translation of *Herfsttij* was published in 1961 under the title *Jesień średniowiecza* (*The Autumn of the Middle Ages*, 1961).[34] The translation was made from the 1953 German edition by Tadeusz Brzostowski, a historian, philologist and translator of Latin and German, while the poetry fragments were translated by Jadwiga Dackiewicz. The edition was published with several paratexts. These include a lengthy foreword by Henryk Barycz, an archivist and professor of Early Modern history at Krakow University, who explores the cultural connections between Poland and the Low Countries as well as providing a biography of Huizinga. The volume also includes a historical essay on *Herfsttij* and cultural history by Stanisław Herbst, a modern historian and professor at the University of Warsaw, as an afterword.[35] The book includes a selection of twenty-four picture plates in black and white and colour and it was reprinted at least eight times.[36]

Jesień średniowiecza was Huizinga's first complete book to be published in Polish. Translations of Huizinga's *Erasmus* and *Homo Ludens* were soon to follow.[37] However, Huizinga had been known to the Polish public before the publication of *Herfsttij*, since the first discussion of the work of 'the famous Dutch humanist' appeared in the period 1946–1948 (Biesiada 2014). In an article devoted to the reception of Huizinga in Poland, Wojciech Lipoński describes how the 1961 publication of the Polish translation marked the end of the Stalinist period in Poland, during which books by humanist thinkers from Western Europe were not published. In an analysis of the lively reactions to the publication of *Jesień średniowiecza*, he distinguishes three types of reactions (Lipoński 2015: 10–15). The first represents the opinion of the dominant communist cultural opinion, according to which Huizinga was a 'catastrophist', whose overall conclusions are erroneous and whose thinking was often contradictory. Polish readers can profit from reading Huizinga's work, but it should be presented with a commentary that highlights the ideological errors in his thinking.[38] In addition to this attitude, however, there were also reactions with a much more positive evaluation, for instance a review by Stanisław Łoś, which allowed for the indirect and figurative expression of the opinions of the Catholic Polish intelligentsia. The fact that such reactions to the book were permitted gave further signals to readers about the thaw in ideological restrictions after the Stalinist period (Łoś 1962: 1–4).[39] A third type of reaction, represented for instance by the philosopher Leszek Kołakowski, was less radically critical and expressed admiration for the breadth of examples from art and literature that Huizinga presented in *Herfsttij*, but also added a methodological critique concerning the lack of an empirical categorization of these examples.[40]

In 2016, the book was retranslated by the polyglot, writer, poet, translator and editor Robert Stiller. In this edition, in stark contrast to the collaborative production visible in the first translation, Stiller not only translated Huizinga's text and the excerpts of poetry, but also wrote the introduction and afterword. In the introduction, Stiller criticizes Brzostowski's translation. He considers this translation to be long-winded, pretentious and careless.[41] Stiller claims to have used an unspecified Dutch version of *Herfsttij* and the second English translation, in case of doubt. Stiller was a polyglot and translated literature from many languages, but Dutch was not one of them. Furthermore, the publication was not printed with the support of the Dutch Foundation of Literature. Since Poland has several good translators from Dutch, the foundation would certainly have required the publisher to contract an experienced Dutch–Polish translator to qualify for the translation subsidy. It remains unclear which was the source language of the second Polish translation, but it can be stated with almost complete certainty that it was not simply based on the Dutch original.[42]

Interestingly, the Polish translation of the title of *Herfsttij* has been incorporated into the realm of pop culture and has started to lead a life of its own that is not directly related to the book.[43] The Polish translator of Quentin Tarantino's 1994 film *Pulp Fiction*,[44] translated the sentence 'I'm gonna get medieval on yo' ass!' as 'Zrobię ci z dupy jesień średniowiecza!', which literally means 'I'll make the autumn of the Middle Ages of your ass!' This ingenious cultural transfer of the phrase 'to get medieval', meaning 'To physically torture or injure someone by means of archaic methods'[45] was incorporated into pop culture, caught on and became part of trendy everyday Polish usage. There are now a growing number of examples from journalistic language in which this phrase is used, ranging, for example, from the context of whether the governing party will make 'the autumn of the Middle Ages' of the opposition, or how a Polish football player from the third league gives the Warsaw club 'the autumn of the Middle Ages'.[46]

The Czech and Slovak reception

Surprisingly, the complete *Herfsttij* was not published in Czech and Slovak until the end of the twentieth century. The first Czech translation appeared in 1999 at the Jinočany publishing house in a translation by Gabriela Veselá under the title *Podzim středověku* (The Autumn of the Middle Ages, 1999).[47] The translation was made from the German authorized translation *Herbst des Mittelalters* by Kurt Köster and Tilly Jolles-Mönckeberg. The translator, Gabriela Veselá was at that time a member of the Czech Literature Institute at the Czech Academy of Sciences and a lecturer at the Department of German Philology at Charles University in Prague (Engelbrecht 2017: 79). The French text fragments were translated by Šárka Belisová. Even though this first Czech edition was published eighty years after the original, it includes neither an explanatory foreword nor an afterword. It does include twelve pages of black and white illustrations. A second edition of this same translation followed in 2010, this time at the literary publisher Pasenka in the series *Historická paměť* (Historical memory), again without an introduction, but this time with eight pages of black and white and coloured illustrations (Huizinga 2010).

The editions were positively received, with a frequent emphasis on the literary qualities of the book, for instance in a review by Ladislav Nagy:

> It is obvious that the book, for the aspects mentioned above, is very close to literature. And indeed, Huizinga is an excellent stylist, an excellent narrator who proves more than favorable to what is emphasized by Hayden White, namely the illusiveness of the distance between historiography and fictional literature. Huizinga's early work is so convincingly accurate especially because of its literary qualities and the delicate harmony between content and form. (Nagy 2000: 20)[48]

The 2010 edition was also received with enthusiasm (Vaverka 2011: 136–137). The reviewers generally did not consider it to be dated, and in one case it was even celebrated for its 'new approach'.[49] In Martin C. Putna's review, it was associated with another book by Huizinga: 'This work also forms the basis for a synthesizing work that was released in 1935 under the title *In the Shadow of Tomorrow*' (Putna 2000: 14). It is significant that he contextualized the new Czech translation by referring to *In the Shadow of Tomorrow*, since this was Huizinga's first book to be translated into Czech in 1938, and it was republished in 1970.[50]

There had been an attempt to make a Czech translation of the *Herfsttij* before the war. In his article about Huizinga's reception in Bohemia, Wilken Engelbrecht writes about three partly overlapping groups of Czech intellectuals who were influenced by Huizinga's oeuvre beginning in the 1920s: Czech historians, who read his work in German, and discussed and wrote reviews of it from the 1920s onward, Protestant scholars who were mainly interested in the philosophical aspects of his writings, and a discernible wave of reception in the 1930s within a group of young historians with a Marxist orientation, *Historická skupina* (the Historical Group). At the end of 1939, this group drew up a plan to publish a series of historical works, both by local historians and studies translated from other languages, in cooperation with the Družstevní práce publishing house. The list included *Herfsttij*, which was to be translated from the French translation of 1932, but the project was aborted due to the outbreak of the Second World War (Engelbrecht 2017: 73).

In an article dedicated to the Slovak reception of Huizinga's oeuvre, Adam Bžoch argues that from 1946 to 1947 onwards the Dutch scholar's writings provoked a vigorous debate in the conservative circle of Catholic intellectuals grouped around the periodical *Verbum*, who were primarily interested in theological, literary and philosophical questions (Bžoch 2017: 87). They were the first to devote attention to Huizinga, when in 1946 they published a review of the French edition of Huizinga's cultural critical political testament, *Geschonden wereld*.[51] This was followed by a longer biographical article about Huizinga in the same periodical, and a Slovak translation of about one third of the first chapter of *Herfsttij* under the title *Napätie života* ('Die Spannung des Lebens') made from the German by Valentín Kalinay in 1947.[52] The translation of the complete *Herfsttij* only followed more than forty years later, in 1990, which nevertheless preceded the Czech translation. It was published in an integral double edition together with *Homo Ludens*. Both works were translated by Viktor Krupa, who used the 1987 English translation of *Herfsttij* for his *Jeseň stredoveku* (The Autumn of the Middle Ages), and the 1944 authorized German translation of *Homo Ludens* as a source text. The edition is accompanied by a lengthy afterword and detailed notes by Vojtech Kopčan (Bžoch 2017: 95).

Conclusion

The definition of Damrosch about how individual works become part of world literature prompted three questions to help analyse the trajectory of Huizinga's

Herfsttij in translation. Questions about the extent to which *Herfsttij* was/is considered literature, about the breadth and time span of its international circulation, and the ways in which it was canonized were addressed, with regard to six different languages. A comparison of the brief summaries of the reception of the translations into Czech, English, German, Hungarian, Polish and Slovak allows significant patterns to emerge.

It is without doubt that not only is Huizinga one of the most important Dutch-speaking authors in translation in the twentieth century (Heilbron 1995: 235–238), this is especially true for his most important work, *Herfsttij*, with thirty-four translations into twenty-six languages. It is also clear that the pace of translation has not declined in the one hundred years since its original publication, since seven (re)translations were published in the twenty-first century, with several new translations in progress.

A repeated feature of the reception in different languages is the reference to the literary qualities of the book. Huizinga's subjective literary style, which seemed to be a flaw and was a recurring point of critique in the first wave of the Dutch reception – an attitude which is in some ways still present in the reactions of Dutch historians – turned out to be one of the enduring qualities of *Herfsttij*.

The literary quality of this work also has influenced the process of canonization. While books of scientific non-fiction generally have a shorter life span than literature, since the progress of knowledge quickly makes information outdated, *Herfsttij* is not considered outdated and has gained the timeless quality of canonized literature. The book is considered a monument of style, of how language can be used to make a period in the past come to life. Retranslation is an emphatic sign of canonization observable in several languages investigated. Canonization is in many cases also signified by embedding the text in editions with multiple paratexts, often compiled by intellectuals and experts of high academic status from the target culture.

Beside the general tendencies important differences also become visible between the two reception histories in German and English on the one hand and the Central-European languages on the other. Translation sociology differentiates between central and peripheral languages according to the percentage of translated books from the different languages in the global market for translations. In contrast to the respective hyper-central and central position of English and German, both the Dutch language and Czech, Hungarian, Polish and Slovak are peripheral languages, with a share of less than 1, or between 1 and 3 percent in the world translation market (Van Es and Heilbron 2015: 297). The centre-periphery structure tends to cause an inverse relation between the centrality of a language and the proportion of translations published in the national book production system, meaning that translations generally flow from centre to periphery. Going against the translations flow by getting a book from a peripheral literature translated in a central literature is a considerable hurdle, as can be seen above, one of the difficulties being the lack of translators with the necessary expertise. However, once the book is translated into central languages this not only makes it available for other peripheral languages, but also bestows on it the cultural prestige of these central languages. It is therefore not surprising that the *Herfsttij* was first translated into

German and English (1924) and French (the first French translation was not published but the second, made by the Belgian medievalist Julia Bastin, was published in 1932) and successively was translated into other peripheral languages, often using one of these three translations as the source text.

It is clear, however, that the trajectory of a text from one peripheral to another peripheral language is even more precarious. This is especially so in the case of Dutch being transferred to Central European languages where the conditions for a larger susceptibility for literature from the other country, such as 'geographical proximity, related languages, extensive trade transaction and professional contacts (including contact between publishers), tourism and migration across borders' often do not exist (Heilbron and Van Es 2015: 81–82).[53] The fact that even modern translations in the investigated Central European languages rely on existing translations in central languages is significant. Despite the excellent literary translators in these countries, Dutch literary texts sometimes still need mediation through the centre to reach another periphery (see e.g. Brems, Réthelyi and Van Kalmthout 2017).

If translation is a mark of a work's evaluation history, then we can conclude that *Herfsttij* has been positively assessed for a century now, throughout many different cultures and languages. It has proven to be a text apt for new languages, editorial interventions and changing publishing conditions; paradoxically, it can take different shapes without losing its monumental status. In her seminal book on adaptations, Linda Hutcheon (2012) takes a Darwinian approach when she compares cultural adaptation to biological adaptation: she sees cultural products successfully migrate to different cultures and times by adapting to their new environments. This seems to be what *Herfsttij* is good at if you follow the tracks of its translation history, as we did in this article. However, it remains uncertain whether it travels as an insightful text about the late Middle Ages in France and the Burgundian Low Countries or as an icon of Western cultural heritage, not so much to be read but to be aware of.

Notes

1 'de meest invloedrijke studie [...] die ooit door een Nederlandse "alfa" werd geschreven.'
2 This contribution was written in the context of the project Eastbound, which investigates the translation and adaptation history of frequently translated oeuvres from Flemish and Dutch literature into German, on the one hand, and into four East-Central European languages, on the other.
3 We wish to thank Theresia Feldmann for her assistance with the digital mapping of the results.
4 In this graph we do not consider Köster's revision of Jolles-Mönckeberg's German translation or the Hungarian revision to be a new translation. We did count the Croatian and the Serbian translation as two different translations.

5   Before 2010, the subsidies were provided by the predecessor of the Foundation for Literature, the Dutch Literary Production and Translation Fund (NLPVF).
6   This information is based on a personal interview with Mireille Berman, a non-fiction specialist at the Dutch Foundation for Literature, representing the Foundation in Amsterdam on 17 April 2018.
7   'Het mag misschien heiligschennis lijken, maar zelfs voor de Nederlandse lezer kan *Herfsttij* toegankelijker lijken in het Duits of het Engels, waarin de eigenaardigheden van de stijl in de vertaling zijn opgelost.'
8   'Of professor Huizinga nu geschiedenis had geschreven of literatuur, want literaire lauweren waren voor een historicus niet weggelegd.'
9   Nevertheless, Huizinga's view of historiography was not unique internationally. However innovative and unconventional Huizinga's essay was, it was aligned with the new sounds that Tollebeek claims were emerging abroad: 'Huizinga's cultural-historical method was closely aligned with the historiographic innovations that were being propagated by the Warburg Institute in London and the *Annales* in France, among others' (1990: 200).
10 'Er verdankt sich zum guten Teil der deutschen Uebersetzung.'
11 'wie es überhaupt ein seltener Glückfall ist, wenn ein grosser Gelehrter zugleich ein grosser Schriftsteller ist.'
12 'Huizinga wurde in Deutschland zu einem "rasch hoch geschätzten" Historiker.'
13 'So schien *Herbst des Mittelalters* schon nach wenigen Jahren zu einem Monument der Geschichtsforschung geworden zu sein, ebenso unumgänglich wie unbeweglich.'
14 'With his *Autumn of the Middle Ages*, however, Huizinga certainly has erected a lasting literary monument. Walking with him through the autumnal Middle Ages is still rewarding, at the least as a literary experience.'
15 'Weshalb sollte man bei dem, was fremden Ursprungs ist, die Spuren des Fremden allzu ängstlich verwischen?'
16 'Ein Werk, das grosse Wirkungen gehabt, kann eigentlich gar nicht mehr beurteilt werden.'
17 Köster writes in his foreword: 'Es erwies sich als notwendig, mit dieser Arbeit der textlichen Angleichung eine durchgreifende sprachliche Ueberarbeitung der älteren übertragung zu verbinden' (XII).
18 'Wat mij betreft, ik zou het hoogst aangenaam vinden, indien van het boek een Engelsche vertaling verscheen, en natuurlijk zeer bereid zijn, tot het welslagen daarvan mee te werken. Gemakkelijk zal het vertalen niet zijn, en ik moet hopen, dat Uw leerlinge er den moed toe vindt. Indien daartoe kan bijdragen, dat ik genegen ben, geregeld over de vertaling te adviseeren, wil ik gaarne, dat U haar daarvan de verzekering geeft' and 'om gedrongen passages te verduidelijken.'
19 And ultimately the publisher decided: 'We should be pleased to undertake the publication of an English translation of your book on "The Decline of the Middle Ages", provided that the English version does not exceed about 110,000 words, which corresponds roughly to the French version you kindly showed us. We think that the majority of the footnotes should be omitted' (Krul et al. 1989: letter 477).
20 Huizinga wrote to Barnouw concerning the London translation: 'Het wordt een verkorte redactie [...]. De vertaling is door Hopman gemaakt, maar ik heb er zelf ook vrij wat aandeel aan, doordat ik met hem op een heel prettige wijze kon samenwerken

en heele passages zelf suggereeren, als mij zijn vertaling niet bevredigde' (It will be an abridged edition [...]. The translation was done by Hopman, but I also had a considerable share in it because I was able to collaborate with him very pleasantly and even suggest whole passages when his translated was not satisfactory) (Krul et al. 1989: letter 526).

21 Shaw's two greatest criticisms were the poetic style and the normative, pedantic character of the book: 'Huizinga reads like a nineteenth-century writer, a restrained romantic stylist fitted with an Enlightenment predilection for judging and the superior tone.' Shaw's greatest compliment was that Huizinga was brave. He was convinced that historians might still learn something from him and encouraged them to adopt his approach: 'Irritate a reader; surprise yourself; show some self. It will make it easier for us all to know what you mean, and why, in resisting your book, we emerge more fully ourselves.'

22 Several years later, Simons and Edward Peters wrote a long and documented critique of the retranslation. They argued in favour of an annotated edition that would incorporate all scholarly literature, since this would provide the double perspective of our own age and that of the book.

23 See, for example, Bellitto 1997, Staples 1999, and Midgley 2012. Krul 1997 offers a well-informed essay on the production history, context, reception, critique, etc. The translation also received extensive attention in the popular press: *The Guardian, London Review of Books, Times Literary Supplement, Observer, The Los Angeles Times Sunday Book Review, The New Yorker, Publishers Weekly, The Wall Street Journal*.

24 They also provide a survey of the reception of the book in the second half of the twentieth century.

25 The Hungarian translation and reception history of *Herfsttij* and Huizinga's complete oeuvre in Hungary is extremely well documented due to the work of two scholars, Tamás Balogh and Krisztina Törő, who have dedicated many publications to the subject over several decades. Tamás Balogh, especially, has revisited different aspects of the Hungarian reception history up to the present day and has meticulously collected philological details to rewrite and clarify certain aspects in ever greater detail. The brief summary of Hungarian reception in this article is deeply indebted to their research.

26 Other volumes in this popular series were, for instance, Frantz Funck-Brentano *L'Ancien régime*, Christopher Dawson *The Making of Europe: An Introduction to the History of European Unity*, etc.

27 'Antal Szerb (1901–45) is chiefly remembered for his widely-read *History of Hungarian Literature* (Kolozsvár, 1934). [...] His last major work was *A History of World Literature* (1941), in which his enthusiasm for the values of European civilization found an outlet in an age when this civilization appeared to be disintegrating. Szerb died of starvation and privation in a forced labour camp in Western Hungary' (Czigány 1984).

28 For the publication history of the Hungarian translations of Huizinga's works up to the Second World War see Balogh 2017.

29 Though the text on the inner cover circumspectly does not specify the extent to which Gábor Dávid reworked the text, the colophon lists both names as translators.

In the same explanation on the inner cover it is specified that the Villon poems were translated by István Vas and the other poetry fragments by István Tótfalusi. The pictures were selected by Zsuzsanna Urbach, an internationally respected art historian and expert on Early Netherlandish painting from the Museum of Hungarian Fine Arts, who also wrote an introduction a detailed catalogue of the picture section (Urbach 1976: 287–316).

30 Quotation translated by RO.
31 Klaniczay was at the time completing his postgraduate studies in Paris with Jacques Le Goff at the École des Hautes Études et Sciences Sociales (EHESS). He would later become an internationally renowned expert on the historical anthropology of European Christendom and comparative cultural and religious history of Hungary and Central Europe.
32 Like Antal Szerb, the critic, essayist and influential intellectual Gábor Halász (1901–1945) was a victim of the Holocaust (Czigány 1984).
33 The 1976 edition was also published in Bratislava by Madách publishers in 1979.
34 We wish to thank Małgorzata Dowlaszewicz and Michal Hynas for their assistance with the Polish material.
35 As well as a chronology by Helena Kahanowa, and an index of the persons by Janina Wiercińska.
36 This edition was reprinted in 1967, 1974, 1992, 1996, 1998, 2002, 2003 and 2005.
37 A single chapter of Huizinga's *Erasmus* had already appeared in 1959, translated from the German (Huizinga 1959).
38 For example, in the review: Grzybowski 1962: 1, quoted in Lipoński 2015: 9–42.
39 Quoted in Lipoński 2015.
40 Kołakowski 1962.
41 Stiller's afterword, in Huizinga 2016b: 377.
42 Unfortunately, the translator cannot be asked to clarify these questions since he passed away in the years of the publication.
43 We wish to thank Małgorzata Dowlaszewicz for drawing our attention to this phenomenon.
44 Elżbieta Gałązka-Salamon.
45 See the phrase 'Go medieval on someone's ass' in Urban Dictionary.
46 For example Walczak 2017 or the sentence 'Dlaczego Rafał Siemaszko, chłopak do niedawna z trzeciej ligi, robi im jesień średniowiecza?,' in Wawrzynowski 2018.
47 We wish to thank Klara Šrejmová for her assistance with the Czech material.
48 See also the review by Martin C. Putna (2000).
49 Cf. Vlnas 2000.
50 For the publication history of the Czech translations of Huizinga's works see Engelbrecht 2017: 71–85.
51 No reaction can be found in the Slovak periodicals either to the German translations of Huizinga's work or to the 1938 Czech translation of *In de schaduwen van morgen* (Bžoch 2017: 86–87).
52 Huizinga 1947. For the publication history of the Slovak translations of Huizinga's works see Bžoch 2017: 98.
53 'Geografische nabijheid, taalverwantschap, omvangrijk handelsverkeer en vele zakelijke contacten (waaronder contacten tussen uitgevers), toerisme en migratie over de grenzen heen' (Heilbron and Van Es 2015: 82; our translation).

References

Balogh, T. (2002), 'Huizinga magyar barátai', in T. Balogh and K. Törő (eds), *Huizinga magyar barátai*, 49–71, Budapest: ELTE Eötvös Kiadó.

Balogh, T. (2009), 'Mélyenszántó gondolat és hűséges megemlékezés. Johan Huizinga és Szerb Antal Huizinga-monográfiájáról', in T. Balogh (ed.), *A holland látóhatár*, 43–65, Budapest: Typotex.

Balogh, T. (2017), *Huizinga Noster: filológiai tanulmányok J. Huizinga magyar recepciójáról*, Budapest: L'Harmattan.

Bellitto, C.M. (1997), 'The Autumn of the Middle Ages', *History: Reviews of New Books* 25 (3): 99–100.

Biesiada, J. (2014), 'Bibliografia prac Johana Huizingi w Polsce po 1945 roku', *Zabawy i Zabawki, Studia Antropologiczne/Plays and Toys Studies in Anthropology* 12: 67–73.

Bouwsma, W.J. (1990), 'The Waning of the Middle Ages Revisited', in W.J. Bouwsma, *A Usable Past. Essays in European Cultural History*, 325–335, Los Angeles: University of California Press.

Brems, E., O. Réthelyi and T. van Kalmthout (2017), 'Dutch on the Move: Studying the Circulation of Smaller Literatures', in E. Brems, O. Réthelyi and T. van Kalmthout (eds.), *Doing Double Dutch. The International Circulation of Literature from the Low Countries*, 11–26, Leuven: Leuven University Press.

Burckhardt, J. (1860), *Die Kultur der Renaissance in Italien*, Basel: Schweihauser.

Bžoch, A. (2017), 'Johan Huizinga in der Slowakei: Lektüren und kritische Auseinandersetzungen in der Zeit von 1946 bis 1990', *World Literature Studies* 9: 86–100.

Czigány, L. (1984), *The Oxford History of Hungarian Literature: From the Earliest Times to the Present*, Oxford: Clarendon Press. Available online: http://mek.niif.hu/02000/02042/html/index.html (accessed 26 February 2019).

Damrosch, D. (2003), *What is World Literature?*, Princeton, NJ: Princeton University Press.

Dunk, H.W. von der (1973), 'Huizinga als kultuurpessimist', *Groniek* 26: 150–154.

Engelbrecht, W. (2017), 'Johan Huizinga in tschechischer Überzetzung', *World Literature Studies* 9: 71–85.

Es, N. Van and J. Heilbron (2015), 'Fiction from the periphery: How Dutch Writers Enter the Field of English-language Literature', *Cultural Sociology* 9 (3): 296–319.

'Go medieval on someone's ass', *Urban Dictionary LLC*. Available online: https://www.urbandictionary.com/define.php?term=GO%20MEDIEVAL%20ON%20SOMEONE%27S%20ASS (accessed 17 February 2019).

Grzybowski, K. (1962), 'Huizinga czyli katastrofizm', *Życie Literackie* 11: 1.

Herrnstein-Smith, B. (1983), 'Contingencies of Value', *Critical Inquiry* 10 (1): 1–35.

Heilbron, J. (1995), 'Nederlandse vertalingen wereldwijd. Kleine landen en culturele mondialisering', in J. Heilbron, W. de Nooy and W. Tichelaar (eds), *Waarin een klein land. Nederlandse cultuur in internationaal verband*, 206–253, Amsterdam: Prometheus.

Heilbron, J. and N. van Es (2015), 'In de wereldrepubliek der letteren', in T. Bevers, B. Colenbrander, J. Heilbron and N. Wilterdink (eds), *Nederlandse kunst in de wereld. Literatuur, architectuur en beeldende kunst 1980–2013*, 20–54, Nijmegen: Vantilt.

Helgesson, S. and P. Vermeulen (2016), 'Introduction: World Literature in the Making', in S. Helgesson and P. Vermeulen (eds), *Institutions of World Literature: Writing, Translation, Markets*, 1–20, New York: Routledge.

Hugenholtz, F.W.N. (1973), 'The fame of a Masterwork', in W.R.H. Koops, E.H. Kossmann and G. van der Plaat (eds), *Johan Huizinga 1872–1972*, 91–103, The Hague: Martinus Nijhoff.

Huizinga, J. (1919), *Herfsttij der Middeleeuwen*, 1st edn, Haarlem: H.D. Tjeenk Willink & Zoon.

Huizinga, J. (1924), *The Waning of the Middle Ages*, trans. F. Hopman, London: Edward Arnold.

Huizinga, J. (1938a), *A középkor alkonya*, trans. A. Szerb, Budapest: Athenaeum. Available online: http://mek.oszk.hu/15300/15381 (accessed 5 June 2018).

Huizinga, J. (1938b), *A holnap árnyékában* [original title *In de schaduwen van morgen, een diagnose van het geestelijk lijden van onzen tijd*, 1935], trans. M.D. Garzuly, Budapest: Egyetemi nyomda.

Huizinga, J. (1947), 'Napätie života ['s Levens felheid/Spannung des Lebens]', *Verbum* II, 1: 23–28.

Huizinga, J. (1949), 'Herfsttij der Middeleeuwen', in J. Huizinga, *Verzamelde werken. Deel 3*, ed. L. Brummel et al., Haarlem: H.D. Tjeenk Willink & Zoon.

Huizinga, J. (1953), *Herbst des Mittelalters*, trans. T. Wolff-Mönckeberg and ed. by K. Köster, Stuttgart: Alfred Kröner Verlag.

Huizinga, J. (1959), *Erasmus: Umysłowość Erazma z Rotterdamu*, trans. H. Migała, Warsaw: Państwowe Wydaw (Naukowe, *Przegląd Humanistyczny* 1 (10) (1959): 126–138.

Huizinga, J. (1961), *Jesień średniowiecza*, trans. T. Brzostowski and J. Dackiewicz, Warszawa: Państwowy Instytut Wydawniczy.

Huizinga, J. (1964), *Erazm*, trans. M. Kurecka, Warsaw: Państwowy Instytut Wydawniczy.

Huizinga, J. (1967), *Homo ludens. Zabawa jako źródło kultury*, trans. M. Kurecka and W. Wirpsza, Warsaw: SW Czytelnik.

Huizinga, J. (1976), *A középkor alkonya. Az élet, a gondolkodás és a művészet formái Franciaországban és Németalföldön a XIV. és XV. Században*, ed. G. Bence and trans. A. Szerb, I. Tótfalusi, I. Vas and G. Dávid, Budapest: Magyar Helikon.

Huizinga, J. (1990), *Jeseň stredoveku/Homo ludens*, trans. V. Krupa, I. Mojík and J. Smrek, Bratislava: Tatran.

Huizinga, J. (1996), *The Autumn of the Middle Ages*, trans. U.H. Mammitzsch and R.J. Payton, Chicago: University of Chicago Press.

Huizinga, J. (1999), *Podzim středověku*, trans. G. Veselá and Š. Belisová, 1st edn, Jinočany: H & H.

Huizinga, J. (2010), *Podzim středověku*, Historická paměť. Velká řada; vol. 19, trans. G. Veselá and Š. Belisová, 2nd edn, Prague: Litomyšl.

Huizinga, J. (2016a), *A középkor alkonya*, Digi-book Magyarország.

Huizinga, J. (2016b), *Jesień średniowiecza*, trans. R. Stiller, Kraków: Wydawnictwo Vis-à-vis Etiuda.

Hutcheon, L. (2012), *A Theory of Adaptation*, New York: Routledge.

Illyés, G. (1992), *Naplójegyzetek, 1977–78*, Budapest: Szépirodalmi.

Klaniczay, G. (1976), 'Utószó [Afterword]', in J. Huizinga (ed.), A *középkor alkonya*, 267–284, Budapest: Magyar Helikon.
Kołakowski, L. (1962), 'Historia jako sztuka piękna. Johan Huizinga: Jesień Średniowiecza', *Nowe Książki* 9: 548–550.
Koskinen, K. and O. Paloposki (2010), 'Retranslation', *Handbook of Translation Studies* 1: 294–298.
Kovács, I. (1999), *Casanova emlékiratai Szerb Antal* fordításában, Budapest: Atlantisz.
Krul, W. (1997), 'In the Mirror of van Eyck. Johan Huizinga's Autumn of the Middle Ages', *Journal of Medieval and Early Modern Studies* 27 (3): 358–363.
Krul, W., A. van der Lem and L. Hanssen, eds (1989), *J. Huizinga, Briefwisseling I*, Utrecht: Uitgeverij L J Veen.
Krumm, C. (2011), *Johan Huizinga; Deutschland und die Deutschen. Begegnung und Auseinandersetzung mit dem Nachbarn*, Studien zur Geschichte und Kultur Nordwesteuropas, vol. 23, Berlin: Waxmann.
Lem, A. Van der (1993), *Johan Huizinga. Leven en werk in beelden & documenten*, Amsterdam: Wereldbibliotheek.
Lem, A. Van der (1997), *Het Eeuwige verbeeld in een afgehaald bed. Huizinga en de Nederlandse beschaving*, Amsterdam: Wereldbibliotheek.
Lipoński, W. (2015), 'Recepcja *Homo ludens* Johana Huizingi w Polsce' [The Impact of Johan Huizinga's *Homo ludens* in Poland], in *Homo Ludens: czasopismo ludologiczne Polskiego Towarzystwa Badania Gier* 1: 9–42.
Łoś, S. (1962), 'Jesień przedwiośnia', *Tygodnik Powszechny* 9: 1–4.
Midgley, A. (2012), 'Book Review: Johan Huizinga, The Autumn of the Middle Ages. Translated by Rodney J. Payton and Ulrich Mammitzsch', *Saber and Scroll* 1 (1): b3.
Moran, S.F. (2016), 'Johan Huizinga, The Waning of the Middle Ages, and the Writing of History', *Michigan Academician* 43 (3): 410–423.
Naaijkens, T., ed. (2010), *Event or Incident. On the Role of Translation in the Dynamics of Cultural Change*, Bern: Peter Lang.
Nagy, L. (2000), 'Huizingův Podzim středověku je úchvatná elegie', *Lidové noviny*, 21 July 2000: 20.
Oostrom, F. Van (1986), 'De oude orde in verval? Hollandse hofliteratuur en Huizinga's 'Herfsttij', *Literatuur* 3 (1): 202–210.
Peters, E. and W.P. Simons (1999), 'The New Huizinga and the Old Middle Ages', *Speculum* 74 (3): 587–620.
Putna, M. C. (2000), 'Podzim středověku jako podobenství o podzimu Evropy', *MF Dnes*, 31 January 2000: 14.
Sellery, G.C. (1925), 'The Waning of the Middle Ages: A Study of the Forms of Life, Thought, and Art in France and the Netherlands in the XIVth and XVth Centuries by J.Huizinga', *The American Historical Review* 31 (1): 113–114.
Senger, H.G. (2004), 'Eine Schwalbe macht noch keine Herbst: Zu Huizingas Metapher vom Herbst des Mittelalters', in J.A. Aertsen and M. Pickavé (eds), '*Herbst des Mittelalters'? Fragen zur Bewertung des 14. und 15. Jahrhunderts*, 3–24, Berlin: De Gruyter.
Shaw, D.G. (1998), 'Huizinga's Timeliness', *History and Theory* 37 (2): 245–258.
Simons, W. (1997), '*About The Autumn of the Middle Ages* by Johan Huizinga, Rodney J. Payton and Ulrich Mammitzsch', *Speculum* 72 (2): 488–491.
Staples, M. (1999), 'The Autumn of the Middle Ages', *Parergon* 16 (2): 343–344.

Tollebeek, J. (1990), *De toga van Fruin. Denken over geschiedenis in Nederland sinds 1860*, Amsterdam: Wereldbibliotheek.

Szerb A. (1941), *A világirodalom története* (The History of World Literature), [Budapest]: Révai.

Törő, K. (1999), 'Fehérek között európai. A holland kultúrtörténész, Johan Huizinga a kortársi Magyarországon', in T. Balogh (ed.), *Huizinga 1999*, 95–108, Budapest: ELTE Germanisztikai Intézet.

Urbach, Z. (1976), 'A képek jegyzéze', in J. Huizinga (ed.), *A középkor alkonya*, 287–316, Budapest: Magyar Helikon.

Vaverka, P. (2011), 'Johan Huizinga – Podzim středověku. 2010', *AntropoWeb* 2: 136–137. Available online: http://www.antropoweb.cz/cs/johan-huizinga-podzim-stredoveku-2010 (accessed 10 February 2019).

Vlnas, V. (2000), 'Solitér a snivec o zlatém věku', *Respekt* 14, 27 March 2000. Available online: https://www.respekt.cz/tydenik/2000/14/soliter-a-snivec-o-zlatem-veku (accessed 5 June 2018).

Walczak, T. (2017), 'Czy PiS zrobi opozycji jesień średniowiecza?', *Online newsagency SE.PL*, 2 September 2017. Available online: http://www.se.pl/wiadomosci/opinie/tomasz-walczak-czy-pis-zrobi-opozycji-jesien-sredniowiecza_1015893.html (accessed 5 June 2018).

Wawrzynowski, M. (2018), 'Prowadzenie Legii przerosło Romeo Jozaka (felieton)', *WP Sportowe Fakty*, 16 April 2018. Available online: https://sportowefakty.wp.pl/pilka-nozna/746587/marek-wawrzynowski-prowadzenie-legii-przeroslo-romeo-jozaka-felieton (accessed 5 June 2018).

13

'Glimpses of a poetic genius': Paul van Ostaijen (1896–1928) and World Literature

Geert Buelens

Paul van Ostaijen's main contribution to world literature must be his 1921 *Bezette Stad* (*Occupied City*, 2016), an extraordinary typographic experimental poetry book about the First World War, designed in collaboration with sculptor Oscar Jespers and his close friend René Victor. At the time it was not received as such. Readers ignored it, and critics dismissed it as secondhand. In *De Stijl* of December 1921 Theo van Doesburg, using his heteronym I.K. Bonset, called it 'leeg hol opgeblazen – dik geïmiteer van fransche literatuursport' (empty hollow inflated – massive imitation of French literary sports, Bonset 1921). Michel Seuphor, still using his birth name Fernand Berckelaers in June of the same year in his Antwerp avant-garde journal *Het Overzicht*, praised the volume's 'spirit' but could not imagine the author having any 'artistieke bedoeling' (artistic meaning/ ambition) with it (Berckelaers 1921: 11). This was the heyday of the avant-garde, after all, with their inescapable turf wars and loud calls for innovation and absolute originality.

Indeed, a quick glance at the volume's remarkable layout might bring French, German and Italian examples to mind, yet a closer look reveals interesting differences and variations. Van Ostaijen's are no *parole in libertà*, because unlike the Futurists he did not really believe in 'freedom' when it comes to poetry; his 'rhythmic typography' obviously does not exclude the visual, but its main aim was aural and musical – the size and position of the words on the page (typeset varying from 10 to 48 pt) were above all supposed to convey the sound of the text. According to Van Ostaijen a printed poem functions like sheet music. Its performance is key.

Some of *Bezette Stad*'s pages contain only a handful of isolated words, one per verse, not unlike Sturm poet August Stramm's dense expressionist lyrics. Van Ostaijen often praised his German colleague, but in *Bezette Stad* his arsenal of poetic means is far richer, juxtaposing expressionist minimalism with a handwritten, multicolour collage, a circus poster making fun of 'Religion, King & State', lyrical *vignettes* full of despair, and expansive proclamations mixing witty intertextual pop cultural statements with scathing political analysis (Van Ostaijen 1979b). These traits betray more than a family resemblance with Dadaist texts from this era, but although he uses the word frequently in this book, Van Ostaijen never gives in to 'nihilism' and his poetics values skilled wordplay over randomness or chance. Commenting on Tristan Tzara's famous instructions to make a Dadaist poem by cutting out words from a newspaper, Van Ostaijen quipped 'this recipe is great. Seulement, il faut savoir découper un journal' (the only thing is that one has to know how to cut up a newspaper, Van Ostaijen 1979d: 522).

From his French contemporaries, Blaise Cendrars's and Guillaume Apollinaire's works seem most directly related to *Bezette Stad*. Both French poets were masters of the *jeu de mots* and of extracting poetic and even sublime moments from the gutters of daily life and the trenches of war. From Cendrars's prose work *La Fin du monde, filmée par L'Ange N.-D.* (1919) Van Ostaijen seems to have taken the idea of presenting the war as an apocalyptic film, produced by God and directed by one of his angels: 'God the Father presents the final act / director archangel Michael / planes blockades submarines strange races'. *Bezette Stad* also contains a few *calligrammes*, the word 'Zeppelin' in the form of a zeppelin, for instance, but the poet later claimed this hadn't been his intention (Van Ostaijen 1979d: 159) as he was more interested in the sound than in the form of words.

With Apollinaire's *Calligrammes* (1918), David Jones's *In Parentheses* (1937) and Paolo Buzzi's posthumous *Conflagrazione. Epopea Parolibera* (1963), *Bezette Stad* ranks as the quintessential experimental poetry volume about the First World War; to some extent these books can even be read as accounts of that war, zooming in on key moments like invasion, siege, assault or retreat. Like Buzzi's, Van Ostaijen's perspective is that of a civilian bystander, a poet with a deep understanding of language and propaganda who uses newspaper headlines and typography to convey the startling modernity of this global conflict. As a citizen of the Belgian city of Antwerp, Van Ostaijen's war experience was not limited to news reports, however. *Bezette Stad* contains a highly autobiographical evocation of the October 1914 German siege of the city and of the exodus of many of its inhabitants to the Netherlands ('Goodbye threatened city / refuge north'), followed by a sobering account of what it was like to return to a city under occupation.

Most striking today is the poet's use of language to convey the multi-diversity of the modern city in war time. As David Colmer points out in the introduction to his English translation, *Bezette Stad* 'includes Dutch, in its Flemish variant the language of both the poet and the populace; French, at the time Belgium's administrative language and the language of the bourgeoisie; German, the language of the occupiers; Latin, the language of the Catholic Church; and English, a presence in this cosmopolitan city even then' (Van Ostaijen 2016). Van Ostaijen uses these languages as a form of mimesis, but also to expose what language conveys about power, class structure and cultural stratification in this multilingual city.

It is only fitting that the main echo of Van Ostaijen in world literature is to be found in the work of South Africa's fiercest experimental white poet and artist, Wopko Jensma (1939–1993?). In its own multilingualism (mixing English, Afrikaans, Portuguese, French, Dutch and German but most strikingly Tswana, Zulu, Fanakalo, the Afrikaans creole sociolect Tsotsi and African-American slang) Jensma's poetry is the epitome of cultural impurity and *métissage* – a provocation of the highest order in apartheid South Africa.

In the late 1960s Jensma became part of an international avant-garde network and a few of his poems were published in Flemish little magazines *De Tafelronde* and *Labris* – the two most important publications to honour and explore Van Ostaijen's legacy at the time (Buelens 2001: 902–912, 942–954). In his volumes from the 1970s Jensma mentioned Van Ostaijen, he included an English variation on one of Van Ostaijen's classic poems, and he positioned himself in the Flemish poet's footsteps by combining typographical experiments, sarcastic collage and jazz-inflicted rhythms.

Van Ostaijen's 1925 poem 'Melopee' is one of the great classics of Dutch language literature. Both highly musical and mysterious, the author tended to use it in his lectures on poetry to illustrate how a poem can communicate through mode and affect, rather than through explicit statements or confession. 'Melopee' was supposed to convey a sense of 'endless fatigue' (*eindeloze moeheid*), he wrote to a friend (Borgers 1971: 966), purely through rhythm, assonance and variation. What he called a 'purely thematic poetry' (Van Ostaijen 1982: 137) was not 'thematic' content-wise but musically. In 'Melopee' that theme consisted of words like 'moon', 'man', 'river', 'canoe' and 'sea'. By juggling them around in this nine-line poem like a composer would (using 'moon' six times, 'sea' five, 'canoe' four, 'river' three times and 'man' twice), he'd build a specifically dense type of poetic tension. Jensma's English version in *Where White is the Colour, Where Black is the Number* (1974) also uses 'man', 'moon' and 'boat' (instead of 'canoe') and brings them together in different constellations (like Van Ostaijen he mentions 'the moon' and 'the man' consecutively), but his main variation – or rather: deviation – pertains to the actual theme of the poem. Jensma does name it explicitly, in the title and no less than five times in the poem itself, and he explores it musically but also on a semantic, psychological and political level:

IN SOLITARY

a man in solitary passes by
passes by me in solitary
the moon caught in tree branches
a boat with a man in it rowing
passes by me in solitary
the moon, the man, confined
it's getting late, far too late
i coined the man, the moon, free
but i remain in solitary
there's another who passes by
but i don't know him but he is
past me confined in solitary.
(Jensma 1974: 44)

To name a poem 'in solitary' in South Africa was, of course, a statement in itself. The repressive apartheid state kept people in solitary confinement all the time, but the way Jensma repeats the phrase 'in solitary' (referring both to the 'man' and the 'i') creates a world defined by social isolation – just like apartheid did.[1]

Jensma, who was treated for mental illnesses throughout his life and who disappeared from the face of the earth around 1993 (Kleyn and Marais 2010), mentions Van Ostaijen in his third and most avant-garde volume, the partly autobiographical scrapbook fittingly titled *i must show you my clippings* (Jensma 1977). Whereas Van Ostaijen tried to write poems without an 'I' Jensma used the letter and subject form throughout, not as a narcissist celebration of his artistic ego but to explore the alienation brought upon people by politics, media and capitalism, but also in an often desperate attempt not to lose himself. White South Africa under apartheid was an extremely conformist society, hostile towards all people and ideas that might have questioned the repressive status-quo. In the Afrikaans poem 'klop en vir jullie sal toegemaak word' (knock and it will be closed for you – a sarcastic reversal of the famous verse from Matthew 7: 'knock, and it shall be opened unto you') Jensma lists artistic outcasts who found themselves excluded and discarded from society because they were loners, often stigmatized and forced within a pathological framework. All these writers, musicians, painters – Europeans as well as Africans – were labelled 'skisofoon', Jensma's word for schizophrenic artists, many of whom died at an early age from disease, suicide or an accident. The 'skisofoon' list starts with Beethoven and Gauguin before moving on to an indented stanza featuring some of the heroes of the historical avant-garde and the sixties counterculture:

> francois villon was
> paul van ostaijen was
> marcel duchamp was
> hendrik marsman was
> tristan tzara was

All of them bad apples who had found the door closed, because they didn't fit into the projected ideal of a community which was supposed to hum like a beehive (Jensma 1977: 24). Van Ostaijen's biography can easily be told following this *poète maudit* template, although his misfortune was not necessarily only society's fault.

When Van Ostaijen died at the age of 32 of TB-related complications scenes followed straight out of the Romantics handbook. Only a handful of people attended his funeral, including poet Gaston Burssens who arranged to put a simple wooden cross on his dear friend's grave with the words 'Here rests the poet of / The First Book of Schmoll / Paul van Ostayen [sic]' (Borgers 1971: 1041). That his friend did not know how Van Ostaijen wanted his name spelled was probably less painful than the simple fact that there was no such thing as *The First Book of Schmoll*. Van Ostaijen had some vague ideas about a collection with that name (*Het eerste boek van Schmoll*), but he had not published a volume of poetry since the fiasco of *Bezette Stad* seven years earlier. Most of his canonical work would be collected posthumously – poems he probably would have included in *Het eerste boek van Schmoll*, but also a complete volume (the multicoloured handwritten *De Feesten van Angst en Pijn*) which would only be published separately in the original Dutch version in 2006, thirty years after a complete English translation had seen the light as *Feasts of Fear and Agony* at New York's prestigious New Directions imprint.

Van Ostaijen's early career had been very different, however. He had started as an art critic at the age of 18 and published his first volume of poetry two years later. Although he was expelled from high school, he was clearly the product of the first Flemish generation that had been allowed to attend most of their classes in Dutch. Guided and encouraged by their teachers, Van Ostaijen and his friends were very active in the student factions of the nationalist Flemish Movement. It might seem inconsistent that he wrote some of his earliest poems in French, wittily rhyming 'sacoche' with 'brioches' and 'mioches' (Van Ostaijen 1979a: 261), but for Flemish intellectuals French would remain the language and culture of reference for decades to come.

Already as a teenager Van Ostaijen was remarkably well read. He was aware of the latest developments in Dutch, French and German literature, and both canonical and popular nineteenth-century authors were part of his repertoire. Some of the poems in his first collection *Music-Hall* (1916) hinted at Symbolists like Jules Laforgue, but also younger Catholic authors Francis Jammes and Charles Péguy left their mark, as did the Austrian poet Richard von Schaukal (Van Ostaijen 1979a). When during the first months of the war the (fake) news circulated that Hugo von Hofmannsthal had died, Van Ostaijen wrote a moving obituary calling him, with Rilke, the quintessential young German poet, the most shining example of the Symbolist tendency he regarded as a crucial regeneration of modern literature at the time. A 'completely pantheist poet', he labelled Von Hofmannsthal (Van Ostaijen 1979d: 417–418) – an appreciation that could also be applied to the only English language writer who had a decisive impact on the young Antwerp poet, Walt Whitman.

'My father Whitman', he called the author of *Leaves of Grass* in the title poem of his second volume *Het Sienjaal* (The Signal), published in the autumn of 1918 (Van Ostaijen 1979a: 149). After four years of carnage and a more than taxing occupation it was a remarkably upbeat work. A new world was coming, Van Ostaijen prophesied, and Walt Whitman was one of its prophets. Here was a poet, inspiring and generous, with a love so overpowering it could break walls and lift people up. Whitman's long meandering lines and stanzas juxtaposing everything and everyone also proved an inspiration. With poems about trams, bike rides and the Jules Romains-inspired title poem about the communal spirit (*unanimisme*) people can experience in a music hall, Van Ostaijen's debut collection had been of its time topically, but on a formal level *Music-Hall* was steeped in nineteenth-century European poetry. *Het Sienjaal* was different: rhyme was largely abandoned, free verse lines could fill a whole page, and its unrelenting rhythm was supposed to overwhelm and excite the reader.

In the meantime Van Ostaijen had explored the European avant-gardes that had followed Symbolism, German expressionism in particular. He welcomed this type of lyricism which, again not unlike Whitman's, did not shy away from ecstasy, despair and explosive feelings of love for mankind. In one of his critical essays Van Ostaijen mentions Johannes R. Becher in this respect and some of the poems in *Het Sienjaal* offer similar expansive moments. The deep Romanticism of expressionism is reflected in Van Ostaijen poems like 'Else Lasker-Schüler', echoing the very precise evocation of wonder which characterize the poems of the main female voice of this movement.

Precision mattered, but to Van Ostaijen the main feature of modern art and literature was 'Dynamism', a feature Apollinaire demonstrated in an exemplary manner, according to his young Flemish colleague in 1917, in 'Zone' (from *Alcools*, 1912): the poem not only discusses modernity, it imitates the way the modern mind works, shifting from one image to another memory and from one rhythmic gear into another, on impulse and association.

Technical finesse and a poetic mindset in itself were not enough to produce modern poetry though. In order to be a great poet, one was also supposed to be a *national* (even nationalist) poet; yet another instance where nineteenth-century Romanticism influenced European culture of the next century. Van Ostaijen presented Franz Werfel, Paul Claudel and, again, Walt Whitman as examples to the new generation of Flemish poets who should 'watch through the prism of the Flemish Movement' (Van Ostaijen 1979d: 10).

And so they did, with Paul van Ostaijen as the herald of a new era in both politics and poetics. His wartime work would be embraced by the young writers and intellectuals for whom dreams of an independent Flanders and free form expressionism went hand in hand. Kurt Hiller's *Aktivismus* proved a major inspiration (he also provided one of the epitaphs of *Het Sienjaal*'s title poem: 'Held ist wer sich opfert, nicht wer geopfert wird' [A hero is who sacrifices himself, not who is sacrificed], Van Ostaijen 1979a: 141), but in Flanders 'activism' also acquired a very specific political meaning during the war. Activists were those who doubted the legitimacy of their native country Belgium and who accepted the German occupier's favours. The main favour – number one on the Flemish wish list for years – was to have a Dutch-language university where a proper Flemish elite could be educated. As he hadn't finished high school Van Ostaijen was not able to study at the Ghent college, but his poetry was studied there, probably making him the youngest poet on the curriculum. Flemish activism was bold but also highly illegal. When the Germans lost the war and Belgian authority was restored, the university in Ghent became French again and students and faculty who had not escaped to the Netherlands or Germany ended up in jail. Van Ostaijen himself would have awaited the same fate, but he left just in time and witnessed the implosion of the German Empire from a Berlin balcony.

The end of his activist dreams, the German November Revolution and its violent crushing by Social-Democrats – including the assassination of Karl Liebknecht and Rosa Luxemburg – proved more than a sobering experience for Van Ostaijen. While his Flemish friends and colleagues, in jail, exile or regrouping in new magazines, hung on to their utopian vision while cherishing *Het Sienjaal* as their generation's greatest poetic achievement, the poet himself felt the need to rebalance his ideals and poetics. The playful irreverence of Dada Berlin and his meetings at Herwarth Walden's Der Sturm gallery with Salomo Friedländer (Mynona) and Paul Scheerbart were to have a decisive influence on his ideas and his own literary activities. He would remain a Flemish nationalist until his death, but in Berlin he lost all his humanitarian inclinations.

'Wrote a novella in which I try to make monkeys of people,' he wrote a friend in April 1919, 'Positive criticism: baloney. Now I like novellas in which you can fool around so marvelously. People aren't worth criticizing. Only material for burlesque novellas' (Beekman 1971: xiii). And thus the celebrated poet became a writer of prose, grotesque prose as a matter of fact, acerbic, cerebral and implacable – half a century later John Updike would call it 'limpid' and the product of 'a visionary' (1975: 371, 374) – but clearly not without criticism. As in *Bezette Stad* he targets some of the key ideals and institutions of modern bourgeois societies: patriotism, hierarchy, marriage, the military, politics, progress, logic and reason. Van Ostaijen is not so much interested in the psychology of his characters (they are puppets, really, ruthlessly manipulated by their creator) as he is in the pathology of the world they inhabit and the way their minds lead them violently astray.

In this climate – enduring the financial hardship and political turmoil of the Weimar Republic years, isolated from his Antwerp political and artistic friends and himself on quite a different artistic road – the part-time Flemish Dadaist turned to a maybe surprising bunch of authors for solace, guidance and inspiration: the mystics Catherine of Siena, Meister Eckhart, Gerlach Peters, Mechtild of Magdeburg, St John of the Cross and the great Brabantian mystic Hadewijch. Their work seemed to accomplish his new creed: presenting a visionary synthesis which would transcend the split between subject (the 'I' of the maker) and object (the external world).

The poetry he wrote in Berlin contains striking flashes of this ideal, but the external world in *Bezette Stad* and the deep-felt individual crisis (full of 'I') in *De Feesten van Angst en Pijn* seem to have had the upper hand. After he returned to Belgium in the Spring of 1921 he developed this new poetics, related to what Henri Bremond around the same time would call 'la poésie pure' and what Van Ostaijen labelled 'pure lyric' (Van Ostaijen 1979d: 349). In his case it envisioned a type of poetry which seems most related to that of a French poet avid namedropper Van Ostaijen never mentioned: Pierre Reverdy. Their poems are short, without storyline, action, let alone politics, the juxtapositions of images connected mainly by sound and unity of vision. Or as Van Ostaijen put it in 1925 in his only interview: 'Il s'agit avant tout de faire apprécier des sonorités rythmiques suggérant des états d'âme, des visions surréelles' (what matters above all is to make you appreciate rhythmic sonorities that suggest states of feeling, surreal visions, Van Ostaijen 1979d: 524). In his final years Van Ostaijen's lyricism turns desperate – no longer a Whitmanesque embrace of each and everyone, but evoking a deep understanding of what his contemporary Maurice Gilliams, referring to Van Ostaijen's work, named a 'pain that encompasses all of man's consciousness' (Gilliams 1943: 18).

There certainly was a lot of pain (his love life was no success and all his siblings succumbed to the same disease that would kill him), but one of the reasons why his poems still sound fresh and alluring today is their playful simplicity. Van Ostaijen felt related to Jean Cocteau in this respect, but his main poetical examples were found much closer to home, in some of the sparkling word play of Guido Gezelle, the nineteenth-century giant of Flemish poetry, and in the children's ditties he could hear on the streets of Antwerp. 'Nous ne sommes pas loin de l'axiome de Verlaine: "De la musique avant toute chose"' (we are not far removed from the axiom of Verlaine: 'music before everything') he used to say (Van Ostaijen 1979d: 289), but he was not thinking of Wagner when he said this: simple songs and popular jazz music and dances like the polka and the charleston set the tone.

Van Ostaijen profoundly disliked Wagner, as a matter of fact, but he felt very much attracted to two other giants of German culture, both born in Prague: Rilke and Kafka. Rilke shared his mystical inclinations and very high expectations of poetry, which led both poets to reject individual romantic outpourings and to expect their colleagues to extract poetry not from specific incidents in their daily lives but from the sum total of their experience. Kafka he read, absorbed and translated long before most of his contemporaries even knew about him. Shortly after Kafka died in 1924 Van Ostaijen introduced him to the Dutch reading public by translating five very short stories from *Betrachtung* (Contemplation, 1912) for the Flemish magazine *Vlaamsche Arbeid* (Flemish Labour), hoping as he pointed out in his postscript, to convey Kafka's 'superior spiritual attitude' (Van Ostaijen 1979c: 371). The translator presented 'Zum Nachdenken für Herrenreiter' ('Reflections for Gentlemen-Jockeys'), 'Wunsch, Indianer zu werden' ('The Wish to be an Indian'), 'Die Vorüberlaufenden' ('Passers-by'), 'Zerstreutes Hinausschaun' ('Absent-minded Window-gazing') and 'Der plötzliche Spaziergang' ('The Sudden Walk') not as stories but as 'poëmata in prose' (371), offering a strong indication as to what might have attracted him in these short pieces in the first place. Plot nor character seem to have preoccupied the writer here. They are minute expressions of very subtle changes in atmosphere and thinking – qualities both Van Ostaijen's poems and prose pieces also possess. These Kafka translations were among the very first in the world – proof of how in tune Van Ostaijen was with some of the major developments of modern European literature.

In the years following his death, Van Ostaijen remained somewhat of a Flemish *Geheimtip* (secret recommendation for connoisseurs), but after the Second World War he became one of the most read and influential poets of Dutch literature. The so-called Fifties generation (the literary counterparts of the COBRA art movement) treasured him as their main precursor, the only Dutch language contemporary to the great French, German and English writers of the historical avant-garde.

He would never quite attain the same status internationally, but when Hans Magnus Enzensberger compiled his epoch-making *Museum der modernen Poesie* (Museum of Modern Poetry, 1960) Van Ostaijen found himself in the company of contemporaries he knew and revered (Apollinaire, Aragon, Breton, Lasker-Schüler, Rilke, Schwitters) and fellow modernists unknown to him (Eliot, Hikmet, Mandelstam, Pessoa, Stevens). With poets like Mihály Babits, Rolf Jacobsen, Miroslav Krleža and Edith Södergran, Van Ostaijen was a representative in the anthology of what would be called *minor literatures* though that was not a label Enzensberger used. These modern poets, he suggested, had created something world literature had never seen: a common transnational language, a poetic 'Weltsprache' (Enzensberger 1960: 17), a product of their constant cross-cultural travelling and cosmopolitan mindset. Van Ostaijen's Berlin years and his acquaintance, critical guidance and in some cases even close friendship with artists like Paul Klee, Heinrich Campendonk, Lyonel Feininger and Georg Muche made the Flemish poet very much a part of this international avant-garde.

Two of the three Van Ostaijen translations in *Museum* were done by Enzensberger himself, the third one by Helmut Heißenbüttel, who would also mention Van Ostaijen's contribution to the history of visual poetry in his essay 'Zur Geschichte des visuellen

Gedichts im 20. Jahrhundert' (On the History of Visual Poetry in the Twentieth Century, 1966: 84). In these years of flourishing concrete poetry experiments Van Ostaijen also reached the English-speaking world. Christopher Levenson (1964) wrote about him for the *Times Literary Supplement* and three years later Herbert Spencer (1967) devoted half of issue 15 of his legendary magazine *Typographica* to Van Ostaijen, presenting *Bezette Stad* and the author's poetics as well as the originals and translations of some of his later poems and some pages of the handwritten volume *De Feesten van Angst en Pijn*. That volume would become the first one to be translated into English – the result of a Van Ostaijen translation workshop at the Poetry International festival in Rotterdam in 1972. 'The Murderers' from this volume would be reprinted in the most ambitious American counterpart to Enzensberger's *Museum* anthology, Jerome Rothenberg and Pierre Joris's *Poems for the Millennium* (1995). The poem was followed by a quote from Van Ostaijen's lecture 'Lyrical Poetry: Directions for Use' and a short introduction to his poetics, comparing him to the Surrealists and Objectivists in his tendency to transform the ordinary into the visionary (Rothenberg and Joris 1995: 450).

The late 1950s, 60s and early 70s saw the publication of the first major academic monographs about Van Ostaijen, in keeping with the autonomist strand in literary studies at the time but also, on a broader level, the upsurge in interest for avant-garde art and literature during a phase in the Cold War where it seemed as if, to set themselves apart from both Nazi's and communists, the connoisseurs in the West were really attuned to these kinds of experiment and even mayhem. On that wave Van Ostaijen's work was also translated in Italian and German (in 1951 a few French translations had been published in Antwerp, still a bilingual city at the time) and he proved to be an inspiration for a major foreign poet who rose to prominence in these years, the South African exile Breyten Breytenbach.

'Oggendlied' (Morning Song) from his third Afrikaans volume *Kouevuur* was not only dedicated to Van Ostaijen, Breytenbach also used the Flemish poet's classic 'Marc groet 's morgens de dingen' (Marc Greets Things in the Morning) as a template for his own early morning musings in Ezulwini (Swaziland) during a journey in his native land (Breytenbach 1969). As in Van Ostaijen's poem the sheer acts of seeing and naming specific elements of the physical world at first seem to empower the person speaking but at the same time these activities reinforce how much he is separated from that world. The 'glimpses of poetic genius' Updike (1975: 374) recognized in Van Ostaijen often have that effect: behind the sparks of joy and wit lies a world of utter forlornness. This quintessentially modern poet longs for any kind of ecstasy if only to forget that he is a stranger in his own world.

Note

1 'Cry me a river', a poem in the form of a spiritual in the same volume (Jensma 1974: 19), is made up of variations on very similar words: 'rowing' (four times), 'boat' (three times), 'without end' / 'without an end' (three times), 'black' (five times) and 'who's that' (six times), but the regular stanza format (four lines, with two and four ending in a question mark) makes it less 'thematic' in the Van Ostaijen sense of the word.

References

Beekman, E.M. (1971), 'Introduction', in P. van Ostaijen, *Patriotism, Inc. and Other Tales*, ix–xix, Amherst: University of Massachusetts Press.
Berckelaers, F. (1921), 'Boeken: Paul van Ostaijen – Bezette Stad', *Het Overzicht* 1 (1): 11–12.
Bonset, I.K. (pseudonym of T. van Doesburg) (1921), 'I.K.Bt's Kritische tesseracts', *De Stijl* 4 (12): 150.
Borgers, G. (1971), *Paul van Ostaijen. Een documentatie*, 2 vols, The Hague: Bert Bakker.
Breytenbach, B. (1969), *Kouevuur*, Capetown: Buren-Uitgewers (Edms) Bpk.
Buelens, G. (2001), *Van Ostaijen tot heden. Zijn invloed op de Vlaamse poëzie*, Nijmegen: Vantilt; Ghent: KANTL.
Enzensberger, H.M. (1960), *Museum der modernen Poesie*, Frankfurt am Main: Suhrkamp.
Gilliams, M. (1943), *De man voor het venster. Aanteekeningen*, Amsterdam: J.M. Meulenhoff.
Heißenbüttel, H. (1966), *Über Literatur*, Olten: Walter.
Jensma, W. (1974), *Where White is the Colour, Where Black is the Number*, Johannesburg: Ravan.
Jensma, W. (1977), *i must show you my clippings*, Johannesburg: Ravan.
Kleyn, L. and J.L. Marais (2010), 'Wopko Jensma en die Soeke na 'n Nuwe (Suid)-Afrikaanse Identiteit', *Tydskrif Vir Letterkunde* 47 (1): 5–24.
Levenson, C. (1964), 'Odes to the Heart and The Hague', *The Times Literary Supplement*, 3 December 1964: 1106.
Ostaijen, P. van (1979a), *Verzameld werk. Poëzie. Music-Hall, Het Sienjaal, De Feesten van Angst en Pijn*, Amsterdam: Bert Bakker.
Ostaijen, P. van (1979b), *Verzameld werk. Poëzie. Bezette Stad en Nagelaten Gedichten*, Amsterdam: Bert Bakker.
Ostaijen, P. van (1979c), *Verzameld werk. Proza. Grotesken en ander Proza*, Amsterdam: Bert Bakker.
Ostaijen, P. van (1979d), *Verzameld werk. Proza. Besprekingen en Beschouwingen*, Amsterdam: Bert Bakker.
Ostaijen, P. van (1982), *The First Book of Schmoll: Selected Poems 1920–1928*, Amsterdam: Bridges Books.
Ostaijen, P. van (2016), *Occupied City*, trans. D. Colmer, Ripon: Smokestack Books.
Rothenberg, J. and P. Joris, eds (1995), *Poems for the Millennium: The University of California Book of Modern & Postmodern Poetry. Vol. 1, From Fin-de-Siècle to Negritude*, Berkeley: University of California Press.
Spencer, H., ed. (1967), special issue of *Typographica* 15 (June).
Updike, J. (1975), 'Satire Without Serifs', in *Picked-Up Pieces. Essays*, 369–374, New York: Alfred A. Knopf.

Van Ostaijen in translation

Van Ostaijen entry on the Poetry International Website:
Buelens, G. (2006), 'Belgium: Paul van Otaijen', *Poetry International Web*, 1 May 2006. Available online: https://www.poetryinternationalweb.net/pi/site/poet/item/6636 (accessed 10 February 2019).

Poetry

Ostaijen, P. van (1951), *Paul van Ostaijen. Introduction à sa poétique*, monograph by E. Schoonhoven, including a selection of French translations, Antwerp: Editions des Cahiers [in French].
Ostaijen, P. van (1966a), *Liriche scelte*, Milan: Gli Amici di Poíesis [in Italian].
Ostaijen, P. van (1966b), *Poesie*, Frankfurt am Main: Suhrkamp [in German].
Ostaijen, P. van (1974), *Homage to Singer and Other Poems*, London: Transgravity Press [in English].
Ostaijen, P. van (1976), *Feasts of Fear and Agony*, New York: New Directions [in English].
Ostaijen, P. van (1982/2015), *The First Book of Schmoll: Selected Poems 1920–1928*, Amsterdam: Bridges Books, 1982/Copenhagen: Green Integer, 2015 [in English].
Ostaijen, P. van (1987), *Poezje wybrane*, Warsaw: Ludowa Spóldzielnia Wydawnicza [in Polish].
Ostaijen, P. van (1990), *Tanec gnómu*, Prague: Odeon [in Czech].
Ostaijen, P. van (1991), *Besetzte Stadt*, Munich: Edition Text + Kritik [in German].
Ostaijen, P. van (1993), *Ville occupée*, Antwerp: Edition de Antwerpen 93 [in French].
Ostaijen, P. van (2001), *Nomenclature: poèmes 1916–1928*, Tours: Farrago [in French].
Ostaijen, P. van (2003), *Le Dada pour cochons*, Paris: Les Editions Textuel [in French].
Ostaijen, P. van (2008), *Music Hall*, Lund: Ellerström [in Swedish].
Ostaijen, P. van (2009), *Prazniki strahu in bolečine*, Ljubljana: Mladinska knjiga [in Slovenian].
Ostaijen, P. van (2016), *Occupied City*, trans. D. Colmer, Ripon: Smokestack Books [in English].

Prose

Ostaijen, P. van (1967), *Grotesken*, Frankfurt am Main: Suhrkamp [in German].
Ostaijen, P. van (1971), *Patriotism, Inc. and Other Tales*, Amherst: University of Massachusetts Press [in English].
Ostaijen, P. van (1996), *Der Pleitejazz*, Berlin: Friedenauer Presse [in German].
Ostaijen, P. van (2003), *Bankerot-jazz*, Copenhagen: Bebop [in Danish].
Ostaijen, P. van (2012), *O jazz da bancarrota e outros contos (nem sempre) grotescos*, Porto: 7 Nós [in Portuguese].
Ostaijen, P. van (2015), *Patriotismo, S.A.*, Mexico-City: San Pedro de los Pinos: Ediciones del Ermitaño [in Spanish].
Ostaijen, P. van (2016), *Trustul patriotismului si alte grotesti*, Piteşti: Editura Paralela 45 [in Romanian].
Ostaijen, P. van (2018a), *Le trust du patriotisme – et autres grotesques*, Brussels: Samsa [in French].
Ostaijen, P. van (2018b), *[Prose]*, Addis Ababa: Hohe Publisher [in Amharic].
Ostaijen, P. van (2018c), *[Prose]*, Giza: Sefsafa Publishing House [in Arabic].

Poetical essays

Van Ostaijen's key text 'Gebruiksaanwijzing der lyriek' has been translated into English twice

Ostaijen, P. van (1982/2015), 'Lyrical Poetry: Directions for Use', in *The First Book of Schmol: Selected Poems 1920-1928*, 125-140, Amsterdam: Bridges Books, 1982/Copenhagen: Green Integer, 2015 [in English].

Ostaijen, P. van (2014), 'A User's Guide to Lyric: Paralipomena', *Chicago Review* 58 (2): 90-122.

Secondary sources [in English]

Beekman, E.M. (1970), *Homeopathy of the Absurd. The Grotesque in Paul van Ostaijen's Creative Prose*, The Hague: Martinus Nijhoff.

Beekman, E.M. (1981), 'The Universal Hue: Paul van Ostaijen's lyrisme à thème', *Dutch Crossing* 5 (13): 42-60.

Berg, H. Van Den (2002), *The Import of Nothing. How Dada Came, Saw, and Vanished in the Low Countries (1915-1929)*, Farmington Hills, MI: Hall.

Bru, S. (2009), *Democracy, Law and the Modernist Avant-Gardes. Writing in the State of Exception*, Edinburgh: Edinburgh University Press.

Buelens, G. (2013), '"The Final Catholic": Paul van Ostaijen and the Catholic Réveil around the First World War', in S. Houppermans, P. Liebregts, J. Baetens and O. Boele (eds), *Modernism Today*, 79-97, Amsterdam: Rodopi.

Buelens, G. (2015), *Everything to Nothing. The Poetry of the Great War, Revolution and the Transformation of Europe*, London/New York: Verso.

D'haen, T. (1989), 'Paul van Ostaijen's Modernism: A Pain that Encompasses All of Man's Consciousness', *Neophilologus* 73 (4): 481-500.

Hadermann, P. (1993), 'From the Message to the Medium. The Poetic Evolution of Paul van Ostaijen', *The Low Countries* 1: 254-261.

Ridder, M. de (2008), 'Europeanism in One Country: August Vermeylen, Paul van Ostaijen, and the International Approach to Nationalism', in N. Bemong, M. Truwant and P. Vermeulen (eds), *Re-thinking Europe: Literature and (Trans)National Identity*, 21-32, Amsterdam: Rodopi.

Spencer, H., ed. (1967), special issue of *Typographica* 15 (June).

Strietman, E. (1985), 'Occupied City: Ostaijen's Antwerp and the Impact of the First World War', in E. Timms and D. Kelley (eds), *Unreal City: Urban Experience in Modern European Literature and Art*, 128-141, Manchester: Manchester University Press.

Versluys, K. (1987), *The Poet and the City. Chapters in the Development of Urban Poetry in Europe and the United States, 1800-1930*, 192-217, Tübingen: Narr Verlag.

14

Dutch Interbellum Poetry and/as World Literature

Theo D'haen

Arguably the most important Dutch interbellum poets are A. Roland Holst (1888-1976), Martinus Nijhoff (1894-1953), J. Slauerhoff (1898-1936) and Hendrik Marsman (1899-1940).[1] Edgar Du Perron (1899-1940), although also of importance as a poet for the period concerned, is better known for his prose, and especially his novel *Het Land van herkomst* (Country of Origin, 1935). The same goes for Simon Vestdijk (1898-1971), who left a voluminous poetic oeuvre – mostly in classical forms – but which is overshadowed by his even more voluminous prose output, with more than fifty novels and numerous collections of novellas, short stories and essays. Other poets that were well known in their own time, such as J.C. Bloem (1887-1966), P.N. Van Eyck (1887-1954), Jan Greshoff (1888-1971), Hendrik de Vries (1896-1989), Herman van den Bergh (1897-1967) and Gerrit Achterberg (1905-1962) are now, for one or another reason, less considered. In fact, even among the four poets of major stature listed the past decades have seen major shifts in appreciation, with Nijhoff now generally considered the most important Dutch Modernist poet, with Slauerhoff and Marsman following, while Roland Holst, whose reputation stood highest of all during the interbellum itself and for some twenty years after the Second World War, has now lost much of his luster.

All writers just mentioned knew of one another, and in most cases actually knew one another. Roland Holst, Nijhoff, Slauerhoff and Marsman at times met one another, and regularly reviewed one another's work. At the same time, the Dutch literary landscape has always been a crossroads open to the major literary cultures surrounding it, and all writers mentioned underwent the influence of the major literary currents emanating from France, England and Germany during the late nineteenth and early twentieth centuries. Next to their indebtedness to these currents, the oeuvres of three of the four major poets mentioned are unusually strongly related to those of some authors unhesitatingly categorized as belonging to world literature considered as a canon of 'greats': W.B. Yeats (1865-1939) in the case of Roland Holst; T.S. Eliot (1888-1965) with Nijhoff, and Chinese, Spanish and Portuguese literature, especially Luís Vaz de Camões (1524-1580), for Slauerhoff. Marsman is a case apart, as we will see.

The clearest case of direct influence is that of Roland Holst and Yeats. Roland Holst first met the poetry of Yeats while a student of Celtic mythology in Oxford. Much later, in 'Eigen achtergronden: Inleiding tot een voordracht uit eigen werk' (Personal Background: Introduction to a Reading from my Own Work; Roland Holst 1981-1983, Proza 2: 345-347),[2] an essay written during the Second World War – when under an assumed name he was living in hiding from the Germans – and published in 1945, he recalled how it seemed as if his reading of the Celtic saga *The Voyage of Bran, Son of Febal* awoke ancient memories in him. He immersed himself in the literature of the Irish Renaissance. He also translated four stories by Lady Gregory (1852-1932) based on Celtic myths, as well as the *Voyage of Bran*. In all of these he found what he called 'een leven dat mythisch en elementair was, een leven dus,waarin het hart voortdurend onderhevig blijft aan de voorpersoonlijke zielskracht' (a mythical and elementary life, a life in which the heart always is in touch with the foreworldly power of the soul; Roland Holst 1981-1983, Proza 1: 355). Roland Holst prefaced his translation of *Voyage of Bran* with a short essay, 'Het Elysisch verlangen' (Longing for Elysium; Roland Holst 1981-1983, Proza 1: 155-163). Man, Roland Holst argues, is estranged from himself on earth, and seeks to be one again with himself and the universe in an otherworld. Most men, caught up in the buzz of daily life, at best are only dimly aware of this longing. The poet, however, feels this longing acutely, and it is his task to find the appropriate symbols to express it. Roland Holst gave definitive shape to this personal myth in the story 'De afspraak' (The Promise, 1923; Roland Holst 1981-1983, Proza 1: 59-98).

From the very beginning, Roland Holst regarded Yeats as the pre-eminent poet of the Irish Renaissance, and in the 1945 essay referred to earlier he expressly stated that the Irish poet had exerted a great influence on him. The early poem 'Klacht van Oisin' (Oisin's plaint; Roland Holst 1981-1983, *Poëzie* 2: 1096-1099), originally published in 1912 in the monthly *De Gids,* but never reprinted during Roland Holst's lifetime, not even in the original *Verzamelde Werken* of 1948 to 1949 (though it is included in the standard 1981 to 1983 edition, published after Holst's death), clearly shows the influence of Yeats, combining materials gleaned from Lady Gregory, Celtic mythology, and Yeats's 'Wanderings of Oisin' (1889). Roland Holst's second collection of poems, *De belijdenis van de stilte* (The Profession of Silence, 1913; Roland Holst 1981-1983, *Poëzie* 1: 145-175), features two epigraphs from Yeats.

Between 1920 and 1955 Roland Holst translated fifteen lyrical poems by Yeats, one dramatic poem and one play. Three lyrical poems are from *The Wind Among the Reeds* (1899): 'The Lover Tells of the Rose in his Heart'('De minnaar verhaalt van de roos in zijn hart'), 'He Hears the Cry of the Sedge' ('De roep in het rietgras') and

'The Fiddler of Dooney' ('De vedelaar van Dooney'). One poem is from *In the Seven Woods* (1904): 'The Withering of the Boughs', ('Hoe de takken verdorden'). *The Green Helmet and Other Poems* (1910) yielded three poems: 'No Second Troy' ('Geen tweede Troje'), 'Reconciliation' ('Verzoening') and 'These Are the Clouds' ('Dit is 't gewolkte'). One poem is from *Responsibilities* (1914): 'Fallen Majesty' ('Gevallen majesteit'). From *The Wild Swans at Coole* (1919) come: 'The Scholars' ('Geleerden'), 'The People' ('Het volk'), and 'A Deep-Sworn Vow' ('Een dure eed'). Three poems again are from *Michael Robartes and the Dancer* (1921): 'The Leaders of the Crowd' ('Volksleiders'), 'The Second Coming' ('De tweede komst') and 'A Prayer for My Daughter' ('Een bede voor mijn dochter'). Finally, one poem is from *The Tower* (1928): 'Leda and the Swan' ('Leda en de zwaan'). The dramatic poem Roland Holst translated is 'The Old Age of Queen Maeve' (1903), rendered in Dutch as 'De ouderdom van Koningin Meve.' All Dutch translations are in Roland Holst, *Poëzie* 2 (1231-1254). Finally, he translated *The Countess Cathleen* (1892) as *De Gravin Catelene* (*Proza* 2, 1143-1193).

The first thing to note from this list of translations is that only one of Yeats's works Roland Holst translated dates from after 1923, the date of 'De afspraak' (The Promise), the story in which Roland Holst's personal myth attained its final shape. In other words, the Yeats that Roland Holst was interested in even in later life continued to be the early and middle Yeats, which is to say largely the Irish Renaissance Yeats, and not the Modernist Yeats preferred by more recent criticism. This is also to say that Roland Holst continued to turn to Yeats to bolster his own personal myth.

Beyond this, though, Roland Holst also turned to Yeats at particular moments in his poetic career, and specifically so when he needed to vanquish periods of relative dearth of poetic inspiration. 'De minnaar verhaalt van de roos in zijn hart', the translation of 'The Lover Tells of the Rose in his Heart', dates from 1920, the year in which *Voorbij de wegen* (Beyond Roads, 1920; Roland Holst 1981-1983, *Poëzie* 1: 177-277) appeared, the collection that is generally considered as the volume in which Roland Holst definitely found his own voice. By far the majority of Roland Holst's Yeats lyrical translations, but also *De Gravin Catalene* (*The Countess Cathleen*), date from 1929 to 1933. 'Een bede voor mijn dochter' ('A Prayer for My Daughter'), 'Hoe de takken verdorden' ('The Withering of the Boughs') and 'Verzoening' ('Reconciliation') are from 1941 to 1942. 'De ouderdom van Koningin Meve' ('The Old Age of Queen Maeve') is dated 1954 to 1955. The periods in which Roland Holst thus seems to have engaged himself most intensively in translating Yeats situate themselves in between the publication of his own collections *De wilde kim* (The wild horizon, 1925; Roland Holst 1981-1983, *Poëzie* 1: 279-308) and *Een winter aan zee* (A winter at the sea-side, 1937; Roland Holst 1981-1983, *Poëzie* 1: 309-397), between the latter collection and *Tegen de wereld* (Against the world, 1947; Roland Holst 1981-1983, *Poëzie* 1: 481-513), and between that collection again and *In gevaar* (In danger, 1958; Roland Holst 1981-1983, *Poëzie* 1: 579-667), all of them collections that are usually seen as marking the various stages of Roland Holst's career.

De wilde kim is often taken as marking a crisis in Roland Holst's belief in his own myth, most revealingly so in 'De nederlaag' (Defeat) and 'Einde' (End or Finish, but Roland Holst rendered it as 'Day of Reckoning' in his own 1955 translation), the second and next to last poems, respectively, of the volume. Roland Holst himself pointed out that in 'Einde' he had borrowed the phrase 'cold and passionate' from Yeats's 'The Fisherman'. *Een winter aan zee*, usually reckoned to be his finest collection and one of the high points of Dutch interbellum poetry, shows Roland Holst vanquishing this crisis by, among other things, forsaking the extreme solitude advocated in the earliest stages of the elaboration of his personal myth. *Een winter aan zee* in fact reaffirms Roland Holst's personal myth by partly re-orientating it. Roland Holst himself said that the rhyme scheme of *Een winter aan zee* was suggested to him by Yeats's 'The Withering of the Boughs', a poem Roland Holst only later translated into Dutch.

Tegen de wereld mainly contains the kind of occasional verse Roland Holst increasingly turned to in the later stages of his career. Still, Yeats again is present here, as the volume also comprises 'Helena's inkeer' (Helena's Repentance), a poem that had already been published separately in 1944. In 1954 to 1955 Roland Holst translated six of his own poems, including 'Helena's inkeer' as 'Helen of Troy', into an English heavily marked by Yeatsian idioms and atmosphere. Also in 1955 he issued a first collection of his Yeats translations, which he re-issued in an enlarged edition in 1958. Moreover, 1955 brings a new Yeats translation: 'De ouderdom van Koningin Meve' ('The Old Age of Queen Maeve'). Rosalinde Supheert (1995), in her dissertation on Roland Holst and Yeats, sees the Dutch poet in his later poems, such as the collection *In gevaar* (1958), as following Yeats's lead in the latter's later poems reflecting on issues of physical decay and death. Van der Vegt (1974), who had heard echoes from Yeats's 'To a Friend' (1914) in Roland Holst's 'Optimistische kunstenaars' (Optimistic artists, 1921), and from the 'The Tower' (1928) in 'Van den droom' (Of a dream, 1931), also detects traces of Yeats's 'The Gyres', from the latter's *Last Poems* (1936-1939), in a late Roland Holst poem such as 'Gefaald' (Failed, 1960), collected in *Onder koude wolken* (Under cold clouds, 1962; Roland Holst 1981-1983, *Poëzie* 2: 717-821).

Roland Holst's poetry and career thus developed in continuous intertextual dialogue with that of Yeats, a 'Yeats' he for the last time discursively remythologized in his 1964 tribute 'William Butler Yeats herdacht' (William Butler Yeats remembered; Roland Holst 1981-1983, *Proza* 2, 767-778) as having been as faithful to his personal myth as Roland Holst believed he had been to his.

The relationship of the work of Martinus Nijhoff to that of T.S. Eliot has always been a contentious one. Many critics have pointed out resemblances between the two oeuvres as far as themes and poetics are concerned, particularly so with respect to the long narrative poem *Awater* (1934), generally taken to be Nijhoff's masterpiece, and Eliot's *The Waste Land*. The narrator-speaker of Nijhoff's poem becomes obsessed with the clerk Awater and trails him through town to the train station. He embarks on an unspecified train journey himself, while Awater stays behind. Most critics deny that there was any direct influence from Eliot. In fact, Nijhoff himself can be said to have gone out of his way to deny such influence.

In a 1935 lecture on the genesis of *Awater* Nijhoff claimed that:

> voorbeelden had ik niet [...] ik had iets aan de geniale jeugdverzen van Jean Cocteau, de Franse dichter, en aan de Amerikaan T.S. Eliot [...] maar dezen

hadden, in tegenstelling tot de surrealisten, hun métier, hun vak, te gering geacht [...] zij hadden op zoek naar abstractie en menigte, hun versvorm zelf als ruiten ingeslagen.

(I had no examples [...] the ingenious early poetry of the French poet Jean Cocteau did something for me, as did the work of the American T.S. Eliot [...] but these poets, other than the surrealists, had not held their trade, their métier, in sufficiently high esteem [...] in their search for abstraction and success, they had smashed their own poetical forms as if of glass.)
(Nijhoff 1961: 1166–1167)

In the same lecture the Dutch poet instead listed four modernist prose writers as having provided some inspiration for *Awater*: Marcel Proust, D.H. Lawrence, Virginia Woolf and James Joyce, with the latter receiving the slightest mention. Yet, as Wiljan van den Akker (1994: 35), co-editor of the standard critical edition of Nijhoff's poetry (Nijhoff 1993) and one of the most astute commentators upon the latter's work, notes and as has been argued by many another critic, it is undoubtedly *Ulysses* (1922) that is most conspicuously present in Nijhoff's poem. Van den Akker in this respect suggests that quite often what is not being said says more than what actually *is* said. Amongst other things, he points out a possible verbal echo from Eliot's 'fragments [...] shored against my ruins' in Nijhoff's 'puinhopen' (heaps of rubble, or 'ruins'!) from the beginning of *Awater*, and also identifies a number of structural parallels: a game of chess, reminiscences of the grail legend, and the motifs of the woman, the desert, the city and water. Van den Akker even makes a very convincing case for considering the character of Awater in Nijhoff's eponymous poem to be an only thinly disguised portrait of T.S. Eliot himself.

In truth, T.S. Eliot is hardly ever discursively mentioned by Nijhoff, at least in what was published during his own lifetime – the 1935 lecture was published only posthumously. However, Nijhoff, who was a gifted translator, did engage directly with T.S. Eliot via translation. Nijhoff worked from French, German and English, translating works by William Shakespeare, Gérard de Nerval, Victor Hugo, Alfred de Musset and Edgar Lee Masters, amongst others. There is no other poet, though, from whom Nijhoff translated as much as from Eliot. In 1950 the Dutch literary periodical *De Gids* featured 'De Hippopotamus', 'De hartekreet van J. Alfred Prufrock' ('The Love Song of J. Alfred Prufrock') and 'Hoe onbehaaglijk het is Mr Eliot te ontmoeten' ('Lines for Cuscuscaraway and Mirza Murad Ali Beg'). In 1951 Nijhoff was commissioned to do *De cocktailparty* (*The Cocktail Party*, 1951; Nijhoff 1982, *Verzameld Werk* 3, Vertalingen: 245–410). The rest of the Eliot translations appeared only posthumously, in the various editions of his collected works: 'De reis van de drie koningen' ('Journey of the Magi') and section I of 'Burnt Norton' from the *Four Quartets*. Nijhoff also left drafts of translations of (parts of) *The Family Reunion* and 'The Rock' (part of *Choruses from 'The Rock'*).

Nijhoff's translations from Eliot, then, both published and unpublished, cover the complete span of the Anglo-American poet's career, and the entire range of the latter's production: from the early 'The Hippopotamus' and 'The Love Song of J.

Alfred Prufrock' to the late *The Cocktail Party* (1949). Because his Eliot translations appeared so late in his life, and because so many of them remained unpublished and even unfinished, they have usually been discounted as having influenced Nijhoff's own creative practice. From the fact that at the poet's death in 1953 his library comprised a 1948 Penguin edition of the *Selected Poems* of T.S. Eliot, containing some pages of handwritten notes by Nijhoff on Eliot's work, several critics, among them the editors of the Critical Edition of Nijhoff's poems, have inferred that he only actively engaged with Eliot's work in the run-up to his commissioned translation of *The Cocktail Party*. Elsewhere (D'haen 2009) I have argued that this is no proof that Nijhoff in fact did not make many of these translations much earlier in his career. That he in some instances chose not to publish at all is borne out by the fact that a translation he made of Oscar Wilde's 'Ballad of Reading Gaol' in 1912 was published only posthumously (Nijhoff 1993, vol. 1: 15–78). The same thing happened with some Baudelaire translations that on the basis of Nijhoff's handwriting have been dated to the 1920s. Nijhoff, then, may have at least tried his hand at translating Eliot well before 1948, and even before 1935, the date of the lecture in which he refers to Eliot. His reason for not 'going public' with such translations at the time may well have been that suggested by Van den Akker for Nijhoff's not mentioning Eliot in his critical writings, and for leaving the 1935 lecture unpublished.

What I want to suggest, then, is that, just as Roland Holst conducted a lifelong dialogue with the work of Yeats, so did Nijhoff with that of Eliot. At the beginning of his career this dialogue may still have been tenuous, or even distant, although, as Sötemann mentions in a footnote, 'about 1950, Nijhoff told J. Kamerbeek Jr. [another Dutch scholar and critic]: "Shortly after the First World War we discovered that Eliot was an important poet"' (Sötemann 1976: 102). With *Awater*, the writing of which Van den Akker and Dorleijn (Nijhoff 2001: 436) date to 1933 or 1934, the dialogue tightens, even if the relation between *The Waste Land* and *Awater* remains on the level of verbal echoes and responses. Nijhoff never tried his hand at translating *The Waste Land* itself. However, if I am correct in surmising that at least some of the unpublished translations found at Nijhoff's death may date from much earlier than 1948, and even 1935, it is not insignificant that 'Lines from Cuscuscaraway and Mirza Murad Ali Beg' appeared in January 1933. Though Nijhoff's translation 'Hoe onbehaaglijk het is Mr Eliot te ontmoeten' was found only in 1953, it may well date from when Nijhoff was working on *Awater*, especially if we bear in mind Van den Akker's suggestion that Awater is a possible avatar of T.S. Eliot.

Reasoning along the same lines, early translations of 'The Journey of the Magi', 'Burnt Norton', *The Rock*, and *The Family Reunion*, may have set Nijhoff on his way towards his own religiously-inspired verse plays of the 1940s, *De ster van Bethlehem*, (The Star of Bethlehem), *De dag des Heren* (The Day of the Lord) and *Des Heilands tuin* (The Savior's Garden). The collective title under which these plays were published, *Het Heilige Hout* (1950; Nijhoff 1978: 253–388), echoes that of Eliot's 1920 collection of essays, *The Sacred Wood* (1920). Though Nijhoff himself cited other influences, surely the spirit of these plays is close to that also found in Eliot's verse plays and later poetry.

J. Slauerhoff (1898–1936) for most of his brief adult life – he died from consumption – worked as a ship's medic on voyages to the South China Seas and to South America. From the very beginning he was drawn to the exotic. Throughout his life he engaged with Chinese, Spanish and Portuguese literature, translating, borrowing and dialoguing, as evidenced by titles of collections or parts of collections such as 'Soleares', 'Tristes', 'Saudades', 'Zambas', 'Coplas', 'Eldorado', 'Oost-Azië' (Far East), 'Macao', 'Korea', 'Islas' and 'Desengaños'.

Chinese poetry is at the heart of Slauerhoff's collection *Yoeng Poe Tsjoeng* (1930; Slauerhoff 2018: 131–205), in which he recreates, on the basis of earlier French, German or English translations, a substantial number of classical Chinese poems, highlighting 'the bitterness of life' he claimed to find in them. He expressed the same feeling in his repeated use of the Portuguese poet Luís Vaz de Camões, with whom he seems to have closely identified. In 'Camões thuiskomst' (Camões's homecoming), from the collection *Eldorado* (1928; Slauerhoff 2018:131–205), the Portuguese poet finds himself and his work, the epic *Os Lusíadas*, singing the Portuguese voyages of discovery, the founding of Macau and the fame of Goa, completely disregarded upon arrival in a Lisbon fearful of the plague, and with a king under the sway of women and religious zealots. In another collection of the same date, *Oost-Azië* (East Asia, 1928; Slauerhoff 2018: 81–129), Camões, in an eponymous poem, listed as having been written in Macau, is pictured as a misfit who in frustration turns to writing *Os Lusíadas*. And in a poem only collected in the posthumous *Al Dwalend* (Roving, or Erring, the Dutch is ambiguous here, 1947; Slauerhoff 2005: 619–822), Camões, again eponymously, is held up as a frightful example of the Muse's victim, dying of poverty, alone and forgotten, an example the poem's speaker, obviously an impersonation of Slauerhoff himself, should never lose sight of, even though he knows he himself has already embarked on the same road. Such depictions of Camões ominously resonate with how Slauerhoff pictures himself in 'In memoriam mijzelf' (In memoriam myself), a poem found among Slauerhoff's papers after his death. The speaker of that poem paints himself as surrounded by enemies, shunned by friends, having known not a single day of good luck, leaving nothing behind, having destroyed whatever he once achieved, and cursing both his ancestors and his successors.

Slauerhoff's most intimately self-identifying use of Camões we find in his major prose work *Het verboden rijk* (Forbidden Empire, 1932; Slauerhoff 1983). The novel recounts the founding of Macau, of Luís Vaz de Camões's part in this, and of the writing of the latter's *Os Lusíadas*. At the same time, it is the story of an early twentieth-century Irish marconist, rather obviously a stand-in again for Slauerhoff himself, who drifts down the social ladder in the South China Seas. In its mixing of time settings, in its use of various first- and third-person narrators, and in the way Camões and the Irish radio officer seem to merge, the officer assuming the role of Camões to the point of sharing the latter's memories and dreams, *Het verboden rijk* almost seems to foreshadow António Lobo Antunes's much later *As naus* (The Return of the Caravels, 1988). The marconist also relives the Lisbon earthquake of 1755, but rather than lamenting it as a disaster he considers it 'de vervulling van een wraak die eeuwen had moeten wachten' (the achievement of a revenge that had been delayed for centuries) and enjoys seeing 'huizen omkrullen, torens omvallen, mensen schroeien' (houses crumbling, towers toppling, people burning, Slauerhoff 1983: 549). The real conflagration of Lisbon during the earthquake and its twentieth-century 'postfiguration' in the Irish marconist's mind picture both the perversion of the individual speaker and the bankruptcy of an entire civilization built on the deeds of conquests as sung in *Os Lusíadas*. Perhaps the 'towers toppling' also constitutes a dim echo of some of the most famous passages in English poetry referring to another civilization going under: the Troy alluded to in Christopher Marlowe's 'Doctor Faustus', with 'Was this the face that launched a thousand ships / And burnt the topless towers of Ilium?' (V.i.97–98). The passage is alluded to in Yeats's 'When Helen Lived', from *Responsibilities and Other Poems* (1916), as again in his 'Long-Legged Fly', from *Last Poems* (1936–1939), and more obliquely again by Pound in *Canto I*, which starts with 'And then went down to the ship', the Greeks setting out on their expedition to destroy Troy in revenge for Paris abducting Helen, or Helen eloping with Paris.

The same message transpires from the posthumous 'Lisboa' (collected in *Verzamelde Gedichten* [1947; Slauerhoff 2005] in the section 'Saudades' of the volume *Soleares*, originally published in a different form in 1933),[3] in which the city never recovered from the earthquake and now only survives as a ghost, its ruins starkly offsetting its former glory. The melancholy inherent in this view Slauerhoff also recognized in the Portuguese *fado*. Still, it is through *fado* that Slauerhoff transcends his Dutch confines and makes it onto the stage of world literature, or in this case rather world music: in the year 2000 one of the best known of the more recent generation of *fadistas*, Cristina Branco (2000), released *Cristina Branco canta Slauerhoff*, a CD with nine poems of Slauerhoff in a Portuguese translation by Mila Vidal Paletti and put to music by Custódio Castelo.

Hendrik Marsman, like Roland Holst, Nijhoff and Slauerhoff, was also deeply influenced by foreign examples, especially by German-language expressionism, with the work of the Austrian Georg Trakl (1887–1914), and its Flemish offshoots in the early works of Wies Moens (1898–1982) and Paul van Ostaijen (1896–1928). Still, no such direct relationship to one specific foreign predecessor or near-contemporary as with the three poets discussed earlier can be traced for Marsman. Rather, Marsman stands out for not only having undergone influence from abroad, but of also having influenced an author in a major language and literature. One of his poetry cycles inspired a volume by an American author that enjoyed a considerable reputation in the second half of the twentieth century: James Dickey (1923–1997). As such, Marsman's poetry fulfils the criterium David Damrosch (2003) defined as decisive for a work or an oeuvre to belong to world literature, i.e. that it circulates, in the original or in translation, beyond its own linguistic or cultural borders.

Marsman debuted in his early twenties with poems influenced by German expressionism and vitalism. Towards the end of his life he adopted a more sober and classical form and diction. It is from this period that dates the cycle 'De dierenriem' (The Zodiac), published in the volume *Tempel en Kruis* (Temple and Cross, 1940; Marsman 1979), the last of his works Marsman himself saw through the press. He died in the Spring of 1940 when the ship with which he tried to flee the German occupation of France, where he had been living since 1936, sank in the English Channel, whether torpedoed by a German U-boat or from some other cause has never been definitively established. 'De dierenriem', true to its title, consists of twelve poems, but the figure twelve is also collated with the twelve apostles and the twelve hours of the clock. This transpires most clearly in the second of the twelve poems, situated in the sign of Cancer, and which ends:

> The while he watches the dial hands creep
> His pride is aware, with a rebellious scorn,
> That even that uncreated vertigo,
> Broken, and barred,
> Is represented to men's eyes
> In the act of Cancer on the tapestry,
> And where once God in the arena stood
> And came to grips with a defiant man,
> Under the banners of a reddening dawn,
> The lobster now kneels round the passion's path
> And prays the dial's stations of the cross. (Marsman 1947)

The poem has as its protagonist 'a man [...] [who] [r]eturned, some time ago, to his native land'. If we know that Marsman himself spent the last years of his life abroad, but had returned briefly to the Netherlands in the Spring of 1939, shortly before the writing of 'De dierenriem', and that the city in which the man in question occupies an apartment over 'peaceful broker's offices' is Utrecht, where Marsman himself had made his living as a lawyer before going abroad, the similarities with Marsman himself are obvious. Marsman was raised in a strictly Protestant household but later lost his faith. That he continued to struggle with this is clear, however, from a passage preceding the lines quoted, in which 'He feels the strokes [of the midnight cathedral tower clock] pass through his aching frame / And thinks: the Father was thus racked in the Son' (Marsman 1947).

James Dickey (1976) introduces his *Zodiac* by referencing Marsman's poem, which he undoubtedly knew from Barnouw's translation, although he does not mention this (Dickey 1992: 345–373). He immediately insists, though, that 'it is in no sense a translation, for the liberties I have taken with Marsman's original poem are such that the poem I publish here, with the exception of a few lines, is completely my own'. That Dickey had only a faint notion of who Marsman was, and what the latter's poem is about, is already clear from the fact that he claims that the twelve sections of Marsman's poem 'are the story of a drunken and perhaps dying Dutch poet who returns to his home in Amsterdam after years of travel and tries desperately to relate himself, by means of stars, to the universe'. As mentioned, the city is Utrecht, not Amsterdam, and Marsman's protagonist is trying to relate himself to God's universe rather than a bare or impersonal universe. In fact, already in this introductory note Dickey is bending Marsman's poem to his own purposes. In the poem this is even more clearly the case when Marsman's he-protagonist is replaced by an I-narrator speaking about himself, and when God is replaced by whiskey as the ultimate cause of Dickey's universe.

Dickey's poem is not divided into twelve clearly-partitioned sections but rather gushes forth as a drunken litany. As illustration I turn to a passage from Dickey obviously inspired by the passage from Marsman quoted earlier, and which with Dickey becomes:

> Where God once stood in the stadium
> of European history, and battled mankind in the blue air
> Of manmade curses, under the exploding flags
> of dawn, I'd put something else now:
> I'd put something overhead ... something new: a new beast
> For the Zodiac. I'd say to myself like a man
> Bartending for God,
> What'll it be?
> Great! The stars are mine, and so is
> The imagination to work them –
> To create.
> Christ, would you tell me why my head
> Keeps thinking up these nit-witted, useless images?
> Whiskey helps
> But it does. It does. And now I'm working
> With *constellations*! What'll it *be*, Heaven? What new creature
> Would you *like* up there? Listen, you universal son-of-a-bitch,
> You're talking to a poet now, so don't give me a lot of shit.
> My old man was a God-damned astronomer
> Of sorts
> – and didn't he say the whole sky's *invented*?
> Well, I am now *inventing*. You've *got* a Crab:
> Especially tonight. I love to eat them: They scare me to death!
> My head is quashed with *aquavit*.
>
> (Dickey 1992: 352)

The ranting content is mirrored in the poem's spatial arrangement, jumping about on the page (actual layout not reproduced here). The critical reception of Dickey's *Zodiac* has not been very positive. The *Kirkus Review* at the poem's publication summed it up as: 'a curious thing: an unsanctified Dutch poet beseeching the sea and stars with deep and melodic Southern intonations. Intense and ardent solipsism, not Dickey at his best.'

Roland Holst, Nijhoff, Slauerhoff and Marsman played distinctive roles in interbellum Dutch literature. Nijhoff, Slauerhoff and Marsman each have left at least one poem that has become an iconic expression of the Dutch landscape and character. For Nijhoff this is 'De moeder de vrouw' (The mother the wife), in which the I-speaker goes to see the 'new bridge' in Bommel, by which 'two opposite sides / that earlier seemed to avoid one another, / become neighbors again'. The I-speaker in Slauerhoff's 'In Nederland' (In the Netherlands) does not want to live in the Netherlands, where 'One always has to curb one's desires / To placate the good neighbors, / That avidly peer through every peephole.' But it is Marsman's 'Herinnering aan Holland' (Reminiscence of Holland) that was voted the most memorable Dutch poem of the twentieth century: 'Thinking of Holland / I see broad rivers / slowly move through unending / low-lying land.' Beyond having thus become part of popular Dutch literary consciousness, these poets, with their work but also in how that work relates to that of foreign contemporaries or (sometimes, as in the case of Slauerhoff remote) predecessors of theirs also participated in the wider European literary currents of their time and even, in the case of Marsman, inspired another poet working in another era, and in a major language. As such, Dutch Modernist poetry also fully plays its role in world literature.

Notes

1. In this essay I summarize some earlier publications of mine as listed in the 'References'. Occasionally I have borrowed a sentence or part of a paragraph from these earlier publications – I do so in full acknowledgement of where these publications earlier appeared, and with the consent of the editors of the originals.
2. All subsequent quotations from Roland Holst 1981–1983 will parenthetically refer to *Poëzie* (Poetry) 1 and 2, or *Proza* (Prose) 1 and 2. All translations of Dutch originals are mine, unless otherwise indicated.
3. The various editions of Slauerhoff's poetry differ considerably, as Lekkerkerker, in the collected poems edition he published in 1947, which was the basis for all further editions until the 2018 edition edited by H. Aalders and M. Voskuil, re-arranged the numerous poems that had remained uncollected or unpublished during the poet's life, into what he thought to be thematically consistent collections. The 2018 edition brings the various collections as published during Slauerhoff's lifetime, followed by the uncollected and posthumously published poems. The poem in question, 'Lisboa', did not originally figure in 'Saudades', but was added to it by Lekkerkerker in 1947.

References

Akker, W. van den (1994), *Dichter in het grensgebied: over de poëzie van M. Nijhoff in de jaren dertig*, Amsterdam: Bert Bakker.

Damrosch, D. (2003), *What is World Literature?* Princeton, NJ: Princeton University Press.

D'haen, T. (1990), 'W.B. Yeats and A. Roland Holst: (S)Elective Affinities', *Yeats: An Annual of Critical and Textual Studies* 8: 49–70.

D'haen, T. (2006), 'Yeats in the Dutch-language Low Countries', in K.P. Jochum (eds), *The Reception of W.B. Yeats in Europe*, 12–24, London: Continuum.

D'haen, T. (2009), 'Mapping Modernism: Gaining in Translation – Martinus Nijhoff and T.S. Eliot', *Comparative Critical Studies* 6 (1): 21–41.

D'haen, T. (2017), 'J.J. Slauerhoff, Dutch Literature and World Literature', in J.L. Jobim (eds), *Literary and Cultural Circulation*, 143–157, Oxford: Peter Lang; also as "J.J.

Slauerhoff, Literatura holandesa e literatura-mundo," in J.L. Jobim (ed.), *A circulação literária e cultural*, 139–152, Oxford: Peter Lang.
Dickey, J. (1992), *The Whole Motion: Collected Poems 1945–1992*, Hanover: Wesleyan University Press.
Lobo Antunes, A. (1988), *As naus*, Lisbon: Dom Quixote.
Marsman, H. (1947), 'The Zodiac', trans. A.J. Barnouw, *The Sewanee Review* 55 (2): 238–251.
Marsman, H. (1979), *Verzameld werk*, Amsterdam: Em. Querido.
Nijhoff, M. (1961), *Verzameld Werk, II: kritisch, verhalend en nagelaten proza, Volumes II.1 and II.2*, Den Haag and Amsterdam: Bert Bakker and G. A. van Oorschot.
Nijhoff, M. (1978), *Verzamelde gedichten*, ed. G. Kamphuis, Amsterdam: Bert Bakker.
Nijhoff, M. (1982), *Verzameld werk 3: Vertalingen*, Amsterdam: Bert Bakker.
Nijhoff, M. (1993), *Gedichten*, Historisch-kritische uitgave, eds W.J. van den Akker and G.J. Dorleijn, vol. 1, Monumenta Literaria Neerlandica, VII, 1 (Teksten), 2 (Commentaar) en 3 (Apparaat), Assen: Van Gorcum, for the Koninklijke Nederlandse Akademie van Wetenschappen.
Nijhoff, M. (2001), *Verzamelde Gedichten*, ed. Wiljan van Den Akker and Gilles J. Dorleijn, Amsterdam: Bert Bakker.
Roland Holst, A. (1981–1983), *Verzameld Werk*, 4 vols, ed. W.J. van Den Akker et al., Amsterdam: Van Oorschot.
Slauerhoff, J. (1983), *Verzameld Proza*, 2 vols, 's Gravenhage: Nijgh & Van Ditmar.
Slauerhoff, J. (2005), *Alle gedichten*, ed. K. Lekkerkerker, Amsterdam: Nijgh & Van Ditmar.
Slauerhoff, J. (2018), *Verzamelde gedichten*, eds H. Aalders and M. Voskuil, Amsterdam: Nijgh & Van Ditmar.
Sötemann, A.L. (1976), '"Non-spectacular" Modernism: Martinus Nijhoff's Poetry in its European Context', in F. Bulhof (ed.), *Nijhoff, Van Ostaijen, 'De Stijl': Modernism in the Netherlands and Belgium in the First Quarter of the 20th Century. Six Essays*, 95–116, The Hague: Martinus Nijhoff.
Supheert, R. (1995), *Yeats in Holland: The Reception of the Work of W.B. Yeats in the Netherlands before World War Two*, Amsterdam: Rodopi.
Vegt, J. van der (1974), *De brekende spiegel: Ontwikkeling, samenhang, achtergronden bij A. Roland Holst*, 's Gravenhage: Nijgh & Van Ditmar.
Yeats, W.B. (1957), *The Variorum Edition of the Poems of W.B. Yeats*, eds P. Allt and R.K. Alspach, New York: Macmillan.

15

Reinventing the Modernist Novel: Louis Paul Boon and Hugo Claus

Kris Humbeeck

Widely translated and critically acclaimed during their lifetime, Louis Paul Boon (1912–1979) and Hugo Claus (1929–2008) were the first Flemish writers to be seriously considered for a Nobel Prize in Literature. After their deaths, their international fame faded and nowadays they are probably only still known to specialists in Dutch-language literature. Boon and Claus themselves had dreamed of shaping the inner life of their community, and projecting it nationally and internationally, with their fiction. Neither writer had an intellectual background or enjoyed an extensive formal education. Both were autodidacts. They were both strongly influenced by expressionism, surrealism and modernism, in particular the works of William Faulkner. Of these isms, surrealism – which Boon and Claus defined in rather different ways – is the most important. Finally, Boon and Claus internalized their literary, artistic and philosophical influences in much the same way. In spite of these similarities, however, there are just as many differences. The latter are in large part due to their diverging personal histories. If Boon is a child of the Great War, Claus is shaped primarily by the Second World War.

Boon's formative years

Boon grew up a restless young man in a petty bourgeois environment in the small Flemish industrial town of Aalst. In the mid-1920s he worked as an assistant to his father, a small-time painting and construction contractor, and as a spray painter for a body shop in Brussels. He had no formal education to speak of but still managed to become acquainted with expressionist and surrealist art, and with big city movies such as *The Crowd* (1928), *The Docks of New York* (1928) and *Die Büchse der Pandora* (Pandora's Box, 1929). He avidly read 'godless' books, with a certain preference for Nobel Prize winners and public intellectuals such as Bjørnstjerne Bjørnson, Rabinadrath Tagore and Bertha von Suttner, but also sympathized and to some extent identified himself with the suffering masses in Emile Zola's *Germinal* (1885). At the same time, he devoured the Bible as a source of stories, ways of storytelling, and mythic patterns. Whereas the latter might explain young Boon's interest in Dante, the fact that he also thought highly of Luigi Pirandello and Cervantes points to an early preoccupation with the deceptive and unstable nature of reality.

In the early 1930s Boon moved in communist circles where Karl Marx, Friedrich Nietzsche and Ernst Haeckel were read, studied and discussed, next to Leninism as well as Buddhism and Taoism. Meanwhile, Oswald Spengler's pessimism still haunts the minds of these children of the Great War, in much the same way that the apocalyptic poetry of Paul van Ostaijen (*Het Sienjaal* [The Signal], 1918; *Bezette stad* [Occupied City], 1921) inspires them. It is in this context that Boon makes his debut.

In his first story, 'De avend vraagt u' (The Night Is Calling You, 1933), an excerpt from the uncompleted novel *Onbekende stad* (Unknown City), Boon called on his rebellious peers to resist all *Wandervogel*-romanticism and confront the metropolis as the product of a misunderstood, failed and derailed modernity. Boon admired Emile Zola's ambition to 'scientifically' map modern society in order to improve 'the system'. This commitment to society is also what Boon appreciated in the works of Leo Tolstoy, Romain Rolland and Henri Barbusse. He worshiped Fyodor M. Dostoevsky, whose *Notes From the Underground* (1864) he regarded as his literary Bible. Reading and rereading Dostoevksy confirmed him in his suspicion that man is by nature a mix of constructive and destructive forces, a vision he also found in the works of Sigmund Freud. It is therefore important to organize society in such a way that the unleashing of the destructive powers is kept to a minimum. From this perspective, utopian as well as unrealistic revolutionary projects are counterproductive, something he learnt from reading Dostoevski as well as Anatole France (*Les Dieux ont soif* [The Gods are Athirst], 1912). The most enduring and at the same time realistic and expressive evocation of the sickening existence in the modern metropolis he found in the first pages of Rainer Maria Rilke's *Die Aufzeichnungen des Malte Laurids Brigge* (The Notebooks of Malte Laurids Brigge, 1910). Initially enchanted with Walt Whitman, by the end of the 1930s he was put off by the epic-solemn tone, the continuing brotherhood pathos and the triumphant vitalism of *Leaves of Grass* ([1855] 1892): 'It seems as if I can constantly hear this amazing, loud marching band pass me by. Raw and massive, but [...] depth? I can't find any.'[1] Eclectic as it may seem, then, the common thread in his reading was his interest in the dynamic life of the big city, the disappearance of traditional interconnections and the rise of the masses. The poetry of Emile Verhaeren (*Les villes tentaculaires* [Tentacular Cities], 1895), Upton Sinclair's novel *The Jungle* (1906), novels about the moral misery of modern man such as Knut Hamsun's *Hunger* (1890), the early novels of Sinclair Lewis, Henrik Ibsen's plays and the prose of Maxim Gorky, all fit in this rickety framework.

De voorstad groeit, or catastrophic modernity

Boon sets his debut novel, *De voorstad groeit* (The suburb grows, 1943), in a nameless metropolis that could be considered the book's main protagonist. In this light, comparisons with John dos Passos and Alfred Döblin are swiftly drawn, but Boon only comes to know and appreciate these writers later on. On closer inspection, Boon's story about a partially allegorical industrial town governed by utilitarianism and efficiency presents itself as an update of Charles Dickens's Coketown, from *Hard Times* (1854), with its ruthless expansion at the cost of dehumanization, leading to an economic crisis in which the metropolis is forced to produce weapons instead of consumer goods. As the story unfolds another influence manifests itself. In his relentless lust for power and success, the metropolis' omnipotent tycoon does not only squeeze the life out of the town's inhabitants, causing a long overdue uprising, he also squanders his personal happiness and moral values. The modern demigod ends up a heartless person, incapable of love and compassion. The sentimental-moralist message and the humanist tone at the end of the novel reveal the influence of Jakob Wassermann, writer of immensely popular novels such as *Caspar Hauser* (1908) and *Christian Wahnschaffe* (1919). In the latter work the German writer denounces the 'Slowness of Heart' of his contemporaries. According to Wassermann, industrial society is essentially heartless. All sense of love, compassion and community has been lost with the rise of industrial capitalism. In contrast with Wassermann's cumbersome prose, though, *De voorstad groeit* is dynamic, spontaneous and refreshingly 'non-literary'. Because of the constant use of colloquialisms, vernacular and at times even patois, critics as well as the writer himself have linked the novel to Louis-Ferdinand Céline's novels *Voyage au bout de la nuit* (Voyage to the End of Night, 1932) and *Mort à crédit* (Death on the Installment Plan, 1936).

Prophetic and utopian: *Abel Gholaerts* and *Vergeten straat*

De voorstad groeit is an omniscient narration. In the intended diptych *Abel Gholaerts*, based on the life of Vincent Van Gogh, Boon attributed himself the role of prophetic guide and seer. However, having published part one (*Abel Gholaerts: The Talent*, 1943), Boon never completed the second volume. His friendship with a group of communist resistance fighters gradually made him aware of the grotesque, out of touch and essentially narcissistic nature of his endeavour. Elated by the German debacle at Stalingrad, Boon began to write a novel in which he wanted to reconcile the utopian idea of a self-sufficient community of free individuals with the reality of big city life. It didn't take long, though, before his idealism started to fade. Disappointed with the events following the end of the Second World War, his utopian experiment in novel form, *Vergeten straat* (Forgotten Street, 1946), acquired dominant dystopian overtones. Still, in spite of the fact that the writer was forced to acknowledge that his view of reality was a limited one, the auctorial narrator remained.

The disruption of history: My Little War

In the autumn of 1945 Boon concluded that instead of heading towards peace, the world was preparing for another war – this time with the additional threat of the atomic bomb. Confronted with this frightening new possibility, Boon faced a double trauma: first as a soldier, a prisoner of war and a citizen in an occupied city, and secondly, as a writer with visionary, prophetic ambitions. Boon's answer was *Mijn kleine oorlog* (My Little War, 1947). At the centre of *My Little War* is Louis, a character that seems to simply scribble down the events around him. But unlike Boon's previous narrators, Louis isn't a reliable narrator: he forgets and repeats things, he jumbles the chronology, and there are gaps in the plot of his story. Moreover, notes, impromptu comments and unspecified *petites histoires* in italics constantly interrupt his chronicle. There is, however, a method to this madness, for the discontinuity of the narration in *My Little War* corresponds with the fundamental discovery that we live in a 'broken time', or to use Hamlet's classic phrase: a 'time out of joint'. There has been an irremediable disruption in the way we experience the world, resulting in a sense of ongoing catastrophe and permanent crisis.

Most contemporaries found *My Little War* so chaotic that they had difficulty identifying it as a novel. Critics lacked any point of reference. Boon himself hinted at Paul van Ostaijen's famous expressionist montage and collage text *Bezette stad* (1921). Perhaps more importantly, the author had discovered Döblin's *Berlin Alexanderplatz* (1929) and the works of Dos Passos and William Faulkner. Especially in the latter's work Boon encountered a similar sense of loss and dislocation combined with a strongly distorted sexuality. Although clearly aware of this modernist tradition, Boon seems to write his story about war and 'liberation' intuitively – out of sheer disgust with the recurrent barbarity of the twentieth century. His sense of revolt is given form in a way that presents clear parallels with *Voyage au bout de la nuit*'s 'psychotic style'. Some passages also reveal how attentively Boon must have read Lautréamonts *Les Chants de Maldoror* (1869) as well. It is no coincidence that Boon was inspired by two writers who contributed to the revolution of the literary language.

Surrealism is the new realism

In the slipstream of his formal experiments, Boon started to publish literary criticism and art reviews. Initially writing for *De roode vaan* (Red Flag), the official newspaper of the Communist Party of Belgium (KPB), Boon provoked furious reactions from his editor-in-chief and the party bosses by enthusiastically embracing the avant-garde. A common thread throughout Boon's criticism is the need for revolutionary new forms of literature and art that can convincingly represent the 'chaos' of post-war reality. Boon started to focus on coincidence as an artistic ordering principle. Omniscience was no longer feasible, in his view, and Boon even began to doubt if the novel as such, being the work of a single mind, can possibly convey the complexities of the world.

After reading Wilhelm von Scholz's *Der Zufall und das Schicksal* (Coincidence and Destiny, 1935), he encouraged his readers to send him as many of their oddest and most unsettling experiences as possible. He published these as a new kind of collective novel, in the hope of revealing, as he put it, new forms of 'beauty'. Such allusions and casual references indicate that after expressionism and modernism, Boon now also embraced surrealism in order to find a new type of realism. A catalyzing moment was his visit to the first post-war surrealist group exhibition 'Surréalisme', in December 1945, in Brussels. Shortly thereafter, the writer met with the man who organized the event, René Magritte. In Boon's view, surrealism essentially offered an alternative, an anti-bourgeois method to give meaning to the world. Citing the surrealists and the work of their medieval forebear Jeroen Bosch, Boon argued that these artists had uncovered a break from the Western logic of identity: in their universes everything that is can just as well be the exact opposite. Those who try to hang on to their faith in a divine order, or in the essence of things, see their world fall apart in a terrible 'chaos'. But for those who cannot believe in order any longer the 'chaotic' state of the world is less of a threat than it is an existential given.

Chapel Road, or exploring our time out of joint

If all had gone to plan, 'Madame Odile', the third novel Boon had started writing near the end of the war, would have been the exemplary story of a lower middle-class girl who, after having survived two world wars, perishes together with her class. Yet the middle-class turned out to be tougher than Boon had predicted in 1943, and the democratic socialism he had so longed for at the time remained a distant dream. Boon dismissed the initial concept of 'Madame Odile' but didn't entirely give up on the novel. In the summer of 1947, he decided to combine the pages he had already written with a series of notes on everyday life he had been working on for about two years, resulting in the modernist classic *De Kapellekensbaan* (Chapel Road, 1953). In this groundbreaking novel, the author of the 'notes' is called Boontje – a diminutive of Boon. Boontje is also the fictional author of the novel-in-the-novel 'Madame Odile', which is presented as a work-in-progress. In *Chapel Road*, chapters of Boontje's novel 'Madame Odile' alternate with Boontje's notes on everyday life as a serial in a newspaper that very well could have been called 'Times Out of Joint'.

Similar to Louis in *My Little War*, Boontje distinguishes himself in his ironic, almost overly conscious awareness of his authorial limitations. Modest in his ambitions, Boontje is constantly overwhelmed by his friends who invade his house and repeatedly rob him of speech, thus undermining his already uncertain authorial status even more. Not only do his friends get a say in what happens to the heroine of Boontje's novel-in-the-novel, one of Boontje's regular visitors even manages to sneak in a novel of his own: an update of *Van den Vos Reynaerde* (Reynard the Fox), the satirical masterpiece of medieval Dutch literature. In this rewrite, the Catholic Party is held responsible for the disastrous restoration of pre-war Belgium, while the Communist Party is considered too sectarian to become a political counterforce. Unusually vivid in its interaction of all 'actors' involved, *Chapel Road* is an essentially dramatic, polyphonic and dialogical novel as Mikhail Bakhtin, in *Problems of Dostoevsky's Poetics* (1984), defines these terms. Some formal aspects of *Chapel Road* show that Boon was still inspired by Dostoevsky. Yet the abundance of voices and narrative strands appear to be a comment, revenge even, on the lack of openness and democracy in life. The novel is wilfully chaotic, as its narrative structure is designed to gather conflicting views on the world.

It is very important to realize that Boon's 'intersubjective' approach is more than just a literary trick or feint. *Chapel Road* is in fact an authentic experiment in depersonalization and de-realization, inspired by surrealism. Boontje's friends are closely modelled after real-life friends of the author. Yet instead of copying their conversations, Boon stages discussions that *could* have taken place. He constantly confronts his own opinions with the imagined opinions of his friends. He does so not in a fully rational way, but rather in a state of controlled daydreaming. This is why Boontje always talks in the second person singular about others and himself, as if he is standing beside himself in a permanent state of contemplation, endlessly ruminating and engaging in internal dialogue. There is indeed a persistent atmosphere of dreamlike alienation in *Chapel Road*, as if the everyday world is suspended and all is open to interpretation.

For all his chagrin caused by his friends' intrusive behaviour, Boontje never claims private ownership over his text. In the end Boontje doesn't consider himself to be in the best position to set out guidelines for interpreting the constantly changing world. In this respect, in *Chapel Road's* sequel, *Zomer in Ter-Muren* (Summer in Ter-Muren, 1956), Boontje outlines a strongly Nietzschean theory about decadence. In a conversation with one of his more educated friends, he finally discovers that modern man is still driven by an unrealistic longing for a paradise on earth. He realizes that this metaphysical longing doesn't just lead to frustration and nihilism, but also to structural violence. Only when man succeeds in overcoming his nihilism – by overcoming the Logic of Decadence underlying history – reasonable alternatives will appear. In the meantime, Boontje maintains, one can only hope that the world will not collapse because of man's metaphysical foolishness.

Next to James Joyce's *Ulysses* (1922) and Samuel Becketts *Molloy* (1951), Boon himself cited Faulkner as an inspiration, claiming he only had to read a few pages of his work to feel empowered to pursue his experiment. He also took a special interest in the work of Henry Miller, whose *Tropic of Cancer* (1934) and *Tropic of Capricorn* (1939) he didn't read as real autobiography, but as partially fictionalized confessions of a degenerate or brutalized man in the concrete jungle. Similarly, he was fascinated by the autobiographical novel *Journal du voleur* (The Thief's Journal, 1949) by Jean Genet. And the fact that in *Summer in Ter-Muren* some of Boontje's friends suddenly get different names probably has something to do with Boon's admiration for Genet's *Notre-Dame-des-Fleurs* (Our Lady of the Flowers, 1951).

Struggling to get *Chapel Road* published, around 1950, Boon tried to fend off cultural marginalization by accepting a seat on the editorial board of a periodical bearing the heavily existentialist title *Tijd en Mens* (Time and Man). Never really able to steer this avant-garde magazine in his desired direction, it didn't take long before Boon started to wonder if his younger fellow editors were really as interested in transforming the world through literature as he was. Some of them seemed to content themselves with strictly poetic interpretations of the world. The most talented and at the same time least obedient representative of this modernist aestheticism was Hugo Claus. Over the next decades, a complicated literary relationship would develop between Boon and Claus.

Remembering a shameful past: The early works of Hugo Claus

Hugo Claus came from a lower middle-class family in the commercial town of Kortrijk. He passed much of his early youth in a very strict, Catholic boarding school. On the eve of the Second Word War he returned to his family in Kortrijk. During the German occupation his mother worked for the occupying forces and became friendly with a German officer. Meanwhile, his father didn't even try to hide his sympathy for Hitler, and neither did some other members of the Claus family.

Claus's formative years

After the war Claus's mother had her civil rights revoked for life, and his father was sent to prison for a year and a half. Hugo himself in early 1941, unknown to his parents, enlisted with the Flemish Youth, a collaborationist youth movement. An avid admirer of Reinhard Heydrich, Claus roamed the streets of Kortrijk in the uniform of the National-Socialist Youth Flanders until the end of the war. Claus later admitted that, at that time, he wanted nothing more than to report himself for duty as an SS-volunteer for the Eastern front. 'Unfortunately' he was too young to enrol.

Even though he came out of the war unharmed and uncharged, Claus's sense of guilt nevertheless lasted a lifetime. Dreaming of conquering the world as an artist, but seeing he was still entangled in social and artistic networks of former collaborators, *Tijd en Mens* primarily offered him an escape route, in anticipation of his artistic breakthrough. In his magnum opus *The Sorrow of Belgium* (1983) he fictionally analysed the unnerving relationship between the romantic Flemish-Nationalism of his youth and his desire to be a Nazi, as well as the questionable innocence of Belgian democracy with regard to the political radicalization process that he and others were subject to. First, though, he had to conquer his shame.

Replacing Heydrich with Artaud

Still in thrall to nationalist themes and motives in the immediate aftermath of the Second World War, Claus found a way out when he discovered surrealism in *Les lettres Françaises*, a French periodical that emerged from the antifascist resistance. In 1947,

Claus met the charismatic 'madman' Antonin Artaud in the latter's favourite bar in Paris, and adopted this surrealist, scarred by alcohol, drugs and electroshocks, as his new role model. While an admirer of Breton and the 'old' surrealists, Claus more closely studied the later proponents of the movement. Jules Supervielle, whose variant of surrealism functions as an antidote to the 'dictatorship of the subconscious', was one of them. René Daumal's influence proved to be even more important, especially after the posthumous publication of his symbolic novel *Le Mont Analogue* (1952). Claus was strongly drawn to Daumal's view that each man irrationally longs for the absolute, to his idea that the poet only gets to know himself through language, and especially to his refusal to lose sight of everyday life in writing. The same combination of a sense of the 'metaphysical' and the fundamental commitment to reality continued to fascinate Claus in Henri Michaux.

Blatantly Faulknerian: *De Metsiers* and *De hondsdagen*

In the summer of 1948, in order to practice his writing and also to earn some much-needed money, Claus wrote the hard-boiled novel *De Metsiers* (1951, variously published in English as *The Duck Hunt* and *Sister of Earth*) in only a few weeks. The masterly use of multiple voices and perspectives in *Sister of Earth* gives away just how well Claus had studied Faulkner's *The Sound and the Fury* (1929) and *As I Lay Dying* (1930). But even though *Sister of Earth* reads like a modernist version of a Flemish naturalist novel, it is not just a weak imitation of Faulkner. Instead, it is a first powerful evocation of personal obsessions. Central in Claus's imagination are the almighty female progenitor, her weak husband and her strong lover, who secures the exclusive love of the mother by eliminating the lawfully wedded husband. More important than the overtly Faulknerian narrative perspective in *Sister of Earth* is the corrupt atmosphere typical of Faulkner's imaginary world, particularly the suggestion of a fundamentally unhinged society, in which even the incest taboo is no longer respected. Just like Boon, Claus connects this breakdown of society to the war. In a world that has defeated fascism, an almost primitive form of violence still lingers, affecting innocent people the most – in this case the mentally disabled boy Bennie, probably inspired by Faulkner's Benjy Compson in *The Sound and the Fury*.

In 1950 Claus moved to Paris, where he occasionally partnered with CoBrA painters like Karel Appel and Corneille, and familiarized himself with Sartre's existentialism. Still trying to reinvent himself as an autonomous artist without a history, Claus starts to feel trapped in a past he cannot forget nor remember. It eventually leads him back in time to the moment he was exiled by his 'treacherous' parents to the boarding school where he spent most of his childhood years. The yearning for a childhood he never had, and the desire for a fresh start, was the starting point of *De hondsdagen* (Dog Days, 1952). In this second novel, Claus symbolizes the lost 'self' in the figure of the boarding school girl Beatrice, who has fled school and is accompanied by a man vaguely familiar to the protagonist. The latter, like Claus at the time, struggles with relationship problems, feeling unable to commit himself fully and terrified of the idea of becoming a father. But above all he is afraid that Beatrice has been kidnapped and is being sexually abused. Yet, however critical the situation may be, it also creates an opportunity for both the protagonist and the schoolgirl to start life anew: by rescuing the girl, the man can save her life and by doing so, construct a self. Beatrice's biography in the meantime reads like a grotesque parody of the author's childhood. She too was dumped by her parents, handed over not to nuns, at least not directly, but to some madam of a city brothel who, after making her feel at home, sent her to a boarding school.

The storyline of Claus's second novel is obviously inspired by Faulkner's controversial masterpiece *Sanctuary* (1931) and James Hadley Chase's hard-boiled novel *No Orchids for Miss Blandish* (1939). But whereas in these two novels a young woman is abducted and subjected to extreme sexual violence, the young lady (a child, still) in *De hondsdagen* is found safe and sound in the end; she doesn't appear to have suffered at all. It's a clear case of much ado about nothing, which makes the return to everyday life for the protagonist all the more upsetting. Neither in his life, nor in that of the 'eternal' boarding school girl, has anything really changed. Even worse, in the course of events the 'new life' he's after, never even announced itself.

Remarkably, throughout the novel, the exemplary modernist story about man's existential shortcomings is interrupted by some completely dysfunctional passages, all of which refer to war, occupation and collaboration – shedding an uncanny light on the seemingly gratuitous mention of Beatrice being Jewish. Considering Claus's traumatizing past, it is not surprising per se that these war memories randomly surface. From a purely aesthetic point of view, however, the fact that these passages were not removed from the text in order to make 'the figure in the carpet' more visible, seems highly inexplicable. But herein lies the author's statement. Claus renounced any attempt to create a realm of existential significance and higher aesthetic order in the face of a world perceived as essentially meaningless and chaotic, if not downright ugly and mean.

Finding a way to confront the past

Although Claus implicitly rejects escape routes from war torn reality, he still hasn't found a way to really confront the past. In *De Oostakkerse gedichten* (The Oostakker Poems, 1955), a wildly experimental collection of poetry, the war is once again a roadblock on the way to an aesthetic understanding of the chaos we call life. Verses such as 'De brandende Jood in het braambos' (The Burning Jew in the Bush) time and again point at the community's deafening silence regarding Flemish collaboration with the Nazi regime.

Having followed his movie star girlfriend to Italy in 1954, Claus gradually found a way to cope with the demons of his past. The mundane film world proved to be the perfect backdrop for a new novel. In *De koele minnaar* (The Distant Lover, 1956)

Claus asks himself the question how someone like him – someone who has been 'betrayed' by his family and by history – is still expected to engage in meaningful relationships. Did 'the war generation' not lose its ability to truly love and connect with someone else? The eventual result of this self-study is mostly positive, despite the fact that at the end of the novel the main protagonist fails to make his latest relationship work.

Along the way, Claus realized that the 'Race of Smiles', as the novel's protagonist describes the film folk, never really show their faces. The insight that we are all actors in life, further developed in *De koele minnaar* with references to *Les Liaisons dangereuses* (Dangerous Liaisons, 1782) by Pierre Choderlos de Laclos and Stendhal's *La Chartreuse de Parme* (The Charterhouse of Parma, 1839), had a profound effect on Claus. A wilful masquerade is a liberating thought. He realized that even when he donned his National Socialist Youth uniform as an adolescent, he was playing a role, albeit in a murderous play. Wearing this uniform, in mimicry of his macho idol Heydrich, was to help reduce the fear of being overwhelmed by the world. For young Claus his fascist uniform was like a suit of armour protecting his fragile self.

De koele minnaar, on the contrary, almost cheerfully embraces the masquerade that is life. In retrospect, this novel plays a pivotal role in Hugo Claus's oeuvre. *De koele minnaar* is the novel in which the writer says goodbye to the epistemological and ontological preoccupations typical of what I call 'classic modernism'. In the literal sense of the word, this is the start of the artist's post-modernist period. Claus was now ready to return home and to take up a socially committed role, utilizing all the means 'modernism' had to offer. In Flanders, this put him at the side of Louis Paul Boon, who by then had formed an entirely different image of his young colleague.

Writing fiction after *Chapel Road*

His groundbreaking modernist novel *Chapel Road* was yet to be published, when Boon described Claus's novel *De hondsdagen* as a suspiciously fashionable kind of modernism. He openly questioned if his young fellow editor of *Tijd en Mens* actually had anything to say about post-war reality. Claus was offended, which prompted Boon to show his reluctant pupil how things should be done.

In *Menuet* (*Minuet* 1955), three narrators tell the same events. The three semi-allegorical characters – a woman whose sole desire is to advance in life, her husband who considers modern life to be meaningless, and a young cynical girl who does not care if the world goes down – are all so closely connected to the post-war period that it is difficult to interpret their story as the function of an abstract epistemological or ontological problem. Together, the three characters represent the moral vacuum and the overall stalemate in which modern man has ended up after two world wars. This situation becomes even more concrete by the presence of a collage of newspaper stories along the top of the pages (resembling a newsreel). There is a strong tension in *Minuet* between the use of multiple perspectives, on the one hand, and the objective feel of the newspaper fragments, on the other, to the extent even that Boon's text seems to parody the classic modernist novel.

It is indeed through parody that Boon found new ways to make even the most indifferent reader aware of 'our broken time'. For example: in 1954, having been recruited by a socialist newspaper to bring a fresh look to the society column, Boon grew fascinated with the celebrity gossip of the day. He was particularly interested in Marilyn Monroe, whom he considered to be the most powerful opiate that postwar Western culture had to offer. To him, the divine MM is the archetypal modern representation of feminine beauty, and at the same time the most grotesque case of religious alienation of the fifties. More than forty years before Joyce Carol Oates's *Blonde* (2000), Boon sets out to write *De paradijsvogel* (1958), a book in which this goddess of the silver screen and the crypto-religious cult surrounding her takes centre stage.

Mingling fact and fiction, Boon presents Monroe as a deeply unhappy woman who, out of dissatisfaction with her public image, wants to destroy herself as well as the modern world. Norma Jean, however, fails to do so, even though her path crosses that of world famous serial killer John Christie. In *De paradijsvogel,* Boon mixes both of their stories with excerpts from his pet project, *De fenomenale feminateek* (The Phenomenal Feminatheque), consisting of over 20,000 pictures of naked women, all categorized according to a makeshift sociological method, as well as with a treatise on the origins of religion, written in a mock-biblical style. Overall, there is some resemblance to the 'expressionist' novels of Klabund (pseudonym of Alfred Henschke, *Rasputin*, 1929). In its representation of urban decline and moral decadence, Boon's novel brings to mind the expressionist film, film noir and Bertolt Brecht's play *Aufstieg und Fall der Stadt Mahagonny* (Rise and Fall of the City of Mahagonny, 1930). Throughout there are references to the Bible, Dante's *Divina Commedia* (Divine Comedy), Charles Baudelaire's *Les Fleurs du Mal* (Flowers of Evil, 1857), and Gustav Meyrink's *Der Golem* (The Golem, 1914).

Fearing he had alienated part of his audience with complex novels like *De paradijsvogel* and the even more grotesque *Vaarwel krokodil* (Goodbye Crocodile, 1959), Boon restored contact with his readership in a daily column he began to write at the end of 1959. The column saw the return of Boontje, who in his new incarnation is a simple man who differs from his contemporaries only in that he happens to produce fiction, some of which he likes to try out in the newspaper. *Het nieuwe onkruid* (The New Weed, 1964) is an example of a novel that actually started as a series of columns. In the book, a nameless older man, who bears a striking resemblance to Boon, confides just how in love he is with a young girl. After a few attempts to get close to her, however, the man has to admit that he will never be able to enter her world or her subculture, which he suspects could provide a counterbalance to the established cultural traditions of the older generation. In order to make his work look authentic, and thus make it more persuasive, Boon presents his case study of the younger generation's morals, values, and cultural practices as a parody of the confessional novel. *Het nieuwe onkruid* shows that Boon is familiar with Nabokov's novel *Lolita* (1955), but his own novel is mostly inspired by his old favourite: Dostoevsky's *Notes from the Underground.*

The difficulty of being a free thinker in the sixties and seventies

After *Het nieuwe onkruid*, it took Boon seven years to write a new novel. In 1971, the author was widely praised for *Pieter Daens* (1971a), a well-documented and highly readable story about the social struggle in his hometown during the last quarter of the long nineteenth century. In his preface, Boon explicitly presents his work as a lesson for a new generation of left-wing idealists who, according to him, got all too easily carried away by revolutionary zeal and rhetoric. In the following years, he authored two more historical novels: *De Zwarte Hand* (The Black Hand, 1976) and *Het Geuzenboek* (The Beggars' Book, 1979), of which the former in particular is an interesting parody of the genre. By this time, Boon could no longer complain about a lack of official recognition or commercial success. *Mieke Maaike's obscene jeugd* (Mieke Maaike's Obscene Youth, 1971b) even became an unlikely bestseller. The book can be seen as a hardcore version of Mason Hoffenberg and Terry Southern's satirical novel *Candy* (1958). Drawing on his knowledge of the works of Rétif de la Bretonne and above all the Marquis de Sade, his female Candide, 'forced by circumstances', undergoes a true transformation and encourages her contemporaries to face the filthy reality hidden behind the facade of morality and normalcy. In *Eros en de eenzame man* (Eros and the Lone Man, 1980), a fake autobiography of a sex-obsessed writer in the vein of Philip Roth's *Deception* (1990) and Bret Easton Ellis's *Lunar Park* (2005), Boon is willing to jeopardize his good name as long as it makes his fiction more unsettling and persuasive.

Towards *The Sorrow of Belgium*, and thereafter

On 15 May 1979, the day Louis Paul Boon is interred, Hugo Claus suggests that he is finally Flanders' most important living author. At that moment, he has already come a long way. In *De Verwondering* (*Wonder*, 1962) Claus faced many of his demons. *Wonder* is set in post-war Flanders. The ruins are still visible, yet a self-proclaimed democratic society is eager to forget and move on. The collaborationist past of tens of thousands of Belgians is actively ignored. On closer examination, this perfect innocence is feigned, bearing all the characteristics of a collective form of *mauvaise foi*. The novel's protagonist challenges this fake innocence. By reopening the seemingly closed case of Nazi collaboration in Belgium, however, he touches on a taboo, for which he will pay dearly.

Wonder's protagonist claims to be interned in a psychiatric hospital against his will. If we are to believe him – although the text contains clues to suggest that is untrue – this is his punishment for disrupting a private gathering in a mysterious castle somewhere in the countryside. Intertextual references to German Romanticism and French Symbolism draw the attention of the more experienced reader to the fact that this trip very well might be an imaginary one. There is no question, though, of an *Au-delà*, an opposite world of ideas. The protagonist's travel destination is more like the wonderland in Henri Michaux's *Au Pays de la Magie* (In the Land of Magic, 1941), a twilight zone between reality as we know it and a romantic dream world. Similarly, in the Victorian age, the dream world of Lewis Caroll's *Alice in Wonderland* (1865) could not be defined as entirely 'unrealistic'. Both *Alice in Wonderland* and *Through the Looking-Glass* (1871), by the way, function as a subtext in *Wonder*.

In Claus's wonderland a yearly gathering of former Flemish Waffen-SS volunteers takes place. Drawing on the implicitly tolerated Flemish subculture former collaborators and their sympathizers had created in the real world, Claus stages the eerie commemoration of a fictitious Nationalist Socialist leader who went missing at the end of the war. A group of boar-headed fascists desperately seeks an answer to the question what befell their political idol – this hero of all heroes. It is only one of the issues that will start to haunt the reader: Is this Flemish S.S.-icon still out there? Or does he only continue to exist in the minds of those who are so desperately longing for his return? And what about the protagonist? Has he really ended up in this semi-illegal Realm of Memory solely by accident? How can one explain the ease with which he manages to access this private ceremony, as if he is one of the regulars? Could he be acquainted with the missing hero? And what if it is all in his mind? What elements in post-collaboration Belgium could have sent him down the rabbit hole?

Juxtaposing the shameless collaborators in the countryside and the vengeful 'democrats' in the city, Claus slowly steers his readers to the conclusion that both the fascists operating on the fringe and the democratic citizens operating in the centre are driven by a similar desire for an absolute identity, fixed boundaries, and 'a house of one's own'. It is exactly this similarity that the citizens of post-war Belgium constantly deny, or at least that is how the story's protagonist perceives it. As a psychiatric patient he even imagines himself to be the victim of a modern scapegoating ritual, when his internment is probably just fiction. As a living memory of Flemish collaboration, however, he is doomed to play the role of a tragic hero who constantly reminds society of its undigested recent past. Claus has structured his novel as a Greek tragedy. Marie Delcourt and Jean-Pierre Vernant read this ancient genre as an attempt by the rationally organized, democratic city-state of Athens to confront its archaic, primitive, past. This is precisely what is supposed to happen here: self-proclaimed democratic Belgium is to confront its neo-pagan, national-socialist past.

A further inquiry into human desire and the psychology of man

In the 1970s, Claus immersed himself in various narcissism theories, as well as in so-called post-structuralism. Especially authors who, in rethinking the concept of desire, as well as the relationship between desire and violence, are moving beyond the Oedipal paradigm earn the writer's particular interest. Along with the works of Jacques Lacan, the pile of books on his nightstand reportedly contained copies of René Girard's *Mensonge romantique et vérité romanesque* (Deceit, Desire and the Novel, 1961), Jacques Derrida's *L'écriture et la différence* (Writing and Difference, 1967), Gilles Deleuze's *Logique du sens* (The Logic of Sense, 1969) and G. Deleuze and Félix Guattari's *L'anti-Œdipe* (Anti-Oedipus, 1972). Furthermore, Claus's fascination with *Ferdydurke* (1937) deepens, mainly because of Witold Gombrowicz's suggestion that modern man is a mentally immature being, forced by society to act like a grown-up, and who is thus doomed to a sense of inferiority, dependency and even voicelessness. In short: a state of cultural infancy. This Gombrowiczian notion plays an important role in Claus's next inquiry into the psychology of man: *Het Verlangen* (Desire, 1978).

Desire is conceived as a loose retelling of the Biblical story of the patriarch Jacob. Two Flemings, regulars of a small-town bar called The Unicorn, head to the modern Canaan to break the bank at a roulette table in Las Vegas. They want it all, and they want it all at once! The duo consists of a slightly foreign-looking, usually sullen man, still living with his mother, and a friendly-looking guy of gigantic proportions. It is the former who takes the initiative to 'conquer the New World', in order to prove to the Unicorn-community that he is not only *a* man, but *the* man. In fact, it is his dream and goal in life to become the new 'Rikkebot', The Unicorn's immortal hero. In reality, however, the late Rikkebot must have been the lousiest gambler the town has ever known. A small-time hustler, wearing the mask of a lady-killer, Rikkebot was constantly overcompensating for his lack of self-esteem. Secretly attracted to physical violence, one of Rikkebot's dearest possessions was an SS knife, a dagger with the well-known inscription 'Meine Ehre heisst Treue.'

The wannabee man-above-all-others in Claus's novel has a similar knife, it may even be the same knife, and just like Rikkebot he is wrestling with his sexual identity. His travelling companion is a natural-born follower, who is as naive as he is big and inert. Eventually, both protagonists are naive in assuming that America awaits them like a mother and will receive them like a virgin bride. As long as the roulette wheels keep spinning and there is money to be spent America is the mythical land of limitless possibilities. In the end, however, this enormous and surprisingly heterogeneous land of plenty triggers an act of violence. The most 'innocent' of the two Flemings – the friendly-looking giant – ends up impulsively murdering a queer variety artist, because he feels this strangely unmanly man threatens his identity. Claus's novel analyses the dangerous desire to be a 'real' man. That is, the fear of psychic disintegration provoked by 'others'. The Unicorn represents a national community that, captivated by an intense longing for a stable identity and absolute autonomy, is unable to explore its own realities, not to mention the big world outside. The failed attempt by the novel's protagonists to 'conquer' America – represented in the text as a mix of simulacra, internalized commodity fetishism, but also authentic cultural diversity – highlights this weakness even more. Even as tourists the two of them are unable to cope with this diversity.

The Sorrow of Belgium, an encyclopedic novel

In retrospect, it is tempting to see *Desire* as a stepping-stone to Claus's magnum opus: *Het Verdriet van België* (The Sorrow of Belgium, 1983). Inspired by Boon's *Chapel Road*, Claus has tried to keep his book open to a heterogeneous and fragmented world, rather than transforming the latter into something more integrated, something only existing in literature and art. One could perhaps say that both Boon and Claus, while writing their respective *chef d'oeuvres*, were no longer 'spurred by the need to recuperate a lost sense of wholeness in self-sustaining orders of art or in the unselfconscious depths of the self' – to refer to Alan Wilde's famous definition of modernism.

Seemingly less fragmented than *Chapel Road*, *The Sorrow of Belgium* takes the reader from 1939 to 1947. The story tells, in chronological order, the events that lead a young man to become an adult as well as a writer. Claus has divided his novel into two parts, respectively titled 'The Sorrow' and 'Of Belgium'. On closer inspection, however, these two parts constantly refer to each other, thus disrupting the chronology of the story. Echoes, mirror effects and semi-déjà-vu experiences interfere with the linear reading to such an extent that reading *The Sorrow of Belgium* ends up being just as uncomfortable, disturbing and engaging as reading Boon's more 'chaotically' looking novel.

The two parts of Claus's novel vary strongly with respect to structure, narrative perspective and style. 'The Sorrow', neatly divided into twenty-eight chapters, is a boarding school novel along the lines of Valery Larbaud's *Femina Márquez* (1917). At the end, the protagonist has to say goodbye to a few childhood fantasies and narcissistic self-images, which is necessary if, at the dawn of the Second World War, he wants to enter the world of adulthood. At the beginning of 'Of Belgium', the protagonist joins a national-socialist youth movement. When he loses faith in the *Führer* and in his role model Heydrich, as well as in the national-socialist myths that initially made the sadly fragmented world so coherent and transparent for him, he chooses to go through life as a writer of fiction. However, one can wonder whether his explicitly modernist-styled boarding school novel 'The Sorrow', which is presented as the protagonist's work and therefore represents this young man's views on fiction and writing, is truly devoid of narcissism. 'The Sorrow' seems to be perfectly organized in order to, again in the words of Alan Wilde, 'recuperate a lost wholeness in a self-sustaining order of art'. The author of 'The Sorrow' is a modernist hero, who, because of his perfect control of literary language and form, manages to rise above the contingencies of daily life. But in doing so, he abandons all references to the ideological battle and the political tensions afflicting Belgium in the late 1930s. The writer of 'The Sorrow' pushes this historical reality as such outside the walls of his literary construction. As if that reality is some sort of background, irrelevant in light of his view on life. Under no circumstances is this historical reality to affect the aesthetically pure form he is working towards as an artist, as this would also cloud his view on life.

Looking at the work in this way, as an attempt to shape the tragic heroism of the human condition as clearly as possible, the first part of *The Sorrow of Belgium* reads like a late offshoot of the kind of modernism Claus embraced in his earliest novels. Particularly ingenious is the fact that 'The Sorrow' systematically undermines its own poetic principles, though the attentive reader only notices this as the novel progresses. Rather than an offshoot of an anti-mimetic modernism, 'The Sorrow' appears to be a parody thereof. This becomes clear as the chronology of the book gets compromised by the fact that everything that happens in the first part – before the war – returns in the second part as events that are firmly set during the occupation and in the post-war period. The eventual suggestion is that the world of adults – the real Belgium – is composed of residues of the infantile fantasies and narcissistic projections of a boy deprived of his mother (whom he consequently idealizes) and betrayed by his weak biological father (whom he consequently tries to replace by heroic role models with superhuman capabilities).

The Sorrow of Belgium displays some remarkable parallels with Klaus Theweleit's study *Männerphantasien* (*Male Fantasies*, 1977–1978), while Claus also touches upon notions introduced by Barbara Spackman in *Fascist Virilities* (1996). Novels comparable to *The Sorrow of Belgium* on an ideological critical level are, amongst others, Paolo Volponi's *Il lanciatore del giavellotto* (The Javelin Thrower, 1981) and Jonathan Littell's *Les Bienveillantes* (The Kindly Ones, 2006). When it comes to actual influence and inspiration, though, it is Carlo Emilio Gadda that should be mentioned. Claus seems to have modelled his extensive study of life in Flanders after his reading of Gadda's psycho-historical analysis of Italian Fascism *Eros e Priapo* (Eros and Priapus, 1967) and his unfinished novel *La cognizione del dolore* (The Experience of Pain, 1963).

Writing fiction after *The Sorrow of Belgium*

The Sorrow of Belgium is the 'novel of commemoration' Claus had been working towards since *De koele minnaar*. When it comes to the Second World War, every literate Fleming now immediately thinks of this 'Great Flemish Novel.' But also in such later novels as *Een zachte vernieling* (A Quiet Destruction, 1988) and *De Geruchten* (*Rumors*, 1996), and the collection of short stories *De mensen hiernaast* (People Next Door, 1985), Claus continues addressing that war. In 2006 Claus was officially diagnosed with Alzheimer's disease, having suffered memory loss since the turn of the century. Six years before this verdict Claus published his last novella, *Een slaapwandeling* (A Sleepwalk, 2000), an experiment in grotesque realism, in which a structural incapacity to identify people and things, and to call them by their right names, fuels the story. Claus seems to detach his terrible affliction from himself. He has managed to turn his accidental brain dysfunction and the practical problems it causes in his personal life into the starting point of a new kind of writing.

His condition prevented Claus from writing the final grand novel that he had planned: 'Wolken' or 'De wolken' (Clouds or The Clouds). What was meant to have been a radical exercise in perspectivism and ambiguous writing threatened to turn into uninspired gibberish. The 75-year-old Claus, whilst still more than lucid enough to realize this, stopped writing fiction. A few years later, having no ambition to be mothered as a babbling child, he decided upon euthanasia. On 19 March 2008, his life was terminated at his own explicit request.

In interviews Claus claimed that the Flemish way of life and the Belgian culture he had tried to capture in *The Sorrow of Belgium* no longer existed. Similarly, since the fall of the Berlin Wall, the world of *Chapel Road* and *Summer in Ter-Muren* had disappeared. But taken as critiques of modernity, focusing on the irrational, if not downright narcissistic and potentially dangerous aspects of modern culture, these Flemish 'modernist classics' have lost none of their relevance. After all, even after the fall of the Berlin Wall, the idea of limitless progress does still hover over the world as a modern myth. Furthermore, who would dare to claim that the construction of individual and collective identities in a globalizing world cannot develop into new forms of totalitarian control and domination? On these grounds alone Claus and Boon deserve far more international critical attention than they have received after their deaths, and a broader international readership. Available in translations in a number of major languages they can rightly be considered 'world literature'.[2]

Notes

1   Louis Paul, Boon, *Brieven aan Morris* (Maastricht: Gerards & Schreurs, 1989), 37.
2   Translated from the Dutch by Marloes Humbeeck.

References

Bakthin, M. (1984), *Problems of Dostoevsky's Poetics*, Minneapolis: University of Minnesota Press.
Boon, L. (1933), 'De avend vraagt u', *De jonge generatie* 1 (2): 9–10.
Boon, L.P. (1943), *De voorstad groeit*, Brussels: A. Manteau.
Boon, L.P. (1944), *Abel Gholaerts*, Brussels: A. Manteau.
Boon, L.P. (1946), *Vergeten straat*, Brussels: A. Manteau.
Boon, L.P. (1947), *Mijn kleine oorlog*, Brussels: A. Manteau.
Boon, L.P. (1953), *De Kapellekensbaan*, Amsterdam: De Arbeiderspers.
Boon, L.P. (1955), *Menuet*, Amsterdam: De Arbeiderspers.
Boon, L.P. (1956), *Zomer te Ter-Muren. Het 2de boek over de Kapellekensbaan*, Amsterdam: De Arbeiderspers.
Boon, L.P. (1958), *De paradijsvogel. Relaas van een amorele tijd*, Amsterdam: De Arbeiderspers.
Boon, L.P. (1959), *Vaarwel krokodil. Een groteske*, Amsterdam: De Arbeiderspers.
Boon, L.P. (1964), *Het nieuwe onkruid*, Amsterdam: De Arbeiderspers.
Boon, L.P. (1971a), *Pieter Daens: of hoe in de negentiende eeuw de arbeiders van Aalst vochten tegen armoede en onrecht*, Amsterdam: De Arbeiderspers.
Boon, L.P. (1971b), *Mieke Maaike's obscene jeugd. Een pornografisch verhaal voorafgegaan door een proefschrift 'in en om het kutodelisch verschijnsel' waarmee de student Steivekleut promoveerde*, Amsterdam: De Arbeiderspers.
Boon, L.P. (1976), *De Zwarte Hand: of het anarchisme van de negentiende eeuw in het industriestadje Aalst*, Amsterdam: De Arbeiderspers.
Boon, L.P. (1979), *Het Geuzenboek*, Amsterdam: De Arbeiderspers.
Boon, L.P. (1980), *Eros en de eenzame man*, Amsterdam: De Arbeiderspers.

Chase, J.H. (1939), *No Orchids for Miss Blandish*, London: Jarrolds.
Claus, H. (1951), *De Metsiers*, Brussels: A. Manteau.
Claus, H. (1952), *De hondsdagen*, Amsterdam: De Bezige Bij.
Claus, H. (1955), *De Oostakkerse gedichten*, Amsterdam: De Bezige Bij.
Claus, H. (1956), *De koele minnaar*, Amsterdam: De Bezige Bij.
Claus, H. (1962), *De verwondering*, Amsterdam: De Bezige Bij.
Claus, H. (1978), *Het verlangen*, Amsterdam: De Bezige Bij.
Claus, H. (1983), *Het verdriet van België*, Amsterdam: De Bezige Bij.
Claus, H. (1985), *De mensen hiernaast*, Amsterdam: De Bezige Bij.
Claus, H. (1988), *Een zachte vernieling*, Amsterdam: de Bezige Bij.
Claus, H. (1996), *De Geruchten*, Amsterdam: De Bezige Bij.
Claus, H. (2000), *Een slaapwandeling*, Amsterdam: De Bezige Bij.
Daumal, R. (1952), *Le Mont Analogue*, Paris: Gallimard.
Deleuze, G. (1969), *Logique du sens*, Paris: Les Editions de Minuit.
Deleuze, G. and F. Guattari (1972), *L'anti-Œdipe. Capitalisme et schizophrénie*, Paris: Les Editions de Minuit.
Derrida, J. (1967), *L'écriture et la différence*, Paris: Editions du Seuil.
Ellis, B.E. (2005), *Lunar Park*, New York: Alfred A. Knopf.
Gadda, C.E. (1963), *La cognizione del dolore*, Turin: Einaudi.
Gadda, C.E. (1967), *Eros e Priapo: da furore a cenere*, Milan: Garzanti.
Girard, R. (1961), *Mensonge romantique et vérité romanesque*, Paris: Editions Bernard Grasset.
Hoffenberg, M. and T. Southern (pseud. Maxwell Kenton) (1958), *Candy*, Paris: Olympia Press.
Klabund (1929), *Rasputin*, Vienna: Phaidon Verlag.
Littell, J. (2006), *Les Bienveillantes*, Paris: Gallimard.
Michaux, H. (1941), *Au Pays de la Magie*, Paris: Gallimard.
Ostaijen, P. van (1918), *Het Sienjaal*, Antwerp: Het Sienjaal.
Ostaijen, P. van (1921), *Bezette stad*, Antwerp: Het Sienjaal.
Roth, P. (1990), *Deception*, New York: Simon & Schuster.
Scholz, W. von (1935), *Der Zufall und das Schicksal*, Leipzig: Paul List Verlag.
Theweleit, K. (1977), *Männerphantasien, 1: Frauen, Fluten, Körper, Geschichte*, Frankfurt am Main: Roter Stern Verlag.
Theweleit, K. (1978), *Männerphantasien, 2: Männerkörper: Zur Psychoanalyse des weissen Terrors*, Frankfurt am Main: Roter Stern Verlag.
Volponi, P. (1981), *Il lanciatore di giavellotto*, Turin: Einaudi.

16

Small Amsterdam and the World Beyond: The Case of the Magazine *Barbarber*

Bart Vervaeck and Dirk de Geest

A functional perspective on small literatures

These days most contemporary scholars seem to agree that national literatures – literatures which are related symbolically to a specific geographical area – can no longer be considered closed universes.[1] On the contrary, they are considered in constant interaction with their cultural and geographical surroundings. Their supposedly specific identity is hence both relative and by definition relational, dependent on the influences (and non-influences) of other literatures. The ongoing process of globalization – stimulated strongly by the digital revolution – has undoubtedly intensified this intrinsic dynamic. Many people are not only reading books from other linguistic traditions and viewing 'hot' imported television series; they also no longer reflect on the national origin of these cultural products. Moreover, a lot of these artefacts have been produced explicitly for the global market, making use of internationally acknowledged formulae and repertoires and along the way bypassing particular regional characteristics (even though a certain degree of regionalism has itself become part of commercial branding). In this respect, we witness in modern culture a complex interaction between national, international (even global) and subnational (regional and sometimes local) dynamics. It is therefore no coincidence that Goethe's concept of 'world literature' – destined to protect a classic pantheon of literary masterworks from erosion – has recently been re-introduced and re-modelled.[2]

Yet, in spite of the fact that this global and multidimensional view on culture seems self-evident today, a longstanding and prestigious tradition of literary histories and university curricula cultivated (and continues to cultivate) the idea of a 'national' literature in society and in education. Obviously, this is also the case in Dutch culture. Even the recent nine-volume *History of Dutch Literature*, instigated by the Dutch Language Union (Nederlandse Taalunie) and subsidized by both the Dutch and Flemish authorities, still tacitly propagates the national perspective, based on the primacy of the Dutch language.[3] This entails that the intra-linguistic differences between Flanders (the Dutch-speaking part of Belgium) and the Netherlands are discussed in detail time and again, whereas the international dimension of Dutch literature (which implies much more than some influences from abroad) tends to recede into the background.

In this respect, the romantic tradition in historiography still prevails in the Low Countries. According to such national(ist) thinking, literatures can (and maybe still should) be defined in terms of a unique language, a common political and social area, one people, a collectively shared history, and finally a well-defined literary canon of undisputable highlights. Especially in the past, these extrinsic characteristics were often called upon to infer the so-called 'essence' of Dutch literature, its 'soul' or its 'unique character'. Subsequently, particular texts and traditions were selected strategically in order to support and promote this very idea of an identifiable 'Dutch literature', both ideologically and artistically. This resulted in a limited and homogeneous canon and, more generally, in all kinds of selection mechanisms dealing with canonization and, inversely, marginalization. This static view is reinforced by institutions such as the Royal Academy, but also by education, prestigious literary collections and literary prizes. To be honest, this view remains influential, not only in public discussions (amongst others in the context of the ongoing globalization and the multiculturality of today's society) but also in a scholarly context (e.g. writing literary history).

This national focus on literature remains prominent in most Western European cultures, but the model is especially dominant in the case of what could be called 'minor' literatures.[4] These literatures may be considered relatively 'young', since they are often rooted in nineteenth-century nationalism; such a pattern still prevails in post-1989 Central Europe. More specifically, the young nation stresses the search for a culture of its own in order to enhance its own political identity. As a matter of fact, Dutch literature has always remained very conscious of its own 'minor' status, its position in between much larger cultural communities: the German and the French language areas, but also British culture. Throughout history, this particular position has necessitated intense interactions with various surrounding language areas: whereas in earlier periods the German and French influences on Dutch literature were very intense, in the post-war era Anglo-American literature has become very dominant (and even more so in music and film).

Generally speaking, the Dutch language area has profited from these 'foreign' influences by being able to integrate an 'international' dimension into its specific tradition and memory. On the other hand, however, this foreign dimension is constantly weighed against both the specificity and the value of the national literature. These comparisons are often thematized in a temporal sense (some Dutch tendencies manifest themselves later or earlier than their foreign counterparts), in a shift in intensity (some phenomena are observed less frequently or in a more moderate form compared to their original manifestation) or in terms of literary quality (Dutch literature being superior or inferior to its foreign equivalents). Rather than taking such a normative stand, however, we advocate a functionalist approach that is not primarily focused on evaluative comparisons but rather on the way in which 'foreign' and 'domestic' literary dynamics are intrinsically related to each other, and on the manner in which they are characterized and legitimized in discourses on literature. In addition to this dynamic interplay between international, national and local components, it is important to keep in mind that the notion of 'influence' is by no means optimal to designate a broad set of phenomena, ranging from translations and inspirations to networks, intertextual allusions or the implicit use of international models and creative formulae.[5]

Consequently, conceiving of Dutch literature as 'world literature' entails much more than a fashionable theoretical makeover or a traditional comparatist perspective on literary phenomena. Instead, it offers entirely new perspectives on smaller literatures by taking the impact of international circulation and negotiation seriously as constitutive factors for the ways in which so-called national literatures are constructed strategically. In other words, adopting the perspective of world literature leads to an innovative view, not only on the multilayered interactions between languages and cultures, but also on literary phenomena which have hardly been discussed in a supra-national frame. To this end, we will discuss the so-called neorealist magazine *Barbarber* (1958–1971), which has often been characterized as a specifically 'Dutch' magazine, in relation to a dynamic international constellation. Inversely, our considerations can also be interpreted as a way of adding some 'local' flavour to various canonized tendencies in English and American literature and art.

Most publications consider *Barbarber* a typical exponent of the roaring sixties, a very productive era in the Dutch context.[6] As such, the magazine tends to be associated with the spirit of anarchistic non-conformism and humour, and with the strong counterculture of rebellion and anti-establishment characteristic of the period, especially in Amsterdam. Yet, *Barbarber* can hardly be seen as an aggressive symptom or an attempt to destroy bourgeois society and culture; rather it opts for a relativistic tone and attitude, 'looking awry' at reality as it were. This quite unique perspective is generally seen as a kind of practical joke, set up by a few amateurs but gradually evolving into a fascinating Dutch phenomenon. This view may be partly accurate, but it hardly takes into account the fact that this relativistic *Barbarber*-practice became very systematic (albeit in a particular, non-conventional way) over the years. What started as a temporary experiment grew into a specific and easily recognizable poetics. In fact, the improvisational character of the magazine conceals a systematic view on literature and art, which can be derived from the short essays and the many mentions in the magazine itself and which can be related to various tendencies in contemporary international neo-avant-garde[7] aesthetics, in literature, in art and in the media.

Barbarber, a case of its own?

From its very first issues, *Barbarber* intentionally displayed an ambiguous identity. On the one hand, it looked like a regular literary magazine. It assembled texts written by both debuting and already established writers. It was led by an editorial team, it published both thematic and anthological issues, and so on. Moreover, starting with issue 36 (1964), the magazine was taken over by one of the major Dutch publishing houses, Querido. Querido not only produced and distributed the magazine, it also published an anthology selected from the first thirty issues, and it even started a separate series of *Barbarber*-books. In short, what started as an inconspicuous youth magazine grew into an established and influential literary institution of its own, the *Barbarber*-industry.

These resemblances with other prestigious literary magazines, such as *Podium* (Podium), *De Gids* (The Guide) or *Maatstaf* (Measure) were, however, radically contradicted by some other features of *Barbarber*. The most obvious peculiar characteristic was undoubtedly its unique format. After the first issue, the magazine received a new look by folding a folio paper vertically. This exceptional form got a lot of attention in the press. At first sight, it simply looks impracticable, since you cannot place a *Barbarber*-issue in a regular bookcase. When you look at collected volumes in which literary texts of the sixties are brought together, you can easily pick out the *Barbarber*-texts as they have this typical, vertical lay-out. Moreover, this long format is hardly suited to present traditional poems and short stories. In addition, the magazine included photographs and illustrations (although often of a rather bad quality), and the table of contents 'forgot' to mention the authors of many contributions.

These characteristics are partly due to the fact that *Barbarber* started as a student magazine at the time of the so-called 'stenciled revolution', when numerous new and experimental magazines were produced by means of manual stencil duplicator machines. The Folio page was current in this type of printing. Typically, these magazines opted for a horizontal orientation of the folded page. *Barbarber*'s first issue followed that rule, but then it changed and became the exception. The stenciling resulted in a deliberately cheap and amateurish outlook, which was even maintained when the magazine was printed in offset by the professionals at Querido. This illustrates how the particular look of *Barbarber* was a programmatic strategy, a visual image of its 'otherness' vis-a-vis the traditional literary landscape. In fact, such peculiarities could be expected from a periodical that 'refused' a normal name: *Barbarber* as a name or a noun does not exist in Dutch, but it resembles the Dutch word 'Rabarber' (rhubarb), hardly suitable for a literary magazine of any prestige. Other associations, such as the bleating of a sheep or the aural proximity to 'Barbarbarian', add to this seeming lack of seriousness.

Indeed, this unconventional format and layout mirror how *Barbarber* positioned itself as an outsider in the landscape of Dutch literature. On the one hand, it clearly avoided traditional poems or short stories, written in accordance with the acknowledged principles of stylistics and composition by established writers. Instead, the extremely narrow format of the magazine encouraged very short lines and vertically-oriented texts. The editors clearly were not interested in producing a conventional literary magazine. In fact, their primary aim was not even literary.

On the other hand, the editors of *Barbarber* refused to follow the radical neo-avant-garde, which deconstructed (or even destroyed) the very principles of literary discourse in an experimental strategy to defamiliarize readers. These writers opted for *Ander Proza* (Other Prose), which was based on anti-realism, intertextuality and the modernist structures of collage and montage in order to criticize the fundamentals of modern capitalist and bourgeois society.[8] In their view, realist poetics was no more than a celebration of bourgeois ideology, and genuine literature had to propagate a shock treatment that would wake up the bourgeoisie by using complex forms not recognizable from everyday reality. These new forms of literature were originally intended to start a democratic struggle against capitalist inequality, but the resulting experimental anti-stories were extremely hermetic and very highbrow. Consequently, they attracted only a small circle of elitist readers and writers.

Barbarber opted clearly for an entirely different view on literature and its role in society. This alternative was, however, not the result of a kind of polemical strategy. Quite on the contrary, it constituted an informal practice, which transcended not only the prevailing conceptions of literature but also the very boundaries between literature and non-literature. In fact, the subtitle of *Barbarber* is programmatically not 'Magazine for literature', but 'Magazine for texts'. The very short and vague editorial statement in the first issue defends this form of so-called new realism and ends with a transcription of some moves taken from a real game of chess. The prevailing frame of literature as fiction was thus jettisoned for a frame in which literature became a game, a play with components taken from everyday reality. Instead of mere fictive imagination, the reader got a new reality; instead of pessimistic social critique, the reader got a relativistic but almost photographic picture of the world; instead of the refined and highbrow language of literature, the reader got everyday texts and signs, easily recognizable from everyday life.

Generally speaking, the poetics of *Barbarber* may be characterized as 'neo-realist' and 'democratic'. In addition, the magazine focused not on the inner world of the lyrical I but on the unadorned representation of reality, on the referential function of language rather than on fictionality, on the naturally given reality rather than on ingenious construction. To this end, the magazine promoted the device of the 'ready-made', as it minimizes the boundary separating literature from everyday language. Indeed, quite explicitly inspired by the Dadaist artist Marcel Duchamp, the magazine concentrated on 'found' rather than 'made' texts.

Each issue of *Barbarber* can thus be seen as an inventory of reality fragments, concrete situations and objects as well as discursive objects, taken from daily conversations, advertisements, letters, clichés and so on. In between those 'found texts', there also feature original poems and anecdotes, but they resemble the ready-mades as closely as possible. In some cases, the magazine even published 'thematic issues', focusing on one particular type of ready-made. The 'frame issue' became quite famous, since it invited readers to insert texts and images of their own choice in empty frames of various sizes and forms.

This may look plain and unartistic. Yet, the very idea of selecting and presenting fragments from reality – and, moreover, transforming these into verbal texts – may be considered a crucial artistic gesture. It involves a creative impulse, an observer who deliberately chooses and frames certain objects or occurrences and turns them into noticeable events. Moreover, the objects originating from reality are turned into textual constructs arranged typographically and in relation to each other; they are presented to readers who are expected to be surprised, intrigued or simply bored. In other words, the 'natural' and 'realistic' impulse of *Barbarber* can be related to the avant-garde ideas of defamiliarization or 'ostranenie', to use the terms of Russian formalists.

The effect of this ready-made strategy is twofold. On the one hand, the volatile and cursory daily experience of reality is frozen, so to speak. In this way, the attention of the reader is drawn to the peculiarity of surprising facts or of banal routine itself. People are invited to see reality differently, almost in an artistic manner. The selection itself is not random. It is made from the *Barbarber* perspective, i.e. it illustrates *Barbarber* poetics. Found objects thus inevitably become construed objects. Simply placing a title above or a subscript below a picture or a text found in a newspaper is enough to transform this picture or text. Both readers and writers are continually aware of this mingling of the found and the construed, and of the tension between them.

This self-reflective awareness of the thin boundaries between the found and the construed becomes even more explicit as the magazine evolves, since later issues deliberately mingle 'found material' with newly written poems or short prose texts, produced by the editors themselves but also by established literary writers. Moreover, as the magazine evolves, its creative texts look more and more like ready-mades. The new and so-called literary texts seem to be an elaboration of the old, given, so-called non-literary texts. The unique form of *Barbarber* is ideally suited for this purpose: as a gallery, a collection and an enumeration it lists found objects and constructed texts in close proximity, thus forcing the reader to think about the difference and likeness between the two. The final issues present only signed contributions, which seems to reflect the awareness of the editors that their magazine has become part of the literary field and establishment.

It is not just the status of the 'text' – including the 'literary text' – that *Barbarber* revolutionizes. Even more important is the new conception of authorship which the magazine promotes. The perspective on the author differs substantially from other literary magazines, which insisted on the so-called author function, by explicitly promoting 'literary writers' and their texts, for instance by providing biographical facts and other titles published (or still unpublished). *Barbarber* claimed to be nothing else than a 'magazine for texts'.

This textual orientation implied a certain marginalization of the author; the author is no longer the god-like figure who creates from scratch by using his imagination. Rather, he is a humble collector, who finds things that already exist. His main activity lies in combining, ranking and listing words and text fragments. This particular view is manifested in the table of contents in the magazine itself. Whereas the title of the contribution is sometimes followed by its author's name, most remain anonymous. The texts themselves often have no signature. Consequently, the stress lies on the message itself (and supposedly on reality) rather than on the authorial function or on the manifestation of a specific style or oeuvre. Various texts are thus in certain respects homogenized.

Yet, in the course of its evolution, several contributors gained prominence and started to develop their own *Barbarber*-oeuvre. In fact, editors like J. Bernlef and K.

Schippers not only wrote a large number of a-poetic poems, their texts and ready-mades were integrated in their own poetry volumes afterwards. Both Schippers and Bernlef became important, well-known and prize-winning authors from the seventies onwards. They never betrayed their *Barbarber* texts and origins but incorporated them in their subsequent works. In this way, too, *Barbarber* gradually became part of the literary field and establishment.

Neo-avant-garde

Most readers and literary critics emphasized the spontaneous perspective of *Barbarber*'s creative impulses, its potential to present a humoristic and relativizing view on man and the world. This attitude was generally seen as typical of *Barbarber*: a genuine concern for the daily events and the banal, which resulted not in a clinical gaze but in a perspective that betrayed real empathy. This view has been taken over by literary historians. *Barbarber* is depicted time and again as a non-conformist magazine that defied the seriousness of the literary field in a typically spontaneous, even 'childish' tone and with an easily understandable language.

However, on closer consideration this perspective completely neglects the way in which *Barbarber* pointed, quite regularly and explicitly, to its literary and artistic precursors and relatives. Indeed, the magazine frequently referred to texts and images that are staples of what they called new realism. This movement embraced both the popular forms of art such as comic books or Laurel and Hardy films, and the more erudite versions, for example the novels of Nabokov (who gets a special issue) and the poetry of Elisabeth Bishop and e.e. cummings. Again, this goes against the naive claim that *Barbarber* gives us direct access to everyday reality. The magazine may reject hermetic intellectual experiments, but it is itself part of a broad international experimental tradition that links the historical avant-garde of the interbellum with the neo-avant-garde of the sixties.

This fragmentary yet crucial combination of art and life, literature and reality, creating and finding, which lies at the core of *Barbarber* poetics, is turned into a central dimension of modern world literature and art in one of the prominent *Barbarber* publications, *Een cheque voor de tandarts* (*A Check for the Dentist*), which appeared in 1967.[9] This is a collection of essays on the origins and the present-day manifestations of modern art and literature, written by the two most famous *Barbarber* founders and editors, Bernlef and Schippers. The title of the book refers to a famous anecdote told by Marcel Duchamp: in 1919 he did not have enough money to pay his dentist, so he gave him a drawing of a check, to be paid by a non-existent bank. The dentist accepted the work of art as a real check. The boundary between art and real object thus disappeared. This is explained in the text on the front cover of the book, transgressing the boundary between text and paratext. On the back cover, Duchamp is quoted, saying that he later bought the drawing from his dentist to complete his personal collection.

A Check for the Dentist emphatically presents Marcel Duchamp (1887–1968) as the prime inspiration of modern art. According to Bernlef and Schippers, he rescued art from its ivory tower and realized that life is art itself. His ready-mades not only destroyed the elitist distinction between art (supposedly non-functional) and everyday objects (supposedly functional). In presenting a bicycle wheel or a fountain as a genuine work of art he also forced the spectators to look anew at objects they thought they knew well and which they regarded as completely unsuited for art. Objects that had so far been neglected now received artistic attention. As such, Duchamp altered our way of viewing and experiencing things. His art is not just about things (all things become artistic) but about vision, experience. This double perspective coincides exactly with the literary program of *Barbarber*.

As a second source of modern art, Bernlef and Schippers point to the Dadaist Kurt Schwitters (1887-1948). Like Duchamp, he used ready-mades and in so doing not only undermined the classical distinctions between art and everyday objects but also forced the spectators to re-examine their way of looking at things. More specifically, Bernlef and Schippers focus on Schwitters's technique of 'merzing', that is, cutting up objects, such as newspapers articles, and reassembling the pieces into a work of art. This aspect of his work is crucial for the avant-garde figures that Bernlef and Schippers held in high esteem: they (re)combine existing materials. The 'combine paintings' by neo-avant-garde artist Robert Rauschenberg (1925-2008), mixing techniques of painting and sculpture, are just one more example of such a form that the two *Barbarber* authors applaud. Indeed, many issues of the magazine may be regarded as literary equivalents of these mixed collages.

Duchamp and Schwitters were associated with Dada, one of the most extreme forms of the historical avant-garde. It was critical of bourgeois art and society, and as such its art staged a form of protest, explicitly so in the case of Duchamp, more implicitly in the case of Schwitters – at least, that is what Bernlef and Schippers claim. In addition, they use this to distinguish the historical avant-garde from the so-called neo-avant-garde of the long sixties. The latter no longer wanted to protest; it embraced modern life and objects: 'The makers of present-day artistic trends such as Pop-Art, Op-art, Zero Art and New Realism are no longer interested in social protest. They are not opposed to the prevailing social order […], they merely want to approach and intensify reality in a new way' (5). This may be a bald and contentious claim, but it is important for the self-positioning of *Barbarber*: as opposed to the highbrow experiments of the previous generation of the so-called 'Fiftiers' (*Vijftigers*) and the contemporary writers of 'Other Prose', they set aside political critique because that would block the reconciliation of life and art.

As to the neo-avant-garde, Bernlef and Schippers point to two major trends that embrace reality in art, French *nouveau réalisme* (a term introduced by Yves Restany) and American pop art. The interesting thing is that the latter is approached with caution, whereas French new realism is embraced whole-heartedly. There are four basic reasons for this. First, pop art is not a clear movement and many of its so-called proponents, including the iconic Roy Lichtenstein (1923-1997), refuse the term. As there is no group identity, Bernlef and Schippers treat pop artists individually, in separate chapters.

Second, new realism uses ready-mades, whereas pop art tends to transform found objects, for example by enlarging drawings found in comic strips or by painting soup cans. As such, pop art still stands in the tradition of 'art transforming life', whereas new realism, and *Barbarber* with it, want to present life without transformation or interpretation. New realists such as Yves Klein (1928–1962) and Daniel Spoerri (1930–) preserve what they find. Again, this statement may be called into question, but it is essential for the positioning of Bernlef, Schippers and *Barbarber*: they claim to present reality without interpretation. The only American artist who comes close to this in the view of Schippers and Bernlef is Robert Rauschenberg. It is no coincidence that they appreciate him more than any other American artist and that they suggest that his work is close to that of the French new realists (100). When Schippers reviews a 1964 exposition by new realists in The Hague, he says: 'It is remarkable that the objects of reality that have been presented in their pure form, without any transformation, leave the deepest impression' (101). The German *Zero* movement and the Dutch *Nul* ('Nil') movement are interpreted along similar lines, not just as forms of art that focus on silence, emptiness and pure possibility, but as movements that leave out all forms of interpretation and focus on the dimension of reality as such.

A third reason why European new realism takes precedence over American pop art lies in the kind of objects embraced by the two movements. Pop art has a preference for objects typical of consumer capitalism, whereas new realism embraces ordinary objects that we typically neglect. The first kind of objects may give rise to the political and critical inspirations of pop art, and as we said social criticism is alien to *Barbarber*. To Schippers and Bernlef, *Barbarber* explicitly deals with the latter kind of objects. The magazine, they contend, presents 'a reality that had hitherto been neglected in art, simply because it was deemed too ordinary, too unimportant, even though it is the part of reality in which we spend most of our lives' (179).

In an interview with Jan Henderikse, who produces boxes filled with everyday objects, a fourth reason is formulated for the precedence of new realism over pop art: 'Pop Art,' he says, 'was unknown in Europe until 1960. We were already active from 1958 onwards' (162). That goes for *Barbarber* too, as the first issue of the magazine was published in 1958. In other words, Bernlef and Schippers try to sketch a dynamic artistic contemporary scene, but at the same time they still continue to trace historical roots and legitimize their own practice by referring to older models from the historical avant-garde as well.

It is very revealing to see how, at the very end of their essay collection *A Check for the Dentist*, Bernlef and Schippers situate their own magazine *Barbarber* within the international neo-avant-garde constellation just mentioned: Dada (especially Duchamp and Schwitters), new realism and, to a lesser extent, pop art. Before we look at this, we want to sum up the positive characteristics – as seen by Bernlef and Schippers – that distinguish the poetics and the practice of this rich avant-garde tradition. First, and most importantly, it tries to do away with the classical distinctions between life and art by embracing everyday objects. This means that all things are works of art (or can be used as such) and that our everyday life should be seen as a work of art. The essential pragmatic effect of these forms of avant-garde lies here: they force the audience to look anew at familiar things and reality. They force us to re-examine the frames we use. The new realists 'try to chop off every fixed world-view and replace it with an open sensibility, working without prejudices' (100).

Time and again, Bernlef and Schippers point to this defamiliarization as the crux of the matter. Duchamp unsettles our routine way of seeing (12); Jasper Johns (1930–) is preoccupied 'with seeing rather than with interpreting the seen object' (97); Yves Klein focuses on 'the content of our consciousness' (107) since reality is always constructed by our perception and consciousness; the French new realist Arman Fernandez (1928–2005) presents 'a nuanced way of observing reality by refusing to restrict seeing to artistic objects' (137); Martial Raysse (1936–), another new realist, makes us realize that 'the material is only important for conveying a vision' (141). The same goes for the *Zero*-artists, 'who force us to look at our senses and thus to look at reality' (150).

A second aspect that Bernlef and Schippers admire in the tradition they present as the bedrock of *Barbarber* is the objectivity of the artists. They do not want to express themselves. They disappear behind their objects and the possible ways of seeing them. Bernlef and Schippers quote Rauschenberg saying: 'I'd really like to think that the artist could be just another kind of material in the picture, working in collaboration with all the other materials' (86). Rauschenberg proposes 'the objectivity of seeing' (91). Daniel Spoerri's so-called topographies of chance are, he says, like police reports of accidents, 'without even the smallest trace of individuality' (118). The music of Erik Satie consists of sounds as objects that leave no trace of its creator (49–50). Something similar goes for John Cage, who has distanced himself 'from the expressive art of other composers' (63). Chance and spontaneity replace intentionality and conscious control. Art is an exploration of possibilities and follows unforeseen paths. The artist is not the guide but is guided by a process he does not control. In Cage's 'aimless music' (65) and 'sounds-not-intended' (67), this attitude of the artists is regarded as the way to imitate nature's way of producing life.

This changes the traditional vocation of art. The new forms of art Bernlef and Schippers defend no longer want to produce unique objects that will last forever. Instead of for unicity they have a preference for seriality and they play with the tension between sameness and difference. In texts, this tendency manifests itself in lists of nearly identical items; in visual arts it can be seen in series. William Carlos Williams used shopping lists as poems (82); Andy Warhol painted the same can over again: 'for the good spectator he makes clear that one object may be just as interesting as ten, and vice versa' (145). Arman 'repeated the same object over and over' (154); in *Vexations* Satie asked the performer(s) to play the same theme 840 times, thus turning boredom into a part of the artistic experience. Jan Henderikse claims that he and the *Zero* movement were characterized 'by what we produced: repetition' (164). The enumerations and lists that are so central for *Barbarber* should be studied from this perspective.

Instead of eternity, the avant-gardes discussed in *A Check for the Dentist* prefer fleeting, perishable objects that associate art with entertainment. Amusement and humour are vital parts of the project. Schwitters, for instance, 'has amused us. He is a friendly man, who has produced something' (40). The music of Satie is 'a commodity, a consumption product' (53). The defamiliarization Schippers and Bernlef approve of, is, as we said before, not a form of political protest or social critique. In paying attention to neglected objects and parts of life, they come close to what Adorno considered as the negativity of modern art, for instance in the works of Franz Kafka. But contrary to Adorno, they did not draw neo-Marxist conclusions from this. Their art is affirmative rather than critical and/or negative.

Apart from unicity and eternity, there is a third traditional dimension of art's vocation that gets lost in the process: the universal value of the work of art. Since the artists promoted by Bernlef and Schippers seek to turn everyday life into art, they must embrace the local rather than the global: they take objects from their immediate surroundings and they tap into everyday life as they experience it, including all sorts of seemingly unimportant anecdotes and *faits divers*. For an understanding of Jasper Johns and Robert Rauschenberg, 'the anecdotal element is indispensable' (86). William Carlos Williams, quoted by Bernlef and Schippers, insists on the 'rediscovery of a primary impetus, the elementary principles of all art, in the local conditions' (83).

Conclusion

So how does the local magazine *Barbarber* tie in with the international avant-gardes, both of the interbellum and the sixties? The final chapter of *A Check for the Dentist* is devoted to 'New Dutch Poetry' (177–185) and describes *Barbarber* as one of the two leading literary periodicals (the other one being *Gard Sivik/De nieuwe stijl*) responsible for this innovation. It is interesting to see that prose fiction is left out here, whereas it features regularly in the magazine. All the avant-garde characteristics we have just summed up (life as art, objective art, spontaneity and chance, series and lists, entertainment, fleeting and local) are present in *Barbarber* and thus function as links between the international movements and the local magazine. The subtitle of the chapter, 'A Moment in the Events of a Day', summarizes the most important of these links, namely the attention for everyday life, the fleeting and the anecdotal (the term 'events' here does not refer to happenings – an avant-garde technique that Bernlef and Schippers do not like as it does not tie in with the humble and self-effacing qualities of the artist). *Barbarber*'s focus on ordinary things which tend to be neglected is the starting point of the discussion. From this point all the rest follows, including the changed authorial function discussed above.

Bernlef and Schippers underscore the importance of intermediality for *Barbarber*, not just in the magazine (which contained photos, drawings, paintings, objects and so on) but also in exhibitions and meetings the editors organized. Objects found in reality were presented in the exhibitions, without any transformation whatsoever – except of course in the context. The idea was that reality itself should be looked at as if it were an artistic exhibition. It is no coincidence that *A Check for the Dentist* is filled with avant-gardists working in the visual arts: *Barbarber* is all about vision (the way we look at reality) and wants to combine language with images.

However, when they focus on new Dutch poetry, Bernlef and Schippers do stress the linguistic system over the visual. The most important ancestors of this new development are poets themselves, namely William Carlos Williams and Marianne Moore, who rejected the difference between 'poetic' and 'ordinary' (177). They reconciled poetic language with everyday speech, using quotations from conversations. Their poems looked like collages. They contented themselves with observations rather than interpretations and left out all sorts of artistic 'egomania' (77).

The paradoxical effect of Bernlef's and Schippers's effort to link up *Barbarber* with the international avant-garde is that it defends the so-called ordinary (non-artistic) by pointing to an extraordinary artistic tradition. It defends the local by appealing to the international (maybe even global) and it claims to present reality-as-it-is, whereas it continually describes reality in terms of avant-garde poetics. This is how *Barbarber* reconciles (or at least: confronts) the world of everyday life with that of World Literature.

Notes

1. See for instance Theo D'haen, *The Routledge Concise History of World Literature* (London: Routledge, 2012), 5–26.
2. Theo D'haen, David Damrosch and Djelal Kadir (eds), *The Routledge Companion to World Literature* (London: Routledge, 2012). Goethe's use of the term 'World Literature' is discussed in this volume by John Pizer, 'Johann Wolfgang von Goethe: Origins and relevance of *Weltliteratur*', in *The Routledge Companion to World Literature*, 3–11.
3. The tenth volume expounds the project's fundamental approach and choices: Arie Jan Gelderblom and Anne Marie Musschoot, *Ongeziene blikken. Nabeschouwing bij de Geschiedenis van de Nederlandse literatuur* (Amsterdam: Bert Bakker, 2017).
4. Gilles Deleuze and Félix Guattari, *Kafka: Toward a Minor Literature*. Translated by Dana Polan, Foreword by Réda Bensmaïa (Minneapolis: University of Minnesota Press, 1986).
5. A classic introduction to the countless problems involved in the theoretical frame of 'literary influence' is *Influence and Intertextuality in Literary History*, eds Jay Clayton and Eric Rothstein (Wisconsin: University of Wisconsin Press, 1991). A recent study combining theory and practice from the viewpoint of 'World Literature' is Mircea Martin, Christian Moraru and Andrei Terian (eds), *Romanian Literature as World Literature* (New York: Bloomsbury, 2018).
6. So far there has been only one full-length monograph on *Barbarber*: Hans Renders, *Barbarber 1958–1971* (Leiden: Martinus Nijhoff, 1986). In the recent overview of postwar Dutch literature (part of the *History of Dutch Literature* mentioned earlier, in note 3), Hugo Brems devotes a lot of attention to *Barbarber* and in passing places it in the context of the international (neo-)avant-garde: *Altijd weer vogels die nesten beginnen: Geschiedenis van de Nederlandse literatuur 1945–2005* (Amsterdam: Bert Bakker, 2006), 214–230.
7. With the term 'neo-avant-garde' we refer to post-war artistic experiments that explicitly referred to the historical avant-garde of the interbellum. A classic example is 'Neo-Dada'. See for instance David Hopkins (ed.), *Neo-Avant-Garde* (Amsterdam: Rodopi, 2006) and Dietrich Scheunemann (ed.), *Avant-Garde/Neo-Avant-Garde* (New York: Rodopi, 2005).
8. See the anthology Sybren Polet (one of the most noted 'Other Prose' writers) published: *Ander proza: Bloemlezing uit het nederlandse experimenterende proza van Theo van Doesburg tot heden (1978)* (Amsterdam: Bezige Bij, 1978). This anthology explicitly linked the new experiments with the interbellum avant-garde.
9. J. Bernlef and K. Schippers, *Een cheque voor de tandarts* (Amsterdam: Querido, 1967). In the rest of the article, all the quotations taken from this essay will be followed by the bracketed page number.

17

Post-war Dutch Fiction

Hans Bertens

Introduction

Judging by Walter Cohen's (2017) *History of European Literature: The West and the World from Antiquity to the Present*, post-war Dutch fiction does not figure prominently in the annals of European literature, let alone world literature. Only two post-war novelists merit a mention: Harry Mulisch, who died in 2010, and Arnon Grunberg. Adding insult to injury – from a Dutch perspective – both are only mentioned in a note. However, another recent book, Michael Orthofer's *The Complete Review Guide to Contemporary World Fiction* (2016a), is more generous. Orthofer singles out novels by Willem Frederik Hermans, Harry Mulisch, Gerard Reve, Cees Nooteboom and Gerbrand Bakker for specific discussion. And calling Arnon Grunberg the 'most promising young Dutch talent', he tells us to also 'keep in mind' Tim Krabbé, Marcel Möring, Leon de Winter, Herman Koch, Connie Palmen, Hella Haasse and Margriet de Moor (Orthofer 2016a). Dutch critics would rank Haasse with Hermans, Mulisch, Reve and Nooteboom, and they would place Bakker, who so far has only published three novels, in his 'keep in mind' category. And they would add a number of writers that Orthofer does not mention. In fact, in another publication Orthofer himself has lavishly praised the fiction of A.F.Th. van der Heijden. However, Van der Heijden's work has not been translated into English and does therefore not feature in the *Complete Review Guide*. For the same reason it is absent from Juri Dilevko et al.'s earlier *Contemporary World Fiction: A Guide to Literature in Translation* (2011), whose selection of Dutch authors overlaps with

Orthofer's, but is again more generous and pays attention to most of the authors that Dutch criticism would add to Orthofer's list (notably Tessa de Loo, Arthur Japin, Renate Dorresteijn and J. Bernlef).

The case of Van der Heijden, whose work has been translated into German, brings us to a first complication. If we define world literature as those literary texts that circulate beyond their culture of origin then a good many, if not most, contemporary Dutch novels qualify as world literature. In the course of the 1980s Cees Nooteboom and Harry Mulisch became fairly big names in Germany and since the Frankfurt Book Fair of 1993, at which Dutch-language literature was a so-called 'Guest of Honour', almost every well-received novel has been translated into German. To illustrate this: practically the whole output of the prolific Maarten 't Hart is available in German, whereas only two of his novels have been translated into English (meeting with little enthusiasm). As the German newspaper *Die Welt* noted in 2002, 'the growth of interest in Dutch literature has been really explosive'. For *Die Welt* that explosive growth was first of all the result of the reading public's changing taste, of 'the renaissance of storytelling' and the 'victory march of realism' after the experimentalism, postmodern or otherwise, of the earlier decades (Wilterdink 2017: 50). Looking back in 2017, Nico Wilterdink summed things up: 'Many more translations of Dutch fiction and literary nonfiction appear in German than in other languages; the translated books are, in general, better sold in Germany than anywhere else, and these books and their authors receive much more media attention than elsewhere' (51).

But does a translation into German – which certainly implies circulation beyond its culture of origin – turn a Dutch novel into world literature? German, with well over 95 million speakers, is after Russian Europe's most prominent language, but it does not have any presence outside Europe. One therefore hesitates to claim novels that have only been translated into German for world literature. But even if a novel is translated into both German and French its readership would still be largely, if not wholly, confined to Continental Europe. Translation into English, then, would seem a necessary condition for entering the pantheon of world literature – but it is, of course, not a sufficient one. Translation does not automatically entail circulation and it certainly does not entail lasting circulation. (Since data on circulation are scarce, I will be guided here by a novel's critical reception.) Still, translation is a crucial first step towards international recognition for Dutch authors and the decades-long invisibility of post-war Dutch fiction in the UK and the USA has much to do with the virtual absence of translations. As Ria Vanderauwera's *Dutch Novels Translated into English: The Transformation of a 'Minority Literature'* (1985) shows, in the first decades after the war contemporary serious fiction was only sporadically translated. There were some exceptions, to which I will return, but the state of affairs is perfectly illustrated by the fate of Simon Vestdijk, until the mid-1950s the most important Dutch novelist, of whose fifty-two novels only two – and not necessarily the best – appeared in English. Even his *De kellner en de levenden* (*The Waiter and the Living*, 1949), which offers a wildly inventive account of a phantasmagoric, Hieronymus Bosch-like trial run for the Day of Judgment, was never translated.

However, compared to that early period, the next two decades were even worse. As Vanderauwera noted, 'the translation of Dutch fiction dramatically declined after 1960' (70), with only Heinemann's Bibliotheca Neerlandica (soon discontinued) and Twayne's Library of Netherlandic Literature (victim of the same fate) carrying the combined flags of Dutch and Flemish fiction. Both publishers largely ignored contemporary Dutch novels (one of the books published by Twayne was Marcellus Emants's *A Posthumous Confession* [(1894) 1975], translated by the later Nobel Prize winner J.M. Coetzee).

It was not until the 1980s that the number of translations into English picked up again, leading to the international success of Nooteboom's *Rituals* (1983; *Rituelen*, 1980) and *In the Dutch Mountains* (1987; *In Nederland*, 1984), and Mulisch's *The Assault* (1985; *De aanslag*, 1982). It is not entirely clear why English interest in contemporary Dutch fiction increased, but an important role must have been played by the independent non-profit organizations funded by the Dutch government that since the mid-1950s had worked to promote Dutch literature and that in 2010 would join forces to create the Dutch Foundation for Literature. The Foundation represents Dutch literature at international Book Fairs, introduces the work of Dutch novelists to foreign publishers, and subsidizes translations. As Nicky van Es and Johan Heilbron claim in a recent study, 'Many works which have been translated with the support of the DFL would probably not have been translated otherwise, as the economic risks involved for foreign publishers to translate books from relatively unknown authors would be too big' (2015: 301). In any case, in the course of the 1990s, Dutch fiction gained a measure of visibility in the anglophone world, in particular in the UK. As *The Independent* noted in 2000:

> A few Dutch novelists made it into English in the early 1990s, the scholarly Cees Nooteboom at their head. Over the past couple of years, a growing stream has been breaching the dyke. Hugo Claus, Renate Dorrestein, Arnon Grunberg, Tessa de Loo, Margriet de Moor, Marcel Möring, Harry Mulisch and Connie Palmen may not be brand names to British readers, but at least some of their work is available in English. (Wilterdink 2017: 45)

With a 2018 budget of €1,769,530, the Foundation has a substantial impact. It subsidized the publication of Mulisch's *The Assault*, Nooteboom's *In the Dutch Mountains*, a new translation of Hermans's *The darkroom of Damocles* (2007; *De donkere kamer van Damocles*, 1958), and Haasse's *The Tea Lords* (2010; *Heren van de thee*, 1992). But it also, and generously, subsidizes less prominent writers. In fact, the international career of all of the writers mentioned by Orthofer and by Dilevko, Dali and Garbutt. was helped along by the Foundation or one of its precursors. All of them had one or more novels translated into German and into English with Foundation subsidies. The aim is to make Dutch fiction more competitive on an international market to which English-language fiction has unimpeded access and where a positive reception in Germany usually plays a role in getting published in the UK or the USA. As Van Es and Heilbron noted, 'Germany is indeed the most significant market for Dutch authors in quantitative as well as in qualitative terms, that is, for obtaining some measure of international visibility' (2015: 305).

The novels

As the 2007 republication of Hermans's *The Dark Room of Damocles* (originally published in 1958) illustrates, the Foundation actively promotes fiction that it considers unjustly neglected. In some cases this has led to unexpected results. When in 2016 Gerard Reve's *De avonden: een winterverhaal* was published in the UK as *The Evenings: A Winter's Tale* (2016), the well-known English writer and critic Tim Parks began his review in *The Guardian* with a rather unusual question: 'It is so rare, as a reviewer, to come across a novel that is not only a masterpiece but a cornerstone manqué of modern European literature, that I hesitate before setting down a response: what can I say, in a world of hype, that will put this book where it belongs, in readers' hands and minds?' Answering his own question, Parks went on to tell his *Guardian* readers that *The Evenings* was 'up there with Henry Green's *Party Going*, and Beckett's *Waiting for Godot*' (2016). This sounds exactly like the sort of hype Parks referred to, but he was only one voice in an admiring chorus. In the *Irish Times* Eileen Battersby called *The Evenings* a 'poised, brilliantly sustained masterwork of comic pathos', 'one of the finest studies of youthful malaise ever written' (2016). For the *Observer* the book was 'a dark masterpiece' (Alberge 2016), for the *Sunday Telegraph* 'an undisputed classic' (Van Loon 2016), for *The Economist* 'an existential masterwork worthy to stand with Beckett and Camus' ('Madness in Words: The Strange Depths of Dutch Fiction' 2017), and for the *TLS* an 'orphaned masterpiece' (Whiteside 2016). In the United States, where *The Evenings* was published the following year, its reception was not much different.

The Evenings was originally published in 1947, when the author was twenty-three years old. Breaking with the intellectualism of the pre-war period the novel set the tone for much of the fiction published in the first couple of decades after the Second World War. Its protagonist, 23-year-old Frits van Egters, who lives with his well-meaning but not particularly inspiring parents in an Amsterdam apartment, tells us in meticulous detail how he struggles to get through the last ten days of 1946. During the day he is distracted by his job, in spite of its monotony, but at night he cannot escape the claustrophobic oppressiveness of his dead-end life. The only relief is sardonic, occasionally sadistic, banter with his brother and with friends, who do not always know how to take his seeming callousness – which does, indeed, often mask grudging affection. Although the novel's apparent nihilism met with a good deal of criticism, it won that year's award for best first novel and has ever since been generally considered one of the best novels of the whole post-war period. In spite of this, it would probably never have reached an English-speaking audience if the Foundation had not contacted Pushkin Press, the novel's British publisher, and had not subsidized its translation.

The case of *The Evenings* is extreme, but a considerable time lag between a novel's publication in Dutch and its publication in English was until fairly recently the rule rather than the exception – if it gets translated at all. As Tim Parks noted in 2011 in the *New York Review of Books*, 'much of the best postwar fiction written in Dutch has only recently become available in English', adding that 'much still remains to be done' (2011). A history of post-war Dutch fiction based on English translations would indeed miss out on some likely contenders for world literature status, but let me (largely) stay with what is actually available in English. Although in *The Evenings* the war is hardly ever mentioned, the almost intolerable bleakness of Frits's sense of things must be traced back to the five-year German occupation of the Netherlands, which ended with a famine that took 18,000 lives in the densely populated western provinces. The war is one of the two most prominent themes in the first post-war period (the other one being life in the Dutch East Indies, the colony that in 1949 gained independence as the Republic of Indonesia, leading to an exodus of repatriating Dutch nationals). The most famous book to come out of the war surely is the diary of 15-year-old Anne Frank, who had died in Bergen-Belsen in 1945 (*The Diary of a Young Girl*, 1952; *Het Achterhuis*, 1947) – Etty Hillesum's *An Interrupted Life* (1984; *Het verstoorde leven*, 1981) is another famous one – but diaries fall outside the scope of this chapter. However, Margo Minco's novellas *Bitter Herbs* (1960; *Het bittere kruid*, 1957) and *The Glass Bridge* (1988; *De glazen brug*, 1986), based as they are on the author's personal experience, give us an equally convincing account of what it was to be Jewish during the German occupation. Minco, the only survivor of an orthodox Jewish family, gives us a sober picture of how the ever more oppressive anti-Jewish policies of the German occupiers, which her family initially shrug off as most of all inconvenient, end in raids and mass arrests. After her fictional alter ego's lucky escape, she is moved from hiding place to hiding place by the Dutch Resistance, her hair bleached to look less Jewish. In *The Glass Bridge* (1988) Minco focuses on the war's long-term effects. After the war her protagonist now retains the new identity the Resistance had given her – that of a deceased Dutch girl whose records it had stolen. Years later, wanting to learn more about the dead girl, she finds a heart-breaking story. The war has destroyed her original identity, which was intimately tied up with her family, but her new one will never be completely hers.

Probably the best novels to deal with the German occupation and the ambiguities, moral and otherwise, of the period, are Hermans's *The Darkroom of Damocles* and Mulisch's *The Assault* (1985). In Hermans' novel a mousy tobacconist, Henri Osewoudt, believes he plays an important role in the Dutch Resistance by acting upon the orders of a certain Dorbeck, to whom he bears an uncanny likeness. When after the war Dorbeck disappears, Osewoudt cannot explain his wartime activities, which included murders, and which would seem to have served the Germans rather than the Resistance. Osewoudt sinks into a nightmare from which there seems no escape. But so does the reader who by then has come to doubt Osewoudt's grasp of reality and no longer knows what or whom to believe. Did Dorbeck really exist or was he the product of Osewoudt's delusions? We cannot know. *The Darkroom* is a gripping thriller that suggests that reality is ultimately unknowable. When the new translation appeared in the UK, the *Telegraph* hailed it as 'A Dutch classic to rival Camus' (Mukherjee 2007) and reviewing the French translation in *Le Monde* Milan Kundera spoke of 'ce roman si riche, si improbablement riche' (this novel, so rich, so improbably rich, 2007). Mulisch's *The Assault* is equally engrossing, but its ambiguities are moral rather than epistemological. In the final stages of the war a notorious collaborator is killed by the Resistance near the home of the novel's protagonist, a boy in his early teens who is the only one of his family to survive the standard German reprisals. But he has seen, before the Germans arrive at the scene, that the family's neighbors carried the victim's body away from their own house to that of his parents, obviously trying to escape the Nazis' revenge. More than thirty years later he finally hears the full story: those neighbours, who had mysteriously kept to themselves, were hiding a Jewish family, saving them from deportation and death. For Mulisch, the war was an endless source of moral ambiguity. He was the son of an Austro-Hungarian father who had served in the First World War and a Jewish mother who, like Mulisch himself, only survived the war because Mulisch senior became a high-ranking collaborator (and was, after the war, sentenced to a substantial prison sentence). No wonder he occasionally claimed that he *was* the war.

However, the war recedes into the background in his magnum opus, *The Discovery of Heaven* (1996; *De ontdekking van de hemel*, 1992). *The Discovery* is a monumental extravaganza that features celestial beings, a cosmic plot, an intense and brilliantly realized intellectual friendship, passionate sexual relationships, but also, as J.M. Coetzee remarked in an otherwise quite favorable review, 'internal squabbles of Dutch politics of the 1970s [that] are largely wasted on the foreign reader' (Coetzee 1997a). The friendship develops between the astronomer Max Delius, whose father was an Austrian-born Dutch Nazi, and the linguist Onno Quist. Celestial conversations in the novel's prologue and in the introductions to its various parts reveal that, apart from everything else, they are pawns in a celestial master plan to end the covenant God made with Moses, a covenant broken anyway because mankind, led astray by Lucifer, has allowed a belief in science and technology to displace its former belief in God. But it is Quinten, the son of either Delius or Quist (the novel does not tell us), who has been chosen for the actual task of stealing Moses's tablets from their hiding place in Rome – here we are getting into Dan Brown territory – so that they can be returned to Heaven and can there be presented to the 'Chief'. Wildly improbable, piling coincidence upon coincidence, *The Discovery of Heaven* yet was internationally acclaimed.

Mulisch returned to the war with *Siegfried* (2003; 2001), which tries to answer fundamental, if not metaphysical, questions about Adolf Hitler, and more in general the war remained and still remains a powerful theme. Let me offer two examples. In Tessa de Loo's *The Twins* (2000; *De tweeling*, 1993) German twin sisters meet again by chance after having been separated for seventy years and, first haltingly, then with increased passion, tell each other the story of their lives. One sister stayed in Germany, opposed Nazism, but still married an SS officer who died in action, the other grew up in the Netherlands and married a Dutch Jew who perished in the camps. Both stories are excruciatingly painful and raise intractable ethical dilemmas. So does, in another illustration of the war's long shadow, Arnon Grunberg's *The Jewish Messiah* (2008; *De joodse messias*, 2004), but in a radically different way. In Grunberg's novel a Swiss adolescent, incited by his grandfather's history as a camp guard, converts to Judaism, intending to dedicate his life to comforting the Jews. But where De Loo opts for detailed realism, Grunberg lets his imagination run wild, with his protagonist becoming the lover of a rabbi's son, learning Yiddish in order to translate *Mein Kampf*, emigrating to Israel where he enters politics and becomes prime minister, and ending in catastrophic self-delusion. Grunberg, whose mother survived Auschwitz, cannot, unlike Mulisch, really believe in the power of literary art to bring us insight or relief. *The Jewish Messiah* is a deliberate exercise in slapstick and caricature that ultimately refuses to take its characters seriously. Still, Grunberg is an extraordinarily inventive and talented writer, as we see in *Tirza* (2013; 2006), the story of a well-intentioned father's obsessive and ultimately fatal love for his daughter.

But to return to the immediate post-war period and its other major theme. Maria Dermoût lived most of her life in the Dutch East Indies and the East Indies dominate her small but exquisite output. Her *The Ten Thousand Things* (1958; *De tienduizend dingen*, 1956) and *Yesterday* (1959; *Nog pas gisteren*, 1951) lead us into a tropical world where all things seem animated and to have a life of their own, sensed but not really understood by the Dutch colonials who remain outsiders in this world in which the natives, whose motives they never fathom, move with natural ease. *The Ten Thousand Things* – in 1958 one of *Time*'s books of the year and republished as a New York Review Book in 2002 – makes clear that for all its sensuous beauty this is not paradise, as is soon realized by Felicia, a young woman who returns with her baby son from Europe to the island where her formidable grandmother still awes the native population. Violence may unexpectedly erupt in this world where reality and myth are a continuum and the past exists side by side with the present. Dermoût is the most uncolonial of writers. As her translator Hans Koning remarks in his introduction to *The Ten Thousand Things*, 'She did not write about her Indies as a Dutch woman, or as a Javanese or an Ambonese. Hers was a near-compassionate disdain for the dividing lines, the hatreds and the fears' (Koning 2002: vi–vii).

This might also be said of another writer born and raised in the Indies, Hella Haasse. Although Haasse ranged far and wide in a long literary career, the East Indies, which she had left forever in 1938, remained a source of fascination. In *The Black Lake* (2012; *Oeroeg*, 1948) a Dutch boy and his Sundanese friend find that the call for independence and the Dutch colonizer's puzzled and hurt reaction irreparably damage their friendship. Haasse allowed herself more scope in *The Tea Lords* (2010; *Heren van de thee*, 1992) which uses letters and other historical materials to present the fortunes of a tea planter and his family in western Java between the 1870s and 1918. As Haasse tells the reader in an afterword: 'The material is not invented, but it has been selected and arranged according to the demands of a fictional approach' so that 'individual fortunes and developments' – Haasse's abiding interest – are highlighted (Haasse 1992: 297; my translation). Still, it takes Haasse's intimate knowledge of the East Indies to make the novel come to life and to make us understand the otherwise puzzling behaviour of the planter's wife, who is Dutch, but unlike him born and raised in the East Indies and far more attuned to native beliefs and superstitions. Having come to doubt the powers of the historical novelist, Haasse had moved away from her earlier, rather traditional historical novels such as *The Scarlet City* (1954; *De scharlaken stad*, 1952), to the almost documentary approach of for instance *Mevrouw Bentinck* (1978; Mrs. Bentinck), which told the stormy life of Countess Bentinck (1715–1800) through her own letters and those of her countless correspondents (among them the royalty of several European nations and that other tireless letter writer Voltaire). In *Mevrouw Bentinck*, which in 2003 was awarded the French Prix du Meilleur Livre Etranger, Haasse abbreviates, offers connecting passages and generally oils the narrative machine, but over 90 per cent of the novel's text comes directly from Countess Bentinck's correspondence.

Dermoût and Haasse had left the Indies before the Japanese invasion that followed the attack on Pearl Harbor, and so escaped internment, but the vast majority of Dutch nationals, women and children included, spent the war under often miserable circumstances in internment camps run by the Japanese army. In *Sunken Red* (1988; *Bezonken rood*, 1981), the French translation of which won the Prix Fémina Etranger, Jeroen Brouwers recreates life in such a camp in his characteristically baroque way, focusing on the way his beloved mother and other Dutch women were stripped of their dignity.

Adriaan van Dis was born after the war in a recently repatriated family, but the war in the East Indies looms large in his fiction. His *My Father's War* (2004; *Indische duinen*, 1994) and *Ik kom terug* (*I'm coming back*, 2014) present the thinly disguised history, both in the East Indies and in post-war Holland, of his traumatized family, with a focus on his emotionally damaged father, who survived a Japanese concentration camp, forced labour, and one of the Second World War's worst shipwrecks, and his formidable and impossible mother.

But of course there is more to post-war Dutch fiction than the German Occupation and life in the Dutch East Indies. Like the rest of the Western world, in the 1960s the Netherlands shook off the shackles of the almost Victorian mores that had reasserted themselves after the war and the Dutch cultural revolution went further than most in the individual liberties, sexual and otherwise, it brought. That revolution has been chronicled extensively. Sometimes the focus is narrow, as in those novels by for instance Maarten 't Hart and Jan Wolkers in which sensitive yet stubborn protagonists face dogmatic Calvinism and emotionally repressed and domineering fathers. At other times the scope is nothing less than panoramic as in the novel cycles of A.F.T. van der Heijden, but there is almost always detailed realism and a strong autobiographical element. A marked exception is the work of Cees Nooteboom, who began publishing in the 1950s, but only won both national and international recognition with *Rituals* (1983), which was awarded the American Pegasus Prize and was later republished with an introduction by A.S. Byatt (2013) that called Nooteboom 'a great European novelist'. *Rituals* contrasts the rather aimless, although quite pleasant life of charismatic protagonist Inni Winthrop with the fanatically regimented lives of father and son Taads, who each in their own way fill the existential emptiness of their days with obsessive rituals (in the case of the younger Taads the Japanese tea ceremony). Nooteboom is the most exhaustively translated of all post-war Dutch novelists, and there should be no doubt that he has an impressive international reputation, but in retrospect his work, which after *Rituals* began to explore metafictional themes, seems to suffer from a lack of substance. Reviewing *In the Dutch Mountains* (1987), an imaginative rewriting of Hans Christian Andersen's 'The Snow Queen,' and taking on board Nooteboom's other work, J.M. Coetzee put his finger on the problem: 'for all the wit, for all the insight into the self and its fictions, for the elegance of the style, there is finally not enough feeling to drive the story forward' (Coetzee 1997b).

It seems to me that Coetzee's criticism goes to the heart of much fiction published in recent decades. As Orthofer notes in an overview, 'in writing what they know, contemporary Dutch authors write from a shared foundation, a perspective of relative security and prosperity [...]. The Netherlands remains a fairly cohesive and homogeneous society, even by European standards, and this is one of the strengths – and, quite possibly, limitations of its fiction' (2010: 185). Hans Koning had earlier offered a similar diagnosis: '[Dutch] fiction reflects the undramatic calm of a well-governed and advanced country' (2002: vi). Indeed, much contemporary fiction is very well done and reaches foreign audiences. But that fiction, accomplished as it is – a quality generously recognized by foreign reviewers – as often as not lacks a sense of urgency. The calm may not be wholly undramatic, but it does lack dramatic intensity. There are, of course, exceptions. Marcel Möring's *In Babylon* (1999; 1997) reconstructs the history of a Jewish family in a magical realist setting and *Bonita Avenue* (2014; 2010) by Peter Buwalda – whose 'brilliance is entirely unique' according to one British reviewer (Saunders 2014) – is a wild ride through contemporary intellectual and sexual culture. Let me mention two more novels that have recently attracted international attention. *These Are the Names* (2015; *Dit zijn de namen*, 2012) by Tommy Wieringa follows the ever more desperate journey of a small group of refugees who have been tricked by smugglers and dumped in an arid no-man's land without any prospect of ever reaching their destination. In a complementary story line an aging chief of police in the same area finally realizes that the songs his mother long ago sang to him were Yiddish songs and that he himself must be Jewish too. In the end the two stories ingeniously merge. In what *Kirkus Review* called 'a quiet masterpiece' ('*These Are the Names by Tommy Wieringa*' 2016). Wieringa confronts one of our age's most urgent problems while avoiding melodrama or easy solutions. Another novel that recently found an international audience was Gerbrand Bakker's *The Twin* (2008; *Boven is het stil*, 2006), which won the International IMPAC Dublin Literary Award. In *The Twin* a middle-aged farmer, who lives alone with his ailing father on an isolated farm, gives us a meticulously detailed account of his daily activities and of his strained relationship with his dying father, who is completely dependent on his help. Gradually his repressed emotional life begins to reassert itself, but Bakker's treatment of that emotional – and possibly sexual – reawakening is so subtle that we are left with a sense of mystery (as is often the case with Haasse too). It is Bakker's refusal to spell things out that lifts *The Twin* above what otherwise would have been the accomplished realism that many contemporary Dutch novelists have mastered.

References

Alberge, D. (2016), 'Dutch to Share Their Dark Masterpiece, 70 Years on', *The Observer*, 23 October 2016. Available online: https://www.theguardian.com/books/2016/oct22/gerard-reve-evenings-first-english-translation.

Bakker, G. (2008), *The Twin*, London: Harvill Secker.

Battersby, E. (2016), 'The Evenings Review: A Masterwork of Comic Pathos,' *The Irish Times*, 12 November 2016. Available online: https://www.irishtimes.com/culture/books/the-evenings-review-a-masterwork-of-comic-pathos/.

Brouwers, J. (1988), *Sunken Red*, New York: New Amsterdam.

Brems, E., O. Réthelyi and T. van Kalmthout, eds (2017), *Doing Double Dutch: The International Circulation of Literature from the Low Countries*, Leuven: Leuven University Press.
Buwalda, P. (2014), *Bonita Avenue*, London: Pushkin.
Byatt, A.S. (2013). Available online: http://www.cees.nooteboom.com/?cat=14&lang=en.
Coetzee, J. M. (1997a), 'Their Man on Earth,' *New York Review of Books*, 6 March 1997. Available online: http://www.nybooks.com/articles/1997/03/06/their-man-earth.
Coetzee, J. M. (1997b), 'Blowing Hot and Cold,' *New York Review of Books*, 17 July 1997. Available online: http://www.nybooks.com/articles/1997/07/17/blowing-hot-and-cold/ (accessed 26 February 2019).
Cohen, W. (2017), *A History of European Literature: The West and the World from Antiquity to the Present*, Oxford: Oxford University Press.
Dermoût, M. (1958), *The Ten Thousand Things*, New York: Simon & Schuster.
Dermoût, M. (1959), *Yesterday*, New York: Simon & Schuster.
Dilevko, J., K. Dali and G. Garbutt, eds (2011), *Contemporary World Fiction: A Guide to Literature in Translation*, Santa Barbara, CA: Libraries Unlimited.
Dis, A. Van (2004), *My Father's War*, London: Heinemann.
Dis, A. Van (2014), *Ik kom terug*, Amsterdam: Atlas Contact.
Emants, M. (1975), *A Posthumous Confession*, Boston, MA: Twayne.
Es, N. Van and J. Heilbron (2015), 'Fiction from the Periphery: How Dutch Writers Enter the Field of English-Language Literature,' *Cultural Sociology* 9 (3): 296–319.
Frank, A. (1952), *The Diary of a Young Girl*, Garden City, NJ: Doubleday.
Grunberg, A. (2008), *The Jewish Messiah*, New York: Penguin.
Grunberg, A. (2013), *Tirza*, Rochester, NY: Open Letter.
Haasse, H.S. (1992), *Heren van de thee*, Amsterdam: Querido.
Haasse, H.S. (2010), *The Tea Lords*, London: Portobello.
Haasse, H.S. (2012), *The Black Lake*, London: Portobello.
Hillesum, E. (1984), *The Interrupted Life: The Diaries, 1941–1943*, New York: Pantheon.
Hermans, W.F. (2007), *The Darkroom of Damocles*, London: Harvill Secker.
Koning, H. (2002), 'Introduction', in M. Dermoût, *The Ten Thousand Things*, v–x, New York: New York Review Books.
Kundera, M. (2007), '*La Poésie noire et l'ambiguïté*,' *Le Monde* 25 January 2007. Available online: http://www.lemonde.fr/livres/article/2007/01/25/la-poesie-noire-et-l-ambiguite_859442_3260.html (accessed 26 February 2019).
Loo, T. De (2000), *The Twins*, New York: Soho.
Loon, A. Van (2016), 'A Life in Ten Evenings,' *Sunday Telegraph*, 13 November 2016.
'Madness in Words: The Strange Depths of Dutch Fiction' (2017), *The Economist*, 9 March 2017. Available online: https://www.economist.com/books-and-arts/2017/03/09/the-strange-depths-of-dutch-fiction (accessed 26 February 2019).
Minco, M. (1960), *Bitter Herbs*, Oxford: Oxford University Press.
Minco, M. (1988), *The Glass Bridge*, London: Peter Owen.
Möring, M. (1999), *In Babylon*, New York: William Morrow.
Mukherjee, N. (2007), '*A Dutch Classic to Rival Camus*,' *The Telegraph*, 13 September 2007. Available online: https://www.telegraph.co.uk/culture/books/fictionreviews/3667861/A-Dutch-classic-to-rival-Camus/.
Mulisch, H. (1985) *The Assault*, New York: Pantheon.
Mulisch, H. (1996), *The Discovery of Heaven*, New York: Viking.
Mulisch, H. (2003), *Siegfried*, New York: Viking.
Nooteboom, C. (1983), *Rituals*, Baton Rouge, LA: Louisiana State University Press.

Nooteboom, C. (1987), *In the Dutch Mountains*, Baton Rouge, LA: Louisiana State University Press.

Orthofer, M.A. (2010), 'A Fundamental Cosmopolitanism in Lomark and the Wieringerwaard: Contemporary Dutch Fiction from a Foreign Perspective', *De Revisor. Jaarboek voor nieuwe literatuur* 1: 177–187.

Orthofer, M.A. (2016a), *The Complete Review Guide to Contemporary Fiction*, New York: Columbia University Press.

Orthofer, M.A. (2016b), 'Michael Orthofer on A.F.Th. van der Heijden', *De Revisor*, Jaargang 2016: 15–19.

Parks T. (2011), 'The Dutch Are Coming!' *New York Review of Books*, 27 October 2011. Available online: http://www.nybooks.com/articles/2011/10/27/dutch-are-coming/ (accessed 26 February 2019).

Parks, T. (2016), 'The Evenings by Gerard Reve Review – A Masterpiece, Translated at Long Last', *The Guardian*, 9 November 1016. Available online: https://www.theguardian.com/books/2016/nov/09/the-evenings-by-gerard-reve-review/ (accessed 26 February 2019).

Saunders, K. (2014), 'Bonita Avenue by Peter Buwalda', *The Times*, 26 April 2014. Available online: https://www.thetimes.co.uk/article/bonita-avenue-by-peter-buwalda-dvtt39x5f35 (accessed 26 February 2019).

'*These Are the Names by Tommy Wieringa*' (2016), *Kirkus Review*, 8 November 2016, http://www.kirkusreviews.com/book-reviews/tommy-wieringa/these-are-the-names/ (accessed 26 February 2019).

Vanderauweraa, R. (1985), *Dutch Novels Translated into English: The Transformation of a 'Minority Literature'*, Amsterdam: Rodopi.

Vestdijk, S. (1949), *De kellner en de levenden*, Amsterdam: Bezige Bij.

Whiteside, S. (2016), 'A Hectic Schedule: A Neglected Dutch Masterpiece, Finally Available in English', *TLS*, 30 November 2016. https://www.the-tls.co.uk/articles/private/a-hectic-schedule/ (accessed 26 February 2019).

Wieringa, T. (2015), *These Are the Names*, London: Scribe.

Wilterdink, N. (2017), 'Breaching the Dyke: The International Reception of Contemporary Dutch Translated Literature', in E. Brems O. Réthelyi and T. van Kalmthout (eds), *Doing Double Dutch: The International Circulation of Literature from the Low Countries*, 45–65, Leuven: Leuven University Press.

18

Expansions Without Affect; Identities Without Globality: Global Novels in Dutch from an Agonistic Perspective

Hans Demeyer

Agonistic global literature

The concept of world literature has been criticized as a 'one-worldist paradigm' or of 'one-worldedness', a literary monoculture homogenizing and absorbing difference (Apter 2013: 77, 83) so many times that by now one might shy away of these claims in fear of predictability. However, to merely acknowledge this threat, Shu-Mei Shih points out with regard to the specific oneworldliness of Eurocentrism, only displaces a problem that should be at the centre of any discussion of world literature. For her it should be 'a literature that critically examines its own construction by suspiciously interrogating all claims to universalisms, while acknowledging that any criteria emerging from these interrogations will be open to new questioning' (2004: 29). Shih's statement can be complemented by Djelal Kadir's focus on 'worlding' as it equally considers world literature less as an object than as an imputable practice: 'the locus where the fixed foot of the compass that describes the globalizing circumscription is placed' (2004: 2). Comparatists need to take into account the position from where they describe, analyse and thus design world literature in order not to produce unwanted and unthought-of effects that confirm and reproduce particular power relations that assimilate and standardize singularity and difference.

We could theorize and organize this relation between the particular locus and the universal totality in the construction of world literature through a model of agonistics as it has been developed by the Belgian political philosopher Chantal Mouffe (e.g. 2013) and has been adapted for literary studies by Sven Vitse and myself (Demeyer and Vitse 2014). Key terms in Mouffe's model, which elaborates on the theoretical framework she developed earlier with Ernesto Laclau (Laclau and Mouffe [1985] 2001), are 'antagonism' and 'hegemony'. The former points to the ineradicable dimension of negativity that pervades each society and that forecloses the possibility of a society beyond conflict and contestation – a society of harmonious totality based on a rational or liberal consensus. From this perspective any social order can only be the result of decisions over its organization. Those articulations that temporarily fix power relations and social meanings are what Mouffe calls hegemonic. Hegemony is accordingly described as the situation in which 'a *particular* social force assumes the representation of a *totality* that is radically incommensurable with it' (x). This particular 'totality', a result of power relations, can always be contested and a healthy democratic society should recognize, legitimize and channel this conflict and pluralism into a democratic debate about society's organization: 'antagonism (struggle between enemies)' is thus transformed into 'agonism (struggle between adversaries)' (Mouffe 2013: 7).

An agonistic approach to literary studies does not only conceive of society as determined by this antagonistic dimension, but the literary field and literary studies as well. Furthermore it does not consider any hegemonic situation – within society, within the literary field – as a neutral situation and perceives of any literary phenomenon as an (implicit or explicit) intervention in that situation. The task of an agonistic literary study is to interpret this intervention with regard to the current hegemony: it can reproduce dominant opinions and political views, criticize them according to different degrees or do both at the same time (Mouffe 2013: 89–90). This analysis has likewise an agonistic character: it can never merely be descriptive or neutral, but is always beset by values and thus holds a particular relation to a social and literary hegemony.[1] Let me clarify these theoretical observations by means of several recurrent topics and dominant attitudes in the debate on world literature.

Within this discussion the hegemonic situation has been alternatively called 'Eurocentrism' or 'Westerncentrism'. Many criticisms of this hegemony are based on the premise that an on-going intercultural dialogue can foster a consensual totality in which particularities coexist without losing their uniqueness. Mariano Siskind identifies this structuring horizon as follows: 'world literature as a cosmopolitan project that aims at articulating cultural difference in order to foster emancipatory goals' (2010: 355). Therefore one needs to 'map the asymmetric interaction of hegemonic and subaltern cultural and economic forces' in order to arrive at the desired representation of 'a diverse globe as a reconciled multicultural totality' (358). From an agonistic perspective this 'reconciled multicultural totality' that is seemingly 'beyond hegemony' (Mouffe 2013: 19–41) is unattainable as it glosses over the antagonistic dimension of the political: the impossibility to reconcile different and conflicting visions within an overriding ensemble; the denial that any identity can only be constructed through difference and that any collective identity ('us') needs another ('them') as its constitutive outside (4–5). This political dimension is lost as Siskind shifts from *socio-economic* inequality toward *cultural* universality: a politics of recognition takes over a politics of the distribution of power (Shih 2004: 22).

The loss of the political can be found as well in advocated modes of reading that revolve around detachment and distance. I think of Franco Moretti's 'distant reading' that wants to replace close reading by scientific data analysis, and Damrosch's understanding of world literature as a mode of disengaged reading: 'not one involving identification or mastery but the discipline of distance and of difference' (2003: 300). In both, although at different levels, there is a stress on disidentification and a turn towards differing degrees of objectivity that claim a certain level of neutrality. From an agonistic point of view, these models underappreciate the 'centrality of collective identities and the crucial role played by affects in their constitution' (Mouffe 2013: 6): attachments cannot be put aside that easily. The modes of reading proposed by Damrosch and Moretti do not acknowledge their own poetics as part of a collective identity in the construction of the (elliptical or world system) literary field in which they read.[2]

In this chapter I would like to contribute to an agonistic study of world literature through an ideological critical reading. The ideological effect of a literary work is never determined – there is no strict relationship between an aesthetic technique and a political or ideological effect – and is thus bound to a contextual interpretation (Demeyer and Vitse 2014: 533–536). The aim of this interpretation is, as said, to demonstrate the way in which literary works intervene in a hegemonic situation. In my reading of two recent novels in Dutch, *Een vorm van vermoeidheid* (*A Form of Weariness*, 2008) by the Flemish author Jeroen Theunissen and *Gebrek is een groot woord* (*Lack Is a Big Word*, 2018) by Dutch writer Nina Polak, their interventions show a disintegration between a Western identity and the (availability of the) global. Making use of Lauren Berlant's notion of genre as an affective contract, I discuss how both novels invoke the genre of the global novel but do not provide the expected affective confirmations. This is related to a more general affective crisis in Western identity.

Genre of the global novel: Affect, historicity

My starting point is Lauren Berlant's definition of genre in *The Female Complaint*:

> a genre is an aesthetic structure of affective expectation, an institution or formation that absorbs all kinds of small variations or modifications while promising that the persons transacting with it will experience the pleasure of encountering what they expected, with details varying the theme. (2008: 4)

I would like to highlight three elements. First, Berlant characterizes genre as an aesthetic way of knowing, a worldview or spirit that generates particular expectations. This definition does not only hold true for aesthetic practices but for ordinary life as well: genre is both 'a mode of cultural creation and interpretation' as well as 'a shaping force in lived experience' (Jackson 2015). If genres function at the level of semiosis and constitute reality-effects (Frow 2015: 20), it is possible to understand that Berlant considers identity or gender as a type of genre. She writes: 'femininity is a genre with deep affinities to the genres associated with femininity' (Berlant 2008: 3). Genres thus become a mental category and offer the means by which people are able to interpret their own experiences and situate them within a meaningful script that creates the expectation that they will attain their goal.

Secondly, genres are collectively acknowledged forms of recognition: our shared classification of genres allows for easy identifications. Applied to everyday experience, this implies that the desire to meet genre expectations can beget a normative character. If women model themselves to dominant genres of femininity, they are performing normative ideas of femininity. Berlant rightfully points out how this normativity can be the central affective expectation as it promises ordinary comfort.

Thirdly, genres are not static but open to all sorts of modification and variation. Therefore, genre can become an 'alternative model for practicing historicism' (Martin 2017: 7). Despite their modifications genres remain identifiable: they offer recognition but at the same time adapt to new cultural situations. This way we can trace through genres tensions between the present and the past, between innovation and repetition. What Berlant's definition adds is a dimension of ideological critique: '[genre] locates real life in the affective capacity to bracket many kinds of structural and historical antagonism on behalf of finding a way to connect with the feeling of belonging to a larger world, however aesthetically mediated' (2008: 4).

Here the accredited influence of Fredric Jameson's work on genre in *The Political Unconscious* ([1981] 2002) is visible. There he famously states that 'the production of aesthetic or narrative form is to be seen as an ideological act in its own right, with the function of inventing imaginary or formal "solutions" to unresolvable social contradictions' (2002: 64). Genre thus becomes a diagnostic method: the analysis of genre is able to track social contradictions and as such offers a way to interpret a literary work's intervention within a hegemonic situation.

In my reading of the novels by Theunissen and Polak I will mostly focus on the work of affect in genre as a method to trace the social and the historical. In *Cruel Optimism* Berlant understands affect theory as a new development in ideology theory and claims that 'the aesthetic or formal rendition of affective experience provides evidence of historical processes' (2011: 16). Affect needs to be understood here as a proprioceptive and corporeal sensibility with which people mediate their relation to the world: how they respond to their environment, adjust themselves to the world and assess their belongings – attachments that need to serve the continuity between themselves and their surroundings and are negotiated through abstractions such as class, gender, race or nation. One way in which one can affectively mediate oneself in relation to the world is genre. Understanding it as an 'affective contract' (275), genres promise 'certain kinds of affective intensities and assurances' that may add to one's sense of belonging to a conventional and recognized (social) world (Berlant 2008: 4).

In discussions of world literature much attention has been paid to the globalization of a genre. Scholars such as Franco Moretti (2013b) and Wai Chee Dimock (2006) make use of genre instead of national literatures or distinct periods as a means to map the evolution, interconnection and movement of literary forms over the globe. In this chapter I would rather focus on genres of the global: not so much using genre as a totalizing concept over literary texts but to look at the aesthetic form of genre through which texts imagine the globe (Hoyos 2015: 11, 22). The genre of the novel has historically always invested in images of the global. Their subject is the '*bourgeois conquérant*' and they put 'into circulation effective accounts of the global reach of the bourgeoisie in terms of the production and reproduction of discourses of universal adventure, exploration, and colonial profit' (Siskind 2010: 343). Under the flag of modernity and the universal these novels represent travels and adventures after which newly discovered spaces across the globe are taken over in order to expand and confirm bourgeois universality. Through transforming the local experience into a global adventure, these novels offer the affective 'intensity and excitement available to those individuals willing to embrace their bourgeois subjectivity and explore its universalizing potential' (343).

Franco Moretti discusses how the pre-modern values of adventure stories are combined in the novel with the opposing bourgeois values of calculation, reasonableness and carefulness (2013a: 25–35). The latter are the values of work that legitimize the new social power (30), whereas the former are part of 'a trope of expansion: capitalism on the offensive, planetary, crossing the oceans' (2013b: 177). Both values are incompatible but nevertheless coexist in the novel without formal integration. For Moretti this points at a structural contradiction within the bourgeois soul between a rational and irrational impulse, a contradiction that will never be resolved (2013a: 35) and, as we will see, is still present as a problem in *A Form of Weariness* and *Lack Is a Big Word*.

In both novels the main characters experience a conflict between a rational impulse to build a home and lead a conventional life, and an irrational impulse to leave that home behind and travel the world. The protagonists suffer from detachment, indifference and weariness, an affective crisis they wish to solve through enacting the genre of the global novel, of travel and adventure. But their affective expectations about the global as 'a bourgeois playing field, ready and available for science, profit and amusement' are not met (Siskind 2010: 343): no assurance of belonging is given. This failure in affective fulfilment points to a historical shift in the hegemonic collective Western identity in relation to the global.

A Form of Weariness

The form of weariness that affects Horacio Gnade, the main character in Jeroen Theunissen's second novel, can be read as an allegory for a form of weariness that characterizes the Western world. The novel presents a conflict between (rational) order and (irrational) romanticism. The desire for ironic distance and control is in a constant struggle with the question of emotional and political engagement. This conflict is staged at the individual level when Horacio leaves behind his ordered and detached life to undertake a romantic flight of which it is unclear if it will lead to any sort of attachment. This is situated within a social and cultural constellation in which the contemporary globalized West implies order, whereas Latin America still symbolizes a romantic possibility. The individual and the global do however not match: globalization, its unequal effects and its resulting political struggles do not allow for an affectively satisfying integration.

Horacio is the prototype of the civilized world-citizen who has been able to achieve what many would consider the conventional good life fantasies that were promised by Western social democratic states after the Second World War. He was born in Argentina, but now lives with his wife and daughter in the German picturesque provincial town of Tübingen, where he is a professor in Spanish Literature. He values measurability and steadiness highly and is 'een burgerlijke man die probeert om werk, hobby's en financiële zekerheid belangrijk te vinden. Hij spaart voor zichzelf, voor zijn gezin en voor zijn kind' (a bourgeois man who tries to find work, hobbies and financial security important. He saves for himself, for his family and for his child) (11). Horacio *tries* – he is well aware that his identification with this perceived norm of normality is unstable and that irrationality is always a possibility: 'Hij is een normale man, maar heeft nu eenmaal chaos in zich. Hij ook, hij beseft dat, dus moet hij opletten voor romantiek' (He is a normal man, but it's so that he has chaos in him. He as well, is aware of that, so he needs to be watchful for romanticism) (9). He resists this tendency through irony and uses it to keep any emotional or political commitment at a distance. This irony betrays a more general detachment. Horacio only identifies with the *form* of the life patterns that he understands to be normal, but does not engage himself with their *content* and thus voids those forms of emotions, ethics or ideals: 'Hij is een man die niet gelooft, maar wel functioneert' (He is a man who does not believe, but does function) (11).

Horacio's domestication of excess returns at the social level. From his secure position in Europe the earth remains the bourgeois' playground:

> Hij is iemand die wordt gebombardeerd met oproepen om op avontuur te gaan, om niet stil te zitten, om het leven op zich af te laten komen, om met overgave en met passie te consumeren, om kosmopoliet te zijn al weet hij dat kosmopolitisme vooral het provincialisme van de rijken is.
> (He is someone who gets bombarded with summons to go on an adventure, to not sit still, to let life get at him, to consume with devotion and passion, to be cosmopolitan although he knows that cosmopolitanism is mostly the provincialism of the rich.) (143)

The scale of the globe becomes provincial. The West does not open its borders but incorporates the global within its own order. In this way it cancels the romantic desire for the unreachable and unattainable through its circulation and consumption of goods and through tourism: 'Toerisme is het einde van de romantiek' (Tourism is the end of romanticism) (10).

Horacio nevertheless does depart after a couple of eccentric events that he cannot rationalize (he shadows the same woman twice; he drunkenly beats up two young men). He claims to be somewhat tired (64), but he actually only experiences a *form* of weariness. It is an unspecified affective state of which he is unable to define the causes or to cure it. His flight is improvised, unsure of what it aims to escape and to acquire, and his inner conflict between irony and desire remains present throughout without arriving at a solution.

Before he left Horacio had counted all his belongings: 'Het is als structuur. Dus streeft hij extreme nauwkeurigheid na' (It is about structure. Thus, he strives for extreme accuracy) (64). This rational measurability is complemented by an irrational adventure, but in contrast to the global novel here this contradiction does not serve the expansion of identity. Its affective expectation is not met, as Horacio's expedition does not result in an accumulation of money nor in an affective fulfilment and accomplishment of an identity. There is no investment and consequently no return. Not surprisingly, the novel ends when Horacio has spent all his money.

The novel represents the other side of the totality of globalization when Horacio ultimately arrives in his home country and more specifically in Patagonia. There he might find what he desires: 'Hij wil alleen maar vermoeid zijn, hij wil rust, hij wil vast kunnen stellen dat hij niets meer na te streven, niets meer te kopen of te doen heeft' (He only wants to be weary, he wants peace, he wants to ascertain that he has nothing left to strive for, to buy or to do) (143). He is however confronted with the West's drive for expansion and investment and the ecological and political problems that creates. In Europe, globalization offered him a 'golden cage' (64); in Latin America globalization imposes a cage: '*La Jaula*', the cage, is the name the Mapuche use for the area that the multinational Grosso (based on Benneton) has (not entirely legally) acquired and fenced off with barbed wire (202). For the Mapuche Indians the land is a sacred area in which a divine creature resides, whereas for the multinational firm it is an investment for profit. These multinationals legitimize their actions in line with century-old practices: in the name of '"vooruitgang", "beschaving" en "toekomst"' ('progress', 'civilization' and 'future') the goals were to make 'de onbewoonde leegte bewoonbaar en exploiteerbaar' (the uninhabited emptiness inhabitable and exploitable) (149).

Horacio gets involved in the struggle against this exploitation of raw materials through his semi-girlfriend Valeria who shoots a documentary about the Mapuche. She is the one who most strongly challenges Horacio's inability to overcome his detachment. Against her rhetorical violence, in which she declares Grosso the enemy, Horacio emphasizes the need for nuance, neutrality and objectivity (205). Valeria responds that it is simply a battle between good and evil: 'en wij zijn verdomme de goeden. "Je gedoe over nuance is alleen maar een deel van je probleem" roept ze' (and we are the good ones for Christ's sake. 'Your going on about nuance is only a part of your problem' she shouts) (205). Because Horacio only responds to the form of Valeria's attack and does not take any political stance, his critique can only perpetuate the status-quo. He falls back upon a formal attachment to normality that continues the affective disconnection from his (global) environment.

Lack Is a Big Word

The 30-year-old Nynke 'Skip' Nauta, the main character in Nina Polak's second novel, considers herself an outsider who likes to shrug off the question 'where is home' and to sail the oceans instead as a means to water down the past (2018: 28). When in Cannes she accidently meets her 'second' family Zeno, she accepts their offer to return 'home' to Amsterdam. Throughout the novel, Skip reflects upon her lack of attachment and connection with a family, a home or a lover, and her desire to roam the earth freely. The novel explores this affective confusion tentatively in both a psychological and social manner, but I will focus here on those aspects that bear upon the relation between a home and the globe and how it constitutes (the affective lack in) Skip's identity.

In *Lack is a Big Word* the bourgeois soul is still torn between rationality and irrationality. Skip's environment takes her sailing mostly as an irrational adventure and tries to persuade her to make a rational choice: to start investing in the good life fantasies of creating a home, getting a mortgage, founding a family. Especially her former boyfriend Borg, with whom she has an adulterous relationship during her return, is prone on getting her to settle. Although Skip expresses at times a desire for peacefulness and order and feels herself for instance attracted to the peace and spaciousness of the Zeno family house, Amsterdam does however not constitute a home for her.

On the one hand she understands Amsterdam as a self-sufficient globe, similar to Horacio's Tübingen, that promises possibility and mobility: 'Waarom zou je, waarom zou *iemand* zo'n centrum van mogelijkheden eigenlijk verlaten, behalve misschien voor een lastminuteweekje magisch Dubrovnik van CheapHolidays.com?' (Why would you, why would *anybody* in fact leave such a centre of possibilities, except maybe for a last-minute week of magical Dubrovnik through CheapHolidays.com?) (34). On the other hand Skip's upbringing in both a working and well-educated middle class makes her attitude towards Amsterdam's cosmopolitan freedom ambiguous. Skip used to live with her ill and depressed mother in Osdorp, a working-class neighbourhood and described as 'de jungle buiten de grachtengordel' (the jungle beyond the Canal District) (119). For her family there has never been any 'CheapTickets.com' nor the realization that the world is available for exploration (224). Even before her mother's death she found a second home in the upper (middle) class area where the cosmopolitan Zeno family lives, but she is also in touch with a Turkish migrant family, which hints at another type of global mobility. This social stratification is not resolved in the personal sphere, and Skip never fully integrates with either one of those communities. At the wedding of the Turkish daughter, her observations move between an exaggerated sensation of collectivity and a faint sense of home, and a feeling of existential nausea and claustrophobia with regard to Amsterdam and a vague longing for the sea. She may participate but always remains a spectator as well. It is the use of theatre imagery that points to this passive and aloof stance.

Skip describes her 'schouwburggevoel' (theatre feeling) as 'alsof me daar in die donkere bonbondoos, in gecomprimeerde vorm het hele bestaan, de hele globe, werd voorgehouden, als een vers, warm koekje, net buiten bereik' (as if in that dark chocolate box, in a compressed form, the whole of existence, the whole globe, was presented to me, like a fresh, warm biscuit, just out of reach) (96). The globe is almost *given* to her. Her desire to sail is not underpinned by an active project to conquer the seas and to beget a sense of identity, but to be passively led on by them: 'om het leven zijn gang met me te laten gaan' (to let life take its course with me) (131).

Already as as a 10-year-old Skip was fascinated by the sea: 'dat de zee ook geeft en dat ze bovendien alles met alles verbindt, overal met overal' (that the sea gives as well and furthermore that it connects everything with everything, everywhere with everywhere) (179). Interestingly, this romantic image is replaced by a vaguely economic discourse in a class speech on sea-containers: they make the circulation of goods possible, and may create employment in other countries. In his novella, Borg's alter-ego criticizes the 20-year-old Skip's desire for the stories and adventures of those first Dutch explorers who were also violent colonizers: 'het kwam niet in haar op om een verbinding te zien tussen haar geromantiseer, haar exotisme en het brute kolonialisme, het paternalisme en de corruptie waarvan de geschiedenissen getuigden' (it did not occur to her to see a connection between her romanticization, her exoticism and the brutal colonialism, the paternalism and the corruption of which these histories testified) (158). In reality Skip is not insensitive to that history, but she remains nostalgically attached to the genre of the *bourgeois conquérant* as they offered and continue to offer her a substitute for the lack of connection she encounters elsewhere: 'alle vergane Hollandse glorie die ik me eigen heb gemaakt omdat ik me toch iets eigen moest maken' (all the lost Dutch glory that I have made my own because I had to make at least something my own) (204). Although sailing is a means to escape the question of a home, it is nevertheless attached to a national self-image and history.

The novel nevertheless does represent a break with these. One of the monuments in honour of this past and which Skip holds dear, the statue of the ship-boys of Bontekoe, after a famous early twentieth-century novel celebrating an early seventeenth-century voyage to the Dutch East Indies, on the quay of the Dutch city of Hoorn, is defiled by anti-colonial activists. This hurts her, although she recognizes the justice of the act:

> Ik weet niet of het de door de activisten beoogde schaamte was, of irritatie omdat mijn geliefde symbolen nu besmeurd waren met een vermoeiende gewetenskwestie. Het was de combinatie waarschijnlijk – hetzelfde verdrietige verzet, de vernedering, waarmee een kind aanhoort dat Sinterklaas een leugen is. Een absurd doodsbericht dat uiteindelijk slechts geaccepteerd en erkend kan worden.
> (I do not know if it was the shame intended by the activists, or irritation, because my beloved symbols were now tainted with a tiring matter of conscience. It was probably the combination – the same sad resistance, the humiliation, with which a child hears that Sinterklaas is a lie. An absurd obituary that in the end can only be accepted and acknowledged.) (201–202)

The novel thus tentatively links this ideological failure of imperialism as a grand narrative with Skip's affective crisis (Vitse 2018). Her attachment is one with desire for the world, but it is unclear if her sailing can deliver upon the affective promises and can confirm her identity. Rather than progressive, her movement is far more stationary: 'Van types zoals ik [...] zou je kunnen beweren dat we rondjes draaien om de illusie van vooruitgang te behouden. Maar het zijn toch zeker glorieuze rondjes. We bewegen, we gaan door' (Of types like me [...] you could claim that we are turning around in circles to maintain the illusion of progress. But they are all the same certainly glorious circles. We move, we continue) (28).

To conclude: Growth without affect

In the opening section of this contribution I advocated reading a literary work as an intervention and I focused on the affective aspects of the global novel in which the local bourgeois experience is expected to be confirmed on a global scale. To conclude I now want to discuss the failure of this promise in *A Form of Weariness* and *Lack Is a Big Word* by situating it in its ideological and socio-economic context.³

In *Cruel Optimism* Lauren Berlant discusses how the good life fantasies of social democracy have dissolved along with the assurance and legitimacy of modernity as a project of socio-economic progress. It continues or finalizes the process that Jean-François Lyotard had previously described in *La condition postmoderne* (1979; *The Postmodern Condition*, 1984): the dismantling of the community and of modernist meta-narratives and the replacement of the true and the just with market efficiency. In a post-ideological context, it seems as if the quantitative accumulation of capital and the qualitative development of civilization now coincide in a dogma of growth – a growth that no longer serves circumscribed ideological needs or aims. As the ecological economist Herman Daly states: "'Anything goes' is a convenient moral stance for a growth economy because it implies that anything also sells. Expanding power and shrinking purpose lead to uncontrolled growth for its own sake' ([1987] 2017: 34). This growth is nevertheless sold as our panacea, as the efficient allocation of accumulated capital through markets that will solve the problems of the world, even those created by the pursuit of capital itself.

At the level of the individual a similar shift has taken place. According to Alain Ehrenberg (1998) the sixties mark a change in our understanding of the individual: no longer constituted through discipline and circumscribed norms, the emphasis is now put on the individual's own responsibility and initiative to make life worthwhile and significant. In this project experience plays an important role. Mark Greif (2016) points at the use of a specific 'concept of experience' as the '*method* of life' to render it meaningful (78). In this frame experience is something we desire: each moment needs to be lived to the fullest and experience can be acquired at any place and at any time. The subject amasses and accumulates them: their 'sheer *quantity*' ('had or missed') becomes more important than their quality (good or bad) (79). Because experience is strived for, however, this specific method creates loss and disappointment: 'The sense that each or any moment might be won for experience, but is lost to time instead, leaves a residue of perpetual loss' (84). This particular 'concept of experience' can thus lead to an affective crisis: the feeling not to exist (sufficiently), to exist without direction. The guilt one felt when the expected norms were not met, Ehrenberg argues, has been replaced by a sense of failure when one feels incapable of taking responsibility for one's own happiness. This feeling of shortcoming can eventually lead to depression and weariness to become oneself.

These affective crises are apparent in Horacio's formal attachment to a form of normality that involves detachment from any system of values or beliefs and in Skip's difficulties to decide to which place and fantasy she wishes to attach herself in a metropolitan community that promises her that 'iedereen kan [...] zelf kiezen wie hij is' (everyone can [...] chose himself who he wants to be) (Polak 2018: 119). Because of the lack of a larger ideological narrative, their 'solutions' to these issues remain affective: the search for absolute weariness that would release Horacio from the bombardment of messages that tell him to '*Live the Life You Imagined*' (Theunissen 2008: 145) and Skip's nostalgic attachment to genres of world exploration in order not to come to terms with the past and future of her own life and those of the nation.

Coda

In *An Ecology of World Literature* (2015) Alexander Beecroft rightfully points at the frequent use of 'economics as a controlling metaphor' to theorize world literature (18). From this perspective it is not difficult to see that a logic of growth and accumulation is implicitly at work in the model. No better example than Franco Moretti who not only wishes to broaden comparative literature's focus from the river Rhine to the globe, but who also wishes to expand the texts under scrutiny: to the canon should be added the 'Great Unread'. His aim is '"to make the literary field longer, larger, and deeper": historically longer, geographically larger, and morphologically deeper' (2013b: 161). But its logic is equally present in Damrosch's conception of world literature as 'writing that *gains* in translation' (2003): it accumulates value within the 'Great Conversation' of world literature (142).

In his polemical study *Literary Criticism: A Concise Political History* (2017) Joseph North discusses the debate on world literature in terms of 'expansion excitement' (180–188). The enthusiasm specifically refers to a breakout from the specialized fields in literary studies narrowly defined by language, time and place to open up to the different periods and contexts that this new scholarly labour brings together and studies in their interconnectivity. Interestingly, North goes on to suggest that the collective work of world literature has 'the structure of a prisoner's fantasies: [...] the real investment has been in the breakout itself, rather than in any specific proposal about what we would do once we were free' (185). As if the quantitative growth in periods, places, literatures, languages is at the same time considered as a qualitative development towards an emancipation of which the aims are unspecified but which might be taken to be similar to the earlier discussed cosmopolitan horizon of a 'reconciled multicultural totality' (Siskind 2010: 358). I would like to suggest that this line of action is structured around the assumption that the development of knowledge and critical consciousness or dialogue is considered as a good in itself. In our post-ideological context the accumulation of this good is deemed positive without assigning it any circumscribed values of truth and justice. There is however no reason to believe that there is a determinate relation between knowledge and righteousness as this depends on the political articulation within a hegemonic situation.

Beecroft suggests that we replace economy by ecology as controlling metaphor and to understand literature 'in an ecological relationship to other phenomena – political, economic, sociocultural, religious – as well as to the other languages and literature with which it is in contact' (2015: 19). From an agonistic perspective this metaphor is to be preferred to an economic one as the incorporation of these ecological dimensions more easily foregrounds difference and inequality across a global scale. These problematize the assumption of a global literary community and may allow for a map of different hegemonic blocks in which literature and knowledge intervene differently. With its emphasis on the mutually interconnected relations between different forms of input, this model also more insistently asks us to determine how we want our knowledge to interact and to make an impact. It foregrounds 'the inescapable moment of decision – in the strong sense of having to decide within an undecidable terrain' (Mouffe 2013: 3); a moment which the mere accumulation of knowledge if not disposes of then at least postpones indefinitely.

Notes

1. The preceding two paragraphs summarize very briefly and translate several sentences from 'Revanche of conflict? Pleidooi voor een agonistische literatuurstudie' (Demeyer and Vitse 2014).
2. Moretti's background is obviously in Marxist poetics, but as Joseph North (2017: 109–116) points out, his arguments in 'Conjectures on World Literature' are only residually political. Shih furthermore questions Moretti's systematic approach that embeds the singular literary work too strongly within systematic laws. 'Although situated in a structure or a system, a literary text also always exceeds its structure or system in the power of its effect and affect,' she writes in terms that are in line with a consideration of the literary work as an intervention within a hegemonic situation (2004: 20).
3. The following repeats some arguments of 'De affectieve dominant: Een ideologiekritische lezing van recent Nederlandstalig proza' (Demeyer and Vitse 2018), but reframes them within a discourse of accumulation and growth. That discourse, which also informs the coda, is informed by a reading of Benjamin Kunkel on 'Steady-State Aesthetics' which can be listened to here: http://theartistsinstitute.org/artists/sept-dec-2017/recordings/ (accessed 17 April 2018).

References

Apter, E. (2013), *Against World Literature: On the Politics of Untranslatability*, New York: Verso.

Beecroft, A. (2015), *An Ecology of World Literature: From Antiquity to the Present Day*, New York: Verso.

Berlant, L. (2008), *The Female Complaint*, Durham, NC: Duke University Press.

Berlant, L. (2011), *Cruel Optimism*, Durham, NC: Duke University Press.

Daly, H. ([1987] 2017), *On the Steady State*, New York: Pocket Institute.
Damrosch, D. (2003), *What Is World Literature?* Princeton, NJ: Princeton University Press.
Demeyer, H. and S. Vitse (2014), 'Revanche of conflict? Pleidooi voor een agonistische literatuurstudie', *Spiegel der letteren* 56 (4): 511–538.
Demeyer, H. and S. Vitse (2018), 'De affectieve dominant: een ideologiekritische lezing van recent Nederlandstalig proza', *TNTL* 134 (3): 220–244.
Dimock, W.C. (2006), 'Genre as World System: Epic and Novel on Four Continents', *Narrative* 14 (1): 85–101.
Ehrenberg, A. (1998), *La Fatigue d'être soi. Depression et société*, Paris: Odile Jacobs.
Frow, J. (2015), *Genre*, 2nd edn. London: Routledge.
Greif, M. (2016), *Against Everything: On Dishonest Times*, New York: Verso.
Hoyos, H. (2015), *Beyond Bolaño: The Global Latin American Novel*, New York: Columbia University Press.
Jackson, V. (2015), 'The Function of Criticism at the Present Time', *Los Angeles Review of Books*, 12 April 2015. Available online: https://lareviewofbooks.org/article/function-criticism-present-time/ (accessed 5 May 2015).
Jameson, F. ([1981] 2002), *The Political Unconscious: Narrative as a Socially Symbolic Act*, London: Routledge.
Kadir, D. (2004), 'To World, To Globalize – Comparative Literature's Crossroads', *Comparative Literature Studies* 41 (1): 1–9.
Laclau, E. and C. Mouffe ([1985] 2001), *Hegemony and Socialist Strategy. Towards a Radical Democratic Politics*, New York: Verso.
Lyotard, J.-F. (1978), *La condition postmoderne*, Paris: Minuit.
Lyotard, J.-F. (1984), *The Postmodern Condition*, Manchester: Manchester University Press.
Martin, T. (2017), *Contemporary Drift: Genre, Historicism, and the Problem of the Present*, New York: Colombia University Press.
Moretti, F. (2013a), *The Bourgeois: Between History and Literature*, New York: Verso.
Moretti, F. (2013b), *Distant Reading*, New York: Verso.
Mouffe, C. (2013), *Agonistics. Thinking the World Politically*, New York: Verso.
North, J. (2017), *Literary Criticism: A Concise Political History*, Cambridge, MA: Harvard University Press.
Polak, N. (2018), *Gebrek is een groot woord*, Amsterdam: Prometheus.
Shih, S.-M. (2004), 'Global Literature and the Technologies of Recognition', *PMLA* 119 (1): 16–30.
Siskind, M. (2010), 'The Globalization of the Novel and the Novelization of the Global. A Critique of World Literature', *Comparative Literature* 62 (4): 336–360.
Theunissen, Jeroen (2008), *Een vorm van vermoeidheid*, Antwerp: Meulenhoff/Manteau.
Vitse, S. (2018), '"Je bent familie of je bent maar weinig". *Gebrek is een groot woord* van Nina Polak', *Dietsche Warande & Belfort*, August 2018. Available online: https://www.uitgeverijvrijdag.be/dw-b/literaire-kritieken/je-bent-familie-of-je-bent-maar-weinig-gebrek-is-een-groot-woord-van-nina-polak (accessed 6 August 2018).

19

Orpheus in the Trenches: Modes of Translation in Stefan Hertmans' *War and Turpentine*

Frank Albers

In October 2017 *The New York Times* asked Simon Schama what the most recent great book was he had read. Schama replied: 'Stefan Hertmans' *War and Turpentine*.' He praised 'the staggering richness' of the novel's language, calling it 'brutal, deep, haunting'. He found the book 'mesmerising from page one, which has the painter-grandfather formally dressed complete with billowing bow tie, sitting on a Belgian beach; later a descent into the hell of World War I. If you think you've had enough of the muddy gore of Flanders Fields, believe me you haven't, not until you've read this book' (Schama 2017).

Schama's accolade epitomizes the critical success this novel by Flemish author Stefan Hertmans (1951–) has enjoyed so far, nationally as well as internationally. Published in Dutch in Amsterdam in 2013, *Oorlog en terpentijn* (2013; *War and Turpentine*, 2016) was instantly hailed by readers and critics alike as a high point in the author's long and distinguished career, and a high point also in contemporary Dutch/Flemish literature. It won several major literary awards in Flanders and the Netherlands,[1] and has sold about 250,000 copies in five years, a rather extraordinary figure for a literary novel in this small market.

Even more exceptional is the international response *War and Turpentine* has garnered and continues to generate. Early translation contracts with Hanser Berlin and Gallimard sparked a more general international interest in Hertmans's novel. As of June 2018, the book has been translated in twenty-five languages. The English and

American edition, translated by David McKay and published by Harvill Secker in the UK, Pantheon Books in the USA and Text in Australia, has marked a pivotal event in the novel's international career. Critics on both sides of the Atlantic heaped praise upon Hertmans's novel, calling it 'a rich, fictionalized memoir' (*The Times*, Wilson 2016), 'a richly detailed excavation of a life and a thoughtful exploration of familial memory' (*Kirkus Review*, 'War and Turpentine' 2016), an 'affecting and unusual book' and 'a masterly portrait of a man's grief over lost love and his commemoration of it in art' (*The Sunday Telegraph*, Crane 2017), a 'masterly book about memory, art, love and war' (*The New York Times*, Schama 2017). According to Neel Mukherjee writing in *The Guardian*, '*War and Turpentine* has all the markings of a future classic.' Several awards and nominations consolidated the novel's international soaring success.[2]

Although exact selling figures are hard to obtain – publishers are reluctant to release commercial data – it seems safe to say that *War and Turpentine* is already one of the most successful Flemish novels ever to hit the English/American book market.[3] This raises the question that informs the first part of this essay: why is this novel in particular doing so well in a market most authors and novels from Flanders – and the Netherlands, for that matter – never reach?

Three reasons why

A first, partial answer has to do with the book's plot. *War and Turpentine* tells the story of Urbain Martien, a Flemish First World War veteran, the son of a poor church painter who had dreamed of becoming an artist himself until history and fate sent him into the trenches of Flanders' Fields. After the war, which he survives in spite of several serious injuries, Urbain Martien settles for a life as a copyist and marries – in what also amounts to an act of copying – his one and only great love's sister – the great love having succumbed to the Spanish flu in 1919. Shortly before his death in 1981, 90-year-old Urbain Martien hands his grandson two notebooks in which he has written down his memories of growing up poor in the Flemish city of Ghent and some of his experiences in the First World War. The grandson – the author's alter ego and the novel's chief narrator – relishes the notebooks ('six hundred manuscript pages in total') for thirty years: 'I had resolved not to read his memoirs until I had plenty of time for them, in the belief that the experience would fill me with the overpowering urge to write his life story' (10).

This is exactly what happens: in 2010, as soon as he retires from his academic career, Hertmans opens the notebooks and discovers a baffling treasure indeed. The cahiers contain a family history that had been largely unknown to the grandson. Transcribing and editing his grandfather's text, Hertmans delves deep into a family past the notebooks both reveal and obfuscate. *War and Turpentine* is the fictionalized report of a genealogical journey undertaken by a reverential grandson who wanted 'to learn to see everything in truer proportions' (15). The novel incorporates, and thus fictionalizes, the true story of its own genesis into the narrative, which makes for a moving account that has been greatly appreciated by readers and critics alike. Indeed, 'moving' is one of the characteristics attributed to Hertmans's book in almost every review and it is certainly one reason why the book became so successful.

A second reason has to do with timing. In the early years of the twenty-first century Hertmans anticipated that the upcoming centennial anniversary of the First World War 'would release a flood of books – a new barrage alongside the almost unscalable mountain of existing historical material' (10). Reluctant though he is to open his grandfather's memoirs, Hertmans overcomes his 'scandalous indolence' and sets about one of the most ambitious, demanding and personal research and writing projects of his entire career. He finishes *War and Turpentine* in time for it to benefit from the massive attention roused by the 'hundredth anniversary of the cataclysm' – before readers would turn away 'with a yawn from yet another book on the blasted First World War' (11). Thus, the success of Hertmans's novel resulted also from the well-timed moment of its publication.

War and Turpentine gained international attention and praise not merely because of its emotional intensity and timely publication, but also and perhaps even principally because of its representation of the First World War. To be sure, libraries teem with books about the First (and the Second) World War, but, as Schama pointed out, 'if you think you've had enough of the muddy gore of Flanders Fields, believe me you haven't, not until you've read this book'. Hertmans's success in the English-speaking world may also be partially due to the fact that, in the USA at least, Flanders is still popularly identified with the First World War. A Flemish novel about the First World War may therefore be received as especially genuine.[4]

In writing about his grandfather's war time experiences - or, more precisely, in writing about his grandfather's writings about his memories of his war time experiences - Hertmans joined one of the largest literary 'families' in the world, to wit, all those readers, writers, survivors, historians and other researchers who are interested in the First World War. When you write a novel about (among other things, for this is more than a war novel) the First World War, one of the most epochal events in modern Western history, your potential audience is much larger than when you focus on, say, your dog's arthritis. Every war morphs into a cultural trauma, shared and suffered by large numbers of people over decades if not centuries. Moreover, every war trauma creates a collective point of reference, or a series of references *available* to the writer and the artist. In tapping this source, writers and artists establish a rapport with an audience that may otherwise – linguistically, historically, geographically – be very distant from them. One could say that in order to break through its linguistic confines, a 'war novel' written in a 'little' language requires *less translation* than most other novels insofar as text and reader already share a common set of references, assumptions, memories and facts. Literary works can enter world literature, as David Damrosch put it, 'by bringing the world directly into the text itself' (2009: 86). This is obviously what happens in *War and Turpentine*. The centrality of the First World War to the book's structure and theme has the novel partake in an ongoing global conversation, as it were, which definitely facilitated its international reach.

What is true for First World War literature is even more true for Second World War literature. The Second World War provides an even more recognizable framework/set of references than the First for the very simple reason that it is closer to us in time. It is not surprising, then, that two fairly recent novels from the Low Countries that were also quite successful in the English/American market and beyond were emphatically situated in the Second World War: *De aanslag* (1982; *The Assault*, 1985) by Dutch writer Harry Mulisch (1927–2010) and *Het verdriet van België* (1983; *The Sorrow of Belgium*, 1990) by his Flemish contemporary Hugo Claus (1929–2008).

So far, we have identified three elements that, taken together, go a long way towards explaining the international success of Hertmans's novel: its moving anecdotage, the strategic timing of its publication, and its often harrowing representation of the First World War horror as experienced and described by the narrator's grandfather and transposed by the author.

However, the lasting significance of *War and Turpentine* must be sought elsewhere. In fact, it may not be Urbain Martien's description (as transposed by his grandson) of 'the muddy gore of Flanders Fields' that makes this book stand out in the vast collection of First World War books as much as the hybrid nature of the text.

As already indicated, Hertmans does not simply copy/reproduce his grandfather's memoirs. He rewrites them thoroughly and extensively. As the author/narrator explains in a highly significant passage:

Like a clerk, I ploughed through the hundreds of handwritten pages, cursing my own mediocre style, the result of my equivocal attempt to remain faithful to him while nevertheless *translating his tale into my own experience*. (15; my italics)

The choice of the verb 'translate' offers a crucial insight into the novel's *modus operandi*. Indeed, I would argue that the entire novel hinges on acts of translation, whereby translation is understood not only as an act of rewriting a text into another language but also as a metaphor for the rather dazzling array of substitutions and exchanges that propel this narration. Already the terms 'substitution' and 'exchange' can be exchanged for congenial terms: transformation, transfer, supplement, displacement – all apply.

Every translated novel substitutes one text for another. To every reader of a translated text who has no knowledge of the text's source language, the translation appears as an orphaned text, a foundling, an 'original copy'. In the case of *War and Turpentine*, much could be said about the relation between the novel's original version – a Flemish variant of Dutch, tinted with regional and sometimes quaint colloquialisms – and David McKay's clear and careful English translation. However, a sustained comparison and interpretation of this relationship would be rather futile in the context of this volume, which means to serve readers who are not necessarily versed in both English and Dutch. Let us therefore confine ourselves here to the question of translation in a wider, metaphorical sense.

Modes of translation

In *War and Turpentine*, acts and modes of translation occur at many levels and on several occasions. Long before the grandson started 'translating' his grandfather's 'tale' into his 'own experience', the grandfather had decided to translate his own experiences into writing. The reason he began to write down his memoirs in 1963, forty-five years after the war ended, is remarkable: Urbain Martien wanted to continue 'telling the story of how his life had been deformed' (12) without annoying 'his family and relatives' who 'had grown tired of his anecdotes and would cut him off, saying, I've heard that one often enough' (12–3). The notebooks signify a transfer from the oral practice of storytelling to the written recording of the same stories. The oral act of storytelling is replaced by writing-as-a-ruse. This primal act of translation served yet another function. Urbain Martien's wife, Gabrielle, 'had died five years earlier; somehow,' the narrator tells us without any further textual evidence to support his claim, 'through the act of writing, he completed his period of mourning' (13). Although the nature of the relationship between mourning and writing remains unexplained, the intimation is that to the grandfather, writing served as an act of mourning by other means. It translated (transformed, transferred) the painful absence of a deceased loved one into text.

In 1981, anticipating his own disappearance, the grandfather gives the notebooks to his grandson. This gift is the foundational transfer, or perhaps the constitutive fiction without which this novel would have been a different book – or non-existent. This reminds one of the etymological affinity between *transfer* and *translation*, the latter being derived from the past particle stem of the Latin verb *transferre*, meaning 'to bear across, carry over, bring through; transfer, copy, translate'.[5] This gift, this transfer, also constitutes an act of translation.

But the gift is not entirely disinterested. The gift is also a charge. 'By entrusting his notebooks to me,' the grandson/narrator felt called upon 'to describe' his grandfather's life, a life 'that spanned nearly a century and began on a different planet' (10). What is called 'to describe' here obviously involves another act of translation-as-transformation: the notebooks will be copied, edited, rewritten and integrated into the novel *War and Turpentine*.

The act of writing-as-translation assumes even greater urgency and complexity when the grandson discovers in his grandfather's first notebook 'the true story' behind another, earlier act of giving that has obliged grandson to grandfather. When his grandson turned 12, Urbain Martien gave him a golden pocket watch. The grandson received it very gratefully, only to let it slide out of his hands and shatter on the ground, which left his grandfather in a daze. The grandson discovers many years later that his grandfather began to write his memoirs two months after this traumatizing incident. The narrator establishes the link emphatically: 'Just before he started writing, in other words, his most valuable keepsake slipped out of my hands and was lost forever' (53). Hence the narrator's nagging understanding: 'I know the debt I incurred to him at that moment can never be repaid' (52).

Years later, while reading the notebooks (the second gift), the grandson grasps the huge significance the watch (the first gift) had had for his grandfather and in his family history:

> The watch had belonged to his father's grandfather, and whenever the family's poverty became too oppressive to bear, his father and mother had their son take a few of their valuables to the pawnshop [...]. One day, his father had reluctantly given him the watch in question, urging him, for God's sake, not to drop it. He entered the gate [...] with this treasure clutched in his hand and placed the watch on the table in front of the scowling nun, who in return gave him some money and a receipt, which he took home. (52)

Later, the family's financial situation having improved, 'the watch was reclaimed' (53). 'After his father's premature death, Urbain's grieving mother placed it in his hands, telling him he was now the man of the house. He put it in his pocket, wore it as a talisman throughout his military training, and kept it with him for all four years of the war' (53).

The passages quoted here reveal the intricate pattern of interfering and interconnected acts of translation/exchange/transfer/transformation that inform and drive Hertmans's novel.

Urbain's writings amount to a threefold act of translation: from oral testimony to written autobiography (the desire to continue 'telling the story of how his life had been deformed'), from grief to resignation ('through the act of writing, he completed his period of mourning'), and then from another grievous incident (the golden watch destroyed by the grandson) to some kind of redemption: the writing of the notebooks, a project he started two months after the family's most precious heirloom had been destroyed. Indeed, one could say that the notebook (gift two) *displaced* the watch (gift one).

Furthermore, to pawn a watch also amounts to an act of translation: it is a form of exchange that transforms/translates a valuable object into a particular amount of money – an exchange that can be compared to an alchemic transformation: a solid object metamorphoses into pecuniary power. When economic hardship decreases, and the family is able to redeem the loan, this alchemic process is reversed and the money changes back, it is *re*translated as it were, into the reclaimed watch that is now no longer a pawn.

Thus, the watch was more than a watch: as a pawn item, it allowed for economic survival. As a talisman during the war, it signified (hope of) physical survival. In destroying it the grandson commits – involuntarily – a symbolic assault on his family's very subsistence. No wonder, then, that the grandson is overcome with a guilt complex and a sense of irredeemable debt.

Writing *War and Turpentine* thus becomes as much an act of penance as an homage to the deceased grandfather, whose notebooks are translated into the central piece of a novel structured as a triptych, which is quite appropriate given the book's preoccupation with painters and paintings and copyists and copies.

Hertmans's (writing a) novel translates his grandfather's (writing) notebooks which translated war time experiences and childhood memories from oral stories into written autobiography. Moreover, both the grandfather's and the grandson's writings make up for multiple and irredeemable losses: the deceased wife (in Urbain Martien's case), the deceased grandfather/hero (in Stefan Hertmans's case) and the shattered watch (in both cases).

The original copy

Years after his grandfather's death, Hertmans 'found in his small library a well-thumbed copy of *Bruges-la-Morte*' (253). Having married his great love's sister after his great love fell victim to the Spanish flu, it is obvious why Urbain Martien identified with Georges Rodenbach's 1892 novella: 'The main character of this tale, Hugues Viane, meets a frivolous double of his dead love and is ultimately forced to conclude that she is no more than a caricature of the woman he once adored' (253). This is the grandson-narrator's summarizing interpretation of Rodenbach's tale:

> It is a story about the impossibility of repeating a great, unique love affair. But it is also a story about a modern Orpheus. Like Orpheus, Hugues descends into the land of the dead to find the specter of his lost love, a mission doomed to catastrophe. (254)

The link with Urbain's own grief is obvious: 'Like the main character in the story, my grandfather secretly erected a mental mausoleum to his lost love' (254).
However: Urbain Martien's mausoleum was not merely mental.
In the opening pages of the novel Hertmans tells us how one day, at a very young age, he found his grandfather – the copyist – in his room 'silently weeping' over a reproduction of a painting torn out of an art book. In a crucial passage, Hertmans writes:

> He holds the picture in his hands; I cannot see what it is, but I see that tears are running down his cheeks and he is silently mouthing words. [...] while he's downstairs having coffee, I slip back up to the room and find the picture on his table. It is a painting of a nude woman with her back to the viewer, a slender woman with dark hair, lying on some kind of sofa or bed in front of a red curtain. Her serene, dreamy expression is visible in a mirror held up for her by a cherub with a blue ribbon over his shoulder; her bare, slender back and round buttocks are prominent. (5–6)

The picture is a reproduction of Velazquez's *Venus at Her Mirror*, 'known as the Rokeby Venus' (27) (Figure 19.1). Many years later, Hertmans discovers in the back of the Rodenbach book something 'that surprised me, because I could not yet see the connection: a torn-out reproduction of Velazquez's Rokeby Venus, the image in front of which I had once found him weeping' (254).

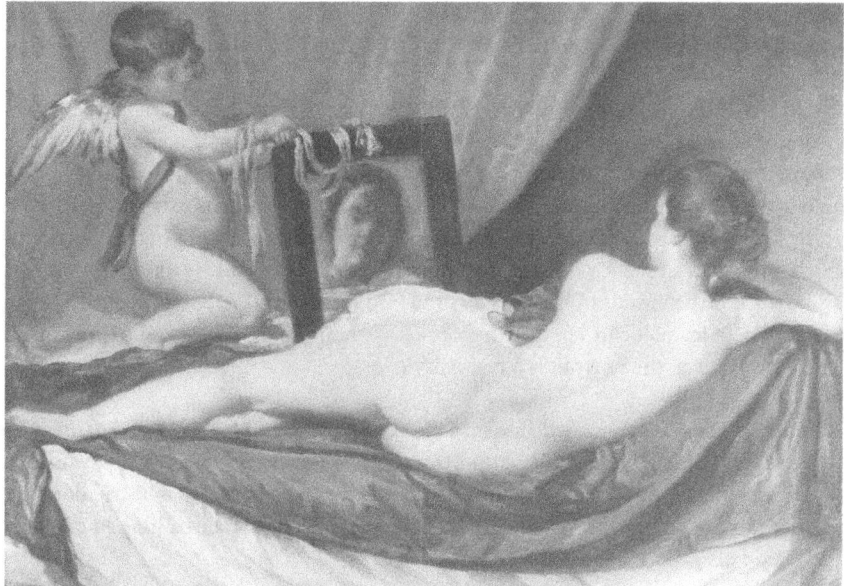

Figure 19.1 Diego Velázquez, *Rokeby Venus*, c. 1647–1651.

The connection had been waiting for him in his father's attic.

During his quest for the truth of his family's past as reconstructed in *War and Turpentine*, Hertmans pays a visit to his 'aged father' – a conspicuously silent character in this novel about (grand)fathers and (grand)sons – who shows him dozens of pictures, found by chance in an old cardboard box, of Urbain's long lost love, Maria Emelia. In the attic, father and son stumble upon the copy of the Velazquez painting made by the grandfather after a reproduction that had him in tears when his grandson entered his room, eons ago. The simultaneous discovery of the Maria Emelia pictures and the Velazquez copy, and of the connection between them, make for the novel's central epiphany:

> The face that regards us in the mirror is not that of Velazquez' model but, unmistakably, the face I have just recently learned to recognize from the grayish photo [...], the face of Maria Emelia. [...] With a dizzying rush, I realize that this copy, however close the resemblance may be, was never a copy, but a concealed act of love; [...] what appeared to be a mere imitation concealed the original of his passion, and the charade of painting thus became the allegory of the hidden love he could never forget. (269–270)

The insertion of Maria Emelia's face into the reproduction of Velazquez's painting reverses the 'logic' of copying: it turns an apparent copy into a new original. But in order to protect 'the hidden love' Urbain Martien could never forget, this new, original painting must necessarily be presented as a copy. It could only exist under the cloak of a putative falsification. Its originality must not be detectable to outsiders. The painting is, in every sense of the word, adulterated.

Urbain Martien's purposeful mystification of the status of his painting – an original in the eyes of the maker, a copy to every other beholder – harks back to a wartime experience described in his notebook as a 'shock of recognition'. Recovering from a bullet wound in Liverpool, Urbain Martien remembers how his own father, the late Franciscus Martien, had been commissioned once to paint a chapel in that same city. During his convalescence he visits just about every church in Liverpool – hoping to find 'a trace of the murals my father was supposed to have restored and extended' (183). Eventually, in a small church, he stumbles across 'a mural that appeared to portray St. Francis'. However, the portrait is a counterfeit:

> The saint's face was, unmistakably, my father's. I could not believe my eyes, but there he stood – he had painted his self-portrait, here, where no one would think worse of him for it, in the certainty that no one would ever know or see what he had done. Here, far from everyone who knew him, my father had immortalized himself in the guise of his patron saint. (183)

A propensity for counterfeiting portraits and copies appears to be a family trait, for several decades later, Urbain Martien will play a similar trick when he immortalizes his unforgettable love Maria Emelia in the guise of Velazquez's model – 'in the certainty that no one would ever know or see what he had done'. The continuity between the great-grandfather's 'modified' portrait of his patron saint and the grandfather's adulteration of Velazquez's Venus is further corroborated by the fact that in his Liverpool mural Franciscus has included his own son in the guise of a shepherd boy. 'It was undeniable: the boy reaching out his hand affectionately to the saint – had my own face' (183–184). Both Urbain and his father Franciscus paint in order to *re*present an absent loved one: the late Maria Emelia (in Urbain's case) and the faraway little son Urbain (in Franciscus's case). In fact, it was the absence of the sorely missed father that pushed the young son to take drawing lessons in the first place: 'he wants to be like his absent father. I want to paint and draw, booms the voice within him' (81). Urbain's life as a copyist springs from his 'memory of the hours spent in churches with his father, whom he finds himself missing more and more' (82). If Hertmans's great-grandfather and grandfather sought to translate/supplement the absent loved one through 'the charade of painting', then the grandson can be said to have pursued a fairly similar goal through writing.

Indeed, one cannot fail to notice the isomorphism between Urbain Martien's painting and his grandson's novel, in that both artefacts rest on a dual falsification: if a copy rests on a (deliberately) false claim to originality, both Urbain Martien's painting and Hertmans's novel pivot on the falsification of this copy status. Both claim to be copies, that is, acknowledged falsifications, but in rewriting and editing his grandfather's notebooks Hertmans exposes the copy status of (t)his text as much as the insertion of Maria Emelia's face turned his grandfather's copy of the Velazquez painting into a new original. Both works can be described, therefore, as *original copies*. To be sure, the grandfather's copy was, as it were, secretly original, 'a concealed act of love' as Hertmans put it, while *War and Turpentine* emphatically problematizes the ambiguity of its 'original copy'-status.[6] In fact, this ambiguity has rattled some critics' nerves for it raises an as yet unanswered question that strikes at the novel's core: what if the notebooks are part of the fiction, rather than the referent 'outside' the novel? What if the source text (Urbain Martien's notebooks) do not exist outside, prior to the novel that claims to have 'merely' edited them? What if the 'copy' is truly an original? Titillating though they may be, these questions are actually quite futile as Hertmans has produced the original notebooks for television cameras on several occasions.

Even so, the ambiguity will persist as long as the nature of the relationship between the text of the notebooks as they appear in the novel ('translated', edited, adulterated, …) and the original text as written by the grandfather and donated to the author remains unexamined. 'I think it's a little early,' Hertmans has stated, 'to begin this dissection,' adding that this study may be undertaken 'after my death' (pers. comm., 19 March 2018). Until then, we will not know how original/adulterated the copy really is.

War and Turpentine is a sophisticated, multilayered novel, at once a personal memoir, a historical testimony, a moving story about hardship and misfortune afflicting a Flemish family of humble origin, a loving portrait of an obliging and devout grandfather by a guilt-ridden grandson, a heartbreaking love-story and a profound comment on the redeeming force of art. It invites important questions about the nature of translation, both as a writing practice and a metaphor for the various acts and modes of displacement and substitution that govern and link the narrative's different levels. Finally, the superior quality of David McKay's translation has certainly contributed to the novel's success in the English-speaking world.[7]

Notes

1 In 2014 *War and Turpentine* won the AKO Literatuurprijs, the Vlaamse Cultuurprijs voor de Letteren and the Lezersjury Gouden Boekenuil. In 2015 Flemish media nominated Hertmans's book 'Best Novel of the Past 25 years.'
2 *War and Turpentine* has been longlisted for the Man Booker Prize International, it was a London *Times*' book of the year, an *Economist* book of the year, an *Irish Times* book of the year, and *The New York Times* ranked it among the ten best books of the year 2016. David McKay's English translation won the Vondel Translation prize, a two-yearly award for the best book translation in English of a Dutch-language work of literature or cultural history. The prize was established in 1996 by the Society of Authors in Britain and is financed by Flanders Literature and the Dutch Foundation for Literature. The prize is worth €5,000.
3 A more detailed reconstruction of the international production, launch and reception of *War and Turpentine* is currently being undertaken by Jack McMartin (KU Leuven). His 'The making of "a future Flemish classic": *War and Turpentine* in English' is to be published in 2019. McMartin is also currently conducting a related study

comparing the various national receptions of the book's twenty-plus translations together with Paola Gentile (KU Leuven).
4   I wish to thank Damon Krukowski for sharing this consideration (pers. comm., 23 May 2018).
5   See 'Transfer', Online Etymology Dictionary.
6   Hertmans's novel can also be said to expose the 'nature' of language in that it thrives on what it effaces, thus flaunting its status as a supplement. I am, of course, alluding to Jacques Derrida's claim that 'all language will substitute itself for that living self-presence of the proper, which, as language, already supplanted things in themselves. Language *adds itself* to presence and supplants it, defers it within the indestructible desire to rejoin it' (1976: 280). Furthermore: 'The verb "supplant" or "to compensate for" *(suppléer)* defines the act of writing adequately' (280).
7   I wish to thank Stefan Hertmans and his wife Sigrid Bousset, translator David McKay and several representatives of Hertmans's English and American publishers, for their generous answers to my questions. I am also grateful to Damon Krukowski, Jonah Raskin and Theo D'haen for their comments upon earlier versions of this essay.

References

Claus, H. (1983), *Het verdriet van België*, Amsterdam: De Bezige Bij.
Claus, H. (1990), *The Sorrow of Belgium*, trans. A.J. Pomerans, New York: Pantheon Books.
Crane, H. (2017), 'A Painter Who Hid Codes in His Copies of Old Masters'. [Review], *The Sunday Telegraph*, 4 June 2017: 27.
Damrosch, D. (2009), *How to Read World Literature*, Chichester: Wiley-Blackwell.
Derrida, J. (1976), *Of Grammatology*, trans. G. Chakravorty Spivak, Baltimore: Johns Hopkins University Press.
D'haen, T. (2012), *The Routledge Concise History of World Literature*, London: Routledge.
Hertmans, S. (2013), *Oorlog en terpentijn*, Amsterdam: De Bezige Bij.
Hertmans, S. (2016), *War and Turpentine*, trans. D. McKay, New York: Pantheon Books.
Mulisch, H. (1982), *De aanslag*, Amsterdam: De Bezige Bij.
Mulisch, H. (1985), *The Assault*, trans. C.N. White, New York: Random House.
Papadima L., D. Damrosch and T. D'haen, eds (2011), *Global Literature: In Search of a Definition*, Amsterdam: Rodopi.
Schama, S. (2017), 'By the Book', [Book Review], *The New York Times*, 19 October 2017. Available online: https://www.nytimes.com/2017/10/19/books/review/simon-schama-by-the-book.html?_r=0 (accessed 19 November 2017).
'Transfer', Online Etymology Dictionary. Available online: https://www.etymonline.com/word/transfer?ref=etymonline_crossreference (accessed 27 November 2017).
'War and Turpentine' (2016), *Kirkus Review*, 1 June 2016. Available online: https://www.kirkusreviews.com/book-reviews/stefan-hertmans/war-and-turpentine/ (accessed 26 February 2019).
Weissbort, D. and A. Eysteinsson, eds (2006), *Translation – Theory and Practice*, Oxford: Oxford University Press.
Wilson F. (2016), 'The Front Line of the 20th Century'. [Review], *The Times*, 16 July 2016: 18.

20

At the Edge of the World and Other Stories: Dutch-Australian Emigration Literature, c. 1945–1990

Ton van Kalmthout

In the period between 1946 and 1992, the Dutch government pursued a targeted and fairly effective emigration policy. It was coordinated by the Ministry of Social Affairs, which in turn delegated its execution to the Dutch Emigration Foundation (Stichting Landverhuizing Nederland). The Foundation, which in 1952 became the Dutch Emigration Service (Nederlandse Emigratiedienst), advertised several destination countries that had migration agreements with the Dutch government, provided information to potential emigrants, and facilitated passage and settlement, including financially. A government commissioner for emigration supervised the entire process. The emigration authorities, including employment offices where one could register prior to departure as well as private and denominational emigration hubs,[1] were assisted in their promotion and information activities by other interest groups and cultural institutions. In liaison with these organizations, the government fine-tuned its emigration policy in its so-called Emigration Board (Emigratiebestuur).[2] The combined efforts helped more than half a million Dutchmen on their way to the United States, Canada, Australia, New Zealand and South Africa.

Key motives for leaving included uncertainty about whether the peace in Europe would last and whether the Netherlands would be able to provide enough food, shelter and employment for all its inhabitants in the future. After the declaration of independence by Indonesia, many Dutchmen from this former Dutch colony were also looking for a safe haven, and over 150,000 Dutch citizens ended up in Australia at the time (Blauw 2006: 171). This essay is about the literature that accompanied Dutch-Australian migration. It is the result of an exploratory study of Dutch-language texts by and for the migrants concerned, dating from the decades after the war until approximately 1990.[3] The latter date saw the beginning of a new era, when the Dutch government stopped its incentive policy and the emigration flow came to a halt for the time being.

The written heritage of emigrants has rarely been studied for its own sake.[4] Yet there are good reasons to examine the nature of the literature that accompanied these migrants' passage and settlement, the social and cultural context in which it was written and received, and the functions it fulfilled. That is what this contribution intends to do. The voyage to Australia brought several categories of Dutch fiction and non-fiction into circulation far beyond the borders of the Netherlands, and this literature, albeit limited in terms of quantity, played an important role in the lives of a large number of Dutchmen and Australians. In a unique and varied way, it documents and represents the motives and experiences of Dutch emigrants, their expectations and illusions, their disappointments and successes, and their views on their new country and on themselves. Consequently, the production and reception of this literature contributed to the establishment of a new individual and group identity: that of the Australian Dutchman.

There are good reasons to study emigration literature as a form of world literature. Following Damrosch's groundbreaking approach, world literature should not so much be regarded as a number of internationally esteemed and canonized works of high artistic value, but rather as a collection of texts that can be read as literature and that have found their way from one linguistic and cultural realm to another (Damrosch 2003: 4–6). Thus considered, the texts available to migrants during their transition to a new homeland can also be classified as world literature, even when their artistic aspirations are modest. Both the Romanist Gaetano Rando (1996: 270) and the historian Bill Jones (2006: 53), who studied the history of Italian-Australian and Welsh-Australian emigration literature, respectively, approach their subjects broadly as consisting of both 'pure' and 'applied' forms. That is to say, not only fictional texts, such as novels, short stories, plays and poetry, but also essays, letters and diaries, prayers, memoirs and biographies, chronicles and historical accounts, guides, travel writing and geographical accounts, both in the original language and in translation.[5] In this chapter, I limit myself largely to published texts in Dutch by correspondents, prose writers and poets, journalists and information officers.

Emigration literature in Dutch

A number of Dutch emigrants recorded their experiences on the far side of the world in writing, and their testimonies form part of the available emigration literature. Emigrants and emigration institutions employed various narratives to give direction and meaning to their new lives, as noted by literary historian Orm Øverland (2000).

He has identified a trio of myths that were cultivated by immigrants in the United States in the decades around 1900: a *foundation myth* that claimed a part in the foundation of the American nation, a *myth of sacrifice* about the sacrifices that had been made for this nation, and an *ideological myth* emphasizing the ideals shared with the new nation. Such myths can also be identified in the stories of Dutch Australians. The latter liked to remind readers, for instance, of Dirck Hartog from Amsterdam, who was the first European to set foot on Australian soil in 1616, or of Abel Tasman, who discovered Van Diemen's Land, today's Tasmania, in 1642. The Australian-Dutch publicist Edward Duyker vigorously refuted similar foundational claims by other nations:

> The Dutch can probably claim the longest European association with Australia of any non-indigenous ethnic group. Evidence suggesting that they were pre-empted by the Portuguese is slender. It was Dutch explorers and cartographers, not Portuguese, who made Australia known to the rest of the world from the beginning of the seventeenth century. Indeed, until the mid-nineteenth century, despite British settlement, Australia was commonly referred to as New Holland.[6]

One such myth of sacrifice was that during the Second World War, it was the Dutch who helped Australia to withstand Japanese aggression: according to Cnossen and Apperloo (1954: 9), by sacrificing their own fleet the Dutch enabled the Americans to regroup and save Australia from Japanese occupation. And in ideological terms, it was easy to emphasize shared values. 'On the whole I think that the Australian has much in common with us Dutchmen,' a Dutch immigrant wrote:

> They also love their children very much, and take them along to the cinema, church, etc., but they never leave them alone at home. O, and good parents can never be bad people, I always say.[7]

In stories written by and about contemporary Dutch-Australian migrants, however, common ingredients are also the strange surroundings in which they suddenly find themselves and the accompanying culture shock: unknown customs, homesickness (especially during the first months), and the unreachability of family back in the Netherlands. At the same time, such stories regularly recall the reasons for leaving the overcrowded Netherlands and emphasize the correctness of that decision. The first generation of Dutch emigrants consisted mainly of farmers and labourers, for whom Australia was their first opportunity to achieve greater prosperity and climb the social ladder. That is why the typical emigration history of this group is summarized as a series of job changes and moves, 'from migrant camps to caravan parks, garages, and shared flats' (Walker-Birckhead 2006: 247). Later on, nostalgia about the country of origin also played a role.

Let us now take a closer look at the most important categories of Dutch-Australian literature.

Prose and poetry

In 1955, the sociologist W.F. Geijl noted that 'Quite a few novels have been written with emigration as the theme.'[8] He must have been referring to novels and stories such as 'Emigratie' (Emigration) by Willem Frederik Hermans (in which the intended emigration never happens).[9] Renowned literary authors who emigrated to Australia, such as Henk Romijn Meijer (1963) and Joop Waasdorp (1965), did situate several stories in their new homeland,[10] but, as is also the case with Dutch-American emigration literature,[11] in Dutch and Australian highbrow literature Dutch-Australian migration is only addressed to a limited extent. Although it is said that Australia developed its own tradition of novel-writing and poetry after the war (Anonymous 1949b: 106; Geursen 1960: 78), the share related to the Netherlands concerned only lesser-known authors such as Margreet de Haan-Woltjes, Lolo Houbein, Reinder P. Meijer, Kosti Simons, Jaap Verduyn and Cornelis Vleeskens (Risseeuw 1965: 124–125; Duyker 1987: 144).

Special mention should be made of another emigrant author, Koos Schuur, who tried his luck in Australia from 1953 to 1961.[12] He was commissioned by the Dutch government to publish a poetry cycle entitled 'Fata morgana voor Nederlanders' ('Fata morgana for Dutchmen', 1956), expressing the feelings of abandonment and homesickness that plagued the emigrant in Australia.[13] Presumably so as not to distress his patron, he added the following justification to the cycle:

> When emigrants in a strange country come together, they criticize their new homeland in a ruthless and often unfair way, and they sing the praises of their land of origin excessively. In trying to give an impression of the emigrants' problems, I have incorporated the mood of these hate-sessions in this cycle.[14]

It is unclear whether Schuur's poetry discouraged many emigrants: as a representative of the experimental movement of Vijftig (Fifty), he probably had a small readership.

Writers such as Klaas van der Geest and Anthony van Kampen, who aimed at a broader audience, could count on having a greater impact. In *Op weg naar de toekomst* (*Towards the future*, 1954b), which, according to its dustjacket, was a 'magnificent, captivating emigration novel, up-to-date from A to Z, and in all respects consistent with the actual situation',[15] Van der Geest described the obstacles that a Frisian farmer's family had to overcome to win a place in Australian society:

> In this captivating story, the readers witness a piece of moving humanity, as reflected in the often emotional events in this family. The conditions frequently inspire the members of the Holwerda family to show a degree of courage one would never have expected from them in different circumstances.[16]

Van Kampen, in turn, reached many readers with his Mary Bryant trilogy (1968, 1969a, 1969b): a series of historical novels about the heroine's exile from late eighteenth-century England, her stay in Australia – at that time still a penal colony – and the pardon and repatriation of Mary and her fellow prisoners.

Around 1990, the next generation made an entrance with *Lege hannen* (*Empty hands*, 1987) by Djoke Weening-Meijer, the story of a 17-year-old girl who stayed behind in the Netherlands when her (once again) Frisian family left for Australia in the 1960s. Just like *Op weg naar de toekomst,* the story is situated in a Protestant milieu, but with themes such as homosexuality, divorce and adultery, the book reflected a new *Zeitgeist*. As it was published in Frisian, *Lege hannen* failed to reach a large audience, unlike Tim Krabbé's international bestseller, *Vertraging* (*Delay*, 1994). Set in the early 1990s, the latter is about a Dutchman who seeks out a childhood love from thirty years ago during a stopover in Sydney. He becomes caught up in her attempt to flee the authorities, who are pursuing her on charges of fraud. Since 1990, however, it has mostly been translated work that has given Dutch readers insights into emigration to Australia in the nineteenth and twentieth centuries, through novels by, among others, the Australian Thomas Keneally and the Dutch-Australian writer Lolo Houbein, who wrote a fictionalized autobiography.

At least as much fiction about Dutch migrants in Australia was written for young readers. Again, there are many similarities between Dutch-Australian and Dutch-American literature; the latter may be more extensive, but it shows comparable tendencies (cf. Krabbendam 2010). After a hesitant start with *Hollandse jongens in Australië* (*Dutch boys in Australia*, 1947), written by the novelist, theatre-maker, filmmaker and painter Nico Molenkamp, Dutch-Australian youth literature more or less kept pace with developments in the emigration flow to Australia: during the 1950s, at least eight titles for boys and girls appeared in Dutch, a number that fell to three per decade in the 1960s and 1970s. After this time, when Dutch children had probably become more accustomed to English-language books, Dutch-language books on Dutch-Australian migration were the exception. Less common were non-fiction youth books, such as J. Abma's *Kees emigreerde toch* (*Kees emigrated anyway,* 1954), a story designed to inform children about the emigration process in general, including that to Australia.[17]

Some youth books were aimed at younger children, such as *Tula de kleine houtsnijder* (*Tula the little woodcarver,* 1956) by Simon Franke; a popular novel about a native boy that also described the lives of European migrants.[18] Youth books for girls were almost exclusively written for adolescents and young adults, and tended to be developmental novels with emigrating heroines aged around 20, who struggle with independence and faithfulness in love.[19] Far more adventurous were the novels for boys, such as *Een truck in de mist* (*A truck in the mist,* 1970) by Elly van Wijmen and *Achter stampende Hoeven* (*Behind stamping hooves,* 1954a) by Klaas van der Geest, mentioned above. In the latter, a thrilling book, a 17-year-old Dutch boy tries to raise money as a cattleman so that his homesick parents can return to the Netherlands. A specific subcategory of novels was written for Protestant boys and girls, such as *Jack en Sheltie* (Jack and Sheltie, 1966) by Piet Prins, a pseudonym of Piet Jongeling. In this novel, already serialized in the *Gereformeerd Gezinsblad* (*Reformed Family Magazine*), Jaap – now called Jack – regains his faith in God, who repeatedly saves him from the heathen native tribes making attempts on his life. This 'truly Christian book,' according to the dustjacket, 'is also the history of a lost son who returns to the Father's house and finds forgiveness.'[20]

Autobiographical writings

A considerable part of the printed emigration literature about Australia consisted of non-fiction texts. Possibly the most important medium for migrants to tell and read their stories was that of autobiographical writings such as letters, recorded interviews, memoirs and autobiographies.[21] Letters form a goldmine of information about emigrants' concerns. In themselves, like other emigrant texts, they served a variety of purposes, such as providing information and inspiration, as a way to pour out one's heart, in order to retrieve memories or to give an account. Until the telephone became the common medium in the 1970s and 1980s, letters were the most widely-used means of communication (Walker Birckhead 2006: 367) and had a great influence on thinking about migration. It is therefore not surprising that these powerful documents on migrant life were regularly collected in edited form, as were interviews with the migrants themselves.

One collection, which consisted entirely of letters from one author, Koos Schuur, was exceptional. It was published in the Netherlands by his fellow artists, Jan Hanlo and Salvador Hertog, as *En de kookaburra lacht* (*And the kookaburra laughs*, 1953). Schuur, a compositor and house painter, wrote to his friends about how difficult he found it to accustom himself to Australian society; a society whose cultural life, in his view, left much to be desired. But compilations were also made of the letters of lesser-known migrants. Usually these were collected purposefully, as was the case in 1959 with the 'correspondence campaign' by the Dutch Women's Committee's Emigration Commission, an initiative that spawned an impressive 1,200 letters after an appeal in the *Dutch Australian Weekly*.[22] Such collections were not only intended for maintaining contact with family and friends or pouring out one's heart. In the 1950s and 1960s, emigration officers also benefitted from what they could learn from letters and interviews.[23]

Some autobiographical writings by migrants also reveal historical interests. In addition to the novel by Lolo Houbein, mentioned above, these include personal and family histories narrated against the broader backdrop of Dutch-Australian history. In a number of cases, the authors self-published these often very informative books, Elizabeth Stukkien's *Hartog's kinderen* (Hartog's children 1990) being one example.

Journalistic travel stories

Closely related to these autobiographical works is a group of prose works of a journalistic nature. Jan Rempt took the lead here; by 1947, he had already written a brochure about the favourable emigration opportunities for the Dutch. This was a world that he also witnessed for himself. In 1951, he left for Australia as a correspondent and contributor to various Dutch and Belgian periodicals. Fifteen years later, he had become editor-in-chief of *The Northern District Times* and *The Leader*.[24]

In 1953, Rempt published *Aan de rand der wereld. Een Hollandse emigrant in Australië* (*At the edge of the world. A Dutch emigrant in Australia*). The dustcover advertised it as 'the first book about Australia written by a Dutch journalist-emigrant, describing the country, people and experiences of Dutch emigrants in an unadorned way, without the writer shying away from things the emigrant finds unpleasant'.[25] Rempt's account was nevertheless overwhelmingly positive, as shown by the sequel, which described Australia in terms of a new Golden Age of Dutch exploration:

> The large development opportunities presented by New Holland are, by comparison, favorable to the degree that the author sees future possibilities for every aspiring emigrant who is made of the right stuff, and that will enable him to make the most out of it. Often, that is more than could be realized in the overcrowded Netherlands.[26]

Aan de rand der wereld offered new Dutch-Australians a versatile and varied perspective on the life that was in store for them. The book contained a lot of matter-of-fact information, but it was written smoothly and embellished with all kinds of anecdotes. Rempt himself had taken the black and white photos that illustrated the book. The introduction was written by none other than Government Commissioner B.W. Haveman, who seized the opportunity to put the journalist's positive reporting to the service of the Dutch policy of stimulating emigration:

> In general, our emigrants are people of magnificent initiative and perseverance. This book has been written for those who wish to emigrate well. I wholeheartedly hope that it will have the effect of holding back the wavering or the insecure. Emigration is only right for those who are suited to it.[27]

In the early 1950s, the government also tried to influence reporting in other ways. In the autumn of 1953, for instance, the Dutch and Australian governments invited nine representatives of major Dutch press organizations to share a study trip to Australia on KLM's 'emigrant airliner' PH-TLW Overloon.[28] The selected representatives included Jan Rempt, who was already working in Sydney at the time; Ans Kamstra, editor of the lady's magazine *Margriet*; and the journalists Martin Duyzings (*Algemeen Handelsblad* and *Maasbode*), Roel Hagoort (*Antirevolutionaire Rotterdammer, Nieuwe Leidsche Courant*), Dick Hendriks (*Trouw, De Tijd*), Huib Koemans (Regionale Dagblad Pers), Jan Onstenk (Unitas-combination, including *Het Binnenhof*), Emile Schil (Algemeen Nederlands Persbureau) and Mathieu Smedts (*Nieuwe Rotterdamse Courant, Het Parool, De Volkskrant*). Their employers only needed to pay for their stay. The trip was a direct response to diminishing Dutch enthusiasm for emigration to Australia, although Koemans maintained that he and his colleagues were not working for the authorities, and that the aim was not to recruit new emigrants. The delegation was simply expected 'to identify the material and spiritual pros and cons associated with emigration; to study the position of women among migrants; to check whether the Dutchman was able, in a strange country and under completely different circumstances, to assimilate with a young people that has not yet established a steady way of thinking and acting in numerous areas'.[29] Koemans and Smedts not only reported in the periodical press, but they also wrote books about the trip based on their articles.[30]

In six chapters, Koemans addressed the various states of Australia, adding personal and at times quite critical comments on what he had seen and heard. Towards the end of the book, he did not hide his impression that the group of journalists, despite having been received hospitably, had not really been welcome. In particular, he had been much annoyed by the efforts of Dutch emigration officials to steer the coverage. They did so by presenting matters in an overly positive light, withholding information, packing the itinerary with preselected interlocutors, and passing on confidential information from the reporters to the Australian government. 'I did not appreciate this system of espionage, because it led me to believe that they wanted to restrict the way we formed our opinions in one way or another.'[31] This, however, was something that Koemans would not allow. He judged the emigration officials' practice to be 'cold and heartless' and, despite its inevitability, found emigration to be a 'particularly uncongenial means [...] to relieve our overcrowded country'. 'But it is too great a stretch for me to present this necessity, for propaganda reasons, as a beautiful expression of the old pioneering spirit that made our dear little country great in the world.' His conclusion, printed in italics, was rather reserved:

The main question was whether a Dutchman who wants to leave his country for whatever reason can become happy in Australia. My answer is 'yes', provided he knows how to make sacrifices of a magnitude that cannot be comprehended here in the Netherlands.[32]

Smedts, in turn, proved to be much more receptive to the influence of both the Dutch and the Australian emigration authorities. His book, entitled *Australië, nieuw vaderland* (*Australia, new fatherland*, 1955), even featured an introduction and warm recommendation by the Australian ambassador to the Netherlands, Alfred Stirling. The journalist conceded that he and his colleagues, following warnings from disappointed emigrants, had initially been wary of the emigration officials who had welcomed them, and that their hosts had painted far too rosy a picture of the migrants' existence. There had been tensions between the journalists and the officials, who in turn begrudged the guests their suspicions. But Smedts went on to say that he had also discovered how well these officials were helping the emigrants to find shelter and work, and, looking back, he stated that he had seen all he wanted to see. In his book's closing lines, he reaffirmed wholeheartedly what the Dutch ambassador had told the group: 'Emigration to Australia has been a success.' It is not surprising that the Australian Minister for Immigration asked Smedts to return, an invitation the journalist gladly accepted.[33]

Several travel reports followed in later years. For instance, 1959 saw the publication of *Kriskras door Australië* (*Criss-cross through Australia*, 1959), J.E.L. Stoffer's Dutch translation of journalist and radio producer Bill Beatty's *Beyond Australia's Cities* (1956), which had been published three years earlier. And in 1965, Christian man of letters Piet Risseeuw devoted part of his book *Overal Hollanders* (*Dutchmen everywhere*, 1965) to those who had ended up in Australia, especially Protestants. 'I hope,' he wrote in the preface, 'that this travel story will help to raise more awareness of the adventures of some of the 400,000 compatriots who have left our shores since the Second World

War.'[34] He had also included past and present emigrants, including to Australia, in his earlier collection of stories *Zover de wereld reikt* (*As far as the world reaches*, 1963), intended for young people.

Information and propaganda material

Many of the travel stories mentioned above, and sometimes novels as well, were recommended in publications that were primarily intended to encourage Dutchmen to leave for Australia and other emigration countries, to prepare for the passage or to familiarize themselves with their new country. These concise guides or manuals formed part of a broader arsenal of promotional and informational media, including oral information, magazines, films and radio broadcasts.[35] For instance, in 1952, the Foundation for Emigrant Interests (Stichting Emigrantenbelangen), based in The Hague, published an *Emigranten zakboekje* (*The emigrant's pocketbook*, 1952). In 1949, the Dutch Emigration Foundation gave *Algemene wenken voor de Nederlandse emigrant in den vreemde* (*General guidelines for the Dutch emigrant abroad*, 1949a), which was meant as a guide 'for emigrants already underway to their destination country or those who have already arrived there'.[36] Now and then, these booklets were little more than outright propaganda. A small guide by Anthony van Kampen, entitled *Een sprong in het duister. Emigreren ... Wat is dat?* (*A jump into the dark. Emigrating ... What is that?*) concluded with the exclamation: 'GAINING HAPPINESS: / THAT'S WHAT EMIGRATING IS!'[37]

Around 1950, both public and private parties identified a market for emigration guides, a market that W. van der Mast, director-inspector of the National Employment Agency in Groningen, defined as broadly as possible in his *Verantwoorde emigratie. Waarom? – Hoe? – Waarheen?* (*Wise emigration. Why? – How? – Where To?*):

> It is a booklet – let it be said in all modesty – that is meant for everybody! Primarily for those who are most closely involved with emigration, but also for those who, in their sphere of action or social activity, form the center – the helpdesk – of a certain milieu, for church councils, administrative bodies and members of employers and employees associations, as well as other social organizations, electoral associations, and furthermore for everyone who is interested in national developments and has a sense of shared responsibility for the future of our Dutch people.[38]

An unusual information booklet was written by the playwright and novelist Ary den Hartog, commissioned by KLM Airlines: *Vluchtige verkenningen zowel van mogelijke emigratie-landen alsook van de menschelijke motieven, welke voor de aanstaande emigrant het besluit en de keuze bepalen, een en ander aan de hand van velerlei aarzelingen en overpeinzingen van een jonkman, die zijn vragenlijst nog moet invullen en daarmee niet wil beginnen voordat hij terdege met zichzelf tot klaarheid is gekomen* (*A brief exploration of potential emigration countries and the human motives that determine the prospective emigrant's decision and choice, based on the many hesitations of a bachelor who is still to complete his questionnaire and doesn't want to make a start until he is completely ready*). It is the story of 25-year-old Herman Cornelis Hollander, who spent the war in hiding and now wants to emigrate, but does not know which destination to fill in on the emigration official's form. He is considering all of the options – including, of course, Australia.

In 1963, B. Degrood, who had emigrated to Australia, and her brother E. Degrood, a Dutch businessman, likewise packaged information in an informative story. Based on their correspondence, in *Australië, het nieuwe vaderland* (*Australia, the new fatherland*, 1963), they view daily life down under through the eyes of an optimistic Dutch immigrant and her family in the vicinity of Melbourne, where she works as a doctor's assistant. According to the back cover, 'even as a manuscript [the book] attracted the attention of the emigration authorities'.[39] This explains why it was published 'in cooperation with the Intergovernmental Committee for European Migration in Geneva and the Dutch Emigration Service in The Hague'.[40]

A rich literature

More research is needed into the various narrative genres of Dutch-Australian emigration literature and the way in which this literature developed. What, for instance, were the differences between the reading practices of first-generation post-war migrants and those of later generations? This literature presumably continued to fulfill various functions: it provided excitement and entertainment, and it often advertised a new life overseas. In addition, it helped migrants to find their way in the place of destination by enlightening them, warning them and sharing experiences, while also informing those who had stayed behind in the Netherlands. In doing so, it contributed significantly to perceptions of emigration and the continent of Australia, and the place a Dutch migrant could find there. In the decades after the Second World War, Dutch and Australian authorities strove to influence these perceptions in various ways in favour of their emigration policies. Consequently, much writing by and for emigrants bears their hallmark.

It was a rich body of literature, sometimes in translation, that accompanied the post-war emigration flow from the Netherlands to Australia: poetry and prose, whether or not accompanied by serious artistic claims, travelogues, letter and interview collections, autobiographies and guides. This essay, however, does not claim to be a complete account of the available reading material; further study is needed of general and specialized newspapers and magazines, songs and prayers, geographical accounts and, most of all, the emigration literature in English that eventually also emerged from the Dutch-Australian community or was aimed at it.

It was to be expected that this literature would mainly be published in English over time; someone who wanted to settle in Australia was expected to adopt that language as soon as possible. Dutch emigrants had relatively little difficulty in mastering the English language and fairly quickly gave up their native tongue. By 1996, almost two thirds of first-generation Dutch migrants had switched to English at home, and almost 100 per cent of the second generation. In the 1990s, in-house spoken Dutch was still one of twenty most common languages in Australia (of a total of about 200), but since the 1970s it had fallen from sixth to seventeenth place.[41] This must have had a strong influence on the language in which migrants read. Around 1980, at least half of the first-generation Dutch-Australian migrants read magazines, newspapers and books in Dutch, although the latter category was no longer very popular (Pauwels 1980: 70–73). The rise of television undoubtedly contributed significantly to this decline, but many Dutch-Australian readers, especially those from the second generation, also chose to read in the language of the new homeland.

Notes

1. The Algemene Emigratie Centrale (General Emigration Center), the Christelijke Emigratie Centrale (Christian Emigration Center) and the Katholieke Centrale Emigratie Stichting (Catholic Central Emigration Foundation), all located in The Hague.
2. On this emigration system, see esp. Van Faassen (2001, 2014).
3. The study was conducted within the framework of the research project *Migrants: Mobilities and Connection*, led by Marijke van Faassen.
4. Tamara Wagner, in particular, has undertaken pioneering research on the nineteenth century. See Wagner (2011, 2014, 2016).
5. Cf. Reece (1988: 1–2), who describes the English-Australian emigration literature from the period 1820–1870 as a 'range of published information and advice' and 'hundreds of books, pamphlets, newspaper accounts, advertisements and official brochures attempted to direct the flood of free emigration from Britain and Ireland'.
6. Duyker (1987: 1). According to the book's cover: 'It tells of the longest proven association with this continent of any non-indigenous people. The Dutch were the first to explore the northern, western and southern (including Tasmanian) coasts.'
7. Ragas (1960: 22): 'Ze houden ook veel van hun kinderen en nemen die mee naar bioscoop, kerk, enz. maar ze zullen ze nooit alleen thuislaten. Och en goede ouders kunnen ook nooit slechte mensen zijn zeg ik maar.'
8. Geijl (1955: 9, ch. 2).
9. The story appeared in Hermans's *Moedwil en misverstand* (1948) and is included in Hermans (2006: 177–182).
10. On Waasdorp's stay in Australia, see: Wierema (1977: 23–27, 33, 38).
11. See Krabbendam (2010: 98–99).
12. On this see *Koos Schuur: Portret van de 71-jarige dichter, die naar Australië emigreerde en weer terug kwam* [audio-cassette] (1986).
13. Schuur (1956: 5–27). On this cycle, among others: Risseeuw (1965: 125–127) and Van der Veen (1988: 86–87).
14. Schuur (1956: 5): 'Wanneer emigranten in een vreemd land samen zijn, bekritiseren zij hun nieuwe vaderland op onbarmhartige en dikwijls oneerlijke wijze en prijzen zij het land van herkomst buitenmate. Trachtend een beeld te geven van de problemen der emigranten, heb ik de sfeer van deze hate-sessions in deze cyclus verwerkt.'
15. 'prachtige, boeiende landverhuizersroman, van A tot Z actueel en in alle opzichten afgestemd op de werkelijkheid.'
16. 'De lezers worden door dit boeiende verhaal getuige van een brok ontroerende menselijkheid, die sterk tot uitdrukking komt in de vaak emotionele gebeurtenissen in dit gezin. De omstandigheden inspireren de leden van het gezin Holwerda vaak tot een moed, die men hun onder andere omstandigheden nooit had toegedacht.'

17 On this book: Krabbendam (2010: 105).
18 Also aimed at younger readers is Simone Schell's *De zevende hemel* (The seventh heaven, 1977). Its main character is a 7-year-old girl who returns to the Netherlands after a five-year stay in Australia.
19 For example, Else Harting's *Stel je voor dat ik ging emigreren* (Imagine that I were to emigrate, 1954), Hella Jansonius's *Emigrante tegen wil en dank* (Emigrant for better or worse, 1955), T. Jager-Meursing's *Een Hollands meisje in Australië* (A Dutch girl in Australia, 1963) and, by the same author, *Tot weerziens in Australië* (See you in Australia, 1964).
20 'echt christelijk boek' – 'is ook de geschiedenis van een verloren zoon die naar het Vaderhuis terugkeert en vergeving vindt'. The book forms a trilogy with Prins's *Speurtocht naar Sheltie* (Hunt for Sheltie, 1971) and *Sheltie en de smokkelaars* (Sheltie and the smugglers, 1972). These two volumes are set in Europe. Other Dutch-Australian children's books of a Protestant-Christian bent include: *Het geluk is vlakbij* (Happiness is nearby, 1956) by Lenie Stafleu-Kruikemeier, *Australisch avontuur* (Australian adventure, 1958) by H. te Merwe (a pseudonym of N. Heiner; author's name on the cover: H. Henszen Veenland) and *Zes weken op de boot* (Six weeks on the boat, 1980) by L. Janse.
21 Published diaries are not represented in my research corpus.
22 Evers-Dijkhuizen (1960: 4) and Wijnstra (1960: 95). Twenty-two of the collected letters were published in *Ons tweede huis* (Anonymous 1960). Comparable collections of letters and interviews: De Rijk-Zaat (1983), *Toen wij uit Nederland vertrokken* (Anonymous 1994), Van der Meel (1994), and Zierke, Smid and Snelleman (1997).
23 See, for example, the letter collection in *Australië. Dagelijks leven van emigranten tegen de achtergrond der Australische economie* (Anonymous 1953a) and the (summaries of) interviews by information officer Heikina R. Scholten (1966).
24 On Rempt, see: Risseeuw (1965: 129–130).
25 'Het eerste door een Nederlandse journalist-emigrant geschreven boek over Australië, waarin land en volk en ervaringen van Nederlandse emigranten worden beschreven op een onopgesmukte wijze, zonder dat de schrijver een blad voor de mond neemt als het er om gaat de vinger te leggen op punten, die een emigrant minder aangenaam treffen.'
26 'De grote ontplooiingsmogelijkheden van Nieuw Holland steken daarbij echter zo gunstig af, dat de auteur voor elke adspirant-emigrant, die uit het goede hout is gesneden, een toekomstmogelijkheid ziet, welke hem gelegenheid biedt uit zijn mars te halen wat er in zit. En dat is veelal meer dan wat in het overbevolkte Nederland kan gebeuren.'
27 Haveman (1953: 7): 'Over het algemeen zijn onze emigranten mensen met prachtig initiatief en doorzettingsvermogen. Voor hen, die goed willen emigreren, is dit boek geschreven. Van harte hoop ik, dat de halfslachtigen en de onzekeren zich er door van emigratie laten weerhouden. / Emigratie is alleen iets voor hen, die ertoe geschikt zijn.'
28 See, among others, Anonymous (1953b, 1953c).
29 Koemans (1954: 9–10): 'moeten speuren naar de materiële en geestelijke voor- en nadelen, aan emigratie verbonden; moeten onderzoeken welke positie de vrouw in de kring van emigranten inneemt; nagaan of de Nederlander in staat is zich in een vreemd land en onder totaal andere omstandigheden te assimileren met een jong volk, dat zelf op tal van gebieden nog geen vaste lijn in doen en denken heeft kunnen vinden.'
30 On both books, see also Elich (1987: 123–125).

31 Koemans (1954: 148-150); quote on 150: 'Dat spionagesysteem kon ik niet waarderen, omdat ik er uit heb afgeleid, dat men op de een of andere manier onze vrije meningsvorming wilde beknotten.'
32 Koemans (1954: 155-156): 'koud en harteloos' - 'een bijzonder onsympathiek middel [...] om ons overbevolkte land te ontlasten' - 'Maar het gaat me te ver deze noodzaak om redenen van propaganda uit te leggen als een prachtige uiting van de oude pioniersgeest, waardoor ons lieve kleine land groot is geworden in de wereld' - *'De vraag was of een Nederlander, die zijn land om welke reden dan ook wil verlaten, in Australië gelukkig kan worden. Daarop antwoord ik "ja", mits hij offers weet te brengen, waarvan hij de zwaarte hier in Nederland niet kan begrijpen.'*
33 Smedts (1955: 44-47, 190, 195-196); quote on 196: 'De emigratie naar Australië is geslaagd.'
34 Risseeuw (1965: 8): 'Ik hoop dat dit reisverhaal ertoe zal medewerken wat meer bekendheid te geven aan de lotgevallen van een aantal der 400,000 landgenoten die ons land na de Tweede Wereldoorlog hebben verlaten.'
35 On the various information channels, see also Elich (1987: 120-123, 125-128). On the driving forces behind emigration information, see: Van Faassen (2006).
36 Anonymous (1949a: 3): 'voor emigranten die reeds op weg zijn naar hun bestemmingsland en voor hen die daar reeds zijn aangekomen.'
37 Van Kampen (1959: 77): 'VERWERVEN VAN LEVENSGELUK: / DAT IS EMIGREREN!'
38 Van der Mast (1951: 9): 'is een boekje - het zij in alle bescheidenheid gezegd - bestemd voor iedereen! In de eerste plaats voor degenen die wel het meest bij de emigratie betrokken zijn, maar daarnevens voor degenen, die in hun werkkring of maatschappelijke bezigheden het centrum - de vraagbaak - zijn van een bepaald milieu, voor kerkeraden, besturen en leden van werkgevers- en werknemersverenigingen en andere maatschappelijke organisaties, voor kiesverenigingen, maar voorts voor een ieder die belangstelling heeft voor het nationale gebeuren en zich mede verantwoordelijk gevoelt voor de toekomst van ons Nederlandse volk.' Earlier examples of such guides include Rempt (1947) and Diederich (1948).
39 'reeds in manuscriptvorm sterk de aandacht van de emigratie-autoriteiten trok.' On this book, see also: Elich (1987: 127).
40 Information at the beginning of the book: 'met medewerking van het Intergovernmental Committee for European Migration te Genève en de Nederlandse Emigratiedienst te 's-Gravenhage.'
41 On the use of Dutch language by Australian immigrants and their shift to English, see: Elich (1985: 66-69), Duyker (1987: 118) and Clyne (2006: 339-342).

References

Abma, J. (1954), *Kees emigreerde toch*, Amsterdam: Duwaer.
Anonymous (1953a), 'Australië: Dagelijks leven van emigranten tegen de achtergrond der Australische economie: Recente emigrantenbrieven, aangevuld met enkele belangrijke artikelen, welke de laatste tijd over Australië het licht zagen', special issue of: *Leven en Werken in den Vreemde* 1 (10): 123-129.

Anonymous (1953b), 'Onze sociale redacteur naar Australië', *Nieuwe Leidsche Courant*, 3 September 1953: 2.
Anonymous (1953c), 'Journalistieke reis naar Australië ten einde', *Nieuwe Leidsche Courant*, 24 November 1953: 2.
Anonymous, ed. (1960), *Ons tweede huis: Emigrantenvrouwen schrijven van verre*, The Hague: Emigratie Commissie van het Nederlandse Vrouwen Comité.
Anonymous (1994), *Toen wij uit Nederland vertrokken: Ervaringen van Nederlandse emigranten in Australië, Nieuw-Zeeland, Canada, Brazilië, Zuidafrika, Frankrijk*, trans. and adaptation N. Schouw-Zaat, final editing J.-W. Elferink, Bedum: Profiel.
Beatty, B. (1956), *Beyond Australia's Cities*, London: Cassell.
Beatty, B. (1959), *Kriskras door Australië*, Utrecht-Antwerp: Het Spectrum.
Blauw, P.W. (2006), 'Explanations of Post-War Dutch Emigration to Australia', in N. Peters (ed.), *The Dutch Down Under 1606-2006*, 168-183, Crawley, Western Australia: University of Western Australia Press.
Clyne, M. (2006), 'The Dutch Language in Australia: Some Comparisons With Other Community Languages', in N. Peters (ed.), *The Dutch Down Under 1606-2006*, 338-349, Crawley, Western Australia: University of Western Australia Press.
Cnossen, T. and M. Apperloo (1954), *Australië en Nieuw-Zeeland*, Wageningen: Zomer en Keuning.
Damrosch, D. (2003), *What is World Literature?*, Princeton, NJ: Princeton University Press.
Degrood, E. and B. Degrood (1963), *Australië: Het nieuwe vaderland*, Utrecht-Antwerp: Prisma-Boeken.
Diederich, J. (1948), *Emigreren waarheen?* Amsterdam: Nederlandsche Keurboekerij.
Dutch Emigration Foundation (1949a), *Algemene wenken voor de Nederlandse emigrant in den vreemde*, The Hague: Dutch Emigration Foundation (Stichting Landverhuizing Nederland).
Dutch Emigration Foundation (1949b), *Australië: Een beschrijving van land en volk ten dienste van emigranten*, The Hague: Dutch Emigration Foundation (Stichting Landverhuizing Nederland).
Duyker, E. (1987), *The Dutch in Australia*, Melbourne: AE Press.
Elich, J.H.W.M. (1985), *De omgekeerde wereld: Nederlanders als etnische groep in Australië: Essays naar aanleiding van een studiereis juli tot december 1994*, Leiden: Centrum voor Onderzoek van Maatschappelijke Tegenstellingen, Faculteit der Sociale Wetenschappen, Rijksuniversiteit te Leiden.
Elich, J.H.W.M. (1987), 'Aan de ene kant, aan de andere kant: De emigratie van Nederlanders naar Australië 1946-1986', PhD thesis, Rijksuniversiteit Leiden.
Emigranten zakboekje (1952) *Emigranten zakboekje, verstrekt door de Stichting Emigrantenbelangen in Den Haag*, s.l.: s.n. (Koninklijke Bibliotheek, The Hague, sign. NL 94 B 1013).
Evers-Dijkhuizen, W. (1960), 'Ten geleide', in Anonymous (ed.), *Ons tweede huis: Emigrantenvrouwen schrijven van verre*, 4-5, The Hague: Emigratie Commissie van het Nederlandse Vrouwen Comité.
Faassen, M. van (2001), 'Min of meer misbaar: Naoorlogse emigratie vanuit Nederland: Achtergronden en organisatie, particuliere motieven en overheidsprikkels, 1946-1967', in S. Poldervaart, H. Willemse and J.W. Schilt (eds), *Van hot naar her: Nederlandse migratie, vroeger, nu en morgen*, 50-67, Amsterdam: Stichting Beheer IISG.
Faassen, M. van (2006), 'Jongens van De Witt: Beeldvorming van twee kanten?: Nederlandse emigratie naar Australie, 1945-1967/Jongens van De Witt: Selling Images

From Both Sides: Dutch Post-war Migration to Australia 1945–1967', paper.Available online: http://www.academia.edu/1418388/Jongens_van_De_Witt_Selling_images_from_both_sides_Dutch_post-war_migration_to_Australia_1945–1967 (accessed 10 July 2018).

Faassen, M. van (2014), *Polder en emigratie: Het Nederlandse emigratiebestel in internationaal perspectief 1945–1967*, unpublished PhD thesis, Rijksuniversiteit Groningen.

Franke, S. (1956), *Tula, de kleine houtsnijder*, illustrated by G. van Straaten, Alkmaar: Kluitman.

Geest, K. van der (1954a), *Achter stampende hoeven: Tom Hoekstra als veedrijver in Australie*, The Hague: Kramers.

Geest, K. van der (1954b), *Op weg naar de toekomst*, Nijkerk: Callenbach.

Geijl, W.F. (1955), *Emigration from the Netherlands*, typescript with handwritten additions, The Hague: s.n. (Koninklijke Bibliotheek, The Hague, sign. NL 94 B 1018).

Geursen, J. (1960), 'Cultuur in aanbouw', in Anonymous (ed.), *Ons tweede huis: Emigrantenvrouwen schrijven van verre*, 76–78, The Hague: Emigratie Commissie van het Nederlandse Vrouwen Comité.

Harting, E. (1954), *Stel je voor dat ik ging emigreren: Een boek voor grotere meisjes*, illustrated by H. Borrebach, Hoorn: West-Friesland.

Haveman, B.W. (1953), 'Ten geleide', in J.D. Rempt (ed.), *Aan de rand der wereld: Een Hollandse emigrant in Australië*, 5–7, Dokkum: Schaafsma & Brouwer.

Hermans, W.F. (2006), *Volledige werken 7: Verhalen en novellen: Moedwil en misverstand, Paranoia, Een landingspoging op Newfoundland en andere verhalen*, ed. J. Gielkens and P. Kegel, Amsterdam: De Bezige Bij – Van Oorschot.

Jager-Meursing, T. (1963), *Een Hollands meisje in Australië (voor oudere Meisjes)*, illustrated by S. Bijlsma, Alkmaar: Kluitman.

Jager-Meursing, T. (1964), *Tot weerziens in Australië: Moderne roman voor meisjes*, illustrated by R. van Giffen, Alkmaar: Kluitman.

Janse, L. (1980), *Zes weken op de boot*, Hendrik Ido Ambacht: Van den Berg.

Jansonius, H. (1955), *Emigrante tegen wil en dank*, illustrated by H. Borrebach, Hoorn: West-Friesland.

Jones, B. (2006), 'Representations of Australia in Mid-Nineteenth-Century Emigrant Literature: *Gwlad Yr Aur* and *Awstralia A'r Cloddfeyd Aur*', *The Welsh History Review* 23 (2): 51–74.

Kampen, A. Van (1959), *Een sprong in het duister ... ?: Emigreren .... Wat is dat?*, Hilversum: De Boer.

Kampen, A. Van (1968), *Het leven van Mary Bryant*, vol. 1, *De verbanning*, Bussum: De Boer.

Kampen, A. Van (1969a), *Het leven van Mary Bryant*, vol. 2: *De open boot*, Bussum: De Boer.

Kampen, A. Van (1969b), *Het leven van Mary Bryant*, vol. 3: *De terugkeer*, Bussum: De Boer.

Koemans, H.M. (1954), *Australië op het eerste gezicht .... en .... bij nader inzien*, Hoorn: West-Friesland.

Krabbé, Tim (1994), *Vertraging*, Amsterdam: Bert Bakker.

Krabbendam, H. (2010), 'Emigration to North America in Dutch juvenile literature', in J.E. Nyenhuis, S.M. Sinke and R.P. Swierenga (eds), *Across Borders: Dutch Migration to North America and Australia*, 97–112, Holland, MI: Van Raalte Press.

Mast, W. van der (1951), *Verantwoorde emigratie: Waarom? – Hoe? – Waarheen?*, Franeker: Wever.
Meel, T. van der (1994), *Geschreven portretten van Nederlandse emigrantenpriesters in Australie*, ed. and adapted by J.W.P. Elferink, Zoetermeer: Katholieke Vereniging van Ouders en Familieleden van Geemigreerden.
Merwe, H. te (name on the cover H. Henszen Veenland; pseud. of N. Heiner) (1958), *Australisch avontuur*, illustrated by Menno, Delft: Meinema.
Molenkamp, N. (1947), *Hollandse jongens in Australië*, illustrated by C. van Kralingen, Barendrecht: Carpe Diem.
Øverland, O. (2000), *Immigrant Minds, American Identities: Making the United States Home, 1870–1930*, Urbana: University of Illinois Press.
Pauwels, A. (1980), 'The Effect of Mixed Marriage on Language Shift in the Dutch Community in Australia', unpublished MA thesis, Monash University. (Koninklijke Bibliotheek, The Hague, sign. NL 94 H 4451).
Peters, N., ed. (2006), *The Dutch Down Under 1606–2006*, Crawley, Western Australia: University of Western Australia Press.
Prins, P. (1966), *Jack en Sheltie*, illustrated by J. Kramer, Groningen: De Vuurbaak.
Prins, P. (1971), *Speurtocht naar Sheltie*, illustrated by J. Kramer, Groningen: De Vuurbaak.
Prins, P. (1972), *Sheltie en de smokkelaars*, illustrated by J. Kramer, Groningen: De Vuurbaak.
Ragas, E.W. (1960), 'Het goede onbekende', in Anonymous (ed.), *Ons tweede huis: Emigrantenvrouwen schrijven van verre*, 18–22, The Hague: Emigratie Commissie van het Nederlandse Vrouwen Comité.
Rando, G. (1996), 'Italian-Australian Literature: A Socio-Historical Survey', in F. Loriggio (ed.), *Social Pluralism and Literary History: The Literature of Italian Emigration*, 269–289, Toronto: Guernica.
Reece, B. (1988), *Australia, the Beckoning Continent: Nineteenth Century Emigration Literature*, London: University of London, Institute of Commonwealth Studies, Australian Studies Centre.
Rempt, J.D. (1947), *Emigratie: Kansen voor jonge Nederlanders in het buitenland?*, Doetinchem: Misset.
Rempt, J.D. (1953), *Aan de rand der wereld: Een Hollandse emigrant in Australië*, foreword by B.W. Haveman, Dokkum: Schaafsma & Brouwer.
Rijk-Zaat, N. de, ed. (1983), *'Toen wij uit Nederland vertrokken': Ervaringen van Nederlandse emigranten in Australië*, The Hague: Katholieke Vereniging van Ouders en Familieleden van Geëmigreerden.
Risseeuw, P.J., with the cooperation of L.H. Stronkhorst (1963), *Zo ver de wereld reikt: Verhalen van Nederlandse pioniers van vroeger en nu*, 2 vols, Baarn: Bosch & Keuning.
Risseeuw, P.J. (1965), *Overal Hollanders: Een reisverhaal*, Baarn: Bosch en Keuning.
Romijn Meijer, H. (1963), *Onder schoolkinderen en andere verhalen*, Amsterdam: De Arbeiderspers.
Schell, S. (1977), *De zevende hemel*, illustrated by Annelies Schoth, Amsterdam: Elsevier.
Scholten, H.R. (1966), 'De teruggekeerde emigrant: Een kwalitatief onderzoek naar de reden van terugkeer in Nederland van Nederlandse emigranten uit Australië ten behoeve van de voorlichting', unpublished thesis, Haagse Sociale Akademie. (Koninklijke Bibliotheek, The Hague, sign. NL 94 B 9000).
Schuur, K. (1953), *En de kookaburra lacht ... : Brieven van een emigrant*, compiled and ed. by J. Elburg, and S. Hertog, Amsterdam: De Bezige Bij.

Schuur, K. (1956), *Fata morgana voor Nederlanders en andere gedichten*, Amsterdam: De Bezige Bij.
Smedts, M. (1955), *Australië, nieuw vaderland*, Voorhout: Foreholte; Antwerp: 't Groeit.
Stafleu-Kruikemeier, L. (1956), *Het geluk is vlakbij*, illustrated by H. Borrebach, Nijkerk: Callenbach.
Stukkien, E. (1990), *Hartog's kinderen*, Groningen: Frieswijk.
Veen, J. van der (1988), *Australie: Het onbekende Zuidland naderbij: Lotgevallen van de Aborigines en van Nederlandse ontdekkingsreizigers en emigranten*, with contributions by D. Grimes and others, Groningen: Volkenkundig Museum Gerardus van der Leeuw.
Waasdorp, J. (1965), *Het naakte leven*, Amsterdam: Meulenhoff.
Wagner, T.S., ed. (2011), *Victorian Settler Narratives: Emigrants, Cosmopolitans and Returnees in Nineteenth-Century Literature*, London: Pickering & Chatto.
Wagner, T.S. ed. (2014), *Domestic Fiction in Colonial Australia and New Zealand*, London: Pickering & Chatto.
Wagner, T.S., ed. (2016), *Victorian Narratives of Failed Emigration: Settlers, Returnees, and Nineteenth-century Literature in English*, Abingdon: Routledge.
Walker-Birckhead, W. (2006), 'A Dutch Home in Australia: Dutch Women Migration Stories', in N. Peters (ed.), *The Dutch Down Under 1606–2006*, 242–253, Crawley, Western Australia: University of Western Australia Press.
Weening-Meijer, D. (1987), *Lege hannen*, Drachten: Osinga.
Wierema, T. (1977), 'Joop Waasdorp: "Ik ben een little loner, die ook door het leven moet"', in *Joop Waasdorp zestig jaar*, 9–43, Amsterdam: De Engelbewaarder.
Wijmen, E. Van (1970), *Een truck in de mist*, Amsterdam: Ploegsma.
Wijnstra, S. (1960), ''t Is wat je er zelf van maakt', in Anonymous (ed.), *Ons tweede huis: Emigrantenvrouwen schrijven van verre*, 95–101, The Hague: Emigratie Commissie van het Nederlandse Vrouwen Comité.
Zierke, E., M. Smid, and P. Snelleman, eds (1997), *Old Ties, New Beginnings: Dutch Women in Australia*, Melbourne: Dutch Care Ltd.

Audio-cassette

Koos Schuur: Portret van de 71-jarige dichter, die naar Australië emigreerde en weer terug kwam (1986), with the cooperation of J. Elburg, audio-cassette of the radio show *Boeken*, broadcasted on 15 July 1986, Hilversum: VPRO Publieksservice. Available online: https://www.vpro.nl/speel~POMS_VPRO_586913~boeken~.html (accessed 8 September 2018).

Index

Abma, J. 299
Achterberg, Gerrit 218
Adorno, Theodor 257
Aesop 13
Akker, Wiljan van den 222-3
Alaiz de Pablo, Felipe 90
Albrecht, Lord of Voorne 46
Aleide of Hainault 45-6, 48
Alexander the Great 15, 45-6, 49
Al-Halool, Musa 94
Almqvist, C.J.L. 87
Amsweer, Doede van 57, 58
Anand, Mulk Raj 147, 152-3, 156, 157-8
Andersen, Hans Christian 2, 267
Anderson, Benedict 97
Andrić, Ivo 2
Antunes, António Lobo 224
Apollinaire, Guillaume 207, 211, 213
Appel, Karel 1, 237
Apperloo, M. 297
Aragon, Louis 213
Arman (Armand Pierre Fernandez) 257
Arnold, Gottfried 27
Artaud, Antonin 236-7
Arthur (King) 5, 6-9, 14-15, 15 n.5, 16 n.12-17 n.27, 46, 50
Asselbergs, W.J.M.A 55
Astafjev, Viktor 92
Aue, Hartmann von 48
Auerbach, Berthold 108
Avianus 13

Babits, Mihaly 213
Bac, Godevaert 62
Bague Jassins, Hans 96
Bakhtin, Mikhail 235
Bakker, Gerbrand 260-8
Bakunin, Mikhail 90
Balduinus Iuvenis 10
Balmont, Konstantin 162
Balogh, Barna 135
Balogh, Tamás 191-2, 200 n.28

Barbier, Felicia, (F. Korpershoek) 136
Barbusse, Henri 231
Bargilesius, Nicolaus 27
Barnouw, Adriaan J. 189, 199 n.20
Bartos, Zoltán 90
Barycz, Henryk 193
Bashir, Ghulam Ahmed 94
Bastin, Julia 198
Battersby, Eileen 263
Baud, Elisabeth 127
Baudelaire, Charles 118 n.18, 223, 240
Beatty, Bill 302
Beaucousin, Richard 27
Becher, Johannes R. 210
Beckett, Samuel 235, 263
Beecroft, Alexander 281-2
Beekman, Eric Montague 86, 90, 94, 97, 212
Beevers, John 155
Belisová, Šárka 195
Bell, Clara 133
Bentsen, Grete 91
Berckelaers, Fernand 206
Bergh, Herman van den 218
Berghe, Jan vanden 60-1
Berlant, Lauren 273-4, 280
Berlant, Lauren 273-4, 280
Bernlef, J. 253-8, 259 n.9, 261
Berrington, Benjamin Shepherd 133-4
Berulle, Pierre de 27
Bette van Zierikzee 46
Birman, Seraphima 169, 173
Bishop, Elisabeth 254
Bittner, W.W. 88
Bjørnson, Bjørnstjerne 231
Blaeu, Willem 74, 77
Bloem, J. C. 218
Blok, Alexander 172
Boendale, Jan van (also: John of Boendale) 13, 21
Boheman, Mauritz 138
Boleslavsky, Richard 167-8, 173
Bölsche, Wilhelm 86
Bom, Emmanuel de 89

Bonaventura 21, 31 n
Boon, Louis-Paul 89, 92, 230–1, 244–6, 246 n.1
Bosch, Jeroen (also: Hieronymus) 1, 234, 261
Botez, N.N. 93
Bouwsma, W.J. 187
Boykova, Irina 178–9
Braak, Menno ter 156–7, 187
Branco, Cristina 225
Brandes, Georg 2, 3, 87
Brandt, Geeraardt 72, 74–5
Brecht, Bertolt 240
Bredero, Gerbrand Adriaenszoon 72–3
Bremond, Henri 212
Breslavskien, Laima 94
Bresson, Louis 135
Breton, André 213, 237
Brett, Vladimír 92
Breytenbach, Breyten 214
Brink, André P. 96
Brouwers, Jeroen 267
Brownlee, K. 38
Bruck, Hans 91
Bryusov, Valery 162
Brzostowski, Tadeusz 193–4
Budde-Lund, Gustav (Henrik Andreas) 87
Buhl, Ingeborg 91
Burckhardt, Jacob 188
Burssens, Gaston 209
Buwalda, Peter 268
Buzzi, Paolo 207
Bžoch, Adam 196

Caers, B. 37
Cage, John 257
Calis, K. 108
Calthrop, Dion Clayton 133
Camões, Luís Vaz de 219, 224
Camus, Albert 264
Cantimpré, Thomas of 47
Cappai, Giovanni Antioco 94
Carlton Dawe, W. 150
Caroll, Lewis (Charles Lutwidge Dodgson) 242
Carrasquer, Francisco 94
Catherine of Siena 212
Cats, Jacob 162
Cats, Nicolaas van 47

Céline, Louis-Ferdinand (Louis Ferdinand Destouches) 232
Cendrars, Blaise 207
Cervantes, Miguel de 94, 231
Charlemagne 15, 16 n.17
Chase, James Hadley (René Lodge Brabazon Raymond) 238
Châtillon, Gautier de 45, 49
Chekhov, Michael 167, 169–71, 173, 179
Chelkowski, Maciej 137
Chi, Myong-Suk 95
Chrétien de Troyes 9
Christie, John 240
Cicero, Marcus Tullius 21
Claudel, Paul 211
Claus, Hugo 230, 236–9, 241–6, 287
Cnossen, T. 297
Cocteau, Jean 212, 221–2
Coetzee, J.M. 262, 265, 267
Cohen, Alexander 86, 88
Cohen, Walter 260
Colmer, David 207
Comestor, Petrus 47
Conrad, Joseph 84, 91, 95, 147, 149, 150–1, 157
Conrat 139
Conscience, Hendrik 104–16, 117 n–18 n, 162, 164
Coornhert, Dirck 58–60
Corneille (Corneille Guillaume Beverloo) 237
Cortese Rossi, Adele 136
Coster, Charles de 164
Coster, Samuel 72
Couperus, Louis 122–39, 147, 149, 151–2, 155–7, 158 n.1, 164
Crespin, Jean 57
Crisafulli, Henri 86
Crispin, C.C. 134
Cruys, Gerard 91
cummings, e.e. 254

Dackiewicz, Jadwiga 193
Dali, K. 262
Daly, Herman 280
Dalziel, James 150
Damascus, John of 49
Damrosch, David 184, 187, 196, 225, 259 n, 273, 281, 286, 296

Dante Alighieri 231, 240
Daumal, René 237
Dávid, Gábor 192, 200 n.29
Davidov, Nešo 93
Debeljanov, Dimčo 93
De Bèze, Theodore 71
Degrood, B. 304
Degrood, E. 304
Deikun, Lidiya 170
Delcourt, Marie 242
Delepierre, Octave 110
Deleuze, Gilles 116 n.5, 243, 259 n.4
Délilah (Lucie van Renesse) 151
Dermoût, Maria 266-7
Derossi, Carl 86
Derrida, Jacques 243, 294 n.6
D'haen, Theo 259 n.1, 294 n.7
Dickens, Charles 87, 105, 118 n.18, 232
Dickey, James 225-7
Diengotgaf, Segher 51
Diepenbrock, Melchior von 109-12, 114, 116 n.6, 117 n.7, 117 n.9-11
Diest, Peter van (also: Peter of, and Petri Diethemii) 59
Dikiy, Alexey 168, 170-1, 173
Dilevko, Juri 260
Dimock, Wai Chee 275
Dis, Adriaan van 267
Döblin, Alfred 232-3
Doesburg, Theo van (I.K. Bonset) 206, 259 n.8
Dorleijn, Gilis 223
Dorresteijn, Renate 261
Dos Passos, John 90, 232-3
Dostoevsky, Fyodor Mihayloviç 231, 235, 240
Dowlaszewicz, Malgorzata 2, 201 n.34, 201 n.43
Draganić, Milan 137
Drápal, Miroslav 92
Du Bartas, Guillaume de Salluste 70-1, 73, 76
Duchamp, Marcel 209, 252, 254-6
Dumas, Alexandre (fils) 165
Dumas, Alexandre (père) 105, 108, 110
Dunk, H. W. von der 188
Duyker, Edward 297, 305 n.6, 307 n.41
Duyzings, Martin 301

Eckhart, Meister 21-2, 212
Edwards, Roy 90, 97
Eeden, Frederik van 133, 164
Ehrenberg, Alain 280-1
Ehrenburg, Ilja 154
Eliot, T.S. 153, 213, 219, 221-3
Ellis, Bret Easton 241
Elsschot, Willem (Alfons de Ridder) 89
Elzen, Peter van 58-9
Emants, Marcellus 262
Ems, Rudof von 44-5, 47-8, 49-51
Engelbrecht, Wilken 196
Enzensberger, Hans Magnus 213-14
Es, Nicky van 115, 118 n.22, 197, 201 n.53, 262
Estienne, Henri 25-6
Euripides 73
Evans, Hubert 87
Even-Zohar, Itamar 108
Eyck, P.N. van 187, 218

Faassen, Marijke van 305 n.3, 307 n.35
Faggin, Giorgio 94
Faltová, Lida 90, 92
Faludy, György 92
Faulkner, William 230, 233, 235, 237-8
Feith, Rhijnvis 161
Feldman, Maria 87
Ferdinand III, Holy Roman Emperor 77
Ferrari, Fulvio 94
Fischer, Manfred S. 91
Flaubert, Gustave 87
Flavius, Josephus 47, 72
Florens V (also Floris, Count of Holland and Zeeland) 7, 44-7, 50, 51
Forman, Ross 149
France, Anatole 231
Franchi, Anna 136
Frank, Anne 28, 264
Franke, Simon 299
Fremann, J. See Frick
Freud, Sigmund 84, 231
Frick, Ida 131
Friedländer, Salomo (Mynona) 211
Frumkin, Abraham 89

Gábor, Ignác 88
Gadda, Carlo Emilio 245

Gandhi, Mahatma 148
Gar, Tommaso 114
Garbutt, G. 262
Garnier, Robert 70, 72
Geest, Klaas van der 298–9
Geijl, W.F. 298, 305 n.8
Genet, Jean 235
Gennep, Jasper van 58–61
Geoffrey of Monmouth 5, 7, 9, 14, 15 n.1
Gera, Judit 92
Gerbert de Montreuil 9
Gerson, John 25–6, 30 n.11, 30 n.14, 30 n.16, 30 n.18
Gezelle, Guido 212
Giatsintova, Sophia 168, 173
Gilliams, Maurice 212
Girard, René 243
Goethe, Johann Wolfgang (von) 14, 248, 259 n.2
Gogh, Vincent Van 1, 232
Gogol, Nikolai 84, 93
Gokhale, Gopal Krishna 148
Goldstein, José 137
Gombrowicz, Witold 243
Gonçalves, Daniel Augusto 94
Gorky, Maxim 231
Gornfeld, Arkady 166
Gosse, Edmund 133, 138
Gottsched, Johan Christoph 14
Goulart, Simon 71–2, 78 n.5
Gray, John 133
Green, Henry 263
Gregory, Isabella Augusta, Lady 219
Greif, Mark 280
Grein, J.T. 133
Greshoff, Jan 135, 218
Grimm, Jacob and Wilhelm 8
Grote, Geert 19–20, 23–6
Grotius, Hugo 74, 75
Grubešlieva, Marija 93
Grunberg, Arnon 260, 262, 265–6
Guattari, Félix 243, 259 n.4
Guillaume de Lorris 35, 38–41
Gürer, Erhan 94

Haan-Woltjes, Margreet de 298
Haasse, Hella S. 260, 262, 266–8
HaCohen, Ran 94

Hadewijch 19, 212
Haeckel, Ernst 231
Hagoort, Roel 301
Hamsun, Knut 2, 231
Hanlo, Jan 300
Hardy, Oliver 254
Hart, Maarten 't 261, 267
Harting, Else 306 n.19
Hartog, Ary den 303
Hartog, Dirck 297
Hauptmann, Gerhart 88
Hauser, Otto 86, 93, 130, 139
Haveman, B.W. 301, 306 n.27
Hedberg, Petrus 87, 91
Heere, Lucas de 71
Hegedűs, Géza 92
Heiden, V. 131
Heijden, A.F.Th. van der 260, 267
Heijermans, Herman 161–80
Heilbron, Johan 115, 118 n.21–22, 123, 197–8, 201 n.53, 262
Heine, Heinrich 87, 93, 157
Heinric 37–42
Heinric van Brussel (Heinric of Brussels) 37–41
Heinrich VII 49
Heißenbüttel, Helmut 213
Hemessen, Jan van 61, 65 n.16
Henderikse, Jan 256–7
Hendriks, Dick 301
Herbst, Stanisław 194
Hergešić, Ivo 94
Hermans, Willem Frederik 84, 260, 262–4, 298, 305 n.9
Hernstein-Smith, Barbara 184
Herp, Henri (also Henry) 23, 26–7
Hertmans, Stefan 284–7, 289–93, 293 n.1, 294 n.6–7
Hertog, Salvador 300
Hertog-Vogt, Martina den 94
Hesse, Herman 188
Heurck, Emile van 89
Heydrich, Reinhard 236, 239, 244
Heyns, Peeter 70
Heyns, Zacharias 71
Hikmet, Nâzım 213
Hiller, Kurt 211
Hillesum, Etty 264

Hoffenberg, Mason 241
Hofmannsthal, Hugo von 56, 210
Honings, Rick 97
Hooft, Pieter Corneliszoon 73–5
Hopkins, David 259 n.7
Hopman, Fritz 190
Horace, Quintus Horatius Flaccus 74, 82
Houbein, Lolo 298–300
Hubert, Antonis de 73–4
Hugenholtz, F. W.N. 187
Hugh of Sint-Victor 21
Huizinga, Johan 183–96, 199 n.8–9, 199 n.12, 199 n.14, 199 n.20, 200 n.21, 200 n.25, 200 n.28, 201 n.37, 201 n.41, 201 n.50–52
Hutcheon, Linda 198
Huygens, Constantijn 69, 74–5

Ibsen, Henrik 2, 88–9, 91, 231
Ignäc, Balla 135
Ignotus (Hugó Veigelsberg) 135
Illyés, Gyula 192
Ipsen, Alfred 87
Ischyrius (Stercken, Christiaan) 55, 58
István, Lendvai 135

Jacobsen, Rolf 213
Jameson, Fredric 274
Jamin, Muhammad 96
Jammes, Francis 210
Jan I of Brabant 6
Japin, Arthur 261
Jean de Meun 35–36, 38–40
Jensma, Wopko 208–9, 214 n.1
Jepsen, Mads 87
Jespers, Oscar 206
Johns, Jasper 256, 258
Jolles, André 187
Jolles-Mönckeberg, Tilly 187–8, 195
Jones, Bill 296
Jones, David 207
Jongeling, Piet 299
Jordaens, Jacob 1
Jordaens, Willem 20, 23–7
Joris, Pierre 214
Joubert, Elsa 96
Joyce, James 222, 235, 240
Julius Caesar 7, 15
Juvenal, Decimus Iunius Iuvenalis 74

Kadir, Djelal 259, 271
Kafka, Franz 213, 257, 259 n
Kalinay, Valentín 196
Kamerbeek, J. Jr. 223
Kampen, Anthony van 298, 303, 307 n.37
Kamper, Jaroslav 138
Kamstra, Ans 301
Kasten, Madeleine 76, 78 n.6
Kastner, Barbara 123
Kaur, Amarjit 148
Keneally, Thomas 299
Keymeulen, Louis van 88
Khmara, Grigory 169–70, 178
Khnopff, Georges 136
Kipling, Rudyard 153, 155, 158
Kirchmayer, Thomas 57
Kiš, Danilo 2
Kisch, Egon 155
Klabund (Alfred Henschke) 240
Klaniczay, Gábor 193, 201 n.31
Klein, Yves 256–7
Koch, Herman 260
Koch, Jerzy 91–2, 97
Koemans, Huib 301–2, 306 n.29, 307 n.31–2
Kołakowski, Leszek 194, 201 n.40
Koning, Hans 266, 268
Koningh, Abraham de 70
Konrad IV 48–50
Kopčan, Vojtech 196
Korsakov, Petr A. 162
Košir, Mirko 93
Koskinen, K. 186
Köster, Kurt 188, 193, 195
Kosterka, Hugo 138
Krabbé, Tim 260, 299
Krejčí, František V. 88
Krijtová, Olga 92
Krleža, Miroslav 213
Krohn, Helmi 136
Krumm, C. 188
Krupa, Viktor 196
Kundera, Milan 2, 264
Kunkel, Benjamin 282 n.3

Lacan, Jacques 243
Laclau, Ernesto 272
Laclos, Pierre Choderlos de 239
Laforgue, Jules 210

Index 317

Lanckveldt, Joris van 55
Landauer, Gustav 86
Langenhoven, C.J. 95
Lapina, Natalia 175
Lasker-Schüler, Else 211, 213
Laurel, Stan 254
Lautréamont, Comte de (Isidore Lucien Ducasse) 233
Lawrence, D.H. 84, 90-1, 222
Lebene, Hans 132
Leerse, Frans 56-7
Leeu, Gheraert 14
Lefèvre, d'Étaples, Jacques 26
Leipoldt, C. Louis 95-6
Lem, A. van der 186-7, 192
Lenin (Vladimir Ilyich Ulyanov) 84, 231
Lennep, Jacob van 83, 85, 91
Lešetický z Lešehradu, Emanuel 90
Levenson, Christopher 214
Lévy, Michel 110-13, 117 n.12, 118 n.18
Lewis, Sinclair 231
Lichtenstein, Roy 255
Liebknecht, Karl 211
Lipoński, Wojciech 194, 201 n.38-39
Littell, Jonathan 245
Loo, Tessa de 261-2, 265
Lorebach, Erich M. 89
Łoś, Stanisław 194
Lubskiy, Vitaly 175
Lundkvist, Artur 91
Luxemburg, Rosa 211
Lu Xun 95
Lyotard, Jean-François 280

Maartens, Maarten 162, 164
Machado de Assis, Joaquim Maria 94
Macropedius, Georgius (Lanckveldt, Joris van) 55, 57, 59
Maerlant, Jacob van 6-7, 10-11, 14, 15 n.3-9, 41-2, 44-51
Maeterlinck, Maurice 28-9, 31 n.29, 115, 164
Magritte, René 234
Májeková, Júlia 92
Mallarmé, Stéphane 90
Malý, Jakub 114
Mammitzsch, Ulrich 190-1
Mande, Hendrik 23
Mandelstam, Osip 213

Mander, Karel van 70-1
Manders, Jo 156-7
Mansfield, Katherine 139
Manzoni, Alessandro 114
Marchlewski, Julian Baltazar 87, 91
Mardzhanov, Konstantin 167
Marès, Roland de 89
Mărgărit, Silvia 93
Markov, Pavel 168
Marlowe, Christopher 225
Marot, Clément 71
Marsman, Hendrik 209, 218, 219, 225-8
Martens, Frederick 134
Martí, José 94
Martini, Martino 77
Marx, Karl 153, 155, 157, 196, 231, 257, 282 n.2
Mary Stuart, Queen of Scots 75
Marzolla, Bernardini 94
Mashuri 96
Mast, W. van der 303, 307 n.38
McKay, David 285, 287, 293, 293 n.2, 294 n.7
McKenna, Stephen 128, 138
Mechtild of Magdeburg 212
Meijer, Maaike 154
Meijer, Reinder P. 298
Menzies-Wilson, Jacobine 134
Mercurian, Everard 27
Merezhkovsky, Dmitri 162
Meulen, Dik van der 97
Meyerhold, Vsevolod 167
Meyners d'Estrey, Henry 89
Meyrink, Gustav 240
Michajlova, Irina 161, 165, 176
Michaux, Henri 237, 242
Michelsen, Carl 87
Michener, James A. 84
Mierlo, Jozef van 29, 31 n.30-31
Migray, József 90
Miller, Henry 235
Miłosz, Czesław 2
Minco, Margo 264
Moens, Wies 225
Molenkamp, Nico 299
Monroe, Marilyn (Norma Jeane Mortenson) 240
Moor, Margriet de 260
Moore, Marianne 258

Moran, Sean Farrell 183, 191
Moretti, Franco 147, 157, 273, 275, 281, 282 n.2
Möring, Marcel 260, 262, 268
Mouffe, Chantal 272
Mühsam, Erich 86
Mukherjee, Neel 285
Mulisch, Harry 260–2, 264, 265, 287
Muller, Samuel 187
Multatuli (Eduard Douwes Dekker) 82–7, 105, 156, 162–4
Muusses, Martha A. 91

Naaijkens, Ton 184
Nabokov, Vladimir 240, 254
Načev, Stefan 93
Nagy, Ladislav 195
Nahuys, Alphonse 85
Naogeorgus (Kirchmayer, Thomas) 57
Naples, Leo of 49
Negrelli, Nicola 114
Nekrasov, Grigory 176, 178
Nettlau, Max 90
Neufeldówna, Bronisława 88, 91
Nevšimalová, Krista 88
Nietzsche, Friedrich 87–9, 231, 235
Nieuwenhuis, A.J. 86
Nieuwenhuys, Rob 84
Nijhoff, Martinus 218–19, 221–3, 225, 227
Nivardus of Ghent 10, 15
Nobelaer, Cornelis 77
Noble, Philippe 94
Noot, Jan van der 71
Nooteboom, Cees 250–2, 267
Nooy, Wouter de 123
Norden, Freia 131
North, Joseph 281, 282 n.2
Novaković-Lopušina, Jelica 94

Oates, Joyce Carol 240
Onstenk, Jan 301
Oostrom, Frits van 15 n.3, 46–7, 50, 183
Orthofer, Michael A. 260–2, 267
Ostaijen, Paul van 89, 206–14, 214 n, 225, 231, 233
Ostuzhev, Alexander 167
Otten, Else 127, 129, 131–3, 139
Öttingen, Konrad II von 49

Ouspenskaya, Maria 173
Øverland, Orm 296
Oversteegen, J.J. 97
Ovidius, Publius Naso [Ovid] 21, 77

Paepe, Cesar de 88
Palladio, Andrea 74
Palmen, Connie 260
Paloposki, O. 186
Parks, Tim 263
Paul, Jean (Johann Paul Friedrich Richter) 84
Paustovsky, Konstantin 84, 92
Pavič, Milorad 2
Pavlovna, Anna, Grand Duchess of Russia (Dutch: Anna Paulowna) 162
Payton, Rodney J. 190–2
Pée, Julius 89–90
Peeters, Gerlach 23
Péguy, Charles 210
Penninc 5, 8, 10
Peraldus, William 63
Perera, S. 153
Perron, E. du 84, 156–7, 218
Pesochinsky, Nikolai 176
Pessoa, Fernando 213
Peter I (Russian Emperor) 161
Peters, Edward 191, 200 n
Peters, Gerlach 212
Pieterse, Saskia 97, 158 n.1
Pirandello, Luigi 231
Plantin, Christophe 1, 70
Polak, Nina 273–4, 278, 281
Porete, Marguerite 19
Posner-Garfeinowa, Malwina 87
Poulaille, Henry 90
Prins, Piet 299, 306 n.20
Proudhon, Pierre-Joseph 90
Proust, Marcel 222
Provoost, Jan 61–2
Putna, Martin C. 196, 201 n.48

Quintilian, Marcus Fabius Quintilianus 24

Raché, Paul Bernhard 86, 130–1, 139
Racine, Jean 77
Radian, H.R. 93–4
Raemdonck, Anne van 90–1, 94

Rando, Gaetano 296
Rauschenberg, Robert 255, 256–8
Ravensburg, Johannes von 49
Raysse, Martial 257
Reael, Laurens 73–4
Rempt, Jan 300–1, 306 n.24, 307 n.38
Rennell Rod, J. 189
Restany, Yves 255
Rétif de la Bretonne 241
Reve, Gerard 260, 263
Reverdy, Pierre 212
Reznik, Lipe 89
Richard of Sint-Victor 21
Richardson, Dorothy 153
Ridder, André de 127
Rilke, Rainer Maria 210, 213, 231
Risseeuw, Piet 302, 305 n.13, 306 n.24, 307 n.34
Rivkin, Baruch 89
Rocker, Rudolf 89, 91
Rodenbach, Georges 115, 290
Rodriguez, Juan Garcia 137
Roelandt, Lode 90
Roland Holst, Adriaan 218–20, 223, 225, 227, 228 n.2
Roland Holst van der Schalk, Henriëtte 164
Rolland, Romain 231
Romains, Jules 210
Romijn Meijer, Henk 298
Róna, Ilona 92
Ronsard, Pierre 71
Roosenburg, S. 136
Roth, Philip 54–5, 63
Rothenberg, Jerome 214
Ruben, Regina 86
Rueter, Gustav 94
Rufus, Quintus Curtius 49
Russell, J.A. 139
Ruusbroec, Jan van (also: John of) 19–29, 29 n.2, 30 n.9, 30 n.13, 31 n.19–21, 31 n.23, 31 n.25–26, 31 n.29–31

Sackville-West, Edward 153
Sade, Marquis de 241
St Aldegonde, Filips van Marnix 71
St Jerome 24
St John of the Cross 212
Saint-Maure, Benoît de 46

Sand, George 105
Sartre, Jean-Paul 237
Satie, Erik 257
Scamozzi, Vincenzo 74
Schama, Simon 284, 286
Schaukal, Richard von 210
Scheerbart, Paul 211
Schil, Emile 301
Schippers, K. 254–9
Schneider, Lina 123, 130
Scholz, Wilhelm von 234
Schoonhoven, Johannes van (also: John of) 25, 30 n.15
Schuur, Koos 298, 300, 305 n.12–14, 311
Schwitters, Kurt 213, 255–7
Scott, Walter 87, 105–6
Seliger, Paul 86
Seneca, Lucius Annaeus 72–4
Senger, H.G. 188
Sepp, Rein 93
Seuphor, Michel (Fernand Berckelaers) 206
Shaw, David Gary 190, 200 n.21
Shi Huiye (also Sie, Jaap) 95
Shih, Shu-Mei 271, 282 n.2
Siebenhaar, Willem 90, 94
Silesius, Angelus (Johan Scheffler) 27
Simons, Kosti 298
Simons, Walter (also W.P.) 190–1, 200 n.22
Sinclair, Upton 231
Siregar, Bakri 96
Siskind, Mariano 272–4
Situmorang, Sitor 96
Slauerhoff, J. 218–19, 224–5, 227–8, 228
Sluyts, Charles 136
Smedts, Mathieu 301–1, 307 n.33
Smyshliaev, Valentin 173
Snell, A.L 135
Snellaert, Ferdinand 109
Södergran, Edith 213
Sophocles 77
Sordevolo, Dina di 136
Sötemann, A.L. 97, 223
Southern, Terry 241
Spackman, Barbara 245
Spencer, Herbert 214
Spengler, Oswald 231
Spoerri, Daniel 256, 257
Spohr, Wilhelm 86–9, 91–5

Stanislavsky, Konstantin 167–8, 172–3, 179–80, 180 n.5
Steinach, Rudolf von 48
Stendhal (Marie-Henri Beyle) 239
Stercken, Christiaan (Ischyrius) 55
Stevens, Wallace 213
Stiller, Robert 194, 201 n.41
Stirling, Alfred 302
Stirner, Max 90
Stoffer, J.E.L. 302
Stoler, Ann 148–9, 154
Stowe, Harriet Beecher 86
Strachey, John 153
Stramm, Augustus 207
Strindberg, August 2, 87
Stromer, Theodor 86
Stück, Erich 91
Stukkien, Elizabeth 300
Suderman, Daniel 27
Sulerzhitsky, Leopold 167
Sunarja, R.T.A. 96
Supervielle, Jules 237
Surius, Laurentius 23–7, 31 n.27
Sushkevich, Boris 173
Suso, Heinrich 22
Suttner, Bertha von 231
Swift, Jonathan 84, 93
Szántó, Rudolf 191
Székely, Lásló 154
Székely-Lulofs, Madelon 147, 152, 154–8
Szerb, Antal 191–3, 200 n.32
Szondi, Béla 92
Szymborska, Maria Wisława 2

Tagore, Rabindranath 231
Taichman, Moyshe 89
Tairov, Alexander 167
Tarantino, Quentin 195
Tasman, Abel 297, 305 n.6
Tasso, Torquato 74
Tauler, Johannes (also: John) 20, 22, 27, 31 n
Tcherkasski, Sergei 172, 174–6, 178, 180 n.2, 180 n.4–5
Teixeira de Mattos, Alexander 129–30, 133
Termorshuizen, Gerard 97
Tersteegen, Gerhard 27
Theunissen, Jeroen 273–5

Theweleit, Klaus 245
Tichelaar, W. 123
Tjitrosuwarno, Urip 96
Toer, Pramoedya Ananta 84, 96, 157
Tolstoy, Leo 87, 165, 231
Trakl, Georg 225
Trübner, Nicholas 110
Twain, Mark (Samuel Langhorne Clemens) 84, 87, 93
Tzara, Tristan 207, 209

Uddgren, Karl Gustaf 138
Uffelen, Herbert van 111, 117 n.7, 118 n.20, 118 n.25
Updike, John 212, 214
Utenhove, Willem 51

Vakhtangov, Evgeny 167, 173
van Alckmer, Hinrek 14
van Nassau, Maurits (also Maurice of Nassau) 72–3
van Veldeke, Hendrik 14
Vanderauwera, Ria 261–2
Veen, L.J. 127–8, 130–1, 133
Velázquez, Diego 290–1
Venuti, Lawrence 72, 76–7, 186
Verduyn, Jaap 298
Verhaeren, Émile 115, 164, 231
Verlaine, Paul 90, 212
Vermeylen, August 89
Vernant, Jean-Pierre 242
Veselá, Gabriela 195
Veselovskaya, Maria 164
Veselý, Josef 90
Vestdijk, Simon 218, 261
Victor, René 206
Vincent of Beauvais 6, 7, 41
Virgil, Publius Vergilius Maro 21, 46, 74–7, 79 n.10
Visscher, Roemer 73
Vitse, Sven 272, 282 n
Vleeskens, Cornelis 298
Volkonsky, Sergei 172
Volponi, Paolo 245
Vondel, Joost van den 2, 68–77, 78 n.2, 161–2, 293 n.2
Vonka, Rudolf Jordan 92
Vorsterman, Willem 62

Vossius, Gerardus 77
Vostaert, Pieter 5, 8
Vries, Hendrik de 218
Vygodskaya, Emma Iosifovna 92

Waasdorp, Joop 298, 305 n.10
Wagner, Richard 212–13
Wagner, Tamara 305 n.4
Wahlenberg, Eva 138
Wahyu, Andi Tenri 97
Walden, Herwarth 211
Wallace, Alfred Russell 84
Walschap, Gerard 89
Warhol, Andy 257
Wassermann, Jakob 232
Webb, Diane 191
Weber, Elizabeth 150
Weening-Meijer, Djoke 299
Wengstein, Mark von (Marie Luise Wanda Olga Gräfin von Wengersky) 131
Werfel, Franz 211
Werner, Alice 87
Westerbaen, Jacob 68–9, 75, 78 n.1, 79 n.11
Whitman, Walt 210–11, 231
Wido 48
Wieringa, Tommy 268
Wijk Adan, Malou Van 94
Wijmen, Elly van 299
Wikén Bonde, Ingrid 91
Wilde, Alan 244

Wilde, Oscar 223
Willaert, Frank 37
Willam 13
Wille, Bruno 86
William of Saint-Thierry 21
Williams, John 184
Williams, William Carlos 257–8
Willem die Madocke maecte 10
William II (also Willem II, Count of Holland and Zeeland) 7, 45
Wilterdink, Nico 261–2
Winius, Andries 161
Winter, Leo de 260
Winterstetten, Konrad von 49–50
Wolff, Maeyken de 69
Wolkers, Jan 267
Woolf, Leonard 153
Woolf, Virginia 153, 222
Worgt, Gerhart 91
Wunschel, Annette 186
Wygosskaja 92. *See also* Vygodskaya, Emma Iosifovna
Wyzewa, Theodor de 88

Yeats, William Butler 219–21, 223, 225

Zentgraaff, Henri Carel 156
Zhou Shuren. *See* Lu Xun
Zielińska, Izabela 88
Zola, Emile 88, 165, 231
Zschokke, Heinrich 108

www.ingramcontent.com/pod-product-compliance
Lightning Source LLC
Chambersburg PA
CBHW070014010526
44117CB00011B/1557